Other books in the *Astrology: A Language of Life* series

Volume I - Progressions

"What it comes down to is that Blaschke's book is strong enough at several different levels—practical, theoretical, esoteric—that one can find good information in it ... I have a feeling that this book, due to its comprehensive treatment of the subject, could easily become a classic."
— Kenneth Irving, *American Astrology*

Volume II - *Sabian Aspect Orbs*

"What the author has uncovered for us is an underlying energy between any two degrees in the Zodiac—no matter what planets may be tenanting them. This precision enables clear distinctions to be drawn between—say—an applying trine of one degree and a separating trine of one degree (or any other combination of aspect and orb). And such precision, which before may have af pealed more to the mathematically-minded than the intuitive, is brought out o the abstract realm of measurement and into the colourful realm of meaning by the inclusion of the Sabian Symbols. What a wonderful world this opens up. Pictures to explain technical measurements. Right brain married to left. A remarkable achievement, a fascinating book, and an invaluable reference."
— Paul F. Newman, *The Astrological Journal (UK)*

Volume III - *A Handbook for the Self-Employed Astrologer*

"This nuts-and-bolts approach to surviving and prospering as a working astrologer gives all the details on making an astrological practice a viable enterprise in the real world. The reader, whether a hopeful astrologer, or anyone interested in becoming an astrologer, is introduced to all the ways an astrologer can make a decent living. Along the way, the reader is also introduced to some of the frustrations, the pitfalls, the joys, successes, and life-style choices that accompany being a professional astrologer. Blaschke's very personal tale is interwoven through the pages of the highly detailed procedures in creating an astrological practice ... The author has made it over the hump, and now enjoys a prosperity that others may also find. This volume shows you how to do it."
— Chris Lorenz, *Dell Horoscope*

Volume IV - *Relationship Analysis*

"Once again Robert Blaschke has written an amazingly comprehensive and useful book for astrologers ... In his usual meticulous and thorough style, Blaschke explains how to use a plethora of techniques for relationship analysis ... *Relationship Analysis* is a valuable resource of astrological methods used for gaining insight into what brings two people together, the types of issues they'll likely be dealing with, and the deeper purpose behind their union. Among the methods discussed are composite and Davison charts, synastry (interchart aspects), house overlays, midpoints, mirror degree synastry, progressions in synastry, and the use of electional astrology to choose a wedding date ... In addition to the more common chart comparison methods, Blaschke explores and explains more esoteric ones, such as using Draconic, Heliocentric and Sidereal zodiacs in synastry, using mutual reception and sole dispositorships in Davison charts, the effects of Astro*Carto*Graphy® on relationships, and using the Sabian Aspect Orb (a technique that Blaschke originated) ... This book contains an enormously useful wealth of information."
— Leda Blumberg, *Considerations Journal*

dedicated to:
the reawakening of astrologers to the central importance of the Sun and
the Zodiac degrees as the spiritual complement to transit technique

Astrology: A Language of Life Volume V

HOLOGRAPHIC TRANSITS

by

Robert P. Blaschke

Second Edition
with an expanded ephemeris

REVELORE PRESS
Olympia WA, 2025

Holographic Transits
Astrology A Language of Life Volume 5

Copyright © 2006 Robert P. Blaschke
First edition published in 2006 by
EARTHWALK SCHOOL OF ASTROLOGY

Second edition published in 2025 by
REVELORE PRESS

All rights reserved. No part of this publication may be reproduced or transmitted in any form or by any means, electronic or mechanical, including photocopy, without permission in writing from the publisher. Reviewers may quote brief passages, as may scholars writing astrological journal articles.

Book and cover design by Jenn Zahrt.
Cover image by Solen Feyissa.
Interior cover image by Carol Cilliers Blaschke

Publisher's Cataloging-in-Publication
(Provided by Cassidy Cataloguing Services, Inc.)
Names: Blaschke, Robert P., author.
Title: Holographic transits / by Robert P. Blaschke.
Description: Second edition, with an expanded ephemeris. | Olympia WA : Revelore Press, 2025. |Series: Blaschke, Robert P. Astrology: a language of life ; v. 5. | Originally published: Ashland, Oregon : Earthwalk School of Astrology, 2006. | Includes bibliographical references.
Identifiers: ISBN: 9781947544772 (paperback)
Subjects: LCSH: Astrology. | Planets--Phases. | Holography. | Progressions (Astrology) | Horoscopes. | Free will and determinism.
Classification: LCC: BF1724 .B53 2025 | DDC: 133.53--dc23

ISBN: 9781947544772

Printed worldwide through Ingram.

Revelore Press
1910 4th AVE E PMB141
Olympia WA 98506
United States
www.revelore.press

Table of Contents

Acknowledgments	*vii*
Foreword to the Second Edition by Rick Levine	*ix*
Introduction	**1**

Chapter One

Holographic Transit Theory and Technique	**5**
Entering the Space-Time Continuum: Free Will and Fate	5
Transits: How Fate is Administered	7
The Solar System as an Immense Clock: Time Cycle Theory	9
Discerning Which Transits Are More Powerful	11
If Fate = Time, Does Free Will = Space?	15
The Dual Holographic Nature of the Nativity	16
The Central Importance of the Sun and its Synodic Cycle	17
Holographic Transits: Aligning the Soul with Higher Self	23
The Supporting Role of the Moon	32
Secondary Progressions Interacting with Phase Angle Returns	35
Recapitulation	37

Chapter Two

Sun-Moon Phase Angle Returns	**39**
Sun-Moon Phase Angle at Birth	39
Pre-Natal Sun-Moon Synodic Cycle	41
Using Sun-Moon Holographic Transits	42

Chapter Three

Sun-Mercury Phase Angle Returns	**47**
Sun-Mercury Phase Angle at Birth	47
Pre-Natal Sun-Mercury Synodic Cycle	58
Using Sun-Mercury Holographic Transits	61

Chapter Four

Sun-Venus Phase Angle Returns	**67**
Sun-Venus Phase Angle at Birth	67
Pre-Natal Sun-Venus Synodic Cycle	77
Using Sun-Venus Holographic Transits	82

Chapter Five

Sun-Mars Phase Angle Returns	**89**
Sun-Mars Phase Angle at Birth	89
Pre-Natal Sun-Mars Synodic Cycle	99
Using Sun-Mars Holographic Transits	107

Chapter Six

Sun-Jupiter Phase Angle Returns	**115**
Sun-Jupiter Phase Angle at Birth	115
Pre-Natal Sun-Jupiter Synodic Cycle	127
Using Sun-Jupiter Holographic Transits	136

Chapter Seven

Sun-Saturn Phase Angle Returns	**143**
Sun-Saturn Phase Angle at Birth	143
Pre-Natal Sun-Saturn Synodic Cycle	159
Using Sun-Saturn Holographic Transits	168

Chapter Eight

Outer Planet Phase Angle Returns	**177**
Outer Planet Phase Angles and Pre-Natal Synodic Cycles	177
Using Outer Planet Holographic Transits	196

Epilogue to First Edition (2006)	205
Epilogue to Second Edition (2025), by Jenn Zahrt, PhD	205

Appendices

I. New Moons + Solar & Lunar Eclipses 1920 to 2120	206
II. Sun-Mercury Inferior + Superior Conjunctions 1920 to 2120	273
III. Sun-Venus Inferior + Superior Conjunctions 1920 to 2120	301
IV. Sun-Mars Conjunctions + Oppositions 1920 to 2120	307
V. Sun-Jupiter Conjunctions + Oppositions 1920 to 2120	312
VI. Sun-Saturn Conjunctions + Oppositions 1920 to 2120	320
VII. Sun-Uranus Conjunctions 1920 to 2120	329
VIII. Sun-Neptune Conjunctions 1920 to 2120	334
IX. Sun-Pluto Conjunctions 1920 to 2120	338
X. Solstice Point Degrees of the Zodiac (Antiscion)	344
XI. Equinox Point Degrees of the Zodiac (Contrascion)	345
Notes	346
Bibliography	355

Acknowledgements

The author gives special thanks to his longtime editor, Patty Laferriere, for her work in editing this book. As in earlier volumes, she has improved the manuscript with her editorial skills and insight. Her Mercury-Saturn-Neptune conjunction trine his Jupiter in Gemini on the Midheaven continues to be an ongoing blessing.

Many thanks go to the author's friend and colleague, Michael Munkasey, for the phone calls they had discussing the cycles and phases of the planets. His original and innovative programming of a lifetime calculation of the progressed planets' synodic cycle phases will help many readers in researching their progressed cycle changes. His astute observations of retrograde Mercury are also appreciated.

To the author's musician daughter, Amy Rose, who released her third CD with her new band, Night Canopy. Congratulations, honey, on your original songwriting and cross-country performance tour. Your angelic voice has touched many hearts. Dad is very proud of you. Your love, support, and affection mean the world to him.

And to Carol Cilliers, who loved and stood by the author through thick and thin during a most difficult year, thank you for your love and steadfastness. This book could not have come out of the spiritual ethers and into concrete form without you. With both of us having hard natal Venus-Saturn aspects, love ain't ever easy, but one thing souls like us *can* do is endure through despair until love prevails again.

Robert P. Blaschke • *Holographic Transits*

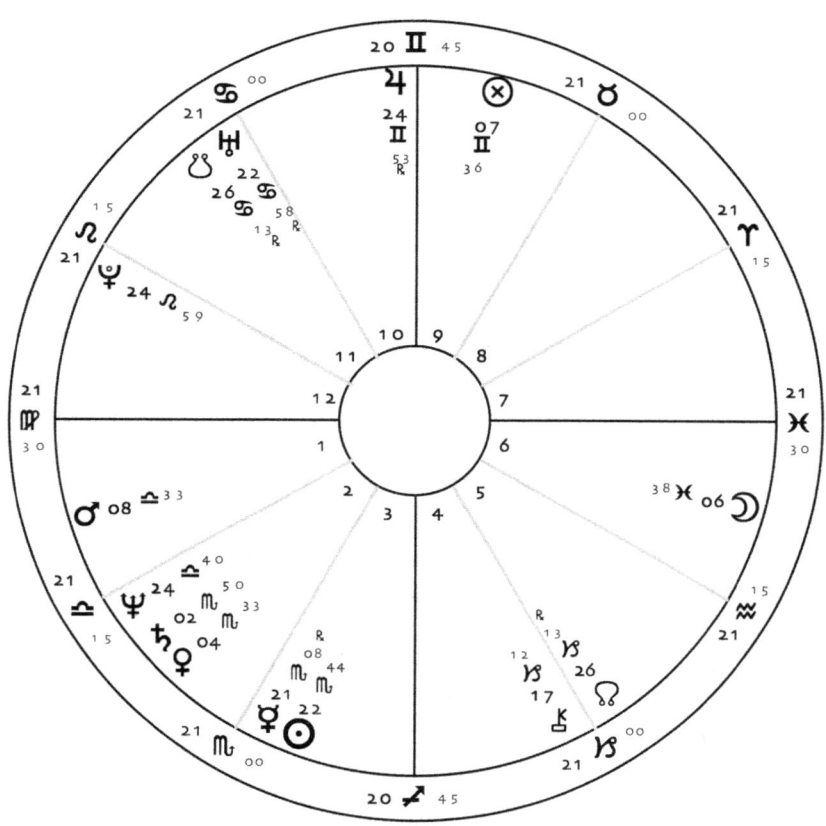

Nativity of the Author

15 November 1953
1:37 AM PST
Santa Monica, California
33N50   118W29
Porphyry Houses
True Node
[*from birth certificate*]

Foreword to the Second Edition (2025)
by Rick Levine

Astrology transforms and evolves along with culture and consciousness. Although many fundamental techniques in the modern astrologer's toolbox originated centuries or even millennia ago, new ones are championed by astrological researchers and pioneers. Although many continue to be presented to the community at large, some actually find their way into widespread use.

One of the great shifts in astrological practice over the last century is the movement away from concrete prediction and toward archetypal description. However, this development is part of a larger transformation that has been powered by breakthroughs in depth psychology and quantum physics. Modern astrology focuses on cycles rather than points, orbital phases rather than isolated moments, and repeating patterns rather than single transits. From Grant Lewi's Saturn cycles to Dane Rudhyar's lunar phases, from Cosmobiology's 90-degree wheels to John Addey's harmonics, the obvious path of modern astrology continues to acknowledge the rising importance of planet waves as a counterbalance to the location of a planet by point on the zodiac.

Johannes Kepler may have been the first astrologer to suggest that the zodiac is not of primary importance but he is surely not the last. He argued that the geometric relationships between the planets were more significant than their zodiacal positions. Furthermore, Kepler was intrigued by the recurrent angular relationships between pairs of planets. Robert Blaschke's *Holographic Transits* pushes Kepler's thinking a giant step ahead, setting the stage for a new generation of astrologers to work with transits in an entirely new manner.

A hologram is a recording of electromagnetic interference patterns that can be brought back to life; it's a three-dimensional image that is created by the interference of light waves, making a realistic, visually immersive experience. The resultant lifelike image is essentially a 3D photograph that captures and recreates an object's appearance in depth. Blaschke makes the case that a natal horoscope is the captured interference patterns of the planetary energy at play at someone's birth moment. The Sun, like a laser used to activate a holographic image, acts as the reference beam in a hologram. However, a second laser is necessary to produce a hologram. A transiting planet can act as the holographic catalyst.

In its simplest form, when the Sun's natal angle of separation to another planet is repeated in the heavens, these so-called "holographic transits" resonate the natal chart *regardless of the degree location of the transiting planets*. For example, someone born with the Sun at 3° Taurus 22' and Jupiter at 7° Taurus 35' has 4° 13' of angular separation between these two planets. Every year when the Sun and Jupiter are separated by exactly 4° 13', this holographic transit catalyzes the hologram of Jupiter, activating the potential for the expression of free will around Jupiterian issues.

Robert Blaschke takes this simple concept of vibrational reactivation to an extraordinary place, revealing through concrete chart examples how the Sun's natal relationship with each of the other planets can be used to unfold a whole new way to understand timing. This basic concept is the jumping off point to a series of specific analytical tools that would be advantageous for all astrologers to have at their disposal.

Rick Levine
April 2025
Redmond, Washington

Introduction

Transit technique has substantially evolved over the last 100 years since Alan Leo published *The Progressed Horoscope* in 1906 in London. The eminent British astrologer, Charles E.O. Carter, further contributed to our knowledge of transits in his writings published from the 1920s through the 1940s. A more sophisticated development of cycle theory was then introduced by Marc Edmund Jones and Dane Rudhyar, with Grant Lewi and Alexander Ruperti coming along later and elevating the understanding of transit technique to its current levels.

More recently, during the 1970s, Robert Hand, Lois Rodden, and Stephen Arroyo wrote exceptional books on delineating the various transiting planets' influences. Then, during the 1980s and 1990s, software containing transit reports was developed and the current generation of professional astrologers use interpretive text files from within these report writers to delineate transits.

Quality rarely arises out of quantity, which is the dilemma that the spiritually oriented astrologer faces when employing transit technique. It appears to this writer that the understanding of transits and cycle theory peaked in the late 1970s and since that time, because of excessive and unnecessary calculations made by computer software, transit technique has actually entered a state of decline.

The intention of this, my fifth volume in the *Astrology: A Language of Life* series, is to propose a theoretical underpinning for transit technique that includes both free will and fate. The essence of a holographic transit is a planet's relationship, or phase angle, to the Sun, the central star of our solar system. They are meant to be used as a complement to standard transit interpretation. Without the Sun, one cannot fully integrate the energies of the planets through the heart into Higher Self.

According to this theory, the nativity contains holograms, or patterns, relative to the Sun that repeat in the Heavens throughout life. By understanding these patterns and cycles, astrologers can choose precise dates for exercising free will. Celestial conditions at the time of a phase angle return reveal how the holographic structure of the soul can be restored to wholeness. The individual nativity is also shown to be part of a larger *soul group*, determined by pre-natal synodic cycles.

This book was written with Jupiter in stationary conjunction with the author's progressed Ascendant, and with transit Pluto stationing opposed his natal Jupiter, activating a Yod. Saturn also transited the progressed Midheaven of the author while he wrote the manuscript. It is hoped that this treatise will be useful to you.

Robert P. Blaschke
12 November 2006
Port Townsend, Washington

Holographic Transits

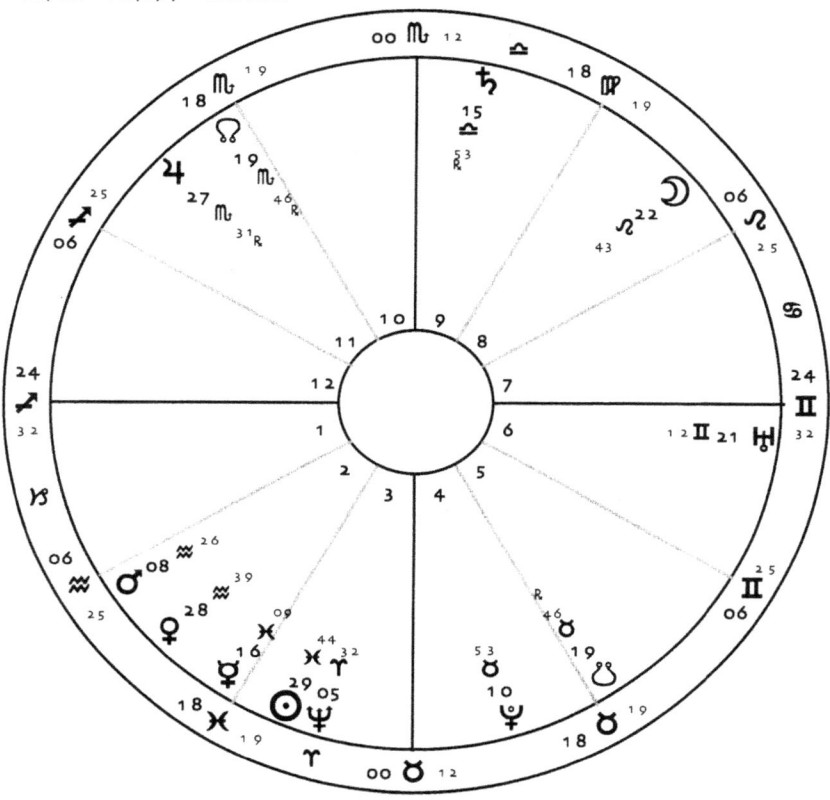

Sagittarius 25 from *La Volasfera*

Three cups of wine standing upon a table in the form of a triangle.

It is the index of a mind that is given to excessive indulgence and undue enthusiasm in matters of a spiritual and mental nature; one who will follow out his projects regardless of consequence, impelled as it were by a species of mental intoxication. The substance and form of this symbol is allied to the higher nature, but should the carnal appetites gain an ascendancy over him, he will in all probability degenerate into a debauchee. Moderation should be his watchword even in spiritual things. It is a degree of EXCESS.

Chapter One
Holographic Transit Theory and Technique

Over time, each astrologer evolves a spiritual context for the practical work that he does. This is necessary in any professional practice, as clients require a meaningful explanation of the forces at work in their nativities and in their progressed horoscopes and transits.

If the astrological language is to truly speak to the client, behind the surface delineation of the Luminaries and the planets must be a spiritual framework through which the birthchart is presented. This level of perspective requires that the astrologer have a clear and refined understanding of a nativity, along with the meaning of the horoscope as it moves through time.

Eventually, this ongoing sophistication of the astrologer's skills brings him to the ultimate spiritual question regarding free will and fate. Unless he faces this query, the astrologer's abilities will stagnate and the quality of his work will not evolve into a deeper spiritual grasp of life's purpose.

Transit technique, being the movement of the Lights and the planets in real time after birth, is the most commonly used method for explaining the changing tides of life. It has been this author's experience that most clients have a real sense of dread about their upcoming transits.

Even when transits are presented along with the secondary progressions, with the latter being explained as necessary inner development taking place in tandem with the external circumstances brought a bout by the transits, most clients still ask questions such as, *"What is going to happen to me?"* or *"When will this all end?"*

This type of expression reveals a perception of helplessness and being trapped at the confusing intersection of free will and fate. Can the astrologer empower the client by explaining how one can align with Higher Self and make choices for the good of his soul? Yes, he can, but to do this he must have a practical philosophy of what the nativity represents, and how to discern free will from fate. Let us now examine a spiritual doctrine that takes into account the twofold nature of a birth.

Entering the Space-Time Continuum: Free Will and Fate

In 1934, when the eminent British astrologer, Charles E.O. Carter, wrote *Some Principles of Horoscopic Delineation* as a companion volume for his classic textbooks, *The Principles of Astrology* and *The Astrological Aspects*, he quoted the sixth-century philosopher, Simplicius (490–560 AD), and his criterion about the spiritual reality of a human birth, as regards the soul:

> Simplicius explained the validity of the nativity by the doctrine that the soul descends into manifestation at a time when the cosmic conditions resemble itself. He also stated that Divine Justice brings souls to birth at times appropriate to their circumstances, that is to say, at times when their nativities would agree with their karma. Simplicius thus touches on the two main fields of astrological interpretation-character and destiny. There is, according to him, a twofold action: the disposition of the soul draws it to a nativity like itself; and karma also attracts a soul to a map that is in agreement with the soul's deserts.

Most astrologers view the nativity as a map of the soul. In the horoscope, an experienced astrologer can perceive the underlying reasons for incarnation into the present life. A picture of the very fabric of the soul can be seen in the birth chart, as well as an understanding of the nature of the karma allotted to that life.

Birth is quite simply the journey of the soul from the heavenly realms into space and time. A definition of the physical universe was given by Albert Einstein, wherein he stated that "everything is related to everything else in a space-time continuum." The astrologer is the spiritual counterpart to the physicist, and he knows that within this space-time continuum lie the mysteries of the relationship between free will and fate. The esoteric Cross of Matter illustrates this reality:

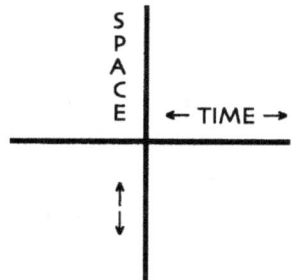

This cross symbolizes the birth of Jesus Christ, the perfect man, who was sent by His Father in heaven into human form to teach humanity about the virtues of love and forgiveness. Entering into the space-time continuum, Jesus took on the fate of an earthly birth, and by ascending into heaven after His resurrection, He also taught mankind about free will and the choice of salvation.

Chapter One • *Holographic Transit Theory and Technique*

This astrologer has had many clients who participated in channeled communication with spiritual beings existing on the other side of the space-time continuum. These regions are commonly referred to by Eastern mystics as the astral or causal planes. What this author has observed is that most of this channeled "spiritual advice" was provided entirely out of context of physical time.

These individuals, usually with Neptune in close aspect to the natal or secondary progressed Luminaries at the time that they received these astral transmissions, in the consultation would describe how much of the spiritual guidance they received would not have relevance until years later. At first, this astrologer thought that this was the necessary time required for the spiritual lessons to sink in. However, he now believes that many of these spirit guides existing on the other side simply cannot see where along the timeline that these messages will come to pass, if at all.

This point of view confirms the essential requirements of earthly perception. Souls who exist outside of a human body, thus beyond the space-time continuum, do not and cannot see the manifestation of human experience through the prism of time. This is not meant to minimize the value of spiritually received guidance, but only to point out that an earthly soul is pretty much on its own for when to apply such direction in its life.

In modern astrology, especially its humanistic philosophy of individual potential being revealed by the nativity, much has been declared about the astrology of free will and choice. If these astrological theories are closely scrutinized, however, they leave the reader feeling as if the assertion of choice and free will is only a feeble counterattack against the fated inevitabilities implied in astrology.

The specifics of how and when choice and free will can be acted on are largely left out of the equation. It is understandable, then, how this branch of astrology can be dismissed as a "feel good" whitewash of reality by the taciturn traditionalists within the profession. Somewhere between idealistic beliefs that one is practicing "the astrology of free will" and the cynical fatalism of the traditionalist practicing "the real astrology," lies a largely unexplored cosmic territory wherein definite spiritual laws combined with precise technique create a sensible and innovative astrology that addresses both matters of free will and fate.

Transits: How Fate is Administered

After some years of practicing astrology, or by studying astrological influences at work during the major events and key changes occurring during one's life, certain repeatable patterns can easily be observed. The deepest impression after seeing these predictable results again and again is that a greater Intelligence is at work which controls the administration of fate.

This writer has come to view transit technique as the chief mechanism involved in this management and command by higher powers of the karma allotted to souls. At birth, certain degrees of the Zodiac are occupied by the Luminaries, planets, and horoscopic angles. Within these specific degree placements lie compressed seeds of fate that have been predetermined for the present incarnation.

Each successive time that these degrees are transited by the solar system bodies, additional energy contained in these seeds of fate is activated and released through events that affect the body, the thoughts, the feelings, or one's fortunes. A seasoned astrologer will come to see that many of life's events are a karmic set up and are interconnected by a thread of purpose, or cosmic design, running through the nativity. This thread can more easily be discerned in the second half of life, defined astrologically as after the Uranus and progressed Moon oppositions.[1]

This way of looking at the mechanics of transits suggests that it is not the natal Light or planet or angle being activated, but rather the imprints left in the degrees of the Zodiac occupied by celestial bodies at the time of birth. In physical terms, heavenly bodies move on in their orbits, leaving the birth positions immediately after the infant draws his first breath. What is a transit activating but the pattern left in that degree at the time of birth?

A close analogy to the mysterious process of transits somehow activating an imprint left by the heavenly bodies that occupied those degrees at birth, is a modern technological invention known as the laser printer. These machines work by using a laser to make an image on a rotating drum and then electrostatically transferring that image to a piece of paper.

The Sun functions as the laser, burning an image into the rotating orbits of the solar system bodies as they pass through specific degrees of the Zodiac at birth. As the individual goes through life an electrostatic process occurs, transferring the image of the soul onto the document of life each time that those degrees are active. It is the opinion of this astrologer that the mysterious power of the Zodiac is the root basis for the functioning of transits, and that the Sun is their principal origin.

During the last thirty years, the planetary archetypes have supplanted the powers of the Sun and the Zodiac as the underlying premise for the workings of astrology. This is inherently wrong as the Sun, being the central star of the solar system that holds the planets in their orbits, must be the primal source in astrology. Any type of attempted modification to the eternal truths of this divine science cannot last longer than a Saturn cycle, as organic forces then enter and correct the falsehoods.

It is no small coincidence that presently, psychological astrology is reaching the end of its Saturn cycle of relevance and that its chief promulgators, born 1946 to 1948 at the Saturn-Pluto conjunction in Leo, are also reaching their second Saturn returns. These souls, having had a stranglehold on the reformulation of the astrological language during the last thirty years, are now experiencing leadership passing to a younger generation of astrologers with new ideas.

There has been a feeling of blasphemy creeping into astrology over the last three decades, as secular proponents of planetary worship and archetypal psychology tried to place themselves at the head of the table. In the Book of Exodus, verse 20:3, the First Commandment states, "You shall have no other gods before me." The Sun is the symbol of God in astrology and perhaps it is now time to restore the star of the solar system to its rightful place.

The Solar System as an Immense Clock: Time Cycle Theory

Several eminent astrologers throughout history have likened the solar system to a very large clock, with the Sun, Moon, planets and horoscopic angles functioning like the hands of a precise timepiece. Some astrologers, such as Alan Leo, proposed that events could be pinpointed to their exact time through the use of multiple chart analysis. In his classic textbook, *The Progressed Horoscope*, published 100 years ago in London, Leo outlined this approach in great detail in his Appendix I.

He included a diagram illustrating the sequence from the general to the particular. At the root of Leo's system was the nativity. From there, he overlaid one chart upon the other, referring to the various horoscopes as lenses of increasing precision. The day-for-a-year secondary progressions were the first level above the nativity, then the month-for-a-year minor progressions, next the diurnal chart for the day of the event, and lastly he showed how the rotation of the angles in the diurnal horoscope pinpointed the event right to the minute of time.[2]

The gist of this method was that when all of the charts aligned like the hour, minute, and second hands of the clock, the event would come to pass. This author, in *Progressions* (Volume I), proposed a similar rationale for the operation of secondary, tertiary, and minor progressions in a 1:13:27 mystic time ratio.

The Nativity Rule and *Law of Excitation* elucidated by C.E.O. Carter, defining the interrelationships between the birth chart and the progressed horoscopes, and how transits trigger progressed aspects into manifestation, were also referenced.

As a departure from the event-orientation of these directional techniques that Leo and Carter wrote about from the 1890s to the 1940s, Dane Rudhyar proposed a humanistic approach alleging that the nativity represents human potential, and that the planetary cycles passing through horoscopic quadrants are responsible for the unfolding of the growth of that capacity lying latent within the soul.

Concurrently with Rudhyar's work, Marc Edmund Jones was investigating the mathematical structure of the Zodiac using the Sabian Symbols and proposing a cyclic mechanism within astrology that contained 72 sequences of 5 degrees each. These two astrologers, along with Leo and Carter, are largely responsible for the genesis of the spiritual and metaphysical tenets of modern astrology.

The key principles of Rudhyar's humanistic astrology were brought to a flowering culmination by Alexander Ruperti who, in his classic text on transit cycles, *Cycles of Becoming*, concisely summarized the planetary patterns of growth. Transits are presented as cycles occurring over an entire lifetime, and a coherent developmental model of personal and social growth is brilliantly delineated in his book.[3]

It is the opinion of this astrologer that since 1978, when the English translation of Ruperti's treatise was first published, no other book on transits has come close to matching the intellectual sophistication of that work and its concise summary of the rather abstract philosophy put forward in Rudhyar's writings.

This astrologer has tried to step back, taking in a sweeping view of the evolution of transit technique over the last century, and while simultaneously contemplating the dichotomy of free will and fate, an interesting perception has arisen.

Regardless of the event-orientation, or the developmental model of human growth put forward by these eminent thinkers, both systems imply astrological fatalism. In the former, events are shown to be the predictable fate of directed horoscopes to an exact moment in time, while in the latter, personal growth is proposed to be the outcome of adjusting one's reactions to fate, and understanding that all difficulties in life can be converted into opportunities for growth if one has the right attitude.

This is not to imply that one system takes technical superiority over the other, or that either astrological predilection sees reality for what it truly is, but rather to serve as a reminder that fate is inescapable when incarnating into human form and no intellectual or philosophical gymnastics can relieve mankind of this burden.

Transits and time cycles, whether used to predict events with impressive certainty or to provide perspective and comfort to struggling souls by helping them to find meaning in difficult moments, are the same mechanism underpinning fate. Schools of thought have appeared over time to propose alternatives to the implied fatalism in astrology, yet these methods generally regard one's attitude toward fate.

Discerning Which Transits Are More Powerful

Some transits, such as the outer planet stations forming conjunctions to natal or secondary progressed Luminaries or angles, are vastly more powerful than others and discernment is called for when evaluating the relative strength of transits.[4] In *Progressions*, this author wrote how transits trigger progressed aspects into manifestation, and also how the progressed aspects themselves are limited by the nativity. Since that book's publication, many readers have inquired if similar laws and rules apply to the transits, irrespective of their links to the progressions.

In the year his mother died, which necessitated a move to the family home to help care for his father, and also the year in which *Relationship Analysis* (Volume IV) was written, the author had the following stationary transits: Jupiter octile Neptune, Jupiter quintile Mercury, Saturn trine Moon, Saturn quintile Mars, Uranus conjunct Moon, Pluto square Ascendant, and Pluto octile Venus. On the angles, Jupiter was conjunct the Ascendant, and Pluto was conjoining the IC. Another transit of import was Saturn trine Sun.[5]

Of these transits, Uranus in stationary conjunction with the natal Moon was by far the most significant, coinciding with an unexpected medical diagnosis of a malignant brain tumor for the author's mother. She died shortly thereafter on 7 September 2004, with Pluto in exact stationary octile with the author's natal Venus. Moving back home to Santa Monica to help his father is seen in the angular transit of Pluto to the IC.

Each of these key 2004 transits were between Luminaries, planets, or angles that are in aspect natally. The author has natal Moon trioctile Uranus, Venus quintile Pluto, and Pluto trine IC. Recalling Carter's *Nativity Rule*:

It is a cardinal rule that no direction can bring to pass what is not shown in the nativity. Exceptions to this are virtually non-existent.

Astrologers may also apply a similar rule to the relative strength of transits:

Pairs of Luminaries or planets in natal aspect that form subsequent stationary aspect by transit will be the stronger transits forming during any given year.

The other transits that year played supporting roles, especially Saturn trine Sun. While his mother was at home in hospice care and dying in late August, the author was able to find the strength and personal discipline to finish the manuscript for Relationship Analysis, getting the book to the printer on time for the planned publication date. This transit also resulted in the feelings of responsibility and duty toward his father, resulting in the decision to end a relationship, move home, and care for him.

Earlier in the year, a sizable portion of the manuscript was written and the creative vision and scope of the book took shape, with Jupiter in stationary quintile to Mercury. The author has these two planets in natal biquintile. Jupiter in stationary octile to Neptune resulted in differences of spiritual understanding with a girlfriend who was a Tibetan Buddhist; the Jupiter trine Neptune in the author's nativity making this a significant transit according to the above rule.

The astrologer should not overlook transits to secondary progressed Luminaries, planets, or angles. It has been the experience of this writer that these transits are very powerful, especially during the second half of life. An outer planet stationing on the secondary progressed Sun, Ascendant, or Midheaven, for example, is quite potent, as is a station on the progressed IC or on the progressed Descendant.

It was the opinion of both Alan Leo and C.E.O. Carter that a spiritually oriented person lived as much through his progressed angles as through his natal angles. It has been this astrologer's experience that transits over the progressed angles are often as powerful as the transits over the natal angles. The tri-wheel chart on the following page shows secondary progressions and transits for the author when his mother passed away.

A progressed solar eclipse had just occurred within the last six weeks, and the chart ruler, Mercury, along with Venus had progressed to a square with Mars. Saturn was in close conjunction with the progressed South Node, and the Ascendant and Saturn were in progressed conjunction.[6] Pluto had just sta-

Robert P. Blaschke

Nov 15 1953 — 1:37 AM PST
Santa Monica — California
33N50 — 118W29
Nov 15 1953 — 09:37:00 GMT
Tropical — Porphyry — True Node

2004 Transit Search

Transiting Planets
Jupiter thru Pluto
Applying Orb 1 Degree
Separating Orb 1 Degree
Sort By Ingress

♃ ∠ ♀	Jan1	Jan3	Jan18
♄ ∠ ♆	Jan1		Jan10
♄ Q AS	Jan1	Jan3	Jan16
♆ ⚺ ☿	Jan1	Jan19	Mar5
♆ ∠ ♀	Jan1		Jan2
♆ Q ♂	Jan1	Jan2	Feb3
♆ ☐ AS	Jan1 Feb1	Mar24	Jun26 May18
♆ ☍ MC	Jan1	Jan8	Feb11
♆ ☌ 4	Jan1	Jan8	Feb11
♄ ☐ ♂	Jan3	Jan15	Jan29
♃ ∠ ♄	Jan10	Jan29	Feb9
♄ ⚼ ☉	Jan13	Jan27	Feb14
♄ △ ☽	Jan28 Feb17	Mar7	Apr15 Mar27
♅ △ ♄	Feb5	Feb23	Mar11
♄ ⚼ ☿	Feb6	Mar7	Apr7
♆ ⚺ ☉	Feb10	Mar24	May8
♃ ⋈ ♆	Feb19	Feb27	Mar6
♃ ⚹ ♅	Feb22	Feb29	Mar8
♆ ⚻ ♅	Feb22	Mar24	Apr25
♃ ⚹ ♀	Mar2	Mar10	Mar18
♅ △ ♀	Mar6	Mar24	Apr15
♃ ⚹ ♄	Mar16	Mar24	Apr3
♃ Q ☉	Mar21	Mar31	Apr11
♄ ⚼ ☉	Mar29	Apr16	Apr29
♃ ∠ ♆	Mar31 Apr12	May5	Jun8 May27
♃ Q ☿	Apr6 Apr23	May5	Jun2 May17
♆ ⚺ ☿	Apr13	Jun2	Jul12
♃ ⚺ ♂	Apr14	May5	May25
♄ ☐ ♂	Apr14	Apr27	May8
♅ ☌ ☽	Apr17 May22	Jun10	Aug6 Jun30
♄ Q AS	Apr26	May8	May17
♃ ∠ ♅	Apr28	May5	May11
♄ ∠ ♆	May2	May12	May22
♆ ☍ MC	May7	Jun16	Aug1
♆ ☌ 3	May7	Jun16	Aug1
♆ Q ♂	May16	Jun24	Aug23
♃ Q ☉	May28	Jun9	Jun18
♃ ⚹ ♄	Jun6	Jun15	Jun24
♄ ⋈ ♆	Jun16	Jun24	Jul2
♃ ⚹ ♀	Jun21	Jun29	Jul6
♆ ∠ ♀	Jun24 Aug23	Aug30	Nov1 Sep7
♃ ⚹ ♅	Jul1	Jul8	Jul14
♃ ⋈ ♆	Jul3	Jul9	Jul15
♃ ∠ ♄	Jul22	Jul28	Aug2
♃ ∠ ♀	Jul31	Aug6	Aug11
♄ ⚺ MC	Jul31	Aug8	Aug16
♄ ☌ 11	Aug2	Aug10	Aug19
♄ △ ☿	Aug3	Aug11	Aug20
♄ ⚹ AS	Aug6	Aug14	Aug23
♃ ☐ MC	Aug7	Aug12	Aug17
♄ ⚼ ☽	Aug7	Aug15	Aug24
♅ △ ♀	Aug8	Sep3	Sep30
♃ ⚹ ☿	Aug9	Aug14	Aug19
♃ ☌ AS	Aug11	Aug16	Aug20
♃ ☌ 1	Aug11	Aug16	Aug20
♄ △ ☉	Aug16	Aug25	Sep4
♃ ⚹ ☉	Aug17	Aug22	Aug26
♃ ⋈ ♄	Aug17	Aug22	Aug27
♃ ⚹ ♅	Aug18	Aug23	Aug28
♄ ☌ ♅	Aug18	Aug27	Sep6
♃ ⋈ ♀	Aug26	Aug30	Sep4
♃ ⚺ ♆	Aug26	Aug31	Sep5
♃ ☐ ♃	Aug27	Sep1	Sep6
♃ ⚺ ♆	Aug28	Sep1	Sep6
♄ ☐ ♆	Sep3	Sep13	Sep26
♄ ⚺ ♃	Sep5	Sep16	Sep29
♄ ⚺ ♆	Sep6	Sep17	Sep30
♆ Q ♂	Sep6	Nov1	Nov30
♃ ⚹ ☿	Sep19	Sep23	Sep28
♅ △ ♄	Sep22	Nov11	Dec30
♄ Q ♂	Sep24 Oct9	Nov8	Dec23 Dec7
♃ ⚹ ☉	Sep26	Oct1	Oct5
♆ ☍ MC	Sep28	Nov8	Dec6
♆ ☌ 4	Sep28	Nov8	Dec6
♃ ⚺ ♄	Oct3	Oct8	Oct13
♃ ⚺ ♀	Oct11	Oct16	Oct21
♃ Q ♅	Oct13	Oct18	Oct23
♃ ⋈ ♆	Oct13	Oct18	Oct23
♆ ⚺ ☿	Oct17	Nov19	Dec16
♃ ∠ ☿	Oct19	Oct24	Oct28
♃ ⚻ ☽	Oct21	Oct26	Oct31
♃ ∠ ☉	Oct26	Oct31	Nov5
♃ ☌ ♂	Oct30	Nov5	Nov10
♆ ☐ AS	Oct31	Nov29	Dec26
♃ ∠ ♆	Nov7	Nov12	Nov17
♃ ⋈ ☿	Nov13	Nov18	Nov24
♃ ⋈ ☉	Nov22	Nov27	Dec4
♆ ⚺ ☉	Dec5	•	Dec31
♆ ⚻ ♅	Dec12		Dec31
♃ ⚹ ♆	Dec15	Dec23	Dec31
♄ ⚺ ♆	Dec17	Dec31	Dec31
♄ ⚺ ♃	Dec18		Dec31
♄ ☐ ♆	Dec22		Dec31
♅ △ ♀	Dec22		Dec31

tioned direct near the IC. The direct station of Neptune at 12° Aquarius 36' six weeks later was exactly conjunct the author's progressed IC as he moved home to take care of his grieving and widowed father. Jupiter was also trine the North Node.

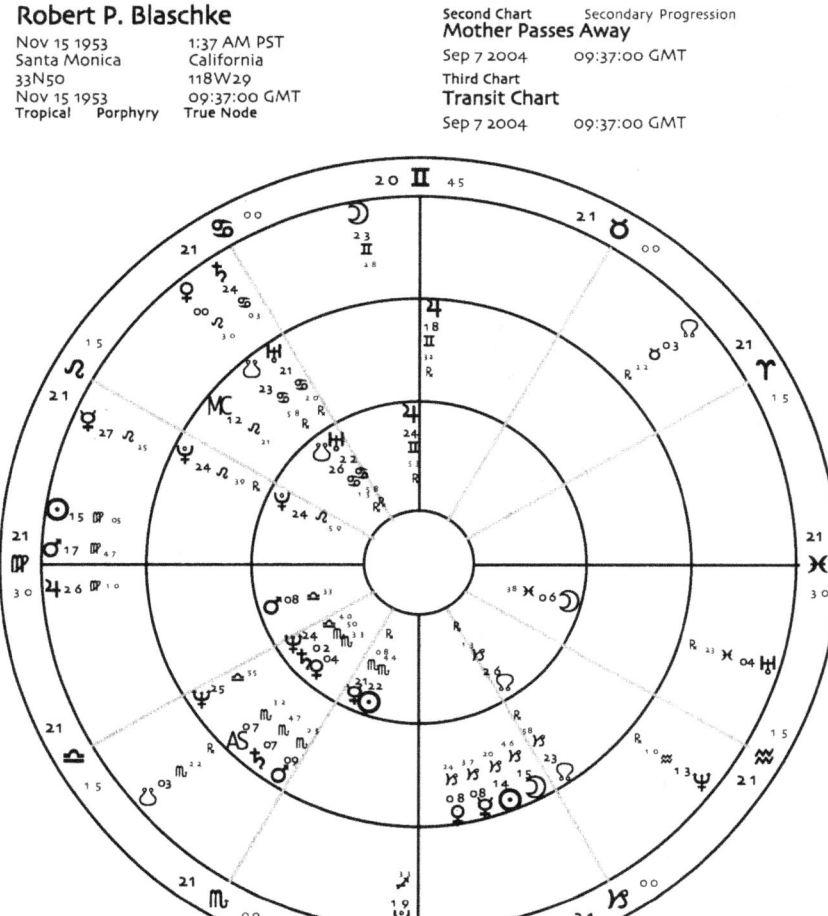

Thus far, the workings of fate after one's birth through the mechanism of transits has occupied our attention. Recalling the doctrine of Simplicius, and the twofold action of the soul as it takes birth in human form, how can astrologers perceive the *"soul descending into manifestation at a time when the cosmic conditions resemble itself?"* Are these cosmic conditions the basic structure of the nativity, such as a Luminary or planet in a particular sign or house, and in aspect to another body? Is there another way to look into the depths of a horoscope and see the very fabric of the soul? Is there also a way to show how the soul is part of the divine whole?

Chapter One • *Holographic Transit Theory and Technique*

If Fate = Time, Does Free Will = Space?

A case has been built so far proposing the time cycles of transits as the chief mechanism administering fate after birth. Einstein defined a space-time continuum existing within the physical universe wherein *"everything is related to everything else."* The probability of free will has been put forth in the doctrine of Simplicius when he states that *"the disposition of the soul draws it to a nativity like itself."*

These three theoretical pillars must necessarily lead to a fourth if a metaphysical basis is to be established for defining the relationship between free will and fate. Asking the Holy Ghost at moments like this to awaken one's mind to an illumined consciousness so that it can grasp these mysteries is the necessary next step.

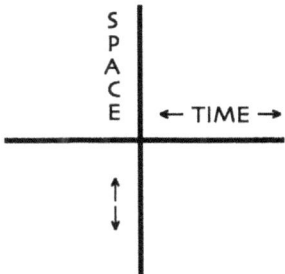

Contemplating the esoteric Cross of Matter, the symbol for the birth of Jesus Christ and for his Ascension, it appears to the seeker that time is horizontal and linear. It is also evident that space is vertical and ennobling, as the root of the Cross travels to its uppermost reaches. If the soul descends into manifestation from the heavenly realms into a human body, then it stands to reason that its free will is preserved and protected by its vertical connection to God within the space-time continuum.

This view of incarnation leads to a logical conclusion: *If the time cycles of transits are the arbiters of fate after one's birth, then spatial configurations and patterns in the nativity must be the mechanism of free will and choice for the soul.* What are these spatial patterns, and how can the astrologer find them in a horoscope? If a blueprint exists within the birth chart whose function is to connect the individual soul with his Creator, would this pattern then need to be of a holographic nature?

The Dual Holographic Nature of the Nativity

For astrology to evolve from its current level of scholarship to a higher plane of theory and technique, this divine science must embrace a multi-dimensional view of reality. One vehicle for this necessary elevation of understanding is the concept of a holographic universe. Within this theoretical framework lies a vast spiritual potential to further enlighten astrological science through the simple premise that the whole can be seen in every part of the creation.

There are two kinds of holographs. In an elegant twist of irony, one refers to fate and the other symbolizes free will. One definition of a holograph is: "*A document, such as a letter or will, handwritten by the person who signed it.*" This description perfectly illustrates the holographic nativity as a signing on to one's karma at birth. In the doctrine of Simplicius, where he states, "*Divine Justice brings souls to birth at times appropriate to their circumstances,*" a contract with fate is implied.

A second definition of holography is a photographic image, or hologram, that is three-dimensional and made without a camera lens by aiming reflected laser beams onto photographic film. When one of these holograms is then cut in halves, thirds, quarters, or into even more minute subdivisions, and another laser is beamed onto the partial image it is subsequently restored into its original form and made whole.

This metaphor is a second illustration of a holographic nativity, one wherein each three-dimensional spatial pattern in the birth chart, having separated from the Creator, requires the Light of God to restore it to wholeness. Here we perceive that no matter how small any part of the horoscope is, it contains our Heavenly Father within it and can be reunited with Him.

According to this metaphysical theory, each nativity has a dual holographic essence. The first reality is a birth document sealing a fate, bound by transits and time cycles after incarnating, while the second entity is a birth chart with spatial patterns requiring the Light of God to awaken the self-realized choice of free will.

The *Solar System Laser*, the restorative Light of God, of course, has to be the Sun. Therefore, in a holographic birth chart it is the planet's unique relationship with the Sun that matters. This is found by measuring precise distance arcs between the Sun and the planets at birth. In any nativity, these Sun-planet holograms are a spiritual opportunity to experience God-realization first-hand.

Although the computer technology is not yet available, this astrologer has been given a future vision of what is to come: a three-dimensional laser-driven computer monitor that displays a dancing holographic image of the nativity. This spherical effigy of the horoscope contained the Zodiacal position of the Luminaries and planets by longitude, their respective declination, and their chains of dispositors.

The Central Importance of the Sun and its Synodic Cycle

As the self-luminous central star of our solar system, the Sun holds each of the planets in their orbits and is the sole source of gravitation, electromagnetism, light, and heat necessary for their physical survival. In spiritual symbolism, the Sun embodies the power, light, and love of almighty God, our heavenly Father.

With its vital role in the formation, operation, and maintenance of the solar system, any kind of astrological theory that does not acknowledge the central importance of the Sun will by necessity have its root assumptions called into question. Even in practical horoscopic delineation, the primacy and sovereignty of the Sun is seen in how the closest aspect to the Sun determines the vocation; in solar return charts where the exact degrees of the angles form precise synastry conjunctions with the important souls arriving in one's life that year; and in the secondary progressions, where the current degree of the Sun and its aspects underpin one's inner evolution.

If the astrologer attempts to unveil the mysteries of free will and fate, he must place the Sun and planets into a system of relative importance. In transit technique, where its entire foundation is based on planetary cycles and the return of these bodies to their natal positions, if the astrologer is to include the Sun as the vital centerpiece of his theory, he must wander outside of conventional wisdom.

Taking this fundamental principle of the supremacy of the Sun in the nativity as the core of our thesis, for the theory to have relevance to transit technique, the astrologer will have to view the relationship between the Sun and planets as a moving pair, a combined unit of spatial motion. This is holographic consciousness.

If one accepts that *fate = time* and *free will = space*, then calculating these spatial holograms in any nativity is essential for viewing the operation of free will within that particular soul's life. In practical terms, the astrologer will have to measure the distance arcs between the Sun and the Moon, between the Sun and the two inferior planets, and between the Sun and the six superior planets.[7]

Once these nine natal holograms are calculated, astrologers have the ability to look into the core of the holographic relationship between the individual soul and his Creator. Recall that in holography, *(when) another laser is beamed onto the partial image it is subsequently restored into its original form and made whole.* A profound spiritual implication in this system is that an astrologer can determine when the restorative Light of God (the Sun) might realign a soul with its Source.

To more fully understand how these holographic moving pairs and spatial units, comprised of the phase angles between the Sun and planets at birth, just may be the horoscopic foundation of the soul's free will, it is important to investigate a form of measurement known as a synodic cycle. This is the period between two consecutive conjunctions of a planet with the Sun, as viewed from the Earth.

Esoterically, when a planet geocentrically conjoins the Sun, it receives its purpose and meaning for the upcoming synodic cycle. One can visualize a planet drinking from the well of light, heat, gravitation, and electromagnetism as it aligns with the Sun. Then, like a camel, it must cross vast spaces of darkness in the solar system in its lonely orbit through the heavens. A planet, if it has any ensouling and any sort of consciousness, must rejoice in its own way when it attains solar alignment. If this Earth is the rare and exclusive habitat of humanity, with souls created in the image of God the Father, then geocentric measurement of planets humanizes them.

The following table shows the Synodic Periods of the solar system planets:[8]

Planet	Distance from Sun	Sidereal Period	Synodic Period
Mercury	36 million miles	87.97 days	115.88 days
Venus	67.2 million miles	224.7 days	583.9 days
Earth	92.9 million miles	365.26 days	n/a
Moon	239,000 miles (Earth)	27.32 days	29.53 days
Mars	141.5 million miles	687 days	779.9 days
Jupiter	483.3 million miles	11.86 years	399 days
Saturn	886.1 million miles	29.46 years	378 days
Uranus	1,783 million miles	84.02 years	370 days
Neptune	2,797 million miles	164.79 years	367.4 days
Pluto	3,670 million miles	248.4 years	366.7 days

In *Relationship Analysis,* this astrologer wrote about the Sun-Venus synodic cycle. Two ways of looking at the cycle were offered. Firstly, the degree in which the inferior conjunction of retrograde Venus and the Sun occurs is quite significant. If this degree of the synodic cycle conjunction conjoins a Luminary, planet or angle in the nativity or in the progressed chart, it heralds the arrival of a significant relationship into one's life.[9]

Secondly, the pre-natal Sun-Venus conjunction, whether inferior or superior, is a determinant for the karmic pattern in relationships throughout one's lifetime. Also, if the degree of the synodic cycle conjunction of the Sun and any planet conjoin a natal or secondary progressed Luminary, planet or angle, the effect would be felt for the entire duration of the synodic cycle. Putting this into a time perspective, a New Moon landing on the Ascendant will hold its influence for 29 ½ days, whereas a conjunction of Mars and the Sun conjoining a natal angle will hold its influence for over two years.

This author also feels that a wealth of insight can be reaped by researching degree symbols for one's nine pre-natal synodic cycle conjunctions. This volume contains tables of these Sun-planet conjunctions by both date and Zodiacal degree for the 200 years from 1920 to 2120. It is also valuable to determine where in the overall cycles one's nine natal holograms lay. In subsequent chapters, pre-natal synodic cycle conjunctions will be shown to represent *soul groups* and collective purpose.

These nine natal Sun-planet holograms are determined by measuring the angular separation between the Sun and the other celestial body. Most astrology software programs can calculate these distance arcs and later in this book, how to perceive the holographic structure of the soul through these patterns will be shown. An examination of the author's nativity will illustrate a summary of his holograms.

From a metaphysical viewpoint, the more holographic phases that a soul possesses in the Oriental half of the synodic cycle, where the planet rises ahead of the Sun, increased openness to new life experience is found. In like manner, the more phases that one has in the Occidental half of the cycle, where a planet sets after the Sun, the more that soul is circumspect and cautious. By researching degree symbols for pre-natal synodic cycle conjunctions, the purpose of one's *soul group* is revealed.[10]

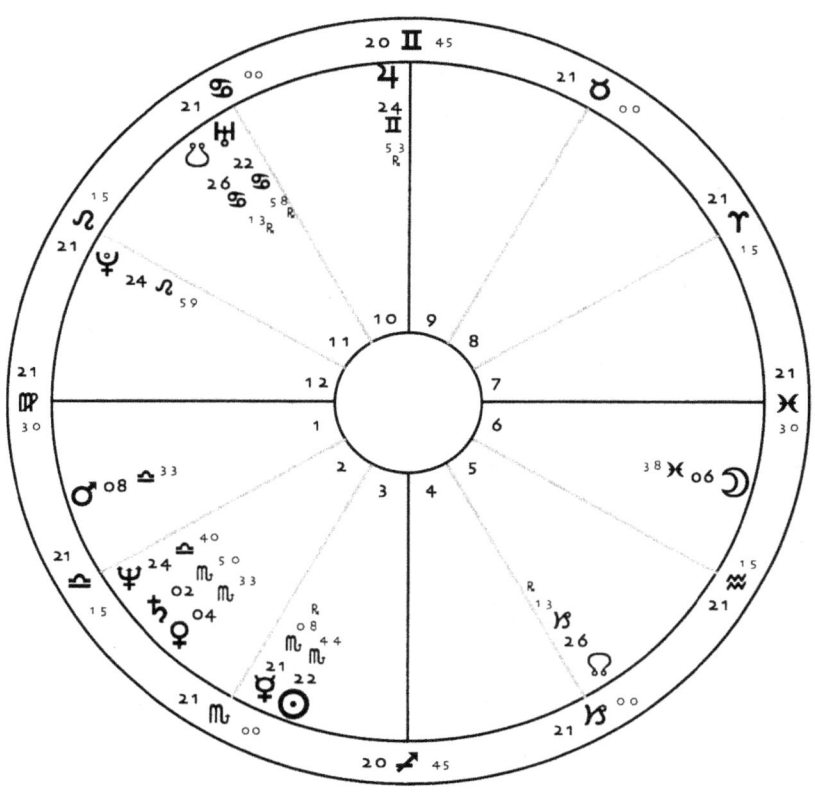

Hologram	Distance Arc	Cycle Phase	Pre-Natal Conjunction[11]	
Sun-Moon	103° 54' 06"	Occidental	Scorpio 15	6 Nov 1953
Sun-Mercury	01° 36' 02"	Combust	Scorpio 23	14 Nov 1953
Sun-Venus	18° 10' 55"	Oriental	Aries 24	13 Apr 1953
Sun-Mars	44° 11' 00"	Oriental	Cancer 17	8 Jul 1953
Sun-Jupiter	147° 51' 15"	Oriental	Gemini 4	24 May 1953
Sun-Saturn	19° 53' 42"	Oriental	Scorpio 1	23 Oct 1953
Sun-Uranus	119° 45' 36"	Oriental	Cancer 19	11 July 1953
Sun-Neptune	28° 03' 47"	Oriental	Libra 24	16 Oct 1953
Sun-Pluto	87° 45' 03"	Oriental	Leo 23	15 Aug 1953

Chapter One • *Holographic Transit Theory and Technique*

Sun-Moon – Scorpio 15
*In unconscious occult symbolism a group of laughing,
joyous children are playing upon five mounds of white sand.*

Sun-Mercury – Scorpio 23
*A little white rabbit rests contentedly in his cage;
before the eyes he metamorphoses into a fairy glade.*

Sun-Venus – Aries 24
*An open window of an old-fashioned room is seen,
the net curtain blowing inward into the shape of a cornucopia.*

Sun-Mars – Cancer 17
*A huge precious stone is so cut that its principal facet
mirrors the whole scene before it in sparkling miniature.*

Sun-Jupiter – Gemini 4
*A series of rooms in a hospitable house, opening one into the other,
are gaily decorated with holly and mistletoe.*

Sun-Saturn – Scorpio 1
*A sight-seeing omnibus is threading its way through crowded city traffic;
its occupants eagerly view the sights.*

Sun-Uranus – Cancer 19
*A fragile miss, representative of proud old blood,
is wed by a pompous priest to an eager youth of the new order.*

Sun-Neptune – Libra 24
*A marvelously colored and figured butterfly is spread before the eyes;
on its left side is an extra third wing.*

Sun-Pluto – Leo 23
*The scene is a circus crowded with spectators,
and in a moment of hush a bareback rider performs extraordinarily.*

What the astrologer is uncovering for himself or for his client by measuring these nine combined units of spatial motion is the precise point within the synodic cycle where the soul incarnated, and the all important Zodiacal degrees at the beginning of those cycles. It is the core thesis of this author that these holograms allow the astrologer to perceive the functioning of free will in the nativity, and to be able to calculate when the Light of God (the Sun) can regenerate the wholeness in a soul.

The ensouled planet obtains its life force energy from the Sun at the conjunction marking the start of a synodic cycle. Then, these Sun-planet celestial pairs become a moving holographic unit distributing Divine Energy throughout the 360 degrees of the Zodiac until their following conjunction occurs. Each soul is born with nine unique pathways connecting it with God, based on where in the synodic cycles birth occurred. This restorative power of the Sun is the love of God in action.

When a soul descends into manifestation, according to the doctrine of Simplicius, it is at a time when cosmic conditions resemble itself. Tragically, however, at the point of incarnation, most memory of past lives is erased, leaving souls without clear recall of their divine origins.[12] This is the human condition, and one form of spiritual service provided by astrologers is to show clients their cosmic imprint.

In the Germanic fable of Hansel and Gretel, wherein the two children leave a trail of breadcrumbs in the forest so as to find their way home, the crumbs are then eaten by animals, leaving the children lost and helpless. Almost tricked by a witch into being baked in an oven and devoured as food, the brother and sister escape, taking jewels from the witch's house with them. They are later reunited with their father.

The nine natal holograms are the breadcrumbs of the soul, placed there in mercy by a Loving Father who wishes all souls to return home to Him. Having been eaten by forest creatures, the lost soul without its trail of crumbs wanders helplessly at times during life, forgetting its way Home. Because its consciousness, once unified in Oneness with its Creator, has become split and divided into many fragments at birth, all souls need assistance in both how and when to realign with Higher Self.

The nine fragmented holograms of human consciousness are:

The Hologram of *Instinct*:	Sun-Moon
The Hologram of *Thought*:	Sun-Mercury
The Hologram of *Attachment*:	Sun-Venus
The Hologram of *Passion*:	Sun-Mars
The Hologram of *Judgment*:	Sun-Jupiter
The Hologram of *Responsibility*:	Sun-Saturn
The Hologram of *Enlightenment*:	Sun-Uranus
The Hologram of *Renunciation*:	Sun-Neptune
The Hologram of *Transformation*:	Sun-Pluto

One can think of these nine holograms as the *Jewels in the Crown of Thorns*. For each painful episode of difficult fate during life that causes a soul to lose its way, as seen in the transits occurring after birth, within the divine justice of God, there is also an equal measure of free will that may be acted on to deal with those fated circumstances. How and when souls can act from free will and become realigned with Higher Self is found by calculating when these holographic spatial patterns are repeating themselves in the heavens throughout life. By doing this for clients, astrologers can show free will and fate to be intertwined and mutually dependent.

Holographic Transits: Aligning the Soul with Higher Self

Astrologers can work with holographic transits in two ways. First, a Sun-planet phase angle in the nativity that cyclically reforms in the heavens can be used as an invaluable counterpart to standard transit technique. If, for example, a client is undergoing a transit of Pluto conjoining the natal Sun and a chapter of life is closing and coming to a painful, yet necessary ending, the current and the next Sun-Pluto holographic return charts can be evaluated side-by-side with the transits.

While the powerful and intense Pluto transit over the Sun is being explained as an inescapable fate to be accepted with guts and courage, astrologers can also enter into a spiritual discussion with the client, explaining that other charts exist that show when alignment of one's free will with Higher Self can be made conscious. In this way, a balance is struck between fate and free will during the delineation.

The second technique for using holographic transits is when spiritually oriented clients wish to know when, through meditation, they can more consciously align with Higher Self. In some cases, there may be no difficult transits or progressions currently in place. Astrologers would then calculate the dates for their upcoming Sun-planet phase angle returns for each of their nine natal holograms.[13]

For the Sun-Moon hologram, these spatial cycles last just a month, but Sun-Mars, for example, would have holographic return horoscopes that are two years apart. The charts can be presented to the client as either a stand-alone horoscope, similar to a solar return, or as a bi-wheel chart in which the holographic transit is placed into the houses of the nativity. In the latter, a more comprehensive view occurs.[14]

The following table shows the frequency of the nine holographic transits:

Hologram	Frequency of Holographic Transit	Synodic Period
Sun-Moon	12 to 13 times per year	29.53 days
Sun-Mercury	3 to 4 times per year	115.88 days
Sun-Venus	once every 19 months	583.9 days
Sun-Mars	once every 25-26 months	779.9 days
Sun-Jupiter	once every 13 months	399 days
Sun-Saturn	once every 12 1/2 months	378 days
Sun-Uranus	once a year	370 days
Sun-Neptune	once a year	367.4 days
Sun-Pluto	once a year	366.7 days

With the inferior planet of Mercury, distance arcs between it and the Sun will actually match the natal hologram six times a year. However, three of these will be when Mercury is either retrograde in the heavens but direct in the natal chart, or direct in the heavens and retrograde in the nativity. The astrologer should only include the Sun-Mercury holograms that match the orbital motion in the nativity.

Likewise, for the inferior planet of Venus, distance arcs between it and the Sun will match the natal hologram twice during the 19-month synodic period. But, as with Mercury, one of these dates will be when Venus is retrograde in the heavens but direct in the natal chart, or when it is direct in the sky and retrograde in the nativity. Limit the once-in-19-month calculation to matching orbital direction.

This bi-wheel chart (*facing page*) is for a female client whose marriage is ending. Transit Pluto stationed retrograde conjunct her natal Sun within 05' of arc. She was under a tremendous amount of emotional duress and psychological pressure. She did not want the marriage to end, and wanted her husband "to be like his old self again."[15]

The consultation revealed that the marriage had been deteriorating for some years, and that during an initial bout of menopausal symptoms, as she became overweight and depressed, her husband had begun a friendship with a woman at work with whom he then had an affair. Despite attempts to reconcile the marriage, and losing weight and feeling better about herself again, her husband had discovered through the affair that he wanted more out of life and had decided to move on from her.[16]

Chapter One • *Holographic Transit Theory and Technique*

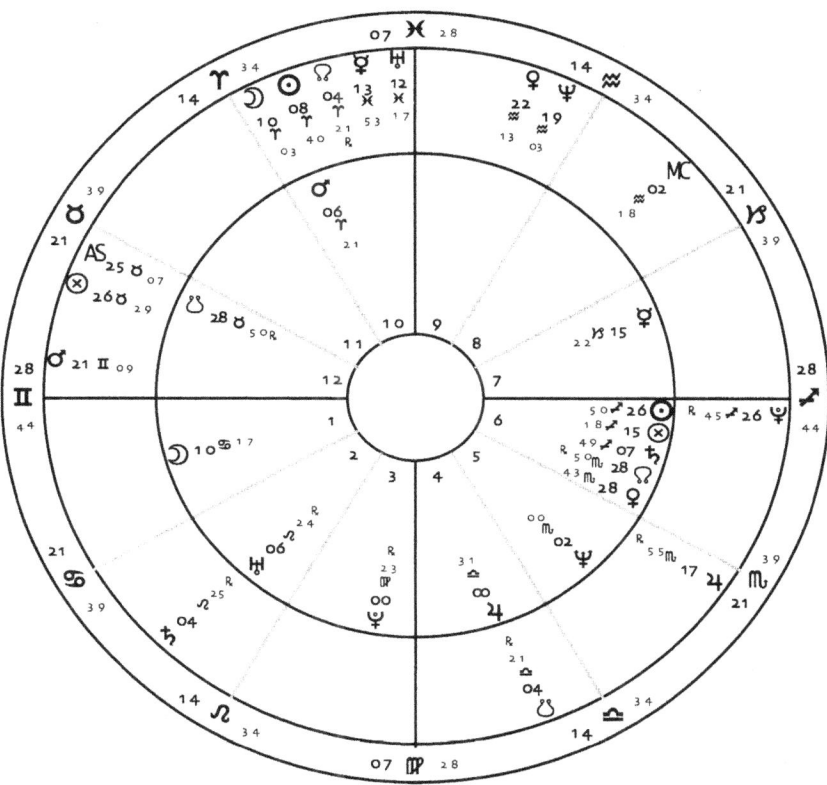

These fated episodes in life are extremely painful, and a professional astrology consultation ought to do more than just point out the obvious planetary correspondences that match what the client is experiencing. There is value, of course, in validating what the client is going through by showing which planetary influences are active by transit. However, a deeper level of understanding can be imparted by using the holographic transits.

This client has a natal Sun-Pluto hologram of 116° 27' 11". Her most recent Sun-Pluto phase angle return had occurred on 13 April 2006, during the very week that she had come to accept the marriage ending. This is that holographic transit:[17]

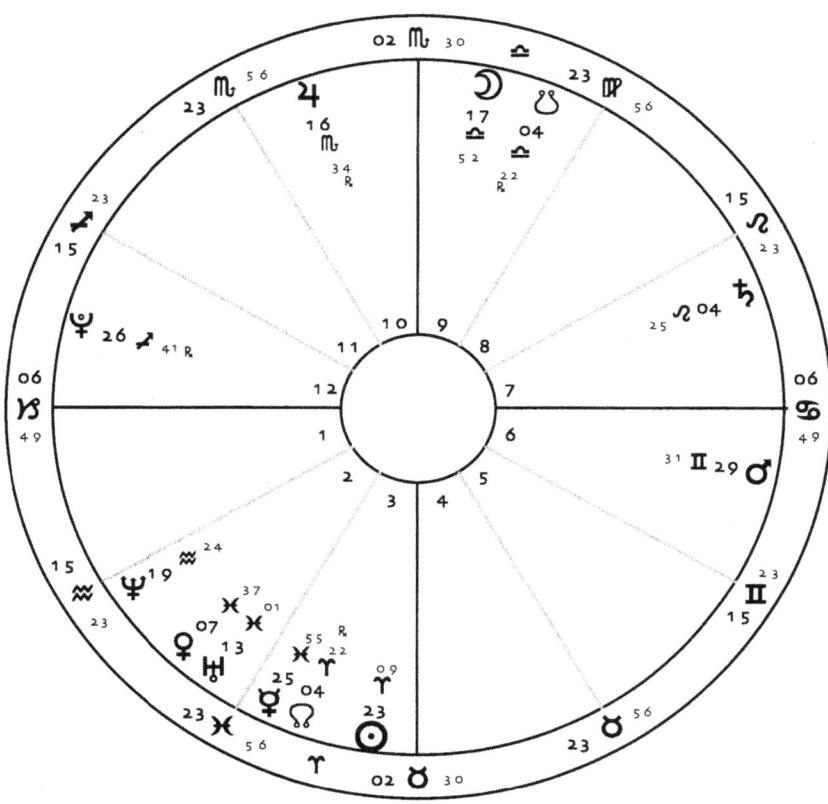

The astrologer sees that the distance arc between the Sun and Pluto has replicated itself in the heavens. The key to understanding these charts is for the astrologer to realize that he is looking at a fragmented hologram of the soul that is longing to be restored to wholeness by the Light of God (the Sun). In this case, it is the desire for transformation that is personified by a Sun-Pluto phase angle. The intercepted Sun in the 3rd house and Pluto in the 12th were both quite relevant for her.

An intense fear of being alone (Pluto in 12th) had submerged her reason and logic (Sun intercepted in 3rd), but on a soul level there was a deep desire for renewal and healing. This level of regeneration was no longer possible within the marriage since much of her essence was compromised obsessing about his relationship with the other woman. When the symbol for the rising degree was revealed to her in the context of it depicting a longing in the soul to become whole again, she wept.

Chapter One • *Holographic Transit Theory and Technique*

From Sepharial's translation of *La Volasfera*, for Capricorn 7:[18]

A heart pierced by a nail.

This is the index of a nature that is capable of strong attachment, both to things and persons, and yet with something of selfish design in all that he espouses. Consequently he cannot fail to meet with trouble, and his chagrin will arouse bitter feelings of resentment against others who may have thwarted his designs. Hence spring various rivalries and feuds, and these operate in his life to produce ruin and desolation, so that in the end he has nothing left but himself to care for and all the world besides to hate and rail against. It is a degree of JEALOUSY.

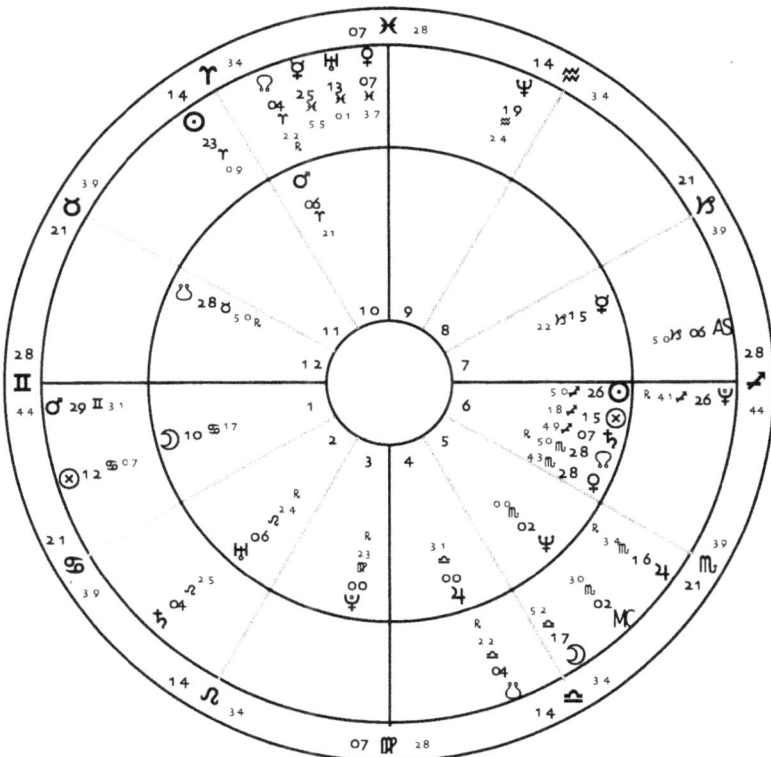

This bi-wheel chart overlays the holographic transit into the houses of the nativity of the client whose marriage is ending. Venus is exactly angular on the Midheaven, and it is her plan now to return to school to pursue a new career to help restore her self-esteem. The holographic Sun in her natal 11th house tells her that she must look to her future in addition to building new friendships. An angular Mars-Pluto opposition on the horizon was explained as an opportunity to rebuild confidence through the letting go of the marriage. When the transit South Node, symbolizing people and things exiting one's life, reached its conjunction with her Descendant ruler, Jupiter, she finally hired a lawyer and initiated the divorce proceedings.

The astrologer knows that a Pluto transit in stationary conjunction with the natal Sun will have an ultimate duration of approximately twenty-two months between the first one degree applying orb and the last separating orb. Rebuilding one's life after a devastating experience such as this requires the transit's entire duration. Within that two-year period two Sun-Pluto holographic transits will occur.

These two key windows of time exist for the holographic realignment of the soul with the Higher Self so that one's free will can be consciously exercised during the painful burden of an unwanted fate. The astrologer using the holographic transits along side standard transit calculations is able to balance the delineation with a discussion of both free will and fate. By first interpreting the holographic transit as a stand-alone phase angle return chart, and then explaining it as part of a bi-wheel chart with the nativity, much valuable insight is imparted to the client.

This astrologer would always look at the symbol for the rising degree of the phase angle return chart, and also at the house position of both the Sun and the planet in question for that specific hologram. Overlaying this chart into the natal houses is a second vantage point from which to view a longing to be restored to wholeness through the Light of God, and to know the free will and fate braided in the soul.

This client also very much benefited from seeing the next holographic transit that occurred within the lengthy two-year influence of transit Pluto conjoining the Sun. It is helpful to define the transformational Sun-Pluto hologram as a dual process. In the first phase there is a dismantling of any existing reality that prevents a soul from knowing its core Self. In the second stage, a rebuilding of the life takes place.

Because a Sun-Pluto synodic period is 366.7 days, replication of natal distance arcs between the Sun and Pluto occur in the heavens once a year. The client can be told that the first holographic transit represents the free will of the soul aligning itself with Higher Self in order to eliminate and dismantle any of the current life conditions preventing transformation. A second holographic transit, occurring the following year, will show the necessary renewal and rebuilding of one's life.

Chapter One • *Holographic Transit Theory and Technique*

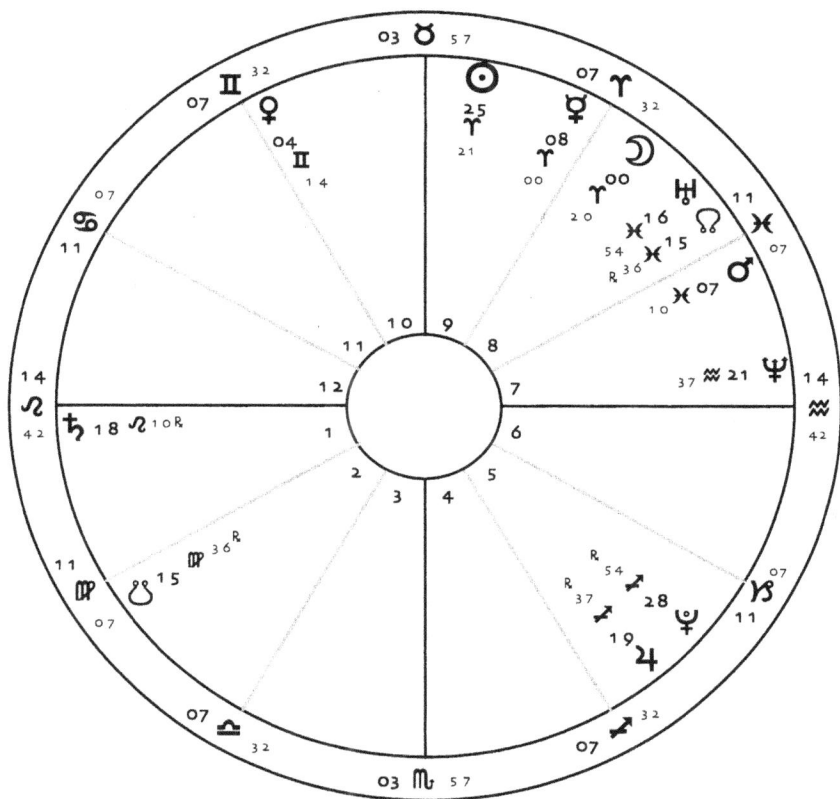

The chart above shows her 15 April 2007 holographic transit of the Sun and Pluto. The astrologer can see that her natal Sun-Pluto distance arc has again replicated itself in the heavens. This chart was explained as the second phase of the two-step hologram of transformation. The 9th-house Sun confirmed the correctness of her choice to return to school to pursue a new career. This alignment of the free will in her soul with Higher Self was additionally validated by Mars being in the precise degree of her natal Midheaven (same degree as Venus in the previous hologram).

The Moon in the powerful 0° Aries Point was presented as proof that her new life would begin to manifest at this time, and the 5th-house Pluto, in the exact degree of her natal Descendant, was stated to be evidence that she would be able to put the ended marriage behind her and become open to a new romantic interest in her life.

But it wasn't until the symbol for the rising degree was shared with her that she began to feel assured that her new life would be on the right track by next year.

Leo 15 from La Volasfera

> *A figure like the angel of the Sun (Michael), standing erect,*
> *and striking the earth with the point of a dazzling sword.*

It indicates a person of very superior ability in some special direction; one in whom the power of government will reside; a mind somewhat ambitious, but conscious of its own powers—which are of no common order—so that no unjust advantage is taken. In some sphere of life the native be an imposing figure, or may do something which may call for wide recognition. Fame and power attend this degree. It is one of SUPERIORITY.

Overlaying this holographic transit into the houses of her natal chart, we observe:

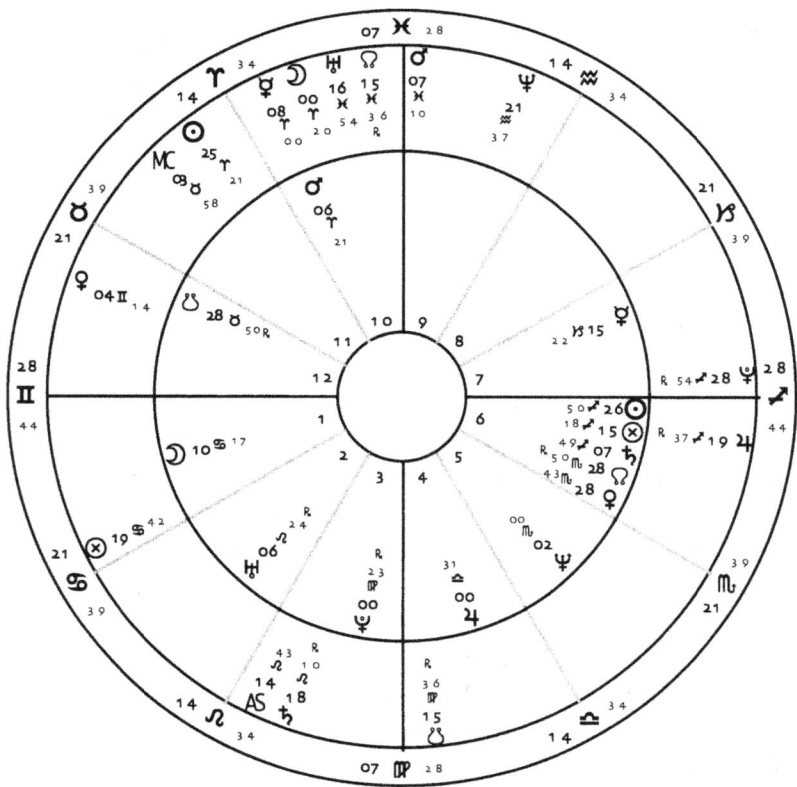

Chapter One • *Holographic Transit Theory and Technique*

The previous year's holographic transit with a paran of Mars and Pluto angular on the horizon will be transformed into a new paran with Mars on the MC and Pluto on the Descendant. In an allegorical fashion, the two consecutive phase angle return charts were communicated to her as the twofold process of the hologram of transformation seeking wholeness via the soul aligning with Higher Self. The Light of God was described as acting through the laser beam of the Sun.

It is hoped that this case study has provided a foundation from which to employ the holographic transit technique and to assimilate its theory.

In this section of the chapter, we have been discussing how holographic transits are an opportunity for aligning one's soul with Higher Self through the mechanism of free will. The fundamental basis for this notion is that the Sun is the necessary divine energy required for the integration of planetary forces into consciousness.

When an astrologer calculates a natal Sun-planet distance arc and then computes when that spatial pattern is reforming in the heavens, he becomes an oracle for his client, seeing into a fragmented hologram of the soul that is longing for the Light of God to restore it to wholeness. The Sun is this Light, and is our divine essence.

When a standard transit interpretation is given based on individual planets aspecting the nativity, *astrologers are watching time structures within the space-time continuum, and are working primarily within the realm of fate.* This is why, despite the best intentions to explain the transit in a way that would offer the client an opportunity for growth, most astrologers will have to admit that the client often just wants to know, *"when will it be over and what will happen to me?"*

It is the opinion of this author that a mirage exists within the world of astrology, one wherein professional astrologers talk among themselves about all of the good that their methods and techniques are doing for clients, yet there is almost a blind assumption made that clients are actually receiving and integrating these benefits.

What if this is not always so? Perhaps the environment created within transit consultations produces temporary relief in which clients are momentarily lifted above the painful challenges of their present fate, but by the next day or the next week they inevitably descend back into pre-consultation levels of awareness, thus not reaping any permanent benefit from the appointment. Yes, they may play the tape over and over again deriving some succor, but the realities of life soon return.

It is the core premise of this volume that the Sun is necessary for integrating transit influences into one's heart so that one takes spiritual responsibility for choosing from an awakened free will, and not from a subconscious reaction to the difficult circumstances of fate. How and when to help clients align with Higher Self and to make conscious choices from free will is found within the holographic transits.

This book recommends adding phase angle return charts to your standard transit interpretations so that the Sun becomes involved in all planetary delineations. In this way, clients are given both an explanation about the transits occurring in the nativity that produce fated circumstances, and are also told how Higher Self can illumine free will when the natal Sun-planet holograms reform in the heavens.

Some astrologers may wonder if one can calculate these holographic transits manually using an ephemeris. *The answer is yes, if one only requires the date of the occurrence, but not the exact time.* These more rudimentary calculations would be for clients who only wished to know on which day a phase angle return was to be exact so that they could meditate and seek alignment with Higher Self.[19]

On page 20, one finds that the author's Sun-Jupiter distance arc is 147° 51' 15". Using an ephemeris, how does one go about locating the day of the year on which his Sun-Jupiter holographic transit, or phase angle return, would occur?

The astrologer would bear in mind that Jupiter is presently transiting Scorpio and that during 2006, for example, Jupiter stations retrograde at 18°, and then stations direct at 8°. Seeing that Jupiter has a natal distance arc of ±148° from his Sun, one could deduce that the Sun would have to be in 6° to 16° of Aries for a holographic transit to occur that year. This narrows our search to late March or early April.

In this midnight ephemeris for April 2006 on the facing page, one sees that late on the 4th, the distance arc between the Sun and Jupiter reaches about 148° (15° Aries to 17° Scorpio). This example shows how, having once calculated the natal phase angle, one can then "eyeball" the exact date of the holographic transit in an ephemeris.[20]

The Supporting Role of the Moon

The Earth and its Moon are held in a joint orbit around the Sun by a combined center of gravity located some one thousand miles beneath the surface of the Earth. Esoterically, the Sun represents spirit, the Moon symbolizes soul, and Earth is an attribute for matter. Through this symbolic relationship,

Chapter One • *Holographic Transit Theory and Technique*

April 2006 — Midnight Ephemeris — Time Zone: **PDT** (07:00 West)

Day	☉	☽	+12 Hr ☽	True ☊	☿	♀	♂	♃	♄	♅	♆	♇
1 Sa	11♈2451	20♉1632	27♉1408	04♈20R	15♓10D	25♒02D	22♊42D	7♏42R	04♌23R	12♓25D	19♒07D	26♐45R
2 Su	12 2404	04♊1105	06 ♊1149	2604	19	15 45	26 04	23 16	7 37	04 23	12 28	19 09	26 44
3 M	13 2315	17 2712	23 5839	04 18	16 25	27 06	23 50	7 32	04 22	12 32	19 10	26 44
4 Tu	14 2224	00♋2407	06♋5435	04 17	17 09	28 09	24 24	7 27	04 22	12 35	19 12	26 44
5 W	15 2131	12 5846	19 0857	04 17D	17 56	29 11	24 59	7 21	04 22	12 38	19 13	26 44
6 Th	16 2035	25 1507	01♌2175	04 17	18 46	00♓14	25 33	7 16	04 22D	12 41	19 14	26 44
7 F	17 1937	07♌2174	13 1514	04 18	19 40	01 18	26 07	7 10	04 22	12 44	19 16	26 43
8 Sa	18 1836	19 1104	25 0544	04 19	20 36	02 21	26 41	7 04	04 22	12 47	19 17	26 43
9 Su	19 1733	00♍5945	06♍5338	04 20	21 36	03 25	27 16	6 58	04 23	12 50	19 19	26 43
10 M	20 1628	12 4750	18 4247	04 22	22 38	04 29	27 50	6 52	04 23	12 52	19 20	26 42
11 Tu	21 1521	24 3854	00♎3632	04 23	23 43	05 33	28 25	6 46	04 24	12 55	19 21	26 42
12 W	22 1412	06♎3600	12 3736	04 23R	24 50	06 37	28 59	6 40	04 24	12 58	19 23	26 42
13 Th	23 1300	18 4134	24 4808	04 22	26 00	07 42	29 34	6 33	04 25	13 01	19 24	26 41
14 F	24 1147	00♏5728	07♏0944	04 20	27 12	08 46	00♋08	6 27	04 26	13 04	19 25	26 41
15 Sa	25 1032	13 2504	19 4335	04 18	28 26	09 51	00 43	6 20	04 27	13 07	19 26	26 40
16 Su	26 0914	26 0522	02♐3029	04 15	29 42	10 57	01 17	6 14	04 28	13 09	19 27	26 40
17 M	27 0755	08♐5902	15 3104	04 11	01♈01	12 02	01 52	6 07	04 30	13 12	19 29	26 39
18 Tu	28 0635	22 0639	28 4549	04 08	02 21	13 08	02 27	6 00	04 31	13 15	19 30	26 38
19 W	29 0513	05♑2839	12♑1509	04 05	03 44	14 13	03 02	5 53	04 32	13 17	19 31	26 38
20 Th	00♉0349	19 0522	25 5918	04 04	05 08	15 19	03 37	5 46	04 34	13 20	19 32	26 37
21 F	01 0223	02♒5655	09♒5809	04 03D	06 34	16 25	04 11	5 39	04 35	13 23	19 33	26 37
22 Sa	02 0056	17 0254	24 1058	04 04	08 03	17 32	04 46	5 32	04 37	13 25	19 34	26 36
23 Su	02 5927	01♓2206	08♓3555	04 05	09 33	18 38	05 21	5 24	04 39	13 28	19 35	26 35
24 M	03 5757	15 5211	23 1011	04 07	11 04	19 45	05 56	5 17	04 41	13 30	19 36	26 34
25 Tu	04 5624	00♈2924	07♈4908	04 07	12 38	20 51	06 31	5 10	04 43	13 33	19 37	26 34
26 W	05 5450	15 0840	22 2710	04 07R	14 13	21 58	07 06	5 02	04 45	13 35	19 38	26 33
27 Th	06 5314	29 4351	06♉5753	04 05	15 51	23 05	07 42	4 55	04 48	13 37	19 38	26 32
28 F	07 5137	14♉0830	21 1500	04 02	17 30	24 12	08 17	4 47	04 50	13 40	19 39	26 31
29 Sa	08 4958	28 1646	05♊1316	03 57	19 10	25 20	08 52	4 40	04 52	13 42	19 40	26 30
30 Su	09 4817	12♊0407	18 4905	03 51	20 53	26 27	09 27	4 32	04 55	13 44	19 41	26 29
1 M	10 4634	25 2802	02♋0100	03 45	22 37	27 35	10 02	4 25	04 58	13 47	19 41	26 28

astrologers perceive the central role that spirit (the Sun) plays in holding both body and soul together.

In our case study, the Sun-Pluto cycle was shown to last for a year. A mechanism takes place between one phase angle return and the next in which transformation assimilates into conscious awareness. Inside the synodic period of the Sun and Pluto, a crucial subcycle also exists. Distance arcs in the nativity between the Moon and Pluto reform monthly in the heavens as well. These lunar holograms show when the soul can assimilate the Light of God as it is entering Higher Self.

As in medical astrology, where the Moon rules the esophagus, stomach, pancreas and the digestive fluids, without which food and its nutritional value would be worthless to the human body, a very important spiritual contribution is also made by the Moon. For the necessary awakening of the soul to the Light of its Higher Self as it perceives distinctions between free will and fate, a reflection must occur.

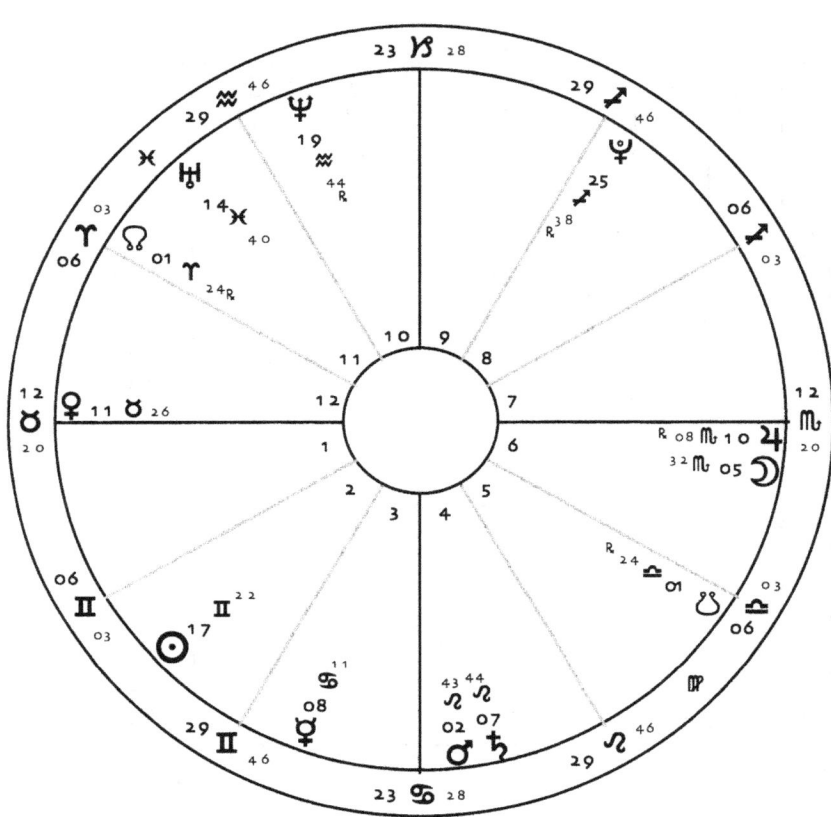

This is that client's Moon-Pluto phase angle return of 8 June 2006. One sees that her natal distance arc of 50° 06' has replicated itself in the heavens. This date, and the dates of the twelve other Moon-Pluto phase angle returns occurring between April 2006 and April 2007 were given to her. These charts were explained as when to meditate and to digest the transformation of her Sun-Pluto holographic cycle. This particular phase angle return occurred when she was feeling quite rudderless in her life, and still coming to grips with her marriage being over. The symbol for the rising degree, mirroring her feelings, was brought to her attention:

Taurus 13 from Charubel

*An anchor unattached to any vessel's chain,
but lying with its hook fast to a rock, the cable broke.*

This supporting role of the Moon when working with holographic transits gives the astrologer incremental dates to present to the client. The lunar holograms that occur on a monthly basis will show when that particular holographic cycle will be digested and assimilated into consciousness. With the longer cycles, such as the 25–26 month Sun-Mars synodic period, or the 19-month Sun-Venus cycle, a larger number of Moon-planet phase angle return charts will require calculation. In the shorter 116-day Sun-Mercury synodic cycle, only four lunar holograms occur.

A core premise of holographic transits is that the Sun is necessary for integrating the planetary forces into consciousness. Using these charts alongside of standard transit calculations allows astrologers to view the interplay of free will and fate taking place within the soul of the client. The theoretical underpinning for this process is that one becomes fragmented into nine holograms at birth, and a longing exists within all souls to be made whole by the Light of God (the Sun). The Moon supports this process, as her separate holograms with the planets reflect that light.

The central theme of the Sun-planet holographic cycle is best perceived by looking at the two consecutive phase angle return charts side by side. This astrologer sees a great deal through the symbolism of the rising degree, and he would always make note of the house positions of the Sun and the relevant planet. An angle in a degree of an upcoming station, or a stationary planet in the chart are also critical factors.

The synastry between these phase angle return charts and the important people in one's life reveals the contribution of others to one's soul growth during a synodic period. As there are nine concurrent holographic cycles in spatial movement at all times, astrologers working with this system will experience a pronounced effect on their consciousness. It is the belief of this astrologer that by acknowledging the eminence of the Sun while delineating transit influences, one's heart opens wider.

Secondary Progressions Interacting with Phase Angle Returns

This author has used secondary progressions for over thirty years. It has become irrefutable to him that the progressed horoscope shows the spiritual evolution of the soul as it fulfills its natal promise, that is to say, unfolds its human potential over a lifetime. Tertiary and minor progressions underpin this evolution on astral and mental levels of consciousness, as the author illustrated in his *Progressions*.

This astrologer has observed a perceptible relationship between the concurrent and synchronous unfolding of life events as secondary progressions and transits become exact by aspect during the identical period of time. The death of his mother, as illustrated in the tri-wheel chart on page 14, showed a progressed solar eclipse and a transit of Uranus over the natal Moon occurring at the same time. Transits also trigger progressed aspects, as was first elucidated by C.E.O. Carter in his *Law of Excitation*.[21] Do secondary progressions also interact with phase angle returns?

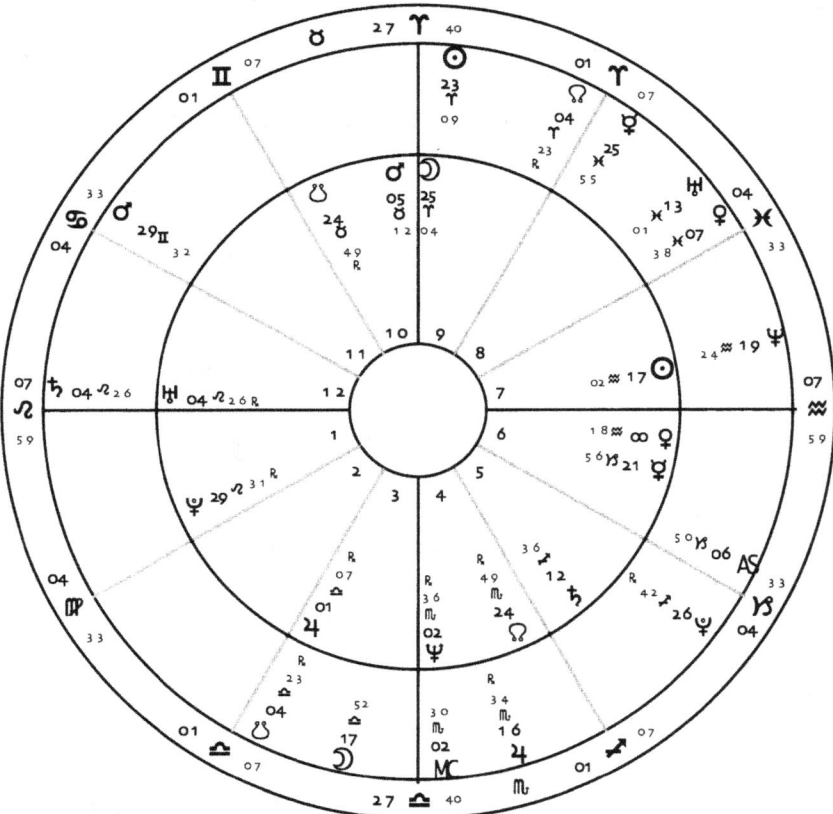

This bi-wheel chart shows the secondary progressions of our case study client for 13 April 2006 in the inner wheel, while her Sun-Pluto holographic transit of that same day has been placed into her progressed houses. The identical GMT is used for both horoscopes. The astrologer sees that a partile (exact to the minute of arc) conjunction of Saturn in 04° Leo 26' has formed with her progressed Uranus.

This aspect was also a prolonged stationary conjunction, as Saturn had turned direct just eight days earlier in 04° Leo 22'. One also observes that the Midheaven in the phase angle return is conjunct her secondary progressed Neptune, exact to 06' of arc. Each of these aspects poignantly illustrate her experience at the time. A coming to terms with the reality of radical change can be seen in Saturn conjoining Uranus, and her anxious despair over a publicly visible scandal emerging during the divorce is evident in the conjunction between Neptune and the Midheaven.[22]

The Sun-Pluto midpoint of 24° Aquarius 55' in the holographic transit is closely square her progressed Lunar Nodes, exact within 06' of arc. One deduces from this aspect that her hologram of transformation was vital to alter her life direction.

Readers also saw on page 27 how this phase angle return chart interacts with her nativity, as Venus was in angular conjunction with her natal MC. It is clear that with her secondary progressed Venus having just ingressed into Aquarius, she is now redefining her femininity for the first time in twenty-four years since her Venus progressed into Capricorn in 1982. With progressed Venus applying to a trine with her natal Jupiter, she stands to financially benefit from this divorce.[23]

Recapitulation

General rules can therefore be laid down for astrologers working with this trio of techniques: basic transits, secondary progressions, and holographic transits. A *Law of Three* is repeatedly evident in the realms of metaphysical inquiry, and an astrologer will see horoscopic factors formerly hidden when adding phase angle return charts to his analytic and intuitive repertoire.

By holding this basic premise in mind-that the soul is a fragmented hologram seeking wholeness through the Light of God-astrologers can then perceive how a client's present fate (basic transits), ongoing spiritual evolution (progressions), and alignment of free will with Higher Self (holographic transits) are interacting as a unified field. Clients can reach an elevated awareness through an awakened free will when they are informed of the timing of these holographic transits.

In this opening chapter, birth has been outlined as the soul entering the space-time continuum and therefore becoming subjected to both physical and spiritual laws. It has also been theorized that free will and fate correspond with space and time, respectively, and that the nativity is comprised of a dual holographic disposition.

The soul is defined as being split into nine fragmented holograms at birth, with the primary importance of the Sun and its synodic cycles being affirmed as necessary for the re-integration of planetary forces into consciousness via the heart center. The Moon has an assimilating role in this alignment of free will with Higher Self.

When employing this system of holographic transits, comprised of solar and lunar phase angle returns, astrologers open a door and step into an interpretive world that balances delineations between fate and free will. In the following chapters, instructions are given for how to understand the various phase angles at birth, as well as for how and when to use different Sun-planet phase angle return charts and their lunar derivatives. Pre-natal synodic cycles and the collective influences of *soul groups* are also discussed. Synodic cycle conjunction tables are included.

Chapter Two
Sun-Moon Phase Angle Returns

Sun-Moon Phase Angle at Birth

The distance arc between the natal Sun and Moon forms the fundamental nature of the soul. This hologram of instinct is critical to one's ability to adapt to changing circumstances in life, as well as being necessary for keeping individuals aligned with their innate and inborn characteristics. Family, and the ancestral bloodline influences, can also be understood by this most basic of all of the natal holograms.

There are several ways for astrologers to study the nature of the Sun-Moon phase angle. The most popular is the eight-phase lunation cycle.[24] Another way is to use this author's Sabian Aspect Orb technique. The degree symbols for angular separations between the Sun and Moon, and between the Moon and the Earth create a three-dimensional hologram for the Luminaries. The easiest way to visualize this is to place the glyph for the Earth into one's tropical nativity.[25] This is the author's horoscope including the glyph for the Earth:

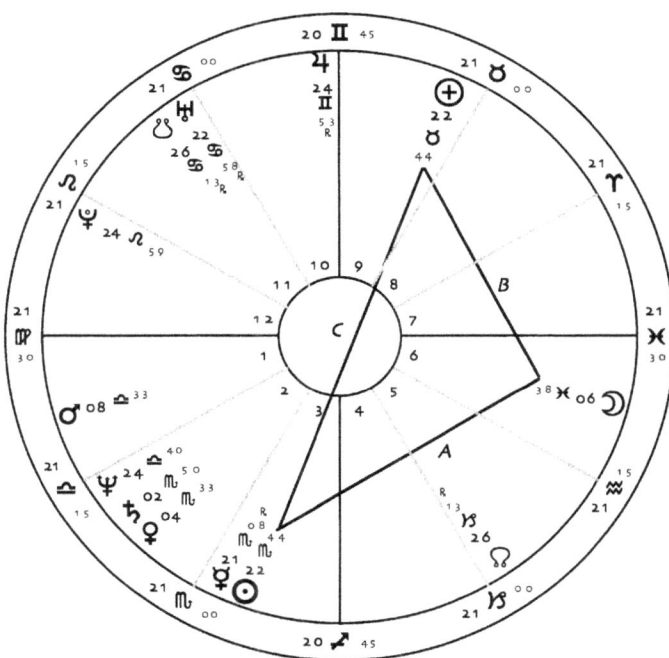

Distance arc *A* is 103° 54' 06", the angular separation between his Sun and Moon. Distance arc *B* is 76° 05' 54", the measurement between his Moon and the Earth. Together, the two arcs total 180° 00' 00". Using his Sabian Aspect Orb technique, arc *A* equates to the 14th degree of Cancer, and arc *B* is equivalent to the 17th degree of Gemini.[26] Observe that these two degrees are antiscia, or solstice points, of one another.[27] Sun-Earth arc *C* is always a constant, measuring exactly 180° 00' 00".

In holography, to create a three-dimensional hologram, a half-silvered mirror is used with two laser beams (reference and object). The first stream of light goes straight to a photographic plate, while a second beam is deflected to the object being photographed and from there, directed onward to the film negative.

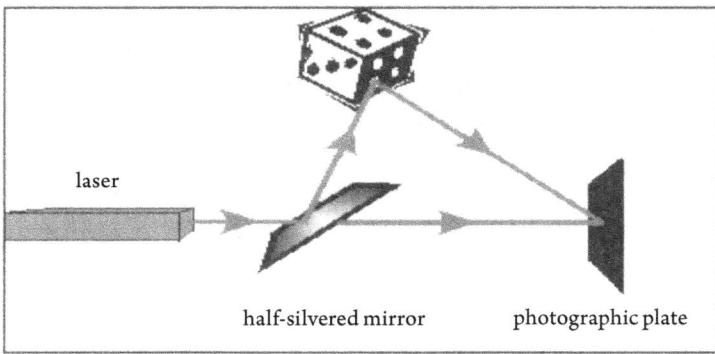

The laser is the Sun, the photographic plate is the soul at birth, and the object being photographed as a three-dimensional image is the Moon (or one of the eight solar system planets). When creating the nine microcosmic natal holograms, this "half-silvered mirror," on a macrocosmic level, is the Zodiac.

To enter this holographic universe, one uses the symbolical dimension of astrology as the "door." The derived degree symbols for arcs *A* and *B* reveal energies in a soul bequeathed by the biological parents, and handed down through the ancestral lineage and family bloodlines. The degree symbols for these distance arcs show how the laser of the Sun permeates a soul with the imprint of the Zodiac. For the author, we find Cancer 14 and Gemini 17 from Charubel to be:

A man, standing before an audience, with all the paraphernalia of a juggler.

This denotes one having all-round accomplishments. He is never at a loss through lack of resources. He is capable of turning his hand or his wits to anything.

Chapter Two • *Sun–Moon Phase Angle Returns*

*A square, containing twelve small squares,
resembling the breast-plate of the Jewish high priest.*

Denotes one of a reverential and devotional disposition. Very secretive, a student of the occult, and one capable of mighty deeds as a magician.

The Sun-Moon hologram at birth is quite often linked to individuals with whom we are connected on a soul level by exact synastry conjunctions. Wives, husbands, children, siblings, parents, and grandparents will have planets, lunar nodes, or horoscopic angles in the same degrees as one's Sun-Moon distance arc, or as one's Moon-Earth distance arc. The opposing degree is also often found in synastry conjunction so both degrees of the axis should be considered.

For the author, Capricorn 14 forms exact synastry conjunctions with his father's ruler, Mercury, and with his former wife's Sun in his marriage of 1983 to 1994. Gemini-Sagittarius 17 are the exact degrees of his younger daughter's MC/IC axis, and are the degrees of his girlfriend's lunar nodes, providing evidence that both of these relationships fall into the "soul-connection" category.

Most astrologers are trained to first look at the Luminaries when interpreting the nativity, and especially so when the Lights form close Ptolemaic aspects. If the Sun and Moon do not form a conventional aspect, note the phase relationship. A special consideration is whether it is in the waxing or waning half of the cycle. Taking this analysis a step further, convert the distance arc between the Lights into a degree symbol to determine one's portal of intuition.

This exact Sun-Moon phase angle calculation is required when using the system of holographic transits, since this precise distance arc is used to compute phase angle return charts. To see the three-dimensional relationship of a Sun-Moon hologram, the position of the Earth needs to be inserted into the tropical nativity, thereby creating the additional distance arc between the Moon and the Earth.

Pre-Natal Sun-Moon Synodic Cycle

The New Moon prior to birth, along with its degree symbol, gives insight about the instinctual nature of the soul being carried over from past lives. Countless souls, of course, incarnate over a lunar month's time and these beings, born within the identical Sun-Moon synodic cycle as ourselves, are part of a larger spiritual family with us. This concept explains the mysterious feeling of fraternity one has when meeting an astrological "time-twin", a soul born during the same lunar cycle.

At the end of this book is a Table of New Moons and Eclipses for the 200 years from 1920 to 2120. Readers can locate their pre-natal Sun-Moon synodic cycle and its conjunction (New Moon) degree. By researching degree symbols for that New Moon, insight about one's past life instinctual nature can be found.

If the New Moon before birth was also a solar eclipse, its effect throughout life is especially pronounced, and its degree symbols should be studied carefully. This author has observed that when the New Moon immediately prior to birth was an eclipse, then that degree is often found in synastric conjunction or opposition with the souls with whom one forms the most transformational relationships.

An example of a past life instinctual tendency being revealed through the degree symbol for a solar eclipse occurring immediately prior to birth, can be found in the horoscope of George W. Bush. Born on 6 July 1946 at 07:26 in New Haven, CT, at the waxing first quarter square of the Sun and Moon, and with a natal distance arc of 92° 56' between the Luminaries, on 29 June 1946, a week before his birth, a solar eclipse occurred in 06° Cancer 48'. The bi-wheel chart on the facing page places this pre-natal solar eclipse into Mr Bush's natal houses. From *La Volasfera*, for Cancer 7:

> *An iron gauntlet, a sword, and a scourge lying together upon the stump of a tree.*

It indicates a person of strong personality, but of a tyrannous nature, who, by force of arms and aggression generally, will press forward regardless of the merits of others and insensible of their feelings. His hand, though strong, is frequently unjust and cruel in its action, impelled by the motive that "might is right"; and, when opposed, is capable of extreme cruelty and selfishness. In certain natures the influence of this degree generates the common-place "bully." It is a degree of SELF-ASSERTION.

Using Sun-Moon Holographic Transits

There are several ways in which Sun-Moon holographic transits can be used:

1. *To pinpoint ovulation dates and times for couples wishing to conceive.* The Sun-Moon phase angle in a woman's horoscope is a key for determining when during the month she is ovulating and ready to conceive. Astrologers can calculate a female's Sun-Moon holographic transits for the next few months and present the dates to the couple for when to have fertile relations. The Moon moves a degree about every two hours, and astrologers should advise clients that there is a four hour window of time for these charts to bear fruit (two hours before and after).[28]

Chapter Two • *Sun–Moon Phase Angle Returns*

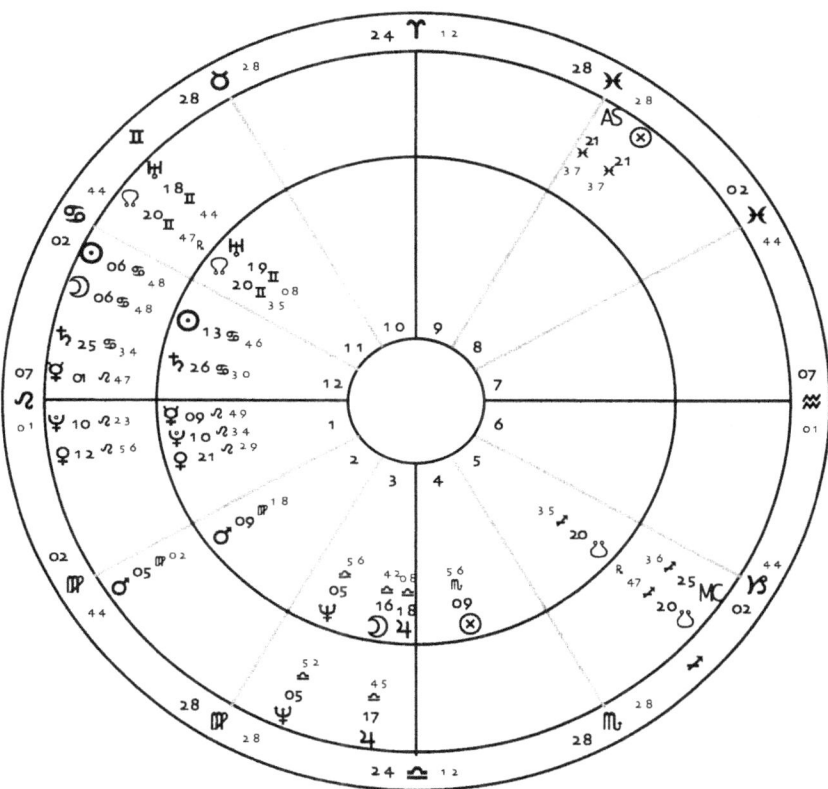

2. ***To align monthly with the instinctual nature and the innate self.*** Sometimes we don't feel as if we are completely ourselves. Illness, stress, worry, the demands of work, heavy responsibilities at home, and fear of the future can all weigh heavily on the soul, obscuring the instinctual nature and causing a person to feel fragmented and separated spiritually from the innate self.

If clients describe these symptoms when scheduling a consultation, astrologers can calculate monthly Sun-Moon phase angle return charts for the client for the next year. At the time of the Sun-Moon phase angle return, advise clients to consciously place their attention on an alignment of instinct with the soul, since this is a time when inner peace is readily achieved.

3. ***To integrate the ancestral energies through the heart into Higher Self.*** Certain talents and virtues are bequeathed by parents and by ancestral lineage. These inherited and genealogical endowments are transmitted through the bloodlines and

bestow upon a soul such diverse gifts as mathematical expertise, musical genius, good looks, or psychic aptitude. Jupiter's exaltation in Cancer is the astrological underpinning for this generational transfer of human treasure.

The monthly Sun-Moon phase angle return is the time when a sincere appreciation can be expressed toward one's biological parents and one's ancestors. Meditating on the day when the Sun-Moon hologram repeats in the heavens can bring further integration of ancestral energies through the heart center and into the Higher Self. Whether the parents are alive or deceased, their spirits, too, will benefit from this.

4. To determine when to act when experiencing difficult transits to the Moon. This astrologer in recent years has experienced the transit of Uranus to his natal Moon in Pisces, which brought havoc and chaos. A marriage ended, a house sold, his mother died suddenly, several moves occurred in a few years, not to mention confrontations with obdurate females. The author has felt like he had entered a wormhole propagated chiefly by antimatter.

However, during such unpredictable and unstable cycles, life goes on and choices must be made. When astrologers work with clients who are experiencing transits of Uranus, Neptune or Pluto in conjunction or opposition to the natal Moon, they can also use the Sun-Moon holographic transits as a complementary technique. Calculate the Sun-Moon phase angle return dates and present these charts as times when the instinctual nature can align with the soul to make empowered choices.

5. To determine when to act during a difficult progressed Moon aspect. In a similar classification, although of shorter duration, are difficult aspects from the secondary progressed Moon to either natal or progressed planets. These lunar directions last for about two months, yet can bring periods of intense upheaval, as for example when a progressed Moon conjoins or opposes Saturn or Pluto. The astrologer can calculate Sun-Moon phase angle returns at the time of these stormy progressed aspects, and give clients the dates on which to make pressing choices.

6. To determine when to make decisions regarding natal or progressed houses with Cancer on the cusp. Sun-Moon holographic transits can also be used in connection with the natal or progressed houses that have the sign of Cancer on the cusp, and with the Moon as the ruler. For example, a Pisces rising individual with Cancer on the 5th could use the Sun-Moon phase angle return to time crucial decisions involving children. Progressed Libra Ascendants with Cancer

Midheavens can make important career choices on the days of their Sun-Moon holographic transits, and so on.

7. *To set a monthly tune-up for balancing masculine and feminine energies.* The Sun and Moon regulate the masculine and feminine forces within a person, and monthly when the Luminaries repeat one's natal hologram, or distance arc, in the heavens, individuals can designate that day for a special "spiritual tune-up." A meditation taking place within the hour of the exact phase angle return will bear much fruit, and one will feel an increase in inner harmony at this time. These dates are vastly more powerful on an individual basis than generic New or Full Moons. It is recommended that the phase angle return chart's rising degree be contemplated.

8. *To pray for the Light of God to regenerate the soul to wholeness.* The condition of human consciousness has been described as becoming fragmented into nine separate holograms at the time of birth. It was also stated that, in holography, a three-dimensional hologram, after being cut into sections, could be restored to its original and complete form by having a laser beam directed onto it.

Once a month, the laser beam of our solar system, the Sun, shines its divine rays onto the Moon from the exact same angle as when we were born. For each of us, this date is the most special day of the month regarding our relationship with God. A sincere prayer at this time can be made for souls to be regenerated to wholeness. These invocations can be timed to the precise moment of the holographic transits.

9. *To time important discussions with spouses or family members.* Another way for clients to benefit from Sun-Moon holographic transits is to use the exact dates of these phase angle returns for timing important subjects to be discussed with spouses, parents, children, or other relatives. Because the Sun symbolizes the husband, and the Moon represents the wife, when one's Sun-Moon hologram reforms monthly in the heavens, spousal matters can be communicated in a most effective way. All other family related discourse can succeed at this time.

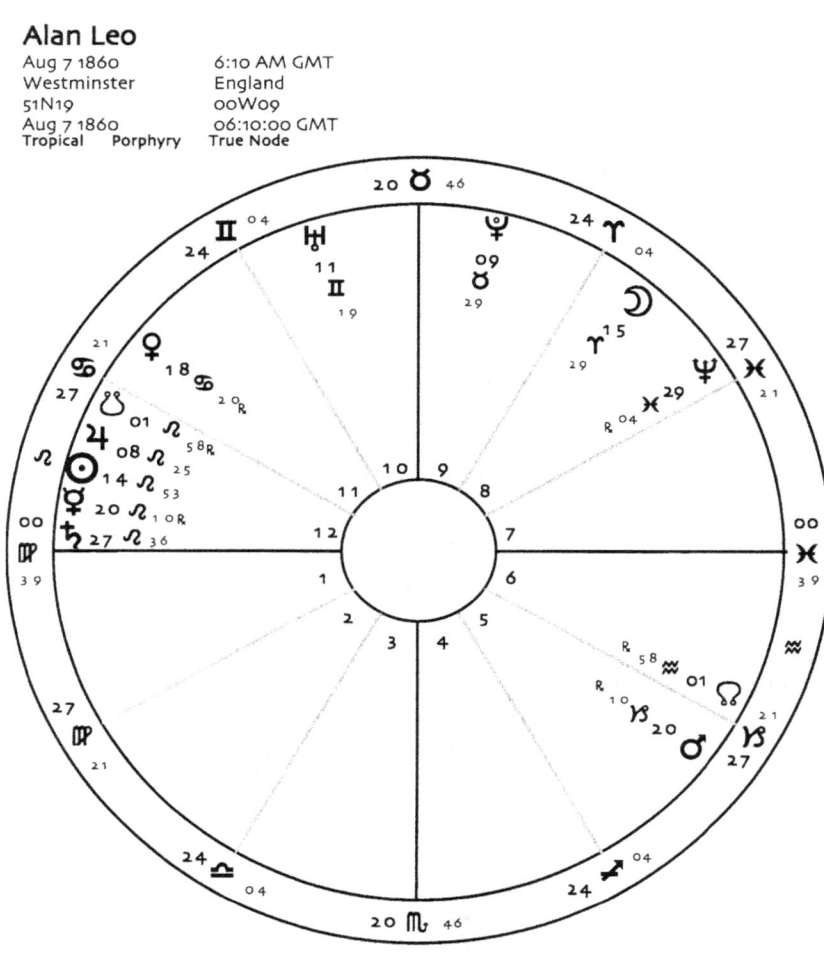

Virgo 1 from *La Volasfera*

A festival or occasion for the assembling together of villagers in gala costume.

It denotes a person of a sociable, friendly and flexible nature; capable of adapting itself to its environment; having a strong taste for pleasures of various kinds, luxuries, festivities, etc. It promises friendships and good fortune to the native, who will be much esteemed for his convivial spirit. It is a degree of FEASTING.

Chapter Three
Sun-Mercury Phase Angle Returns

Sun-Mercury Phase Angle at Birth

The Sun-Mercury phase angle forms the specific nature of the mind. This hologram of thought governs the functions of observation, perception, discernment and speech. It also fashions the composition of the nervous system. The Sun-Mercury synodic cycle is divided into ten distinct phases, beginning with the inferior conjunction of retrograde Mercury and the Sun. The average length of this cycle is 115–116 days, so it recurs three times a year. Its pattern is quite variable.

The most detailed research about the cycles and phases of the planet Mercury has been conducted by astrologer Michael Munkasey. His calculations include the four heliacal risings and settings, stationary points, greatest elongation east or west for this planet, and inferior or superior conjunctions with the Sun. These ten computations establish the phase angle transition points for the Sun and Mercury. The diagram on the facing page illustrates these phases of the Sun-Mercury synodic cycle:

Most astrologers learn early on in their studies that Mercury can never be greater than 28° from the Sun in a nativity. These greatest elongation points in Mercury's orbit are referenced as #4 or as #8 in the illustration. However, when at its perihelion at elongation, Mercury's maximum angle from the Sun can be as little as 18°.[29] Further scrutiny of the Sun-Mercury synodic cycle reveals other patterns.

In the Mercury retrograde cycle, a sequence of three repeats itself over time. Retrograde Mercury increases in duration from 20 days to 24 days, while at the same time Mercury decreases in the number of Zodiac degrees through which its retrogression travels. This deceleration degree range is from approximately 16° to 9°. A net result is that the fastest daily orbital travel for Mercury[30] in retrograde motion ranges from 0° 37' to 1° 21' (see tables in *Progressions* Chapter Three: Progressed Planetary Motion). By secondary progression, this is the range of Zodiac distance that Mercury retrogrades per year. The shorter the retrograde Mercury period, the faster Mercury's orbital movement.[31]

Munkasey found that the more difficult retrograde Mercury periods overall are those that have the longest duration (24-day) and the least range of degree travel (± 9°). During these Mercury retrograde periods, the Winged

Messenger has slowed to a maximum degree travel of 0° 37' per day between stations. It is this deceleration of degree movement that amplifies the Mercury retrograde effect.

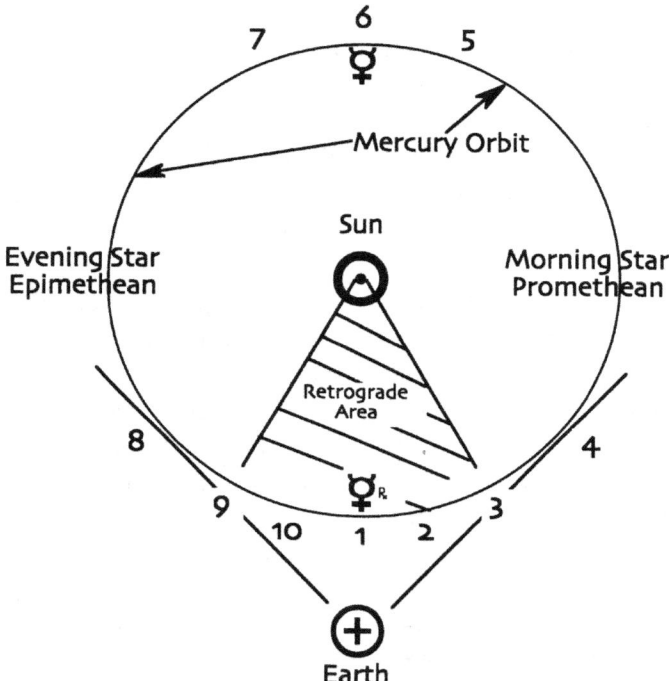

Cycles and Phases of the Planet Mercury

1. Inferior Conjunction
2. Heliacal Rising
3. Stationary Direct
4. Greatest Elongation East
5. Heliacal Setting
6. Superior Conjunction
7. Heliacal Rising (Emerging from Sun's rays)
8. Greatest Elongation West
9. Stationary Retrograde
10. Heliacal Setting (Disappears into Sun)

Chapter Three • *Sun–Mercury Phase Angle Returns*

Further extrapolating from Munkasey's observations, individuals born during the one Mercury retrograde period in three with the longest duration and the least degree movement between stations, may have the most difficulty with the natal retrograde Mercury. On the other hand, as in the author's case, where one is born during a short retrograde period with greater degree travel between stations, the retrograde Mercury in the nativity is perhaps more facile and can resuscitate knowledge from past lives, bringing information through into the current lifetime.[32]

Author and astrologer, Erin Sullivan, in her book, *Retrograde Planets*, wrote of a pattern in the Mercury cycle wherein four to six consecutive periods of retrograde Mercury fall in the same element. This sequence of retrogradation occurs opposite to the pattern of signs in the Zodiac, going from Water to Air to Earth to Fire. Her research showed that this elemental cycle of Mercury lasts a little over six years.

What the astrologer may deduce from Sullivan's work is that the four elements can fall into two categories. In the former, Mercury consecutively retrogrades in the air and earth elements for three years, bringing a mental and deliberative climate into the collective consciousness. In the latter, successive retrogradation of Mercury in the fire and water elements for three years produces an emotional and instinctual atmosphere in the mass magnetics of human consciousness.

Each soul incarnates at a precise point within the Sun-Mercury phase angle cycle, and one's nervous system and mental type is influenced by this. A distinction was made by Dane Rudhyar, and later elaborated on by Alexander Ruperti, between the opening and closing halves of the Mercury cycle. From the inferior conjunction to the superior conjunction, with Mercury as the morning star, Rudhyar called *Mercury-Prometheus*; it is said to give one a quality of forethought.

From the superior conjunction back to the inferior conjunction, with Mercury as an evening star, is called *Mercury-Epimetheus* and bequeaths one with the gift of afterthought. The Promethean mind is the future-oriented introvert, dealing with ideals and abstractions, whereas the extroverted Epimethean mind has superior hindsight and a capacity for review and assessment of what has already occurred.

It appears that the most powerful point in the Sun-Mercury cycle is where the *reversal of polarity in the electromagnetic field occurs*.[33] Souls born at the inferior conjunction (where the Epimethean cycle transitions to the Promethean, and where the Mercury orbit is closest to Earth) have extremely high-strung nervous systems and minds that phase back and forth from hindsight to forethought.

This erratic reversing of mental polarity is like a magnet flipping its poles. One explanation of severe bipolar disorder is a Sun-Mercury inferior conjunction in the nativity, especially if the birth was during a 24-day Mercury retrograde period, with only 9° of retrogression between the retrograde and direct stations.

Recalling the illustration on page 48, each of the ten Sun-Mercury phase angle positions at birth have distinct features from which the nervous system and one's hologram of thought are derived. To give readers an idea of just how long Mercury remains in any of these ten phases, and of the variability of this pattern, three years of retrograde Mercury periods from 2005 to 2008 are summarized, detailing the duration and degree movement of retrogradation, and overall length of each synodic cycle. The following are nine consecutive inferior conjunctions:[34]

Nov 24 2005	02° Sg 28' R	20 days/16°	111 days (from 8/5/05)
Mar 12 2006	21° Pi 23' R	23 days/13°	108 days
Jul 18 2006	25° Cn 32' R	24 days/10°	<u>128 days</u>
			347 days ÷ 3 = 115 ⅔ avg.
Nov 8 2006	16° Sc 20' R	20 days/16°	113 days
Feb 23 2007	04° Pi 11' R	22 days/15°	107 days
Jun 28 2007	06° Cn 42' R	24 days/9°	<u>125 days</u>
			345 days ÷ 3 = 115 average
Oct 23 2007	00° Sc 12' R	20 days/16°	117 days
Feb 6 2008	17° Aq 20' R	21 days/15°	106 days
Jun 7 2008	17° Ge 15' R	24 days/9°	<u>122 days</u>
			345 days ÷ 3 = 115 average

As you can see, the synodic cycle of Mercury has a three-part pattern. The length of each synodic period is variable, but when taken as a whole, the overall duration is similar, totaling 345–47 days for three synodic cycles in a row, with an average cycle length of 115–16 days each. One also observes a transition from the fire to the water to the air elements. Six continuous inferior conjunctions in the same element is the maximum, and four is the minimum.

Within Mercury's synodic cycle, measured from one inferior conjunction to the next, are ten phases of varying length. See the illustration on page 48. To determine at which Sun-Mercury cycle phase a birth occurred, Munkasey has published the *Ephemerides: Cycles and Phases of Venus & Mercury*. It has exact calculations for the dates of each of the ten phase changes within the Sun-Mercury cycle from 1600 to 2100. This publication was once obtainable through the NCGR website.[35]

As with all things Mercurial, variations abound, and the individual phase lengths are no exception. In the following summary, based on just four consecutive synodic cycles of the Sun and Mercury in 2005–2007, readers will see that it is impossible to attempt to "eyeball" the length of each of the ten phases within these overall cycles:

Phase 1. Inferior Conjunction to Heliacal Rising = from 4 to 7 days
Phase 2. Helical Rising to Stationary Direct = from 4 to 8 days
Phase 3. Stationary Direct to Greatest Elongation East = from 8 to 14 days
Phase 4. Greatest Elongation East to Heliacal Setting = from 14 to 31 days
Phase 5. Heliacal Setting to Superior Conjunction = from 10 to 20 days
Phase 6. Superior Conjunction to Heliacal Rising = from 8 to 16 days
Phase 7. Heliacal Rising to Greatest Elongation West = from 14 to 35 days
Phase 8. Greatest Elongation West to Stationary Retrograde = 6 to 13 days
Phase 9. Stationary Retrograde to Heliacal Setting = from 4 to 7 days
Phase 10. Heliacal Setting to Inferior Conjunction = from 5 to 7 days

Astrologers who work extensively with secondary progressions, as does this author, will bear in mind that the above figures *are identical in years* for Mercury progressing from one phase to the next. How should one interpret the ten phases?

The Sun-Mercury synodic cycle was divided into two hemicycles by Rudhyar, the Promethean (forethought) and Epimethean (afterthought). Maximum subjectivity is thought to occur at the inferior conjunction, as Mercury is both retrograde and conjoined to the Sun, thus causing the mind to be influenced by the feelings and to be lacking in objectivity. Retrogradation exerts an effect on the intellect, causing it to be more internalized and self-referencing. One sees forethought originating here, as the ability for planning and preparation requires a strong inner compass.

Objectivity and detachment are mental attributes when a soul is born near greatest elongation of Mercury. In these nativities, one finds Mercury as either a morning star or an evening star, about 18° to 28° away from the Sun, and frequently in a different sign than the Sun as well. Perception is minimally affected by one's pride or feelings; these individuals could excel as book reviewers, or as analysts. At the superior conjunction, a direct motion Mercury is conjoined with the Sun. It is also at this point in the Mercury cycle where the Winged Messenger reaches its fastest possible orbital motion through the Zodiac, as much as 02° 11' per day. At this phase in Mercury's cycle, knowledge is shared freely and openly with others. The intellect has a trace of pride, as at the inferior conjunction, yet a direct motion Mercury renders the mind less self-conscious, with more confidence and poise.[36] A nearly partile example of a *cazimi* superior conjunction is shown in this nativity:[37]

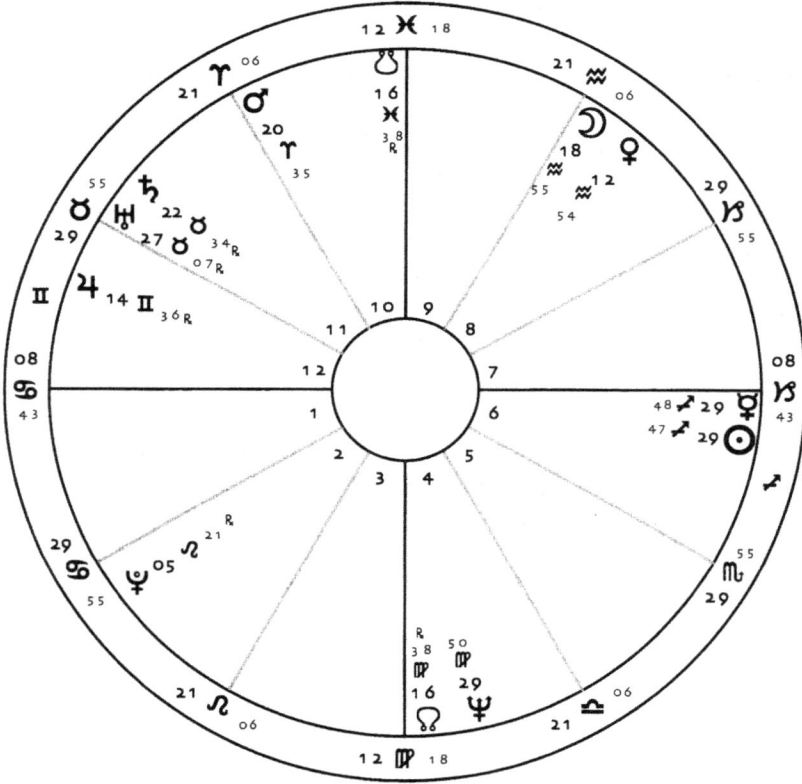

This is the horoscope of the most powerful healer that this astrologer has ever had as a client. She was a Lakota Sioux medicine woman who did "psychic surgery," a procedure that involved extricating and cutting diseased bloodlines that caused mental illness or insanity.

When she worked with patients, a common occurrence would be a presence of evil spirits in the room, having been trapped in the DNA of the bloodlines of the poor soul undergoing spiritual exorcism. This woman had a laser-like focus. She would not flinch nor crack when these twisted entities would fill the room with their hideous presence. This Sun-Mercury conjunction made her mind very powerful and heart-centered and many souls were healed of family trauma by her work. Alas, she is now deceased.

At the superior conjunction, again a reversal of polarity in the electromagnetic field occurs, this time with the Promethean phase transitioning into Epimethean. Forethought is replaced by afterthought, and the matrix of the mind for those born in the second half of the Mercury cycle becomes one of assessment and review, as opposed to the Promethean mind of planning, preparation and futuristic idealism.

Those born near a heliacal rising or setting of retrograde Mercury, between the inferior conjunction and stationary, may possess the gift of prophecy. The mind is emerging from, or disappearing into, the rays of the Sun. As Mercury is inward, one's radiant inner vision can be preserved, such as lucid recall of a vivid dream. One theorizes that the better predictive astrologers have this, as did Nostradamus:

The symbol for his rising degree, Pisces 28, from *La Volasfera*, attests to his ability as a physician who treated those with the Plague, and as a prophetic astrologer:

A serpent standing erect within a circle of fire.

> This is the index of a mind of more than usual powers of intellect and a soul disposed to the searching out of the deeper secrets of nature. Such an one will manifest much wisdom and will attain to high distinction in the pursuit of scientific study, but more particularly such as is related to the art of healing, as chemistry, medicine and anatomical science. From him, as through a lens, the rays of a higher truth and deeper understanding will converge and be dispersed again for the better instruction of the world and its manifest and manifold advantage. He will take life at the crisis and turn it back from the Gates of Death. It is a degree of KNOWLEDGE.

A nativity with a stationary Mercury makes for a powerful orator, especially so at a direct station. If other factors support this, such as a trine from the Moon or Uranus to Mercury, the intellectual powers can be quite pronounced and speaking or writing ability may be exceptional. The American president, John F. Kennedy, was born less than eight hours after a direct station of Mercury on 29 May 1917.

Here we have a true Promethean mind, forward looking and filled with visions for the future. Mercury rising ahead of the Sun as the morning star functions like an Indian scout at dawn, scanning the horizon to see what is over

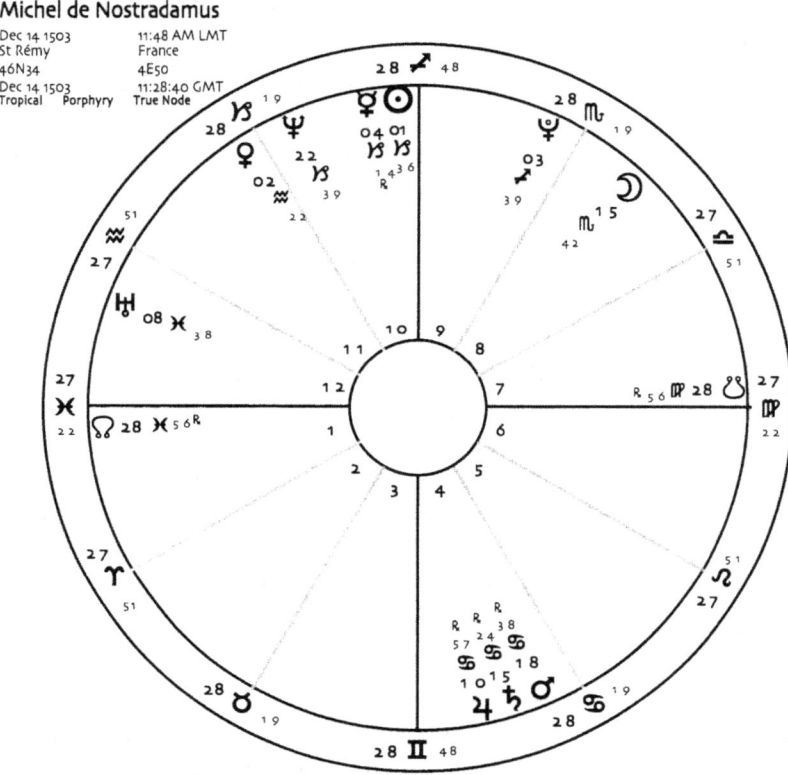

the next hill. President Kennedy, in a speech in 1962, set the goal for the US to put a man on the Moon by the end of that decade. It was accomplished on 20 July 1969. He was author of *Profiles in Courage*, winning a Pulitzer Prize for biography in 1957.[38]

For those born at the heliacal setting of a direct motion Mercury, the lifetime is of strengthening the mind through a deeper belief in one's intellectual capacity. The author had his secondary progressed Mercury enter this phase at the end of 1993, when Mercury in Sagittarius 23 became combust with the Sun in Capricorn 4 by secondary progression. Since that time, he has learned much about the process of mental creativity, as progressed Mercury draws nearer to the Sun.

Souls born at the heliacal rising of a direct motion Mercury, occurring about one to two weeks after the superior conjunction, experience lifetimes of how to use their minds in more effective and productive ways. Perhaps having spent many lives with Promethean minds, pondering the future while missing

Chapter Three • *Sun–Mercury Phase Angle Returns*

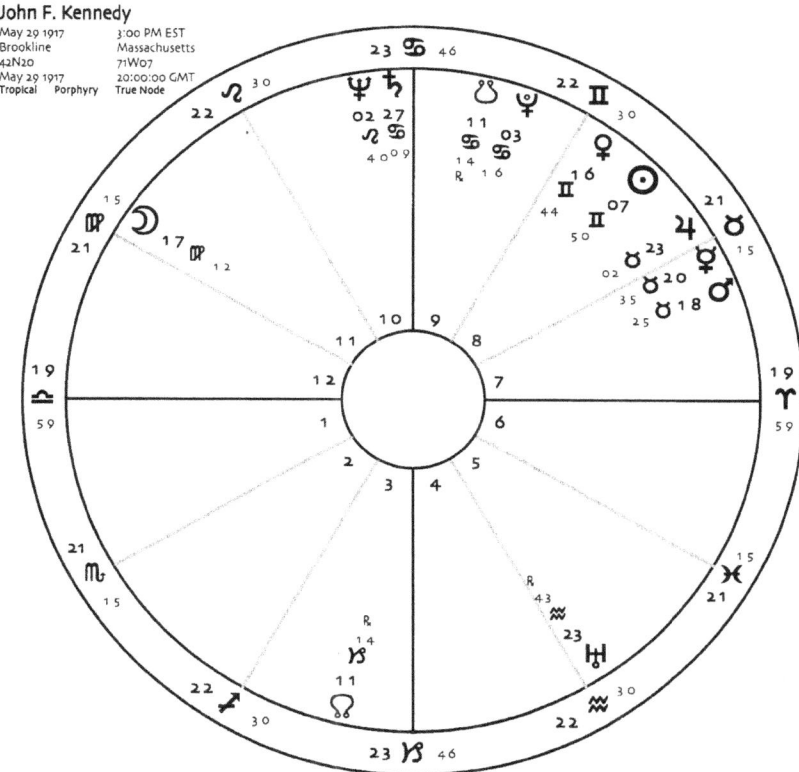

opportunities in front of them, these souls are learning how to review and reassess their past experiences to be better prepared for the next episode in life.

Several distinguished scientists are born near the retrograde station of Mercury. This is understandable as the Epimethean mind, in effect during the evening star period of the Mercury cycle, is one of review and assessment, which attributes serve an analytic thinker quite well. Some of these scientists, such as Marie Curie, who received Nobel Prizes for Physics and Chemistry, and René Descartes, a philosopher and mathematician responsible for the foundations of analytic geometry, were born between four and seven days before the retrograde station.

It is as if a Mercury slowing for its retrograde station can focus on a research endeavor until a breakthrough is achieved. Another facet of this point in a Mercury cycle is the ability to swim against the prevailing tide intellectually, as did Nicolaus Copernicus, who was born the day before a retrograde station.

Copernicus, a Prussian Pole, who was educated in medicine, law and mathematics, hypothesized that the Earth rotated on its axis and orbited around the Sun. His heliocentric theory of the solar system superseded the existing Ptolemaic world-view of the planets and the Sun orbiting about the Earth. His revolutionary book, *De revolutionibus orbium coelestium* (*On the Revolutions of the Celestial Spheres*), was published in 1543, the year of his death. It was not until the early 17th century with Galileo and Kepler, that his theories were verified.

Copernicus' Sun-Mercury phase angle was between points #8 and #9 in the illustration on page 48. Mercury was within 03' of arc of its retrograde station the day after his birth. His remarkable life, during which astronomy was only an avocation while he performed other duties as a soldier, governor, jurist and physician, is perfectly summed up by the symbolism for his rising degree. From *La Volasfera*, for Virgo 3:

> *A man in a skull-cap, busy at work with some scientific instruments.*
>
> It denotes a person of industrious habits; quick insight into natural laws; an investigator in the chemical or other scientific world; fond of experiment, eager in his undertakings, very hopeful, though during life will be hardly used at the hands of fortune. The native will, however, eventually succeed in his endeavors, and will assuredly reap the fruit of long and earnest labors. It is a degree of RESEARCH.

The Sun-Mercury midpoint for Copernicus, 18° Pisces 56', fills in a Mutable Grand Cross. The square to Saturn is exceptionally close, with the Moon and Pluto forming the remainder of this Mental Cross. For a soul to wield such power so as to cause scientific tenets to come into question and to be transformed, suggests an aspect such as Saturn square Pluto, which forms only about every 17 years. The research of C.E.O. Carter showed that *22° Gemini-Sagittarius was especially connected to mathematics, being also aspected from the two other airy signs.* Copernicus had a Mars at 22° Aquarius, in perfect trine to this *mutable axis of mathematical talent.*[39]

The Winged Messenger in a nativity derives its meaning and relevance through its relationship with the Sun. The hologram of thought is cast in place by the distance arc between the Sun and Mercury, and by the position of Mercury in either its opening (Promethean) or closing (Epimethean) halves of the orbital cycle, relative to its successive conjunctions with the Sun.

During life, the secondary progression of Mercury will cause its orbital cycle to change phases. In *Progressions*, this author wrote about Mercury's progressed stations and their impact on the thought patterns, perceptions, and style of communication. If progressed Mercury reaches superior or inferior conjunction with a progressed Sun (not with the natal Sun), that year will be

Chapter Three • *Sun–Mercury Phase Angle Returns*

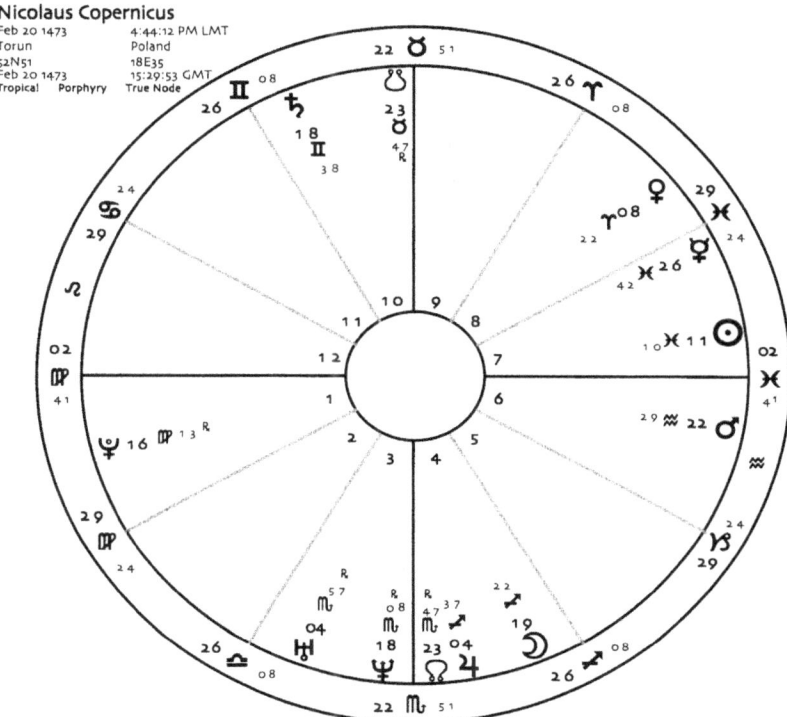

highly significant, especially for souls with Gemini or Virgo rising, or these signs on the MC, or if the Luminaries are in these Mercury-ruled signs. Others will also notice its effect, too.

Progressed Mercury reaching greatest elongation or heliacal rising or setting is also very significant. When the author's secondary progressed Mercury reached its greatest eastern elongation in 1971, he began his serious study of astrology. As mentioned on page 54, the author's progressed Mercury reached heliacal setting in 1993, disappearing into the Sun's rays, as his creative writing output increased.

A lifetime calculation of the eight progressed planets' synodic cycle phase changes (Mercury through Pluto) can be obtained through Munkasey. He programmed an unique software calculation that measures the changing phase angles between the Sun and the planets, and which produces a lifetime report for when a planet's synodic cycle changes phases, *i.e.*, from greatest elongation to heliacal setting.[40] It is also illuminating to determine when a Sun-Mercury phase angle shifts phases by tertiary or minor progression as well.

Pre-Natal Sun-Mercury Synodic Cycle

The inferior conjunction of retrograde Mercury and the Sun prior to birth, along with its degree symbols, provides insight about the collective thought patterns and mental inclinations that one shares with his "soul group," and which is being carried over from past lives. As mentioned in Chapter Two on the pre-natal Sun-Moon synodic cycle, wherein countless souls are, of course, incarnating over a lunar month's time, it is the belief of this astrologer that one's individual hologram of thought emanates from an immense "mental matrix," of which one is just a part. It is presumed that this record is on the causal plane, mirroring world conditions in previous eras that affected the thinking of those living during that time.[41]

At the end of this book is a Table of Sun-Mercury conjunctions for the 200 years from 1920 to 2120. Readers can locate their pre-natal Sun-Mercury synodic cycle and its inferior conjunction degree (retrograde Mercury conjunct Sun). One may also determine from the table whether a birth occurred during the Promethean phase (from inferior to superior conjunction) or during an Epimethean phase (from superior to inferior conjunction). Direct is shown by a "D", and retrograde by "R".

The degree symbols for one's pre-natal inferior conjunction can produce insight about past life conditions existing in the collective mental ethers. It should be borne in mind that we share these past life factors with other souls incarnating during the same 116-day Sun-Mercury synodic cycle as ourselves. The author has found that certain inferior conjunctions of the Sun and Mercury are quite exceptional, and several souls born into that synodic cycle attain eminence.

Abraham Lincoln and Charles Darwin are well-known astrological time twins, both born 12 February 1809 within nine-and-a-half hours of each other. Their pre-natal Sun-Mercury inferior conjunction was quite rare, as it occurred at a solar eclipse that was in close conjunction with Saturn. The inferior conjunction after birth for each of them was also very powerful, as it was exactly conjunct Pluto.

The degree symbol for the Sun-Mercury inferior conjunction just after the birth of Lincoln and Darwin, which each arrived at by secondary progression at age 20, is quite poignant in its relevance to the US Civil War. Pisces 15 from Charubel:[42]

> *A hand with a sword in it. Just rising in the ascendant, a halo of golden light envelopes it. That sword is not for indiscriminate slaughter. It is to defend the right.*

Chapter Three • *Sun–Mercury Phase Angle Returns*

Abraham Lincoln
Feb 12 1809   6:54 AM LMT
Hodgenville   Kentucky
37N34   85W44
Feb 12 1809   12:36:56 GMT
Tropical   Porphyry   True Node

Second Chart   Natal Chart
Sun-Mercury Inferior Conjunction
Nov 18 1808   02:57:47 GMT
Third Chart   Natal Chart
Sun-Mercury Inferior Conjunction
Mar 5 1809   06:15:06 GMT

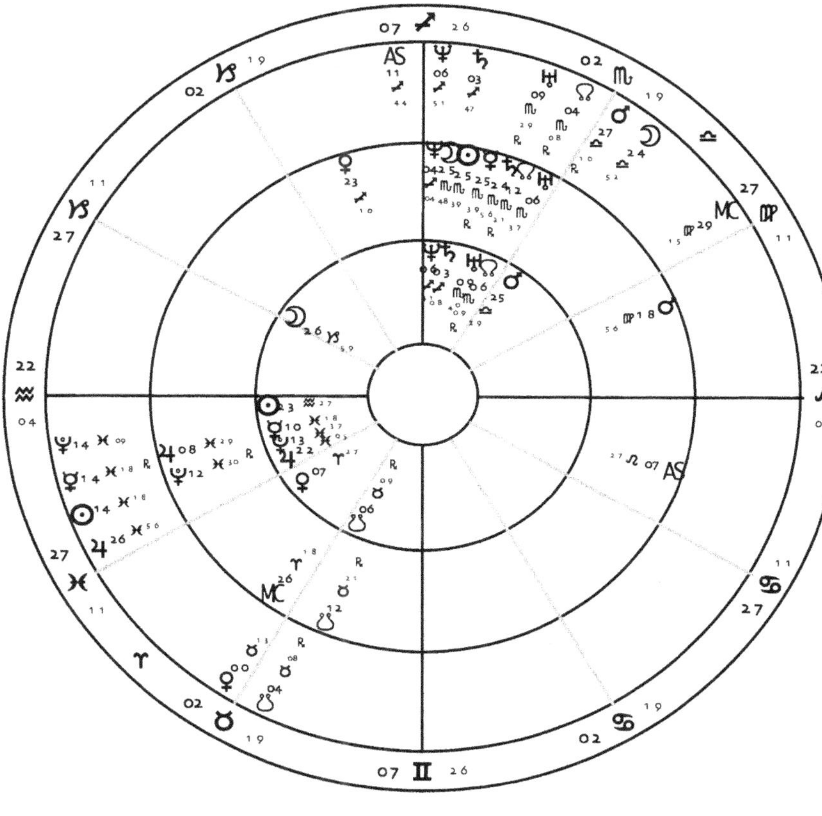

As regards the profession of astrology, about every 15 years there is a conjunction of Uranus and the North Node. It would be reasonable to hypothesize that certain souls incarnate at these times with a life purpose to seed the future of astrology in some significant way. Any Sun-Mercury synodic cycle originating at a Uranus-North Node conjunction would thus affect the intellectual evolution in astrology.

A conjunction of Uranus and the North Node occurred on 25 July 1946 and eight days later, on 2 August 1946, an inferior conjunction of retrograde Mercury and the Sun in Leo 10, and conjunct Pluto, started a new 111-day synodic period. Two celebrated astrologers, Liz Greene and Stephen Arroyo, were born into this cycle. One observes Saturn in the final minute of arc of Cancer, at the cusp of a new era.

Ms Greene was born 4 September 1946 during the Promethean half of this synodic cycle. Her natal Sun-Mercury phase angle was at the heliacal setting of a direct motion Mercury, ten days before the superior conjunction in Virgo 22. Mr Arroyo was born a month later on 6 October 1946 during the Epimethean half of the cycle. His natal Sun-Mercury phase angle was between the heliacal rising and greatest western elongation of a direct motion Mercury. Remarkably, their Mercuries are each other's Contrascion (Equinox Point). Not only did these two superb authors greatly contribute to their generation's astrological knowledge, but they are also male and female exemplars, the morning and evening stars of an astrological era.[43]

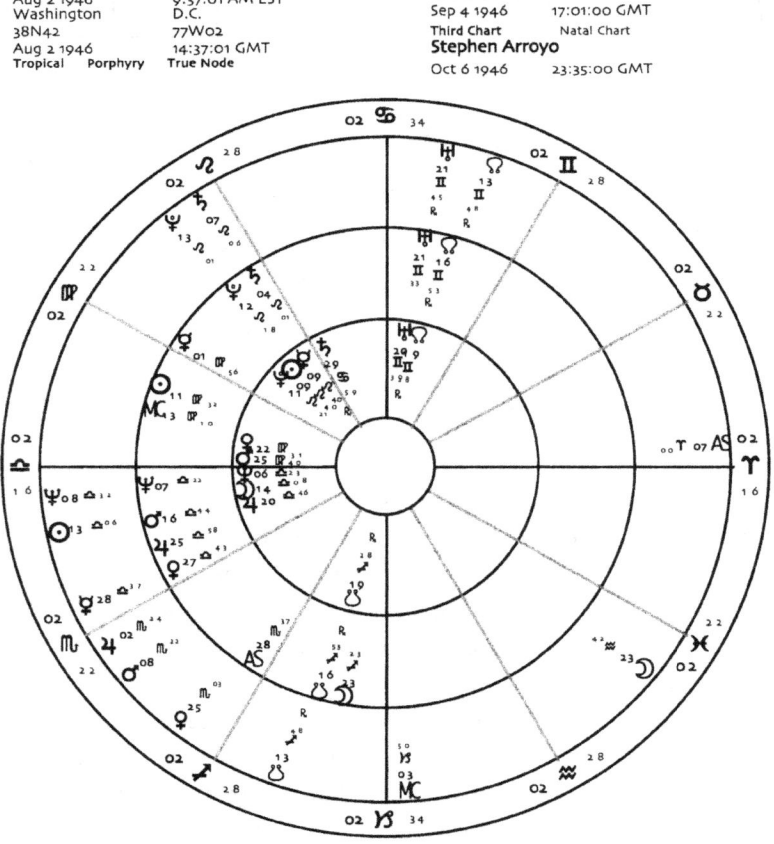

Chapter Three • *Sun–Mercury Phase Angle Returns*

An examination of degree symbols for the Sun-Mercury conjunctions prior to their births provides insight into the mental matrices out of which their minds formed. Ms Greene's hologram of thought is symbolized by Leo 10, degree of the inferior conjunction occurring prior to her birth. From Marc Jones, the Sabian Symbol is:

> *Everywhere there is a sparkle, and nature is revealed in pastel colors;*
> *the early morning dew salutes the sunlight.*

Rudhyar's analysis of the degree befits a Jungian analyst plunging into the *shadow*:

> The exalted feeling that rises within the soul of the individual who has successfully passed through the long night which has tested his strength and his faith.

Mr Arroyo's hologram of thought is illustrated by Virgo 22, degree of the superior conjunction of the Sun and Mercury on 14 September 1946, just before his birth and at the shift of the Promethean cycle into the Epimethean cycle. From Charubel:

> *An extensive forest; in the distance, the sun just peeping above the*
> *horizon and flooding the tops of the trees with his glowing rays.*

This denotes what the Greek cynic, Diogenes, was looking for with his lantern. A man. Yes, a man among men. One who will spontaneously elicit the goodwill and plaudits of his fellow-men. Thousands will look up to him for light and for guidance. It is possible he may initiate a new epoch, or prove himself the founder of a new philosophy.

From this, one sees that degree symbols for the pre-natal superior conjunction can also provide insight for those born into the Epimethean half of the Mercury cycle. The degree of the inferior conjunction is still important and should also be studied.

Using Sun-Mercury Holographic Transits

A Sun-Mercury holographic transit occurs when the precise distance arc between the natal Sun and Mercury forms again in the heavens, *and is also in the identical phase as the natal Mercury cycle, i.e., Promethean or Epimethean.* The Sun-Mercury phase angle return occurs three times a year, and on these days one can align with Higher Self and gain insight into upcoming mental activity and decision-making.

Harry S. Truman

May 8 1884   4:00 PM CST
Lamar   Missouri
37N30   94W17
May 8 1884   22:00:00 GMT
Tropical   Porphyry   True Node

Second Chart   Natal Chart
Sun/Mercury Phase Angle Return
Apr 5 1945   07:04:03 GMT

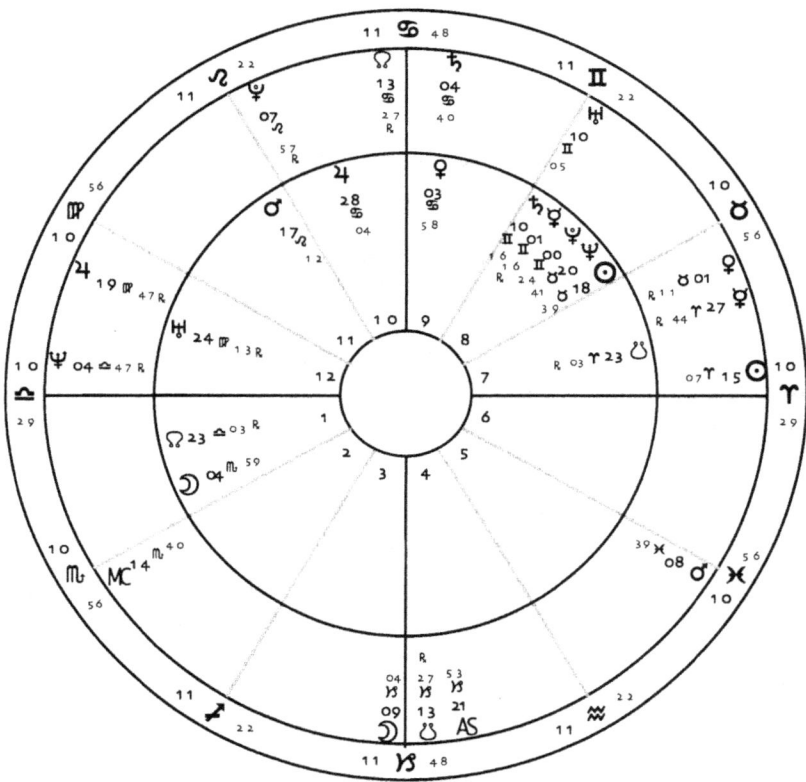

One of the most difficult decisions made in recent history was by Harry S. Truman, who became US president when Franklin Roosevelt died on 12 April 1945 during the waning months of World War II. In the Potsdam Declaration of 26 July 1945, terms of surrender were given to the Japanese. After their rejection, Truman made an historical decision to drop atomic bombs on Japan to end the war and spare the countless casualties of an invasion by American forces of the Japanese mainland.

Born two days after a retrograde station of Mercury conjoining Pluto, Truman had experienced a fateful Sun-Mercury phase angle return only a week before his elevation to the American presidency. The length of this holographic transit lasted until 13 August 1945, when his next phase angle return occurred just four days after the second atomic bomb was dropped on Japan, thus ending World War II.

This bi-wheel chart places that Sun-Mercury phase angle return into the natal houses of President Truman. The astrologer sees that a rare double Yod formed in the heavens on 5 April 1945. Uranus is sextile Pluto, and the first Yod pointed at the Moon in 09° Capricorn 04', 03' of arc from the precise Uranus/Pluto midpoint.

The bomb dropped on Hiroshima contained 130 pounds of Uranium-235; the bomb dropped on Nagasaki was comprised of 4.1 pounds of Plutonium-239. 145,000 Japanese civilians were instantly incinerated in both cities. The second Yod had an apex Pluto, and was in the most powerful class of *Fingers of Fate*, ones wherein the apex planet is both the slowest of the three and in a fixed sign, therefore rendering the two 150° aspects from quincunxes into the more potent inconjuncts.[44]

One also observes that Truman's sudden and unexpected presidency occurred as transit Uranus formed the third and final conjunction to his natal Saturn. At the time of this fateful Sun-Mercury phase angle return, the North Node was in the very degree of the US Sun, 13° Cancer. In a portentous twist of fate, the greater malefic, Saturn, was in the exact midpoint of the US benefics, Venus and Jupiter. As if remarkably pre-ordained by fate from the late 1800s, President Truman had his Moon in 04° Scorpio 59', the exact degree of the Japanese horoscope's Vertex.[45]

A superior conjunction of the Sun and Mercury occurred prior to Truman's birth on 30 March 1884 in 09° Aries 58'. From *La Volasfera*, for Aries 10, we find:

> A man on horseback standing alone in the middle of a battlefield
> where around him lie the dead and dying.

It denotes a person who will occupy some singular position in life; one whose career will be remarkable, if not unique, and noted for its daring and hazardous exploits. It gives success in undertakings and much prestige. It is a degree of VICTORY.

This abridged case study illustrates the significance of planetary positions at the time of one's Sun-Mercury phase angle return. During these holographic transits, one's mental matrix is set in place for the next four months. The conditions in the heavens at this time set the mold for one's upcoming thought patterns and decision-making during the entire length of the personal Sun-Mercury synodic cycle.[46]

The author has found that the Zodiac degree of Mercury at the time of the phase angle return is highly significant. When using Sun-Mercury holographic transits with clients, a reading of the degree symbol for Mercury is instructional. While writing the present volume, the author had a Sun-Mercury phase angle return on 12 March 2006 (See Chart below). Mercury was in 20° Pisces 35'. From Charubel, for Pisces 21:

> *A man walking in darkness with an old-fashioned lantern in his hand.*
>
> Denotes one who possesses much individuality; very conservative in his predilections; one who will experience much adversity; at the same time one who will find his way out of every difficulty, ever guided by a divine instinct, having an implicit faith in those religious truths as taught and practised by his forefathers.

The author's experience during this Sun-Mercury synodic cycle, lasting until July 18th, was exactly as the degree symbol inferred. Saturn was rising and opposite Venus, and several relationship challenges knocked him off his balance and made the writing of this manuscript rather difficult. Yet, despite the predicament of his personal life, a "way was found out of every difficulty," and a

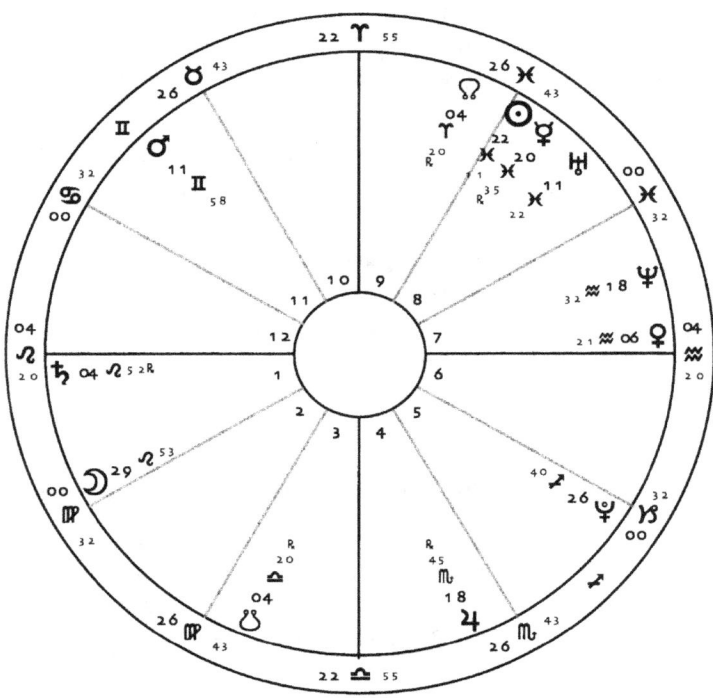

"divine instinct" did indeed guide him forward as he was writing this volume. Faith was his "lantern."[47]

Clients may also benefit by being informed of Moon-Mercury phase angle returns occurring monthly within the overall personal Sun-Mercury synodic cycle. As the author wrote in Chapter One, the Moon has a supporting role in the assimilation of the Light of the Sun, reflecting those divine rays and helping spiritual digestion.

During his Sun-Mercury cycle lasting from March until July of 2006, the author had a monthly Moon-Mercury phase angle return on May 4th. At that time, it was becoming clear that he needed to change his environment for this book to be written and published on schedule. His relationship appeared to be hindering his writing, and his resoluteness to get the book finished was causing distress in his personal life. Competing priorities reached a stalemate.

The author's natal Moon-Mercury distance arc of 105° 30' 09" had replicated itself in the heavens. Like any soul facing a personal challenge, he sought perspective and understanding through this monthly Moon-Mercury phase angle return. The Water Grand Trine and Kite, along with the Fixed Grand Cross, informed the author that something of creative and spiritual beauty was trying to come through, but that a very heavy price would have to be paid for it to be born.

The author moved to Port Townsend later that month to have the solitude to work on this book, yet the separation from his girlfriend proved quite painful. The degree of his natal Neptune was culminating in this phase angle return, so he chose to follow his vision and to accept the sacrifice necessary to bring it about. A careful study of the symbolism for the rising degree, Capricorn 4, was undertaken:

A vestal lamp burning brightly. (La Volasfera)

This is an indication of an elevated and superior mind, given to the study of things that are essentially spiritual. There are aspiration and intuition in a superior degree, and such an one will probably seek and find in the silence of his own chamber the key to many of the higher mysteries of life and thought. In any capacity he will attain to a superior position and will be an acknowledged leader of men and moulder of human minds. From all that is essentially mundane and sordid his thoughts will be estranged. He will have an intuitive perception of eternal verities. It is a degree of INITIATION.

If astrologers see clients experiencing difficult aspects from secondary progressed Mercury to their natal planets, or if they have hard transits to natal or progressed Mercury, these Sun-Mercury and Moon-Mercury phase angle return charts can be calculated and presented to clients as when to align free will with Higher Self to make empowered choices and difficult decisions. In this way, the consultation has a balanced delineation, with a discussion of both free will and fate. It is always pertinent to include the degree symbols for the Ascendant and Mercury.

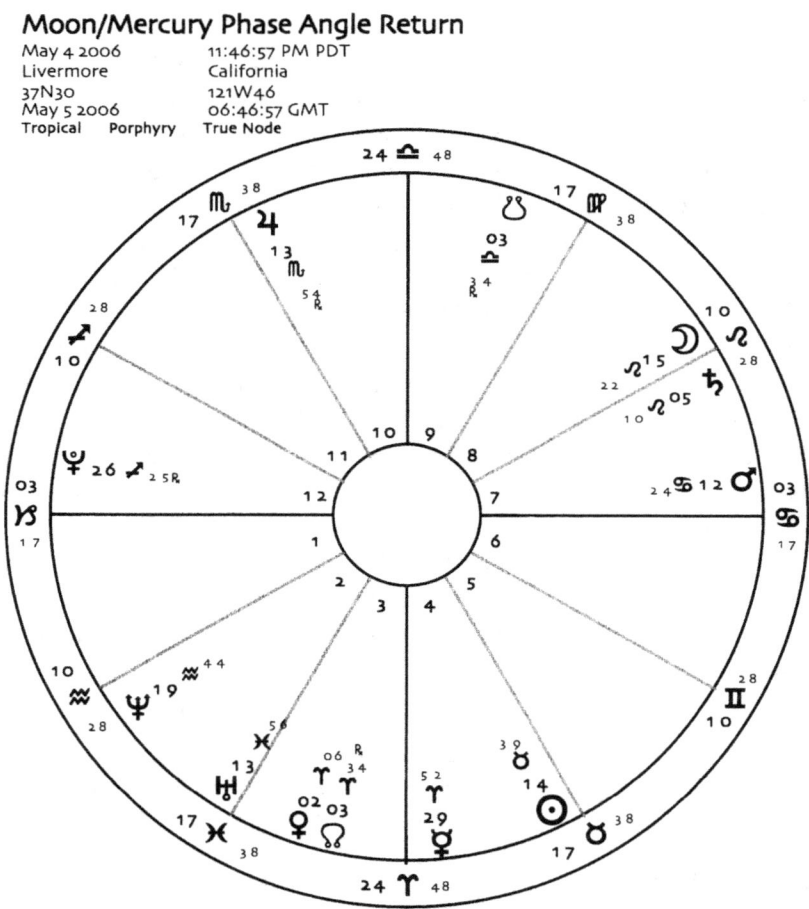

Chapter Four
Sun-Venus Phase Angle Returns

Sun-Venus Phase Angle at Birth

The Sun-Venus phase angle at birth creates the specific nature of the feelings. This hologram of attachment establishes one's approach to personal relationships, and how a person perceives the relative value of the material and spiritual worlds. If astrologers view the primary function of Venus through her exaltation in Pisces, a lucid picture emerges of two fishes swimming in opposite directions—one toward earthly comfort and sensual pleasure, the other away from this world.

The two fishes are inescapably bound to one another. The search for love becomes an impetus, ideally for unifying and synthesizing matter and spirit. The greatest example of this, of course, is knowing God through loving another soul. It is the ultimate irony in life that only through deep attachment and subsequent loss can the soul understand spiritual verities.

Cycles and Phases of the Planet Venus

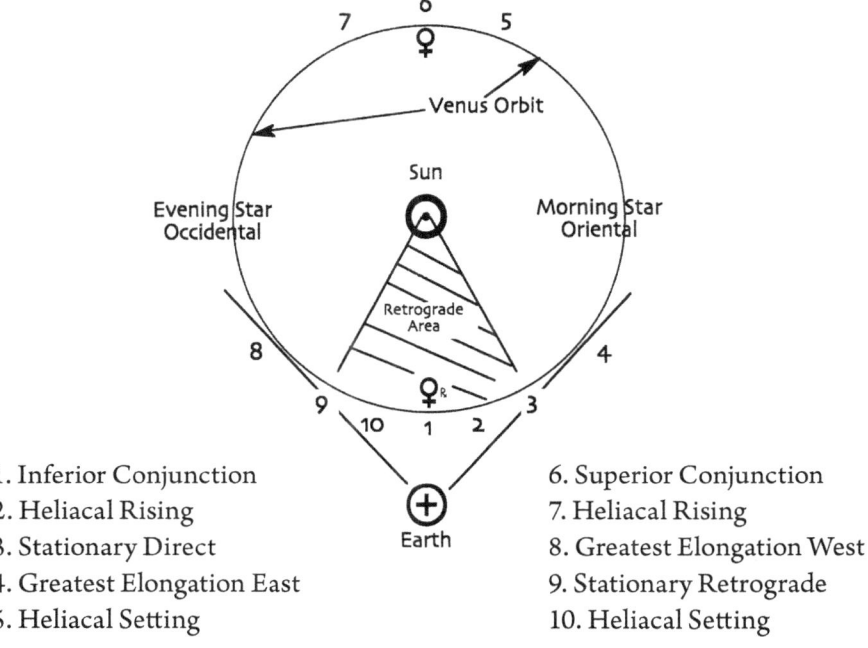

1. Inferior Conjunction
2. Heliacal Rising
3. Stationary Direct
4. Greatest Elongation East
5. Heliacal Setting

6. Superior Conjunction
7. Heliacal Rising
8. Greatest Elongation West
9. Stationary Retrograde
10. Heliacal Setting

In the solar system, Venus, as does Mercury, orbits between the Earth and the Sun, and is the second inferior planet. Her maximum angle from the Sun, as measured from Earth, cannot exceed 48° and, thus, Venus can only be in one of five signs in any nativity—the same as the Sun, or one or two signs before or after the Sun.

As with the Mercury cycle, the Sun-Venus synodic period has ten similar phases. Broadly speaking, it is divided into halves, with the orbital period from inferior to superior conjunction making Venus the morning star, rising ahead of the Sun. In the second half of the cycle, Venus sets after the Sun and is the evening star. Venus Oriental and Venus Occidental refer to the morning and evening star, respectively.

As with Mercury, the most powerful point in the Sun-Venus synodic cycle is at the inferior conjunction, when Venus is both retrograde and closest to the Earth. This is the beginning of the 584-day synodic period, and five of these cycles occur every eight years. Plotting the inferior conjunction degrees of retrograde Venus and the Sun onto the Zodiac, one finds a five-pointed star inscribed in the heavens.

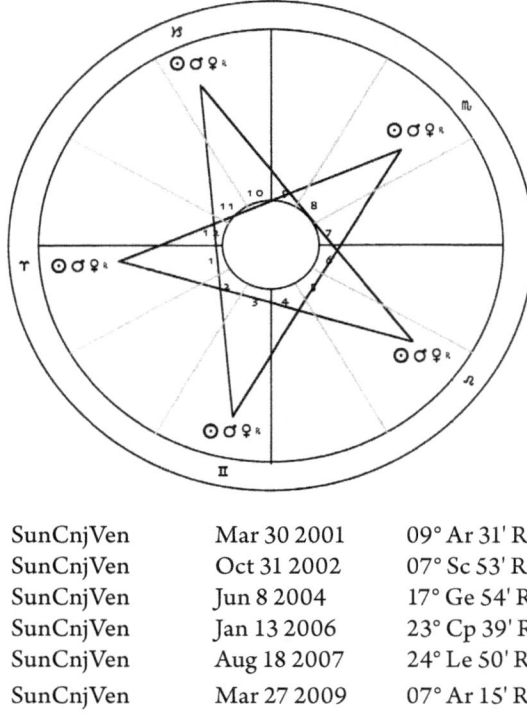

SunCnjVen	Mar 30 2001	09° Ar 31' R
SunCnjVen	Oct 31 2002	07° Sc 53' R
SunCnjVen	Jun 8 2004	17° Ge 54' R
SunCnjVen	Jan 13 2006	23° Cp 39' R
SunCnjVen	Aug 18 2007	24° Le 50' R
SunCnjVen	Mar 27 2009	07° Ar 15' R

Chapter Four • *Sun–Venus Phase Angle Returns*

As the astrologer can see in the illustration of the inferior conjunctions of retrograde Venus and the Sun for this decade, a beautiful star is formed in the heavens. One observes that the five synodic cycles of Venus equal almost exactly eight years, and that the opening and closing conjunctions are within two degrees.

The author has found that those born with a Sun-Venus phase angle as a morning star are more likely to proceed with their feelings and think about consequences later. Additionally, these souls had the inferior conjunction prior to birth and as such, are much more prone to repeat difficult karmic lessons in their relationships.

On the other hand, those born with Venus setting after the Sun as the evening star are more circumspect about personal relationships, and similar to an Epimethean Mercury, appear to have better skills for personal reflection and for learning from love's lessons. This is especially the case when natal Venus is in a different sign than the Sun. In these nativities, the superior conjunction of Venus precedes the birth and a repeating of karmic lessons in love is nowhere near as predominant.[48]

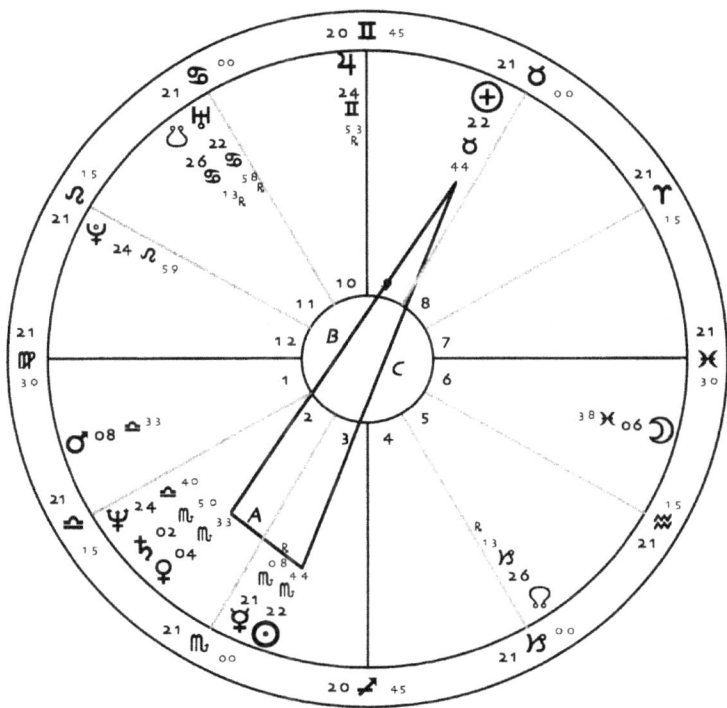

To better perceive the Sun-Venus hologram of attachment, the glyph for the Earth can be added into the horoscope, thus creating a three-dimensional likeness. In the author's nativity, his Sun-Venus distance arc A is 18° 10' 55", and the Venus-Earth distance arc B is 161° 49' 05". Together, these two arcs total 180° 00' 00". Using his Sabian Aspect Orb technique, arc A equates to the 19th degree of Aries, and arc B is equivalent to the 12th degree of Virgo. As with the illustration on page 39, astrologers observe that these two degrees are antiscia, or solstice points, of one another. Sun-Earth arc C is always a constant, measuring exactly 180° 00'.

From Sepharial's translation of *La Volasfera*, for Virgo 12:

A woman blindfold, and a man leading her.

It denotes a person of a weak yet seductive nature, one who will have much influence upon the other sex, and who may be led into dangerous relations with them, so that the life may be compared only to a tangled skein in which the complications are more various than the materials which enter into them. It is a degree of ENTANGLEMENT.

And from *La Volasfera*, for Aries 19:

An old man, dressed in a simple and much worn gown,
carrying two bags of gold clasped at his breast with nervous hands.

It denotes one who worships gold; a stingy and misanthropic nature. One who acquires to no purpose: self-centered and reclusive; whose constant fear is loss, a fear that is sure to be realised. It is a degree of ACQUISITIVENESS.

Hard to admit, yet the author can see his relational and financial experiences in this degree symbolism for the distance arcs of his natal Sun-Venus hologram. In the former, his life experience of entanglement in relationships is starkly depicted, and in the latter, financial fears as a self-employed astrologer are amusingly revealed. To further understand this hologram, degree symbols from Charubel are consulted:

Several figures of eight in a row, thus: 8 8 8 8 8 8 8 8.

Thus you see the square of eight. Denotes a man, or woman, of mystery; a lover of the mystical; a student of the mystical; a secretive person; a profound understanding; he will leave for himself a name in history. (Virgo 12)

A country site at the foot of a mountain, with many small dwellings thereon.
There are coal-pits in the locality. A poor woman is nursing a baby;
she is weeping, having just been made a widow.

This denotes that the native will be engaged in mining operations, and will lose his life thereby. (Aries 19)

After contemplating these degree symbols, and viewing his three-dimensional Sun-Venus hologram as the celestial pattern out of which his feelings and attachments were created, this astrologer found insight into the probability of his past karma.

In some past lives, his mystical absorption eliminated his material attachments, yet wreaked havoc in his personal relationships, where normal human bonding was necessary. In other past lives, perhaps dying young and leaving behind grieving widows with fatherless infants, explains his estranged and antagonistic relations with the mothers of his two daughters in this lifetime. How enigmatic is karma!

By measuring distance arcs between the Sun and Venus, and between Venus and the Earth, then converting these arcs into their derived Zodiac degrees, a door into the holographic universe opens by using the symbolical dimension of astrology. It is the belief of this author that the Sun-Venus hologram characterizes not only the nature of one's attachments in life, but that it also delineates karmic inclinations.

Besides being either the morning or evening star, Venus can also be retrograde or direct in the nativity. Since Venus is in retrogression 40–43 days out of every nineteen months, only 7.7% of the population have this celestial circumstance. Just as Mercury undergoes a reversal of polarity in its electromagnetic field at both the inferior and superior conjunctions with the Sun, Venus experiences a mutation of her energies as well when forming inferior or superior conjunctions to the Sun.

Bound fishes swimming in opposite directions in Pisces, sign of the exaltation of Venus, represent this reversal of polarity inherent in the Venusian cycle when the transition from Oriental to Occidental occurs. The same applies *mutatis mutandis* to the passage of Venus from evening to morning star. These powerful conjunctions with the Sun, one when Venus is direct, the other when retrograde, symbolize the periodicity of matter and spirit upon the collective level of human consciousness.

When Venus is direct and reaches a superior conjunction with the Sun, the bound fish swimming toward the material world prevails. With the Venus Occidental phase angle at birth, one therefore is more prone to materialism and the seduction of consumerism. When Venus is retrograde and forms an inferior conjunction with the Sun, the constrained fish swimming toward the spiritual world predominates. The morning star half of the cycle retains this influence until superior conjunction. With a Venus Oriental phase angle, the spiritual world thus has a stronger allure.

A cazimi superior conjunction of the Sun and Venus is found in the horoscope of Oprah Winfrey, a modern heroine of materialism. As the astrologer can see in her nativity below, her superior conjunction falls in the sign of Aquarius, ruling television and radio broadcasting. Her Moon is in the exact degree of the US Sibly chart Ascendant, attesting to her popularity with the American public. With a reported net worth of $1.4 billion, she is the richest black person in the world. Having been born poor in the rural South to unwed teenage parents, a remarkable manifestation of the fish swimming in material waters has transpired.

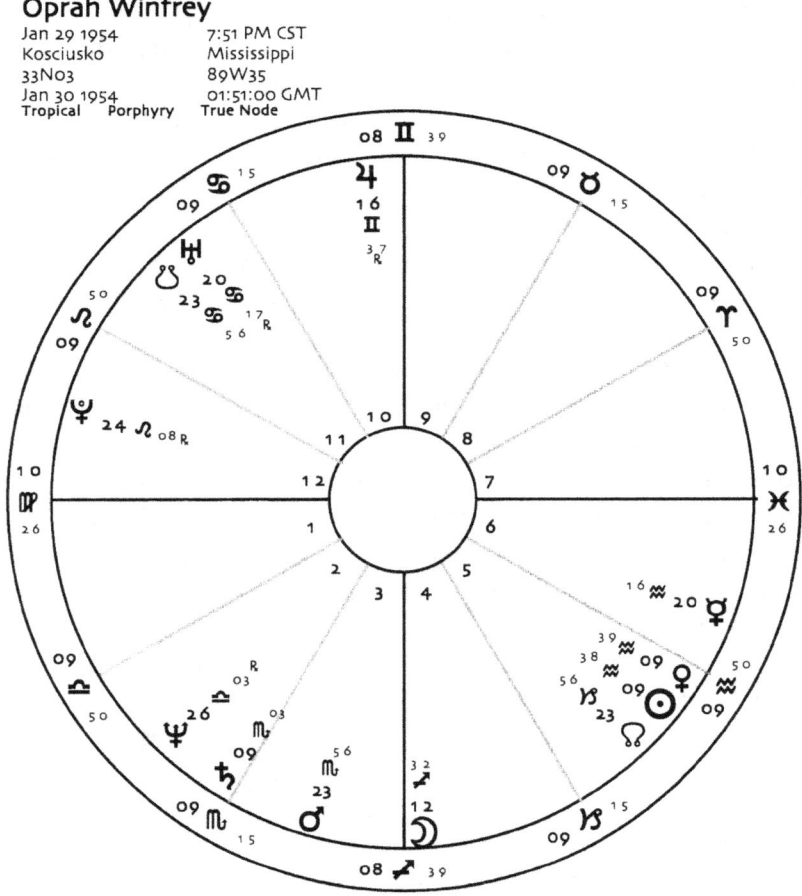

Chapter Four • *Sun–Venus Phase Angle Returns*

	Long	Lat	Decl	R.A.
☉	09 ♒ 38 33	00 N 00	17 S 50	312 05
☽	12 ♐ 32	03 S 29	25 S 46	250 34
☿	20 ♒ 16	01 S 41	16 S 19	323 14
♀	09 ♒ 39	01 S 09	18 S 57	312 25
♂	23 ♏ 56	01 N 00	17 S 47	231 49
♃	16 ♊ 37 ℞	00 S 22	22 N 24	075 31
♄	09 ♏ 03	02 N 27	12 S 11	217 28
♅	20 ♋ 17 ℞	00 N 29	22 N 24	112 01
♆	26 ♎ 03 ℞	01 N 42	08 S 28	204 47
♇	24 ♌ 08 ℞	10 N 03	22 N 56	150 03

For Ms Winfrey to have a nativity devoid of planets in Earthy signs,[49] save a Virgo Ascendant, one further admires how her cazimi Sun-Venus conjunction has been a progenitor of such wealth. A befitting testimony to the power of declination is found in her Sun-Mars parallel, exact to 03', bestowing an exceptional will, and in a partile Jupiter-Uranus parallel, conferring an ability to grow into a colossal public authority in this life.

At the other end of the spectrum is the pitiable life of Amedeo Clemente Modigliani, an Italian painter and sculptor. Born into poverty in a Sephardic Jewish family at the inferior conjunction of the Sun and Venus, he was dead at 35, penniless and destitute. His was a carnal life filled with countless love affairs, alcoholism, and hashish addiction, yet also a creative life which produced fabulous and beautiful paintings, nude drawings, and for a time, some original and innovative sculpture.

He died on 24 January 1920 with Saturn exactly on his Ascendant, shortly after his third Jupiter return. His early life was tormented by health problems, starting with enteric fever at age 14, and then tuberculosis at 16.[50] During his adult life as an artist in Paris, where he lived at times in Bohemian communes, he would give away his sketches or paintings for cafe meals, never getting ahead financially. In contrast to Winfrey's Venusian fish swimming in material waters, Modigliani had retrograde Venus at the inferior conjunction and swam only in waters of spirit. It is his Sun in exact sextile to the 8th-house ruler, Mars, that preserved his legacy.[51]

When a natal Sun-Venus angle changes phases by secondary progression, it marks an important year in the life for any person. The author, whose Sun-Venus natal phase angle was between points 4 and 5 in the illustration on page 67, in 1983 progressed into the heliacal setting of Venus, disappearing into the Sun's rays. His longest marriage began that year. At age 75, he will reach superior conjunction.[52]

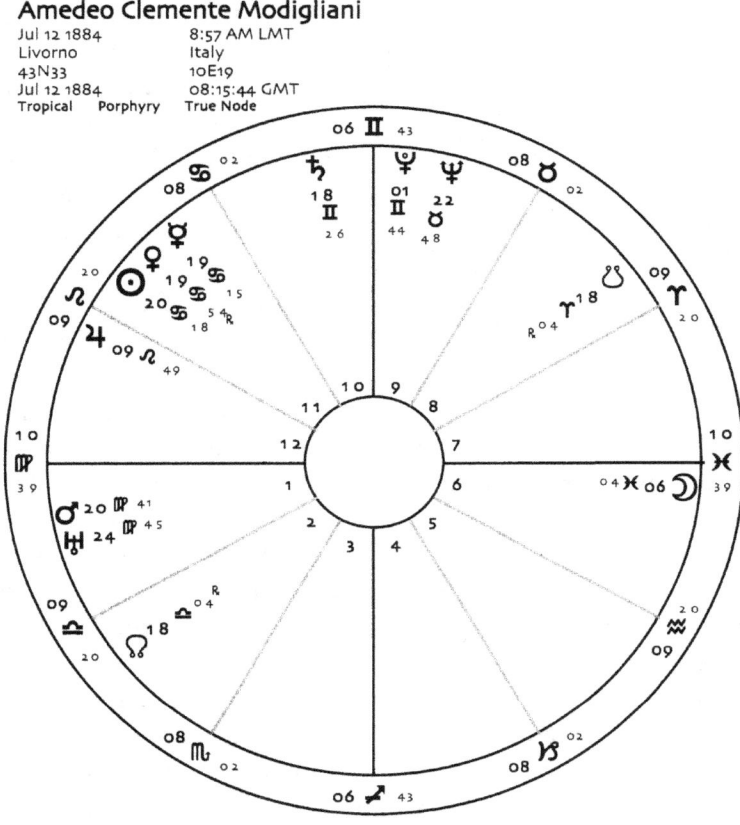

In the following list, based on consecutive synodic cycles of the Sun and Venus from 1966 to 2015, readers will see that Venus has a fairly uniform orbital cycle:

Phase 1. Inferior Conjunction to Heliacal Rising = from 6 to 7 days
Phase 2. Heliacal Rising to Stationary Direct = from 13 to 15 days
Phase 3. Stationary Direct to Greatest Elongation East = from 48 to 53 days
Phase 4. Greatest Elongation East to Heliacal Setting = from 174 to 184 days
Phase 5. Heliacal Setting to Superior Conjunction = from 39 to 45 days
Phase 6. Superior Conjunction to Heliacal Rising = from 38 to 44 days
Phase 7. Heliacal Rising to Greatest Elongation West = from 173 to 187 days
Phase 8. Greatest Elongation West to Stationary Retrograde = 47 to 54 days
Phase 9. Stationary Retrograde to Heliacal Setting = from 14 to 15 days
Phase 10. Heliacal Setting to Inferior Conjunction = from 7 to 8 days

Chapter Four • *Sun–Venus Phase Angle Returns*

A complete synodic cycle of Venus between two consecutive inferior conjunctions ranged from 578 to 589 days, with an average cycle of 584 days. Astrologers working extensively with secondary progressions will realize that *the above phase lengths in days translate into years in the progressed horoscope.*

A close scrutiny of this summary of the cycles and phases of the planet Venus reveals that many souls who are born just after greatest eastern elongation, or just after the heliacal rising of a direct motion Venus, could live to be 90 or 100 years old and never experience a progressed phase angle change. However, souls born just before the retrograde station of Venus will pass through five phase changes in their secondary progressions by the age of 40 to 50. This includes two stations of Venus, a heliacal setting and rising, and the inferior conjunction. It is no wonder that these souls have the most harrowing stories to tell about their personal lives.

A textbook example of one born just prior to a retrograde station of Venus having a wild ride during the first forty or so years of life is found in the nativity of Heidi Fleiss, the infamous Hollywood Madam.

Born only six days before Venus turned retrograde, Fleiss was the daughter of a prominent pediatrician in Los Angeles who started her career as a Capricorn entrepreneur with a baby-sitting business at 13, employing other young neighborhood girls to handle her overflow of work.

Dropping out of high school in the 10th grade, she worked for a time in retail and in real estate. After meeting the owner of the most successful prostitution business in Los Angeles at a nightclub, she went to work for her as manager and sextupled the monthly gross income from $50,000 to $300,000 in her first month on the job. She later went out on her own and built a lucrative business providing sexual services to an "A" list of wealthy businessmen, foreign royalty, and movie stars.

The tri-wheel on the next page shows that her secondary-progressed Venus stationed retrograde just before she was six years old. She reached the progressed inferior conjunction at the age of 26, right when her prostitution business was at its peak. Ominously, however, that inferior conjunction conjoined her natal 12th-house Mars, exact to 04' of arc. By the next Spring, she was caught in the act of pandering by the Los Angeles County Sheriff Department in an elaborate plot involving an undercover Beverly Hills police officer who posed as a wealthy Japanese client looking to procure sexual services for himself and three other men for a total of $6,000.

She eventually served a three-year prison term, and while in jail had to

Robert P. Blaschke • *Holographic Transits*

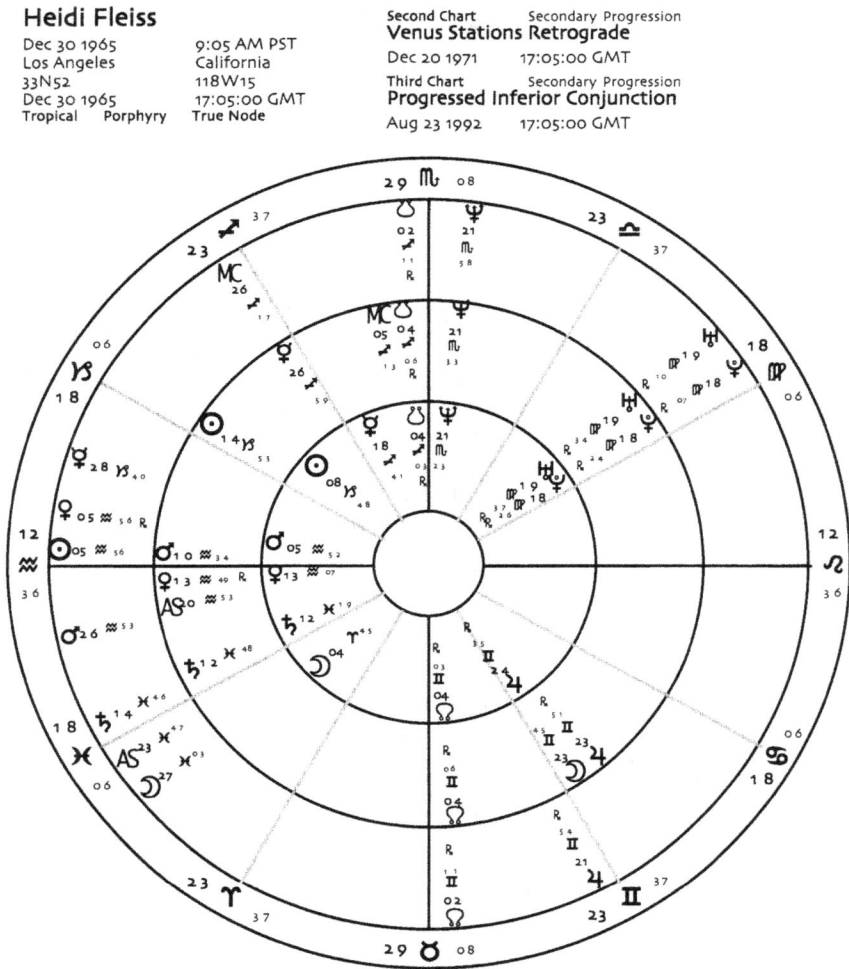

violently defend herself from physical assault by aggressive lesbian inmates. After release from prison, she entered into a relationship with a male actor and became a victim of domestic violence. Since writing a book and having her life story developed into a movie, she is now constructing an all-male brothel in Nevada for female patrons. All this wild living and she still hasn't even reached her progressed direct station.

The astrologer is struck by the Uranus-Pluto conjunction exactly on her 8th cusp, as well as the anaretic 30th degree of the sexual sign, Scorpio, on the Midheaven. From Sepharial's translation of *La Volasfera*, for Scorpio 30:

Chapter Four • *Sun–Venus Phase Angle Returns*

A woman in trailing robes waving a wand around which is coiled a serpent.
It is the index of a nature that is both clever and cunning; capable of asserting its power over others by persuasion or fascination. To such will be given some lofty command or position of trust, and success will be achieved by personal charm and magnetic power. It is a degree of ATTRACTION.

It has been this author's personal experience that women born near the greatest eastern or western elongation of Venus have substantial detachment toward their personal lives, similar to an objectivity one finds with a Sun-Mercury phase angle at greatest elongation. This appears to be especially the case when Venus is two signs apart from the Sun. One was a Libra wife with Venus in Leo, another was a Scorpio girlfriend with Venus in Virgo, and a third was a Gemini girlfriend with Venus in Leo. In each case, the woman as an individual (Sun) appeared separated from her identity as a wife or lover (Venus). In consultation with like male clients, *i.e.*, a Cancer Sun with Venus in Virgo, a similar detachment in love was observed.

Of all the points around the Sun-Venus phase cycle, it has been this astrologer's experience that the most intense in terms of personal relationship are between the heliacal setting and rising. This, of course, includes both the inferior and superior conjunctions of the Sun and Venus. From the time Venus disappears into the rays of the Sun until she re-emerges and is again visible as either a morning or evening star, is a journey into the heart of love wherein a soul is burned in the fires of the Sun, purifying attachments until the soul's spiritual essence is known.

Pre-Natal Sun-Venus Synodic Cycle

The inferior conjunction of retrograde Venus and the Sun prior to birth, along with its degree symbols, produces insight about the collective feeling patterns and romantic inclinations that one shares with his "soul group," which is carried over from past lives. As stated in the previous chapters on the Moon and Mercury, countless souls will incarnate during the 584-day synodic cycle of Venus. It is the belief of this astrologer that one's individual hologram of attachment emerges from an extensive "feeling matrix," of which one is but a part. It is assumed that these records are on the astral plane, epitomizing conditions in previous eras of history that deeply affected the feelings and attachments of those living during that time.

At the end of this book is a Table of Sun-Venus conjunctions for 200 years from 1920 to 2120. Readers can locate their pre-natal Sun-Venus synodic cycle and its inferior conjunction degree (retrograde Venus conjunct Sun). One may also determine from the table whether a birth occurred during the Oriental phase (from inferior to superior conjunction), or during the Occidental phase (from superior to inferior conjunction). Direct is shown by a "D", and retrograde by "R".

By researching the degree symbols for one's pre-natal inferior conjunction, insight about past life conditions existing in the collective ethers can be found. It should be borne in mind that we share these past life factors with the other souls incarnating during the same 584-day Sun-Venus synodic cycle as ourselves. It has also been this astrologer's experience that these other souls, born within the same Sun-Venus synodic cycle as ourselves, have similar relational experiences to ours.

The following bi-wheel has the author's pre-natal Sun-Venus inferior conjunction, which was about seven months prior to his birth, overlaid into his natal houses. Souls born between 13 April 1953 and 15 November 1954, when the subsequent inferior conjunction took place, share collective relational and financial dynamics set into place at the time of that new Sun-Venus synodic cycle. The degree symbol for the inferior conjunction, Aries 24, defines the collective conditions of the cycle, whereas the rising degree for the inferior conjunction calculated for an individual birth location symbolizes the personal experience of that cycle. For the author, his rising degree for the inferior conjunction cast for Santa Monica is Capricorn 9.

The author has scores of clients born between April 1953 and November 1954, many for whom he has been personal astrologer for over twenty-five years. In listening to their stories about hardship in love and broken hearts and failed marriages, he has felt the heavy weight in his heart of a soul group learning some hard Sun-Venus lessons during this lifetime.

If the astrologer carefully examines that April 1953 inferior conjunction shown in the preceding page, he will find that the Sun-Venus conjunction is exactly opposite a retrograde Saturn-Neptune conjunction, and also part of a massive six-planet Tetradic Yod anchored by a Mercury in detriment sextile to Jupiter. A prophetic omen was there for all souls born during this 19-month synodic cycle—a Mutual Reception in detriment is found between Venus in Aries and Mars in Taurus. It is clear that all who incarnated during this synodic cycle have been severely tested. As an avowal to the resiliency of this soul group, with Venus opposite Neptune, they never quite give up the hope for love despite the repetitive Saturnian failings.

Chapter Four • Sun–Venus Phase Angle Returns

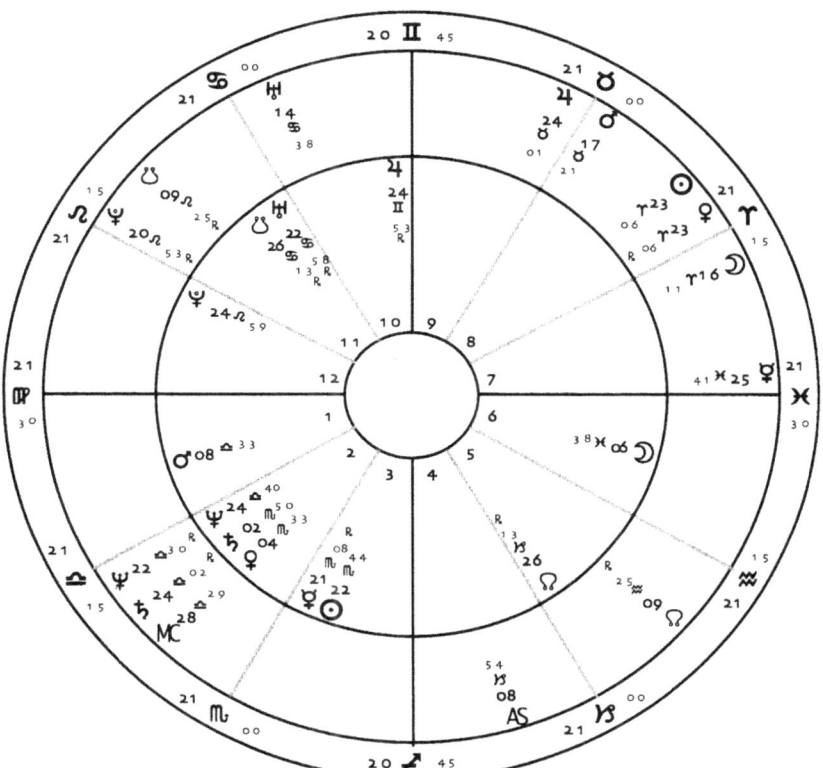

As the lunation cycle was in the Balsamic phase at the time of inferior conjunction, one can plainly see that this was an especially karmic synodic cycle. Perhaps this soul group is completing karma from many past lives, and yet, with that Mercury in sextile to Jupiter at the base of the Yod, much spiritual understanding will come out of it all, despite the confusion and thoughts of victimization brought on by a Mercury in detriment in Pisces. The Sun and Saturn are in exalted opposition, and this soul group will, before the end of their lives, attain maturity and stability.

From Sepharial's translation of *La Volasfera*, for Aries 24, a collective definition:

A man playing with coloured balls, an immodest woman standing behind him.

This indicates one of a playful but careless nature, given over to pleasures and unprofitable pursuits. One who will be crossed in life by the opposite sex, and meet with troubles thereby. One with very little force of character or worthy ambition. It is a degree of FOOLISHNESS.

For the author, born seven months after the inferior conjunction when that Venus conjoined Saturn, Capricorn 9 was rising at the place of his birth when that new synodic cycle began. The symbols for this rising degree tell his personalized story:

From Charubel, for Capricorn 9:

> *A man climbing a steep hill, a road consisting of steps; an angel form at the top giving words of cheer with a golden crown awaiting him.*

Denotes one who will be inspired to pursue an object worthy of his ambition, and one who will labour hard and suffer much in the fulfillment of his mission.

And from *La Volasfera*, for Capricorn 9:

> *A cross and a broken key.*

This is the index of a nature that is aspiring and eager to penetrate into the experiences of life, but doomed by an adverse fate to failure and disappointment. The broken key is the sign of those abortive enterprises in which he will engage to his undoing and loss of reputation. Where he should knock and wait in patience he will essay an entry by craft and worldly wisdom, and even as he turns the key in the lock it will break off short in his hand. If he should restrain his impetuosity and daring, and cultivate humility of spirit, haply his cross will not be found too heavy for him to bear. With that as key to the treasures of this world he may enter the Gates of the Temple of Wisdom. It is a degree of IMPOTENCE.

So, the reader can see that an angel is encouraging the author to write his seven astrology books, but though the hill is steep, that "golden crown" keeps beckoning. One also sees that the author's "craftiness and impetuosity" has broken his key off in the lock on the "Gate of the Temple of Wisdom," and that if he cultivates humility of spirit by acknowledging his mistakes and character defects, he may one day be granted admission into that Sacred Place on the other side of the Locked Gate.[53]

Some readers may wonder just how to ascertain from which "feeling matrix" on the astral plane one's individual hologram of attachment has emerged, and from what "previous era of history that deeply affected the feelings and attachments of those living during that time" is the soul in this lifetime connected to

Chapter Four • *Sun–Venus Phase Angle Returns*

from past lives? The author has contemplated this question, and during research found the following.

Examining the Sun-Venus synodic cycle over a period of 2500 years, he found that inferior conjunctions occur in the same degree of the Zodiac every 251 years, and repeat from two to eight times, and then the sequence of exact conjunctions leaves that degree. For example, a Sun-Venus inferior conjunction occurred in Aries 24 in April of the years (all AD) 447, 698, 949, 1200, 1451, 1702, 1953, and will occur for an eighth and final time in 2204. The inferior conjunctions just before and after this time sequence, *i.e.*, in 196 and in 2455, fall in Aries 23 (22° 59' in 196 AD).

It is this author's thesis that these dates are the "previous eras of history" in which souls born between 13 April 1953 and 15 November 1954 took birth during their prior incarnations, thus resulting in the identical pre-natal Sun-Venus inferior conjunction degree as in the present life. Specifically, these are past lives that are directly connected to the present life in regard to personal relationships, use of artistic or creative propensities, and memories of financial success or failure in past incarnations. All are departments of life that are Venus-ruled.

A subsequent Sun-Venus inferior conjunction occurred on 15 November 1954 in 22° Scorpio 24'. This particular sequence only has three repeating conjunctions in that identical degree of Scorpio 23; the first in 1703, then in 1954, with the final one in 2205. The implication is that Venusian karma can last from two to eight consecutive lifetimes. The gist of this reincarnation theory is that souls come back to Earth when the synodic cycle of the Sun and any planet originates in the exact same Zodiac degree as in previous lifetimes. These pre-natal synodic cycles determine one's *soul group*, and also link the past to the present.

The artistic and creative Sun-Venus "soul group" to which this author and his fellow beings born between April 1953 and November 1954 belong, is no chopped liver. During the Sun-Venus synodic cycle of April 1451 to November 1452, which began with the inferior conjunction in Aries 24, we find Leonardo da Vinci born on 14 April 1452. Additionally, during that cycle, Christopher Columbus was born on an unspecified date between August and October 1451. The prior synodic cycle of April 1200 to November 1201 had Aries 24 as its inferior conjunction degree as well. On 3 May 1201 Thibaut IV of Champagne, the King of Navarre, was born. He is considered one of the great lyrical poets of the thirteenth century.

The astrologer employing these techniques can research for his client the pre-natal inferior conjunction degree of the Sun and retrograde Venus. Then, by calculating forwards and backwards in time in multiples of 251 years, one can determine for how many lifetimes this sequence of karma lasts. For some souls, the succession of identical inferior conjunction degrees will go back for 502, 753, 1004, 1255, 1506, or 1757 years. Others are in their first or second lifetimes of these karmic chains. The author is in his 7th consecutive incarnation of a sequence begun in 447 AD.[54]

Using Sun-Venus Holographic Transits

A Sun-Venus holographic transit occurs when the exact distance arc between the natal Sun and Venus forms again in the heavens, *and is also in the identical phase as the natal Venus cycle, i.e., Oriental or Occidental.* The Sun-Venus phase angle return occurs every nineteen months, and at these times one can align with Higher Self and make crucial choices about relationships, finances, or creative endeavors.

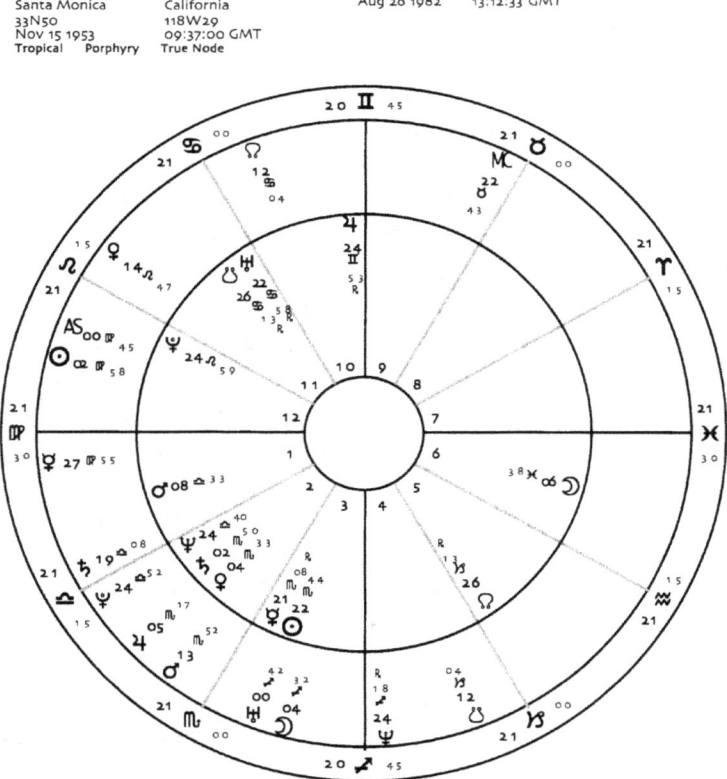

Chapter Four • *Sun–Venus Phase Angle Returns*

The author has found that these holographic transits are highly portentous, with exact synastry conjunctions regularly occurring between these phase angle return charts and the planets or angles in one's own nativity, or in the nativities of souls who are about to enter your life during the next nineteen-month Sun-Venus synodic period. Synastric aspect configurations between the charts are common.

The bi-wheel on the previous page shows the Sun-Venus holographic transit for the author of 26 August 1982. One sees that his Sun-Venus distance arc of 18° 10' 55" has reformed in the heavens, and that the Sun-Venus phase is Oriental, as it was at his birth. Three months later in November of 1982, the author met his wife with whom he would be wed until early 1994. The Descendant of the phase angle return chart is 00° Pisces 45', the exact degree of the author's natal Vertex. The IC of the holographic transit is 22° Scorpio 43', conjunct his Sun within 01' of arc. As if to prognosticate a serious cycle of karma, the rising degree was the Saturn/North Node midpoint.[55]

This next bi-wheel chart is the author's Sun-Venus phase angle return of 14 June 1995. In November 1995, he reconnected with an old friend (he was the godfather of her two grown children). Now divorced, she and the author became involved and eventually had a child, a daughter born in September 1997. Their relationship was filled with a deep love; however, it was also extremely unstable, resulting in many painful separations and chaotic uncertainty. It was a life-changing episode.

Astrologers see that the Sun and Venus have again replicated his natal distance arc in the heavens. As a prophetic omen of the intense spiritual transformation the author would be undergoing during the next nineteen months, three exact synastric Yods form between his nativity and this Sun-Venus holographic transit, all in 24°. The rulers of the author's horizon, Mercury and Jupiter, were configured in a tight Mutable T-Cross with an apex Mars, ruling planet of separation and strife. Again prognosticating serious karma, Saturn/North Node= the author's Sun/Moon.[56]

In his ensuing Sun-Venus holographic transit of 17 January 1997, which preceded the birth of his younger daughter that following September, the author had quite a Stellium falling into his 5th house of children. Unfortunately for him, however, a second child is ruled by the 7th house and here we find both the lesser and greater malefics, Mars and Saturn, on the Nodes in the 1st and 7th houses. It is without exaggeration to say that the loss of that child was the most painful experience of the author's life. Phase angle return Moon/Pluto and Sun/Saturn = his Vertex.[57]

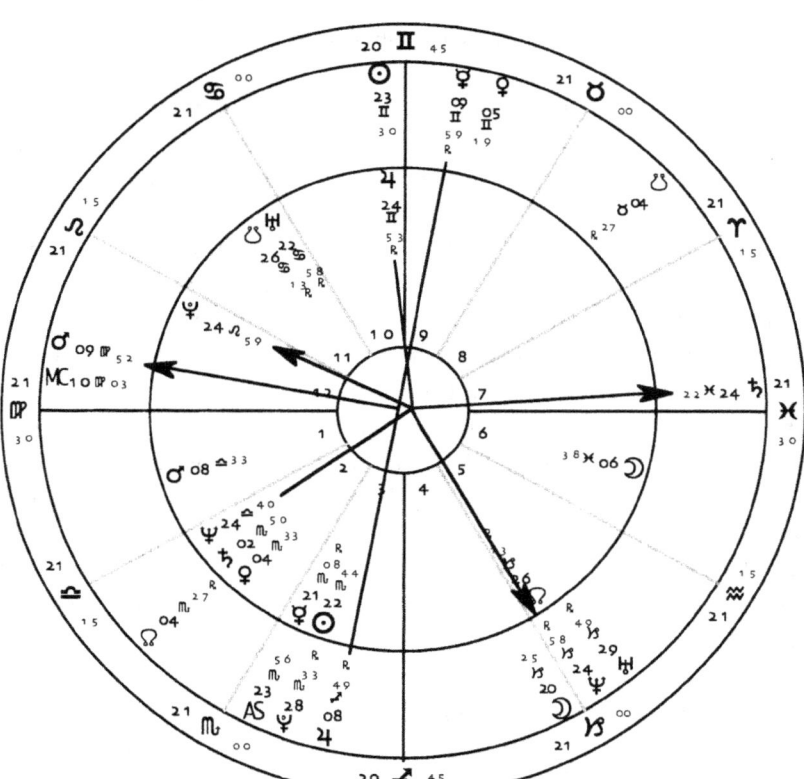

The astrologer can also observe from this tri-wheel chart (shown on the next page) how phase angle returns interact with secondary progressions. Uranus is exactly conjunct the progressed IC, and part of an exact Fixed T-Cross with natal Venus and progressed Mars. The phase angle return IC in 00° Scorpio 24' is conjunct the author's progressed Ascendant. His crisis in consciousness is seen in a progressed Last Quarter Moon.

From these examples, astrologers can see the interaction between the nativity and the celestial conditions in place at the time of the phase angle return. The author is of the opinion that holographic transits represent an alignment of free will with Higher Self, as the natal Sun-planet hologram has replicated itself in the heavens. It is at these times that the rays of the Sun duplicate the

Chapter Four • *Sun–Venus Phase Angle Returns*

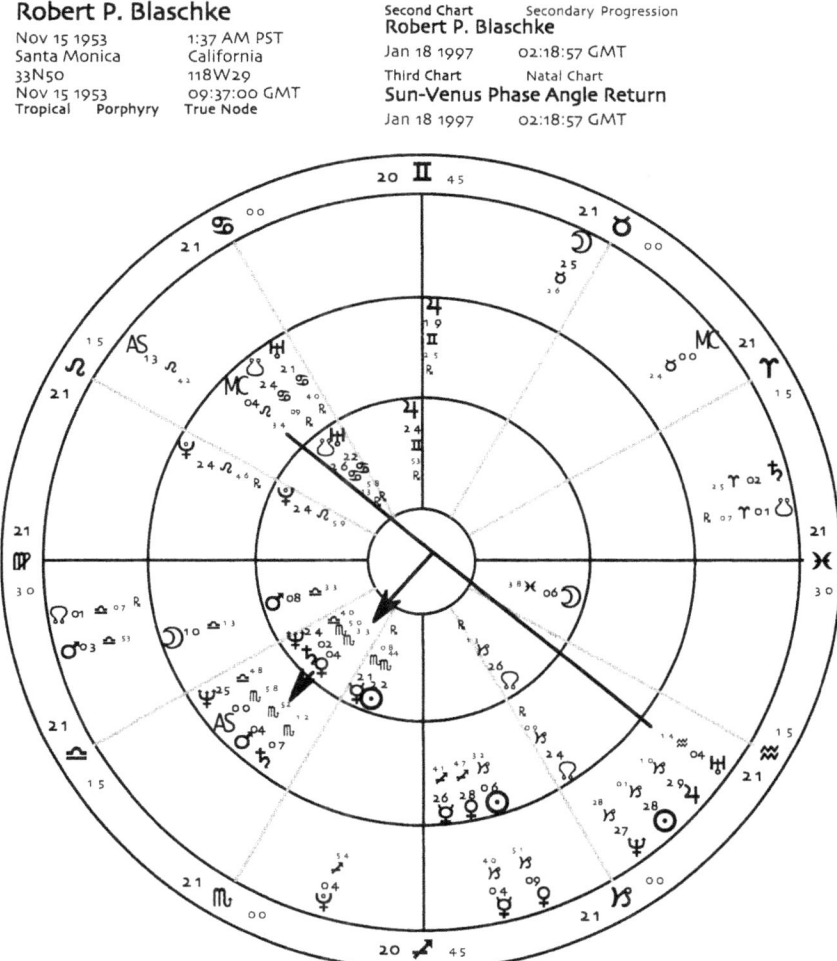

birth angle with Venus. In these episodes from the author's life, one sees that free will can also choose peril.

This tri-wheel chart illustrates exact synastric conjunctions that exist between a phase angle return and the nativity of a soul who is about to arrive in one's life. In January of 2005, the author had a Sun-Venus holographic transit occur with the Sun in 25° Capricorn. Later that year, in August, he met his partner who has, you guessed it, her natal Sun in that very degree. In a remarkable twist of fate, his wife in 1982 had a natal Mercury-Venus conjunction in 7° Capricorn, as in this chart.

Robert P. Blaschke

Nov 15 1953   1:37 AM PST
Santa Monica   California
33N50   118W29
Nov 15 1953   09:37:00 GMT
Tropical   Porphyry   True Node

Second Chart   Natal Chart
Sun-Venus Phase Angle Return
Jan 15 2005   12:27:34 GMT
Third Chart   Natal Chart
Female
Jan 16 1956   20:50:00 GMT

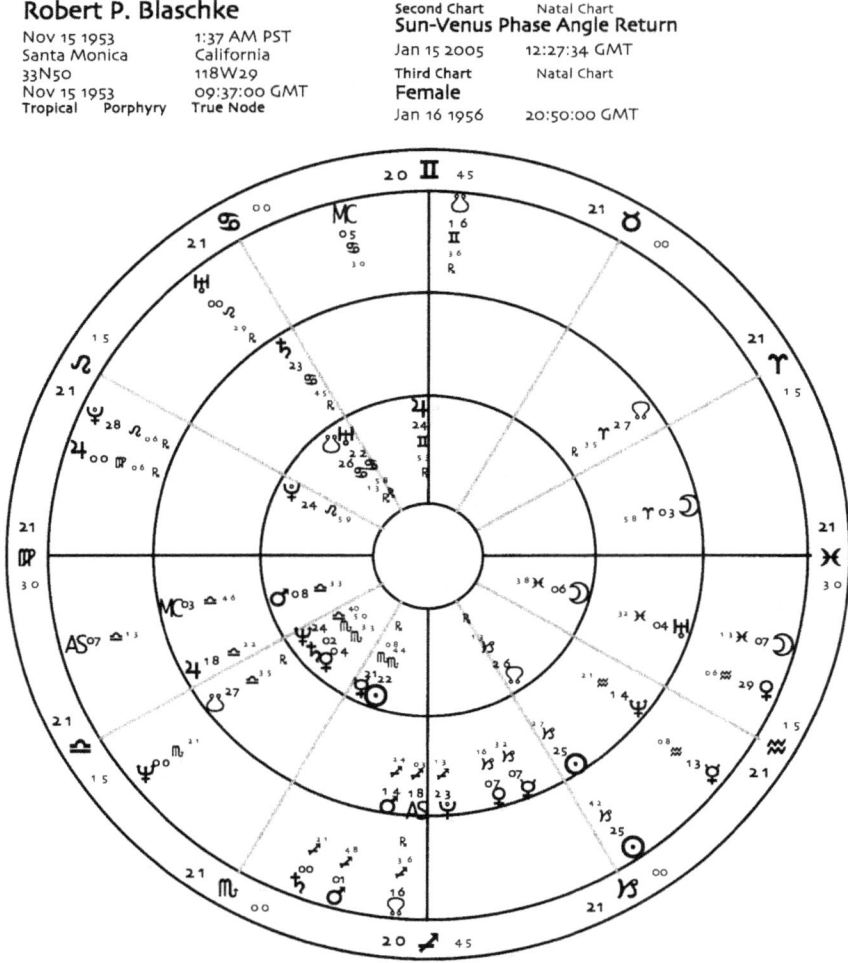

Readers are no doubt thinking about how to use Sun-Venus holographic transits in a practical way. The author recommends viewing these once-in-nineteen-month phase angle return charts as the recurring divine essence of one's true love nature. On the day that the Sun's rays form the same phase angle to Venus as when one took birth is, for this astrologer, a very special spiritual opportunity to align with Higher Self. One takes comfort in the fact that on these days, celestial conditions are such that one is assured that his free will is aligned with his divine essence.

Chapter Four • *Sun–Venus Phase Angle Returns*

To give a personal example of what is meant by this, in the tri-wheel shown on the previous page, the author and his partner have conjunct Moons in Pisces. Their synastrically conjoined Moons had transit Uranus station on them when the two first met. Needless to say, the first year of their relationship was a case study in instability, unpredictable turns of events, and unexpected and unanticipated surprises. Many times, the two considered ending their relationship yet, when they searched their hearts, they both agreed they still loved each other.

The author saw in his phase angle return chart a sign from above that he was to be with her, as the Sun on the day of the holographic transit conjoined her Sun. He took this as evidence that she was the one, despite the difficulties that confronted them during the first year. The philosophical underpinning of this belief system is based on a precise astrological technique—what is in the heavens on the day of a phase angle return is the same as one's essence—*to thine own self be forever true.*

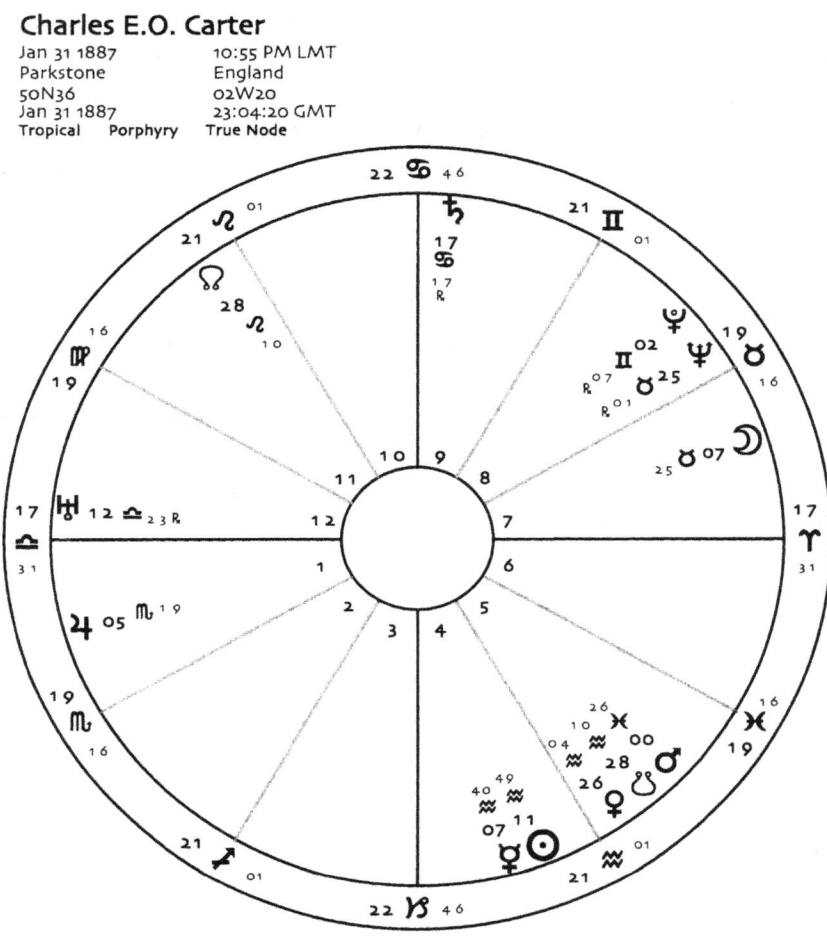

Libra 18 from *La Volasfera*

A well-lighted house with open door.

It denotes a person of hospitable and homely nature, ever ready with the best of fare to entertain friends and acquaintances. The native will grow to be much beloved for his open-handedness and sincerity of feeling. He will be both prosperous and happy, and will rejoice in the company of his friends. It is a degree of HOSPITALITY.

Chapter Five
Sun-Mars Phase Angle Returns

Sun-Mars Phase Angle at Birth

The Sun-Mars phase angle at birth forms the specific nature of one's determination and drive. This hologram of passion establishes the pattern of action, leadership, courage, and endurance within the mature soul, yet during youth, the personality must wrestle with its demons to overcome base passions that bring a destructive self-centeredness into a life. Mars can be understood best through its exaltation in Capricorn. If the entity is able to discipline itself and channel passion into accomplishment, like a fine wine, life will improve with age.

The Ram, the Scorpion/Eagle, and the Mountain Goat are three representations of Mars. In Matthew 25:31–33, Jesus says in the parable of *The Sheep and the Goats*, "When the Son of Man comes in his glory, and all the angels with him, he will sit on his throne in heavenly glory. All the nations will be gathered before him, and he will separate the people one from another as a shepherd separates the sheep from the goats. He will put the sheep on his right and the goats on his left."

Jesus then says to those on his right (Aries, the Ram, a male sheep), "Come, you who are blessed by my Father; take your inheritance (Scorpio, the Eagle), the kingdom prepared for you since the creation of the world. For I was hungry and you gave me something to eat, I was thirsty and you gave me something to drink, I was a stranger and you invited me in, I needed clothes and you clothed me, I was sick and you looked after me, I was in prison and you came to visit me ... I tell you the truth, whatever you did for one of the least of these brothers of mine, you did for me."

To those on his left (Capricorn, the Mountain Goat) He says, "Depart from me, you who are cursed, into the eternal fire prepared for the devil (Scorpio, the Scorpion) and his angels. For I was hungry and you gave me nothing to eat ... I tell you the truth, whatever you did not do for one of the least of these, you did not do for me."

Pondering these passages from Scripture about the sheep and the goats (Aries and Capricorn), signs of Mars' masculine dignity and exaltation, how to understand what Jesus meant? To the author, the mystery has its answer in the lower and higher natures of Scorpio, sign of Mars' feminine dignity.

Recalling the essays of C.E.O. Carter on the planets and signs, he wrote regarding Mars and Aries,[58] "... *in the case of an evolved Martian, may produce a valiant and idealistic fighter on behalf of the weak; this, indeed, is the highest type produced by Mars*" and "*in good types (Aries) the courage and vigour are devoted to sensible and useful ends, and the native may achieve much as a reformer or advocate of the weak.*"

Regarding the worst of Capricorn, Carter wrote, "... *the failings which may occur in weak examples are such as worldliness, snobbishness, a tendency to manage and even to make use of others for private ends ... there may be downright selfishness and craftiness in pursuit of personal advantage.*" One need only look at corporations.

When Jesus *separates the sheep from the goats*, he is rewarding those who fight for the poor with entry into the kingdom of Heaven (peace and happiness in the heart). By saying *depart from me* to those who have succumbed to worldliness, and who are attached to social status and conspicuous consumption at the expense of social conscience and a concern for the poor, Jesus speaks of the eternal fire of hell on Earth, wherein one can never have enough, get enough, or find contentment within.

In this allegory, between Aries (the sheep) and Capricorn (the goat), lies Scorpio, sign of either the plebeian Scorpion or the evolved Eagle. A key spiritual question thus is asked of any individual: *How will you use your Mars?* The author believes that a true understanding of one's Sun-Mars phase angle will help to answer this moral inquiry, and fathoming one's natal hologram is the key.

To visualize one's natal Sun-Mars hologram, the glyph for the Earth is added into the horoscope, thus creating the three-dimensional image. In the author's nativity, his Sun-Mars distance arc A is 44° 11' 00", and the Mars-Earth distance arc B is 135° 49' 00". Together, these two arcs total 180° 00' 00". Using his Sabian Aspect Orb technique, arc A equates to the 15th degree of Taurus, and arc B is equivalent to the 16th degree of Leo. These two degrees are antiscia, or solstice points, of one another. Sun-Earth arc C is always a constant, measuring exactly 180° 00' 00".

From Sepharial's translation of *La Volasfera*, for Taurus 15:

A venerable man seated in an uncertain light;
before him are several books, and various scientific instruments surround him.

It denotes a studious and intuitive nature, whose mental vision will see where others are in the darkness; one devoted to the inner meaning of Nature's workings, and acting from obscure motives; one of much self-reliance, inclined to

Chapter Five • *Sun–Mars Phase Angle Returns*

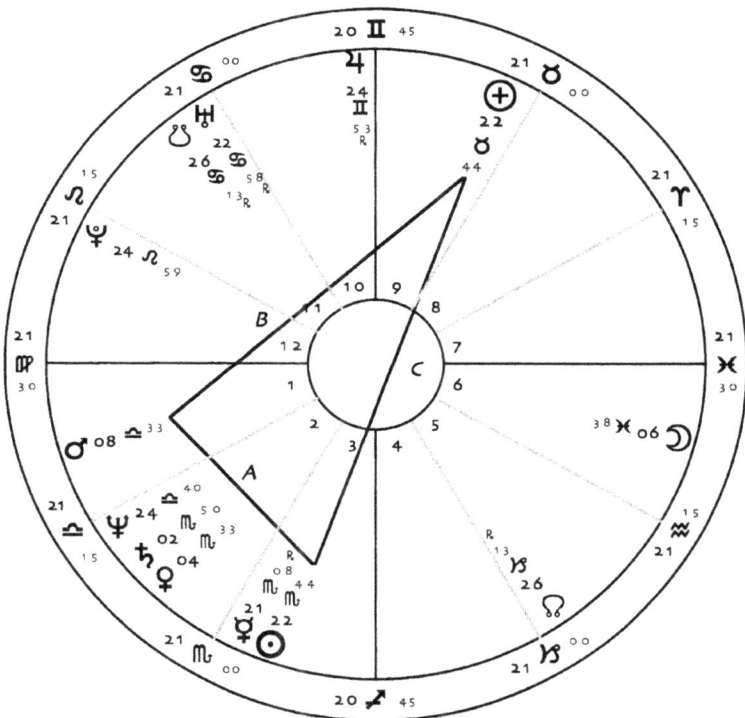

solitariness, and yet always surrounded by friends; one who will be sought after while himself seeking none. It is a degree of MYSTERY.

And from *La Volasfera*, for Leo 16:

A ram standing upon a barren rock, pawing the ground.

It indicates a person of a headstrong and rash disposition, extremely given to impulse; difficult to restrain; a formidable opponent and a warm-hearted, generous friend. The native is effusive, enthusiastic and restless, but capable of subsisting upon small fare and in all probability he will be poor though in some sense eminent. It is a degree of IMPULSE.

The author could not have found a more apt description of his lower and higher natures. Readers familiar with *A Handbook for the Self-Employed Astrologer* know that this astrologer has indeed "subsisted upon small fare" for years. For further insight, Charubel for Taurus 15:

A natural well surrounded with moss, low shrubs, and briars. The water is clear as crystal and cold as ice. The immediate locality is dry and barren.
A person possessing wonderful abilities, numerous accomplishments, and, above all, a revealer of secrets, much given to researches in nature.

A giant amusing himself with a child's doll.
Denotes one who possesses great abilities; a mind, which, if rightly directed, could accomplish, or at least assist in bringing about, great and beneficial changes on the earth. But in place of this, he condescends to employ his time and his energies in the pursuit of what is childish, whimsical, and worthless; by which he not infrequently makes himself the laughing-stock of his contemporaries. (Leo 16)

As with all of the three-dimensional natal holograms, these Sun-Mars and Mars-Earth distance arcs, when converted into their derived degree symbols, open up a window into the holographic dimensions of one's soul. The very fact that the two combined arcs total 180°, and the derived degrees are antiscion of one another, informs the astrologer that the divine symmetrical rays of the Sun are at their core.

The Sun-Mars phase angle at birth is part of an overall synodic cycle lasting for an average of 779 days, or 25–26 months.[59] The cycle begins with a conjunction of the Sun and direct motion Mars, reaches its halfway point at the opposition of the Sun and retrograde Mars, and has quarter points when the Sun squares Mars. All souls incarnate at a specific point within the cycle, and with a unique phase angle.

Some readers may be wondering where in the orbital cycle of Mars the sextile, trine, and quincunx aspects occur. A heliacal setting and rising of Mars occurs at an angle of about 10° to 11° from the Sun. The illustration on the next page shows both the rising and setting of the Earth as if observed from Mars (points 5 and 7), and the heliacal rising and setting of Mars as measured from the Earth (points 2 and 10).

Therefore, the waxing sextile of the Sun and Mars would occur between points 2 and 3 in the cycle, and waning sextiles between points 9 and 10. The waxing trine occurs between points 3 and 4, the waning trine between points 8 and 9. As with all superior planets, any body quincunx or opposite the Sun has to be retrograde. The waxing quincunx occurs between points 4 and 5, the waning between 7 and 8.

Regarding direct or retrograde stations of Mars, the geocentric distance between the Sun and stationary Mars varies from a minimum angular separation of 127° to a maximum of 148°. This fluctuation is caused by Mars being at aphelion (furthest from Sun in its elliptical orbit), or at perihelion (closest to Sun).

Chapter Five • Sun–Mars Phase Angle Returns

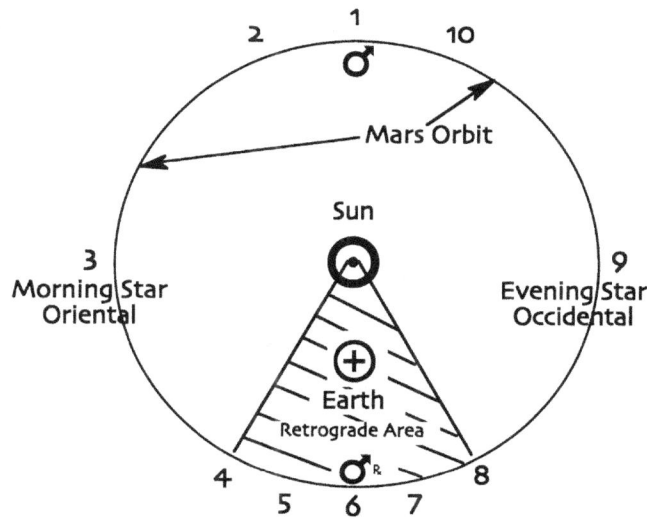

Cycles and Phases of the Planet Mars

1. Sun-Mars Conjunction
2. Mars' Heliacal Rising
3. Waxing Square
4. Stationary Retrograde
5. Earth's Heliacal Setting
6. Sun-Mars Opposition
7. Earth's Heliacal Rising
8. Stationary Direct
9. Waning Square
10. Mars Heliacal Setting

This astrologer has observed that if the retrograde station of Mars forms an exact aspect to the Sun while stationing, such as a 135° trioctile or 144° biquintile, that retrograde period of Mars is more destructive than usual. A recent example of this was in March 1999, when Mars stationed retrograde 135° from the Sun. The NATO bombing of Serbia occurred during that particular retrogression of Mars.[60]

The natal Sun-Mars phase angle can be used when providing vocational guidance. The cycle of Mars relative to the Sun can be divided into four quarters, similar to the lunation cycle. Referring to the diagram above, these four quadrants are:

Quadrant	Cycle Span	Ruler	Vocational Inclinations
1st (1 to 3)	0° to 90°	Sun	Creative Self-Employment
2nd (3 to 6)	90° to 180°	Jupiter	Protection & Preservation
3rd (6 to 9)	180° to 270°	Saturn	Design, Art, Law & Order
4th (9 to 1)	270° to 360°	Mars	Leadership & Management

These rulerships are based on the exaltations of the Luminaries and planets. Aries symbolically starts the cycle at the conjunction, with the Sun exalted in this sign. The waxing square occurs at the Cancer ingress, and here we have Jupiter exalted. Libra, the exaltation of Saturn, corresponds with the opposition. And at the Third Quarter square, during the Capricorn ingress, we have Mars in its exaltation.

Using the cycles and phases of the planet Mars for vocational insight, those born between the conjunction and the 90° square will be happiest with self-employment in a creative and independent capacity. Having a morning star Mars in this opening quadrant, which lasts on average for 283 days, gives much pride in one's work. The will has a strong desire to prove itself, and favors owning a business.[61]

A natal Sun-Mars phase angle between the waxing square and opposition falls in the second quadrant, and partly when Mars is retrograde. Lasting on average 106 days, this section of the cycle is ruled by Jupiter and favors employment in professions that provide protection and preservation for others. This includes child care, real estate, hotel or restaurant work, food services, catering, military service, guidance counselors and therapists, and the clergy doing religious work.

At the retrograde opposition to the Sun, Mars reverses polarity from oriental to occidental and becomes the evening star. This third quadrant lasts on average 105 days until the 270° square, and is ruled by Saturn. Souls born with a Sun-Mars phase angle in this part of the cycle will be happiest in professions such as music and art, or architecture and graphic design. You will find them working in places of culture, such as galleries and museums. Also favored in this Sun-Mars quadrant is work in the criminal justice system, such as law enforcement.

A natal phase angle between waning square and the end of the cycle falls in the Mars-ruled fourth quadrant. Souls born during this phase, lasting for an average of 285 days, will do best in positions of leadership and management, and are capable of working in hierarchical corporate structures, where rules, regulations, and strict codes regarding personal appearance apply. Since this quadrant is also when Mars is the evening star, taking directions from others is tolerated more readily, as opposed to the self-starting morning star types who disdain authority.

If a Sun-Mars phase angle changes by secondary progression during the adult life, individuals may experience declining interest in their careers, and a

Chapter Five • Sun–Mars Phase Angle Returns

midlife change of profession should be recommended by the consulting astrologer. Of course, this will be most disorienting at the progressed conjunction or opposition of Mars and the Sun, where a reversal of polarity from morning star to evening star occurs, or *mutatis mutandis* when Mars shifts from occidental to oriental.[62]

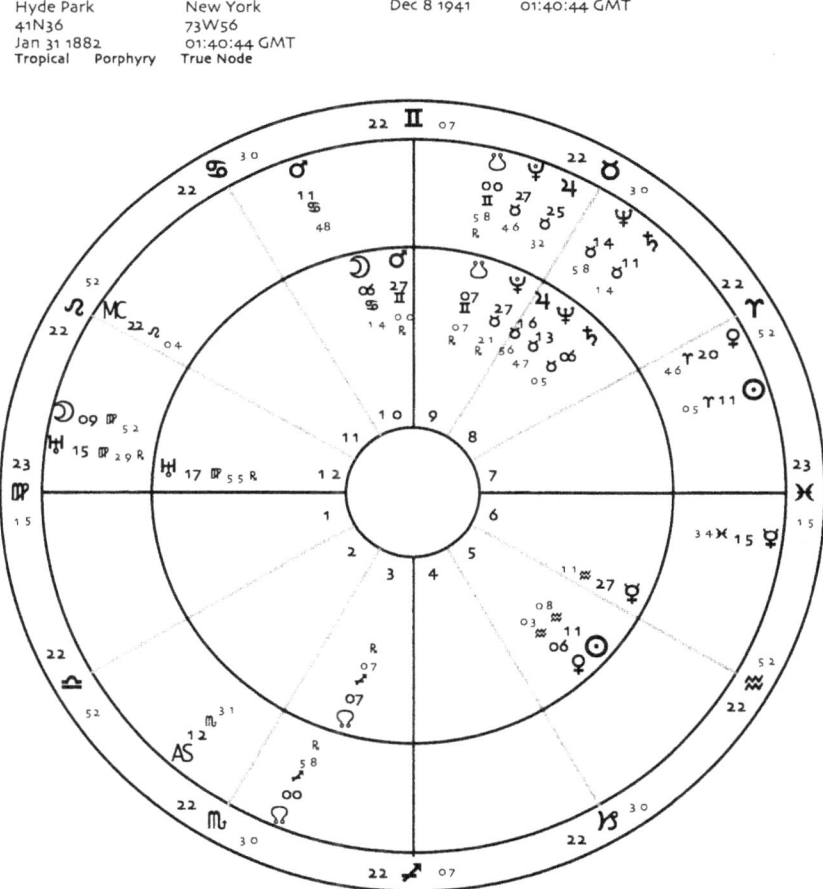

The phase changes at the Sun-Mars progressed waxing or waning squares are significant, but generally result in different circumstances in an existing career, rather than resulting in a total change of the profession. A textbook example of this occurred in the life of President Franklin D. Roosevelt. In the biwheel chart, note that at the time of the Pearl Harbor attack in December 1941,

FDR had his secondary progressed Sun and Mars applying to a waning square. President Roosevelt was born less than three days before the direct station of Mars on 2 February 1882, and when the involvement of the US in World War II became necessary after the attack by the Japanese, his Sun-Mars natal phase angle had progressed from a trioctile to the waning square.[63]

A tragic example of one born near the retrograde station of Mars, and Mars in hard aspect to the Sun, is John F. Kennedy, Jr. Mars had stationed on 20 November 1960 in 18° Cancer 39', just a few days before his birth. The Sun and Mars in his nativity are in a 135° trioctile aspect, exact to 33' of arc. During his abbreviated life, Kennedy had two progressed phase changes of the Sun and Mars. He died on 16 July 1999 at 38 in a plane crash. An inexperienced pilot, he was trying to land at night in hazy conditions.

Reaching his progressed Sun-Mars opposition in 1996,[64] Kennedy experienced a reversal of polarity from the oriental morning star to the occidental evening star, and married his wife, Carolyn Bessette, that year. In a poignantly symbolic way, when his plane crashed into the ocean, Mars was in the sky as the evening star. In his hologram, Mars-Earth distance arc B is 45° 33'. From *La Volasfera*, Taurus 16:

> *Two white cows are standing together in a jungle;*
> *behind them is a tiger ready to spring.*

It denotes that one born under this sign will have many advantages in early life, will make a prosperous marriage, but through a false sense of security will afterwards come to ruin and sorrow. It is a degree of RELAXATION.

In a rueful representation of the higher nature of his Sun-Mars hologram, and a testimony to what he would have been capable had he lived longer, consult his Sun-Mars distance arc A of 134° 27'. Leo 15 from *La Volasfera*:

> *A figure like the angel of the Sun (Michael), standing erect,*
> *and striking the earth with the point of a dazzling sword.*

It indicates a person of very superior ability in some special direction; one in whom the power of government will reside; a mind somewhat ambitious, but conscious of its own powers-which are of no common order-so that no unjust advantage is taken. In some sphere of life the native will be an imposing figure, or may do something which may call for wide recognition. Fame and power attend this degree. It is one of SUPERIORITY.

The solar eclipse of 16 February 1999, immediately prior to Kennedy's death, was in 27° Aquarius 08', conjunct his natal Moon. This is also the degree

Chapter Five • *Sun–Mars Phase Angle Returns*

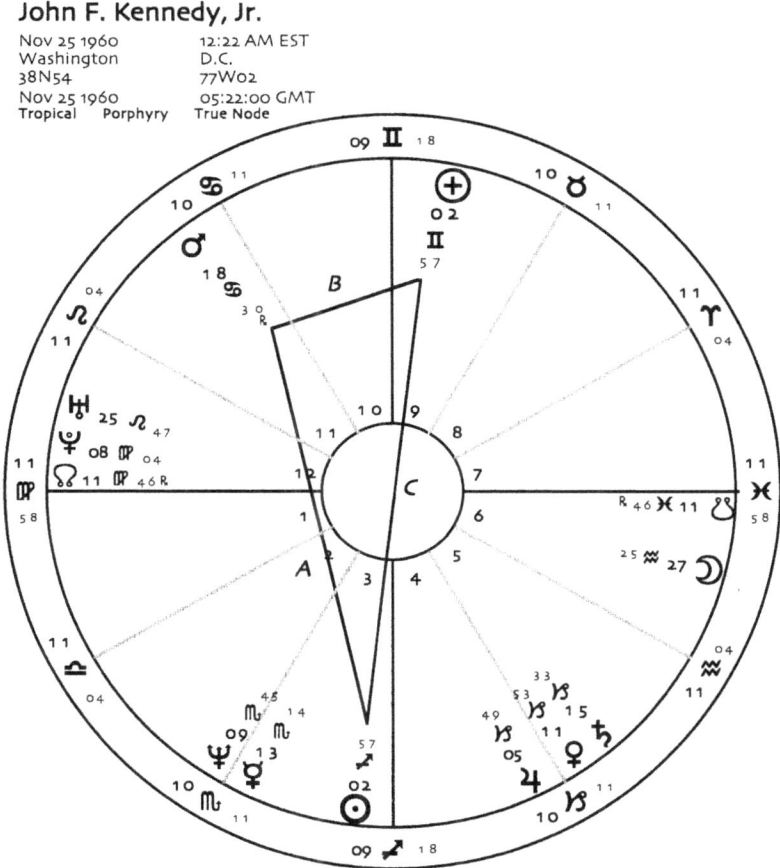

John F. Kennedy, Jr.
Nov 25 1960 12:22 AM EST
Washington D.C.
38N54 77W02
Nov 25 1960 05:22:00 GMT
Tropical Porphyry True Node

of the US Sibly Moon, and the public outpouring of grief over his death was quite heartfelt.

As with the Sun-Mercury phase angle, where a reversal of polarity occurs at both the inferior and superior conjunctions, in the Sun-Mars cycle, a mutation of energy occurs with conjunctions and oppositions at phase shifts between occidental and oriental. Just as those born at the inferior conjunction of the Sun and Mercury experience a reversal in the electromagnetic field (Mercury is both retrograde and closest to the Earth in its orbit), souls born when retrograde Mars opposes the Sun, and is nearest to the Earth in its cycle, can be more predisposed to violence.

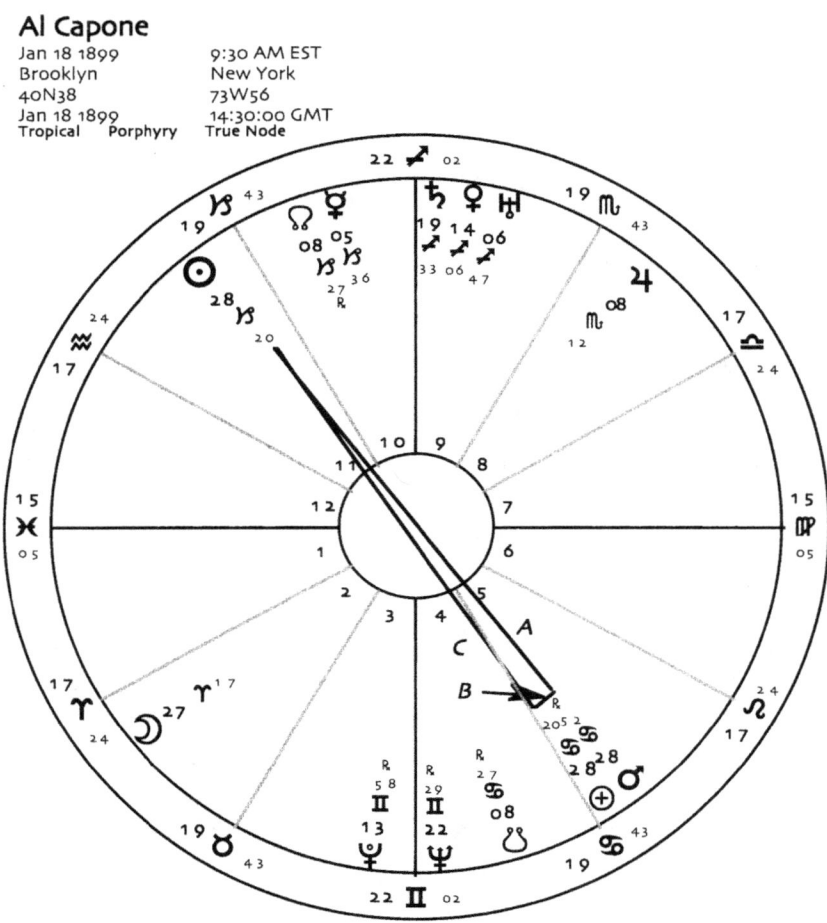

The most infamous example of this is the nativity of Al Capone, the notorious and violent Chicago gangster known as "Scarface." With a Sun conjunct the US Pluto, and his Neptune conjunct the US Mars, he is a glamorized symbol of violence. Capone was born at the exact opposition of retrograde Mars and the Sun, where Mars was closest to Earth in its 26-month synodic cycle. His Aries Moon fills in a Cardinal I-Cross, pointing at the 2nd house, and it was thought that he earned as much as $100 million a year in the 1920s from illegal prostitution and alcohol.

Capone organized "The Saint Valentine's Day Massacre" of 14 February 1929. Gangsters from his Italian Chicago South Side turf set up rival thugs from the Irish and German North Side of Chicago, who were in competition with Capone for the control of the lucrative underworld businesses made so profitable by Prohibition. Seven members of the rival gang were gunned down in cold blood, horrifying the country with the severity of the reckless violence. Capone's progressed Saturn had conjoined his MC, and he then became a marked man for arrest by federal officials.

In 1931, he was indicted on tax evasion charges and sentenced to eleven years in federal prison. He was transferred to Alcatraz and denied any contact with the outside world because he was running his underworld businesses from the inside.

His mental health began to decline while in prison, brought on by dementia caused by syphilis contracted during youth. Reports of an obsessive-compulsive disorder circulated, where he would make his bed and then unmake it for hours on end. It is also reported that he was haunted by the ghost of one of the Saint Valentine's Day Massacre victims. The final year of his sentence was spent in a mental institution.

In Al Capone's natal hologram, his Sun-Mars distance arc A is 179° 28', analogous with the final degree of Virgo. From *La Volasfera*, for Virgo 30:

> A man standing, either headless, or with the head shrouded in black cloth.
>
> It denotes a person of a very melancholy disposition and eccentric mind, a searcher of secret things, and fond of midnight studies; a recluse. It threatens the native with some mental affliction, or danger of wounds in the head.[65] The native will have to exercise great care in his mental efforts or he will end his days in chaos and confusion of mind. It is a degree of OBSCURATION.

Pre-Natal Sun-Mars Synodic Cycle

The conjunction of Mars and the Sun prior to birth, along with its degree symbols, can reveal the collective leadership abilities and pioneering inclinations that one shares with his "soul group," and which is carried over from past lives. As the author has written in previous chapters, countless souls will, of course, incarnate during the average 779-day synodic cycle of Mars. It is the thesis of this book that one's individual hologram of passion emanates from an immense "desire matrix," of which one is a part. It is the opinion of this astrologer that this chronicle is on the astral and causal planes, and condenses conditions in previous eras affecting those living during those times into a karmic seed one carries into this life.

At the end of this book is a Table of Sun-Mars conjunctions and oppositions for the 200 years from 1920 to 2120. Readers can locate their pre-natal

Sun-Mars synodic cycle and its conjunction degree. One may also determine from these tables whether a birth occurred during the Oriental phase (from conjunction to opposition), or during the Occidental phase (from opposition to conjunction).

Degree symbols for the pre-natal conjunctions can reveal past life conditions. Remember that we share these past life factors with the other souls incarnating during the same 779-day Sun-Mars synodic cycle as ourselves. It has also been the author's experience that the other souls born within the same synodic cycle have similar karmic inclinations and tendencies, as well as similar leadership abilities.

This bi-wheel chart shows the author's pre-natal Sun-Mars conjunction, which occurred a little over four months before his birth, overlaid into his natal houses. Souls born from 8 July 1953 to 17 August 1955, when the following conjunction took place, share this same matrix of drive and determination set into place at the time of that new synodic cycle. The degree symbol for the conjunction, Cancer 17, delineates the collective conditions of that cycle, whereas the rising degree for the conjunction calculated for the individual birth location symbolizes the personal experience of the cycle. For the author, his Santa Monica rising degree is Libra 28.

In light of Uranus conjoining the author's pre-natal Sun-Mars conjunction of July 1953, at the start of the 25-month synodic cycle, and which was followed just two days later by a solar eclipse conjunct that Mars and Uranus, one can delight in the symbolism that defines its collective dynamics. From *La Volasfera*, for Cancer 17:

> *A lightning flash.*
>
> It indicates a person of extreme nervous energy and force of character, who, by reason of his executive ability and great fund of energy, will take a leading part in the affairs of his community. The native of this sign will, among other things, be a great reformer. He will clear doubts as lightning rends the clouds, and will, while overturning much of existing belief, become a source of illumination to many. It is a degree of PIONEERING.

All souls born into this Sun-Mars synodic cycle have the potential to be reformers within their chosen profession, and to be a source of illumination to others. This approach to astrology, wherein the pre-natal synodic cycles are viewed as a sort of collective mold out of which an individual incarnates, reduces the primacy of the nativity to a degree, and elevates the collective influence of one's soul group. In the writings of C.E.O. Carter, he spoke of a similar

Chapter Five • *Sun–Mars Phase Angle Returns*

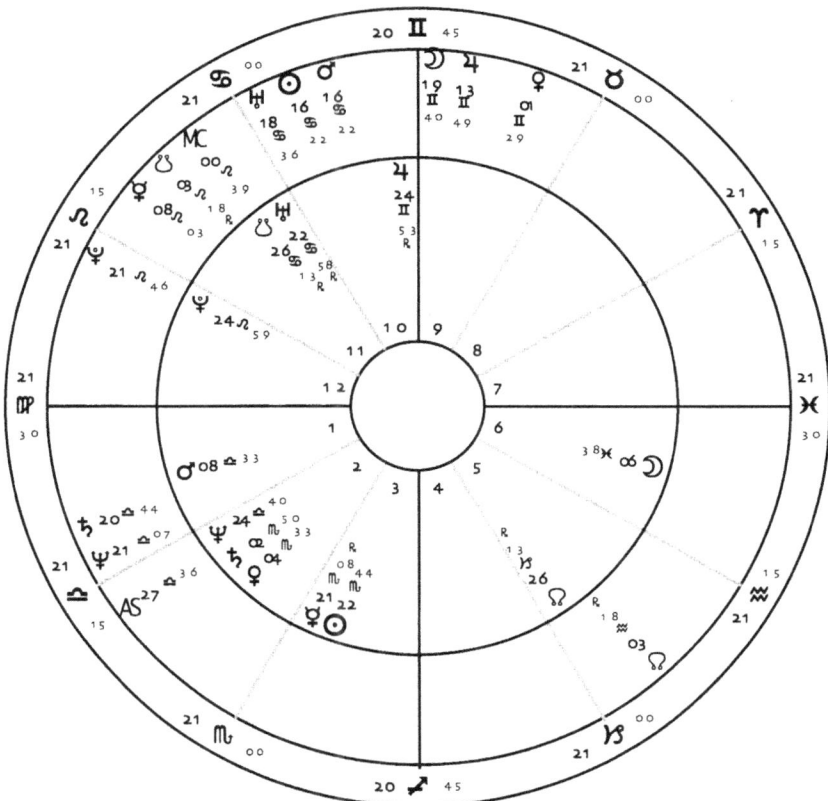

Law of Subsumption, wherein the birth chart is subsumed, *i.e.,* by the horoscopes of one's city and one's country.

By overlaying the pre-natal Sun-Mars conjunction into the houses of the nativity, one can see in which department of life its energies will prevail. For the author, it fell into his 10th house of career. The Moon in the new synodic cycle chart is also elevated and closely conjunct his Midheaven, and in a case such as this, the soul is destined to take on more of a visible and public role in its professional capacity. A look at the Sabian Symbol for Cancer 17 sheds even more light on this soul group:

> *A huge precious stone is so cut that its principal facet*
> *mirrors the whole scene before it in sparkling miniature.*

Marc Jones' analysis of this degree in his 1931 Lecture-Lessons:

This is a symbol of the gathering of all life values and experience in the concentrated compass of intelligence, consciousness as the ordering factor in creativity. Positively, it is a degree of higher vision; negatively, superficial love of knowledge. The keyword is BRILLIANCE.

By contemplating degree symbols for these pre-natal synodic cycle conjunctions, one can identify with the specific qualities of his soul group. For the astrologer wishing to personalize the collective influence of the pre-natal synodic cycle's conjunction, he need only to cast the chart for the location of birth. In this way, the personal symbolism for the degree of the Ascendant can be shared with the client.

For the author, Libra 28 was rising in Santa Monica. The Sabian Symbol is:

> *A man stands alone in surrounding gloom*
> *were his eyes open to spirit things he would see helping angels arriving.*

> *An ass tethered to the shaft of a grinding mill.* (La Volasfera)

> *A man with a crown on his head, and a spear in his hand.* (Charubel)

As the Sun-Mars phase angle and its overall synodic cycle have direct relevance with one's occupation, the rising degree symbolism for the pre-natal conjunction is a glimpse into the personal work habits of any soul. From the preceding symbols for the author, we see a self-employed astrologer who for years has lived on the edge of financial gloom, and has at times felt like a tethered ass in his business by having to work seven days a week in order to write books while earning a living. At least when he heads out the door on speaking trips, he has a crown on his head.

Mars, as a malefic, is also relevant to life experiences that wound one and bring pain and suffering. Past life karma is at the root of these episodes, which teach one valuable lessons, and the author has found that key individuals in life who *wield the knife* have exact synastry with the angles in these pre-natal Sun-Mars synodic cycle conjunction charts. As it is written in Galatians 6:7: "*Be not deceived. God is not mocked: for whatsoever a man soweth, that shall he also reap.*" If one has caused pain in past lives, these individuals will eventually show up to balance the ledger.

Chapter Five • Sun–Mars Phase Angle Returns

In the bi-wheel chart below, the nativity of the mother of the author's younger daughter, with whom he underwent some very sorrowful karma, is overlaid into his pre-natal Sun-Mars conjunction chart. Astrologers note a *partile* conjunction forms from her Moon to the Descendant, as well as a South Node conjunct Venus.[66]

As written in Chapter Three regarding the Sun-Mercury inferior conjunction just before the births of Lincoln and Darwin, certain synodic cycle conjunctions are in an exceptional category. The Sun-Mars conjunction of 17 August 1955 falls into this classification, as it included a six-planet Stellium with a partile Moon-Jupiter conjunction. The richest man in the world, Bill Gates, had it fall in his 2nd house.

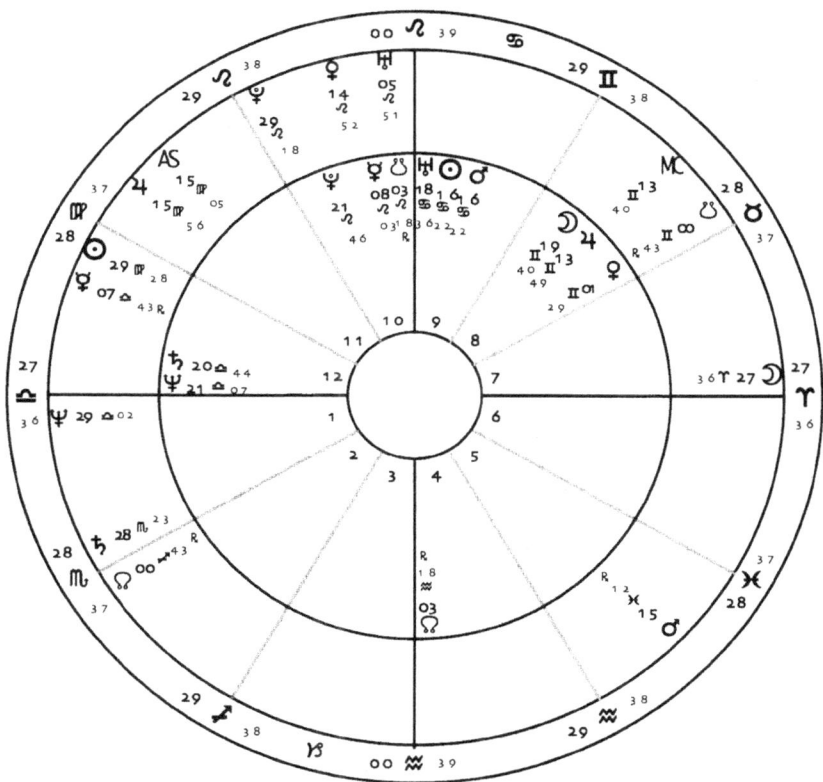

Robert P. Blaschke • *Holographic Transits*

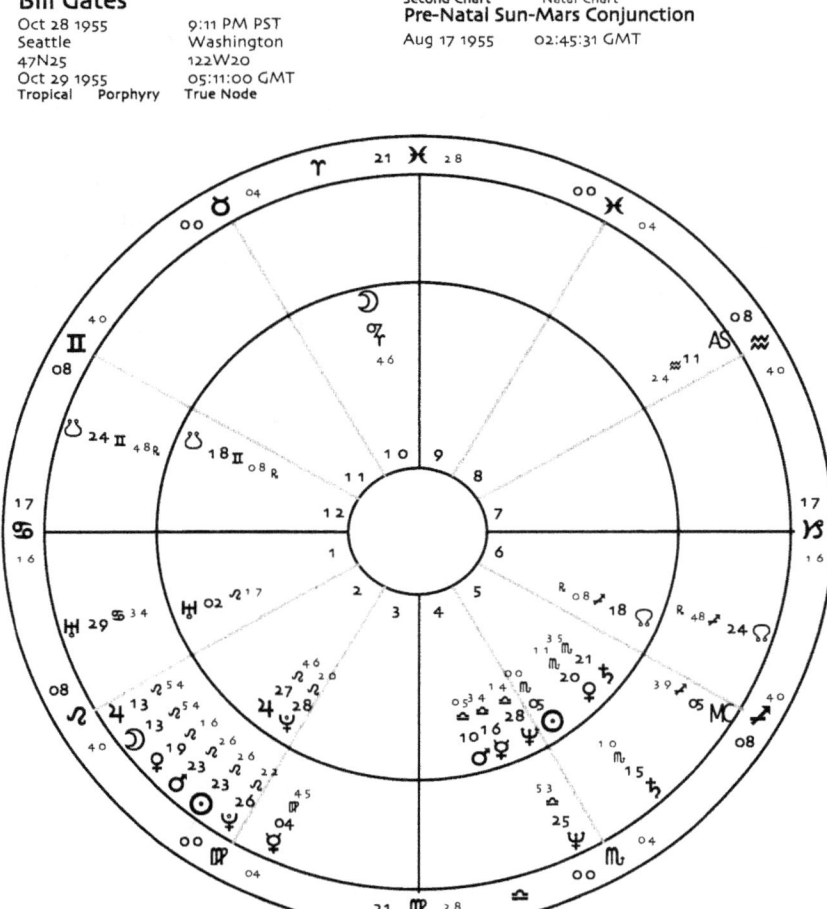

Bill Gates
Oct 28 1955　9:11 PM PST
Seattle　　　Washington
47N25　　　122W20
Oct 29 1955　05:11:00 GMT
Tropical　Porphyry　True Node

Second Chart　　Natal Chart
Pre-Natal Sun-Mars Conjunction
Aug 17 1955　02:45:31 GMT

This particular synodic cycle, lasting until 21 September 1957, has, in the author's experience, produced an abnormally high percentage of spiritually-oriented souls, especially those incarnating during the matching Leo stellium of July 1957. The Sabian Symbol for Leo 24, degree of the conjunction, explains this phenomenon:

> *A strange figure is revealed, outwardly unprepossessing, untidy, unkempt;*
> *he is a yogi of transcendent powers.*

One can only wonder if Mr Gates' material success in this life is a karmic reward for having assiduously meditated in Himalayan caves in past lives until reaching Samadhi. There are two competing times of birth for him: 9:15 and

10:00 PM. The author rectified his nativity to put Pisces 22 on the Midheaven. Its Sabian Symbol:

> *Down the man-made mountain of industry, in allegorical representation, comes the prophet with the tablets of new law.*

To gain insight into the relationship between Mr Gates as an individual and the collective energies of this synodic cycle, one calculates the Sun-Mars conjunction for Seattle, his place of birth. Aquarius 12 rises, and from *La Volasfera*, we find:

> *A lion raging against the bars of its cage.*

This symbol imports a nature of considerable native strength and dignity, yet unfortunate and in danger of being carried away by his passions and love of freedom. Hard though it may be to force his spirit into submission it will be well with him should he early learn that his compeers and superiors are equally jealous as himself of their rights and privileges. At some time in his life he will be the victim of a nature superior to his own and will suffer restraint and curtailment of liberty thereby. Let him adapt himself to his environment. His will else be the hard fate of those who are born of free spirit into the bonds of necessity. It is a degree of RESTRAINT.

Readers may wonder, as does the author, how Mr Gates may experience some sort of "curtailment of liberty" during his remaining years. One can also consider when using these pre-natal techniques, that everyone born in Seattle from August 1955 until September 1957 would have this rising degree for the pre-natal conjunction. What allows a soul like Mr Gates to rise to such eminence, while others born near to him along the timeline would have rather ordinary and undistinguished lives?

To answer this question, one must next examine the relative strength or weakness of the individual Sun-Mars hologram. For Gates, his natal Sun-Mars distance arc is 24° 55', equivalent to the 25th degree of Aries. From *La Volasfera*, for Aries 25:

> *A man of powerful form, riding upon a restive horse, whose mouth is curbed.*

It denotes a man of strong character, capable of maintaining his dignity and position by means of his natural powers. One of strong and independent nature, who will so far have his own way as to be at times tyrannous and unjust. One who will brook no opposition, nor give quarter to an enemy. It is a degree of DOMINION.

Readers may ponder, as in the previous chapter on Venus, just how to establish from which collective "desire matrix" on the astral/causal planes one's individual hologram of passion has emanated, and from what "previous eras of history" is the soul in this lifetime connected to? The author believes that this can be found by researching synodic cycles of Mars with the same conjunction degree.

Examining the Sun-Mars synodic cycle over a period of 3,500 years, he found that conjunctions occur in the identical degree of the Zodiac every 205 years, recurring between two and eight times (as did Venus), and then the sequence of conjunctions leaves that degree. For example, a Sun-Mars conjunction occurred in Cancer 17 in the years (all AD) 1543, 1748, 1953, and will occur in 2158, 2363, 2568, and in 2773. The Sun-Mars conjunctions just before and after this time sequence, *i.e.*, in 1338 and in 2978, fall in the adjacent degree of Cancer 16. This is a karmic string of seven consecutive conjunctions to which the author's soul group belongs, with the implication that this is the third lifetime in that chain of karma.

These years are the "previous eras of history" in which souls born between 8 July 1953 and 17 August 1955 took birth during prior incarnations, thus resulting in the same pre-natal Sun-Mars conjunction degree as in the present life. Specifically, these are past lives that are directly connected to the present life in regard to one's occupation, one's experiences of pain, loss or separation, and the use of drive and determination to accomplish goals. All are spheres of life that are Mars-ruled.

The Sun-Mars conjunction subsequent to the author's birth occurred on 17 August 1955 in 23° Leo 26'. This is a new synodic cycle sequence of only two occurrences, with just one repeating conjunction in that degree to come in 2160. Similar to the Saros cycle of eclipses that repeat like clockwork every 18 years and 10 days, or like the Metonic cycle of lunations repeating every 19 years, these Sun-Mars synodic cycles originating in the identical degree depict scenarios of related karma lasting between two and eight consecutive lifetimes.[67] Perhaps Bill Gates intuits this, and will give away all of his money in this life, creating good karma for 2160.

Astrologers using these techniques can research the client's pre-natal conjunction degree for the Sun and Mars. Then, by calculating forwards and backwards in time in multiples of 205 years, one determines for how many lifetimes this sequence of karma lasts. For some souls, if they are in the 8th and final lifetime of the chain, the succession of identical conjunction degrees will go back as far as 1,435 years.

This astrological reincarnation theory employs a precise technique to spe-

Chapter Five • *Sun–Mars Phase Angle Returns*

cifically date where along the timeline a soul previously incarnated. Those interested in exploring these methods are advised to study the periods of history during which their identical pre-natal conjunction degrees have formerly occurred. The author, who has his progressed Sun applying to a conjunction with Chiron while writing this book, hopes that some readers will be doing some shamanic time-traveling.

The Sun-Mars "soul group" to which this author and his fellow beings born from July 1953 to August 1955 belong, contains a few historical big guns.[68] The greatest German writer, Johann Wolfgang Goethe, was born 28 August 1749, and had his pre-natal Sun-Mars conjunction of 8 July 1748 also fall in Cancer 17. His nativity (shown on the next page) is a work of art in and of itself, with a Jupiter-Neptune-Pluto Water Grand Trine and a Kite to Venus, a Virgo Sun in mutual reception with Mercury and in trine to an exalted Mars, and a Pisces Moon trine to Saturn in the power degree of 15° Scorpio. Contemplating his horoscope, one surmises that in any particular synodic cycle of Mars, those born with the sextile or trine to the Sun are its human zenith.

Using Sun-Mars Holographic Transits

A Sun-Mars holographic transit occurs when the exact distance arc between the natal Sun and Mars forms again in the heavens, *and is also in the identical phase as the natal Mars cycle, i.e., Oriental or Occidental*. The Sun-Mars phase angle return occurs every 25–26 months, and at these times one can align with Higher Self and make important choices about one's work, physical activity, goals and ambitions.

The author has found that Sun-Mars phase angle returns are superior to the Mars return charts. He has observed that the sidereal cycle of Mars, *i.e.*, from the birth position one revolution and back again, *is a marker in time for the chapters of life*, but the Mars return horoscope itself, cast for the location of residence, is dubious.

This bi-wheel is the Sun-Mars holographic transit for the author of 25 January 2005, under which influence he is writing the present volume. Note that his Sun-Mars distance arc of 44° 11' has replicated in the heavens, and that the Sun-Mars phase is Oriental, as it was in his nativity. The astrologer also notes that Saturn is conjunct his Uranus by 01' of arc, and Mercury in the phase angle return chart is opposing that degree. A Gibbous Full Moon makes an exceedingly tight Fixed T-Cross with his natal Venus, exact to the midpoint of the Luminaries by 01' of arc.

107

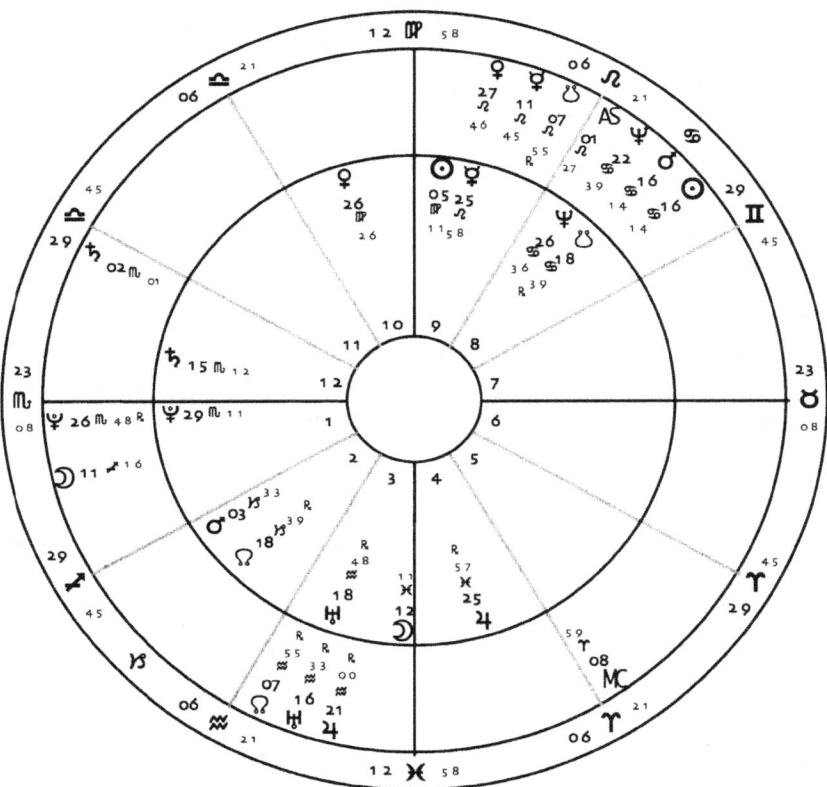

During this current Sun-Mars cycle, the author has been through hell and high water to get this book written. The Mercury-Saturn opposition in this phase angle return placed tremendous mental pressure on him to hold to the focus of the book, despite every conceivable disruption and distraction repeatedly knocking him off track. With the Lights in this holographic transit forming a T-Cross to Venus, the principal source of the unpredictable upheaval has, of course, been relational.

It is the primary contention of this book that, at the time of a holographic transit, one's free will is aligned with Higher Self, and that celestial conditions in place at the phase angle return are a divine reflection of the holographic

Chapter Five • *Sun–Mars Phase Angle Returns*

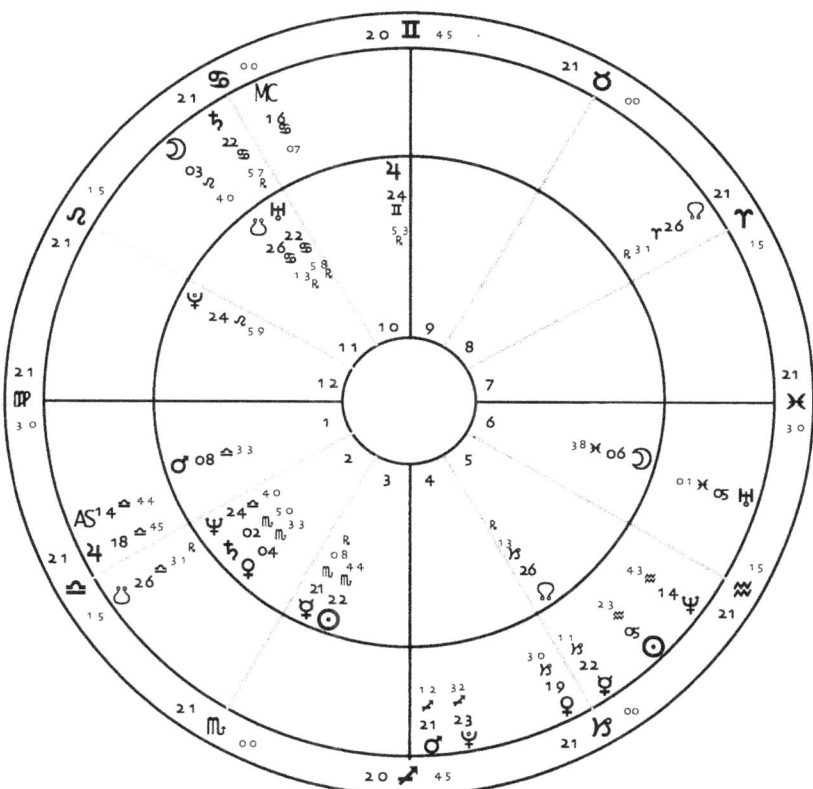

nature of the soul. What this means in practice is that rather than delineating the standard transits as what is happening to you (such as transit Uranus conjunct Moon), one instead interprets the holographic transit as the blueprint of the soul seeking realization.

This is a radical shift in emphasis away from fate and towards free will. There is much strength to be drawn from the phase angle return chart, not least of which is that the divine rays of the Sun are illuminating the particular planet from the same angle as at birth. It is comparable to the laser discussed in Chapter One, wherein a restoration is made of the fragmented three-dimensional object back to wholeness.

Astrologers will also note that the Lunar Nodes at 26° Aries-Libra in the phase angle return make an exact Cardinal Grand Cross with the author's nodal axis in 26° Cancer-Capricorn. The way he has encountered this aspect configuration is by undergoing a seemingly impossible tug-of-war at times between his goal of writing this book and his efforts to build a lasting personal relationship with his partner. The Cross is akin to a crucifixion experience, where peace is only found within. A closer scrutiny of this chart finds Neptune trine the Ascendant within 01' of arc.[69]

The rising degree in the phase angle return chart, cast for one's place of residence, provides insight into the conditions of that particular personal synodic cycle.[70] From Sepharial's translation of *La Volasfera* for the chart's Ascendant, Libra 15:

A man walking with two women, their arms linked in his.

It denotes a person of untrustworthy nature: frivolous, insincere, capable of duplicity: of a light, joyous spirit sometimes running away with the reason. The native will be given to self-indulgence, and to the flattery of women. There will be trouble in love affairs and in marriage. It is a degree of VACILLATION.

The author must admit that he has been repeatedly accused of vacillation by his girlfriend for the variance in his priorities during this year. This book, according to the symbolism, has been *the woman on one arm*, while she was on his other arm. Ah, the inopportune absurdities of being born with Mars in detriment in Libra.

Part of the spiritual philosophy implied in the use of holographic transits is that the soul has become fragmented at birth, and is seeking to be restored to wholeness through the divine rays of the Sun. This basic reality is what makes phase angle return charts so powerful, and so indicative of what the soul chooses to actualize. The author has found that there are links between past and present phase angles, and that exact synastry exists between the holographic transits and the nativity.

This bi-wheel chart shows the operative holographic transit of Mars, when the author was completing his *Progressions*, overlaid into his natal houses. Observe that the degree of the Sun in this phase angle return is matching the rising degree, Libra 15, from the January 2005 chart. Does history, or should one say, *karma*, repeat itself? Are partially-learned lessons destined to happen until one becomes sufficiently conscious? It would appear so.

An almost identical experience was occurring for the author in the Fall of 1998. In his attempt to finish writing his first book, he realized that he had to

Chapter Five • *Sun–Mars Phase Angle Returns*

stop dating and retreat into solitude to complete that manuscript. In the 1998 phase angle return, his Sun-Mars oriental distance arc of 44° 11' formed in the heavens, and that Mars was exactly conjunct the North Node. The South Node in 00° Pisces was precisely conjunct the author's natal Vertex, and Venus on the day of the holographic transit is conjunct his natal Mars, exact within 07' of arc.

With his Cancer-Capricorn nodal axis, this author has had numerous experiences wherein he felt *no choice but to choose between* emotional attachment (Cancer) and completing a professional accomplishment (Capricorn). Needless to say, these life scenarios rattle one's cage on a soul level, as circumstances involved literally are designed to induce one to reverse his unconscious inclinations of many past lives.

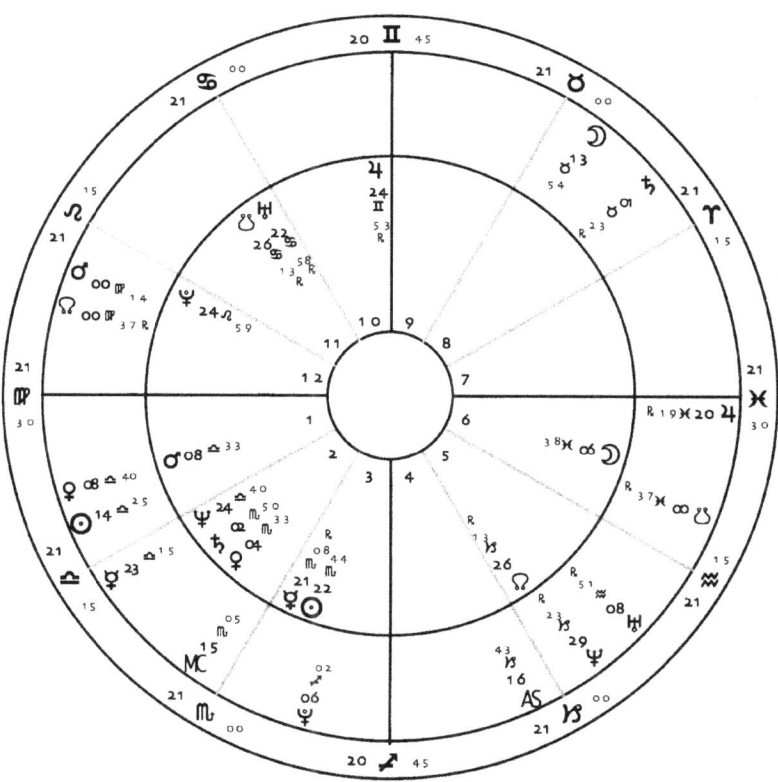

If one subscribes to the theory that celestial conditions at the time of a holographic transit are a blueprint for what the soul intends to actualize and fulfill, and to go against this would be akin to *a spiritual crime*, then one must delineate these phase angle return charts as the process of free will aligning with Higher Self to live up to one's karmic destiny. It is hoped that the reader can take this concept to heart, and view these horoscopes as an ally and as a protective benefactor.

For the author, in 1998, with phase angle Venus conjunct Mars, a separation was necessary to complete his book. With the South Node on his Vertex, by letting the relationship go, he, unbeknownst at that time, opened the door for another soul to enter his life after the book was finished, a woman with her Venus in 00° Pisces.

It has become clear to the author that the phase angle return chart is connected to one's spiritual essence at birth, specifically the pre-natal synodic cycle's degree of conjunction. If the reader recalls the chart on page 103, Cancer 17 is the degree of his pre-natal Sun-Mars conjunction. In the 2005 phase angle return, that degree was culminating on the Midheaven, and in the 1998 chart, it is on the Descendant.

Regarding the author's choice in 1998 to stop dating and complete *Progressions*, from *La Volasfera*, the phase angle return chart's rising degree, Capricorn 17:

A lyre lying upon a wreath of flowers.

It denotes one who will show some remarkable powers of expression, and by the power of sound will persuade where others cannot compel by force. He may become a poet or musician, and in the gentler offices of life will show considerable talent. His nature will be docile, tractable, harmless and inoffensive. He will be constant in his attachments and will undergo some singular persecutions and tests of his fidelity, emerging therefrom victorious and undismayed. Should he follow the highest expressions of his faculty he will be capable of enunciating in language that is harmonious, persuasive and subtly compelling, a new body of doctrine or a new phase of philosophic truth. It is a degree of PERSUASION.

Because the Sun-Mars synodic cycle has a duration of 25–26 months, phase angle returns of the Sun and Mars will only occur about every two years. If delineating Sun-Mars holographic transits that are one or two years old, it is recommended that Moon-Mars phase angle returns for the time of the consultation are included. These subcycle charts show how souls are presently assimilating and digesting the choices that were made by aligning free will with

Chapter Five • *Sun–Mars Phase Angle Returns*

Higher Self at the time of their last Sun-Mars phase angle return, from as long as two years ago.

Readers may get a laugh at the author's expense by examining his Moon-Mars phase angle return for the time that he was completing this part of the manuscript, shown below. Nervously deliberating as he was over revealing this much personal information to explain these astrological techniques, rather than using celebrity case histories to illustrate phase angle returns, he decided that this lunar subcycle would be the determining factor. Sure enough, phase angle Mercury is in 4° Scorpio, and exactly conjunct his natal Venus. The rising degree is indeed most sobering, and the listing vessel carrying his relationship baggage had better cast its anchor in one port.[71]

From Sepharial's translation of *La Volasfera* for the chart's Ascendant, Cancer 21:

> *A waning moon, amid a bank of clouds, dimly reveals a ship at sea, but all disabled.*

> It indicates a person of roving, unsettled habits, whose ill-fortune will lead him to many pursuits in quest of wealth, but who eventually will be badly placed, and with little hope of improvement. It indicates that the native will have much aptitude and versatility, but not much perseverance or hopefulness, and this continually, passing from one bad thing to something worse, instead of improving that which he holds. It is a degree of INSTABILITY.

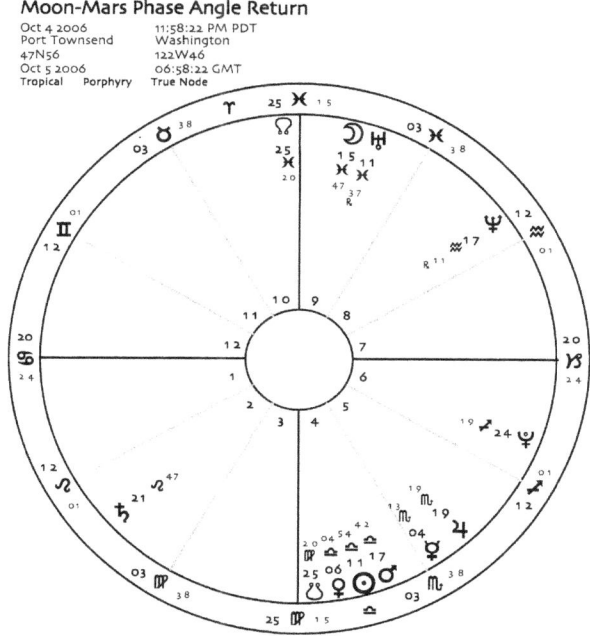

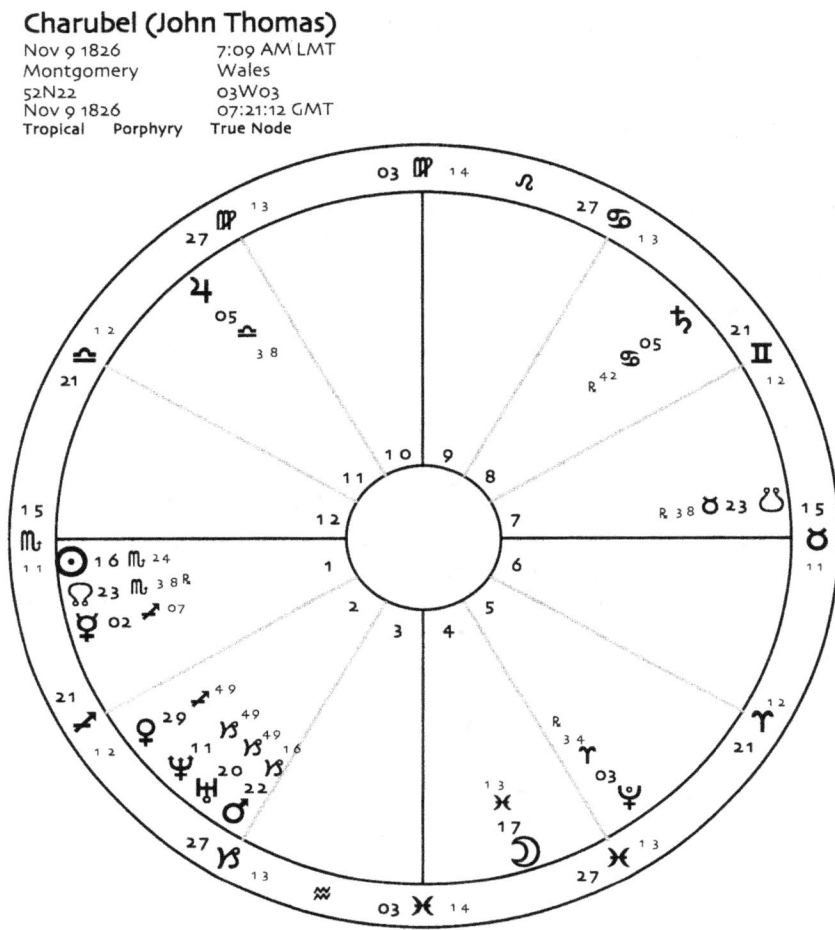

Scorpio 16 from *La Vofasfera*

A cup or goblet from which rays of ruddy light are emitted.

It is the index of a kind and benevolent nature; a generous and humane disposition; ever eager to befriend and comfort those who may be in distress of body or mind. The grandeur and spiritual loftiness of this soul will attract many friends, and the work of charity and benevolence will increase continually, gathering volume as it goes, till it reaches the ocean of human life, and enfolds all mankind. It is a degree of HUMANENESS.

Chapter Six
Sun-Jupiter Phase Angle Returns

Sun-Jupiter Phase Angle at Birth

The Sun-Jupiter phase angle at birth creates the expansive capacity of one's mind. This hologram of judgment develops throughout life, starting with early religious training, then through one's education, augmented by cultural exploration and travel, and is brought to its culmination through the aptitude to develop wisdom and a moral conscience that distinguishes between right and wrong.

The phase angle of the Sun and Jupiter provides insight into whether one's impulse for growth and expansion is aimed towards achieving prosperity in the material world, or if the urge to grow is towards the mental spheres of philosophy, spirituality, classical literature, scientific research, or into speculative thought. A spirit of generosity and a desire to share is present within every human heart, and the exaltation of Jupiter in Cancer is one's need to belong to a larger cosmic family.

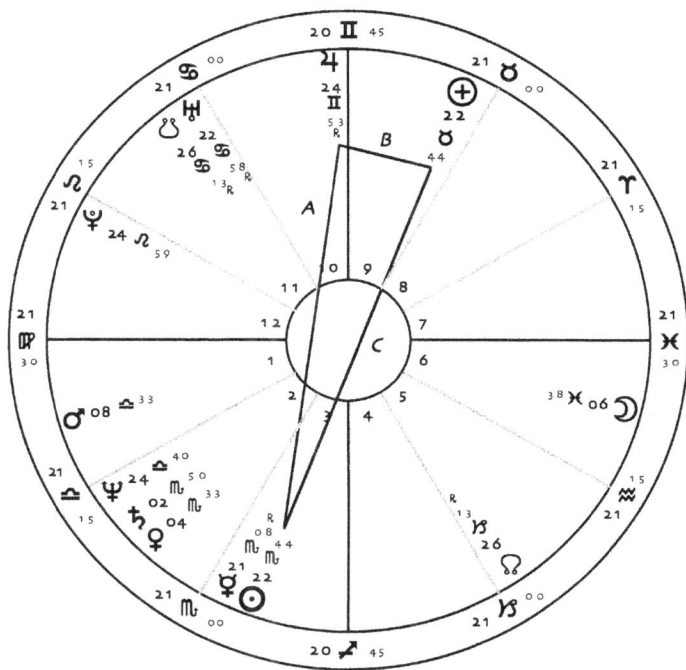

To visualize one's natal Sun-Jupiter hologram, the glyph for the Earth is placed in the horoscope, thus creating a three-dimensional image. In the author's nativity, his Sun-Jupiter distance arc A is 147° 51' 15", and the Jupiter-Earth distance arc B is 32° 08' 45". Together, these two arcs total 180° 00' 00". Using his Sabian Aspect Orb technique, arc A equates to the 28th degree of Leo, and arc B is equivalent to the 3rd degree of Taurus. These two degrees are antiscia, or solstice points, of one another. Sun-Earth arc C is always a constant, measuring exactly 180° 00' 00".

From Sepharial's translation of *La Volasfera*, for Leo 28:

Two hands linked in a close grip of friendship.

It denotes a person of a very amiable and sociable nature, filled with concord and goodwill towards his fellows. A rich, unselfish nature, capable of those little greatnesses in daily life which make a man beloved, if not remarkable. It is probable that the native will be instrumental in forming some large associations for social cooperation, or intellectual improvement. The native is essentially constructive, harmonising and humane. It is a degree of SUSTAINING.

And from *La Volasfera*, for Taurus 3:

A woman is gathering grapes, with which she fills many baskets.

It denotes a person whose interests will be greatly enhanced in the autumn of life, who will reap benefits from old age and pleasures from maturity; whose chief characteristic is acquisitiveness, and whose designs will meet with much success. It is a degree of acquirement, of GATHERING TOGETHER.

When the author founded a school of astrology in 1992, his Sun-Jupiter hologram opened to a higher level of community expression. It was a public business, with a sign on the outside of the leased commercial office space. It was also a social environment for the students who attended classes and workshops, with many new friendships taking root at the school. And it was an intellectual and academic milieu wherein astrological and spiritual knowledge was freely shared.

Regarding "the autumn of life" and "the gathering of grapes," this astrologer was told in the 1970s that with Jupiter in the 10th house, success would come towards the latter part of life. Knowing this has allowed him to weather many lean years, without disposable income while he worked as a self-employed astrologer, built a practice, a school, a small publishing company, and a lecturing career.

Chapter Six • *Sun–Jupiter Phase Angle Returns*

Earthwalk School of Astrology Lake Oswego, Oregon circa 1993

The Sun-Mars, Sun-Jupiter, and Sun-Saturn holograms are the foundation of one's life work and professional contribution. If an individual can channel passion into accomplishment, the exaltation of Mars in Capricorn will reward one with personal satisfaction and feelings of purpose and conviction. However, the exaltation of Jupiter in Cancer will reward the soul who shares his blessings with others with the feeling of security of belonging to a larger spiritual family.

As with all of the three-dimensional natal holograms, these Sun-Jupiter and Jupiter-Earth distance arcs, when converted into their derived degree symbols, reveal the holographic dimensions of the soul. It must also be stated that Jupiter is not immune to negative manifestation, despite its status as the Greater Benefic, frequently resulting in wastefulness, recklessness, and wanton self-indulgence. If astrologers using these techniques find unflattering degree symbols for the Sun-Jupiter hologram, it is recommended that this *shadow* side of Jupiter be discussed.

The natal Sun-Jupiter phase angle is part of an overall synodic cycle that lasts for an average of 399 days, or 13 months. The cycle begins with a conjunction of the Sun and direct-motion Jupiter, reaches its halfway point at the opposition of the Sun and retrograde Jupiter, and has quarter points when the Sun squares Jupiter. All souls incarnate with a unique phase angle at a specific point within this cycle.

Those born after the conjunction of the Sun and Jupiter, but before the Sun-Jupiter opposition, have Jupiter as the morning star in their nativities, rising ahead of the Sun. During the latter part of this oriental half of the synodic cycle, Jupiter is retrograde and closer to Earth than at any other point in its orbital cycle. Because of this, its karmic influence from past lives is stronger, peaking at the opposition.

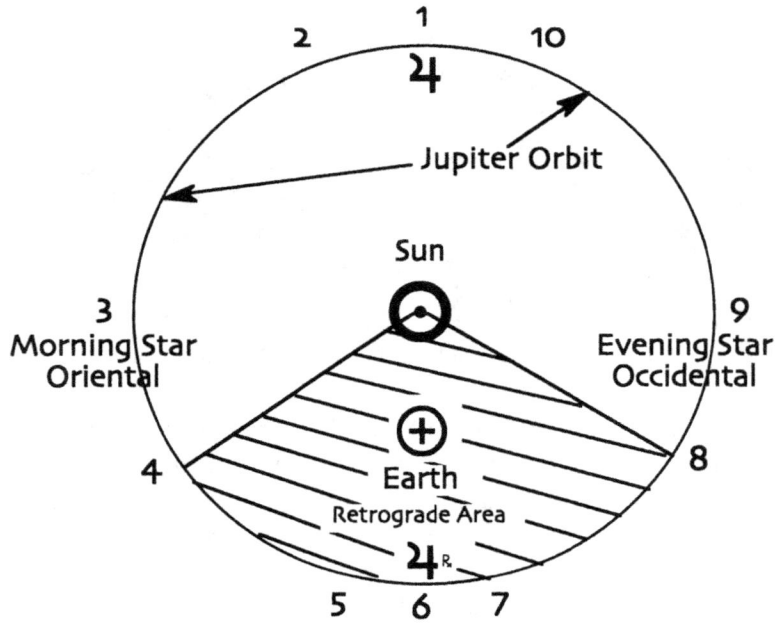

Cycles and Phases of the Planet Jupiter

1. Sun-Jupiter Conjunction
2. Jupiter Heliacal Rising
3. Waxing Square
4. Stationary Retrograde
5. Earth's Heliacal Setting
6. Sun-Jupiter Opposition
7. Earth's Heliacal Rising
8. Stationary Direct
9. Waning Square
10. Jupiter Heliacal Setting

Those born after the Sun-Jupiter opposition, but before the next conjunction, have Jupiter as the evening star, setting after the Sun. For the first part of this occidental half of the synodic cycle, Jupiter is retrograde. The most powerful points in the Sun-Jupiter cycle are at the conjunction when Jupiter shifts from occidental to oriental, and again at the opposition, when retrograde Jupiter also has a reversal of polarity from oriental to occidental. The ability to realize one's full potential of material prosperity or scientific achievement peaks at the Sun-Jupiter conjunction.

Researching direct and retrograde stations of Jupiter, one finds that the distance between the Sun and stationary Jupiter varies from a minimum angular separation of 114° to a maximum of 118°. Jupiter is retrograde when trine, trioctile, biquintile, inconjunct, triseptile, or opposite the Sun. These are all highly karmic phase angles. It has been the experience of this astrologer that a retrograde Jupiter is powerful when also in close aspect to the Sun. In this case, the orb is limited to under 2 ½°.

Throughout life, secondary progressions evolve the Sun-Jupiter relationship, often resulting in important phase changes, depending on where in the orbital cycle one is born. The author has a waxing inconjunct[72] between his Sun and a retrograde Jupiter, with an orb of 02° 09'. In the illustration on page 118, this places his birth between points #4 and #5. During his adult life, the author has progressed through the heliacal setting of the Earth (#5), the Sun-Jupiter opposition (#6), and Earth's heliacal rising (#7). He started with an oriental Jupiter, which is now occidental.

Consequential events occurred in the author's life during each of these progressed phase changes. In 1971, when his Sun-Jupiter cycle progressed into heliacal setting of the Earth, he began his serious studies in astrology. In March 1982, as shown in this chart, he reached a progressed Sun-Jupiter opposition.

The astrologer sees that, right as his Sun-Jupiter synodic cycle transitioned from oriental to occidental, the author also had a progressed First Quarter Moon. This Mutable T-Cross was very close to exact, the Moon having perfected squares simultaneously to the Sun and Jupiter just three days earlier on 27 February 1982.

The author's marriage dissolved exactly at this progressed Sun-Jupiter opposition at the end of February 1982, and ultimately resulted in his identity shifting from husband and father to mystic, astrologer, and visiting Dad for the remainder of his child's upbringing. While he paid child support for the next 19 years, not ever missing a month, never again did he feel like a family man. Jupiter rules both his natal IC and Descendant.

Overlaying those secondary progressions from 2 March 1982 into the natal houses of the author, the progressed Moon is angular and conjunct his Descendant within 01' of arc, thus creating a 21° Mutable Grand Cross, including his natal Ascendant. It is of note that his progressed Venus was in 10° Sagittarius 04', having just ingressed into the Aries decanate, and was also applying to octiles with a progressed Mars-Neptune conjunction, ruling the 7th. In addition, that progressed Moon was applying to a Yod with Mars-Neptune-Pluto.

When the author's Sun-Jupiter synodic cycle progressed into the Earth's heliacal rising (#7) in 1989, he became a full-time self-employed professional astrologer. If he lives to be 87 years old, in November 2040, the author will

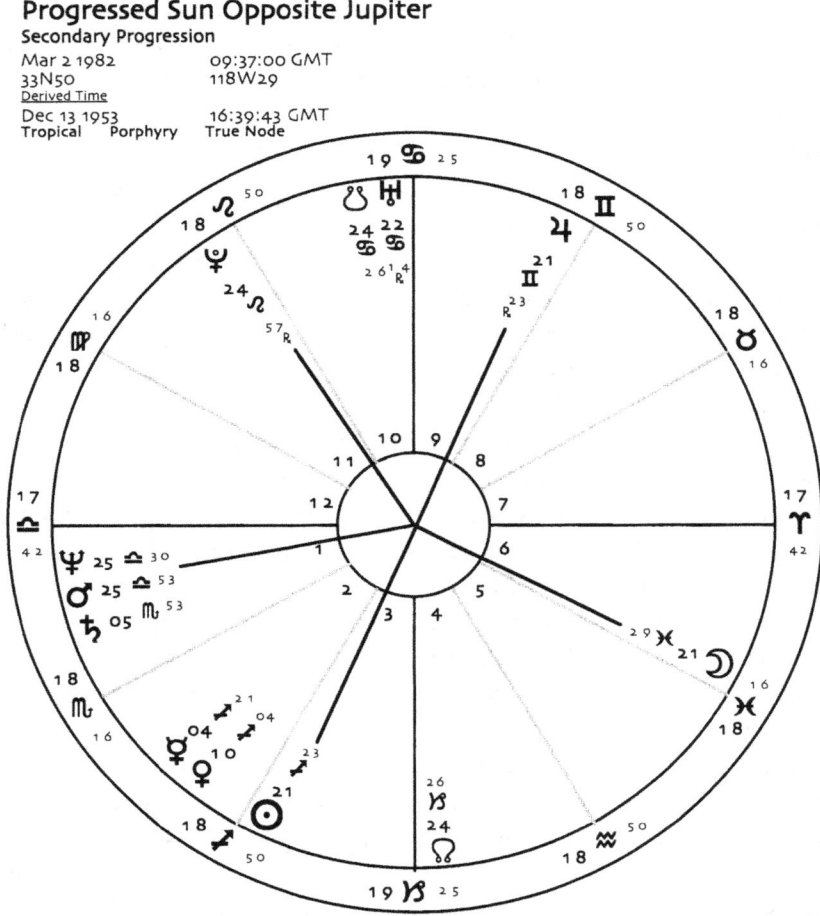

arrived at the direct station of his progressed Jupiter, having passed through a trine to the Sun in 2036.

From this history, readers can see that the 1982 progressed Sun-Jupiter opposition was a watershed year for the author, with a reversal of polarity in his synodic cycle of Jupiter from oriental to occidental. For him, with Jupiter ruling the IC, there was a fundamental shift in his emotional identity. With time, he viewed this personal experience as a karmic, or fated change in life's direction. Regarding free will, even though he has felt like a failure as a husband and father, the author chose to do the best he could, making a professional contribution to astrology by establishing a school, consulting, teaching, writing, and lecturing.[73]

Chapter Six • *Sun–Jupiter Phase Angle Returns*

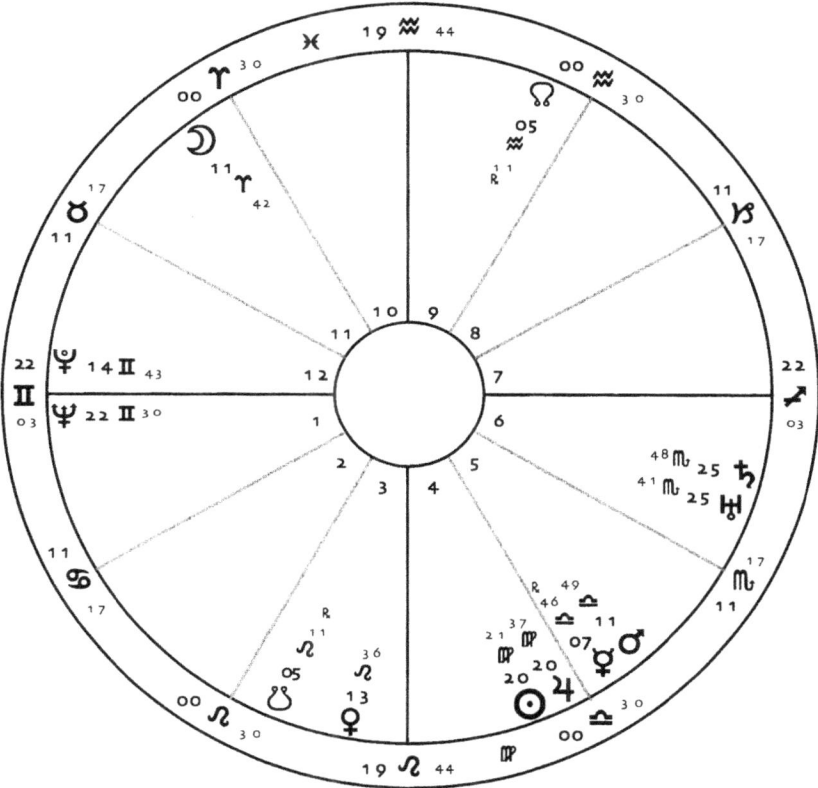

A textbook example of realizing one's full potential of scientific achievement when born at the Sun-Jupiter conjunction is found in the nativity of Irène Joliot-Curie. Daughter of Nobel Prize winners, Marie and Pierre Curie, she first worked as a lab assistant for her mother. In 1935, with her husband, Frédéric Joliot, she shared the Nobel Prize in Chemistry. With her Sun-Jupiter conjunction in Virgo and with Neptune rising, she literally sacrificed her life for her work, dying of leukemia contracted while conducting her lab research. In her distinguished career, she was Chair of Nuclear Physics at the Sorbonne, and an Officer of the *Legion of Honour*.[74]

A tragic example of Jupiter's karmic influence from past lives being the strongest at the retrograde opposition is found in the nativity of Nicole Brown

Nicole Brown Simpson

May 19 1959　　2:00 AM CET
Frankfurt　　　Germany
49N56　　　　08E40
May 19 1959　　01:00:00 GMT
Tropical　Porphyry　True Node

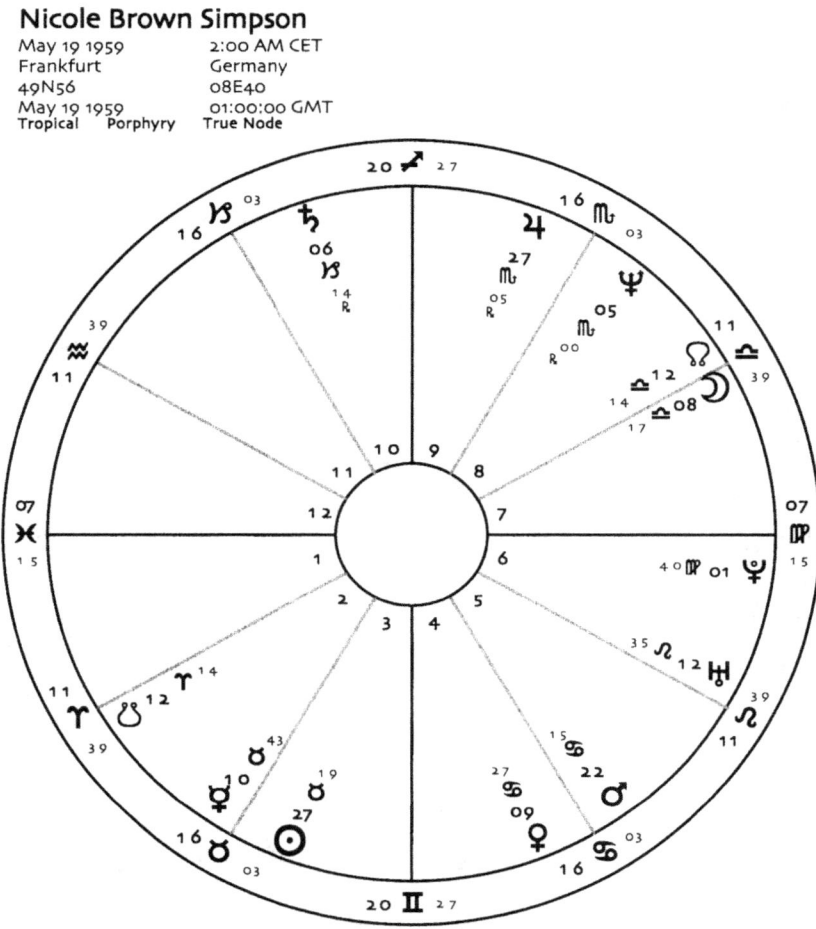

Simpson, slain ex-wife of former football star and actor, O.J. Simpson. Born with Jupiter within 14' of arc of exactly opposing the Sun, she was brutally murdered on 12 June 1994.

Divorced in 1992 after seven years of marriage and two children, she stated that it had been an abusive relationship. The astrologer sees that Nicole Simpson has a Cardinal T-Cross inimical to marriage, with Venus opposite Saturn and the Moon at its apex. Proving C.E.O. Carter's research about marital troubles being found when certain Zodiacal areas are occupied by, or involved in afflictions from, the malefics (8° Aries–Libra, 25° Virgo, 19° Leo–Aquarius, and 27° Leo–Aquarius), she had the Moon in 8° Libra and in square to Saturn. Her Sun is also conjunct Algol.

Chapter Six • Sun–Jupiter Phase Angle Returns

This astrologer has observed that retrograde planets in close aspect to the Sun are highly karmic, and that the influence appears to peak at the opposition, either when in the nativity, such as Mrs Simpson had, or when the opposition is reached by secondary progression, as occurred with the author.

Regarding the acute triangles involved in the natal holograms, recall the nativity of Al Capone on page 98, who was born with a very close opposition of the Sun and retrograde Mars. Natal holograms for an exact opposition create a triangle of extreme narrowness.

In the case of Nicole Simpson, her Jupiter-Earth distance arc will be less than 10. When interpreting derived degree symbols for the angular separation between the Sun and planet, the author has used the shorter of the two distance arcs, i.e., the arc that is less than 180°. In many cases, he has also found that the degree symbol for the longer of these two distance arcs has been quite relevant.[75] The angular separation from Jupiter to her Sun is 180° 14'. From *La Volasfera*, for Libra 1:

> *A man with a drawn sword in an aggressive attitude.*
>
> It denotes a person of martial and quarrelsome character, ever ready to pick a quarrel and to rush into danger. Such an one will fight his way through life with little regard to the feelings and prejudices of others, and though he may become notorious for his executive readiness, he will meet with disgrace and trouble through his impetuosity. There is danger of a fatality at the hands of the native. He will do well to keep his action under control. It is a degree of WOUNDING.

Jupiter remains retrograde for four months a year, traversing about 10° in the Zodiac during retrogression, hence around one third of the population is born with this condition. Jupiter travels approximately 40° through the Zodiac each year when direct, and so two-thirds of humanity have this in their nativity.

The author has found that retrograde Jupiter is highly fateful when also in a close aspect to the Sun. This will occur at the 120° trine, 135° trioctile, 144° biquintile, 150° quincunx, 154° 17' triseptile, or the 180° opposition, with orbs less than 2.5°. If the astrologer is delineating one of these Sun-Jupiter phase angles for his client, the discussion of free will takes on greater importance, as it is probable that these individuals, by the time they reach middle age, will have undergone experiences of life-changing intensity to a much greater extent than those without a close aspect.

This phenomenon, of course, is explained by the Jupiterian impulse for growth and expansion, and what better way to fulfill spiritual development than by crossing the threshold into the dark night of the soul. The Sun-Jupiter phase angle at birth tells a story, illustrated by the derived degree symbols for its hologram, about how the soul is attempting to holographically evolve its moral conscience and judgment.

This type of spiritual evolution is rarely accomplished in a single lifetime, and as the author has written previously about one's pre-natal synodic cycle conjunction degrees that repeat for two to eight consecutive lifetimes, one sees that this process can be a gradual and arduous one. It can also be said that pain, tragedy and death are as much a part of one's spiritual evolution as inner peace gotten by meditation. Two aspects forming in the retrograde Jupiter phase of its cycle stand out in this regard: a fated 154° 17' triseptile and the creative/self-destructive 144° biquintile.

This is the chart for the late Princess Diana. Examining her Sun-Jupiter hologram, the Sun-Jupiter distance arc *A* is found to be 154° 33' 59", a very close triseptile with an orb of 00° 17', and her Jupiter-Earth distance arc *B* measures 25° 26' 01".[76] Arc *A* is equivalent to the 5th degree of Virgo, and arc *B* the 26th degree of Aries. Her life was most certainly fated; from *La Volasfera*, for Aries 26:

> *A kingly person, presenting a sceptre to one kneeling.*
>
> It denotes one who, whether by his merits, or by the influence of persons in power and authority, will rise above the level of his birth. The nature is one of merit allied to ambition, which will effect great things, not however without assistance. It is a degree of ATTAINMENT.

Diana died suddenly and unexpectedly in an automobile crash on 31 August 1997. Her progressed Jupiter had retrogressed to 00° Aquarius 38', and had formed yet another fated triseptile to her progressed Uranus/North Node at the time of her death. Born with her Sun-Jupiter phase angle in the oriental half of the synodic cycle, she reached a progressed Sun-Jupiter opposition, becoming occidental, on 27 February 1985, just months after her second son, Prince Harry, was born. It was at this time that her marriage began to disintegrate, with she and Prince Charles both commenting on the failed wedlock in leaks to the press through their friends. One can only imagine how she felt about her life.

The triseptile from her Sun to her ruler, Jupiter, was a most influential aspect, as was her rising degree. From Sepharial's translation of *La Volasfera*, for Sagittarius 19, one can see that despite being the most famous woman in the world, privately it was hell on Earth:

Chapter Six • *Sun–Jupiter Phase Angle Returns*

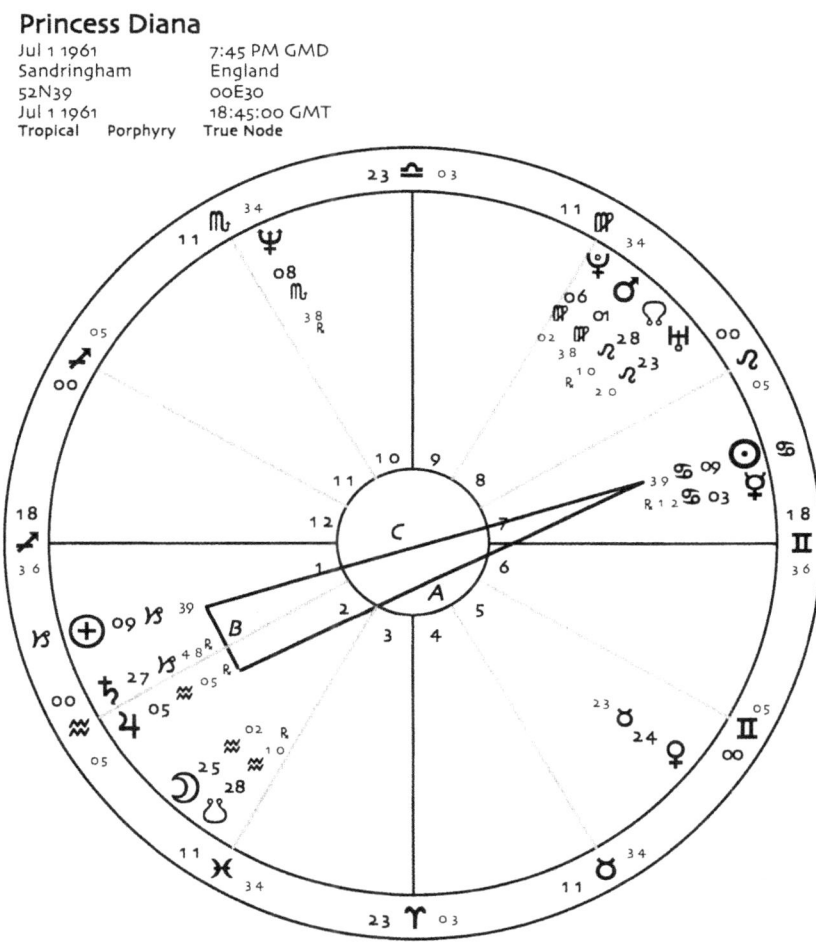

A serpent surrounded by a circle of fire.

This symbol denotes one whose mind is subtle and tortuous, resentful and passionate. He will be continually involved in difficulties, and surrounded by dangers. At some time in life he may find himself in a beleaguered city, or in a cruel distraint, from which he will escape only with some hurt to his person or• fortunes. In one form or another he will be called upon to pass through a fiery ordeal, and throughout life his mind will be chafed and tortured by stress and limitations. It is a degree of CAPTIVITY

The other highly karmic aspect forming between the Sun and retrograde Jupiter is the 144° biquintile. Both this aspect and the nearby triseptile are

Robert P. Blaschke • *Holographic Transits*

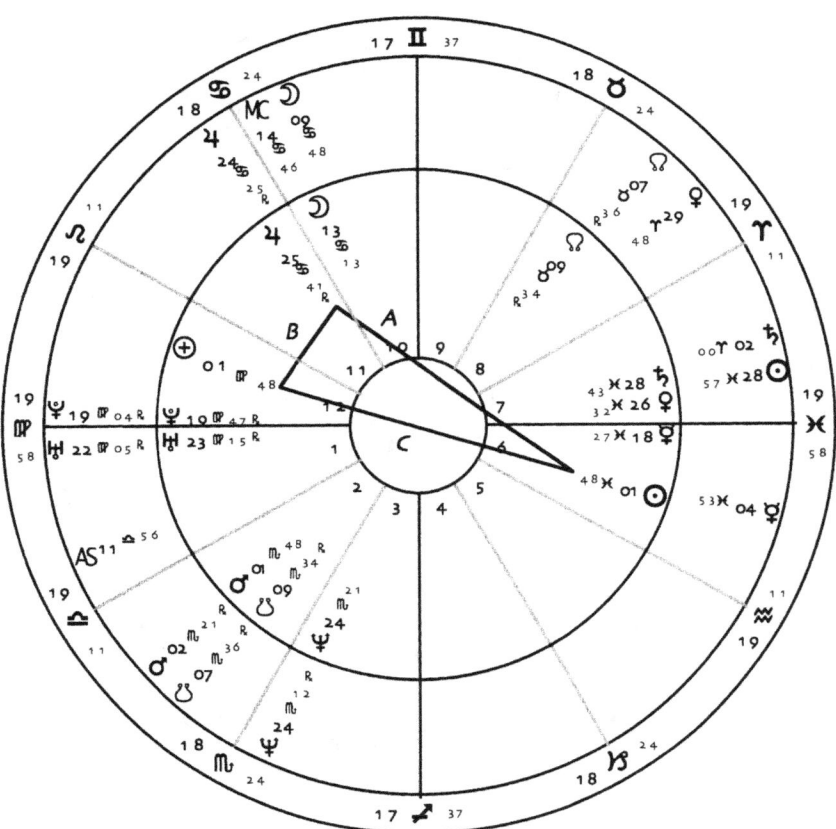

often mistaken by professional astrologers *for an inconjunct with a wide orb*. Each of these two aspects bounds the 150° quincunx on either side, and therefore the inconjunct's orb should be limited to a maximum of 3°. A biquintile is of the 5th harmonic, wherein the circle is divided by five and then multiplied by two. Along with its root aspect, the 72° quintile, a biquintile is known for both creativity and self-destructiveness.

This bi-wheel chart has the nativity of the deceased musician, Kurt Cobain, in the inner wheel, and the secondary progressions at his death from a self-inflicted gunshot wound to the head on 5 April 1994, in the outer wheel. His Sun-Jupiter hologram distance arc A is 143° 53' 27", a nearly exact biquintile with an orb of 00° 07'. His Jupiter-Earth distance arc **B** is 36° 06' 33". Arc **A** equates to the 24th degree of Leo, and distance arc **B** is equivalent to the 7th degree of Taurus.[77]

Cobain was a singer and songwriter for the popular band, Nirvana. He struggled with drug addiction and depression, and the astrologer sees that he was a highly sensitive soul with eight planets in the water element, of which four made a Grand Trine and a Kite to the rising Uranus-Pluto conjunction. His progressed Sun had conjoined his Saturn in the year before his suicide, compounding his pre-existing depression and melancholia. The creative bi-quintile between his Sun and Jupiter had a *shadow* side, one in which his mind regularly had self-destructive thoughts.

From *The Degrees of the Zodiac Symbolised* by Charubel, Taurus 7, the symbol for his Jupiter-Earth distance arc, is descriptive of his demise:[78]

A horrid sight ! a naked man suspended by the feet, to a cross-beam, mutilated, and the blood running down the body.

His fame had come from the secondary progressed Sun first in trine with Neptune, then trine to Jupiter, and next conjoining his natal Venus, all within three years. It is a pity that his life was cut short at age 27, just before a progressed Moon return, as his progressed Jupiter was stationary direct, and his spirits would have lifted.

Pre-Natal Sun-Jupiter Synodic Cycle

The conjunction of Jupiter and the Sun before birth, along with its degree symbols,· reveals the collective philosophical orientation and spiritual understanding that one shares with his soul group, and which is carried over from past lives. As mentioned in previous chapters, countless souls incarnate during the average 399-day synodic cycle of Jupiter. One's individual hologram of judgment originates from a vast wisdom matrix, of which one is but a part. These thought forms flow out of the causal plane, condensing attitudes and beliefs from prior eras of history that affected those living during that time, into a karmic seed carried into this life.

At the end of this book is a Table of Sun-Jupiter conjunctions and oppositions for the 200 years from 1920 to 2120. Readers can locate their pre-natal Sun-Jupiter synodic cycle and its conjunction degree. One may also determine from these tables whether a birth occurred during the Oriental phase (from conjunction to opposition), or during the Occidental phase (from opposition to conjunction).

By researching degree symbols for one's pre-natal conjunction, recollection and recognition of past life experiences can penetrate the veils between lives. It should be remembered that we share these past life factors with other souls incarnating during the same 399-day Sun-Jupiter synodic cycle as ourselves. Other souls born within this same synodic cycle have matching karmic inclinations and tendencies.

The bi-wheel chart on the facing page shows the author's pre-natal Sun-Jupiter conjunction, which occurred a little less than six months before his birth, overlaid into his natal houses. Souls born from 25 May 1953 until 30 June 1954, when the subsequent conjunction took place, share a collective matrix of philosophical orientation and spiritual understanding that was set into place at the time of that new synodic cycle. The degree symbol for the conjunction, Gemini 4, delineates the aggregated conditions of that cycle, whereas the rising degree for the conjunction calculated for the individual birth location symbolizes the personal expression of the cycle. For the author, its rising degree in Santa Monica was Sagittarius 14.

Note that the author's pre-natal Sun-Jupiter conjunction was also conjoined by Mercury and fell into his natal 9th house, appropriate indeed for the owner of a small publishing company and an astrology school, as well as for one who always aspired to be an international lecturer. In the heavens on that day is also a second triple conjunction of the Moon, Saturn, and Neptune, all in 21° Libra and exactly opposed by Venus in 21° Aries. This imposing opposition falls across the author's 2nd and 8th cusps, right to the degree,[79] and through the contention of a pre-natal Sun-Jupiter conjunction having relevance to one's spiritual growth, it is perhaps understandable why the author has passed through so many relational endings, while at the same time remaining ever dedicated to his astrology business.

It is certainly of note that Uranus, at the time of this Sun-Jupiter conjunction was in Cancer 17, the degree of the author's pre-natal Sun-Mars conjunction, and he is a career astrologer. To gain insight into the collective conditions of this cycle, one researches the symbols for its conjunction degree. From *La Volasfera*, for Gemini 4:

> *A man dressed like a Minister of State, of venerable and kindly aspect.*
>
> This degree will produce a person of kind and noble disposition; one who will occupy positions of trust, and, by his own merits, rise to eminence in his own sphere of work. It is a degree of DIGNITY.

Chapter Six • *Sun–Jupiter Phase Angle Returns*

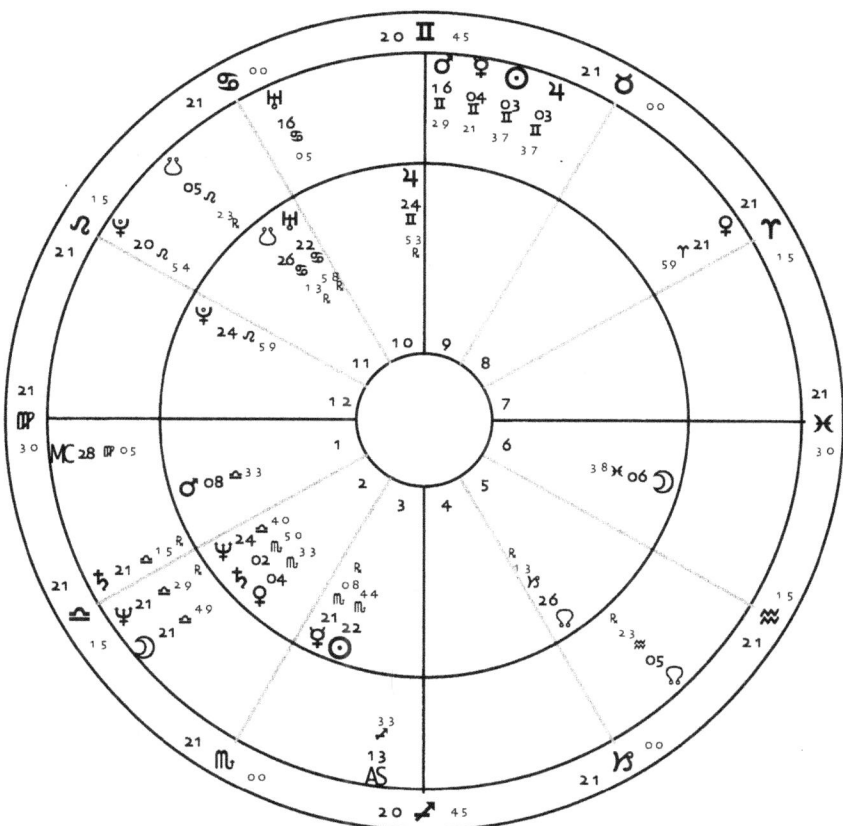

And from *The Degrees of the Zodiac Symbolised* by Charubel, for Gemini 4:

A profile, with only one eye in view.

Great powers of perception. An active, sharp intellect; an exact or accurate observer of men and things. He would make a good detective; a practical mind; no mere theoriser.

Souls born into this Sun-Jupiter synodic cycle have a capacity to rise to eminence professionally as a result of their abilities, and by working hard. Studying the degree symbols for a pre-natal synodic cycle conjunction, one can

Pre-Natal Sun-Jupiter Conjunction

May 24 1953	8:37:14 PM PDT	**Second Chart**	Natal Chart
Santa Monica	California	**Brother**	
33N50	118W29	Jul 15 1951	23:10:00 GMT
May 25 1953	03:37:14 GMT	**Third Chart**	Natal Chart
Tropical Porphyry	True Node	**Daughter**	
		Oct 19 1980	13:03:00 GMT

identify with the distinctive attributes of his soul group. In order to personalize the influences of the pre-natal synodic cycle, calculate this chart for the location of birth and refer to its rising degree. For the author, from *La Volasfera*, for Sagittarius 14:

A quantity of books and papers in disorder.

It is the index of a mind given to the study of literature, history and other intellectual pursuits. The literary and scientific taste will be cultivated and trained to useful but somewhat unpopular or novel ends. The memory will be highly retentive, and the imagination lively but well under control. Such an one may become a prolific writer, combining science and invention with a facile power of romantic fancy. A strenuous worker and temperate liver, he will not fail to meet with due distinction. It is a degree of INTELLECT.

And from *The Degrees of the Zodiac Symbolised* by Charubel, for Sagittarius 14:

> *A magician in his sacerdotal vestments, standing in a magic circle, performing some magic rites.*

The Sun-Jupiter phase angle and its overall synodic cycle have a direct impact on one's pattern of personal growth and self-improvement. Rising degree symbolism for the local pre-natal conjunction provides insight into one's personal expression of the cycle's collective energies. For the author, from the preceding symbols we see a soul immersed in intellectual pursuits, happy as a clam to be at his desk in an office surrounded by books and papers, writing for several hours each day.

Because of Jupiter's exaltation in Cancer, the pre-natal Sun-Jupiter conjunction is connected by synastric aspect to the nativities of family members who are the most supportive of one's personal growth and self-improvement. In the above tri-wheel, the author's pre-natal Sun-Jupiter conjunction chart is in the innermost wheel, his older brother's horoscope in the middle wheel, and his elder daughter's birthchart is in the outer wheel. Of all the family members in this incarnation, these two souls are always consistently supportive of his aims.

The author's daughter has Jupiter in the exact degree of his pre-natal Sun-Jupiter conjunction chart's Midheaven, and his brother's Saturn is conjunct the MC by 1°. His daughter's Saturn is in exact trine to the pre-natal conjunction degree, and his brother's Mercury and Jupiter trine the chart's Ascendant. His daughter's Pluto in 21° Libra conjoins the Moon-Saturn-Neptune; she is always there for his rebirths.

When one thinks of Jupiter, one must, of course, think of philosophers. Of the great thinkers throughout history, among the most eminent is Immanuel Kant, the last major philosopher of the Enlightenment. In the 18th century he was peerless, and his 1781 *Critique of Pure Reason* is widely regarded as one of the greatest works in the history of philosophy. His writing coincided in time with the discovery of the planet Uranus, and it is fitting that Kant had a Sun-Uranus opposition with a close orb of 00° 09'. He was born with an oriental morning star Jupiter in an exact trine to his 3rd-house ruler, Venus. His pre-natal synodic cycle is truly impressive.

From Sepharial's translation of *La Volasfera*, the conjunction degree, Capricorn 21:

> *An ancient hieroglyphic manuscript with a retort and crucible upon it.*

This symbol is the index of one who will essay the Magnum Opus or great work of alchemical science. It may be that he will attempt the solution of some scientific problems, and in such would be successful beyond his belief. On the other hand its scope may be restricted to the world of commerce, or even extended to the spiritual world, so that the transmutation of the gross and external body of the soul may be effected. In any case the native will be a deep researcher and will study ancient methods and principles with benefit to himself and advantage to the world. He will begin a new school of thought and his mind will be set upon reforms in the scientific and philosophic worlds. It is a degree of RENOVATION.

Personalizing this Sun-Jupiter cycle for Kant, Libra 20 was rising in Königsberg:

> *A man in the robe of a priest standing in the cloister beneath the light of a window.*

It denotes a person of sincere, religious tendencies: a taste for ecclesiastical work, in which he will probably indulge. The life will be quiet, peaceful and free from much of event, perhaps secluded. The native will have protection and favour from persons of high position and intellectual dignity. It is a degree of RELIGION.

Kant was raised in a Lutheran reform movement known as the *Pietists*. It was a strict and austere upbringing (Moon square Saturn), stressing personal humility and an intense religious devotion. He never married, he lived a scholarly life, yet he also enjoyed socializing at dinner parties (Venus trine Jupiter). The gist of his philosophy was that humans make an autonomous choice (Sun opposite Uranus) to act from rational moral principles, and that moral law is the basis of reason. A case can be made for Jupiter in Aquarius as underpinning his *science of morality*.[80]

Of all of the group of souls incarnating during any given Sun-Jupiter synodic cycle, how can one know which individual souls will bring to realization the intent of that cycle's conjunction degree? The author has pondered this question, and feels that the conjunction's local rising degree is one of the spiritual filters, and that other reciprocities also exist between the collective and the individual.

In the 18th century, the *Rationalist* and *Empiricist* movements exalted reason and experience as their root principles. In that *Age of Reason*, Kant reintroduced moral law as the necessary third pillar of knowledge and understanding.

Chapter Six • *Sun–Jupiter Phase Angle Returns*

Immanuel Kant
Apr 22 1724　　3:00 AM LMT
Königsberg　　Germany
49N54　　10E34
Apr 22 1724　　02:17:44 GMT
Tropical　Porphyry　True Node

Second Chart　　Natal Chart
Pre-Natal Sun-Jupiter Conjunction
Jan 10 1724　　23:50:08 GMT

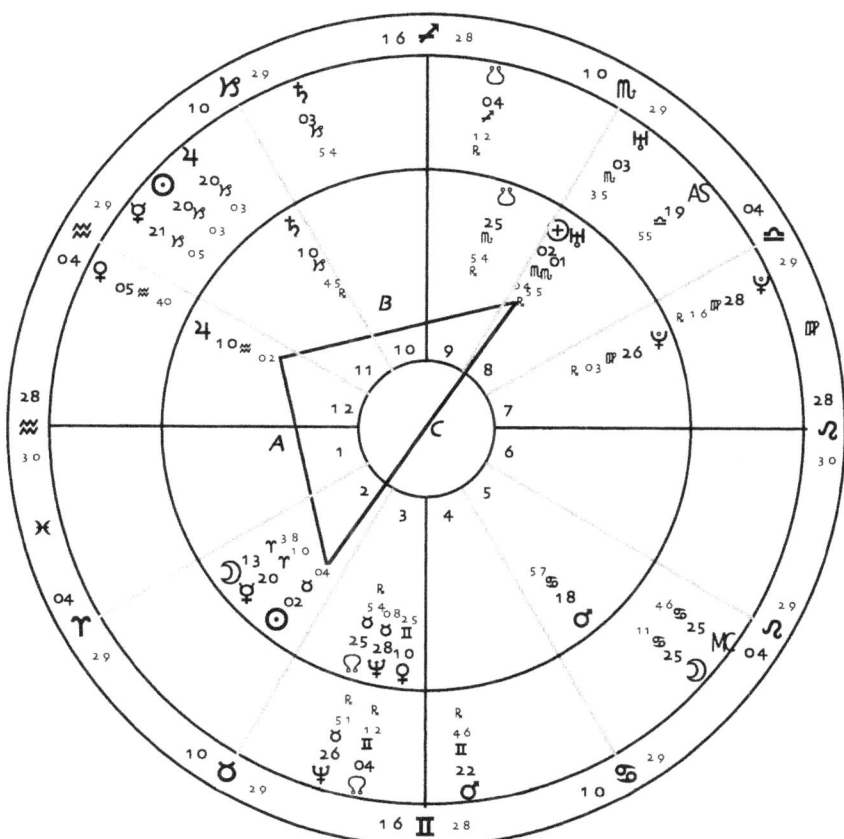

It was as if he could see into a future (Balsamic natal Sun-Moon phase) where the diminishment of the soul at the hands of reason would have degraded humanity and morality.

As an individual, was he sensitive to a potentially amoral future of mankind? His personal rising degree illustrates his consciousness. From Charubel, Aquarius 29:

> *A man with open breast, showing enlarged heart overflowing with blood.*

By examining Kant's natal Sun-Jupiter hologram of judgment, the astrologer can get a glimpse into the holographic structure of his soul. His Sun-Jupiter distance arc *A* is 82° 01' 59", equivalent to the 23rd degree of Gemini. Synchronously, Mars in the pre-natal Sun-Jupiter conjunction chart is in this very degree. This is also the midpoint of Kant's Mars/North Node, idiosyncratic of his life work. The symbols for Gemini 23 illustrate Kant's prophetic visions into a troubled future wherein blind reason had triumphed over moral law and sympathy with divine order:

> *A man standing on a lonely plain, weeping.*

This denotes one who is liable to give up in the struggle of life to despondency; very much wanting in energy, and destitute of moral courage. (*Charubel*)

> *An old oak, without leaf or bark, splintered by the storms*
> *through which it has passed, stands alone upon a desolate moorland.*

It denotes one who through his own actions, or the force of circumstances, will be deserted by kith and kin, and will pass through many trials. The storms of life will sear his heart and blight his nature ere the young world of his dreams can grow up around him to shelter and protect his years of falling leaf. It is a degree of ABANDONMENT. (*La Volasfera*)

His nearly exact Sun-Uranus opposition was the lightning strike *splintering the oak*, and his *Critique of Pure Reason* was published in 1781 at Uranus' discovery. As a further illustration of his individual karmic mission to awaken and alert the thinkers who succeeded him to the dangers of the seductive power of reason to kill the spirit of Man, his Jupiter-Earth arc *B* is 9° 58' 01", and equates to Cancer 8:[81]

> *A dove lies upon the ground, while over it a snake is poised in an attitude of attack.*
> *A man pulling at a rope attached to a bell suspended near the top of a high tree.*

Examining the Sun-Jupiter synodic cycle over a period of 5,000 years, the author found that a Sun-Jupiter conjunction occurs in the same degree of the Zodiac every 83 years to the day. A total of 76 synodic cycles recur during this periodicity. The mathematics behind this is as follows: 83 years x 365.26 days = 30,316.58 days. This product of days is then divided by the number of days in a synodic cycle of Jupiter. 30,316.58 days+ 398.9 days/ cycle= exactly 76 synodic cycles.

Each successive conjunction of the Sun and Jupiter advances from 390° to 397° in the Zodiac. Eleven consecutive conjunctions of the Sun and Jupiter complete a cycle around the Zodiac. The next conjunction occurs about 4.3°

Chapter Six • *Sun–Jupiter Phase Angle Returns*

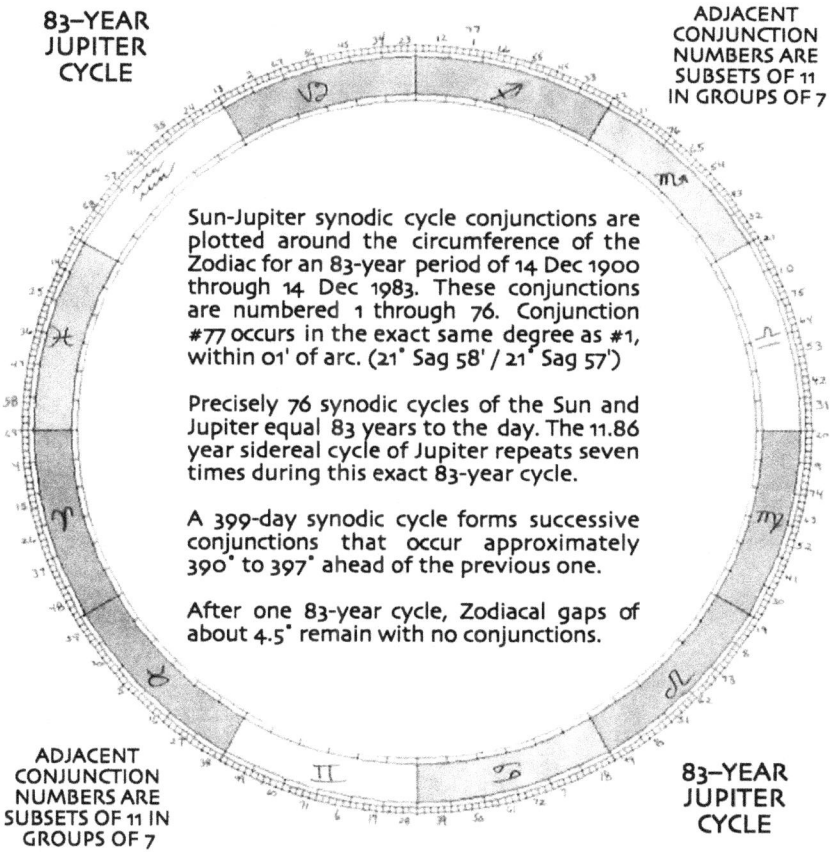

past where the finishing subcycle originally began. After seven 11.86-year sidereal cycles, the 83-year period is complete, and the conjunction degree is identical to 83 years ago. The above illustration shows the 76 conjunctions forming around the Zodiac.

The Zodiac degrees in which Sun-Jupiter conjunctions recur remain in place for thousands of years, repeating cycle after cycle. Then, the recurring conjunctions shift a degree and begin to fall in the adjacent degrees for another extremely long period of time. The geometric perfection of this 83-year cycle causes the conjunctions to cluster in the same Zodiac degrees, with a gap of about 4–5° between clusters. For example, Sun-Jupiter conjunctions occurred in 19° and 24° Capricorn for almost three and one half millenniums. Rarely, conjunctions will occur once in an adjacent degree to the repeating cluster, and then revert back.

The pre-natal Sun-Jupiter synodic cycle that Immanuel Kant was born into occurred in one of these *rare degrees,* Capricorn 21, *that had not hosted a synodic cycle conjunction since 1016 BC, and will not host another conjunction until 2471 AD, a span of 3,487 years.*[82] His pre-natal cycle is a rarity, as is the phenomenal symbol for Capricorn 21. These can be called *Rare Conjunctions.*

Metaphysical astrologers, such as the author, must, of course, theorize that Kant was reincarnated from the mystical Shang Yin dynasty in China from the eleventh century BC, which was historically supplanted by the rational philosophy of the Chou dynasty around the time of the last Sun-Jupiter conjunction in Capricorn 21. It can be predicted that, in the late 25th century and beyond, Kantian philosophy will underpin contemporary society with its moral laws as the basis of reason.[83]

Using Sun-Jupiter Holographic Transits

A Sun-Jupiter holographic transit occurs when the exact distance arc between the natal Sun and Jupiter forms again in the heavens, *and is in the identical phase as the natal Jupiter cycle, i.e., Oriental or Occidental.* A Sun-Jupiter phase angle return occurs every 13 months, and at these times celestial conditions show how spiritual understanding, personal growth, and self-improvement can occur. The chart is a useful complement to the progressions or standard transits affecting natal Jupiter.

The facing bi-wheel chart is the Sun-Jupiter holographic transit for the author of 4 April 2006. His Sun-Jupiter distance arc of 147° 51' 15" has replicated itself in the heavens, and the Sun-Jupiter phase angle is Oriental, as it was in his nativity. There is also a nearly partile conjunction from Mars in the phase angle return chart to his natal Jupiter. The chart was cast for Pacific Grove, California, his residence briefly at that time, and has a rising degree of Scorpio 2.

During this period, the author was undergoing the transit of Pluto in opposition to his natal Jupiter, ruler of his Descendant and IC. He was not able to concentrate nor write in the environment in which he was living and working at the time. That Pluto transit, as is normally the case, intensified his decision-making process into a black or white point of view. He became convinced that he had to move to write this volume, and his personal relationship had become severely strained.

The author reluctantly chose to move to the coast of California and rent an office, thinking that being near the ocean would be best. From *La Volasfera,* Scorpio 2:

Chapter Six • *Sun–Jupiter Phase Angle Returns*

Robert P. Blaschke
Nov 15 1953   1:37 AM PST
Santa Monica   California
33N50   118W29
Nov 15 1953   09:37:00 GMT
Tropical   Porphyry   True Node

Second Chart   Natal Chart
Sun-Jupiter Holographic Transit
Apr 5 2006   03:48:28 GMT

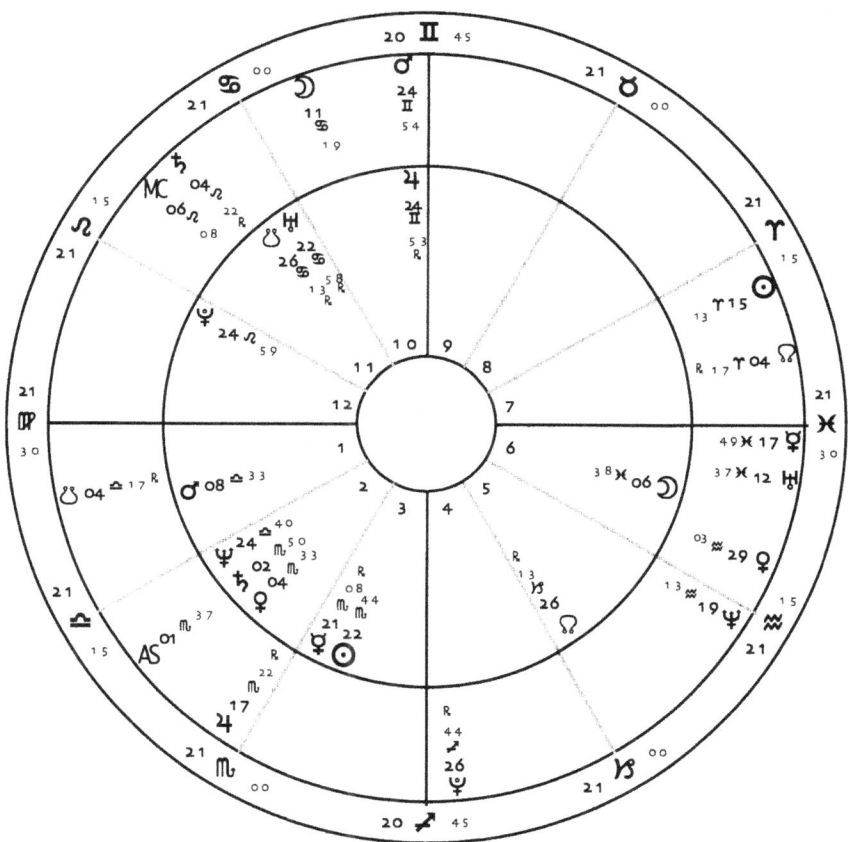

A great headland over which the Sun is rising. It overhangs the sea.

After leasing an office, but unable to find a living space, the mission was aborted ten days later, and he moved back to his previous home, but with still no progress made on the book. With Pluto opposing the IC and Descendant ruler, the author confronted fears of abandonment. If he went off to write his book, would she still want to be with him? If he stayed to preserve the relationship, would the book be written? He was caught between the proverbial rock and a hard place.

On the day of his Sun-Jupiter phase angle return, he was staring at the walls in his new office on the coast, feeling torn and still unable to write. Venus in 29° Aquarius was conjunct his girlfriend's natal Venus, exact to 03' of arc. The interpretation: for the next 13-month Sun-Jupiter cycle, spiritual understanding, personal growth, and self-improvement would come through keeping her in his life.

Mars conjunct the ruler of both his IC and Descendant, Jupiter, was taken to mean that a separation was necessary to finish writing this manuscript. The dignified Moon in the phase angle return chart applies to trines with Mercury, Jupiter and Uranus, the three bodies that are retrograde in the author's nativity. It was also clear that with stationary direct Saturn in square to his Venus, no easy decision was to be found, and a burdensome choice would have to be made.

The choice was made to move to Port Townsend, to be nearer to his elder daughter who lives in Seattle. With the phase angle return Moon trine Uranus, and his progressed Moon trine natal Mars, the author went on the Internet, found on-line classifieds, and called to schedule appointments to look at office space and an apartment. He flew to Seattle, rented a car, drove to Port Townsend and leased office space and an apartment in one day. Would he now be able to write?

It is one of the primary contentions of this book that the celestial conditions at the time of a phase angle return show free will aligning with Higher Self through the holographic structure of the soul. Because the Sun is sending its divine rays to the planet from the exact same phase angle as at birth, the soul is being restored to a state of wholeness during a holographic transit, and the chart can be read as such.

The chart on the facing page relocates the author's Sun-Jupiter phase angle return to his new home in Port Townsend. In a remarkable twist of fate, the Ascendant is Libra 28, the very same degree as his pre-natal Sun-Mars conjunction's rising degree for Santa Monica. From page 102, recall the degree symbols for Libra 28:

> *A man stands alone in surrounding gloom; were his eyes open to spirit things he would see helping angels arriving.*
>
> *An ass tethered to the shaft of a grinding mill.*

The author is pleased to inform the reader that he has indeed been a tethered ass since arriving here five months ago, working seven days a week to write the book. Helping angels have been all around him. With the new angles, the

Chapter Six • *Sun–Jupiter Phase Angle Returns*

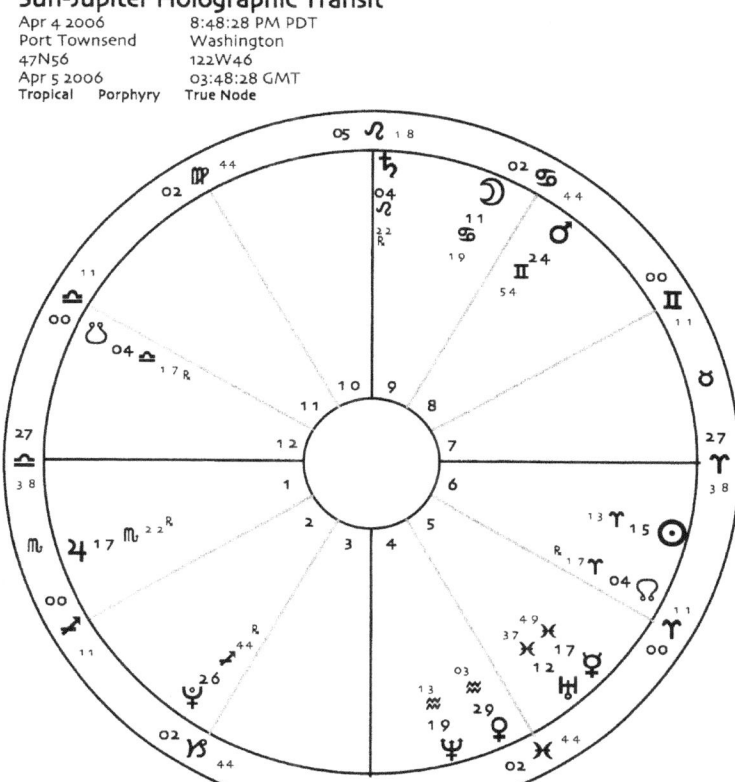

Sun-Jupiter Holographic Transit
Apr 4 2006   8:48:28 PM PDT
Port Townsend   Washington
47N56   122W46
Apr 5 2006   03:48:28 GMT
Tropical Porphyry True Node

1st-house Jupiter reverted back within an interception. It has been like a fountain of inner strength for the author, and with Jupiter trine Mercury, he has been able to travel back and forth between the technique and the theory. A happy ending is always heartwarming: a house on a bluff overlooking the sea has been rented, and she moves here to join him this month. Yes, it faces the rising Sun.

This next bi-wheel shows the Sun-Jupiter holographic transit of 16 February 2001 for George W. Bush overlaid into his natal houses. Occurring just after taking office as president, this is also his operative phase angle return for the terrorist attack of 11 September 2001. Because a Sun-Jupiter hologram forms one's judgment, which for this president with a Sun-Jupiter square, is called into question repeatedly, it will be an expedient endeavor to investigate the holographic structure of his soul.

George W. Bush

Jul 6 1946　　7:26 AM EDT
New Haven　　Connecticut
41N07　　72W56
Jul 6 1946　　11:26:00 GMT
Tropical　Porphyry　True Node

Second Chart　　Natal Chart
Sun-Jupiter Holographic Transit
Feb 16 2001　　05:59:58 GMT

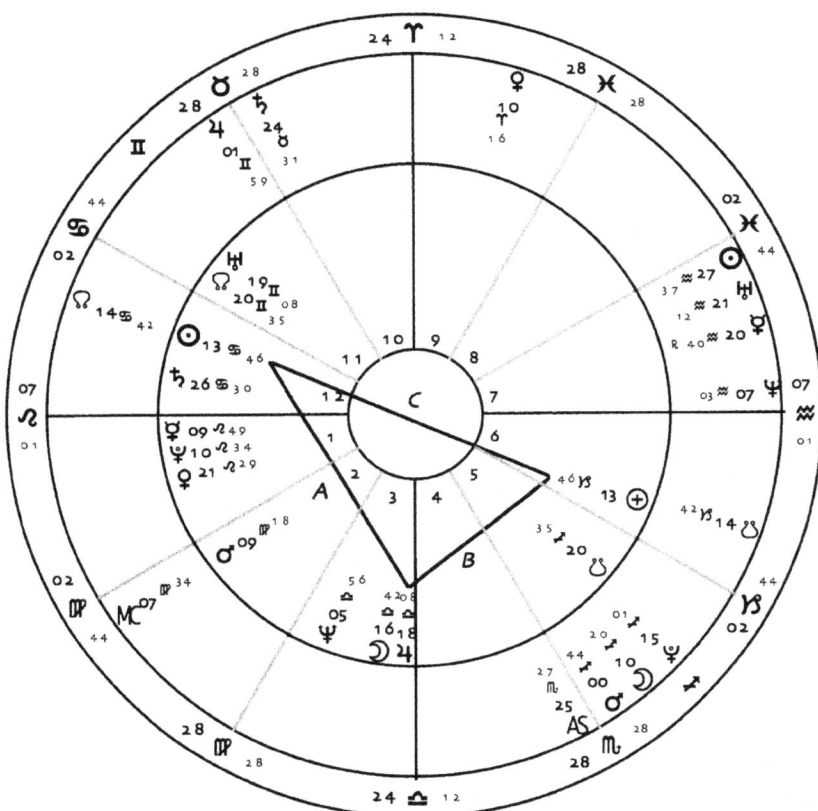

The astrologer sees that his Sun-Jupiter distance arc *A* is 94° 21' 55", equivalent to the 5th degree of Cancer. Jupiter-Earth distance arc *B* is 85° 38' 05", and equates to the 26th degree of Gemini, both degrees being the antiscion of the other. The Sabian Symbol for Cancer 5, and its spiritual analysis by Marc Jones, provides insight:

> *A man in an automobile, maddened by the lust for speed,*
> *races with a fast train and loses; he is killed.*

This is a symbol of the bringing of individual man to account for his obligation to society, it is the closing of old books of outer life. Positively it is a degree of curbed recklessness; negatively, it is the bringing of life's loose ends to justice.

Chapter Six • *Sun–Jupiter Phase Angle Returns*

From Sepharial's translation of *La Volasfera*, Cancer 5:

> *A young tree or sapling, bent about the middle, and thence growing awry.*

It indicates a person of warm affections, but incautious nature; who confides, without sufficient grounds, in those around him; and is apt to misplace his trust. To those of the female sex it is a baneful degree. In general, it shows a loving and trustful nature without much knowledge of human weaknesses. It is apt to be bent, and perhaps broken, by the storms of passion, and to lean where there is no real support. It is a degree of BETRAYAL.

In the Sabian Symbol, one sees that there can be a recklessness within his soul that obscures his judgment. And from Sepharial, we learn that he has an inclination to receive bad advice from trusted confidants in his inner circle. Though he may be warm and affectionate, misplaced trust and vulnerability to being manipulated by those with whom he leans on for support and guidance, makes him prone to error.

From Sepharial's translation of *La Volasfera*, for Gemini 26, his Jupiter-Earth arc:

> *A market place, in which several young men are in dispute, and asserting their respective opinions by the free use of cudgels.*

It signifies a person of a stubborn, willful nature, easily persuaded of the merits or rights of others, litigious and quarrelsome, of few sympathies, jealous and revengeful. It denotes a life of many dangers and perhaps death by the hands of a man. It is a degree of CONTEST.

It has been reported that bad news and negative policy assessments are withheld from this president by his staff and subordinates, due to his adverse reaction upon hearing such communications. This symbol leaves one wondering just what kind of discord exists inside the White House, despite the surface appearance of decorum, protocol and formality. For a Tecumseh's Curse president, this symbolism is grim.[84]

Less than a month after taking office for his first term, Mr Bush had a Sun-Jupiter phase angle return with Neptune conjunct his Descendant within 02' of arc (see bi-wheel chart on page 140). In the heavens, as the Sun[85] and Jupiter replicated his natal distance arc of 94° 21' 55", several other exact aspects formed. Opposing his natal Venus was Uranus, and the Moon and Venus make a Fire Grand Trine with his natal Pluto, exact to the degree. The Lunar Nodes are about to conjoin his Sun-Earth axis, and as a warning of what was to come on 9/11, Mars opposes Jupiter.

The celestial conditions of 16 February 2001, at the time of his Sun-Jupiter phase angle return, set into place the holographic structure of how Mr Bush responded to the terror attacks in September. With Neptune conjunct the cusp of his 7th house of open enemies, his initial reaction as a 21st-century Crusader is understandable.

Regarding that exact Fire Grand Trine activating Pluto, the planet associated with the use or misuse of power, it is instructive to recall the analysis of C.E.O. Carter:

> Such a configuration was considered evil by medieval writers and unfortunately this view appears to be not without foundation. Often the fortunes seem to be greatly involved in those of others, both for good and evil, and the character may tend to weakness and lack of moral fibre. The element in which the grand trine falls may be too prominent in the temperament.[86]

One observes that the Grand Trine was not only in the fire signs, but also in his fiery 1st, 5th and 9th houses of identity. Mr Bush repeatedly refers to himself as a "War President;" his identity and self-image having been utterly impacted by those events of 9/11. Perhaps the fire element became *too prominent in the temperament.*[87]

Uranus opposing his IC ruler, Venus, was a shocking realization on a personal level that matched what the country was feeling: *We are not as safe anymore as we thought.* The elevated Venus in Aries in his 9th house can be seen to symbolize his feelings about a foreign culture attacking the US with its declaration of *jihad.* Aries 11 from Charubel insinuates a bewildered and indiscriminate perspective:

> *A man with a large telescope, which he employs chiefly in looking at things in his immediate surroundings, and what lies on the Earth. The most remarkable thing is, that he is looking at the large end of the instrument.*

From this study, astrologers can see that the celestial conditions at the time of the phase angle return provide insight into the holographic structure of the soul. How one makes choices, acting from their free will, can also be read in these charts. It is recommended that astrologers overlay holographic transits into the natal houses.

Chapter Seven
Sun-Saturn Phase Angle Returns

Sun-Saturn Phase Angle at Birth

The Sun-Saturn phase angle at birth forms one's inborn sense of reliability and duty. This hologram of responsibility is parallel to the lunar hologram of instinct, and from the phase angles of the Sun with both Saturn and the Moon, one is able to see how the karmic potential of an individual is set in motion by one's family bloodlines and ancestry, and by the discipline received during one's upbringing.

The phase angle of the Sun and Saturn reveals how a soul is inclined to bring into concrete and practical form that of which he is capable. The exaltation of Saturn in Libra is commonly overlooked by astrologers, and substantiates why there is a strong artistic, musical and creative side to Saturn, besides its kinship to business, finance, mathematics, and science. *The propensity of the greater malefic for causing limitations may be the soul choosing to narrow its focus.*

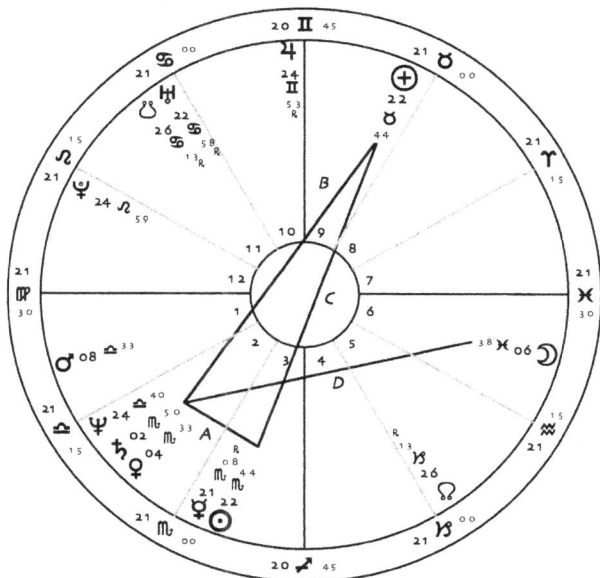

To visualize one's natal Sun-Saturn hologram, the glyph for the Earth is placed in the nativity, thus creating a three-dimensional image. In the author's horoscope, his Sun-Saturn distance arc *A* is 19° 53' 42", and the Saturn-Earth distance arc *B* is 160° 06' 18". Together, the two arcs total 180° 00' 00". Using his Sabian Aspect Orb technique, arc *A* is equivalent to the 20th degree of Aries, and arc *B* equates to the 11th degree of Virgo. These two degrees are antiscia, or solstice points, of one another. Sun-Earth arc *C* is always a constant, measuring exactly 180° 00' 00".

From Sepharial's translation of *La Volasfera*, for Aries 20:

A man equipped for a rough journey, belted and armed.

This degree signifies one of adventurous nature, fond of discovery and of travel. A pioneer in whatever field of labour he may undertake to work in; one who will open up new roads of knowledge and research; active, aggressive, bold and fearless; one who will travel into distant countries and gain applause for his discoveries. It is a degree of INQUISITIVENESS.

And from *La Volasfera*, for Virgo 11:

A man's hand, with the index finger pointing upward as if in command.

It denotes a nature of the most high utility. A flexible nature, capable of fulfilling many and various positions in life; a generous and kind disposition; a high order of intelligence; always seeking after the uses of things; ingenious, inventive; one who will succeed in life, and will have many tributes to his intelligence and usefulness. It is a degree of UTILITY.

The author appears to have set the former symbolism in motion by running away from home in December 1969 at the age of barely 16, and hitchhiking to Cleveland, Ohio, after an emotionally devastating break-up with his first girlfriend, who had left him for another boy. That transformation of hurt and rejection into an opening to travel and explore the wider world has been a foundation of his nature. It also put into motion an adolescent social identity that carried on into adulthood—to come back from an adventure, physical or intellectual, reporting his findings.

The latter symbolism reflects the author's cadent Sun and ruler, Mercury, in the 3rd house, along with the useful and practical Virgo rising. The gesture of a hand with the index finger pointing upward is a common behavior by the author during lectures and workshops. Reviewers have described books in this series as *useful*.

The relationship between the Sun-Moon and Sun-Saturn holograms is vital for the understanding of *karma*. Whether the vicissitudes of life break one's will or spur the soul on, is a key spiritual question. One's ingrained responsibility in the Saturnian hologram will be tested throughout life by the lunar hologram.

Chapter Seven • *Sun–Saturn Phase Angle Returns*

Referring to the author's Sun-Moon hologram on page 39, recall that the two relevant distance arcs were equivalent to Cancer 14 and Gemini 17. The degree symbols from Sepharial's translation of *La Volasfera*, respectively, are:

*A bunch of spring flowers, over which is set a bright star
which flashes and sparkles in a deep blue atmosphere.*

It indicates a person of poetical and gentle disposition, fond of sublime subjects and the study of nature in its gentler phases; may be a botanist or astronomer, or one with a strong taste for such associations. In early life this individual will rise to a good position, and if not born into an illustrious family will marry a person of high rank or fame. In all cases the native attains a good position and generally marries early into a family devoted to the fine arts. It is a degree of SUCCESS.

A broken pitcher lying upon the ground with spilled fruit around it.

It denotes one who will come to some untimely end through the hands of another. It shows the nature to be unpractical and the pursuits of the native to be mostly vain and of no lasting benefit. It shows loss of powers during lifetime, and perhaps loss of faculties. It is a degree of IMPOTENCE.

These two symbols, for the author, remarkably illustrate the vulnerabilities of his lunar hologram, and accurately encapsulate the history of his personal life. Early on, when in his 20s and 30s, opportunities for marriage came easily and his third wife, especially, was from a family of refinement, education, and social elegance.

In the visual second symbol, one sees broken marriages and divorces, and it raises the core karmic question of his Moon-Saturn relationship: Will repeated personal failures eventually ruin the capacity for the achievement and accomplishment suggested by the symbols for Aries 20 and Virgo 11?

The Moon and Saturn are especially prominent in the karmic interpretation of any nativity, and the derived degree symbols for their natal holograms are insightful. It takes an objective mind to look at one's karma in this way, and some transparency is called for when sharing private details to explain subtle techniques. It is also probable that the Moon-Saturn distance arc D, as shown on page 143, has a derived degree symbol that resembles the other holograms. For the author, that arc is 123° 47' 49". From Charubel, for Leo 4, useful, practical, and on the move:

A carrier's waggon (sic); one of those with the tarpaulin overhead.

Denotes an active person; one who is always on the move. In his case the saying is true: "The grass is not allowed to grow under his feet." A practical person, always engaged in what is useful to himself or others. A business man, he will at a glance take in what may be to his own advantage or otherwise.

The Sun-Saturn phase angle at birth is part of an overall synodic cycle lasting for an average of 378 days, or about 12 ½ months. The cycle begins with a conjunction of the Sun and direct motion Saturn, reaches its halfway point at the opposition of the Sun and retrograde Saturn, and has quarter points when the Sun squares Saturn. This synodic cycle functions as a counterbalancess to the Muslim calendar of 354 days, consisting of 12 Sun-Moon synodic cycles of 29.5 days each.

Those born after the conjunction of the Sun and Saturn, but before the Sun-Saturn opposition, have Saturn as the morning star in their nativities, rising ahead of the Sun. During the latter part of this oriental half of the synodic cycle, Saturn is retrograde and closer to Earth than at any other point in its orbital cycle. Because of this, its karmic influence from past lives is stronger, peaking at the opposition.

Those born after the Sun-Saturn opposition, but before the next conjunction, have Saturn as the evening star, setting after the Sun. For the first part of this occidental half of the synodic cycle, Saturn is retrograde. The most powerful points in the Sun-Saturn cycle are at the conjunction when Saturn shifts from occidental to oriental, and again at the opposition, when retrograde Saturn also has a reversal of polarity from oriental to occidental. At a Sun-Saturn conjunction, the necessity of standing for a principle in life, despite rejection and ridicule, is at its strongest.

With direct and retrograde stations of Saturn, the distance between the Sun and stationary Saturn is rather consistent, between 108° to 109°. Saturn is retrograde when sesquiquintile, trine, trioctile, biquintile, inconjunct, triseptile, or opposite the Sun. These are all highly karmic phase angles. As with Jupiter, it has been the experience of this astrologer that a retrograde Saturn is powerful when also in close aspect to the Sun, and with an orb of less than 2 ½°.

Throughout life, secondary progressions evolve the Sun-Saturn relationship, often resulting in important phase changes, depending on where in the orbital cycle one is born. Especially karmic is a natal Sun-Saturn phase angle shifting from oriental to occidental at the opposition of the progressed Sun and progressed Saturn. This is certainly the case with a natal waxing inconjunct of retrograde Saturn and the Sun, as a karmic lesson in responsibility usually occurs about age 27, near to the progressed Moon return. It lasts another 2–4°, until the Sun opposes natal Saturn.

Chapter Seven • *Sun–Saturn Phase Angle Returns*

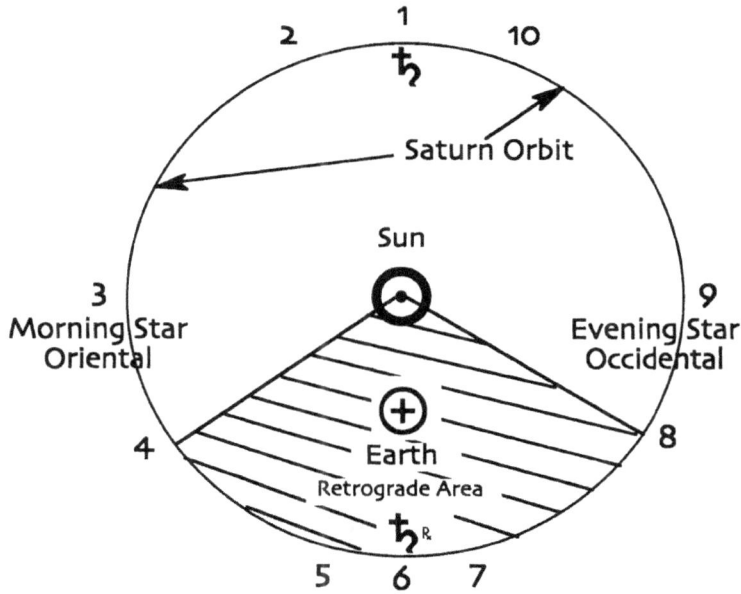

Cycles and Phases of the Planet Saturn

1. Sun-Saturn Conjunction
2. Saturn Heliacal Rising
3. Waxing Square
4. Stationary Retrograde
5. Earth's Heliacal Setting
6. Sun-Saturn Opposition
7. Earth's Heliacal Rising
8. Stationary Direct
9. Waning Square
10. Saturn Heliacal Setting

The following tri-wheel chart shows the nativity of the actress, Winona Ryder, in the inner wheel, her progressed Sun-Saturn opposition of 13 February 1999 in the middle wheel, and her arrest for shoplifting on 12 December 2001 in the outer wheel. Note that Ryder was born with an exact waxing inconjunct of the Sun and Saturn, separating by only 28' of arc. Her progressed Sun-Saturn opposition occurred at age 27 years and 3 ½ months, exactly at her secondary progressed Moon return.

At her progressed opposition in 1999, she became executive producer for the film, *Girl, Interrupted*, in which she starred in the role of a character with borderline personality disorder, with Angelina Jolie playing the sociopathic supporting role. This increase in responsibility as the film's producer, in addition to acting, was concomitant with the Sun-Saturn cycle's phase change from oriental to occidental.

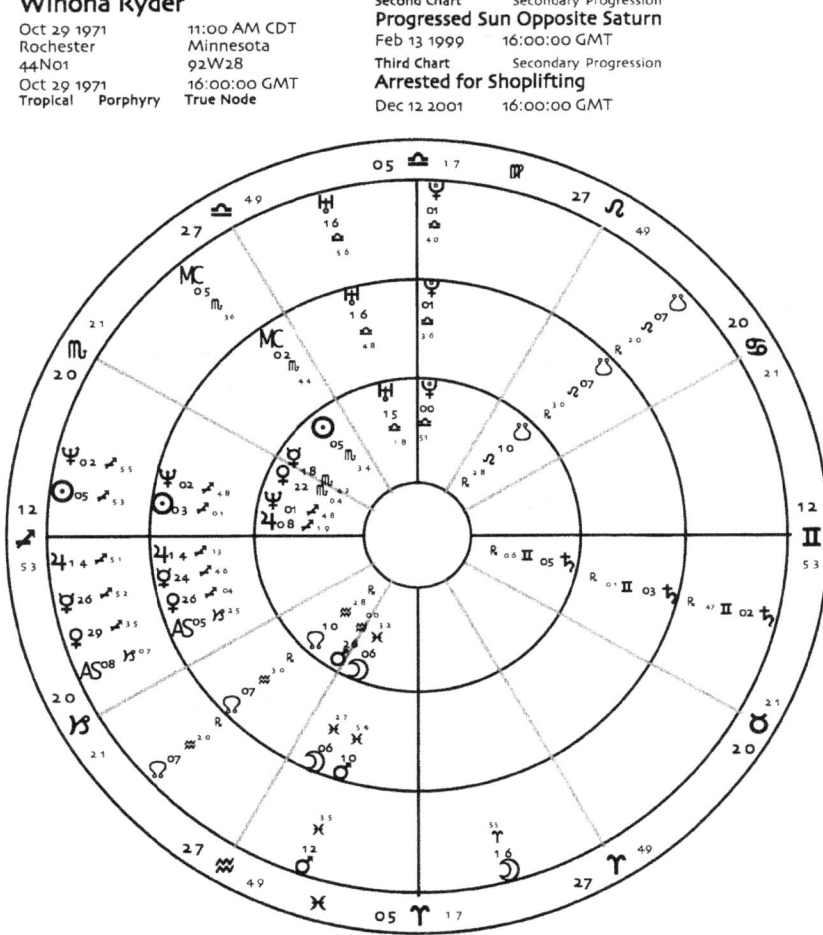

Winona Ryder
Oct 29 1971   11:00 AM CDT
Rochester   Minnesota
44N01   92W28
Oct 29 1971   16:00:00 GMT
Tropical   Porphyry   True Node

Second Chart   Secondary Progression
Progressed Sun Opposite Saturn
Feb 13 1999   16:00:00 GMT
Third Chart   Secondary Progression
Arrested for Shoplifting
Dec 12 2001   16:00:00 GMT

Because her progressed Saturn had retrogressed about 2° behind its natal position by age 27, it would be another three years before this shift in the Saturn cycle was concluded—not until her progressed Sun finished its opposition to natal Saturn.

It was around 1999 that Ms Ryder began to develop an addictions[89] to prescription medications. In December 2001, she was arrested for shoplifting several thousand dollars worth of designer clothes at a Saks Fifth Avenue store in Beverly Hills. Her reputation was badly damaged by the arrest, and the disclosure during her trial that she had 37 prescriptions filled by 20 doctors in a 3-year period, using six different aliases, exposed the extent of the problem. Right as she was arrested, her progressed Midheaven was conjunct her natal Sun, and it was all very public.

In December 2002, she was sentenced to three years' probation, community service, fines were levied, and she had to pay restitution to the department store. The judge also ordered her to undergo drug counseling and psychotherapy. This was a hard and very karmic Saturnian lesson, and it came as her cycle shifted phases at the progressed opposition. Her life is back on track, with three films due out in 2007.

Some readers may wonder how Ryder, convicted of two felonies, grand theft and vandalism, was able to avoid a prison sentence, and instead receive probation. An investigation into her rising degree is revealing. From *La Volasfera*, Sagittarius 13:

> *A large portcullis guarding the entrance to a prison.*[90]
>
> It is the symbol of a nature doomed to seclusion and separateness of life, either on account of some incurable hurt to the flesh or by reason of a mind that is misanthropic and perverse. Such an one will move in narrow limits, and his walk in life will be circumscribed by a stern necessity. He will be in danger of restraint, captivity, or imprisonment, and his life will be full of dangers. It is a degree of RESTRAINT.

One hopes that the holographic structure of her soul has evolved into a greater degree of Saturnian responsibility after the shoplifting incident, and that she will not have to further manifest the above symbolism, either privately or publicly.

The Sun-Saturn conjunction in the nativity of Tipper Gore, wife of former Vice-President Al Gore, provides a textbook example of the necessity of standing for a principle despite rejection or ridicule. In the mid-1980s, Mrs Gore launched a campaign protesting the explicit sex, drug use, and the glorification of violence in rock music lyrics. She received a lot of ridicule for being prudish, but with her nearly partile Sun-Saturn conjunction in Leo, the sign of children, she stood by her principles. She wrote a book entitled *Raising PG Kids in an X-Rated Society*, published in 1987. Hers is a strong will, shown in the rising degree. From *The Degrees of the Zodiac Symbolised* by Charubel, Cancer 10:

> *A bulbous plant, just pushing its way upward from beneath the sod, and beginning to unfold itself in order to show forth its beauties.*
>
> This denotes one possessed of a great amount of soul-force; in whom the principle of life is very strong. He will make a powerful magnetist, as he will have a strong will.

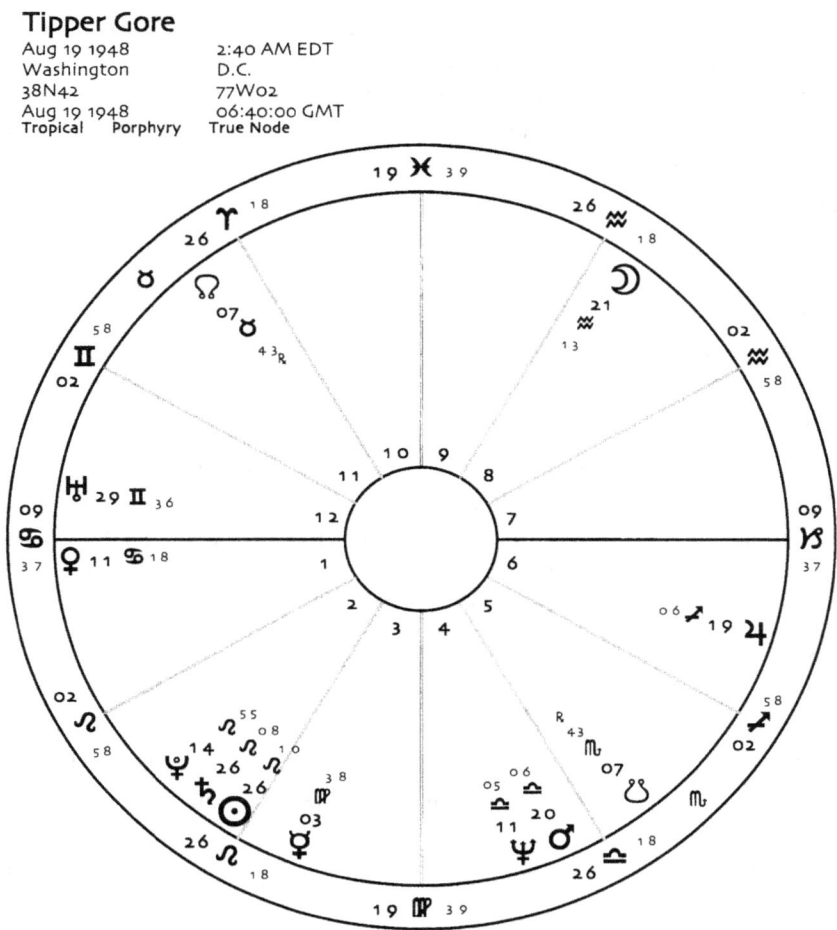

Tipper Gore
Aug 19 1948 2:40 AM EDT
Washington D.C.
38N42 77W02
Aug 19 1948 06:40:00 GMT
Tropical Porphyry True Node

An example of a retrograde Saturn in opposition to the Sun reaching its peak of karmic transformational power is found in the complex life of Eldridge Cleaver (*chart on facing page*). Bringing in a violent nature from past lives, with Pluto rising conjunct the South Node, Cleaver was convicted of assault with intent to murder in 1957 and sentenced. While in San Quentin and Folsom prisons, he wrote a series of essays on racial issues and revolutionary violence that was published after his parole in 1968 as *Soul on Ice*, the book helping to define the fledgling Black Power movement.

With Sun trine radical Uranus, and with an antisocial retrograde Venus, Cleaver wrote of his raping white women as an act of insurrection, and said "*it delighted me that I was defying and trampling upon white man's law ... defiling*

Chapter Seven • *Sun–Saturn Phase Angle Returns*

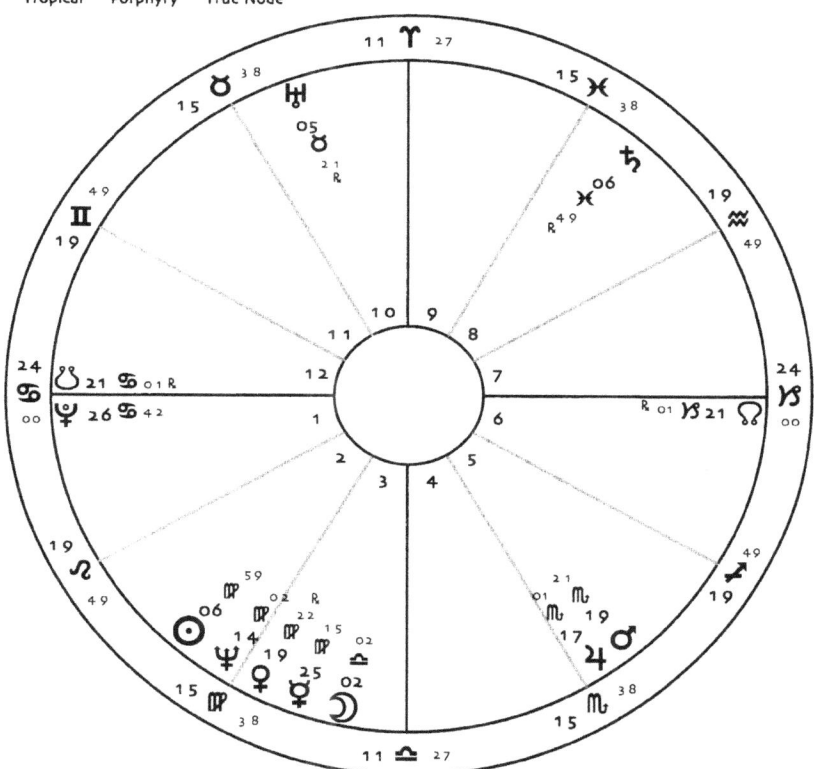

Eldridge Cleaver
Aug 31 1935   2:15 AM CST
Wabbaseka   Arkansas
34N11   91W48
Aug 31 1935   08:15:00 GMT
Tropical Porphyry   True Node

his women." It is evident that with his Sun in exact opposition with retrograde Saturn, Cleaver had karmic authority issues that were to undergo fundamental transformation.

Released from prison in 1966 with his progressed Venus stationary direct in 6° Virgo and exactly on his Sun-Saturn opposition, Cleaver helped found the militant Black Panthers group in Oakland. In 1968, while running for president on the obscure *Peace and Freedom Party* ticket, his progressed Venus perfected its second opposition to natal Saturn, and he jumped bail and fled the country after he was wounded in a shootout with the Oakland police and arrested. He lived first in exile in Cuba and Algeria, and then fled to France. In 1975, living underground in Paris, he had a conversion experience and became a born-again Christian.[91]

Returning to the US, Cleaver renounced the Black Panthers, receiving probation instead of a prison sentence for his outstanding arrest warrant. In the ultimate Saturnian transformation, he went on to become a conservative Republican and unsuccessfully ran for the US Senate in 1986. Not quite through yet with a life of radical changes, Cleaver then became addicted to crack cocaine in the late 1980s.

Convicted of drug possession and burglary in 1992 at his secondary progressed New Moon, two years later progressed Sun opposed Uranus and Cleaver nearly died from a drug-related assault. Finally, his progressed Venus conjoined his natal Venus and moved ahead of it for the first time in his life, and he overcame his habit and got involved in health foods and nutrition. Cleaver died in 1998 from prostate cancer at age 62 with progressed Ascendant conjunct Neptune. If he had lived just a few more years, progressed Saturn would have stationed direct, changing phase.

Readers can viscerally feel the intensity of Cleaver's life, as his retrograde Saturn opposite the Sun reached a peak of transformational power in this incarnation. It is open to debate where his soul goes from here, but one would have to theorize a dark night of the soul has been concluded, and his transition from morning star to evening star of Saturn has set his evolutionary course in a new direction. Cleaver was highly intelligent with Sun trine Uranus, and his rising degree defined his life:

> *A strong castle on a high rock, and upon the battlements*
> *of the castle a flag with a crown upon it is seen extended in the wind.*
>
> It denotes a strong, masterly character, of great endurance, stability and daring; ambitious of honour and capable of withstanding his enemies while achieving greatness and fame for himself. It is a degree of MASTERY. (Cancer 24; *La Volasfera*)

The Sun-Saturn phase angle at birth also has relevance in the lives of men who are fathers. The author has discovered that a "holographic synastry" exists between a man's natal Sun-Saturn hologram and women who bear his children. Unlike the aspects in conventional synastry, where one planet conjoins, opposes or trines a body in the second chart, *holographic synastry* is geometric. It involves certain degrees in a nativity that are unoccupied by the Luminaries or planets, yet when a body from a second chart occupies that degree, it transforms the natal hologram.

Chapter Seven • *Sun–Saturn Phase Angle Returns*

Robert P. Blaschke
Nov 15 1953   1:37 AM PST
Santa Monica   California
33N50   118W29
Nov 15 1953   09:37:00 GMT
Tropical   Porphyry   True Node

Second Chart   Natal Chart
Mother of Elder Daughter
Jun 3 1954   13:10:00 GMT

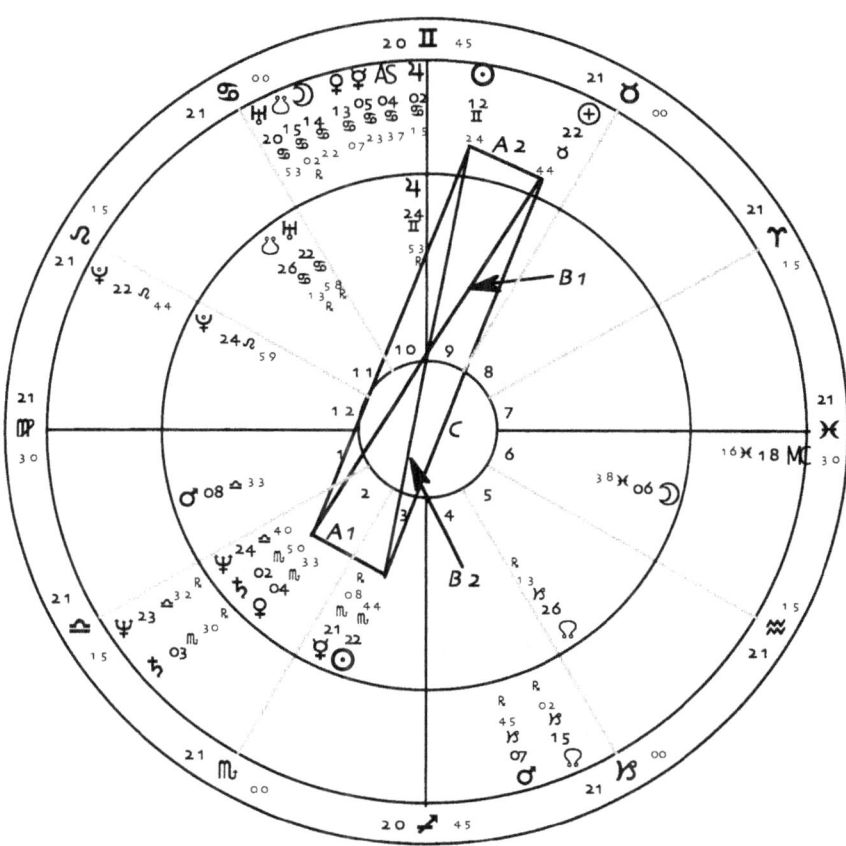

This bi-wheel chart shows the nativity of the author in the inner wheel, and the horoscope for the mother of his older daughter in the outer wheel. His Sun-Saturn hologram is shown by distance arcs *A1*, *B1*, and *C*. The mother has a natal Sun in 12° Gemini 24', and distance arc *A2* between her Sun and his Earth completes a *geometric transformation of the three-sided triangle into a four-sided rectangle*. *A2* is 19° 40', and shares the same degree symbol, Aries 20, with arc *A1* of 19° 53' 42". Saturn-Earth arc *B1* is 160° 06' 18", and *B2* from her Sun to his Sun is 160° 20' and shares the same degree symbol, Virgo 11, as *B1*. *This is spatial geometry synastry.*

The author has found that retrograde or stationary direct Saturn[92] is quite fateful when also in a close aspect to the Sun. This can occur at the 108° tridecile,[93] 120° trine, 135° trioctile, 144° biquintile, 150° inconjunct, 154° 17' triseptile, or the 180° opposition, when orbs are less than 2.5°. Retrograde Saturn in general is less so.[94]

Here is the nativity for Joan Baez, a folk singer and songwriter with a beautiful three-octave soprano voice who was very active in the civil rights movement. In 1959, she performed at the Newport Folk Festival and went on to become a leading folk musician in the early 1960s. She had a personal relationship with Bob Dylan in 1963–64, and later married a prominent anti-war protester, David Harris, with whom she had a son. Born with stationary direct Saturn in a close tridecile aspect with her Sun, she also has the rare Grand Conjunction of Jupiter and Saturn.[95]

Investigating her natal hologram, astrologers find Sun-Saturn arc *A* to be 108° 52' 24", and Saturn-Earth distance arc *B* is 71° 07' 36". Arc *A* is equivalent to the 19th degree of Cancer, and arc *B* equates to the 12th degree of Gemini. As a singer who is known more for performing other songwriter's music, such as Jackson Browne, Paul Simon, and Natalie Merchant, from *La Volasfera*, for Cancer 19, we see why:

> *An escutcheon containing a harp and a gauntlet.*
>
> It denotes a person of noble aspirations and refined tastes. One whose family is connected with the musical or military worlds, and who will have tastes in one or the other direction. In either he will show much aptitude, but in music the executive powers will transcend the ability to compose. As an interpreter of others' works he would shine. In the character there is a peculiar admixture of gentleness and irritability, of playfulness and gravity, which will render the native difficult to deal with. It is a degree of EXECUTION.

Her father, Albert Baez, was a Mexican physicist and inventor who turned down contracts from the US Department of Defense to work on the Manhattan Project to build an atomic bomb during World War II. With her Sun-Uranus trine perfectly symbolizing such a father, his principled decisions had a profound effect on her. A stationary direct Saturn is fateful in that the soul is called to stand for something.

In 1956, at the age of 15, young Baez attended a speech by Martin Luther King in which he spoke about civil rights and non-violent social change. Moved by his words, the pull of her stationary direct Saturn to take a principled stand began to well up inside of her. Her progressed Sun in the sign of

Chapter Seven • *Sun–Saturn Phase Angle Returns*

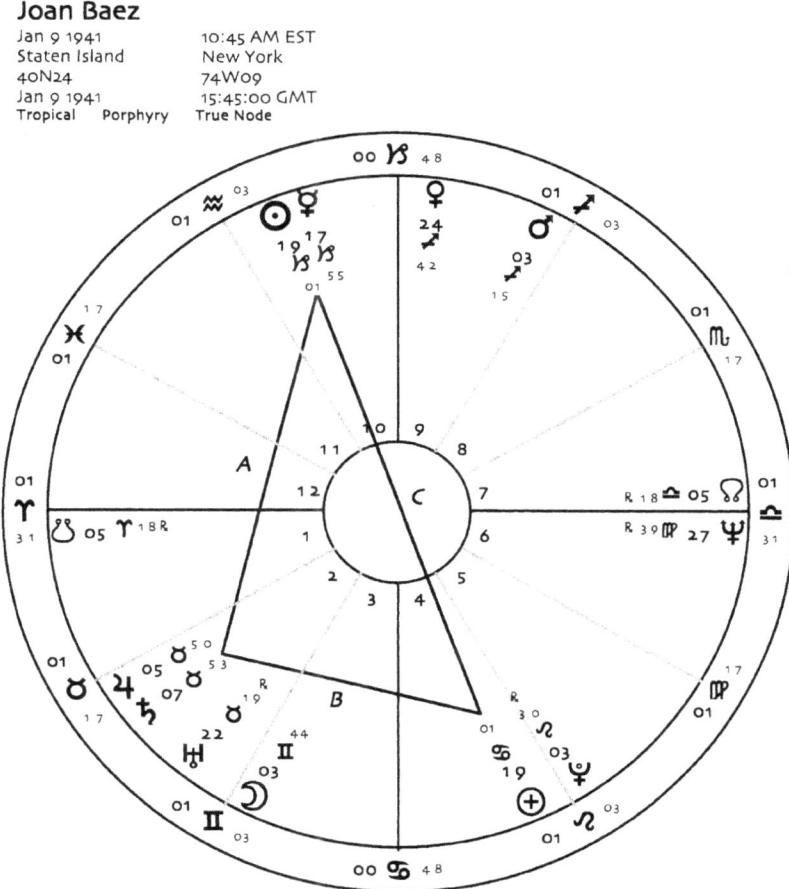

social justice, Aquarius, was forming a trine to her North Node in Libra when she first heard King speak. Years later, she and he would march and demonstrate together in the movement.

As with all Sun-Saturn holograms, the derived degree symbols tell stories of both accomplishment and acclaim, and of private losses and disappointments. For Baez, the ending of her love affair with Bob Dylan was one such heartache, eloquently chronicled in her 1975 album, *Diamonds & Rust*. From *La Volasfera*, for Gemini 12:

> *A young laurel tree, broken by the wind and withered.*

The native will be of a hopeful and honourable character, full of projects for the future, but will lose many opportunities through misfortunes unforeseen. His affections will be sincere, but fate will be against him in this respect, and few things in his life will come to maturity. Expected honours will be snatched from him, and the flowers of life will wither in his hand. Let him practice self-restraint and encourage contentment. This is a degree of SPOLIATION.

In a remarkable and literal manifestation of this holographic symbolism, Baez has been nominated for a Grammy Award six times, but she has never won. *A peculiar admixture of gentleness and irritability, of playfulness and gravity, which will render the native difficult to deal with*, can be seen with a Moon-Mars opposition.

Her natal hologram changed phases only once in her life, in 1959 at the progressed Sun-Saturn square. It was that year when she first performed at the Newport Folk Festival, launching her career. In 1960, she was awarded a recording contract.

The author has found that two aspects forming in the retrograde Saturn part of its cycle are exceptionally fated: the 154° 17' triseptile and the 144° biquintile. A Sun-Saturn hologram appears to peak in karmic influence at its progressed opposition.

The next bi-wheel shows the nativity of Beach Boys drummer, Dennis Wilson, in the inner wheel and his progressed Sun-Saturn opposition in the outer wheel. With his two brothers, Brian and Carl, and cousin Mike Love, Wilson was a founding member of the famous California surfing culture band. After forming the group in 1961, their first album, *Surfin' Safari*, was recorded in 1962 when he was only 17. The author can recall a summer vacation when he was a lad of 8 or 9, at the Sea Sprite motel with his family on Hermosa Beach's oceanfront strand, seeing the Beach Boys practicing in a house with a big bay window directly facing the sea.

In the natal hologram for Wilson, his Sun-Saturn arc A is 153° 48' 50", a very close triseptile with an orb of 00° 28', and his Saturn-Earth arc B is 26° 11' 10". Arc A equates to the 4th degree of Virgo, arc B is equivalent to the 27th degree of Aries. Dennis Wilson died tragically at 39 from an alcohol-related drowning on 28 December 1983, with transit Uranus opposite natal Uranus, exact to 04'. From *La Volasfera*, for Aries 27:

A man, richly attired, having lost his foothold, is falling to the ground.

It denotes one whose nature will not sustain the reverses of fortune to which he will be subjected. Attaining to considerable dignity and influence, most likely as the accident of birth, he will not continue therein to the end of his days, but will fail for want of judgment and persistence. This degree signifies the breaking up of families and the loss of their traditions. It is a degree of DECADENCE.

Chapter Seven • *Sun–Saturn Phase Angle Returns*

Dennis Wilson
Dec 4 1944 10:56 PM PWT
Inglewood California
33N47 118W21
Dec 5 1944 05:56:00 GMT
Tropical Porphyry True Node

Second Chart   Secondary Progression
Progressed Sun Opposite Saturn
Oct 27 1968   05:56:00 GMT

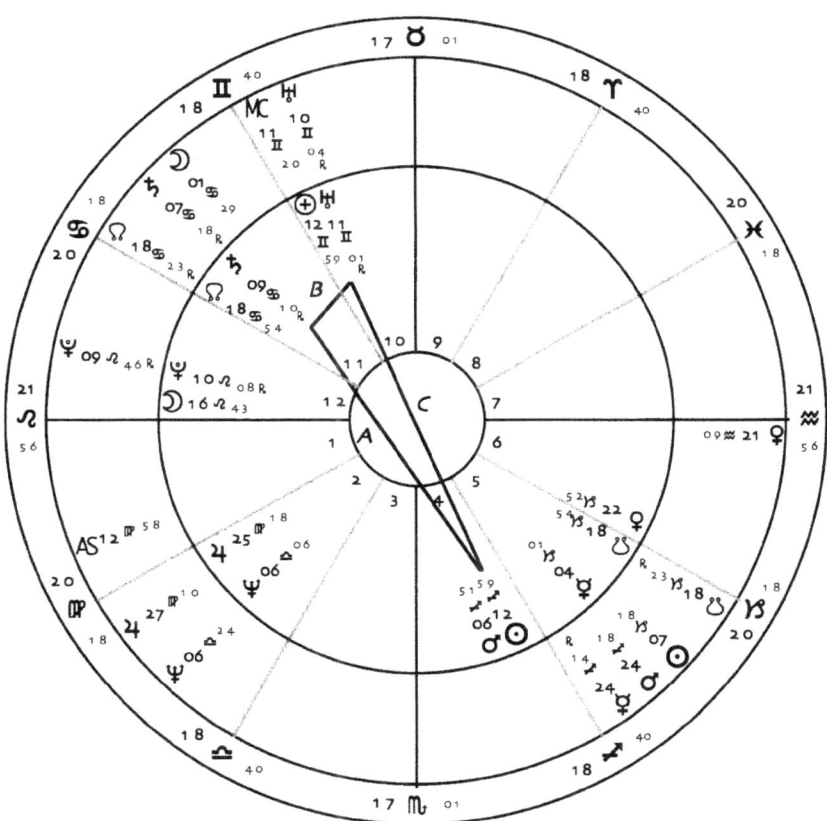

With the Sun and Mars opposite Uranus, Wilson was described as rebellious and hyperactive. Yet, with his Venus trine Jupiter, he is also remembered as loving and generous, with a heart of gold. Being the younger brother of Brian, the musical prodigy of the band, kept Dennis in the background for the first several years of the group's existence. He was born with a retrograde Saturn in triseptile aspect to his Sun, and in 1968 he arrived at his progressed Sun-Saturn opposition, shifting from the oriental phase to occidental. This point in the Sun-Saturn synodic cycle has been described by the author as its *peak in karmic influence*. Two significant experiences in Dennis Wilson's short and tragic life illustrate this phenomenon.

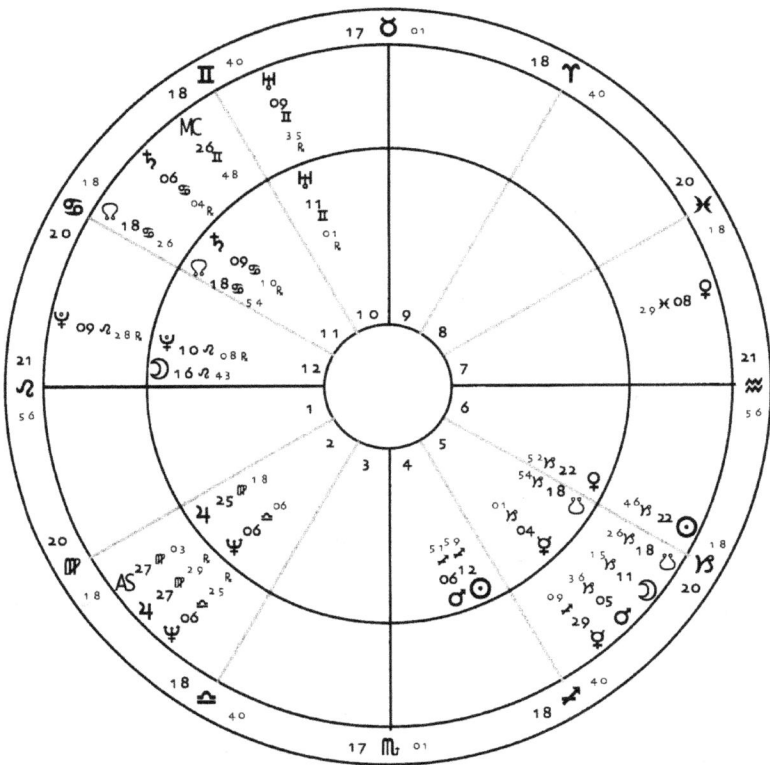

Dennis Wilson
Dec 4 1944　　10:56 PM PWT
Inglewood　　California
33N47　　118W21
Dec 5 1944　　05:56:00 GMT
Tropical　Porphyry　True Node

Second Chart　　Secondary Progression
Accidental Drowning While Drunk
Dec 29 1983　　05:56:00 GMT

Starting in 1968, Dennis became the second most important composer in the Beach Boys. Right at his progressed Sun-Saturn opposition, he stepped out of the creative shadow of his older brother, and began to more extensively showcase his talents as a multi-instrumentalist, playing the piano and guitar in addition to drumming. A progressed Venus, ruler of the Midheaven and angular on his Descendant, coming above the horizon for the first time, clearly illustrates this increased exposure.

A second karmic experience that Wilson had in 1968 at his progressed Sun-Saturn opposition was of a highly fated nature. Driving on the Pacific Coast Highway in Malibu, he picked up two female hitchhikers. Later that day, he picked up the same two girls a second time, and wound up taking them to his home. He left them there while he was at a recording session and when he came home in the middle of the night, he was met by a male stranger and a dozen others. It was Charles Manson.

It was reported that over the next year, until the abominable 1969 Tate/LaBianca murders, Dennis Wilson became friends with Manson, living in the same home. The horrid crime haunted him for the rest of his life, and was a contributing factor in a downward spiral of alcohol, cocaine addiction, and with the Moon and Pluto in the 12th house, an aching loneliness and depression that never went away. His Cardinal T-Cross, with Mercury afflicted by both depressive planets, Saturn and Neptune, gives astrologers insight into the mental demons with which he struggled.

Wilson died with his progressed Sun in 22° Capricorn 46', conjunct natal Venus[96] within 06' of arc, and at the Earth's heliacal rising in his Sun-Saturn cycle. A progressed Jupiter-Ascendant conjunction also occurred at the time of his death.

Wilson's death confirms C.E.O. Carter's research into drowning.[97] Carter wrote, *"peril from the water is shown by an affliction of Neptune either to the ruler or to the lord or occupant of the 4th ... there are (natal) contacts between Mercury and Saturn in every case save two."* His IC ruler, Mars, also in his 4th house, progressed to a square with Neptune at his death, and he has a natal Mercury opposing Saturn.[98]

Pre-Natal Sun-Saturn Synodic Cycle

The conjunction of the Sun and Saturn before birth, along with its degree symbols, represents ingrained attitudes towards social customs and conventions that one shares with his soul group, and which are carried over from past lives. One's individual hologram of responsibility emanates from a vast socialization matrix, of which one is a part. These foundational values of personal dignity and honor are stored on the astral plane, and result from social conditions in previous eras of history that affected the value systems of the souls living during that time.

At the end of this book is a Table of Sun-Saturn conjunctions and oppositions for the 200 years from 1920 to 2120. Readers can locate their pre-natal Sun-Saturn synodic cycle and its conjunction degree. One may also determine from these tables whether a birth occurred during the Oriental phase (from conjunction to opposition), or during the Occidental phase (from opposition to conjunction).

By researching degree symbols for one's pre-natal conjunction, memories of past life experiences can be brought into conscious awareness. It should be remembered that we share these past life factors with the other souls incarnating during the same 378-day Sun-Saturn synodic cycle as ourselves. The souls born within this same period have similar karmic lessons and evolutionary priorities as we do.

The bi-wheel chart on the facing page shows the author's pre-natal Sun-Saturn conjunction, which occurred less than a month before his birth, overlaid into his natal houses. Souls born from 23 October 1953 until 4 November 1954, when the subsequent conjunction took place, share a group pattern of social customs that was set into place at the time of that new synodic cycle. The degree symbol for the conjunction, Scorpio 1, delineates collective conditions for that cycle, whereas the rising degree for the conjunction calculated for the individual birth location symbolizes the personal expression of the synodic cycle. For the author, its rising degree in Santa Monica was Capricorn 27, the degree of his North Node.

This particular Sun-Saturn synodic cycle is unusual, as it commenced at a waning square of stationary retrograde Uranus and Neptune, an aspect occurring twice in 172 years, and which is the "seed point" of the subsequent conjunction of these two bodies that took place in February 1993. Many souls born into this cycle began to pursue their life work in the late 1980s and early 1990s as Uranus and Neptune conjoined in Capricorn. There is also a Mutual Reception of Mercury and Mars in sextile, and from this we see that competent thinkers and writers are in this group.

From *The Degrees of the Zodiac Symbolised* by Charubel, for Scorpio 1, we find:

> *A heart.*

Affectionate, confiding, unselfish; much influenced by others.

And from Sepharial's translation of *La Volasfera*, for Scorpio 1:

> *A nomadic warrior, equipped with javelin and firearms.*

It denotes a character that is ever ready for the fray, liable to become involved in many strifes and quarrels, and to resort to force rather than reason for his victories over others. Such an one is liable to become subject to the accusation of violence towards others, and will hardly pass through life without wounding some one or more of his fellow-creatures. In body robust and in mind offensive to the peace of others he will not fail to make numerous enemies. It is a degree of OFFENCE.

Chapter Seven • Sun–Saturn Phase Angle Returns

Robert P. Blaschke
Nov 15 1953　　1:37 AM PST
Santa Monica　　California
33N50　　118W29
Nov 15 1953　　09:37:00 GMT
Tropical　Porphyry　True Node

Second Chart　Natal Chart
Pre-Natal Sun-Saturn Conjunction
Oct 23 1953　　20:38:12 GMT

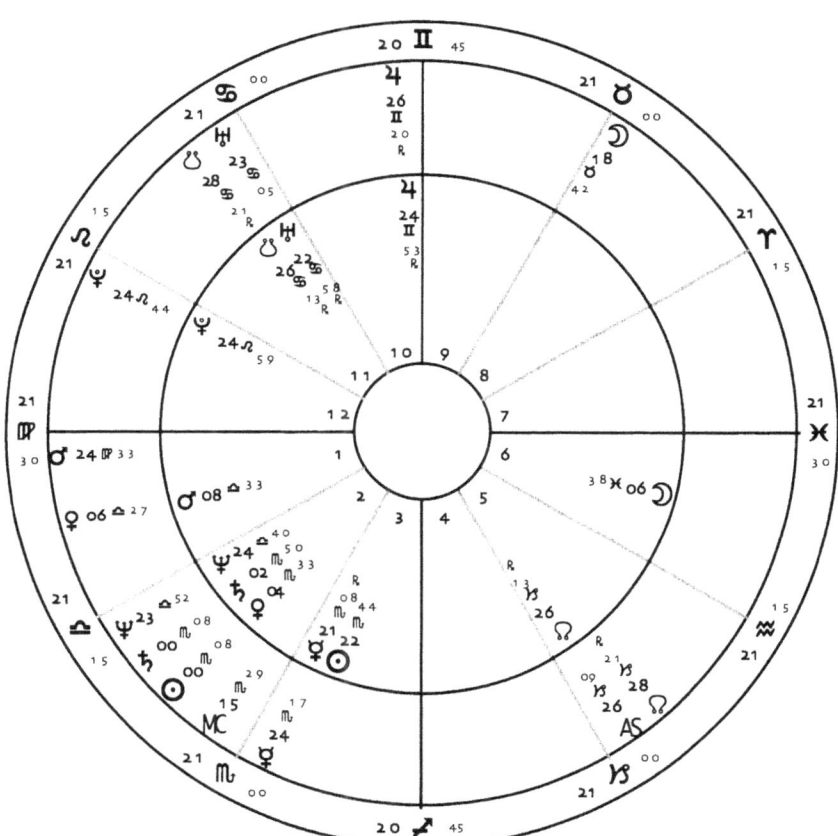

From this symbolism, ones sees that the soul group to which the author belongs has a complicated duality. With an exalted Moon in Taurus and Venus in dignity in Libra at the time of the cycle's conjunction, the artistic and receptive qualities of these souls are highly evolved. However, if their hearts are wounded by social or personal rejection, or by ridicule of their talents, an offensive aggressiveness can come out as a reaction, thus resulting in the accumulation of *numerous enemies*.

By researching degree symbols for a pre-natal synodic cycle's conjunction, one can identify with the distinctive attributes of his soul group. In order to personalize the influence of a pre-natal synodic cycle, calculate the chart for the place of birth and refer to its rising degree. For the author, from *La Volasfera*, for Capricorn 27:

> A stretch of broken country with a fringe of woodland.

This symbol denotes a nature that is rugged and natural in its expression and wholly devoid of the superficialities and polish of conventional life. Left to himself he will prefer a life of quiet retirement and rustic work, but in the busier haunts of men he will pass for one who is ungracious and uncouth, though none will question his sincerity and genuineness. He may be disposed to seek his living in the cultivation of the soil, or the sale of its produce. His temper will be uneven, and at times morose and lowering, but a certain off-hand gruffness of expression will only veil a kind and ingenuous nature. It is a degree of RUSTICITY.

The Sabian Symbol for Capricorn 27, and its spiritual analysis by Marc Jones:

> A party of anchorites are making a mountain pilgrimage;
> in view lie both the busy world and the quiet way ahead.

This is a symbol of the constructive double life which the seeker is expected to lead, the living in both objective and subjective realms. Positively it is a degree of balance in response to inner and outer values; negatively, stimulation by inner stirrings.

For the author, both symbols represent a withdrawal from the material world and its social conventions to the more reclusive life of a mystic where the mind remains uninfluenced by the ephemeral trends and superficialities of the changing seasons. It is certainly a life lesson in learning how to be in the world, but not of the world. The *La Volasfera* symbolism also refers to the author's lack of formal education. As the son of a father with a PhD in mechanical engineering (UCLA, 1953), he has no education beyond Saint Monica High School, and is thus lacking academic polish.

The degree of the pre-natal Sun-Saturn conjunction will also connect by synastry with the Luminaries or planets of other souls born into different synodic cycles. If a beneficial planet, such as Venus or Jupiter, forms a synastric conjunction to the pre-natal degree, these individuals will usually be supportive of one's career and professional achievements. If synastry involves disruptive or undermining bodies such as Uranus or Neptune, the effect can be one of being knocked off track.

Chapter Seven • *Sun–Saturn Phase Angle Returns*

Pre-Natal Sun-Saturn Conjunction
Oct 23 1953   12:38:12 PM PST
Santa Monica California
33N50   118W29
Oct 23 1953   20:38:12 GMT
Tropical Porphyry True Node

Second Chart   Natal Chart
Astrological Colleague
Sep 29 1946   14:27:00 GMT

Third Chart   Natal Chart
Female Friend
Jan 16 1956   20:50:00 GMT

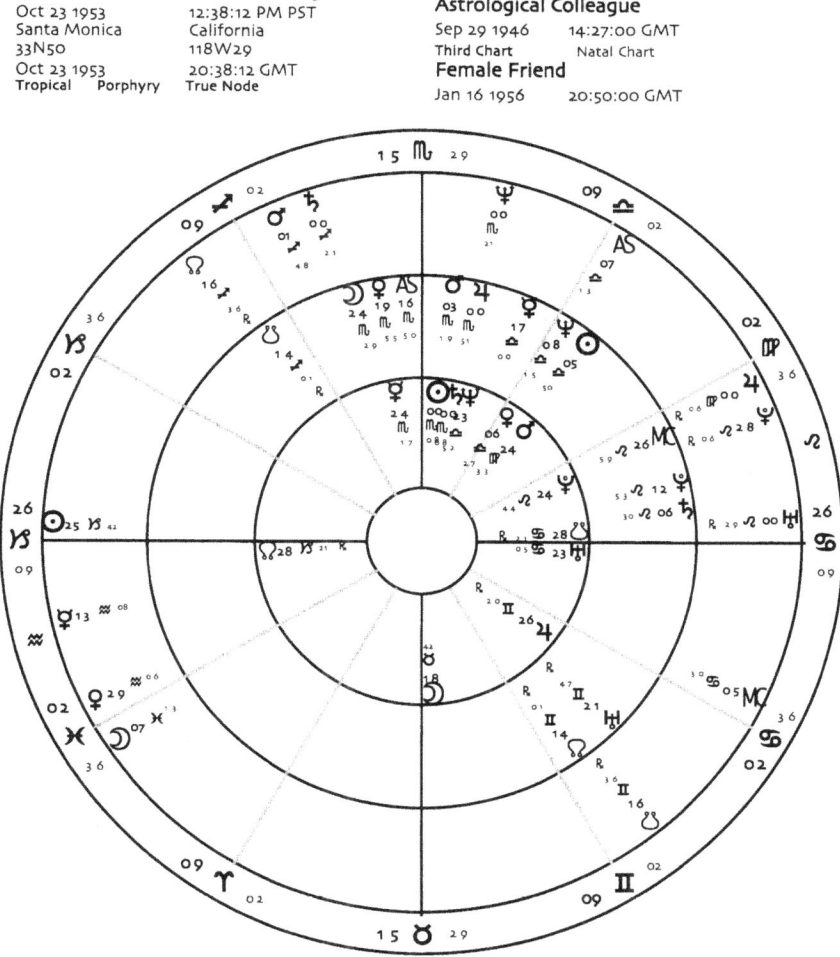

This tri-wheel chart has the pre-natal Sun-Saturn conjunction for the author in the inner wheel, the nativity of an astrological colleague in the middle wheel, and the horoscope of a female friend in the outer wheel. Jupiter in the colleague's chart is in 00° Scorpio 51', and conjunct the pre-natal degree. This individual has been very supportive of the author's career, arranging for him to speak to his local astrology group on the East Coast on two different occasions.

On the other hand, in the outer wheel, Neptune in the horoscope of the female friend is in 00° Scorpio 21', and also conjunct the pre-natal degree. Despite the best of intentions to be loving and supportive of the author's work and goals, the actual effect was one of disorder, loss of focus, and erosion of confidence. The end result of this technique is that synastry from other nativities to these pre-natal synodic cycle conjunction degrees will, for better or worse, affect one's profession.

The bi-wheel chart on the next page has the nativity of US President George Washington in the inner wheel, and his pre-natal Sun-Saturn conjunction in the outer wheel. Prior to becoming president, Washington had a long military career, commanding troops in the French and Indian War of 1754–1763. He was also commander-in-chief of the Continental Army during the Revolutionary War against Britain. One sees that the degree of his pre-natal conjunction is Pisces 25. From *La Volasfera*, its symbol:

> *A crown through which is set an upright sword.*
>
> It is the index of a mind set upon high resolves and capable of sustaining the assaults of its enemies in such a degree as to achieve its purposes without loss of fortune, prestige or honour. Such an one may prove to be a great warrior, a man of the sword, to whom honours will be given without stint. A king, he will sustain his throne by the use of aggressive measures and by victories gained over all his enemies; while one of lowly birth will gain his crown in the service of his king. His mind will be upright, astute, aspiring and sustained by an unswerving faith. It is a degree of VICTORY.

His ruler, Venus, is exalted in Pisces and in Mutual Reception with Jupiter. One of the remarkable connections Washington has to his nation's chart, in addition to his Uranus-Neptune opposition on its horizon, and Mercury conjunct the South Node, is that the rulers of his Ascendant and MC, Venus and Saturn, are conjunct and their midpoint, 01° Aries 03', is the Sibly chart IC, exact to the minute of arc.

When George Washington's pre-natal Sun-Saturn conjunction is calculated for his place of birth, Popes Creek Plantation, Virginia, 06° Leo 24' culminates on the MC, the exact degree of the US North Node. From *La Volasfera*, the symbol for Leo 7:

> *A sceptre, on the crest of which shines a diamond like a magnificent star.*
>
> The native is born to power, eminence, fame. He will, by the use of his many talents, supplemented by a powerful will, rise to a foremost position in his sphere of life. There is in the character a large amount of courage, nobility, energy and endurance, and the free use of such qualities will, under a benign fate, bring the native into a field of life where he will be a central figure. It is a degree of SUPERIORITY.

Chapter Seven • *Sun–Saturn Phase Angle Returns*

George Washington
Feb 22 1732 10:00 AM LMT
Popes Creek Virginia
38N11 76W56
Feb 22 1732 15:07:44 GMT
Tropical Porphyry True Node

Second Chart   Natal Chart
Pre-Natal Sun-Saturn Conjunction
Mar 15 1731   02:14:18 GMT

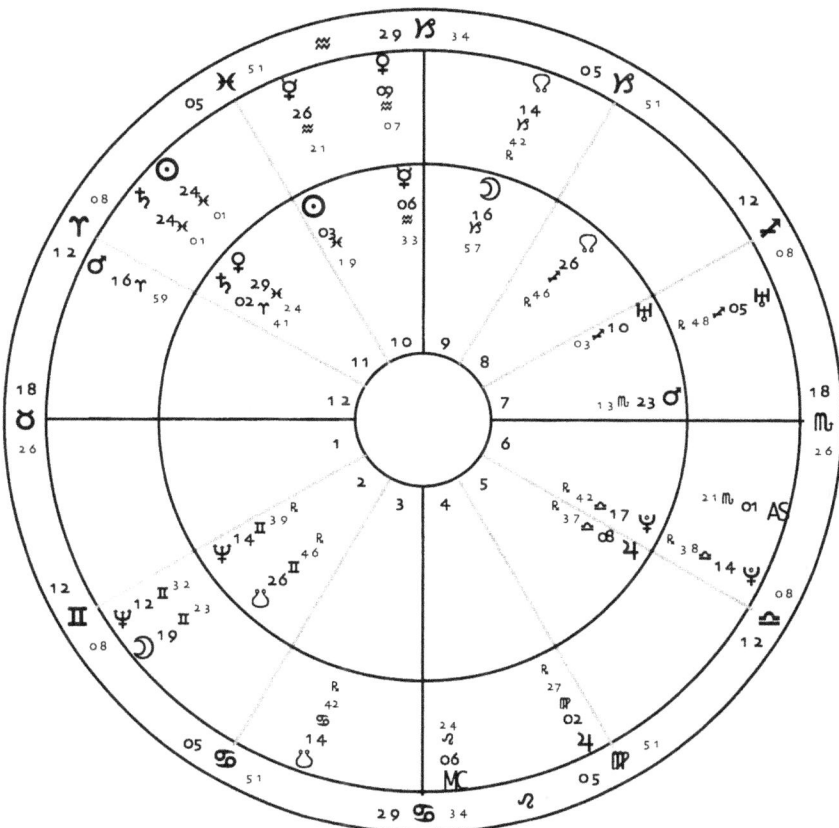

This symbol confirms the destiny of the United States, as does Charubel for Leo 7:

> *A pyramidal figure with a Maltese cross at the top, or rather on the apex.*
> THIS IS POSSIBLY AS GLORIOUS A DEGREE AS ANY IN THE ZODIAC. This degree is impinged by a ray from a transcendental sun, one of those suns which with our sun revolves round the grand central sun. Denotes the greater good; the sublime; gives prophetic inspirations; rules the wonderful; and fills the soul with a flood of celestial glory. This degree throbs sympathetically with the seventh degree of Libra.

Robert P. Blaschke • *Holographic Transits*

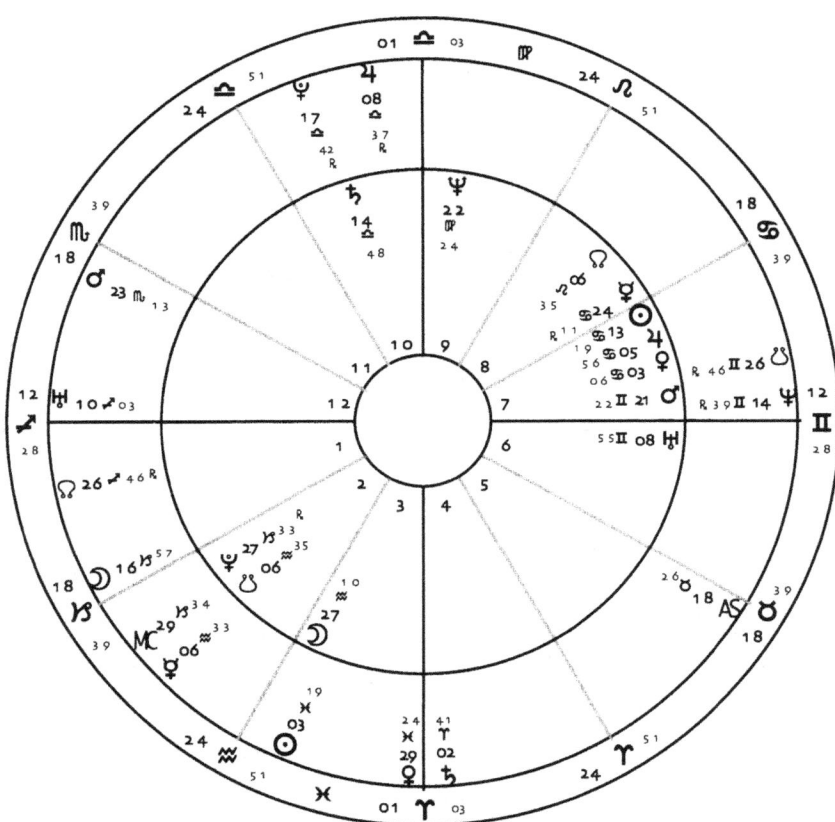

United States of America
Jul 4 1776 5:10 PM LMT
Philadelphia Pennsylvania
39N46 75W10
Jul 4 1776 22:10:40 GMT
Tropical Porphyry True Node

Second Chart Natal Chart
George Washington
Feb 22 1732 15:07:44 GMT

This synodic cycle into which George Washington was born has reincarnational connections with certain periods of history. A Sun-Saturn conjunction occurred in Pisces 25 in the year 1525, and identifies exactly when his *soul group* was last on Earth. One spiritual purpose of this *soul group* can be understood through the Sabian Symbol for Pisces 25, and what actually occurred at that point in history:

> *Ecclesiastical reform of a drastic nature is in progress,*
> *a priestcraft purged and purified opens a new ministry.*

Chapter Seven • *Sun–Saturn Phase Angle Returns*

In 1525–26, during the synodic cycle of the Sun and Saturn with its conjunction in Pisces 25, the Protestant Reformation was in full bloom, about seven years after Martin Luther posted his 95 theses on the door of Wittenberg's Palast Church in Germany. The purging of the Roman Catholic church in 1525 resulted in Prussia becoming a secular duchy, and also in English translations of the New Testament.

Examining the Sun-Saturn synodic cycle over a period of 3,000 years, the author found that Sun-Saturn conjunctions can occur in the same degree of the Zodiac every 147 years. A total of 142 synodic cycles recur during this periodicity. The mathematics behind this are as follows: 147 years × 365.26 days = 53,693.22 days. This product of days is then divided by the number of days in a synodic cycle of Saturn. 53,693.22 days ÷ 378.1 days/cycle = exactly 142 synodic cycles.

The author also found in his research that this recurring cycle *floats in the Zodiac*, with Sun-Saturn conjunctions in the identical Zodiac degree sometimes repeating only every 206, 265, or 353 years. In these cases, the conjunctions in the 147-year periodicity would drift from 1–3° from being exact. One observes that some of these sums are either 59 or 88 years apart, and equal two or three 29.46-year sidereal periods of Saturn. (147 + 59 = 206; 206 + 59 = 265; 265 + 88 = 353).

Each successive conjunction of the Sun and Saturn advances from 371° to 375° in the Zodiac; 29 consecutive conjunctions of the Sun and Saturn complete a cycle around the Zodiac. The next conjunction occurs about 7° past where the finishing subcycle originally began. After five[99] 29.46-year sidereal cycles, the 147-year period is complete, and the conjunction degree is identical to that of 147 years ago. The following illustration shows the 142 conjunctions forming around the Zodiac.

From these research findings, the author theorizes that one's structural framework for reincarnation follows a 147-year pattern between births. An interval between lives, of course, is variable, depending on the length of the lifetime, but it appears that the time between successive births is fixed by this 147-year Saturn cycle. The other recurring periodicities of 249 or 394 Mercury synodic cycles in 79 or 125 years, respectively, 157 Venus synodic cycles in 251 years, 96 Mars synodic cycles in 205 years, and 76 Jupiter synodic cycles in 83 years, are all part of a complex reincarnation matrix that this astrologer does not fully comprehend.[100]

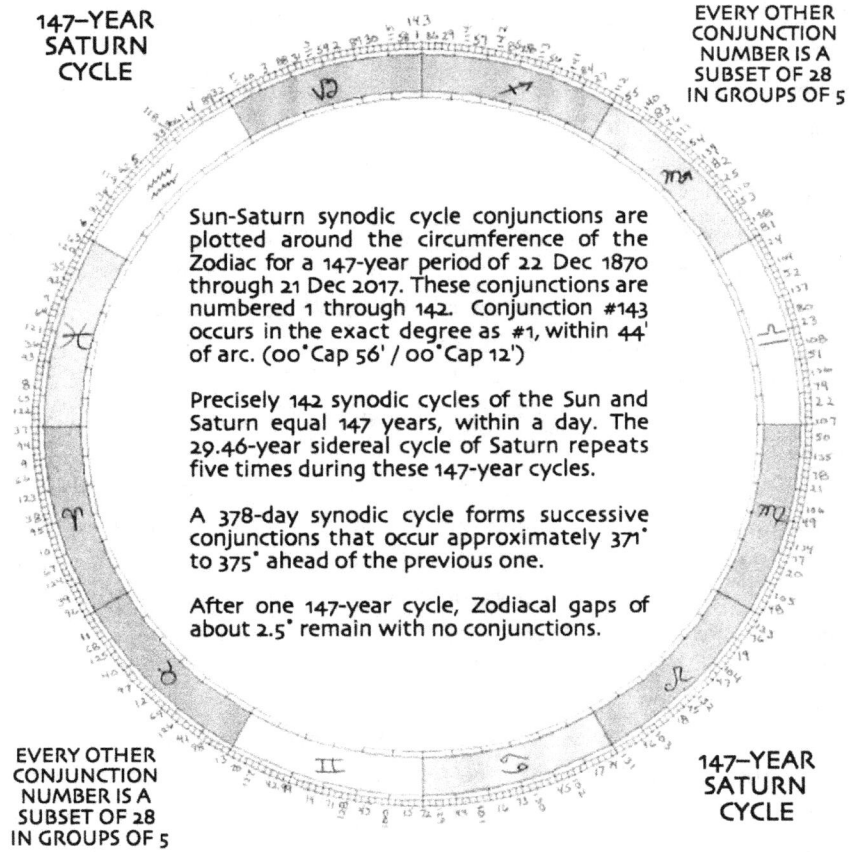

Using Sun-Saturn Holographic Transits

A Sun-Saturn holographic transit occurs when the exact distance arc between the natal Sun and Saturn forms again in the heavens, *and is in the identical phase as the natal Saturn cycle, i.e., Oriental or Occidental*. A Sun-Saturn phase angle return occurs every 12½ months, and at this time the alignment of free will with Higher Self can be seen in the celestial conditions. The effort one chooses to make towards goals and accomplishments can be understood through this horoscope, and choices regarding personal responsibility are also illuminated by the study of this chart.

Here is the Sun-Saturn holographic transit for the author of 16 August 2005. Note that his Sun-Saturn distance arc of 19° 53' 42" has replicated in the heavens, and that the Sun-Saturn phase angle is Oriental, as it is in his nativity.

Chapter Seven • *Sun–Saturn Phase Angle Returns*

Sun-Saturn Holographic Transit

Aug 16 2005   09:06:19 AM PDT
Santa Monica   California
33N50   118W29
Aug 16 2005   16:06:19 GMT
Tropical   Porphyry   True Node

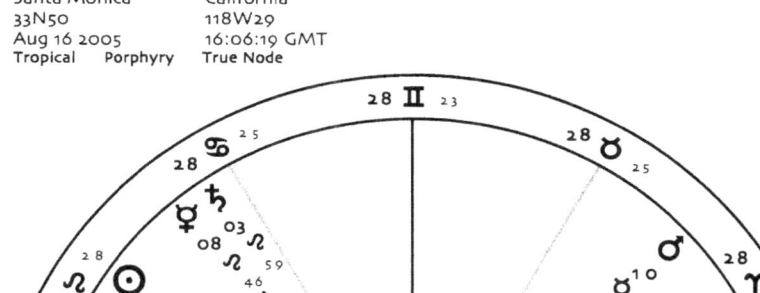

The ruler, Mercury, is stationary direct and at the finger of a Yod, with the Moon-Uranus sextile as its base. The author had just met his girlfriend a week earlier on the 9th, and Venus is rising in the exact degree of their composite Ascendant. Little did he know just what he was getting into with this personal choice, as he had also just started to write this volume. The Moon was wildly out-of-bounds at 28° S 07'.[101]

With a Saturnian goal of writing another book set in place at the time of the holographic transit, the author made his choice, and the aim was now his responsibility to fulfill.

	Long	Lat	Decl	R.A.
☉	23 ♌ 52 48	00 N 00	13 N 33	146 11
☽	10 ♑ 18	05 S 05	28 S 07	281 39
☿	08 ♌ 46	02 S 42	15 N 27	130 27
♀	29 ♍ 27	00 N 46	00 N 55	179 48
♂	10 ♉ 28	02 S 48	12 N 17	038 57
♃	15 ♎ 45	01 N 08	05 S 08	194 57
♄	03 ♌ 59	00 N 19	19 N 34	126 23
♅	09 ♓ 23 R	00 S 48	08 S 47	341 16
♆	15 ♒ 59 R	00 S 08	16 S 10	318 29
♇	21 ♐ 53 R	08 N 02	15 S 09	261 41

Every conceivable kind of disruption took place during the 12½ months until the following phase angle return occurred, as portended by the square of Mars to Mercury, and the out-of-bounds Moon.

Yet, the celestial conditions at the time of a phase angle return show how free will has aligned with *Higher Self, and what the soul must do to holographically receive its restoration through the divine rays of the Sun.* For the author, with Mercury at the apex of a Yod, no matter how many times he was knocked off track while writing this book, he would pick up again and press forward.

This present volume has been by far the most difficult to write in the *Language of Life* series, and the author has felt at times that he was overreaching in his attempt to decipher the mechanics of free will and fate inside the space-time continuum. The Sabian Symbol for the rising degree of this holographic transit, Virgo 29:

> *A scholar has just succeeded in deciphering an archaic manuscript;*
> *it holds an idea for which he has long sought.*

Astrologers can interpret holographic transits as a spiritual renewal. If the client is made aware that his soul has holographically realigned with its blueprint from birth when a phase angle recurs, then he can consciously choose to set his goals at that time, knowing that his free will is in direct alignment with Higher Self. This is a most valuable source of spiritual certainty about one's direction and aims in life.

The karmic result of one's efforts, and of one's exercise of personal responsibility, can be ascertained in the succeeding Sun-Saturn phase angle return. Occurring 12½ months after the prior holographic transit, each successive phase angle return has a spiritual connection to its predecessor. These *personalized synodic cycles* of 378 days symbolize an evolutionary spiral throughout the course of one's life.

Chapter Seven • *Sun–Saturn Phase Angle Returns*

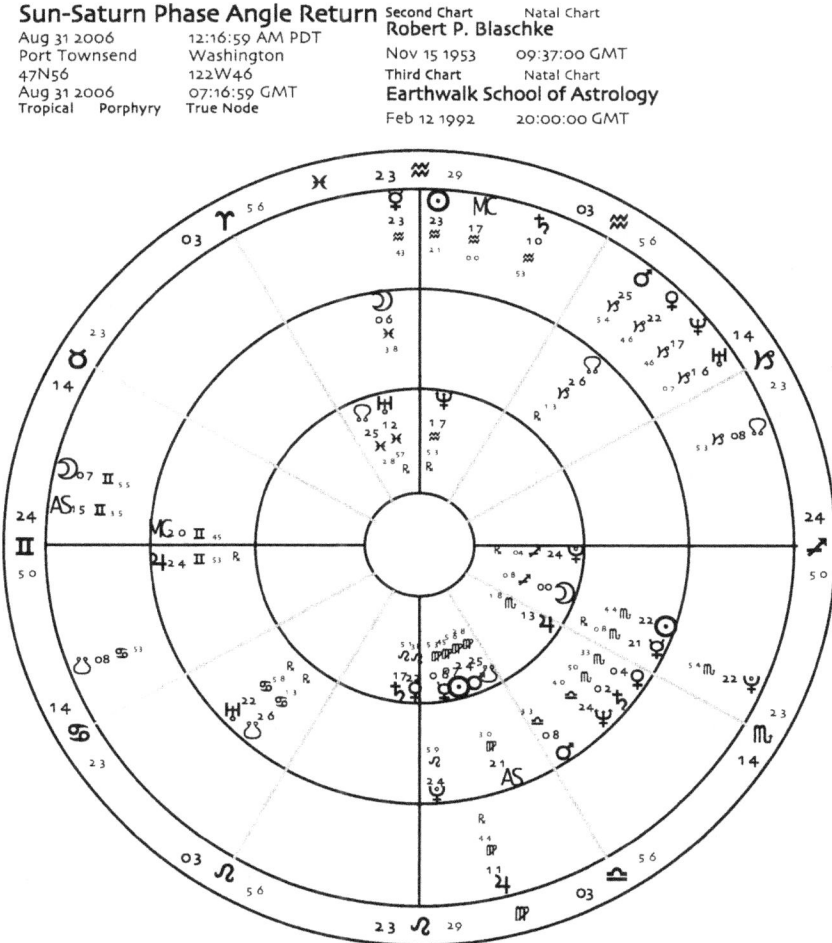

This tri-wheel chart has the author's subsequent Sun-Saturn phase angle return of 31 August 2006 in the inner wheel, his nativity in the middle wheel, and the chart of his astrology school in the outer wheel. This holographic transit represents the karmic result of the efforts made, and of the personal responsibility taken to attain the goals and aims chosen at the previous phase angle return in August 2005.

The Ascendant is conjunct the author's natal Jupiter, and the Midheaven is in the exact degree of the Earthwalk School of Astrology Sun-Mercury superior conjunction. On the day of this phase angle return, the once-in-35-year Saturn-Neptune opposition perfected exactly conjunct the MC/IC axis in his school's horoscope. This is a surprising number of angular conjunctions, and all are exact to the degree. It is also remarkable that his girlfriend's natal Saturn is in 00° Sagittarius 21', making an exact synastry conjunction to this chart's Moon. Her natal Moon is in 07° Pisces 13', exactly opposing the phase angle return Sun.

The author has repeatedly found phase angle return charts forming exact synastry conjunctions with one's own nativity, with the horoscopes of other souls playing an important role in the holographic renewal of one's soul, and with the chart of one's business. In this case, Jupiter conjunct the holographic transit rising degree is a sign of victory in the effort to complete this book, and with the Midheaven in the degree of the Earthwalk Astrology Sun-Mercury conjunction, one hopes that this book will instruct other astrologers to use these techniques to help their clients.

With Saturn exactly opposite Neptune on the day of this holographic transit, one sees how the spiritual subtleties contained within the space-time continuum, and which comprise the holograms of free will and fate, were seeking to be expressed in concrete form. After what the author went through trying to grasp these elusive spiritual concepts and render them into a practical and usable technique, not for another 35 years would he dare tackle a project as absurd as this one has been.

The Sun-Moon opposition and the Moon-Saturn conjunction between this phase angle return chart and his girlfriend's nativity illustrates the central role that she has played in the holographic regeneration of his soul. Putting up with his artistic temperament during the writing of this manuscript, and his creative frustration in attempting to peer into the Neptunian fog of the astral plane and then articulate in a concrete Saturnian way that which he saw, has not been easy for her. The Moon and Saturn conjoined speak volumes about holding it together no matter what.

It is rather ironic that the author had chosen the degree symbol for his Jupiter to be the cover art for this book, and to have that degree rising in the phase angle return as the writing concluded. From Sepharial's translation of *La Volasfera*, Gemini 25:

An old book lying open upon a table, and beside it a burning lamp.

It signifies a person of some exceptional mental powers, whose mind will be well stored with ancient learning. One of a studious and retiring nature, whose greatest happiness and whole wealth will be in the conquests of the mind. He will achieve something of importance to the world by dint of close and patient study. It is a degree of CULTIVATION.

Chapter Seven • *Sun–Saturn Phase Angle Returns*

In a relevant allegory, the rising degree for the previous holographic transit, at the time that this present work was launched, is a testimony to the many sides of the author's temperament that were brought out by the writing of this manuscript.

A man attired as a cardinal of the church.[102]

It denotes one of a quick and energetic nature, short temper, reclusive habits; highly imaginative and capable of much creative work; inclined to religion of a ceremonial nature; subject to spells of sensuousness, but of strong self-commanding faculty. It is a degree of ECCLESIASTICISM.

Using Sun-Saturn holographic transits enables astrologers to see the outcomes of choices made from free will. This hologram of responsibility is highly karmic and underpins the laws of cause and effect. From Galatians 6:7: "Be not deceived. God is not mocked: for whatsoever a man soweth, that shall he also reap." A recent historical example of this is seen in the Clinton-Lewinsky scandal of 1998.

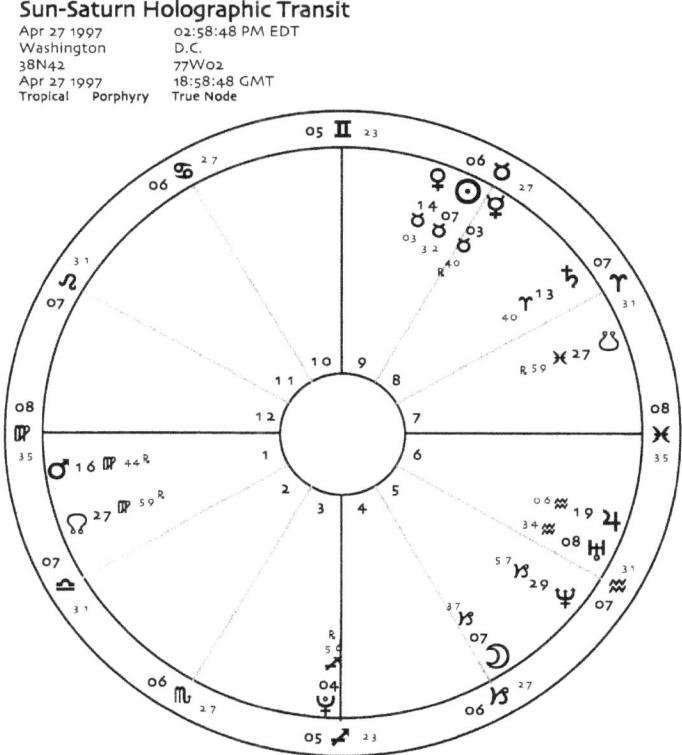

The chart on the previous page shows the Sun-Saturn phase angle return for President Clinton of 27 April 1997, and is his operative 12½ month holographic transit when the Monica Lewinsky scandal broke on 21 January 1998. Mr Clinton's natal Sun-Saturn distance arc is 23° 52' 00", and this phase angle has recurred in the heavens.

When the president began a secret dalliance with Ms Lewinsky, the rising degree for his phase angle return was indeed prophetic. From *La Volasfera*, Virgo 9:

> *A stagnant pool filled with weeds and rank verdure.*

> It denotes a person of an indolent and wasteful character, prone to let duties slide and to procrastinate with fortune. It further indicates that the native will form an alliance with a female which will be to his detriment. In general, the native will be unfortunate, his marriage especially so. It is a degree of STAGNATION.

The planet of scandal, Neptune, was in the final minutes of arc in the anaretic 30th degree of Capricorn, the sign of government. The magnitude of this affair was even affected by the yet to come Fixed Grand Cross Solar Eclipse of 11 August 1999.

In a once-in-658-year Grand Cross Solar Eclipse for Washington DC, the angles are found to be in the exact degrees of Mr Clinton's Luminaries. This could have only happened for about four minutes (clock time) on that day. In the natal Sun-Saturn hologram for Mr Clinton, his distance arc *A* is 23° 52' 00", equivalent to the 24th degree of Aries. From *La Volasfera*, for Aries 24:

> *A man playing with coloured balls, an immodest woman standing behind him.*

> This indicates one of a playful but careless nature, given over to pleasures and unprofitable pursuits. One who will be crossed in life by the opposite sex, and meet with troubles thereby. One with very little force of character or worthy ambition. It is a degree of FOOLISHNESS.

President Clinton's subsequent Sun-Saturn holographic transit occurred on 11 May 1998, and was the operative phase angle return when Congress voted on his impeachment. In remarkable synchronicity, the vote against conviction came on the exact day of Jupiter entering Aries, and leaving behind scandal-ridden Pisces. The very public, contentious and humiliating airing of Mr Clinton's dirty laundry is seen in the Full Moon opposite Mars, with that Moon being exact to the minute of arc of the Sun/Mars midpoint. The cusp of the 7th house of open enemies is in the same degree as scandalous Neptune in the April 1997 phase angle return chart.[103]

Chapter Seven • *Sun–Saturn Phase Angle Returns*

Bill Clinton
Aug 19 1946
Hope
33N40
Aug 19 1946
Tropical   Porphyry

8:51 AM CST
Arkansas
93W35
14:51:00 GMT
True Node

Second Chart   Natal Chart
Grand Cross Solar Eclipse
Aug 11 1999   11:04:00 GMT

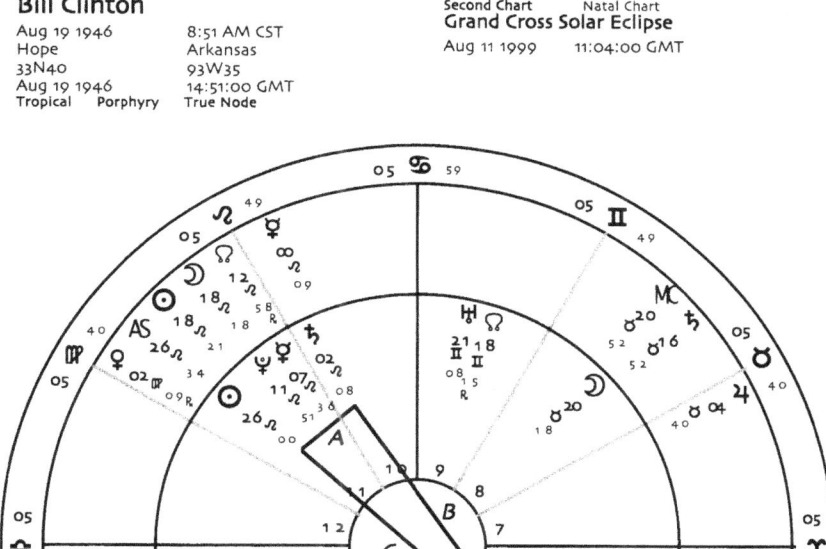

The author has observed that the applying lunar aspects in phase angle return charts depict a sequence of events. In this case, the Moon applies first to an opposition with Mars, ruling the MC. Public opinion turned against the president, and his reputation was badly damaged as a result of the sex scandal and his flagrant lies and pathetic denials. The Moon next applied to a trine with a dignified Jupiter, also in accidental dignity in the 9th house of legal proceedings, and Mr Clinton in the end was not convicted in the Senate's impeachment trial.[104]

175

Cancer 30 rising illustrates Mr Clinton's relief over evading absolute disgrace:

> *A young horse running across a field with a leading cord in trail;*
> *it lifts its head against the breeze and sniffs the air.* (La Volasfera)

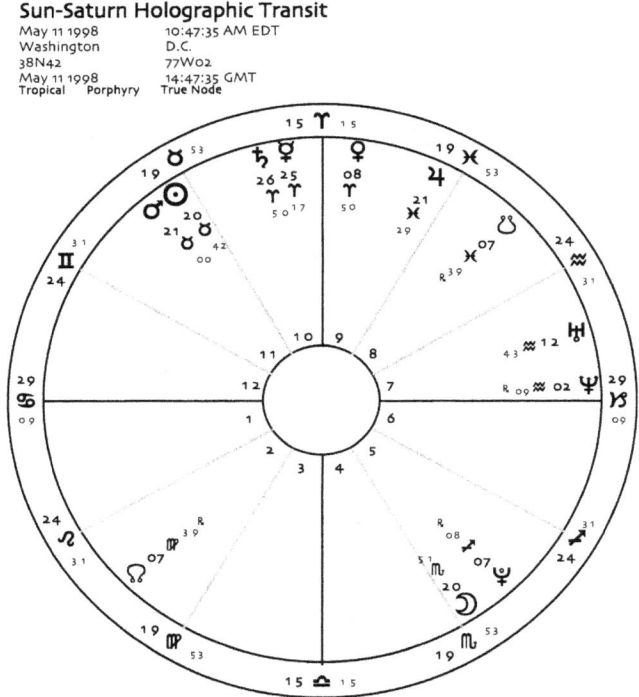

Chapter Eight
Outer Planet Phase Angle Returns

Outer Planet Phase Angles and Pre-Natal Synodic Cycles

Phase angles between the Sun and the outer planets holographically represent the potential to reach states of universal consciousness after one has passed through two lower levels of personal and social development. Dividing consciousness into a triadic hierarchy is necessary for comprehending these multidimensional layers.

At the personal level, instinct, thought, and attachment are holographic soul-forces consisting of the Sun-Moon, Sun-Mercury, and Sun-Venus holograms, respectively. At the social level, passion, judgment, and responsibility are the holographic soul-forces produced by the Sun-Mars, Sun-Jupiter, and Sun-Saturn holograms. At the universal level, enlightenment, renunciation, and transformation are holographic soul-forces created by the Sun-Uranus, Sun-Neptune, and Sun-Pluto holograms.

Triadic Hierarchy of Multidimensional Soul Forces

PATH	MYSTIC	SCHOLAR	HOUSEHOLDER
Universal Level	Enlightenment	Renunciation	Transformation
Social Level	Passion	Judgment	Responsibility
Personal Level	Instinct	Thought	Attachment

Triadic Hierarchy of Natal Sun-Planet Holograms

Universal Level	Sun-Uranus	Sun-Neptune	Sun-Pluto
Social Level	Sun-Mars	Sun-Jupiter	Sun-Saturn
Personal Level	Sun-Moon	Sun-Mercury	Sun-Venus

Within this theoretical model, the grouping of the solar system bodies with the Sun in this way reveals hidden relationships between the three levels of soul-forces. If one is to reach enlightenment, the soul-forces of instinct and passion must be fully opened. This is the mystic's path to God.

If one is to embrace renunciation as a spiritual goal, the soul-forces of thought and moral judgment need to be completely developed. This is the scholar's path to God. If transformation is one's spiritual objective, the soul-forces of attachment and responsibility will have to be fully surrendered to. This is the householder's path to God.[105]

These three pathways to higher consciousness each require an awakening by the soul to the cause-and-effect relationships between personal, social, and universal levels of earthly existence. Each of the three paths to God will extract a painful price from the soul. The mystic, the scholar, and the householder all must ascend a mountain path of commensurate steepness. How can one know what path to take?

To discern one's path to God, a careful study should be undertaken of one's three natal outer planet holograms, and of one's pre-natal outer planet synodic cycles. The realization of only one of the three universal states of consciousness is a life-changing experience. At these levels, karma is mitigated and the soul becomes free. *In holographic astrology, derived degree symbols awaken one to his karmic forces.*

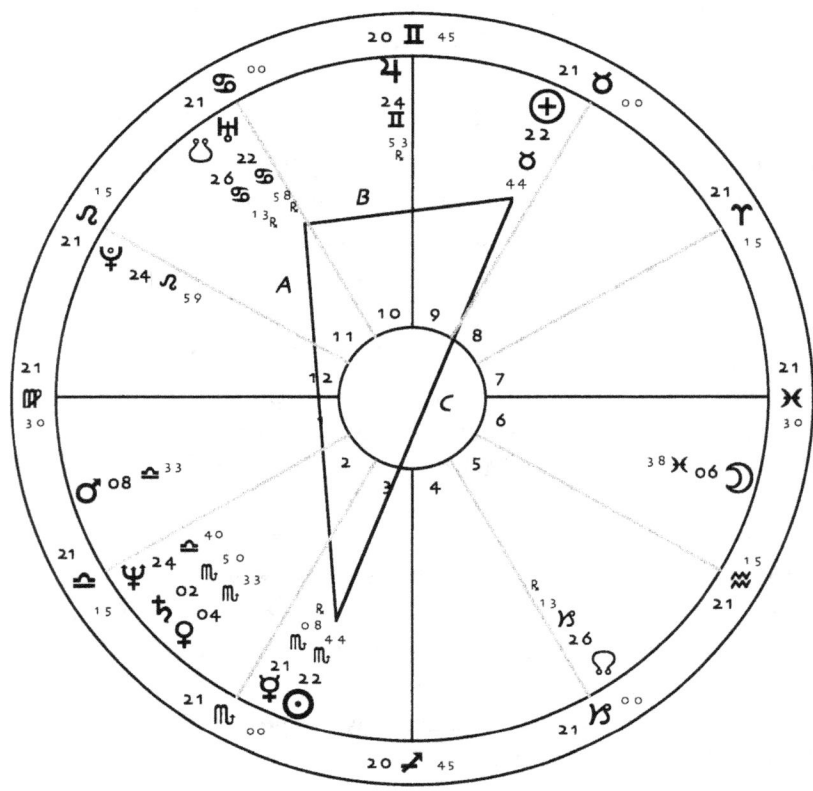

To visualize one's natal Sun-Uranus hologram, the glyph for the Earth is placed in the horoscope, thus creating this three-dimensional image. In the author's nativity, Sun-Uranus distance arc A is 119° 45' 36", and Uranus-Earth distance arc B is 60° 14' 24". Together, these two arcs total 180° 00' 00". Using the Sabian Aspect Orb technique, arc A equates to the 30th degree of Cancer, and arc B is equivalent to the 1st degree of Gemini. These two degrees are antiscia, or solstice points, of one another. Sun-Earth arc C is always a constant, measuring exactly 180° 00' 00".

From Sepharial's translation of *La Volasfera*, for Gemini 1:

Two yellow flowers growing beneath the shade of a luxuriant tree.

It indicates a life of security, peace and prosperity. The native will make friendships that will prove sincere and advantageous; and by means of his friends he will meet with success in life. He will be protected by someone greater than himself, whose influence will be widespread and beneficent. The native will have a kind nature, trustful disposition, and his domestic life will be happy and prosperous. It is a degree of SECURITY.

The author's contrasting karmic forces are revealed by Gemini 1 from Charubel:

A white oval figure on a very black background.
The background contains no forms or shapes of any kind.

This is an important degree; whoever may have this degree on his or her ascendant will be unfortunate through marriage. If a female, should she ever become a mother, the labour will be attended with much suffering, and possibly death. A very negative person, open to evil influences.

Within the juxtaposition of the two symbols, both the author's karmic opportunity for a life of domestic happiness and security, and a past history of marital trouble, can clearly be seen. The awakening of his free will so that it may align with Higher Self and choose the positive path will be accomplished by his awareness of being protected by someone greater than himself, whose influence is beneficent.

Concurrent and coexistent with karmic awakening in his personal life, a different holographic awareness exists in the author's professional life. The Sabian Symbol for Cancer 30, and its spiritual analysis by Marc Edmund Jones, provides insight:

A "Daughter of the American Revolution" walks proudly to the rostrum;
it is the meeting of some women's society.

This is a symbol of that necessary ingrained and thoroughly established background in all dominant human society, the will and ability to maintain supremacy of position. Positively it is a degree of inner aristocracy; negatively, it is outer elevation.

Throughout his career as a lecturing and teaching astrologer, this author has been committed to upholding an astrological tradition dating back to Sepharial, Alan Leo, and Charles E.O. Carter, who, in his view, articulated astrological theory and technique far superior to that of his modern psychological contemporaries.[106]

These outer planet phase angles at birth are part of overall synodic cycles lasting from 367 to 370 days, or just over a year. These cycles begin with a conjunction of the Sun and the direct motion outer planet, and reach their halfway points at the opposition of the Sun and the retrograde outer planet. Quarter points in the cycles occur when the Sun forms squares to Uranus, Neptune, or Pluto.

Those born after the conjunction of the Sun and an outer planet, but before the opposition, have that outer planet as the morning star in their nativities, rising ahead of the Sun. During the latter part of this oriental half of the synodic cycle, the three outer planets are retrograde and closer to Earth than at any other point in their orbital cycles. Karmic influence is stronger, and peaks at the opposition.

Those born after a Sun-outer planet opposition, but before the next conjunction, have that outer planet as the evening star, setting after the Sun. For the first part of this occidental half of the synodic cycle, the outer planet is retrograde. The most powerful points in these cycles are at the conjunction when an outer planet shifts from occidental to oriental, and again at the opposition, when a retrograde outer planet also has a reversal of polarity from oriental to occidental. It is the author's experience that retrograde outer planets in close aspect to the Sun are very potent.

With direct and retrograde stations of the outer planets, the distance arc between the Sun and that stationary outer planet is about 101° to 104°. Outer planets are retrograde when biseptile, sesquiquintile, trine, trioctile, biquintile, inconjunct, triseptile, or opposite the Sun. These are all highly karmic phase angles.

The fact that the outer planets station both direct or retrograde when forming the reality-suspending biseptile aspects of 102° 51' or 257° 09' with the Sun, speaks volumes about the shifts in consciousness that can occur at the

Chapter Eight • Outer Planet Phase Angle Returns

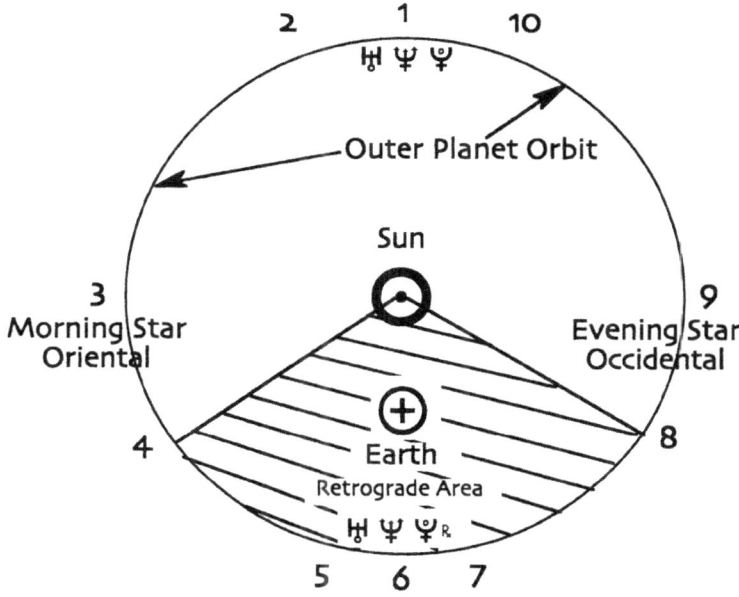

Cycles and Phases of the Planet Saturn

1. Conjunction with Sun
2. Planet Heliacal Rising
3. Waxing Square
4. Stationary Retrograde
5. Earth's Heliacal Setting
6. Opposition with Sun
7. Earth's Heliacal Rising
8. Stationary Direct
9. Waning Square
10. Planet Heliacal Setting

time of a stationary Uranus, Neptune, or Pluto. These arcs equate with Cancer 13 and Sagittarius 18.[107]

From Sepharial's translation of *La Volasfera*, Cancer 13, the retrograde station:

> *A caduceus between two moons, one crescent and the other gibbous.*

It denotes a person of extreme capacity in the pursuit of knowledge, a penetrating mind, and retentive memory; the native will accomplish wonders in the pursuit of the subtle sciences. The temper is changeful like the moon, and subject to fits of hope and despondency of more or less rapid alternation. The native is likely to travel much and to be subject to many changes of fortune. But the chief characteristic is versatility and aptitude in the gaining of knowledge. With the symbol of Hermes dominant the native will either be a linguist, doctor, or a distinguished scholar. It is a degree of KNOWLEDGE.

It is certainly of interest to the metaphysically inclined astrologer that the septile aspect of 51° 26' falls in the crescent phase of the lunation cycle, and the triseptile aspect of 154° 17' occurs in its gibbous phase. In this allegory, the derived degree symbol for a biseptile is the caduceus between the other two 7th harmonic aspects. This winged staff with two snakes wrapped around it refers to kundalini energy stored at the base of the spinal column, which carries the power to heal or harm.

The author has three biseptiles in his nativity: between Sun and Moon, Venus and Uranus, and between Mars and Jupiter. Because this aspect correlates with the retrograde station of an outer planet, occurring as it does about 102° to 103° past a conjunction, it connotes the scholar turning inward in the pursuit of knowledge. It is presumed that these intellectual activities are carried over from past lives.

And again from *La Volasfera*, Sagittarius 18, corresponding with the direct station:

> *A man's face painted with grotesque scrolls,*
> *and surrounded by a mass of tangled hair.*

> It is the index of a mind that is without proper balance, given over to vain and wild projects, neither useful nor fortunate. Such an one is in danger of losing his reason by disappointment of foolish and inconsequent efforts. His mode of life will be eccentric, and the expression of his thought touched with a singular grotesqueness and peculiarity. There may be genius; but, if so, of an unpractical and fruitless type: more probably there will be lack of reason. It is a degree of DISORDER.

In this hideous imagery, coming as it does after five months of retrogression of the outer planets, we see a soul who has lost his mind and his reason after an intense inward journey into the retrograde province of universal forces. Disheveled and crazed, he has been on a wild ride through the subatomic realms of his Creator.

Lastly, we discover a third symbol for the stationary outer planet phenomenon. In a purely mathematical context, we find: 257° 09' − 102° 51' = 154° 18'. This figure is the symbolic number of degrees that the Sun travels between outer planet stations.

It correlates with the 5th degree of Virgo; its symbols illustrate the experience:[108]

> *A soldier prepared for battle.* (La Volasfera)

> *A man lies dreaming in the shade of an Irish countryside;*
> *his dream brings to him the playful "little people".* (Sabian Symbol)

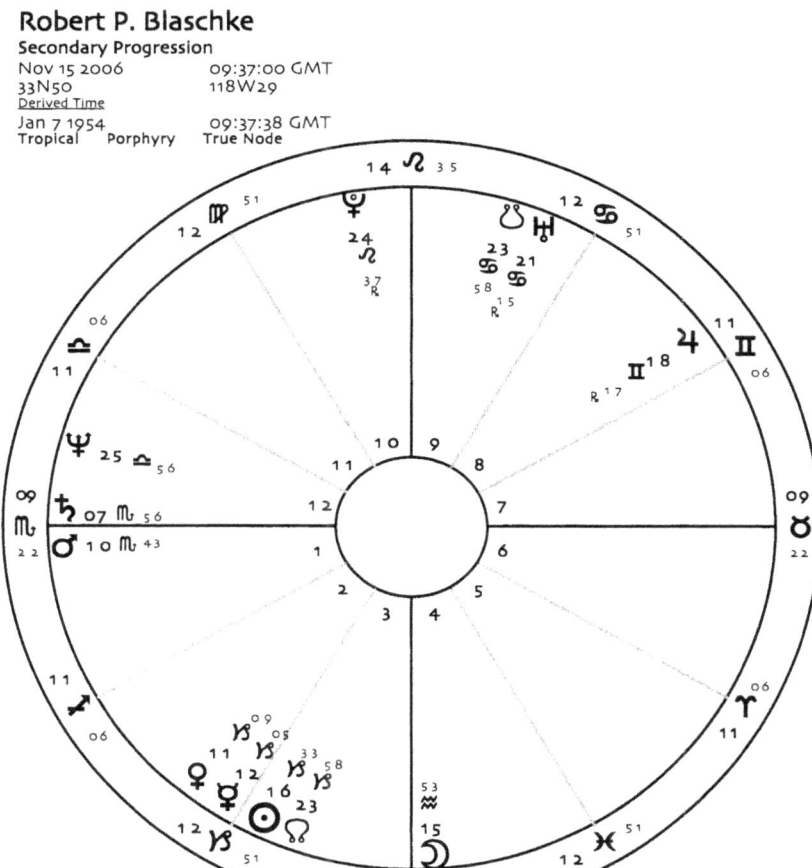

Throughout life, progressions will evolve the Sun-outer planet relationship, often resulting in important phase changes, depending on where in these orbital cycles one is born. Especially karmic is a natal phase angle shifting from oriental to occidental at an opposition of the progressed Sun to a progressed outer planet. The author's Sun-Uranus phase angle progressed to Earth's heliacal setting in the year that he published *Progressions*; it will soon reach the opposition.

In the progressed horoscope for the author's 53rd birthday, his Sun-Uranus phase angle is between points #5 and #6 in the orbital diagram shown on page 181.

Further insight into the Sun-Uranus hologram of enlightenment, and clues pointing to whether this is one's path to take, can be found in a careful study of one's pre-natal Sun-Uranus synodic cycle. The conjunction of Uranus and the Sun prior to birth, along with its degree symbols, reveals collective potential for awakened consciousness that one shares with his *soul group* from past lives. *Personalized expression of these energies out into the world is seen through the local Midheaven.*

At the end of this book is a Table of Sun-Uranus conjunctions for the 200 years from 1920 to 2120. Readers can locate their pre-natal Sun-Uranus synodic cycle and its conjunction degree, and then from there, research its degree symbols. A hint to the reader: the Sun-Moon and Sun-Mars holograms are also ancillary.

This facing bi-wheel chart has the author's nativity in the inner wheel, and his pre-natal Sun-Uranus conjunction in the outer wheel. Souls born from 11 July 1953 until 16 July 1954, when the subsequent conjunction took place, share a group pattern of awakening to higher consciousness that was set into place at the time of that new synodic cycle. The degree symbol for its conjunction, Cancer 19, shows collective conditions for that cycle, whereas the culminating degree for this conjunction calculated for the birth location symbolizes the individual expression of this synodic cycle. For the author, the Midheaven in Santa Monica was Aquarius 9.

From *The Degrees of the Zodiac Symbolised* by Charubel, Cancer 19:

> A man with a very old-looking book before him.
> It has the appearance of some ancient record.

This denotes a studious person, a profound thinker, one capable of grappling with abstruse studies. He loves his books, and his studies are more for self-amusement than with the object of appearing in print. He is free from that craze.

Souls born from July 1953 to July 1954, and into this Sun-Uranus synodic cycle, have the capacity to awaken to higher consciousness not through contemporary spiritual teachers, who at all costs should be ignored, but rather through patient study of ancient spiritual texts such as the Bible, and of other esoteric treatises.

By studying degree symbols of pre-natal synodic cycle conjunctions, one identifies the collective characteristics of his *soul group*. *To master the individual expression of a pre-natal outer planet synodic cycle*, calculate the chart for the birth location and refer to its culminating degree. For the author, Aquarius 9 from *La Volasfera*:[109]

Chapter Eight • Outer Planet Phase Angle Returns

Robert P. Blaschke
Nov 15 1953   1:37 AM PST
Santa Monica   California
33N50   118W29
Nov 15 1953   09:37:00 GMT
Tropical   Porphyry   True Node

Second Chart   Natal Chart
Pre-Natal Sun-Uranus Conjunction
Jul 11 1953   09:22:58 GMT

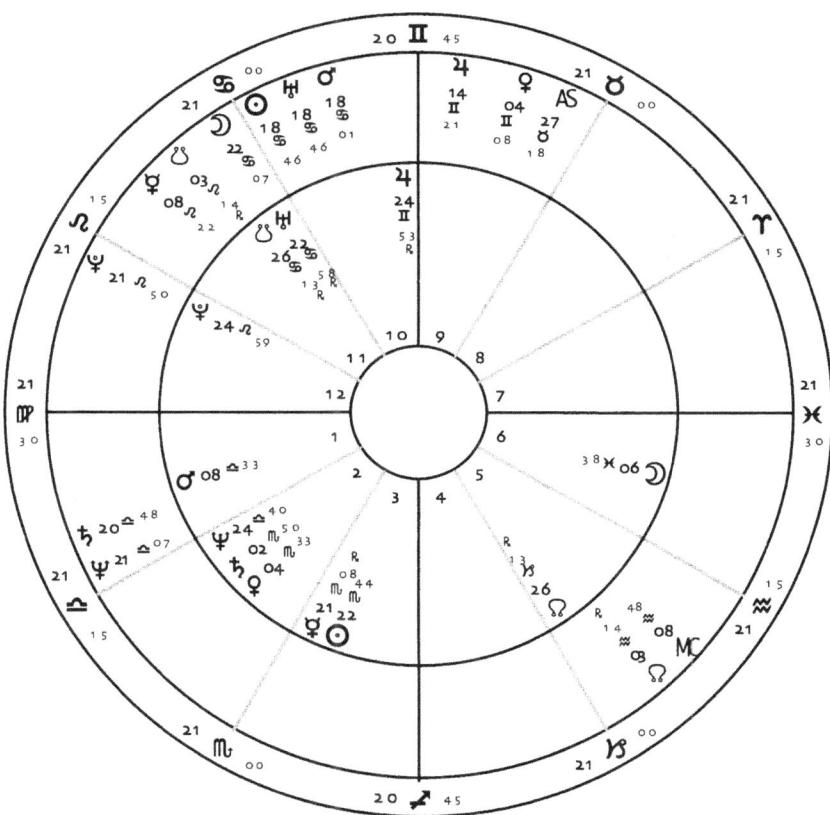

A huge rock rent by a flash of lightning.

This symbol denotes one who has a powerful, aggressive, forceful, and executive nature, capable of driving his way through all obstacles, however hard and enduring they may be. Quick, energetic, and alert, he will make considerable progress in his particular walk in life, and may be the means of convincing the most sceptical concerning certain matters of a celestial and ethereal nature. His spirit is too intense and forceful, too incisive and critical not to be the occasion of much reviling and bitterness of spirit in others. He will do his work in the world with celerity of action and directness of execution, and he will let light into dark places. His departure will be sudden, but will not transpire till he has done some work of magnitude. It is a degree of CONVERSION.

For the author's Sun-Uranus *soul group*, Mercury was stationary retrograde at the time of their synodic cycle conjunction, and a solar eclipse had occurred just a few hours earlier. In a word, this conjunction was a *fuseblower*. That stationary retrograde Mercury is an indication of an inner reservoir of knowledge waiting to be accessed and shared for others' benefit. For the author, lightning struck for a second time, as documented on page 100 for his pre-natal Sun-Mars conjunction.[110]

This is the nativity of F. Scott Fitzgerald, one of the great American writers of the 20th century, and author of *The Great Gatsby*. Born with a stationary retrograde Neptune in a fated biseptile aspect with the Sun, Fitzgerald experienced his natal Sun-Neptune hologram through severe alcoholism, a mentally

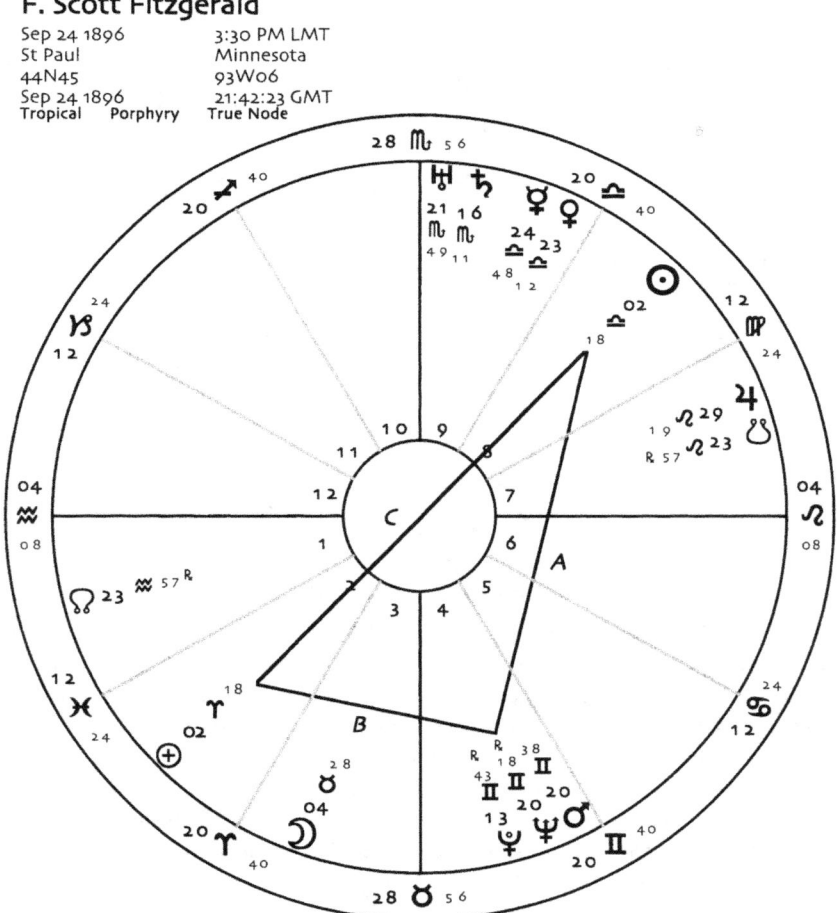

ill wife who became institutionalized with schizophrenia, as a spokesperson for the "Lost Generation" of Americans just after World War I, and through death at the age of 44 from two heart attacks brought on by unhealthy living habits and addictive excesses.

His captivation with the Neptunian glamour of the "Jazz Age" in America during the Roaring Twenties, with its glorification of celebrity and wealthy lifestyles, is the antithesis of the Neptunian hologram of renunciation and serves as a reminder of how Neptune can also weave webs of illusion, seducing one into materialism.[111]

Examining Fitzgerald's natal hologram, observe that his Sun-Neptune distance arc *A* is 102° 00' 16", equivalent to the 13th degree of Cancer, and the arc of the fated biseptile. The mental breakdown of his wife was one its karmic manifestations. His Neptune-Earth arc *B* is 77° 59' 44", and equates to the 18th degree of Gemini. An aspiring, yet unfulfilled, nature is seen in Gemini 18 from *La Volasfera*:

A flying arrow.

It indicates a person of lofty aspirations, keen mental powers, penetration and executive ability. One who will cut out his own line in life and excite attention, but who may, by his destiny, fail in achieving the result aimed at. It is a degree of EXECUTION.

If a soul is a spokesperson for the collective, as was Fitzgerald with publication of his first novel about the Flapper generation, *This Side of Paradise*, in 1920, that person must have *an astrological link between the individual and his soul group*. A close scrutiny of his pre-natal Sun-Neptune synodic cycle conjunction reveals that it occurred in Gemini 18, the exact same degree of his hologram distance arc *B*.

The Great Gatsby was published in 1925 at Fitzgerald's Saturn return, and was his third novel. After attending Princeton University for three years, he dropped out in 1917 and enlisted in the Army when the United States entered World War I. He did not serve in combat in Europe, and actually wrote the draft of his first book while at an officer training camp. His early success and his tragically short life are seen in his rising degree. From Charubel, for Aquarius 5:

A cherry tree in full blossom.

One who is very precocious, with early promise of genius, but who rarely lives to maturity.

F. Scott Fitzgerald

Sep 24 1896　　3:30 PM LMT
St Paul　　　　Minnesota
44N45　　　　93W06
Sep 24 1896　　21:42:23 GMT
Tropical　Porphyry　True Node

Second Chart　　Natal Chart
Pre-Natal Sun-Neptune Conjunction
Jun 8 1896　　02:44:10 GMT

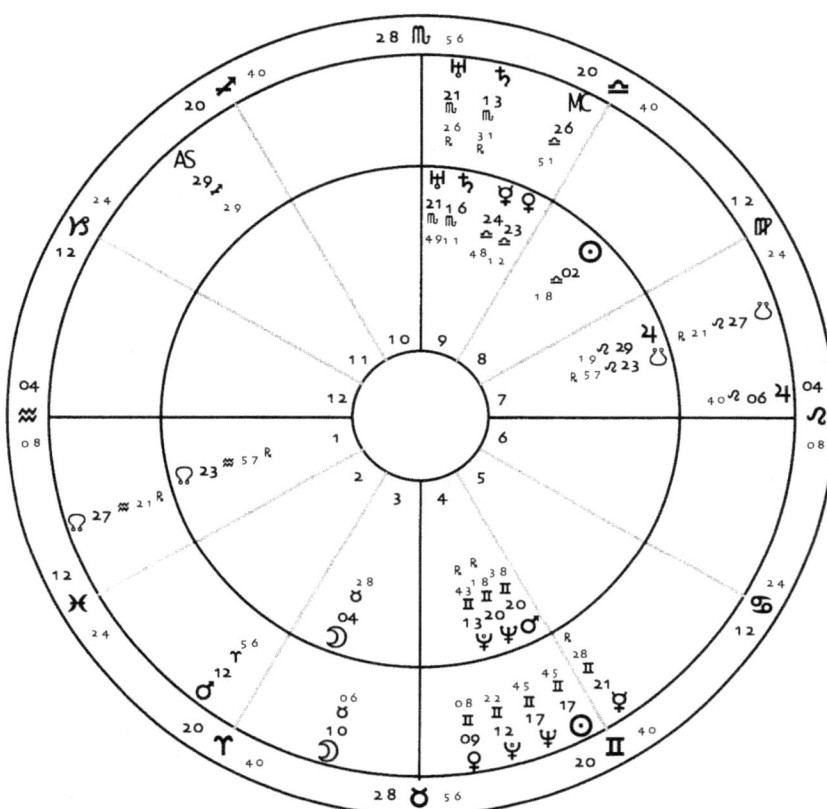

Fitzgerald died after his second heart attack with progressed Sun conjunct Saturn within 04' of arc. Also alluding to his demise was a progressed Ascendant exactly conjunct the IC of his pre-natal Sun-Neptune synodic cycle chart.

One's pre-natal Sun-Neptune conjunction and its degree symbols should be studied carefully to understand how choosing the path of renunciation leads to spiritual consciousness within one's soul group. The Midheaven calculated for the location of birth, and its degree symbol, provides insight into *how a person can best express the collective energies of his soul group in an individualized manner.*

F. Scott Fitzgerald

Sep 24 1896 3:30 PM LMT
St Paul Minnesota
44N45 93W06
Sep 24 1896 21:42:23 GMT
Tropical Porphyry True Node

Second Chart — Secondary Progression
Death From Second Heart Attack
Dec 21 1940 21:42:23 GMT

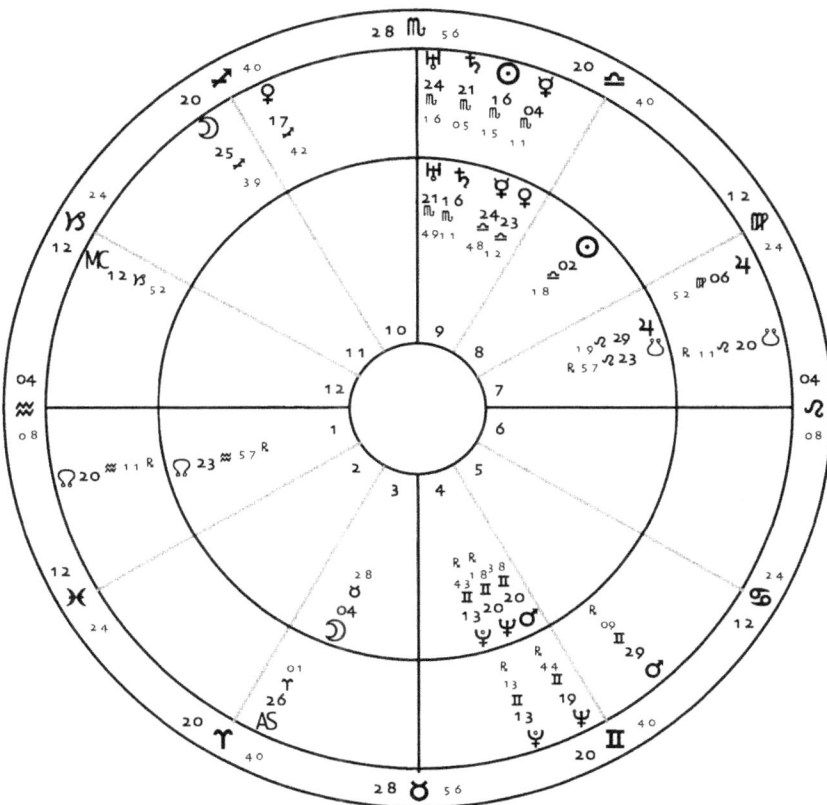

The biwheel on the next page shows that the author's soul group has Libra 24 as its pre-natal Sun-Neptune conjunction degree. From Sepharial's translation of *La Volasfera*, for Libra 24:

> *A solitary tree upon a rocky height, behind which is a dark and threatening cloud.*

It denotes a person of much independence of spirit, self-confidence, pride, and no little love of distinction. The native will suffer on account of his isolated feelings, and will be in danger of betrayal by the machinations of perfidious enemies. At a time when he has reached a height of isolated distinction, he will fall under the jealous hand of his enemies. It is a degree of PRIDE.

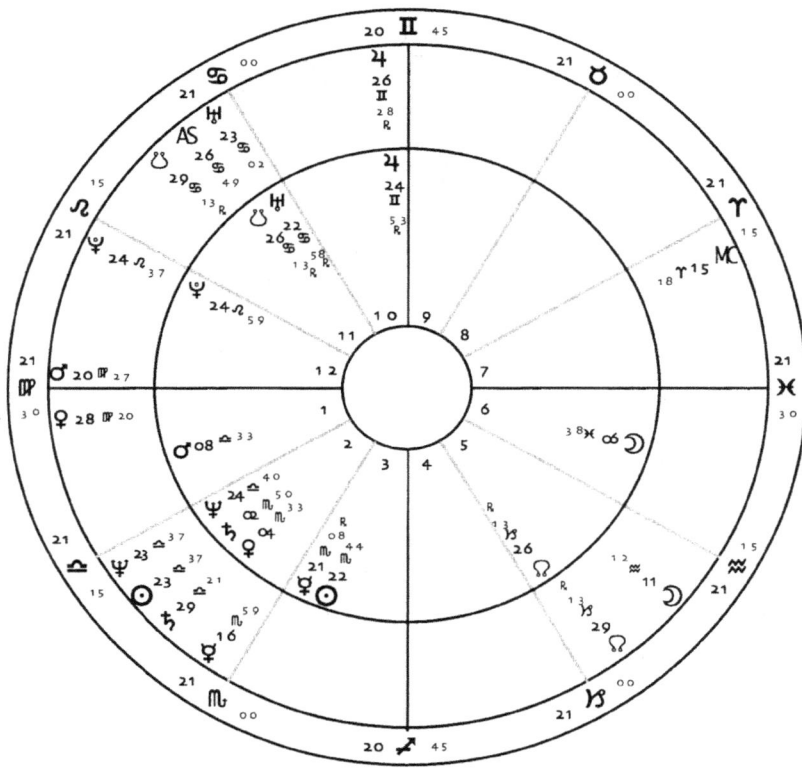

It appears that the central issue within this soul group is the professional envy of colleagues and associates who cannot function with an equivalent independence of spirit and self-confidence that these souls possess in their careers and creative endeavors. The scholar's path to spiritual consciousness through renunciation is achieved by renouncing the ego's desire for individual recognition for work, and to instead devote proficiency to the betterment of one's profession.

With Saturn in exact square to the lunar nodes as this Sun-Neptune synodic cycle commenced, it is evident that this lifetime is pivotal for this soul group to grasp the spiritual essence of its collective purpose. For the author to consciously awaken to his individualized manner of expressing these collective

Chapter Eight • *Outer Planet Phase Angle Returns*

energies, he has to take to heart the degree symbolism for his local Midheaven at the time of this pre-natal conjunction. From Sepharial's translation of *La Volasfera*, for Aries 16:

> *A youth, book in hand, wanders apparently through a glade overhung with the branches of surrounding trees. The sunlight is slanting through the trees, and falling upon the figure of the student.*

> It denotes one who is fond of nature, and studious of her laws; loving the peaceful contemplation of natural beauty; devoted to the higher interests of his soul; and of a reclusive disposition. Such would be successful in his pursuits of natural history, whether in one department or another, but would not apply his knowledge to the attainment of fame. This is a degree of PASSIVE BEAUTY.

It is clear from this symbolism that the author attains a universal level of spiritual consciousness by choosing to share his knowledge with his fellow astrologers in the spirit of making a professional contribution. Renunciation on a scholar's path therefore takes the form of removing personal desires for the attainment of fame.[112]

At the end of this book is a Table of Sun-Neptune conjunctions for the 200 years from 1920 to 2120. Readers can locate their pre-natal Sun-Neptune synodic cycle and its conjunction degree, and then from there, research its degree symbols. A hint to readers: the Sun-Mercury and Sun-Jupiter holograms are also relevant.

While this book was being written, the International Astronomical Union (IAU) voted on 24 August 2006 in Prague in the Czech Republic to reclassify Pluto as a *dwarf planet*, essentially reducing the solar system to the Sun and the eight planets, Mercury through Neptune. It is unclear at this time if the vote on the resolution is going to become a permanent change in status for Pluto, as of the 2,411 scientists in attendance at the Assembly, only 424 members actually voted on this resolution.

Regardless of Pluto's future solar system status, its hologram of transformation is a powerful soul-structure in any nativity, and should be studied carefully. It also has an immediate relationship with one's Sun-Venus and Sun-Saturn holograms.

To visualize one's natal Sun-Pluto hologram, the glyph for the Earth is placed in the horoscope, thus creating this three-dimensional image. In the author's nativity above, Sun-Pluto distance arc A is 87° 45' 03", and Pluto-Earth distance arc B is 92° 14' 57". Together, the two arcs total 180° 00' 00". Using his Sabian Aspect Orb technique, arc A equates to the 28th degree of Gemini, and

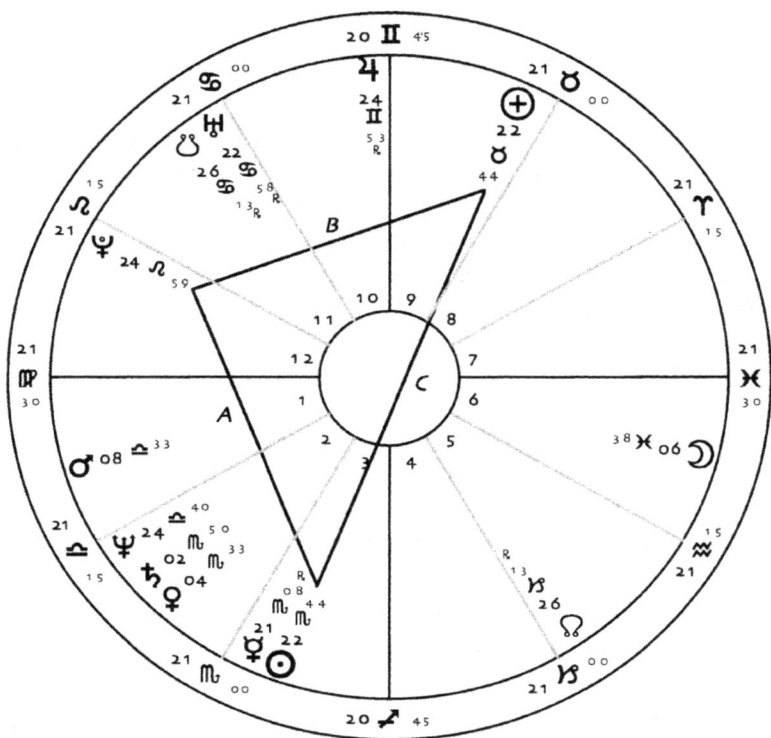

arc *B* is equivalent to the 3rd degree of Cancer. These two degrees are antiscia, or solstice points, of one another. Sun-Earth arc *C* is always a constant, measuring exactly 180° 00' 00".

From Sepharial's translation of *La Volasfera*, for Cancer 3:

> A woman seated in an attitude of grief, her clothes disordered and her hair unkempt, holding some faded flowers in her hands; among the flowers are lilies and roses.
>
> It indicates a person of fateful inclinations and strong passions, whose life will be subject to the influence of the opposite sex, and who, if not extremely cautious in those relations, will suffer injury and perhaps disgrace. It points to one of weak will, but strong feelings which are apt to over-rule reason and experience. It is a degree of SPOLIATION.

Hard to admit, yet obvious with his marital history; the author certainly could not have written a more apropos commentary on his personal life in this incarnation. The Sun-Pluto hologram is the path of transformation which leads through earlier states of attachment at the personal level, and of responsibility at the social level. The counterbalancing degree symbol within this hologram can awaken one to how the alignment of free will with Higher Self can result in transformational choices.

The Sabian Symbol for Gemini 28, and its spiritual analysis by Marc Jones, will provide additional insight into the author's karmic struggle to transform his soul:

> *A man is leaving a courtroom with mixed feelings of relief and determination; he has just passed through bankruptcy.*

This is a symbol of the release of the self from pressure which it would have been unable to bear, of the regathering of the forces of the being for a new struggle towards achievement. Positively it is a symbol of realignment; negatively, of protection. The keyword is EXEMPTION.

If one were to get on the elevator at this county courthouse and go from the fourth floor of bankruptcy court to the fifth floor of divorce court, this revised symbolism would be a tailored fit for the author's personal failure in marriage. It can be said in all honesty that, each time he experienced a marriage ending in divorce, "*the release of the self from pressure which it would have been unable to bear, and the regathering of the forces of the being for a new struggle towards achievement,*" is a literal and verbatim description of the feelings he had about those experiences. His square from the Sun to Pluto in the 12th shows karmic forces beyond one's control.

A careful study of one's natal holograms and their derived degree symbols can be a humbling experience, cutting like a surgeon's knife through the illusions of the self-image. However, the holographic structure of a soul is revealed by this technique, and though not for the faint of heart, those committed to the spiritual path of truth, and committed to the spiritual transformation of their astrology clients, will find a magical doorway opening into a holographic universe when using degree symbols.

If life is to be fully lived, one must know his motivation at the soul level. The natal Sun-Pluto hologram reveals this primal drive within the depths of one's soul. For the author, the Sabian Symbol for Cancer 3, and spiritual analysis by Marc Jones:

> *Through the cold darkening depths of a Northern canyon a man all bundled up in furs leads a shaggy reindeer.*

This is a symbol of the pioneer and trail-blazing instinct in the human heart, the desire to get out beyond all things. Positively it is a degree of the plunging of self into virgin possibilities of existence; negatively, it is the idle visioning of adventure. The keyword is IMMERSION.

The pre-natal Sun-Pluto conjunction and its degree symbols can be examined with the nativity to perceive how the path of transformation affects one's soul group, and how a person can express the collective energies of his soul group in an individualized manner. By calculating pre-natal conjunctions for the location of birth, the Midheaven and its degree symbol reveal this particularized expression.

The author's soul group has the 23rd degree of Leo as their pre-natal Sun-Pluto conjunction. From Sepharial's translation of *La Volasfera*, for Leo 23:

> *A bright, pale blue star, shining over a clear lake.*
>
> It indicates one of a quick, refined, and well-trained intelligence, who will gain distinction by his mental powers. The nature will be peaceful, harmonious, and beneficent. The mind is highly intuitive, and capable of lofty and sustained flights. Withal there is a good knowledge of character and a quiet but potent reserve of diplomatic power. The native will shine like a star in his sphere of life, and will have many followers. It is a degree of INTELLIGENCE.

At the time of this Sun-Pluto conjunction, the Moon was in exact square to the lunar nodes. From this, it can be determined that the soul group to which the author belongs is experiencing evolutionary pressure at a deep level to face karmic issues of immaturity, dependence, and a loss of self-reliance. This group is called to fully develop intuitive faculties to achieve transformation in this lifetime.

Souls born from 15 August 1953 to 17 August 1954, when the ensuing conjunction took place, share this collective pattern of refined intelligence and karmic issues. A conjunction of Mercury and the South Node shows this mental acumen carrying over from past lives. This Sun-Pluto synodic cycle in sextile to the Saturn-Neptune conjunction at its start reveals a purpose of making concrete spiritual obscurities.

At the end of this book is a Table of Sun-Pluto conjunctions for the 200 years from 1920 to 2120. Readers can locate their pre-natal Sun-Pluto synodic cycle and its conjunction degree, and research the meaning of its degree symbols.

For the author, the 2nd degree of Sagittarius was culminating on the Midheaven in Santa Monica at this pre-natal Sun-Pluto conjunction. To understand how he can best express the collective energies of his soul group in an individualized manner, a study of the degree symbol for Sagittarius 2 is undertaken. From *La Volasfera*:

Chapter Eight • Outer Planet Phase Angle Returns

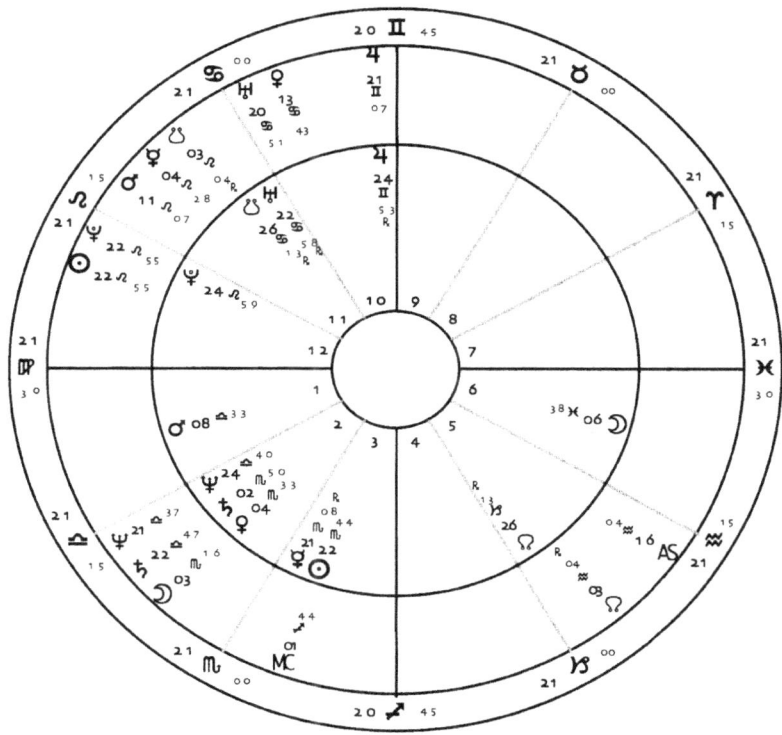

A man standing with drawn sword.

This indicates a character that is given to strife and aggression, whether in assaults-at-arms or in polemics. He will lead a life of continual warfare, and litigation, and will be in danger of wounding and of being wounded. Wherever he goes he will make enemies and will be in peril of his life thereby. Armed, he is yet unshielded, and this is a challenge which even gods will not ignore. It is a degree of WOUNDING.

By taking this symbolism to heart, the author can learn an important karmic lesson on the path of transformation. Intelligence, no matter its refinement or capacity for quick articulation, if used in aggressive ways, wounding the feelings of others, is not in alignment with God's Will. Effort must thus be made to develop impartiality, and to put back into its scabbard the strife-producing sword of the mind's powers.

Using Outer Planet Holographic Transits

An outer planet holographic transit occurs when the exact distance arc between the natal Sun and an outer planet forms in the heavens, *and is in the identical phase as its natal cycle, i.e., Oriental or Occidental*. Outer planet phase angle returns come once a year, and at this time the alignment of free will with Higher Self can be seen in the celestial conditions. The universal forces of enlightenment, renunciation and transformation are holographically regenerating the soul-structure at these times, and a careful study of these charts will illuminate realignment with God's Will.

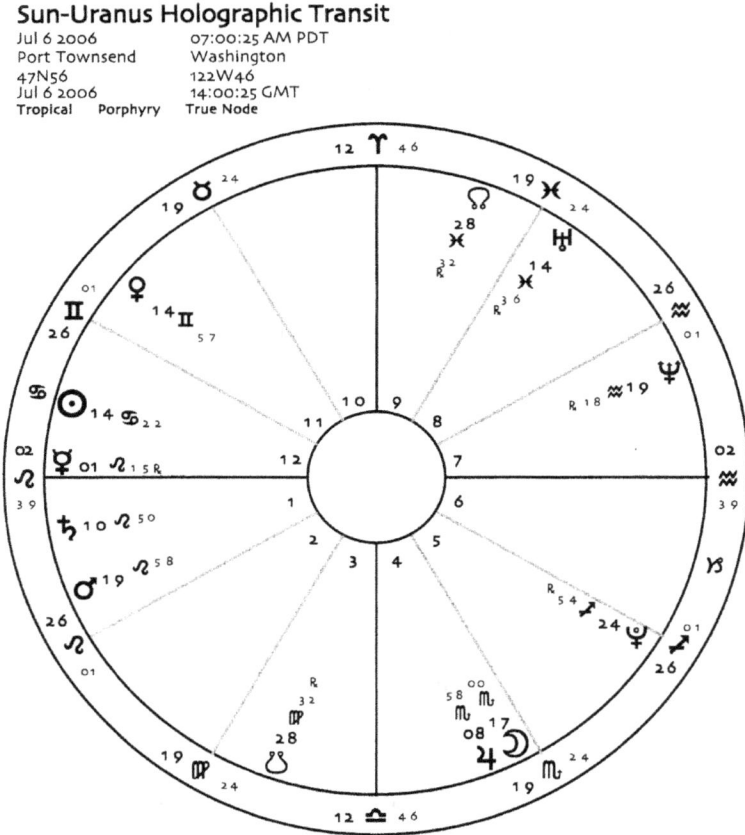

This is the Sun-Uranus holographic transit for the author of 6 July 2006. Observe that his Sun-Uranus distance arc of 119° 45' 36" has replicated in the heavens, and that the Sun-Uranus phase angle is Oriental, as in his nativity. This astrologer is of the opinion that the universal forces represented by the outer planets cannot be harnessed through acts of will, nor comprehended at the personal or social levels.

The spiritual energy of these forces comes straight down from the heavenly realms and into one's crown chakra when the divine rays of the Sun repeat their identical phase angles with the outer planets as at birth. The entry point into consciousness is through the culminating degree, or Midheaven of the chart cast for a phase angle return. *The uppermost degree of this horoscope is the "God degree," as esoterically it symbolizes the fusion of the soul with its Higher Self through the overhead Sun.*

For the author, this is the operative Sun-Uranus holographic transit as he finished the writing of this manuscript. Any universal forces of enlightenment coming into his soul during the one-year period of July 2006 until July 2007 can be perceived through celestial conditions at this time, and by the degree of the Midheaven. From *The Degrees of the Zodiac Symbolised* by Charubel, for Aries 13:

> *An inverted triangle immersed in a dark fog; slowly this fog clears away, and the triangle becomes a bright blue, imbedded in gold.*

> This is a most significant degree. It denotes great native powers or abilities which, by some occult power, bring about a host of heart-rending trials for the native during his earlier days. This may be noted in a number of instances, where there is a born genius; and it has proved a puzzle to the philosopher. The question has been asked again and again, "Why should such persons be the subjects of such trials?" The answer I give is that by virtue of pre-natal conditions, combined with the natal, the psychic nature of that person being more open to outside influence than the ordinary, there is a rush of the unfavourable and malignant powers to that sphere, with the object of extinguishing that luminary, or otherwise bringing on a total eclipse.

And from Sepharial's translation of *La Volasfera*, for Aries 13:

> *A man at the summit of a mountain, illumined by the setting sun; holding a staff in his right hand, in his left a crown.*

> It denotes one who through suffering, pain, and hard work, will at the close of life rise to much dignity and receive many honours. This degree is capable of lifting the native from obscurity to prominence as the reward of enduring effort. It is a degree of REWARD.

The Sun in 14° Cancer 22' at the time of this phase angle return was opposite the author's secondary progressed solar eclipse of 29 July 2004 in 14° Capricorn 13', exact to 09' of arc. The intercepted Sun in the 12th house, which is part

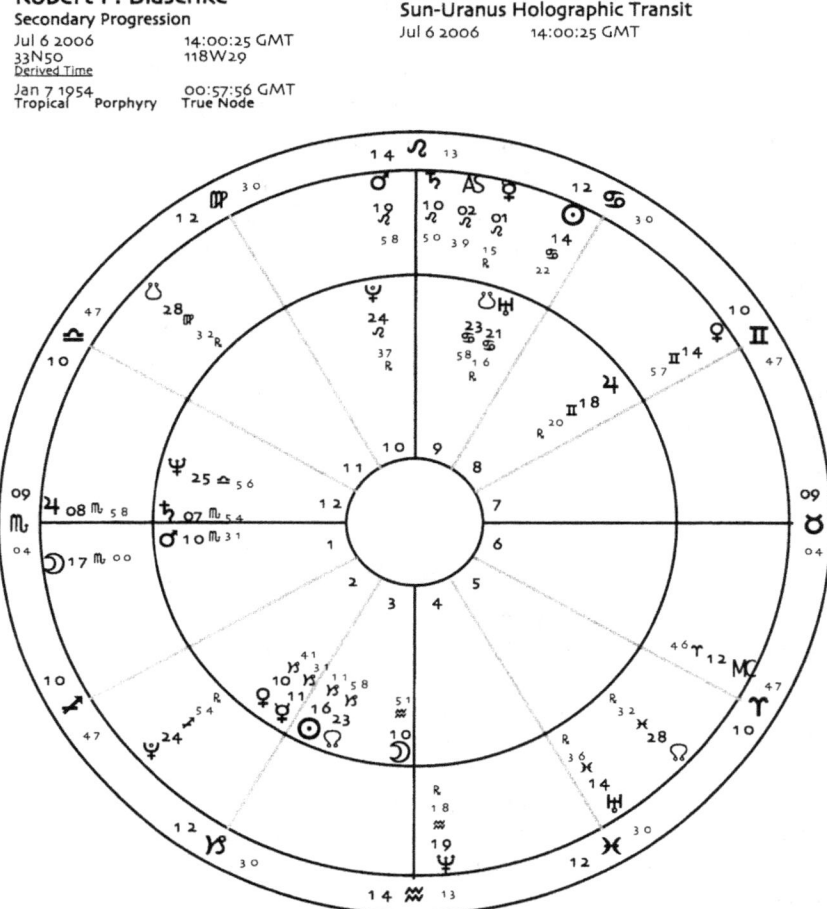

of a Grand Water Trine with the Moon and Jupiter, illustrates an important lesson in how a hidden aspect configuration such as this can become useful. Without Mars and Neptune forming a Fixed T-Cross with that Moon, inspiring the author to fight to finish this volume, all these ideas and techniques would have stayed buried.

    Astrologers using outer planet holographic transits with clients can interpret the horoscopes as stand-alone charts, paying special attention to the degree of the MC and its symbols, and to the house positions of the Sun and the outer planets. It has been the author's experience that when overlaying these holographic transits into the houses of the nativity, or into the houses of the progressed horoscope, some very exact aspects are formed between the

Chapter Eight • *Outer Planet Phase Angle Returns*

two charts. The aspects illustrate how universal forces in place at the time of a phase angle return are holographically entering the soul-structure, and regenerating individuals through their solar rays.

The facing bi-wheel chart illustrates how an outer planet holographic transit interacts with the secondary progressed horoscope. At the time of the author's Sun-Uranus phase angle return, Saturn was opposing his progressed Moon within 01' of arc. Jupiter had stationed direct less than eight hours earlier, and was in stationary conjunction with his progressed Ascendant. These close aspects inform one how universal forces holographically enter the soul-structure at a phase angle return.

Saturn opposing the ruler of the progressed 9th house was necessary for bringing into concrete form the spiritual abstractions of this material. Jupiter stationing on the author's progressed Ascendant was essential for him to enlarge his perspective and be open to the universal forces coming through the crown chakra at that time. The author can testify to the discomfort he felt while writing this volume, as with Uranus in an exact inconjunct with his progressed Midheaven at the time of that phase angle return, he felt as if his mind was navigating a space-time wormhole.[113]

When using outer planet holographic transits with clients, one effective technique is to bring to their attention the interplay between free will and fate. The author recommends using the standard transits side-by-side with the holographic transits so that the relationship between these two realms of consciousness is seen. The tri-wheel chart on the next page has the author's nativity in the inner wheel, his next Sun-Neptune phase angle return of March 2007 in the middle wheel, and stationary retrograde Neptune in transit square to his Sun, due to occur in May 2007, in the outer wheel.

The outer planet transit that the author will experience in 2007 is not unlike what the professional astrologer observes when doing his pre-consultation preparation work for a client. It is common to find at least one transit conjunction, opposition, or square from Uranus, Neptune, or Pluto to the natal or progressed Luminaries, or to the natal or secondary progressed Mercury, Venus, Mars, Jupiter, or Saturn. A key question is: *How does one's soul actualize these universal forces consciously?*

Three important astrological factors to analyze and synthesize are:

1. The nature of the natal Sun-Neptune hologram.
2. The nature of the current secondary progressed Sun-Neptune hologram.
3. Celestial conditions at the time of the Sun-Neptune holographic transit.

Robert P. Blaschke • *Holographic Transits*

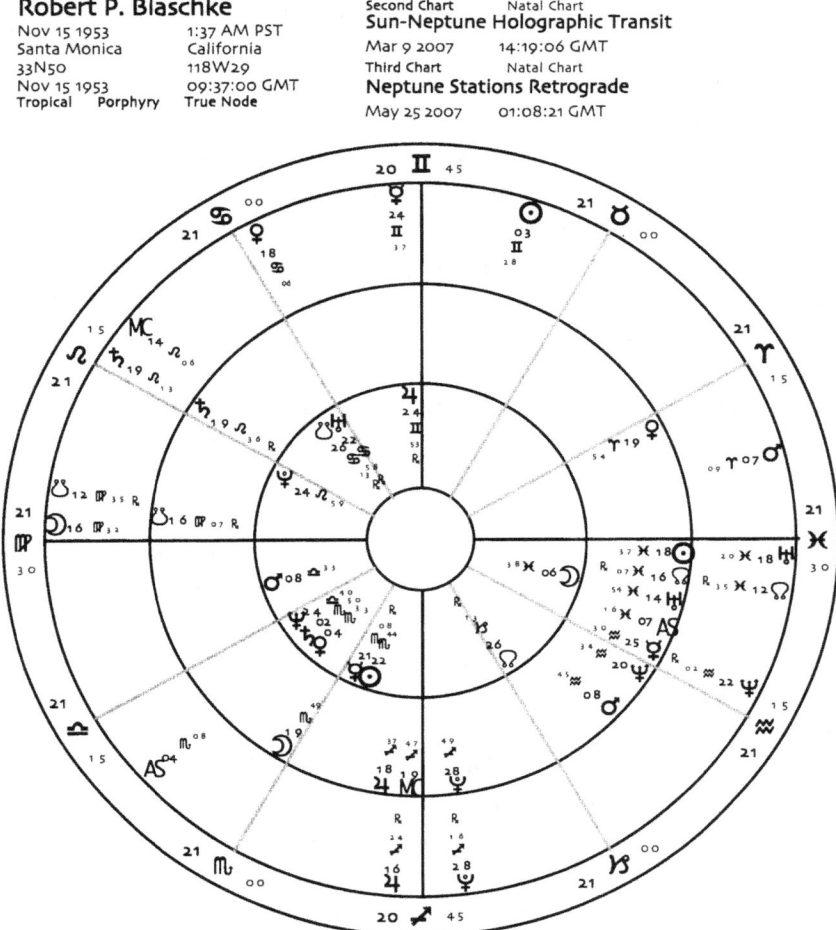

Robert P. Blaschke
Nov 15 1953　　1:37 AM PST
Santa Monica　　California
33N50　　　　　118W29
Nov 15 1953　　09:37:00 GMT
Tropical　Porphyry　True Node

Second Chart　　Natal Chart
Sun-Neptune Holographic Transit
Mar 9 2007　　14:19:06 GMT

Third Chart　　Natal Chart
Neptune Stations Retrograde
May 25 2007　　01:08:21 GMT

Starting with his *natal hologram*, the author's Sun-Neptune distance arc A of 28° 03' 47" equates to the 29th degree of Aries. Its Sabian Symbol from Marc Jones is:

A celestial choir has arisen to sing.

This is a symbol of the underlying consciousness of all life or expression in rapport with the upbuilding or constructive forces of the cosmos. Positively it is a degree of response to the Pythagorean music of the spheres, inherent harmony with all real being; negatively, it is a sense of lack of harmony, a tendency towards conflict. The keyword is FAITH.

Chapter Eight • Outer Planet Phase Angle Returns

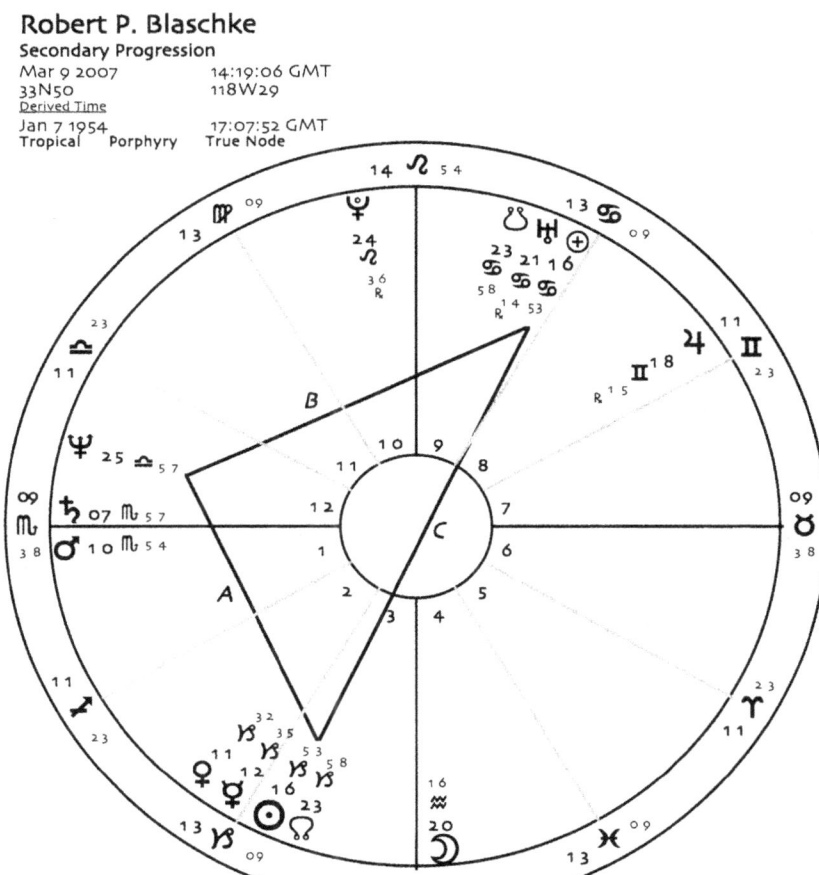

Next, we look at his progressed hologram. Sun-Neptune distance arc A in the chart above has at the time of that phase angle return progressed to 80° 55' 57", equivalent to the 21st degree of Gemini, the author's natal Midheaven. His career and reputation are therefore being actualized by these universal forces.

To further understand how his holographic soul-structure has progressed thus far, look at progressed Neptune-Earth distance arc B of 99° 04' 03", equivalent to the 10th degree of Cancer. From Sepharial's translation of *La Volasfera*:

> A wide-spreading oak tree, around the roots of which are many young shoots, while the birds of the season sing among its branches.

> It indicates a steady, strong, and reliable nature, which by much industry comes at length to the fruits of its labour, and in the autumn of life will be surrounded by

the most grateful evidences of its own energy and perseverance. While sustaining itself it will afford shelter and comfort to others, both among its own kindred and among strangers, so that with integrity and competence there will go honour and esteem to enrich a good old age. It is a degree of FRUITFULNESS.

Third, look at celestial conditions at the time of the Sun-Neptune holographic transit. In the middle wheel of the tri-wheel chart on page 200, observe that the Midheaven calculated for his place of residence in Port Townsend is the 20th degree of Sagittarius. This is the exact point in the Zodiac directly overhead when the divine rays of the Sun shine their energy on Neptune at a matching phase angle. The symbolism of this degree enters the soul through the crown chakra in the head.

From Sepharial's translation of *La Volasfera*, for Sagittarius 20, one finds:

A garden of many-hued flowers.

It is the index of a mind that is genial, kindly, and sociable. Such an one will find many friends and admirers. His life will be filled with happy and fortunate associations, and his mind will be devoted to the artistic, ornamental, and æsthetic. The beautiful in nature will attract him, and his life will be surrounded with elements of concord and amity. It is a degree of CONCORD.

The astrologer also observes that a perfect Fire Grand Trine forms in the heavens at that time, with Venus in the 20th degree of Aries, and Saturn in Leo 20. Neptune in 20° Aquarius 34' fills in a Kite configuration in the exact degree of the author's progressed Moon for that day. The Sun is in a partile square with Jupiter, exact to the minute of arc. Once again, there is a Fixed T-Cross with the Moon, activating the Grand Trine. One hopes that this is an indication of this volume's fruitfulness.

In synthesizing these three astrological factors, the author, through his natal Sun-Neptune hologram, is responsive to the Pythagorean music of the spheres, which is the Sacred Geometry underpinning this science of astrology. He also needs to deepen his faith, and to further open his connection to the divine.

The author's progressed Sun-Neptune hologram at this stage in his life has evolved one of its distance arcs to the derived degree of his natal Midheaven, suggesting a level has been reached where his work can be like the comfort of a wide oak tree. For this force to manifest, there must be a renunciation of the desire for fame.

When his Sun-Neptune phase angle return occurs in 2007, a Fire Grand Trine and Kite form in the heavens, and are conjoined by his progressed

Moon. Recalling C.E.O. Carter's admonition about the Grand Trine,[114] *"Often the fortunes seem to be greatly involved in those of others, both for good and evil,"* the author can set the intention in his heart to align his free will with Higher Self, humbly receive these universal forces sustained by the Sun, and create his *garden of many-hued flowers.*

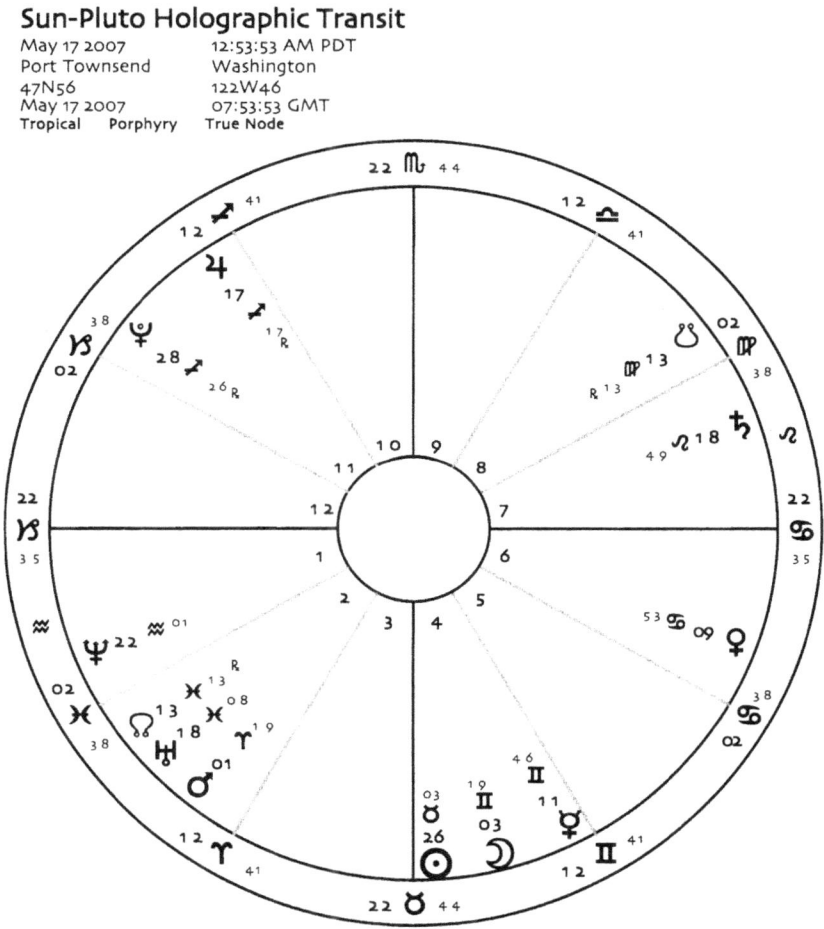

Many times throughout life, universal forces enter our soul-structure through another's love for us. We also serve as spiritual conduits by giving our love. Perhaps we can only know the love of God by giving and receiving love. This astrologer has repeatedly seen that we find ourselves in the outer planet holographic transits of others. Knowing this, we awaken to a higher level of transformation: what we do, what we say, and what we think are circuits of energy touching other lives, other minds, other hearts, and other souls.

In the chart on the previous page is the upcoming Sun-Pluto phase angle return for the author's girlfriend. Her natal Sun-Pluto distance arc of 147° 36' 45" will form again in the heavens. Now living with the author in Port Townsend, after a year in which her father died, her home of many years was leased to a business, and in which she and the author endured lengthy separations while she was abroad in South Africa, they rented temporarily an historical home on a bluff overlooking the sea. Without her, this book could not have been written. With her, it has life.

At the moment next May when her Sun-Pluto holographic transit becomes exact, and the divine rays of the Sun are in the same angle to Pluto as during her birth, a sight to behold occurs on the local Midheaven. That culminating degree is the same as the author's Sun, exact to the minute of arc. Coming into her crown chakra will be holographic soul forces of transformation, and through the author they travel on their way into her. Love is never easy, but one must always reach for the Light.

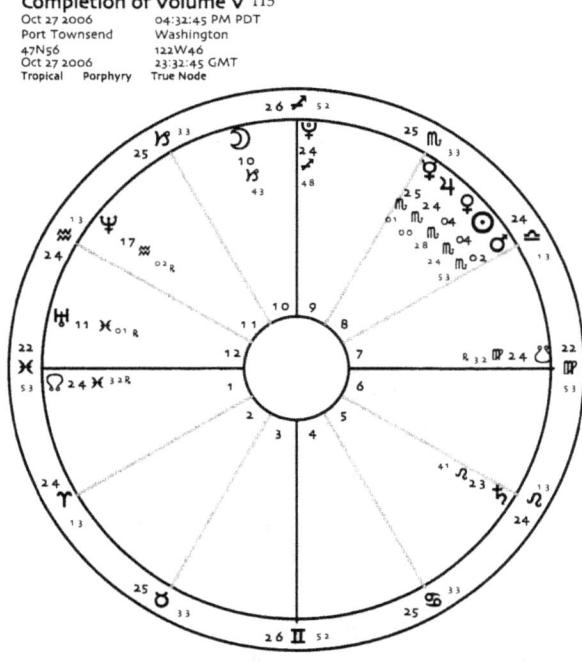

Epilogues

Epilogue to the First Edition (2006)

All worthy endeavors in life come at a cost. On 2 November 2006, just a few days after the completion of this manuscript, the author was diagnosed with cancer. He will be undergoing radiation treatments and chemotherapy shortly, followed by surgery. After that, more chemotherapy will be administered to prevent recurrence.

With Saturn stationing on his Pluto within 05' of arc, the author knew something serious was coming, but never did he dream of a fate such as this. Life is fleeting, and when one is reminded of his mortality, all priorities are instantly rearranged. Now he must apply these holographic methods of free will to his own life. Please say a prayer for this old warrior to make it through and write Volumes VI and VII for you on the other side of this impending ordeal. God bless you, my friend.

Epilogue to the Second Edition (2025)

Tragically, Robert P. Blaschke would not live to write volumes VI and VII. It's not clear what he had planned to write in those volumes. He left few hints. He did, however, posthumously win the prestigious Regulus Award for Discovery, Innovation, and Research at the United Astrology Congress held in New Orleans in 2012, which happened to be this publisher's first astrology conference, after half a Saturn cycle of private mentorship in astrology. Another half–Saturn cycle later, it is my honor to give Robert's work new life at Revelore Press, just as Jupiter transits his natal Jupiter/MC in Gemini.

As I write this, the garden surrounding the Celestial Arts Education Library (CAELi) teems with young shoots, tender leaves reaching for the Cascadian forest canopy, a literal manifestation of Sepharial's image of the stable Oak tree that Robert shared (on page 201) for his progressed Neptune-Earth arc when he finished his final, quite mystical book. At CAELi, we carry on his legacy of pioneering research through labs and live teaching. If any of the ideas in Blaschke's five-volume series pique your curiosity, I invite you to join a community of astrologers who continue to actively work with and expand upon his techniques: www.caeli.institute.

Jenn Zahrt, PhD
May 14, 2025
Olympia, WA

Appendices

The tables in these appendices were calculated using Solar Fire for Windows, v.9.0.29
© 2014–2019 Astrolabe Inc.
Time given is GMT

Appendix I

New Moons + Solar & Lunar Eclipses 1920 to 2120

Mon Cnj Sun	Jan 21 1920	05:26	29° Cp 53'
Mon Cnj Sun	Feb 19 1920	21:34	29° Aq 57'
Mon Cnj Sun	Mar 20 1920	10:55	29° Pi 32'
Mon Cnj Sun	Apr 18 1920	21:43	28° Ar 32'
Lunar Eclipse	May 3 1920	01:47	12° Sc 19'
Solar Eclipse	May 18 1920	06:25	26° Ta 59'
Mon Cnj Sun	Jun 16 1920	13:41	25° Ge 04'
Mon Cnj Sun	Jul 15 1920	20:25	22° Cn 59'
Mon Cnj Sun	Aug 14 1920	03:44	21° Le 01'
Mon Cnj Sun	Sep 12 1920	12:51	19° Vi 26'
Mon Cnj Sun	Oct 12 1920	00:50	18° Li 23'
Lunar Eclipse	Oct 27 1920	14:09	03° Ta 51'
Solar Eclipse	Nov 10 1920	16:05	17° Sc 58'
Mon Cnj Sun	Dec 10 1920	10:04	18° Sg 04'
Mon Cnj Sun	Jan 9 1921	05:26	18° Cp 26'
Mon Cnj Sun	Feb 8 1921	00:36	18° Aq 43'
Mon Cnj Sun	Mar 9 1921	18:09	18° Pi 38'
Solar Eclipse	Apr 8 1921	09:05	17° Ar 59'
Lunar Eclipse	Apr 22 1921	07:49	01° Sc 38'
Mon Cnj Sun	May 7 1921	21:01	16° Ta 43'
Mon Cnj Sun	Jun 6 1921	06:14	14° Ge 58'
Mon Cnj Sun	Jul 5 1921	13:36	12° Cn 57'
Mon Cnj Sun	Aug 3 1921	20:17	10° Le 54'
Mon Cnj Sun	Sep 2 1921	03:33	09° Vi 06'
Solar Eclipse	Oct 1 1921	12:26	07° Li 46'
Lunar Eclipse	Oct 16 1921	22:59	23° Ar 02'
Mon Cnj Sun	Oct 30 1921	23:38	07° Sc 00'
Mon Cnj Sun	Nov 29 1921	13:25	06° Sg 48'
Mon Cnj Sun	Dec 29 1921	05:39	06° Cp 59'
Mon Cnj Sun	Jan 27 1922	23:48	07° Aq 17'
Mon Cnj Sun	Feb 26 1922	18:47	07° Pi 24'
Lunar Eclipse	Mar 13 1922	11:14	22° Vi 06'

Appendix I • *New Moons + Solar & Lunar Eclipses 1920 to 2120*

Solar Eclipse	Mar 28 1922	13:03	07° Ar 04'
Lunar Eclipse	Apr 11 1922	20:43	21° Li 10'
Mon Cnj Sun	Apr 27 1922	05:03	06° Ta 09'
Mon Cnj Sun	May 26 1922	18:04	04° Ge 40'
Mon Cnj Sun	Jun 25 1922	04:19	02° Cn 49'
Mon Cnj Sun	Jul 24 1922	12:47	00° Le 48'
Mon Cnj Sun	Aug 22 1922	20:34	28° Le 56'
Solar Eclipse	Sep 21 1922	04:38	27° Vi 24'
Lunar Eclipse	Oct 6 1922	00:58	11° Ar 59'
Mon Cnj Sun	Oct 20 1922	13:40	26° Li 22'
Mon Cnj Sun	Nov 19 1922	00:06	25° Sc 52'
Mon Cnj Sun	Dec 18 1922	12:20	25° Sg 48'
Mon Cnj Sun	Jan 17 1923	02:41	25° Cp 58'
Mon Cnj Sun	Feb 15 1923	19:07	26° Aq 05'
Lunar Eclipse	Mar 3 1923	03:23	11° Vi 32'
Solar Eclipse	Mar 17 1923	12:51	25° Pi 54'
Mon Cnj Sun	Apr 16 1923	06:28	25° Ar 15'
Mon Cnj Sun	May 15 1923	22:38	24° Ta 03'
Mon Cnj Sun	Jun 14 1923	12:42	22° Ge 25'
Mon Cnj Sun	Jul 14 1923	00:45	20° Cn 33'
Mon Cnj Sun	Aug 12 1923	11:16	18° Le 42'
Lunar Eclipse	Aug 26 1923	10:29	02° Pi 09'
Solar Eclipse	Sep 10 1923	20:52	17° Vi 06'
Mon Cnj Sun	Oct 10 1923	06:05	15° Li 54'
Mon Cnj Sun	Nov 8 1923	15:27	15° Sc 12'
Mon Cnj Sun	Dec 8 1923	01:30	14° Sg 56'
Mon Cnj Sun	Jan 6 1924	12:48	14° Cp 56'
Mon Cnj Sun	Feb 5 1924	01:38	14° Aq 59'
Lunar Eclipse	Feb 20 1924	16:07	00° Vi 46'
Solar Eclipse	Mar 5 1924	15:58	14° Pi 49'
Mon Cnj Sun	Apr 4 1924	07:17	14° Ar 15'
Mon Cnj Sun	May 3 1924	23:00	13° Ta 12'
Mon Cnj Sun	Jun 2 1924	14:34	11° Ge 45'
Mon Cnj Sun	Jul 2 1924	05:35	10° Cn 02'
Solar Eclipse	Jul 31 1924	19:42	08° Le 16'
Lunar Eclipse	Aug 14 1924	20:19	21° Aq 43'
Solar Eclipse	Aug 30 1924	08:37	06° Vi 40'
Mon Cnj Sun	Sep 28 1924	20:16	05° Li 24'
Mon Cnj Sun	Oct 28 1924	06:57	04° Sc 35'
Mon Cnj Sun	Nov 26 1924	17:15	04° Sg 11'
Mon Cnj Sun	Dec 26 1924	03:46	04° Cp 07'
Solar Eclipse	Jan 24 1925	14:45	04° Aq 07'
Lunar Eclipse	Feb 8 1925	21:49	19° Le 39'
Mon Cnj Sun	Feb 23 1925	02:12	03° Pi 58'

Mon Cnj Sun	Mar 24 1925	14:03	03° Ar 25'
Mon Cnj Sun	Apr 23 1925	02:28	02° Ta 25'
Mon Cnj Sun	May 22 1925	15:48	01° Ge 00'
Mon Cnj Sun	Jun 21 1925	06:17	29° Ge 20'
Solar Eclipse	Jul 20 1925	21:40	27° Cn 36'
Lunar Eclipse	Aug 4 1925	11:59	11° Aq 33'
Mon Cnj Sun	Aug 19 1925	13:15	26° Le 00'
Mon Cnj Sun	Sep 18 1925	04:12	24° Vi 43'
Mon Cnj Sun	Oct 17 1925	18:06	23° Li 50'
Mon Cnj Sun	Nov 16 1925	06:58	23° Sc 24'
Mon Cnj Sun	Dec 15 1925	19:05	23° Sg 18'
Solar Eclipse	Jan 14 1926	06:35	23° Cp 21'
Lunar Eclipse	Jan 28 1926	21:35	08° Le 14'
Mon Cnj Sun	Feb 12 1926	17:20	23° Aq 15'
Mon Cnj Sun	Mar 14 1926	03:20	22° Pi 47'
Mon Cnj Sun	Apr 12 1926	12:56	21° Ar 51'
Mon Cnj Sun	May 11 1926	22:55	20° Ta 28'
Mon Cnj Sun	Jun 10 1926	10:08	18° Ge 45'
Lunar Eclipse	Jun 25 1926	21:13	03° Cp 31'
Solar Eclipse	Jul 9 1926	23:06	16° Cn 56'
Lunar Eclipse	Jul 25 1926	05:13	01° Aq 30'
Mon Cnj Sun	Aug 8 1926	13:49	15° Le 14'
Mon Cnj Sun	Sep 7 1926	05:45	13° Vi 50'
Mon Cnj Sun	Oct 6 1926	22:13	12° Li 53'
Mon Cnj Sun	Nov 5 1926	14:34	12° Sc 25'
Mon Cnj Sun	Dec 5 1926	06:11	12° Sg 21'
Lunar Eclipse	Dec 19 1926	06:09	26° Ge 35'
Solar Eclipse	Jan 3 1927	20:28	12° Cp 28'
Mon Cnj Sun	Feb 2 1927	08:54	12° Aq 31'
Mon Cnj Sun	Mar 3 1927	19:25	12° Pi 13'
Mon Cnj Sun	Apr 2 1927	04:24	11° Ar 26'
Mon Cnj Sun	May 1 1927	12:40	10° Ta 08'
Mon Cnj Sun	May 30 1927	21:06	08° Ge 26'
Lunar Eclipse	Jun 15 1927	08:19	23° Sg 14'
Solar Eclipse	Jun 29 1927	06:32	06° Cn 31'
Mon Cnj Sun	Jul 28 1927	17:36	04° Le 37'
Mon Cnj Sun	Aug 27 1927	06:45	03° Vi 00'
Mon Cnj Sun	Sep 25 1927	22:11	01° Li 50'
Mon Cnj Sun	Oct 25 1927	15:37	01° Sc 13'
Mon Cnj Sun	Nov 24 1927	10:09	01° Sg 08'
Lunar Eclipse	Dec 8 1927	17:32	15° Ge 38'
Solar Eclipse	Dec 24 1927	04:13	01° Cp 21'
Mon Cnj Sun	Jan 22 1928	20:19	01° Aq 35'
Mon Cnj Sun	Feb 21 1928	09:41	01° Pi 31'

Appendix I • *New Moons + Solar & Lunar Eclipses 1920 to 2120*

Mon Cnj Sun	Mar 21 1928	20:29	00° Ar 58'
Mon Cnj Sun	Apr 20 1928	05:25	29° Ar 53'
Solar Eclipse	May 19 1928	13:14	28° Ta 17'
Lunar Eclipse	Jun 3 1928	12:13	12° Sg 38'
Solar Eclipse	Jun 17 1928	20:42	26° Ge 21'
Mon Cnj Sun	Jul 17 1928	04:35	24° Cn 20'
Mon Cnj Sun	Aug 15 1928	13:48	22° Le 27'
Mon Cnj Sun	Sep 14 1928	01:20	20° Vi 58'
Mon Cnj Sun	Oct 13 1928	15:56	20° Li 03'
Solar Eclipse	Nov 12 1928	09:35	19° Sc 46'
Lunar Eclipse	Nov 27 1928	09:05	04° Ge 53'
Mon Cnj Sun	Dec 12 1928	05:06	19° Sg 56'
Mon Cnj Sun	Jan 11 1929	00:28	20° Cp 18'
Mon Cnj Sun	Feb 9 1929	17:55	20° Aq 31'
Mon Cnj Sun	Mar 11 1929	08:36	20° Pi 17'
Mon Cnj Sun	Apr 9 1929	20:32	19° Ar 29'
Solar Eclipse	May 9 1929	06:07	18° Ta 07'
Lunar Eclipse	May 23 1929	12:50	01° Sg 52'
Mon Cnj Sun	Jun 7 1929	13:56	16° Ge 18'
Mon Cnj Sun	Jul 6 1929	20:47	14° Cn 15'
Mon Cnj Sun	Aug 5 1929	03:40	12° Le 13'
Mon Cnj Sun	Sep 3 1929	11:47	10° Vi 28'
Mon Cnj Sun	Oct 2 1929	22:19	09° Li 13'
Solar Eclipse	Nov 1 1929	12:01	08° Sc 35'
Lunar Eclipse	Nov 17 1929	00:14	24° Ta 10'
Mon Cnj Sun	Dec 1 1929	04:48	08° Sg 31'
Mon Cnj Sun	Dec 30 1929	23:42	08° Cp 49'
Mon Cnj Sun	Jan 29 1930	19:07	09° Aq 10'
Mon Cnj Sun	Feb 28 1930	13:33	09° Pi 14'
Mon Cnj Sun	Mar 30 1930	05:46	08° Ar 48'
Lunar Eclipse	Apr 13 1930	05:48	22° Li 34'
Solar Eclipse	Apr 28 1930	19:08	07° Ta 45'
Mon Cnj Sun	May 28 1930	05:37	06° Ge 09'
Mon Cnj Sun	Jun 26 1930	13:47	04° Cn 12'
Mon Cnj Sun	Jul 25 1930	20:42	02° Le 09'
Mon Cnj Sun	Aug 24 1930	03:37	00° Vi 14'
Mon Cnj Sun	Sep 22 1930	11:41	28° Vi 44'
Lunar Eclipse	Oct 7 1930	18:55	13° Ar 46'
Solar Eclipse	Oct 21 1930	21:48	27° Li 46'
Mon Cnj Sun	Nov 20 1930	10:21	27° Sc 22'
Mon Cnj Sun	Dec 20 1930	01:24	27° Sg 26'
Mon Cnj Sun	Jan 18 1931	18:35	27° Cp 43'
Mon Cnj Sun	Feb 17 1931	13:11	27° Aq 55'
Mon Cnj Sun	Mar 19 1931	07:51	27° Pi 45'

Lunar Eclipse	Apr 2 1931	20:05	12° Li 07'
Solar Eclipse	Apr 18 1931	01:00	27° Ar 02'
Mon Cnj Sun	May 17 1931	15:28	25° Ta 45'
Mon Cnj Sun	Jun 16 1931	03:02	24° Ge 00'
Mon Cnj Sun	Jul 15 1931	12:20	22° Cn 02'
Mon Cnj Sun	Aug 13 1931	20:27	20° Le 06'
Solar Eclipse	Sep 12 1931	04:26	18° Vi 27'
Lunar Eclipse	Sep 26 1931	19:45	02° Ar 44'
Solar Eclipse	Oct 11 1931	13:06	17° Li 15'
Mon Cnj Sun	Nov 9 1931	22:55	16° Sc 34'
Mon Cnj Sun	Dec 9 1931	10:16	16° Sg 22'
Mon Cnj Sun	Jan 7 1932	23:29	16° Cp 28'
Mon Cnj Sun	Feb 6 1932	14:45	16° Aq 37'
Solar Eclipse	Mar 7 1932	07:44	16° Pi 32'
Lunar Eclipse	Mar 22 1932	12:37	01° Li 40'
Mon Cnj Sun	Apr 6 1932	01:21	16° Ar 02'
Mon Cnj Sun	May 5 1932	18:11	15° Ta 00'
Mon Cnj Sun	Jun 4 1932	09:16	13° Ge 30'
Mon Cnj Sun	Jul 3 1932	22:20	11° Cn 43'
Mon Cnj Sun	Aug 2 1932	09:42	09° Le 51'
Solar Eclipse	Aug 31 1932	19:55	08° Vi 09'
Lunar Eclipse	Sep 14 1932	21:06	21° Pi 48'
Mon Cnj Sun	Sep 30 1932	05:30	06° Li 50'
Mon Cnj Sun	Oct 29 1932	14:56	05° Sc 59'
Mon Cnj Sun	Nov 28 1932	00:43	05° Sg 35'
Mon Cnj Sun	Dec 27 1932	11:22	05° Cp 31'
Mon Cnj Sun	Jan 25 1933	23:20	05° Aq 34'
Lunar Eclipse	Feb 10 1933	13:00	21° Le 21'
Solar Eclipse	Feb 24 1933	12:44	05° Pi 28'
Lunar Eclipse	Mar 12 1933	02:46	21° Vi 05'
Mon Cnj Sun	Mar 26 1933	03:20	05° Ar 01'
Mon Cnj Sun	Apr 24 1933	18:38	04° Ta 06'
Mon Cnj Sun	May 24 1933	10:07	02° Ge 46'
Mon Cnj Sun	Jun 23 1933	01:22	01° Cn 07'
Mon Cnj Sun	Jul 22 1933	16:03	29° Cn 21'
Lunar Eclipse	Aug 5 1933	19:31	12° Aq 53'
Solar Eclipse	Aug 21 1933	05:48	27° Le 42'
Lunar Eclipse	Sep 4 1933	05:04	11° Pi 12'
Mon Cnj Sun	Sep 19 1933	18:21	26° Vi 20'
Mon Cnj Sun	Oct 19 1933	05:45	25° Li 23'
Mon Cnj Sun	Nov 17 1933	16:24	24° Sc 53'
Mon Cnj Sun	Dec 17 1933	02:53	24° Sg 44'
Mon Cnj Sun	Jan 15 1934	13:37	24° Cp 44'
Lunar Eclipse	Jan 30 1934	16:31	10° Le 07'

Appendix I • *New Moons + Solar & Lunar Eclipses 1920 to 2120*

Solar Eclipse	Feb 14 1934	00:43	24° Aq 38'
Mon Cnj Sun	Mar 15 1934	12:08	24° Pi 13'
Mon Cnj Sun	Apr 13 1934	23:57	23° Ar 21'
Mon Cnj Sun	May 13 1934	12:30	22° Ta 02'
Mon Cnj Sun	Jun 12 1934	02:11	20° Ge 25'
Mon Cnj Sun	Jul 11 1934	17:06	18° Cn 41'
Lunar Eclipse	Jul 26 1934	12:08	02° Aq 48'
Solar Eclipse	Aug 10 1934	08:46	17° Le 01'
Mon Cnj Sun	Sep 9 1934	00:20	15° Vi 38'
Mon Cnj Sun	Oct 8 1934	15:05	14° Li 38'
Mon Cnj Sun	Nov 7 1934	04:44	14° Sc 05'
Mon Cnj Sun	Dec 6 1934	17:25	13° Sg 55'
Solar Eclipse	Jan 5 1935	05:20	13° Cp 57'
Lunar Eclipse	Jan 19 1935	15:44	28° Cn 39'
Solar Eclipse	Feb 3 1935	16:27	13° Aq 55'
Mon Cnj Sun	Mar 5 1935	02:40	13° Pi 36'
Mon Cnj Sun	Apr 3 1935	12:10	12° Ar 48'
Mon Cnj Sun	May 2 1935	21:36	11° Ta 32'
Mon Cnj Sun	Jun 1 1935	07:52	09° Ge 53'
Solar Eclipse	Jun 30 1935	19:44	08° Cn 04'
Lunar Eclipse	Jul 16 1935	05:00	22° Cp 44'
Solar Eclipse	Jul 30 1935	09:32	06° Le 17'
Mon Cnj Sun	Aug 29 1935	01:00	04° Vi 46'
Mon Cnj Sun	Sep 27 1935	17:29	03° Li 40'
Mon Cnj Sun	Oct 27 1935	10:15	03° Sc 03'
Mon Cnj Sun	Nov 26 1935	02:36	02° Sg 54'
Solar Eclipse	Dec 25 1935	17:49	03° Cp 01'
Lunar Eclipse	Jan 8 1936	18:15	17° Cn 18'
Mon Cnj Sun	Jan 24 1936	07:18	03° Aq 08'
Mon Cnj Sun	Feb 22 1936	18:42	02° Pi 59'
Mon Cnj Sun	Mar 23 1936	04:14	02° Ar 22'
Mon Cnj Sun	Apr 21 1936	12:32	01° Ta 13'
Mon Cnj Sun	May 20 1936	20:34	29° Ta 37'
Solar Eclipse	Jun 19 1936	05:14	27° Ge 43'
Lunar Eclipse	Jul 4 1936	17:34	12° Cp 31'
Mon Cnj Sun	Jul 18 1936	15:19	25° Cn 46'
Mon Cnj Sun	Aug 17 1936	03:21	24° Le 01'
Mon Cnj Sun	Sep 15 1936	17:41	22° Vi 40'
Mon Cnj Sun	Oct 15 1936	10:20	21° Li 52'
Mon Cnj Sun	Nov 14 1936	04:42	21° Sc 38'
Solar Eclipse	Dec 13 1936	23:25	21° Sg 48'
Lunar Eclipse	Dec 28 1936	04:00	06° Cn 15'
Mon Cnj Sun	Jan 12 1937	16:47	22° Cp 05'
Mon Cnj Sun	Feb 11 1937	07:34	22° Aq 10'

Mon Cnj Sun	Mar 12 1937	19:32	21° Pi 49'
Mon Cnj Sun	Apr 11 1937	05:10	20° Ar 54'
Mon Cnj Sun	May 10 1937	13:18	19° Ta 27'
Lunar Eclipse	May 25 1937	07:38	03° Sg 40'
Solar Eclipse	Jun 8 1937	20:43	17° Ge 36'
Mon Cnj Sun	Jul 8 1937	04:13	15° Cn 34'
Mon Cnj Sun	Aug 6 1937	12:37	13° Le 36'
Mon Cnj Sun	Sep 4 1937	22:53	11° Vi 57'
Mon Cnj Sun	Oct 4 1937	11:58	10° Li 50'
Mon Cnj Sun	Nov 3 1937	04:16	10° Sc 19'
Lunar Eclipse	Nov 18 1937	08:10	25° Ta 34'
Solar Eclipse	Dec 2 1937	23:11	10° Sg 22'
Mon Cnj Sun	Jan 1 1938	18:58	10° Cp 43'
Mon Cnj Sun	Jan 31 1938	13:35	11° Aq 02'
Mon Cnj Sun	Mar 2 1938	05:40	10° Pi 59'
Mon Cnj Sun	Mar 31 1938	18:52	10° Ar 24'
Mon Cnj Sun	Apr 30 1938	05:28	09° Ta 12'
Lunar Eclipse	May 14 1938	08:39	22° Sc 53'
Solar Eclipse	May 29 1938	14:00	07° Ge 31'
Mon Cnj Sun	Jun 27 1938	21:10	05° Cn 31'
Mon Cnj Sun	Jul 27 1938	03:53	03° Le 27'
Mon Cnj Sun	Aug 25 1938	11:17	01° Vi 35'
Mon Cnj Sun	Sep 23 1938	20:34	00° Li 08'
Mon Cnj Sun	Oct 23 1938	08:42	29° Li 17'
Lunar Eclipse	Nov 7 1938	22:23	14° Ta 51'
Solar Eclipse	Nov 22 1938	00:05	29° Sc 01'
Mon Cnj Sun	Dec 21 1938	18:07	29° Sg 13'
Mon Cnj Sun	Jan 20 1939	13:27	29° Cp 36'
Mon Cnj Sun	Feb 19 1939	08:28	29° Aq 48'
Mon Cnj Sun	Mar 21 1939	01:49	29° Pi 33'
Solar Eclipse	Apr 19 1939	16:35	28° Ar 43'
Lunar Eclipse	May 3 1939	15:15	12° Sc 17'
Mon Cnj Sun	May 19 1939	04:25	27° Ta 18'
Mon Cnj Sun	Jun 17 1939	13:37	25° Ge 27'
Mon Cnj Sun	Jul 16 1939	21:03	23° Cn 24'
Mon Cnj Sun	Aug 15 1939	03:53	21° Le 25'
Mon Cnj Sun	Sep 13 1939	11:22	19° Vi 46'
Solar Eclipse	Oct 12 1939	20:30	18° Li 36'
Lunar Eclipse	Oct 28 1939	06:42	03° Ta 56'
Mon Cnj Sun	Nov 11 1939	07:54	18° Sc 01'
Mon Cnj Sun	Dec 10 1939	21:45	17° Sg 56'
Mon Cnj Sun	Jan 9 1940	13:53	18° Cp 09'
Mon Cnj Sun	Feb 8 1940	07:45	18° Aq 24'
Mon Cnj Sun	Mar 9 1940	02:23	18° Pi 22'

Appendix I • *New Moons + Solar & Lunar Eclipses 1920 to 2120*

Lunar Eclipse	Mar 23 1940	19:33	03° Li 01'
Solar Eclipse	Apr 7 1940	20:18	17° Ar 51'
Lunar Eclipse	Apr 22 1940	04:37	01° Sc 53'
Mon Cnj Sun	May 7 1940	12:07	16° Ta 46'
Mon Cnj Sun	Jun 6 1940	01:05	15° Ge 10'
Mon Cnj Sun	Jul 5 1940	11:28	13° Cn 15'
Mon Cnj Sun	Aug 3 1940	20:09	11° Le 17'
Mon Cnj Sun	Sep 2 1940	04:15	09° Vi 32'
Solar Eclipse	Oct 1 1940	12:41	08° Li 10'
Lunar Eclipse	Oct 16 1940	08:15	22° Ar 49'
Mon Cnj Sun	Oct 30 1940	22:03	07° Sc 20'
Mon Cnj Sun	Nov 29 1940	08:42	06° Sg 59'
Mon Cnj Sun	Dec 28 1940	20:56	07° Cp 00'
Mon Cnj Sun	Jan 27 1941	11:03	07° Aq 08'
Mon Cnj Sun	Feb 26 1941	03:02	07° Pi 08'
Lunar Eclipse	Mar 13 1941	11:47	22° Vi 30'
Solar Eclipse	Mar 27 1941	20:14	06° Ar 46'
Mon Cnj Sun	Apr 26 1941	13:23	05° Ta 54'
Mon Cnj Sun	May 26 1941	05:18	04° Ge 33'
Mon Cnj Sun	Jun 24 1941	19:22	02° Cn 51'
Mon Cnj Sun	Jul 24 1941	07:39	01° Le 00'
Mon Cnj Sun	Aug 22 1941	18:34	29° Le 14'
Lunar Eclipse	Sep 5 1941	17:36	12° Pi 44'
Solar Eclipse	Sep 21 1941	04:38	27° Vi 48'
Mon Cnj Sun	Oct 20 1941	14:20	26° Li 48'
Mon Cnj Sun	Nov 19 1941	00:04	26° Sc 16'
Mon Cnj Sun	Dec 18 1941	10:18	26° Sg 07'
Mon Cnj Sun	Jan 16 1942	21:32	26° Cp 08'
Mon Cnj Sun	Feb 15 1942	10:02	26° Aq 05'
Lunar Eclipse	Mar 3 1942	00:20	11° Vi 47'
Solar Eclipse	Mar 16 1942	23:50	25° Pi 45'
Mon Cnj Sun	Apr 15 1942	14:33	24° Ar 59'
Mon Cnj Sun	May 15 1942	05:45	23° Ta 45'
Mon Cnj Sun	Jun 13 1942	21:02	22° Ge 11'
Mon Cnj Sun	Jul 13 1942	12:03	20° Cn 27'
Solar Eclipse	Aug 12 1942	02:28	18° Le 45'
Lunar Eclipse	Aug 26 1942	03:46	02° Pi 16'
Solar Eclipse	Sep 10 1942	15:53	17° Vi 17'
Mon Cnj Sun	Oct 10 1942	04:06	16° Li 13'
Mon Cnj Sun	Nov 8 1942	15:19	15° Sc 35'
Mon Cnj Sun	Dec 8 1942	01:59	15° Sg 20'
Mon Cnj Sun	Jan 6 1943	12:38	15° Cp 19'
Solar Eclipse	Feb 4 1943	23:29	15° Aq 17'
Lunar Eclipse	Feb 20 1943	05:45	00° Vi 43'

Mon Cnj Sun	Mar 6 1943	10:34	14° Pi 58'
Mon Cnj Sun	Apr 4 1943	21:53	14° Ar 14'
Mon Cnj Sun	May 4 1943	09:43	13° Ta 03'
Mon Cnj Sun	Jun 2 1943	22:33	11° Ge 29'
Mon Cnj Sun	Jul 2 1943	12:44	09° Cn 45'
Solar Eclipse	Aug 1 1943	04:06	08° Le 02'
Lunar Eclipse	Aug 15 1943	19:34	22° Aq 05'
Mon Cnj Sun	Aug 30 1943	19:59	06° Vi 33'
Mon Cnj Sun	Sep 29 1943	11:29	05° Li 26'
Mon Cnj Sun	Oct 29 1943	01:59	04° Sc 46'
Mon Cnj Sun	Nov 27 1943	15:23	04° Sg 30'
Mon Cnj Sun	Dec 27 1943	03:50	04° Cp 30'
Solar Eclipse	Jan 25 1944	15:24	04° Aq 32'
Lunar Eclipse	Feb 9 1944	05:29	19° Le 21'
Mon Cnj Sun	Feb 24 1944	01:59	04° Pi 20'
Mon Cnj Sun	Mar 24 1944	11:36	03° Ar 42'
Mon Cnj Sun	Apr 22 1944	20:43	02° Ta 34'
Mon Cnj Sun	May 22 1944	06:12	01° Ge 00'
Mon Cnj Sun	Jun 20 1944	17:00	29° Ge 12'
Lunar Eclipse	Jul 6 1944	04:27	13° Cp 57'
Solar Eclipse	Jul 20 1944	05:42	27° Cn 21'
Lunar Eclipse	Aug 4 1944	12:39	11° Aq 58'
Mon Cnj Sun	Aug 18 1944	20:25	25° Le 43'
Mon Cnj Sun	Sep 17 1944	12:37	24° Vi 28'
Mon Cnj Sun	Oct 17 1944	05:35	23° Li 43'
Mon Cnj Sun	Nov 15 1944	22:29	23° Sc 27'
Mon Cnj Sun	Dec 15 1944	14:35	23° Sg 31'
Lunar Eclipse	Dec 29 1944	14:38	07° Cn 47'
Solar Eclipse	Jan 14 1945	05:07	23° Cp 41'
Mon Cnj Sun	Feb 12 1945	17:33	23° Aq 39'
Mon Cnj Sun	Mar 14 1945	03:51	23° Pi 12'
Mon Cnj Sun	Apr 12 1945	12:30	22° Ar 13'
Mon Cnj Sun	May 11 1945	20:21	20° Ta 45'
Mon Cnj Sun	Jun 10 1945	04:26	18° Ge 55'
Lunar Eclipse	Jun 25 1945	15:08	03° Cp 39'
Solar Eclipse	Jul 9 1945	13:35	16° Cn 57'
Mon Cnj Sun	Aug 8 1945	00:32	15° Le 05'
Mon Cnj Sun	Sep 6 1945	13:44	13° Vi 35'
Mon Cnj Sun	Oct 6 1945	05:22	12° Li 35'
Mon Cnj Sun	Nov 4 1945	23:11	12° Sc 10'
Mon Cnj Sun	Dec 4 1945	18:07	12° Sg 14'
Lunar Eclipse	Dec 19 1945	02:17	26° Ge 49'
Solar Eclipse	Jan 3 1946	12:30	12° Cp 32'
Mon Cnj Sun	Feb 2 1946	04:43	12° Aq 44'

Appendix I • *New Moons + Solar & Lunar Eclipses 1920 to 2120*

Mon Cnj Sun	Mar 3 1946	18:01	12° Pi 33'
Mon Cnj Sun	Apr 2 1946	04:37	11° Ar 50'
Mon Cnj Sun	May 1 1946	13:16	10° Ta 33'
Solar Eclipse	May 30 1946	20:49	08° Ge 48'
Lunar Eclipse	Jun 14 1946	18:42	23° Sg 04'
Solar Eclipse	Jun 29 1946	04:06	06° Cn 48'
Mon Cnj Sun	Jul 28 1946	11:54	04° Le 47'
Mon Cnj Sun	Aug 26 1946	21:07	03° Vi 00'
Mon Cnj Sun	Sep 25 1946	08:45	01° Li 40'
Mon Cnj Sun	Oct 24 1946	23:32	00° Sc 57'
Solar Eclipse	Nov 23 1946	17:24	00° Sg 49'
Lunar Eclipse	Dec 8 1946	17:52	16° Ge 03'
Mon Cnj Sun	Dec 23 1946	13:06	01° Cp 06'
Mon Cnj Sun	Jan 22 1947	08:34	01° Aq 29'
Mon Cnj Sun	Feb 21 1947	02:00	01° Pi 36'
Mon Cnj Sun	Mar 22 1947	16:34	01° Ar 12'
Mon Cnj Sun	Apr 21 1947	04:19	00° Ta 13'
Solar Eclipse	May 20 1947	13:44	28° Ta 41'
Lunar Eclipse	Jun 3 1947	19:27	12° Sg 21'
Mon Cnj Sun	Jun 18 1947	21:26	26° Ge 46'
Mon Cnj Sun	Jul 18 1947	04:15	24° Cn 42'
Mon Cnj Sun	Aug 16 1947	11:12	22° Le 44'
Mon Cnj Sun	Sep 14 1947	19:28	21° Vi 07'
Mon Cnj Sun	Oct 14 1947	06:10	20° Li 03'
Solar Eclipse	Nov 12 1947	20:01	19° Sc 35'
Lunar Eclipse	Nov 28 1947	08:45	05° Ge 16'
Mon Cnj Sun	Dec 12 1947	12:53	19° Sg 39'
Mon Cnj Sun	Jan 11 1948	07:45	20° Cp 00'
Mon Cnj Sun	Feb 10 1948	03:02	20° Aq 17'
Mon Cnj Sun	Mar 10 1948	21:15	20° Pi 13'
Mon Cnj Sun	Apr 9 1948	13:17	19° Ar 35'
Lunar Eclipse	Apr 23 1948	13:28	03° Sc 17'
Solar Eclipse	May 9 1948	02:30	18° Ta 22'
Mon Cnj Sun	Jun 7 1948	12:55	16° Ge 39'
Mon Cnj Sun	Jul 6 1948	21:09	14° Cn 39'
Mon Cnj Sun	Aug 5 1948	04:13	12° Le 38'
Mon Cnj Sun	Sep 3 1948	11:21	10° Vi 50'
Mon Cnj Sun	Oct 2 1948	19:42	09° Li 30'
Lunar Eclipse	Oct 18 1948	02:23	24° Ar 37'
Solar Eclipse	Nov 1 1948	06:03	08° Sc 43'
Mon Cnj Sun	Nov 30 1948	18:44	08° Sg 29'
Mon Cnj Sun	Dec 30 1948	09:45	08° Cp 37'
Mon Cnj Sun	Jan 29 1949	02:42	08° Aq 52'
Mon Cnj Sun	Feb 27 1949	20:55	08° Pi 57'

Mon Cnj Sun	Mar 29 1949	15:11	08° Ar 36'
Lunar Eclipse	Apr 13 1949	04:08	22° Li 54'
Solar Eclipse	Apr 28 1949	08:02	07° Ta 42'
Mon Cnj Sun	May 27 1949	22:24	06° Ge 16'
Mon Cnj Sun	Jun 26 1949	10:02	04° Cn 27'
Mon Cnj Sun	Jul 25 1949	19:33	02° Le 29'
Mon Cnj Sun	Aug 24 1949	03:59	00° Vi 39'
Mon Cnj Sun	Sep 22 1949	12:21	29° Vi 09'
Lunar Eclipse	Oct 7 1949	02:53	13° Ar 30'
Solar Eclipse	Oct 21 1949	21:23	28° Li 08'
Mon Cnj Sun	Nov 20 1949	07:29	27° Sc 39'
Mon Cnj Sun	Dec 19 1949	18:56	27° Sg 33'
Mon Cnj Sun	Jan 18 1950	08:00	27° Cp 39'
Mon Cnj Sun	Feb 16 1950	22:53	27° Aq 42'
Solar Eclipse	Mar 18 1950	15:20	27° Pi 27'
Lunar Eclipse	Apr 2 1950	20:49	12° Li 32'
Mon Cnj Sun	Apr 17 1950	08:25	26° Ar 45'
Mon Cnj Sun	May 17 1950	00:54	25° Ta 33'
Mon Cnj Sun	Jun 15 1950	15:53	23° Ge 57'
Mon Cnj Sun	Jul 15 1950	05:05	22° Cn 08'
Mon Cnj Sun	Aug 13 1950	16:48	20° Le 21'
Solar Eclipse	Sep 12 1950	03:29	18° Vi 48'
Lunar Eclipse	Sep 26 1950	04:21	02° Ar 30'
Mon Cnj Sun	Oct 11 1950	13:34	17° Li 39'
Mon Cnj Sun	Nov 9 1950	23:25	16° Sc 59'
Mon Cnj Sun	Dec 9 1950	09:29	16° Sg 44'
Mon Cnj Sun	Jan 7 1951	20:10	16° Cp 43'
Mon Cnj Sun	Feb 6 1951	07:54	16° Aq 43'
Lunar Eclipse	Feb 21 1951	21:12	02° Vi 26'
Solar Eclipse	Mar 7 1951	20:51	16° Pi 28'
Lunar Eclipse	Mar 23 1951	10:50	02° Li 00'
Mon Cnj Sun	Apr 6 1951	10:52	15° Ar 50'
Mon Cnj Sun	May 6 1951	01:36	14° Ta 44'
Mon Cnj Sun	Jun 4 1951	16:40	13° Ge 14'
Mon Cnj Sun	Jul 4 1951	07:48	11° Cn 32'
Mon Cnj Sun	Aug 2 1951	22:39	09° Le 48'
Lunar Eclipse	Aug 17 1951	02:59	23° Aq 24'
Solar Eclipse	Sep 1 1951	12:50	08° Vi 16'
Lunar Eclipse	Sep 15 1951	12:38	21° Pi 51'
Mon Cnj Sun	Oct 1 1951	01:57	07° Li 05'
Mon Cnj Sun	Oct 30 1951	13:55	06° Sc 20'
Mon Cnj Sun	Nov 29 1951	01:00	05° Sg 59'
Mon Cnj Sun	Dec 28 1951	11:43	05° Cp 56'
Mon Cnj Sun	Jan 26 1952	22:26	05° Aq 55'

Appendix I • *New Moons + Solar & Lunar Eclipses 1920 to 2120*

Lunar Eclipse	Feb 11 1952	00:28	21° Le 13'
Solar Eclipse	Feb 25 1952	09:16	05° Pi 43'
Mon Cnj Sun	Mar 25 1952	20:13	05° Ar 07'
Mon Cnj Sun	Apr 24 1952	07:27	04° Ta 03'
Mon Cnj Sun	May 23 1952	19:28	02° Ge 34'
Mon Cnj Sun	Jun 22 1952	08:45	00° Cn 51'
Mon Cnj Sun	Jul 21 1952	23:31	29° Cn 06'
Lunar Eclipse	Aug 5 1952	19:40	13° Aq 17'
Solar Eclipse	Aug 20 1952	15:20	27° Le 31'
Mon Cnj Sun	Sep 19 1952	07:22	26° Vi 17'
Mon Cnj Sun	Oct 18 1952	22:42	25° Li 29'
Mon Cnj Sun	Nov 17 1952	12:56	25° Sc 07'
Mon Cnj Sun	Dec 17 1952	02:02	25° Sg 05'
Mon Cnj Sun	Jan 15 1953	14:08	25° Cp 09'
Lunar Eclipse	Jan 29 1953	23:44	09° Le 48'
Solar Eclipse	Feb 14 1953	01:10	25° Aq 03'
Mon Cnj Sun	Mar 15 1953	11:05	24° Pi 34'
Mon Cnj Sun	Apr 13 1953	20:09	23° Ar 35'
Mon Cnj Sun	May 13 1953	05:06	22° Ta 08'
Mon Cnj Sun	Jun 11 1953	14:55	20° Ge 22'
Solar Eclipse	Jul 11 1953	02:28	18° Cn 29'
Lunar Eclipse	Jul 26 1953	12:21	03° Aq 12'
Solar Eclipse	Aug 9 1953	16:10	16° Le 45'
Mon Cnj Sun	Sep 8 1953	07:48	15° Vi 21'
Mon Cnj Sun	Oct 8 1953	00:41	14° Li 26'
Mon Cnj Sun	Nov 6 1953	17:58	14° Sc 02'
Mon Cnj Sun	Dec 6 1953	10:48	14° Sg 02'
Solar Eclipse	Jan 5 1954	02:21	14° Cp 13'
Lunar Eclipse	Jan 19 1954	02:37	28° Cn 29'
Mon Cnj Sun	Feb 3 1954	15:55	14° Aq 17'
Mon Cnj Sun	Mar 5 1954	03:11	14° Pi 00'
Mon Cnj Sun	Apr 3 1954	12:25	13° Ar 12'
Mon Cnj Sun	May 2 1954	20:22	11° Ta 52'
Mon Cnj Sun	Jun 1 1954	04:03	10° Ge 07'
Solar Eclipse	Jun 30 1954	12:26	08° Cn 10'
Lunar Eclipse	Jul 16 1954	00:29	22° Cp 57'
Mon Cnj Sun	Jul 29 1954	22:20	06° Le 14'
Mon Cnj Sun	Aug 28 1954	10:21	04° Vi 34'
Mon Cnj Sun	Sep 27 1954	00:50	03° Li 23'
Mon Cnj Sun	Oct 26 1954	17:47	02° Sc 46'
Mon Cnj Sun	Nov 25 1954	12:30	02° Sg 42'
Solar Eclipse	Dec 25 1954	07:33	02° Cp 58'
Lunar Eclipse	Jan 8 1955	12:44	17° Cn 28'
Mon Cnj Sun	Jan 24 1955	01:07	03° Aq 16'

Mon Cnj Sun	Feb 22 1955	15:54	03° Pi 15'
Mon Cnj Sun	Mar 24 1955	03:42	02° Ar 44'
Mon Cnj Sun	Apr 22 1955	13:06	01° Ta 37'
Mon Cnj Sun	May 21 1955	20:59	00° Ge 01'
Lunar Eclipse	Jun 5 1955	14:08	14° Sg 08'
Solar Eclipse	Jun 20 1955	04:12	28° Ge 04'
Mon Cnj Sun	Jul 19 1955	11:35	26° Cn 01'
Mon Cnj Sun	Aug 17 1955	19:58	24° Le 07'
Mon Cnj Sun	Sep 16 1955	06:19	22° Vi 36'
Mon Cnj Sun	Oct 15 1955	19:32	21° Li 40'
Mon Cnj Sun	Nov 14 1955	12:02	21° Sc 20'
Lunar Eclipse	Nov 29 1955	16:50	06° Ge 41'
Solar Eclipse	Dec 14 1955	07:07	21° Sg 30'
Mon Cnj Sun	Jan 13 1956	03:01	21° Cp 54'
Mon Cnj Sun	Feb 11 1956	21:38	22° Aq 09'
Mon Cnj Sun	Mar 12 1956	13:37	21° Pi 57'
Mon Cnj Sun	Apr 11 1956	02:39	21° Ar 11'
Mon Cnj Sun	May 10 1956	13:04	19° Ta 50'
Lunar Eclipse	May 24 1956	15:26	03° Sg 24'
Solar Eclipse	Jun 8 1956	21:29	18° Ge 01'
Mon Cnj Sun	Jul 8 1956	04:38	15° Cn 58'
Mon Cnj Sun	Aug 6 1956	11:25	13° Le 57'
Mon Cnj Sun	Sep 4 1956	18:57	12° Vi 11'
Mon Cnj Sun	Oct 4 1956	04:25	10° Li 55'
Mon Cnj Sun	Nov 2 1956	16:44	10° Sc 14'
Lunar Eclipse	Nov 18 1956	06:45	25° Ta 54'
Solar Eclipse	Dec 2 1956	08:13	10° Sg 08'
Mon Cnj Sun	Jan 1 1957	02:14	10° Cp 24'
Mon Cnj Sun	Jan 30 1957	21:25	10° Aq 45'
Mon Cnj Sun	Mar 1 1957	16:12	10° Pi 49'
Mon Cnj Sun	Mar 31 1957	09:19	10° Ar 23'
Solar Eclipse	Apr 29 1957	23:54	09° Ta 22'
Lunar Eclipse	May 13 1957	22:34	22° Sc 52'
Mon Cnj Sun	May 29 1957	11:39	07° Ge 49'
Mon Cnj Sun	Jun 27 1957	20:53	05° Cn 54'
Mon Cnj Sun	Jul 27 1957	04:28	03° Le 52'
Mon Cnj Sun	Aug 25 1957	11:33	01° Vi 59'
Mon Cnj Sun	Sep 23 1957	19:18	00° Li 29'
Solar Eclipse	Oct 23 1957	04:43	29° Li 30'
Lunar Eclipse	Nov 7 1957	14:32	14° Ta 55'
Mon Cnj Sun	Nov 21 1957	16:19	29° Sc 06'
Mon Cnj Sun	Dec 21 1957	06:12	29° Sg 07'
Mon Cnj Sun	Jan 19 1958	22:08	29° Cp 20'
Mon Cnj Sun	Feb 18 1958	15:38	29° Aq 29'

Appendix I • *New Moons + Solar & Lunar Eclipses 1920 to 2120*

Mon Cnj Sun	Mar 20 1958	09:50	29° Pi 17'
Lunar Eclipse	Apr 4 1958	03:45	13° Li 52'
Solar Eclipse	Apr 19 1958	03:23	28° Ar 34'
Lunar Eclipse	May 3 1958	12:23	12° Sc 33'
Mon Cnj Sun	May 18 1958	19:00	27° Ta 19'
Mon Cnj Sun	Jun 17 1958	07:59	25° Ge 37'
Mon Cnj Sun	Jul 16 1958	18:33	23° Cn 42'
Mon Cnj Sun	Aug 15 1958	03:33	21° Le 48'
Mon Cnj Sun	Sep 13 1958	12:02	20° Vi 11'
Solar Eclipse	Oct 12 1958	20:52	19° Li 01'
Lunar Eclipse	Oct 27 1958	15:41	03° Ta 43'
Mon Cnj Sun	Nov 11 1958	06:34	18° Sc 21'
Mon Cnj Sun	Dec 10 1958	17:23	18° Sg 09'
Mon Cnj Sun	Jan 9 1959	05:34	18° Cp 12'
Mon Cnj Sun	Feb 7 1959	19:22	18° Aq 16'
Mon Cnj Sun	Mar 9 1959	10:51	18° Pi 07'
Lunar Eclipse	Mar 24 1959	20:02	03° Li 26'
Solar Eclipse	Apr 8 1959	03:29	17° Ar 33'
Mon Cnj Sun	May 7 1959	20:11	16° Ta 30'
Mon Cnj Sun	Jun 6 1959	11:53	15° Ge 02'
Mon Cnj Sun	Jul 6 1959	02:00	13° Cn 16'
Mon Cnj Sun	Aug 4 1959	14:34	11° Le 27'
Mon Cnj Sun	Sep 3 1959	01:56	09° Vi 49'
Lunar Eclipse	Sep 17 1959	00:52	23° Pi 23'
Solar Eclipse	Oct 2 1959	12:31	08° Li 33'
Mon Cnj Sun	Oct 31 1959	22:41	07° Sc 45'
Mon Cnj Sun	Nov 30 1959	08:46	07° Sg 23'
Mon Cnj Sun	Dec 29 1959	19:09	07° Cp 19'
Mon Cnj Sun	Jan 28 1960	06:15	07° Aq 20'
Mon Cnj Sun	Feb 26 1960	18:23	07° Pi 10'
Lunar Eclipse	Mar 13 1960	08:26	22° Vi 46'
Solar Eclipse	Mar 27 1960	07:37	06° Ar 38'
Mon Cnj Sun	Apr 25 1960	21:44	05° Ta 40'
Mon Cnj Sun	May 25 1960	12:26	04° Ge 16'
Mon Cnj Sun	Jun 24 1960	03:27	02° Cn 36'
Mon Cnj Sun	Jul 23 1960	18:31	00° Le 52'
Mon Cnj Sun	Aug 22 1960	09:15	29° Le 15'
Lunar Eclipse	Sep 5 1960	11:19	12° Pi 52'
Solar Eclipse	Sep 20 1960	23:12	27° Vi 58'
Mon Cnj Sun	Oct 20 1960	12:02	27° Li 05'
Mon Cnj Sun	Nov 18 1960	23:46	26° Sc 39'
Mon Cnj Sun	Dec 18 1960	10:47	26° Sg 32'
Mon Cnj Sun	Jan 16 1961	21:30	26° Cp 32'
Solar Eclipse	Feb 15 1961	08:10	26° Aq 25'

Lunar Eclipse	Mar 2 1961	13:35	11° Vi 44'
Mon Cnj Sun	Mar 16 1961	18:51	25° Pi 57'
Mon Cnj Sun	Apr 15 1961	05:37	25° Ar 01'
Mon Cnj Sun	May 14 1961	16:54	23° Ta 38'
Mon Cnj Sun	Jun 13 1961	05:16	21° Ge 57'
Mon Cnj Sun	Jul 12 1961	19:11	20° Cn 10'
Solar Eclipse	Aug 11 1961	10:36	18° Le 30'
Lunar Eclipse	Aug 26 1961	03:13	02° Pi 38'
Mon Cnj Sun	Sep 10 1961	02:50	17° Vi 09'
Mon Cnj Sun	Oct 9 1961	18:52	16° Li 14'
Mon Cnj Sun	Nov 8 1961	09:58	15° Sc 45'
Mon Cnj Sun	Dec 7 1961	23:52	15° Sg 39'
Mon Cnj Sun	Jan 6 1962	12:35	15° Cp 43'
Solar Eclipse	Feb 5 1962	00:10	15° Aq 42'
Lunar Eclipse	Feb 19 1962	13:18	00° Vi 25'
Mon Cnj Sun	Mar 6 1962	10:31	15° Pi 22'
Mon Cnj Sun	Apr 4 1962	19:45	14° Ar 33'
Mon Cnj Sun	May 4 1962	04:25	13° Ta 14'
Mon Cnj Sun	Jun 2 1962	13:27	11° Ge 31'
Mon Cnj Sun	Jul 1 1962	23:52	09° Cn 38'
Lunar Eclipse	Jul 17 1962	11:41	24° Cp 24'
Solar Eclipse	Jul 31 1962	12:24	07° Le 48'
Lunar Eclipse	Aug 15 1962	20:09	22° Aq 30'
Mon Cnj Sun	Aug 30 1962	03:09	06° Vi 16'
Mon Cnj Sun	Sep 28 1962	19:39	05° Li 11'
Mon Cnj Sun	Oct 28 1962	13:05	04° Sc 37'
Mon Cnj Sun	Nov 27 1962	06:29	04° Sg 31'
Mon Cnj Sun	Dec 26 1962	22:59	04° Cp 42'
Lunar Eclipse	Jan 9 1963	23:08	18° Cn 58'
Solar Eclipse	Jan 25 1963	13:42	04° Aq 52'
Mon Cnj Sun	Feb 24 1963	02:06	04° Pi 44'
Mon Cnj Sun	Mar 25 1963	12:10	04° Ar 07'
Mon Cnj Sun	Apr 23 1963	20:29	02° Ta 57'
Mon Cnj Sun	May 23 1963	04:00	01° Ge 19'
Mon Cnj Sun	Jun 21 1963	11:46	29° Ge 23'
Lunar Eclipse	Jul 6 1963	21:55	14° Cp 05'
Solar Eclipse	Jul 20 1963	20:43	27° Cn 24'
Mon Cnj Sun	Aug 19 1963	07:35	25° Le 36'
Mon Cnj Sun	Sep 17 1963	20:51	24° Vi 14'
Mon Cnj Sun	Oct 17 1963	12:43	23° Li 25'
Mon Cnj Sun	Nov 16 1963	06:50	23° Sc 11'
Mon Cnj Sun	Dec 16 1963	02:06	23° Sg 23'
Lunar Eclipse	Dec 30 1963	11:04	08° Cn 01'
Solar Eclipse	Jan 14 1964	20:43	23° Cp 43'

Appendix I • *New Moons + Solar & Lunar Eclipses 1920 to 2120*

Mon Cnj Sun	Feb 13 1964	13:01	23° Aq 51'
Mon Cnj Sun	Mar 14 1964	02:14	23° Pi 32'
Mon Cnj Sun	Apr 12 1964	12:37	22° Ar 37'
Mon Cnj Sun	May 11 1964	21:02	21° Ta 10'
Solar Eclipse	Jun 10 1964	04:22	19° Ge 18'
Lunar Eclipse	Jun 25 1964	01:08	03° Cp 30'
Solar Eclipse	Jul 9 1964	11:31	17° Cn 15'
Mon Cnj Sun	Aug 7 1964	19:17	15° Le 16'
Mon Cnj Sun	Sep 6 1964	04:34	13° Vi 36'
Mon Cnj Sun	Oct 5 1964	16:20	12° Li 26'
Mon Cnj Sun	Nov 4 1964	07:16	11° Sc 54'
Solar Eclipse	Dec 4 1964	01:18	11° Sg 55'
Lunar Eclipse	Dec 19 1964	02:41	27° Ge 14'
Mon Cnj Sun	Jan 2 1965	21:07	12° Cp 17'
Mon Cnj Sun	Feb 1 1965	16:36	12° Aq 37'
Mon Cnj Sun	Mar 3 1965	09:56	12° Pi 37'
Mon Cnj Sun	Apr 2 1965	00:21	12° Ar 03'
Mon Cnj Sun	May 1 1965	11:56	10° Ta 53'
Solar Eclipse	May 30 1965	21:13	09° Ge 13'
Lunar Eclipse	Jun 14 1965	01:59	22° Sg 48'
Mon Cnj Sun	Jun 29 1965	04:52	07° Cn 13'
Mon Cnj Sun	Jul 28 1965	11:45	05° Le 10'
Mon Cnj Sun	Aug 26 1965	18:51	03° Vi 18'
Mon Cnj Sun	Sep 25 1965	03:18	01° Li 50'
Mon Cnj Sun	Oct 24 1965	14:11	00° Sc 57'
Solar Eclipse	Nov 23 1965	04:10	00° Sg 39'
Lunar Eclipse	Dec 8 1965	17:21	16° Ge 25'
Mon Cnj Sun	Dec 22 1965	21:03	00° Cp 49'
Mon Cnj Sun	Jan 21 1966	15:46	01° Aq 09'
Mon Cnj Sun	Feb 20 1966	10:49	01° Pi 21'
Mon Cnj Sun	Mar 22 1966	04:46	01° Ar 06'
Mon Cnj Sun	Apr 20 1966	20:35	00° Ta 18'
Lunar Eclipse	May 4 1966	21:00	13° Sc 55'
Solar Eclipse	May 20 1966	09:42	28° Ta 55'
Mon Cnj Sun	Jun 18 1966	21:09	27° Ge 07'
Mon Cnj Sun	Jul 18 1966	04:30	25° Cn 06'
Mon Cnj Sun	Aug 16 1966	11:48	23° Le 09'
Mon Cnj Sun	Sep 14 1966	19:13	21° Vi 30'
Mon Cnj Sun	Oct 14 1966	03:52	20° Li 21'
Lunar Eclipse	Oct 29 1966	10:00	05° Ta 31'
Solar Eclipse	Nov 12 1966	14:26	19° Sc 45'
Mon Cnj Sun	Dec 12 1966	03:13	19° Sg 38'
Mon Cnj Sun	Jan 10 1967	18:06	19° Cp 48'
Mon Cnj Sun	Feb 9 1967	10:44	19° Aq 59'

Mon Cnj Sun	Mar 11 1967	04:30	19° Pi 54'
Mon Cnj Sun	Apr 9 1967	22:20	19° Ar 22'
Lunar Eclipse	Apr 24 1967	12:03	03° Sc 37'
Solar Eclipse	May 9 1967	14:55	18° Ta 17'
Mon Cnj Sun	Jun 8 1967	05:13	16° Ge 44'
Mon Cnj Sun	Jul 7 1967	17:00	14° Cn 53'
Mon Cnj Sun	Aug 6 1967	02:48	12° Le 58'
Mon Cnj Sun	Sep 4 1967	11:37	11° Vi 15'
Mon Cnj Sun	Oct 3 1967	20:24	09° Li 55'
Lunar Eclipse	Oct 18 1967	10:11	24° Ar 20'
Solar Eclipse	Nov 2 1967	05:48	09° Sc 06'
Mon Cnj Sun	Dec 1 1967	16:10	08° Sg 46'
Mon Cnj Sun	Dec 31 1967	03:38	08° Cp 45'
Mon Cnj Sun	Jan 29 1968	16:29	08° Aq 50'
Mon Cnj Sun	Feb 28 1968	06:56	08° Pi 45'
Solar Eclipse	Mar 28 1968	22:48	08° Ar 19'
Lunar Eclipse	Apr 13 1968	04:52	23° Li 19'
Mon Cnj Sun	Apr 27 1968	15:21	07° Ta 24'
Mon Cnj Sun	May 27 1968	07:30	06° Ge 03'
Mon Cnj Sun	Jun 25 1968	22:24	04° Cn 22'
Mon Cnj Sun	Jul 25 1968	11:49	02° Le 34'
Mon Cnj Sun	Aug 23 1968	23:57	00° Vi 52'
Solar Eclipse	Sep 22 1968	11:08	29° Vi 29'
Lunar Eclipse	Oct 6 1968	11:46	13° Ar 16'
Mon Cnj Sun	Oct 21 1968	21:44	28° Li 33'
Mon Cnj Sun	Nov 20 1968	08:02	28° Sc 04'
Mon Cnj Sun	Dec 19 1968	18:19	27° Sg 55'
Mon Cnj Sun	Jan 18 1969	04:59	27° Cp 56'
Mon Cnj Sun	Feb 16 1969	16:25	27° Aq 50'
Solar Eclipse	Mar 18 1969	04:51	27° Pi 25'
Lunar Eclipse	Apr 2 1969	18:45	12° Li 50'
Mon Cnj Sun	Apr 16 1969	18:16	26° Ar 34'
Mon Cnj Sun	May 16 1969	08:26	25° Ta 17'
Mon Cnj Sun	Jun 14 1969	23:09	23° Ge 40'
Mon Cnj Sun	Jul 14 1969	14:11	21° Cn 56'
Mon Cnj Sun	Aug 13 1969	05:16	20° Le 16'
Lunar Eclipse	Aug 27 1969	10:32	03° Pi 58'
Solar Eclipse	Sep 11 1969	19:56	18° Vi 53'
Lunar Eclipse	Sep 25 1969	20:21	02° Ar 34'
Mon Cnj Sun	Oct 11 1969	09:39	17° Li 53'
Mon Cnj Sun	Nov 9 1969	22:11	17° Sc 20'
Mon Cnj Sun	Dec 9 1969	09:42	17° Sg 09'
Mon Cnj Sun	Jan 7 1970	20:35	17° Cp 08'
Mon Cnj Sun	Feb 6 1970	07:13	17° Aq 05'

Appendix I • *New Moons + Solar & Lunar Eclipses 1920 to 2120*

Lunar Eclipse	Feb 21 1970	08:19	02° Vi 17'
Solar Eclipse	Mar 7 1970	17:42	16° Pi 44'
Mon Cnj Sun	Apr 6 1970	04:09	15° Ar 56'
Mon Cnj Sun	May 5 1970	14:51	14° Ta 41'
Mon Cnj Sun	Jun 4 1970	02:21	13° Ge 03'
Mon Cnj Sun	Jul 3 1970	15:18	11° Cn 16'
Mon Cnj Sun	Aug 2 1970	05:58	09° Le 32'
Lunar Eclipse	Aug 17 1970	03:15	23° Aq 48'
Solar Eclipse	Aug 31 1970	22:01	08° Vi 04'
Mon Cnj Sun	Sep 30 1970	14:32	07° Li 00'
Mon Cnj Sun	Oct 30 1970	06:28	06° Sc 25'
Mon Cnj Sun	Nov 28 1970	21:14	06° Sg 14'
Mon Cnj Sun	Dec 28 1970	10:43	06° Cp 17'
Mon Cnj Sun	Jan 26 1971	22:55	06° Aq 20'
Lunar Eclipse	Feb 10 1971	07:41	20° Le 55'
Solar Eclipse	Feb 25 1971	09:49	06° Pi 08'
Mon Cnj Sun	Mar 26 1971	19:23	05° Ar 29'
Mon Cnj Sun	Apr 25 1971	04:02	04° Ta 18'
Mon Cnj Sun	May 24 1971	12:32	02° Ge 41'
Mon Cnj Sun	Jun 22 1971	21:57	00° Cn 49'
Solar Eclipse	Jul 22 1971	09:15	28° Cn 55'
Lunar Eclipse	Aug 6 1971	19:42	13° Aq 41'
Solar Eclipse	Aug 20 1971	22:53	27° Le 15'
Mon Cnj Sun	Sep 19 1971	14:42	26° Vi 00'
Mon Cnj Sun	Oct 19 1971	07:59	25° Li 16'
Mon Cnj Sun	Nov 18 1971	01:46	25° Sc 03'
Mon Cnj Sun	Dec 17 1971	19:03	25° Sg 11'
Solar Eclipse	Jan 16 1972	10:52	25° Cp 24'
Lunar Eclipse	Jan 30 1972	10:58	09° Le 39'
Mon Cnj Sun	Feb 15 1972	00:29	25° Aq 25'
Mon Cnj Sun	Mar 15 1972	11:35	24° Pi 59'
Mon Cnj Sun	Apr 13 1972	20:31	24° Ar 00'
Mon Cnj Sun	May 13 1972	04:08	22° Ta 29'
Mon Cnj Sun	Jun 11 1972	11:30	20° Ge 37'
Solar Eclipse	Jul 10 1972	19:39	18° Cn 36'
Lunar Eclipse	Jul 26 1972	07:24	03° Aq 23'
Mon Cnj Sun	Aug 9 1972	05:26	16° Le 43'
Mon Cnj Sun	Sep 7 1972	17:28	15° Vi 10'
Mon Cnj Sun	Oct 7 1972	08:08	14° Li 09'
Mon Cnj Sun	Nov 6 1972	01:21	13° Sc 43'
Mon Cnj Sun	Dec 5 1972	20:24	13° Sg 49'
Solar Eclipse	Jan 4 1973	15:42	14° Cp 09'
Lunar Eclipse	Jan 18 1973	21:28	28° Cn 40'
Mon Cnj Sun	Feb 3 1973	09:23	14° Aq 25'

Mon Cnj Sun	Mar 5 1973	00:07	14° Pi 17'
Mon Cnj Sun	Apr 3 1973	11:45	13° Ar 35'
Mon Cnj Sun	May 2 1973	20:55	12° Ta 17'
Mon Cnj Sun	Jun 1 1973	04:34	10° Ge 32'
Lunar Eclipse	Jun 15 1973	20:35	24° Sg 34'
Solar Eclipse	Jun 30 1973	11:39	08° Cn 31'
Lunar Eclipse	Jul 15 1973	11:56	22° Cp 50'
Mon Cnj Sun	Jul 29 1973	18:59	06° Le 29'
Mon Cnj Sun	Aug 28 1973	03:25	04° Vi 41'
Mon Cnj Sun	Sep 26 1973	13:54	03° Li 19'
Mon Cnj Sun	Oct 26 1973	03:17	02° Sc 33'
Mon Cnj Sun	Nov 24 1973	19:55	02° Sg 24'
Lunar Eclipse	Dec 10 1973	01:35	17° Ge 51'
Solar Eclipse	Dec 24 1973	15:07	02° Cp 40'
Mon Cnj Sun	Jan 23 1974	11:02	03° Aq 03'
Mon Cnj Sun	Feb 22 1974	05:34	03° Pi 13'
Mon Cnj Sun	Mar 23 1974	21:24	02° Ar 51'
Mon Cnj Sun	Apr 22 1974	10:16	01° Ta 54'
Mon Cnj Sun	May 21 1974	20:34	00° Ge 23'
Lunar Eclipse	Jun 4 1974	22:10	13° Sg 53'
Solar Eclipse	Jun 20 1974	04:56	28° Ge 30'
Mon Cnj Sun	Jul 19 1974	12:07	26° Cn 26'
Mon Cnj Sun	Aug 17 1974	19:02	24° Le 29'
Mon Cnj Sun	Sep 16 1974	02:45	22° Vi 51'
Mon Cnj Sun	Oct 15 1974	12:25	21° Li 46'
Mon Cnj Sun	Nov 14 1974	00:53	21° Sc 16'
Lunar Eclipse	Nov 29 1974	15:10	07° Ge 01'
Solar Eclipse	Dec 13 1974	16:25	21° Sg 16'
Mon Cnj Sun	Jan 12 1975	10:20	21° Cp 35'
Mon Cnj Sun	Feb 11 1975	05:17	21° Aq 51'
Mon Cnj Sun	Mar 12 1975	23:47	21° Pi 46'
Mon Cnj Sun	Apr 11 1975	16:39	21° Ar 10'
Solar Eclipse	May 11 1975	07:05	19° Ta 59'
Lunar Eclipse	May 25 1975	05:51	03° Sg 25'
Mon Cnj Sun	Jun 9 1975	18:49	18° Ge 18'
Mon Cnj Sun	Jul 9 1975	04:10	16° Cn 21'
Mon Cnj Sun	Aug 7 1975	11:57	14° Le 22'
Mon Cnj Sun	Sep 5 1975	19:19	12° Vi 36'
Mon Cnj Sun	Oct 5 1975	03:23	11° Li 16'
Solar Eclipse	Nov 3 1975	13:05	10° Sc 29'
Lunar Eclipse	Nov 18 1975	22:28	25° Ta 57'
Mon Cnj Sun	Dec 3 1975	00:50	10° Sg 13'
Mon Cnj Sun	Jan 1 1976	14:40	10° Cp 18'
Mon Cnj Sun	Jan 31 1976	06:20	10° Aq 30'

Appendix I • *New Moons + Solar & Lunar Eclipses 1920 to 2120*

Mon Cnj Sun	Feb 29 1976	23:25	10° Pi 30'
Mon Cnj Sun	Mar 30 1976	17:08	10° Ar 07'
Solar Eclipse	Apr 29 1976	10:19	09° Ta 13'
Lunar Eclipse	May 13 1976	20:04	23° Sc 10'
Mon Cnj Sun	May 29 1976	01:47	07° Ge 49'
Mon Cnj Sun	Jun 27 1976	14:50	06° Cn 03'
Mon Cnj Sun	Jul 27 1976	01:39	04° Le 09'
Mon Cnj Sun	Aug 25 1976	11:01	02° Vi 21'
Mon Cnj Sun	Sep 23 1976	19:55	00° Li 54'
Solar Eclipse	Oct 23 1976	05:10	29° Li 55'
Lunar Eclipse	Nov 6 1976	23:15	14° Ta 40'
Mon Cnj Sun	Nov 21 1976	15:11	29° Sc 26'
Mon Cnj Sun	Dec 21 1976	02:08	29° Sg 20'
Mon Cnj Sun	Jan 19 1977	14:11	29° Cp 24'
Mon Cnj Sun	Feb 18 1977	03:37	29° Aq 22'
Mon Cnj Sun	Mar 19 1977	18:33	29° Pi 02'
Lunar Eclipse	Apr 4 1977	04:09	14° Li 16'
Solar Eclipse	Apr 18 1977	10:35	28° Ar 16'
Mon Cnj Sun	May 18 1977	02:51	27° Ta 03'
Mon Cnj Sun	Jun 16 1977	18:23	25° Ge 28'
Mon Cnj Sun	Jul 16 1977	08:36	23° Cn 41'
Mon Cnj Sun	Aug 14 1977	21:31	21° Le 57'
Mon Cnj Sun	Sep 13 1977	09:23	20° Vi 28'
Lunar Eclipse	Sep 27 1977	08:17	04° Ar 06'
Solar Eclipse	Oct 12 1977	20:31	19° Li 24'
Mon Cnj Sun	Nov 11 1977	07:09	18° Sc 47'
Mon Cnj Sun	Dec 10 1977	17:33	18° Sg 33'
Mon Cnj Sun	Jan 9 1978	04:00	18° Cp 32'
Mon Cnj Sun	Feb 7 1978	14:54	18° Aq 28'
Mon Cnj Sun	Mar 9 1978	02:36	18° Pi 10'
Lunar Eclipse	Mar 24 1978	16:20	03° Li 40'
Solar Eclipse	Apr 7 1978	15:15	17° Ar 26'
Mon Cnj Sun	May 7 1978	04:47	16° Ta 16'
Mon Cnj Sun	Jun 5 1978	19:02	14° Ge 44'
Mon Cnj Sun	Jul 5 1978	09:50	13° Cn 01'
Mon Cnj Sun	Aug 4 1978	01:01	11° Le 18'
Mon Cnj Sun	Sep 2 1978	16:09	09° Vi 49'
Lunar Eclipse	Sep 16 1978	19:01	23° Pi 33'
Solar Eclipse	Oct 2 1978	06:41	08° Li 43'
Mon Cnj Sun	Oct 31 1978	20:07	08° Sc 02'
Mon Cnj Sun	Nov 30 1978	08:19	07° Sg 46'
Mon Cnj Sun	Dec 29 1978	19:36	07° Cp 44'
Mon Cnj Sun	Jan 28 1979	06:20	07° Aq 43'
Solar Eclipse	Feb 26 1979	16:45	07° Pi 29'

Lunar Eclipse	Mar 13 1979	21:14	22° Vi 41'
Mon Cnj Sun	Mar 28 1979	02:59	06° Ar 50'
Mon Cnj Sun	Apr 26 1979	13:15	05° Ta 42'
Mon Cnj Sun	May 26 1979	00:00	04° Ge 10'
Mon Cnj Sun	Jun 24 1979	11:58	02° Cn 23'
Mon Cnj Sun	Jul 24 1979	01:41	00° Le 35'
Solar Eclipse	Aug 22 1979	17:10	29° Le 00'
Lunar Eclipse	Sep 6 1979	10:59	13° Pi 15'
Mon Cnj Sun	Sep 21 1979	09:47	27° Vi 49'
Mon Cnj Sun	Oct 21 1979	02:23	27° Li 05'
Mon Cnj Sun	Nov 19 1979	18:04	26° Sc 48'
Mon Cnj Sun	Dec 19 1979	08:23	26° Sg 49'
Mon Cnj Sun	Jan 17 1980	21:19	26° Cp 55'
Solar Eclipse	Feb 16 1980	08:51	26° Aq 50'
Lunar Eclipse	Mar 1 1980	21:00	11° Vi 26'
Mon Cnj Sun	Mar 16 1980	18:56	26° Pi 20'
Mon Cnj Sun	Apr 15 1980	03:46	25° Ar 19'
Mon Cnj Sun	May 14 1980	12:00	23° Ta 49'
Mon Cnj Sun	Jun 12 1980	20:38	21° Ge 59'
Mon Cnj Sun	Jul 12 1980	06:46	20° Cn 03'
Lunar Eclipse	Jul 27 1980	18:54	04° Aq 51'
Solar Eclipse	Aug 10 1980	19:09	18° Le 16'
Lunar Eclipse	Aug 26 1980	03:42	03° Pi 03'
Mon Cnj Sun	Sep 9 1980	10:00	16° Vi 52'
Mon Cnj Sun	Oct 9 1980	02:50	15° Li 58'
Mon Cnj Sun	Nov 7 1980	20:43	15° Sc 36'
Mon Cnj Sun	Dec 7 1980	14:35	15° Sg 39'
Mon Cnj Sun	Jan 6 1981	07:24	15° Cp 54'
Lunar Eclipse	Jan 20 1981	07:39	00° Le 10'
Solar Eclipse	Feb 4 1981	22:14	16° Aq 01'
Mon Cnj Sun	Mar 6 1981	10:31	15° Pi 46'
Mon Cnj Sun	Apr 4 1981	20:19	14° Ar 58'
Mon Cnj Sun	May 4 1981	04:19	13° Ta 36'
Mon Cnj Sun	Jun 2 1981	11:32	11° Ge 49'
Mon Cnj Sun	Jul 1 1981	19:03	09° Cn 49'
Lunar Eclipse	Jul 17 1981	04:39	24° Cp 30'
Solar Eclipse	Jul 31 1981	03:52	07° Le 51'
Mon Cnj Sun	Aug 29 1981	14:43	06° Vi 09'
Mon Cnj Sun	Sep 28 1981	04:07	04° Li 56'
Mon Cnj Sun	Oct 27 1981	20:13	04° Sc 19'
Mon Cnj Sun	Nov 26 1981	14:38	04° Sg 15'
Mon Cnj Sun	Dec 26 1981	10:10	04° Cp 33'
Lunar Eclipse	Jan 9 1982	19:53	19° Cn 14'
Solar Eclipse	Jan 25 1982	04:56	04° Aq 53'

Appendix I • *New Moons + Solar & Lunar Eclipses 1920 to 2120*

Mon Cnj Sun	Feb 23 1982	21:13	04° Pi 55'
Mon Cnj Sun	Mar 25 1982	10:17	04° Ar 26'
Mon Cnj Sun	Apr 23 1982	20:29	03° Ta 20'
Mon Cnj Sun	May 23 1982	04:40	01° Ge 44'
Solar Eclipse	Jun 21 1982	11:52	29° Ge 46'
Lunar Eclipse	Jul 6 1982	07:32	13° Cp 54'
Solar Eclipse	Jul 20 1982	18:57	27° Cn 43'
Mon Cnj Sun	Aug 19 1982	02:45	25° Le 48'
Mon Cnj Sun	Sep 17 1982	12:09	24° Vi 16'
Mon Cnj Sun	Oct 17 1982	00:04	23° Li 17'
Mon Cnj Sun	Nov 15 1982	15:10	22° Sc 55'
Solar Eclipse	Dec 15 1982	09:18	23° Sg 04'
Lunar Eclipse	Dec 30 1982	11:33	08° Cn 26'
Mon Cnj Sun	Jan 14 1983	05:08	23° Cp 27'
Mon Cnj Sun	Feb 13 1983	00:32	23° Aq 43'
Mon Cnj Sun	Mar 14 1983	17:43	23° Pi 34'
Mon Cnj Sun	Apr 13 1983	07:58	22° Ar 49'
Mon Cnj Sun	May 12 1983	19:25	21° Ta 29'
Solar Eclipse	Jun 11 1983	04:38	19° Ge 42'
Lunar Eclipse	Jun 25 1983	08:32	03° Cp 14'
Mon Cnj Sun	Jul 10 1983	12:19	17° Cn 41'
Mon Cnj Sun	Aug 8 1983	19:18	15° Le 40'
Mon Cnj Sun	Sep 7 1983	02:35	13° Vi 55'
Mon Cnj Sun	Oct 6 1983	11:16	12° Li 37'
Mon Cnj Sun	Nov 4 1983	22:21	11° Sc 55'
Solar Eclipse	Dec 4 1983	12:26	11° Sg 46'
Lunar Eclipse	Dec 20 1983	02:00	27° Ge 36'
Mon Cnj Sun	Jan 3 1984	05:16	12° Cp 00'
Mon Cnj Sun	Feb 1 1984	23:46	12° Aq 18'
Mon Cnj Sun	Mar 2 1984	18:31	12° Pi 22'
Mon Cnj Sun	Apr 1 1984	12:10	11° Ar 57'
Mon Cnj Sun	May 1 1984	03:45	10° Ta 57'
Lunar Eclipse	May 15 1984	04:29	24° Sc 31'
Solar Eclipse	May 30 1984	16:48	09° Ge 26'
Lunar Eclipse	Jun 13 1984	14:42	22° Sg 44'
Mon Cnj Sun	Jun 29 1984	03:18	07° Cn 33'
Mon Cnj Sun	Jul 28 1984	11:51	05° Le 34'
Mon Cnj Sun	Aug 26 1984	19:26	03° Vi 42'
Mon Cnj Sun	Sep 25 1984	03:11	02° Li 13'
Mon Cnj Sun	Oct 24 1984	12:08	01° Sc 15'
Lunar Eclipse	Nov 8 1984	17:43	16° Ta 30'
Solar Eclipse	Nov 22 1984	22:57	00° Sg 49'
Mon Cnj Sun	Dec 22 1984	11:47	00° Cp 49'
Mon Cnj Sun	Jan 21 1985	02:28	00° Aq 59'

Mon Cnj Sun	Feb 19 1985	18:43	01° Pi 04'
Mon Cnj Sun	Mar 21 1985	11:59	00° Ar 49'
Mon Cnj Sun	Apr 20 1985	05:22	00° Ta 04'
Lunar Eclipse	May 4 1985	19:53	14° Sc 16'
Solar Eclipse	May 19 1985	21:41	28° Ta 50'
Mon Cnj Sun	Jun 18 1985	11:58	27° Ge 11'
Mon Cnj Sun	Jul 17 1985	23:56	25° Cn 19'
Mon Cnj Sun	Aug 16 1985	10:06	23° Le 28'
Mon Cnj Sun	Sep 14 1985	19:20	21° Vi 54'
Mon Cnj Sun	Oct 14 1985	04:33	20° Li 46'
Lunar Eclipse	Oct 28 1985	17:38	05° Ta 14'
Solar Eclipse	Nov 12 1985	14:20	20° Sc 08'
Mon Cnj Sun	Dec 12 1985	00:54	19° Sg 56'
Mon Cnj Sun	Jan 10 1986	12:22	19° Cp 57'
Mon Cnj Sun	Feb 9 1986	00:55	19° Aq 58'
Mon Cnj Sun	Mar 10 1986	14:52	19° Pi 44'
Solar Eclipse	Apr 9 1986	06:08	19° Ar 06'
Lunar Eclipse	Apr 24 1986	12:46	04° Sc 02'
Mon Cnj Sun	May 8 1986	22:10	18° Ta 00'
Mon Cnj Sun	Jun 7 1986	14:00	16° Ge 31'
Mon Cnj Sun	Jul 7 1986	04:55	14° Cn 47'
Mon Cnj Sun	Aug 5 1986	18:36	13° Le 02'
Mon Cnj Sun	Sep 4 1986	07:10	11° Vi 28'
Solar Eclipse	Oct 3 1986	18:55	10° Li 15'
Lunar Eclipse	Oct 17 1986	19:22	24° Ar 07'
Mon Cnj Sun	Nov 2 1986	06:02	09° Sc 31'
Mon Cnj Sun	Dec 1 1986	16:43	09° Sg 11'
Mon Cnj Sun	Dec 31 1986	03:10	09° Cp 08'
Mon Cnj Sun	Jan 29 1987	13:45	09° Aq 06'
Mon Cnj Sun	Feb 28 1987	00:51	08° Pi 53'
Solar Eclipse	Mar 29 1987	12:46	08° Ar 17'
Lunar Eclipse	Apr 14 1987	02:31	23° Li 37'
Mon Cnj Sun	Apr 28 1987	01:34	07° Ta 15'
Mon Cnj Sun	May 27 1987	15:13	05° Ge 48'
Mon Cnj Sun	Jun 26 1987	05:37	04° Cn 06'
Mon Cnj Sun	Jul 25 1987	20:38	02° Le 22'
Mon Cnj Sun	Aug 24 1987	11:59	00° Vi 47'
Solar Eclipse	Sep 23 1987	03:08	29° Vi 34'
Lunar Eclipse	Oct 7 1987	04:12	13° Ar 21'
Mon Cnj Sun	Oct 22 1987	17:28	28° Li 46'
Mon Cnj Sun	Nov 21 1987	06:33	28° Sc 24'
Mon Cnj Sun	Dec 20 1987	18:25	28° Sg 19'
Mon Cnj Sun	Jan 19 1988	05:26	28° Cp 20'
Mon Cnj Sun	Feb 17 1988	15:54	28° Aq 12'

Appendix I • *New Moons + Solar & Lunar Eclipses 1920 to 2120*

Lunar Eclipse	Mar 3 1988	16:01	13° Vi 17'
Solar Eclipse	Mar 18 1988	02:02	27° Pi 41'
Mon Cnj Sun	Apr 16 1988	12:00	26° Ar 42'
Mon Cnj Sun	May 15 1988	22:11	25° Ta 16'
Mon Cnj Sun	Jun 14 1988	09:14	23° Ge 31'
Mon Cnj Sun	Jul 13 1988	21:53	21° Cn 41'
Mon Cnj Sun	Aug 12 1988	12:31	20° Le 00'
Lunar Eclipse	Aug 27 1988	10:56	04° Pi 22'
Solar Eclipse	Sep 11 1988	04:49	18° Vi 40'
Mon Cnj Sun	Oct 10 1988	21:49	17° Li 48'
Mon Cnj Sun	Nov 9 1988	14:20	17° Sc 24'
Mon Cnj Sun	Dec 9 1988	05:36	17° Sg 22'
Mon Cnj Sun	Jan 7 1989	19:22	17° Cp 29'
Mon Cnj Sun	Feb 6 1989	07:37	17° Aq 30'
Lunar Eclipse	Feb 20 1989	15:32	01° Vi 58'
Solar Eclipse	Mar 7 1989	18:19	17° Pi 09'
Mon Cnj Sun	Apr 6 1989	03:33	16° Ar 18'
Mon Cnj Sun	May 5 1989	11:46	14° Ta 57'
Mon Cnj Sun	Jun 3 1989	19:53	13° Ge 11'
Mon Cnj Sun	Jul 3 1989	04:59	11° Cn 15'
Mon Cnj Sun	Aug 1 1989	16:06	09° Le 22'
Lunar Eclipse	Aug 17 1989	03:07	24° Aq 11'
Solar Eclipse	Aug 31 1989	05:45	07° Vi 48'
Mon Cnj Sun	Sep 29 1989	21:47	06° Li 43'
Mon Cnj Sun	Oct 29 1989	15:27	06° Sc 11'
Mon Cnj Sun	Nov 28 1989	09:41	06° Sg 08'
Mon Cnj Sun	Dec 28 1989	03:20	06° Cp 22'
Solar Eclipse	Jan 26 1990	19:20	06° Aq 35'
Lunar Eclipse	Feb 9 1990	19:16	20° Le 46'
Mon Cnj Sun	Feb 25 1990	08:54	06° Pi 29'
Mon Cnj Sun	Mar 26 1990	19:48	05° Ar 53'
Mon Cnj Sun	Apr 25 1990	04:27	04° Ta 42'
Mon Cnj Sun	May 24 1990	11:47	03° Ge 03'
Mon Cnj Sun	Jun 22 1990	18:55	01° Cn 05'
Solar Eclipse	Jul 22 1990	02:54	29° Cn 03'
Lunar Eclipse	Aug 6 1990	14:19	13° Aq 51'
Mon Cnj Sun	Aug 20 1990	12:39	27° Le 14'
Mon Cnj Sun	Sep 19 1990	00:46	25° Vi 50'
Mon Cnj Sun	Oct 18 1990	15:37	25° Li 00'
Mon Cnj Sun	Nov 17 1990	09:05	24° Sc 45'
Mon Cnj Sun	Dec 17 1990	04:22	24° Sg 57'
Solar Eclipse	Jan 15 1991	23:50	25° Cp 20'
Lunar Eclipse	Jan 30 1991	06:10	09° Le 50'
Mon Cnj Sun	Feb 14 1991	17:32	25° Aq 31'

Mon Cnj Sun	Mar 16 1991	08:11	25° Pi 14'
Mon Cnj Sun	Apr 14 1991	19:38	24° Ar 21'
Mon Cnj Sun	May 14 1991	04:36	22° Ta 54'
Mon Cnj Sun	Jun 12 1991	12:06	21° Ge 02'
Lunar Eclipse	Jun 27 1991	02:58	04° Cp 59'
Solar Eclipse	Jul 11 1991	19:06	18° Cn 58'
Lunar Eclipse	Jul 26 1991	18:24	03° Aq 16'
Mon Cnj Sun	Aug 10 1991	02:28	16° Le 59'
Mon Cnj Sun	Sep 8 1991	11:01	15° Vi 18'
Mon Cnj Sun	Oct 7 1991	21:39	14° Li 07'
Mon Cnj Sun	Nov 6 1991	11:11	13° Sc 32'
Mon Cnj Sun	Dec 6 1991	03:56	13° Sg 31'
Lunar Eclipse	Dec 21 1991	10:23	29° Ge 02'
Solar Eclipse	Jan 4 1992	23:10	13° Cp 51'
Mon Cnj Sun	Feb 3 1992	19:00	14° Aq 12'
Mon Cnj Sun	Mar 4 1992	13:22	14° Pi 13'
Mon Cnj Sun	Apr 3 1992	05:01	13° Ar 41'
Mon Cnj Sun	May 2 1992	17:44	12° Ta 33'
Mon Cnj Sun	Jun 1 1992	03:57	10° Ge 54'
Lunar Eclipse	Jun 15 1992	04:50	24° Sg 20'
Solar Eclipse	Jun 30 1992	12:18	08° Cn 56'
Mon Cnj Sun	Jul 29 1992	19:35	06° Le 54'
Mon Cnj Sun	Aug 28 1992	02:42	05° Vi 02'
Mon Cnj Sun	Sep 26 1992	10:40	03° Li 35'
Mon Cnj Sun	Oct 25 1992	20:34	02° Sc 41'
Mon Cnj Sun	Nov 24 1992	09:11	02° Sg 20'
Lunar Eclipse	Dec 9 1992	23:41	18° Ge 10'
Solar Eclipse	Dec 24 1992	00:43	02° Cp 27'
Mon Cnj Sun	Jan 22 1993	18:27	02° Aq 45'
Mon Cnj Sun	Feb 21 1993	13:05	02° Pi 55'
Mon Cnj Sun	Mar 23 1993	07:14	02° Ar 40'
Mon Cnj Sun	Apr 21 1993	23:49	01° Ta 52'
Solar Eclipse	May 21 1993	14:07	00° Ge 31'
Lunar Eclipse	Jun 4 1993	13:02	13° Sg 54'
Mon Cnj Sun	Jun 20 1993	01:52	28° Ge 45'
Mon Cnj Sun	Jul 19 1993	11:24	26° Cn 47'
Mon Cnj Sun	Aug 17 1993	19:28	24° Le 53'
Mon Cnj Sun	Sep 16 1993	03:10	23° Vi 16'
Mon Cnj Sun	Oct 15 1993	11:36	22° Li 07'
Solar Eclipse	Nov 13 1993	21:34	21° Sc 31'
Lunar Eclipse	Nov 29 1993	06:31	07° Ge 03'
Mon Cnj Sun	Dec 13 1993	09:27	21° Sg 23'
Mon Cnj Sun	Jan 11 1994	23:10	21° Cp 30'
Mon Cnj Sun	Feb 10 1994	14:30	21° Aq 37'

Appendix I • *New Moons + Solar & Lunar Eclipses 1920 to 2120*

Mon Cnj Sun	Mar 12 1994	07:05	21° Pi 28'
Mon Cnj Sun	Apr 11 1994	00:17	20° Ar 53'
Solar Eclipse	May 10 1994	17:07	19° Ta 48'
Lunar Eclipse	May 25 1994	03:39	03° Sg 43'
Mon Cnj Sun	Jun 9 1994	08:26	18° Ge 17'
Mon Cnj Sun	Jul 8 1994	21:37	16° Cn 28'
Mon Cnj Sun	Aug 7 1994	08:45	14° Le 37'
Mon Cnj Sun	Sep 5 1994	18:33	12° Vi 57'
Mon Cnj Sun	Oct 5 1994	03:55	11° Li 41'
Solar Eclipse	Nov 3 1994	13:35	10° Sc 54'
Lunar Eclipse	Nov 18 1994	06:57	25° Ta 42'
Mon Cnj Sun	Dec 2 1994	23:54	10° Sg 34'
Mon Cnj Sun	Jan 1 1995	10:56	10° Cp 33'
Mon Cnj Sun	Jan 30 1995	22:48	10° Aq 35'
Mon Cnj Sun	Mar 1 1995	11:48	10° Pi 25'
Mon Cnj Sun	Mar 31 1995	02:09	09° Ar 54'
Lunar Eclipse	Apr 15 1995	12:08	25° Li 03'
Solar Eclipse	Apr 29 1995	17:36	08° Ta 56'
Mon Cnj Sun	May 29 1995	09:27	07° Ge 33'
Mon Cnj Sun	Jun 28 1995	00:50	05° Cn 53'
Mon Cnj Sun	Jul 27 1995	15:13	04° Le 07'
Mon Cnj Sun	Aug 26 1995	04:31	02° Vi 29'
Mon Cnj Sun	Sep 24 1995	16:55	01° Li 10'
Lunar Eclipse	Oct 8 1995	15:52	14° Ar 53'
Solar Eclipse	Oct 24 1995	04:36	00° Sc 17'
Mon Cnj Sun	Nov 22 1995	15:43	29° Sc 51'
Mon Cnj Sun	Dec 22 1995	02:22	29° Sg 44'
Mon Cnj Sun	Jan 20 1996	12:50	29° Cp 44'
Mon Cnj Sun	Feb 18 1996	23:30	29° Aq 36'
Mon Cnj Sun	Mar 19 1996	10:45	29° Pi 07'
Lunar Eclipse	Apr 4 1996	00:07	14° Li 30'
Solar Eclipse	Apr 17 1996	22:49	28° Ar 11'
Mon Cnj Sun	May 17 1996	11:46	26° Ta 50'
Mon Cnj Sun	Jun 16 1996	01:36	25° Ge 11'
Mon Cnj Sun	Jul 15 1996	16:15	23° Cn 26'
Mon Cnj Sun	Aug 14 1996	07:34	21° Le 47'
Mon Cnj Sun	Sep 12 1996	23:07	20° Vi 26'
Lunar Eclipse	Sep 27 1996	02:51	04° Ar 16'
Solar Eclipse	Oct 12 1996	14:14	19° Li 31'
Mon Cnj Sun	Nov 11 1996	04:16	19° Sc 03'
Mon Cnj Sun	Dec 10 1996	16:56	18° Sg 55'
Mon Cnj Sun	Jan 9 1997	04:26	18° Cp 57'
Mon Cnj Sun	Feb 7 1997	15:06	18° Aq 53'
Solar Eclipse	Mar 9 1997	01:15	18° Pi 30'

Lunar Eclipse	Mar 24 1997	04:45	03° Li 35'
Mon Cnj Sun	Apr 7 1997	11:02	17° Ar 40'
Mon Cnj Sun	May 6 1997	20:47	16° Ta 21'
Mon Cnj Sun	Jun 5 1997	07:04	14° Ge 39'
Mon Cnj Sun	Jul 4 1997	18:40	12° Cn 48'
Mon Cnj Sun	Aug 3 1997	08:14	11° Le 01'
Solar Eclipse	Sep 1 1997	23:52	09° Vi 33'
Lunar Eclipse	Sep 16 1997	18:50	23° Pi 55'
Mon Cnj Sun	Oct 1 1997	16:52	08° Li 32'
Mon Cnj Sun	Oct 31 1997	10:01	08° Sc 01'
Mon Cnj Sun	Nov 30 1997	02:14	07° Sg 54'
Mon Cnj Sun	Dec 29 1997	16:57	08° Cp 01'
Mon Cnj Sun	Jan 28 1998	06:01	08° Aq 06'
Solar Eclipse	Feb 26 1998	17:26	07° Pi 54'
Lunar Eclipse	Mar 13 1998	04:34	22° Vi 23'
Mon Cnj Sun	Mar 28 1998	03:14	07° Ar 14'
Mon Cnj Sun	Apr 26 1998	11:41	06° Ta 02'
Mon Cnj Sun	May 25 1998	19:32	04° Ge 23'
Mon Cnj Sun	Jun 24 1998	03:50	02° Cn 27'
Mon Cnj Sun	Jul 23 1998	13:44	00° Le 30'
Lunar Eclipse	Aug 8 1998	02:10	15° Aq 21'
Solar Eclipse	Aug 22 1998	02:03	28° Le 47'
Lunar Eclipse	Sep 6 1998	11:21	13° Pi 40'
Mon Cnj Sun	Sep 20 1998	17:02	27° Vi 31'
Mon Cnj Sun	Oct 20 1998	10:09	26° Li 48'
Mon Cnj Sun	Nov 19 1998	04:27	26° Sc 37'
Mon Cnj Sun	Dec 18 1998	22:42	26° Sg 48'
Mon Cnj Sun	Jan 17 1999	15:46	27° Cp 04'
Lunar Eclipse	Jan 31 1999	16:07	11° Le 19'
Solar Eclipse	Feb 16 1999	06:39	27° Aq 08'
Mon Cnj Sun	Mar 17 1999	18:48	26° Pi 43'
Mon Cnj Sun	Apr 16 1999	04:22	25° Ar 44'
Mon Cnj Sun	May 15 1999	12:05	24° Ta 13'
Mon Cnj Sun	Jun 13 1999	19:03	22° Ge 19'
Mon Cnj Sun	Jul 13 1999	02:24	20° Cn 17'
Lunar Eclipse	Jul 28 1999	11:25	04° Aq 57'
Solar Eclipse	Aug 11 1999	11:08	18° Le 21'
Mon Cnj Sun	Sep 9 1999	22:02	16° Vi 46'
Mon Cnj Sun	Oct 9 1999	11:34	15° Li 43'
Mon Cnj Sun	Nov 8 1999	03:53	15° Sc 17'
Mon Cnj Sun	Dec 7 1999	22:32	15° Sg 22'
Mon Cnj Sun	Jan 6 2000	18:14	15° Cp 43'
Lunar Eclipse	Jan 21 2000	04:40	00° Le 26'
Solar Eclipse	Feb 5 2000	13:03	16° Aq 01'

Appendix I • *New Moons + Solar & Lunar Eclipses 1920 to 2120*

Mon Cnj Sun	Mar 6 2000	05:17	15° Pi 56'
Mon Cnj Sun	Apr 4 2000	18:12	15° Ar 16'
Mon Cnj Sun	May 4 2000	04:12	14° Ta 00'
Mon Cnj Sun	Jun 2 2000	12:14	12° Ge 15'
Solar Eclipse	Jul 1 2000	19:20	10° Cn 14'
Lunar Eclipse	Jul 16 2000	13:55	24° Cp 19'
Solar Eclipse	Jul 31 2000	02:25	08° Le 11'
Mon Cnj Sun	Aug 29 2000	10:19	06° Vi 22'
Mon Cnj Sun	Sep 27 2000	19:53	05° Li 00'
Mon Cnj Sun	Oct 27 2000	07:58	04° Sc 12'
Mon Cnj Sun	Nov 25 2000	23:11	03° Sg 59'
Solar Eclipse	Dec 25 2000	17:22	04° Cp 14'
Lunar Eclipse	Jan 9 2001	20:24	19° Cn 39'
Mon Cnj Sun	Jan 24 2001	13:07	04° Aq 36'
Mon Cnj Sun	Feb 23 2001	08:21	04° Pi 46'
Mon Cnj Sun	Mar 25 2001	01:21	04° Ar 27'
Mon Cnj Sun	Apr 23 2001	15:26	03° Ta 31'
Mon Cnj Sun	May 23 2001	02:46	02° Ge 02'
Solar Eclipse	Jun 21 2001	11:58	00° Cn 10'
Lunar Eclipse	Jul 5 2001	15:04	13° Cp 38'
Mon Cnj Sun	Jul 20 2001	19:44	28° Cn 08'
Mon Cnj Sun	Aug 19 2001	02:55	26° Le 12'
Mon Cnj Sun	Sep 17 2001	10:27	24° Vi 35'
Mon Cnj Sun	Oct 16 2001	19:23	23° Li 29'
Mon Cnj Sun	Nov 15 2001	06:40	22° Sc 57'
Solar Eclipse	Dec 14 2001	20:47	22° Sg 56'
Lunar Eclipse	Dec 30 2001	10:41	08° Cn 47'
Mon Cnj Sun	Jan 13 2002	13:29	23° Cp 11'
Mon Cnj Sun	Feb 12 2002	07:41	23° Aq 24'
Mon Cnj Sun	Mar 14 2002	02:03	23° Pi 18'
Mon Cnj Sun	Apr 12 2002	19:21	22° Ar 42'
Mon Cnj Sun	May 12 2002	10:45	21° Ta 32'
Lunar Eclipse	May 26 2002	11:51	05° Sg 03'
Solar Eclipse	Jun 10 2002	23:47	19° Ge 54'
Lunar Eclipse	Jun 24 2002	21:42	03° Cp 11'
Mon Cnj Sun	Jul 10 2002	10:26	18° Cn 00'
Mon Cnj Sun	Aug 8 2002	19:15	16° Le 03'
Mon Cnj Sun	Sep 7 2002	03:10	14° Vi 20'
Mon Cnj Sun	Oct 6 2002	11:18	13° Li 01'
Mon Cnj Sun	Nov 4 2002	20:34	12° Sc 14'
Lunar Eclipse	Nov 20 2002	01:34	27° Ta 32'
Solar Eclipse	Dec 4 2002	07:34	11° Sg 58'
Mon Cnj Sun	Jan 2 2003	20:23	12° Cp 01'
Mon Cnj Sun	Feb 1 2003	10:48	12° Aq 09'

Mon Cnj Sun	Mar 3 2003	02:35	12° Pi 05'
Mon Cnj Sun	Apr 1 2003	19:19	11° Ar 38'
Mon Cnj Sun	May 1 2003	12:15	10° Ta 43'
Lunar Eclipse	May 16 2003	03:36	24° Sc 52'
Solar Eclipse	May 31 2003	04:20	09° Ge 19'
Mon Cnj Sun	Jun 29 2003	18:39	07° Cn 36'
Mon Cnj Sun	Jul 29 2003	06:53	05° Le 45'
Mon Cnj Sun	Aug 27 2003	18:26	04° Vi 01'
Mon Cnj Sun	Sep 26 2003	03:09	02° Li 37'
Mon Cnj Sun	Oct 25 2003	12:50	01° Sc 41'
Lunar Eclipse	Nov 9 2003	01:13	16° Ta 12'
Solar Eclipse	Nov 23 2003	22:59	01° Sg 13'
Mon Cnj Sun	Dec 23 2003	09:43	01° Cp 07'
Mon Cnj Sun	Jan 21 2004	21:05	01° Aq 09'
Mon Cnj Sun	Feb 20 2004	09:18	01° Pi 04'
Mon Cnj Sun	Mar 20 2004	22:41	00° Ar 39'
Solar Eclipse	Apr 19 2004	13:21	29° Ar 49'
Lunar Eclipse	May 4 2004	20:33	14° Sc 41'
Mon Cnj Sun	May 19 2004	04:52	28° Ta 33'
Mon Cnj Sun	Jun 17 2004	20:27	26° Ge 57'
Mon Cnj Sun	Jul 17 2004	11:24	25° Cn 12'
Mon Cnj Sun	Aug 16 2004	01:24	23° Le 31'
Mon Cnj Sun	Sep 14 2004	14:29	22° Vi 06'
Solar Eclipse	Oct 14 2004	02:48	21° Li 05'
Lunar Eclipse	Oct 28 2004	03:07	05° Ta 02'
Mon Cnj Sun	Nov 12 2004	14:27	20° Sc 32'
Mon Cnj Sun	Dec 12 2004	01:29	20° Sg 21'
Mon Cnj Sun	Jan 10 2005	12:03	20° Cp 21'
Mon Cnj Sun	Feb 8 2005	22:28	20° Aq 16'
Mon Cnj Sun	Mar 10 2005	09:10	19° Pi 53'
Solar Eclipse	Apr 8 2005	20:32	19° Ar 05'
Lunar Eclipse	Apr 24 2005	10:06	04° Sc 19'
Mon Cnj Sun	May 8 2005	08:45	17° Ta 51'
Mon Cnj Sun	Jun 6 2005	21:55	16° Ge 16'
Mon Cnj Sun	Jul 6 2005	12:03	14° Cn 30'
Mon Cnj Sun	Aug 5 2005	03:05	12° Le 48'
Mon Cnj Sun	Sep 3 2005	18:45	11° Vi 21'
Solar Eclipse	Oct 3 2005	10:28	10° Li 18'
Lunar Eclipse	Oct 17 2005	12:14	24° Ar 13'
Mon Cnj Sun	Nov 2 2005	01:25	09° Sc 43'
Mon Cnj Sun	Dec 1 2005	15:01	09° Sg 31'
Mon Cnj Sun	Dec 31 2005	03:12	09° Cp 32'
Mon Cnj Sun	Jan 29 2006	14:15	09° Aq 32'
Mon Cnj Sun	Feb 28 2006	00:31	09° Pi 16'

Appendix I • New Moons + Solar & Lunar Eclipses 1920 to 2120

Lunar Eclipse	Mar 14 2006	23:35	24° Vi 14'
Solar Eclipse	Mar 29 2006	10:15	08° Ar 35'
Mon Cnj Sun	Apr 27 2006	19:44	07° Ta 24'
Mon Cnj Sun	May 27 2006	05:26	05° Ge 48'
Mon Cnj Sun	Jun 25 2006	16:05	03° Cn 57'
Mon Cnj Sun	Jul 25 2006	04:31	02° Le 07'
Mon Cnj Sun	Aug 23 2006	19:10	00° Vi 30'
Lunar Eclipse	Sep 7 2006	18:42	15° Pi 00'
Solar Eclipse	Sep 22 2006	11:45	29° Vi 20'
Mon Cnj Sun	Oct 22 2006	05:14	28° Li 39'
Mon Cnj Sun	Nov 20 2006	22:18	28° Sc 27'
Mon Cnj Sun	Dec 20 2006	14:01	28° Sg 32'
Mon Cnj Sun	Jan 19 2007	04:01	28° Cp 41'
Mon Cnj Sun	Feb 17 2007	16:14	28° Aq 36'
Lunar Eclipse	Mar 3 2007	23:17	12° Vi 59'
Solar Eclipse	Mar 19 2007	02:43	28° Pi 07'
Mon Cnj Sun	Apr 17 2007	11:36	27° Ar 05'
Mon Cnj Sun	May 16 2007	19:27	25° Ta 33'
Mon Cnj Sun	Jun 15 2007	03:13	23° Ge 40'
Mon Cnj Sun	Jul 14 2007	12:04	21° Cn 41'
Mon Cnj Sun	Aug 12 2007	23:03	19° Le 51'
Lunar Eclipse	Aug 28 2007	10:35	04° Pi 45'
Solar Eclipse	Sep 11 2007	12:44	18° Vi 24'
Mon Cnj Sun	Oct 11 2007	05:01	17° Li 30'
Mon Cnj Sun	Nov 9 2007	23:03	17° Sc 09'
Mon Cnj Sun	Dec 9 2007	17:40	17° Sg 15'
Mon Cnj Sun	Jan 8 2008	11:37	17° Cp 33'
Solar Eclipse	Feb 7 2008	03:45	17° Aq 44'
Lunar Eclipse	Feb 21 2008	03:31	01° Vi 52'
Mon Cnj Sun	Mar 7 2008	17:14	17° Pi 30'
Mon Cnj Sun	Apr 6 2008	03:55	16° Ar 43'
Mon Cnj Sun	May 5 2008	12:18	15° Ta 22'
Mon Cnj Sun	Jun 3 2008	19:23	13° Ge 34'
Mon Cnj Sun	Jul 3 2008	02:19	11° Cn 32'
Solar Eclipse	Aug 1 2008	10:13	09° Le 31'
Lunar Eclipse	Aug 16 2008	21:16	24° Aq 21'
Mon Cnj Sun	Aug 30 2008	19:58	07° Vi 48'
Mon Cnj Sun	Sep 29 2008	08:12	06° Li 33'
Mon Cnj Sun	Oct 28 2008	23:14	05° Sc 54'
Mon Cnj Sun	Nov 27 2008	16:55	05° Sg 49'
Mon Cnj Sun	Dec 27 2008	12:22	06° Cp 07'
Solar Eclipse	Jan 26 2009	07:55	06° Aq 29'
Lunar Eclipse	Feb 9 2009	14:49	20° Le 59'
Mon Cnj Sun	Feb 25 2009	01:35	06° Pi 35'

Mon Cnj Sun	Mar 26 2009	16:06	06° Ar 07'
Mon Cnj Sun	Apr 25 2009	03:23	05° Ta 03'
Mon Cnj Sun	May 24 2009	12:11	03° Ge 27'
Mon Cnj Sun	Jun 22 2009	19:35	01° Cn 30'
Lunar Eclipse	Jul 7 2009	09:21	15° Cp 24'
Solar Eclipse	Jul 22 2009	02:35	29° Cn 26'
Lunar Eclipse	Aug 6 2009	00:55	13° Aq 43'
Mon Cnj Sun	Aug 20 2009	10:02	27° Le 31'
Mon Cnj Sun	Sep 18 2009	18:44	25° Vi 59'
Mon Cnj Sun	Oct 18 2009	05:33	24° Li 58'
Mon Cnj Sun	Nov 16 2009	19:14	24° Sc 34'
Mon Cnj Sun	Dec 16 2009	12:02	24° Sg 39'
Lunar Eclipse	Dec 31 2009	19:13	10° Cn 14'
Solar Eclipse	Jan 15 2010	07:11	25° Cp 01'
Mon Cnj Sun	Feb 14 2010	02:51	25° Aq 17'
Mon Cnj Sun	Mar 15 2010	21:01	25° Pi 10'
Mon Cnj Sun	Apr 14 2010	12:29	24° Ar 27'
Mon Cnj Sun	May 14 2010	01:04	23° Ta 09'
Mon Cnj Sun	Jun 12 2010	11:15	21° Ge 23'
Lunar Eclipse	Jun 26 2010	11:30	04° Cp 46'
Solar Eclipse	Jul 11 2010	19:40	19° Cn 23'
Mon Cnj Sun	Aug 10 2010	03:08	17° Le 24'
Mon Cnj Sun	Sep 8 2010	10:30	15° Vi 40'
Mon Cnj Sun	Oct 7 2010	18:44	14° Li 23'
Mon Cnj Sun	Nov 6 2010	04:52	13° Sc 40'
Mon Cnj Sun	Dec 5 2010	17:36	13° Sg 28'
Lunar Eclipse	Dec 21 2010	08:13	29° Ge 20'
Solar Eclipse	Jan 4 2011	09:03	13° Cp 38'
Mon Cnj Sun	Feb 3 2011	02:31	13° Aq 53'
Mon Cnj Sun	Mar 4 2011	20:46	13° Pi 55'
Mon Cnj Sun	Apr 3 2011	14:32	13° Ar 29'
Mon Cnj Sun	May 3 2011	06:51	12° Ta 30'
Solar Eclipse	Jun 1 2011	21:03	11° Ge 01'
Lunar Eclipse	Jun 15 2011	20:14	24° Sg 23'
Solar Eclipse	Jul 1 2011	08:54	09° Cn 12'
Mon Cnj Sun	Jul 30 2011	18:40	07° Le 15'
Mon Cnj Sun	Aug 29 2011	03:04	05° Vi 27'
Mon Cnj Sun	Sep 27 2011	11:09	04° Li 00'
Mon Cnj Sun	Oct 26 2011	19:56	03° Sc 02'
Solar Eclipse	Nov 25 2011	06:10	02° Sg 36'
Lunar Eclipse	Dec 10 2011	14:36	18° Ge 10'
Mon Cnj Sun	Dec 24 2011	18:06	02° Cp 34'
Mon Cnj Sun	Jan 23 2012	07:39	02° Aq 41'
Mon Cnj Sun	Feb 21 2012	22:35	02° Pi 42'

Appendix I • *New Moons + Solar & Lunar Eclipses 1920 to 2120*

Mon Cnj Sun	Mar 22 2012	14:37	02° Ar 22'
Mon Cnj Sun	Apr 21 2012	07:18	01° Ta 35'
Solar Eclipse	May 20 2012	23:47	00° Ge 20'
Lunar Eclipse	Jun 4 2012	11:12	14° Sg 13'
Mon Cnj Sun	Jun 19 2012	15:02	28° Ge 43'
Mon Cnj Sun	Jul 19 2012	04:24	26° Cn 54'
Mon Cnj Sun	Aug 17 2012	15:54	25° Le 08'
Mon Cnj Sun	Sep 16 2012	02:11	23° Vi 37'
Mon Cnj Sun	Oct 15 2012	12:03	22° Li 32'
Solar Eclipse	Nov 13 2012	22:08	21° Sc 56'
Lunar Eclipse	Nov 28 2012	14:46	06° Ge 46'
Mon Cnj Sun	Dec 13 2012	08:42	21° Sg 45'
Mon Cnj Sun	Jan 11 2013	19:44	21° Cp 45'
Mon Cnj Sun	Feb 10 2013	07:20	21° Aq 43'
Mon Cnj Sun	Mar 11 2013	19:51	21° Pi 24'
Mon Cnj Sun	Apr 10 2013	09:35	20° Ar 40'
Lunar Eclipse	Apr 25 2013	19:57	05° Sc 45'
Solar Eclipse	May 10 2013	00:28	19° Ta 31'
Lunar Eclipse	May 25 2013	04:25	04° Sg 08'
Mon Cnj Sun	Jun 8 2013	15:56	18° Ge 00'
Mon Cnj Sun	Jul 8 2013	07:14	16° Cn 17'
Mon Cnj Sun	Aug 6 2013	21:51	14° Le 34'
Mon Cnj Sun	Sep 5 2013	11:36	13° Vi 04'
Mon Cnj Sun	Oct 5 2013	00:35	11° Li 56'
Lunar Eclipse	Oct 18 2013	23:38	25° Ar 45'
Solar Eclipse	Nov 3 2013	12:50	11° Sc 15'
Mon Cnj Sun	Dec 3 2013	00:22	10° Sg 59'
Mon Cnj Sun	Jan 1 2014	11:14	10° Cp 57'
Mon Cnj Sun	Jan 30 2014	21:39	10° Aq 55'
Mon Cnj Sun	Mar 1 2014	08:00	10° Pi 39'
Mon Cnj Sun	Mar 30 2014	18:45	09° Ar 58'
Lunar Eclipse	Apr 15 2014	07:42	25° Li 15'
Solar Eclipse	Apr 29 2014	06:14	08° Ta 51'
Mon Cnj Sun	May 28 2014	18:40	07° Ge 21'
Mon Cnj Sun	Jun 27 2014	08:08	05° Cn 37'
Mon Cnj Sun	Jul 26 2014	22:42	03° Le 51'
Mon Cnj Sun	Aug 25 2014	14:13	02° Vi 18'
Mon Cnj Sun	Sep 24 2014	06:14	01° Li 07'
Lunar Eclipse	Oct 8 2014	10:51	15° Ar 05'
Solar Eclipse	Oct 23 2014	21:57	00° Sc 24'
Mon Cnj Sun	Nov 22 2014	12:32	00° Sg 07'
Mon Cnj Sun	Dec 22 2014	01:36	00° Cp 06'
Mon Cnj Sun	Jan 20 2015	13:14	00° Aq 08'
Mon Cnj Sun	Feb 18 2015	23:47	29° Aq 59'

Solar Eclipse	Mar 20 2015	09:36	29° Pi 27'
Lunar Eclipse	Apr 4 2015	12:06	14° Li 24'
Mon Cnj Sun	Apr 18 2015	18:57	28° Ar 25'
Mon Cnj Sun	May 18 2015	04:13	26° Ta 55'
Mon Cnj Sun	Jun 16 2015	14:05	25° Ge 07'
Mon Cnj Sun	Jul 16 2015	01:24	23° Cn 14'
Mon Cnj Sun	Aug 14 2015	14:53	21° Le 30'
Solar Eclipse	Sep 13 2015	06:41	20° Vi 10'
Lunar Eclipse	Sep 28 2015	02:51	04° Ar 40'
Mon Cnj Sun	Oct 13 2015	00:06	19° Li 20'
Mon Cnj Sun	Nov 11 2015	17:47	19° Sc 00'
Mon Cnj Sun	Dec 11 2015	10:29	19° Sg 02'
Mon Cnj Sun	Jan 10 2016	01:31	19° Cp 13'
Mon Cnj Sun	Feb 8 2016	02:39	19° Aq 15'
Solar Eclipse	Mar 9 2016	01:54	18° Pi 55'
Lunar Eclipse	Mar 23 2016	12:01	03° Li 17'
Mon Cnj Sun	Apr 7 2016	11:24	18° Ar 04'
Mon Cnj Sun	May 6 2016	19:30	16° Ta 41'
Mon Cnj Sun	Jun 5 2016	03:00	14° Ge 53'
Mon Cnj Sun	Jul 4 2016	11:01	12° Cn 53'
Mon Cnj Sun	Aug 2 2016	20:45	10° Le 57'
Lunar Eclipse	Aug 18 2016	09:27	25° Aq 51'
Solar Eclipse	Sep 1 2016	09:03	09° Vi 21'
Lunar Eclipse	Sep 16 2016	19:06	24° Pi 19'
Mon Cnj Sun	Oct 1 2016	00:11	08° Li 15'
Mon Cnj Sun	Oct 30 2016	17:38	07° Sc 43'
Mon Cnj Sun	Nov 29 2016	12:18	07° Sg 42'
Mon Cnj Sun	Dec 29 2016	06:53	07° Cp 59'
Mon Cnj Sun	Jan 28 2017	00:07	08° Aq 15'
Lunar Eclipse	Feb 11 2017	00:33	22° Le 28'
Solar Eclipse	Feb 26 2017	14:58	08° Pi 12'
Mon Cnj Sun	Mar 28 2017	02:57	07° Ar 37'
Mon Cnj Sun	Apr 26 2017	12:16	06° Ta 27'
Mon Cnj Sun	May 25 2017	19:44	04° Ge 46'
Mon Cnj Sun	Jun 24 2017	02:31	02° Cn 47'
Mon Cnj Sun	Jul 23 2017	09:46	00° Le 44'
Lunar Eclipse	Aug 7 2017	18:11	15° Aq 25'
Solar Eclipse	Aug 21 2017	18:30	28° Le 52'
Mon Cnj Sun	Sep 20 2017	05:30	27° Vi 27'
Mon Cnj Sun	Oct 19 2017	19:12	26° Li 35'
Mon Cnj Sun	Nov 18 2017	11:42	26° Sc 19'
Mon Cnj Sun	Dec 18 2017	06:30	26° Sg 31'
Mon Cnj Sun	Jan 17 2018	02:17	26° Cp 54'
Lunar Eclipse	Jan 31 2018	13:27	11° Le 37'

Appendix I • *New Moons + Solar & Lunar Eclipses 1920 to 2120*

Solar Eclipse	Feb 15 2018	21:05	27° Aq 07'
Mon Cnj Sun	Mar 17 2018	13:12	26° Pi 53'
Mon Cnj Sun	Apr 16 2018	01:57	26° Ar 02'
Mon Cnj Sun	May 15 2018	11:48	24° Ta 36'
Mon Cnj Sun	Jun 13 2018	19:43	22° Ge 44'
Solar Eclipse	Jul 13 2018	02:48	20° Cn 41'
Lunar Eclipse	Jul 27 2018	20:20	04° Aq 44'
Solar Eclipse	Aug 11 2018	09:58	18° Le 41'
Mon Cnj Sun	Sep 9 2018	18:01	17° Vi 00'
Mon Cnj Sun	Oct 9 2018	03:47	15° Li 48'
Mon Cnj Sun	Nov 7 2018	16:02	15° Sc 11'
Mon Cnj Sun	Dec 7 2018	07:20	15° Sg 07'
Solar Eclipse	Jan 6 2019	01:28	15° Cp 25'
Lunar Eclipse	Jan 21 2019	05:16	00° Le 51'
Mon Cnj Sun	Feb 4 2019	21:04	15° Aq 45'
Mon Cnj Sun	Mar 6 2019	16:04	15° Pi 47'
Mon Cnj Sun	Apr 5 2019	08:50	15° Ar 17'
Mon Cnj Sun	May 4 2019	22:46	14° Ta 10'
Mon Cnj Sun	Jun 3 2019	10:02	12° Ge 33'
Solar Eclipse	Jul 2 2019	19:16	10° Cn 37'
Lunar Eclipse	Jul 16 2019	21:38	24° Cp 04'
Mon Cnj Sun	Aug 1 2019	03:12	08° Le 36'
Mon Cnj Sun	Aug 30 2019	10:37	06° Vi 46'
Mon Cnj Sun	Sep 28 2019	18:26	05° Li 20'
Mon Cnj Sun	Oct 28 2019	03:38	04° Sc 25'
Mon Cnj Sun	Nov 26 2019	15:06	04° Sg 03'
Solar Eclipse	Dec 26 2019	05:13	04° Cp 06'
Lunar Eclipse	Jan 10 2020	19:21	20° Cn 00'
Mon Cnj Sun	Jan 24 2020	21:42	04° Aq 21'
Mon Cnj Sun	Feb 23 2020	15:32	04° Pi 28'
Mon Cnj Sun	Mar 24 2020	09:28	04° Ar 12'
Mon Cnj Sun	Apr 23 2020	02:26	03° Ta 24'
Mon Cnj Sun	May 22 2020	17:39	02° Ge 04'
Lunar Eclipse	Jun 5 2020	19:12	15° Sg 34'
Solar Eclipse	Jun 21 2020	06:41	00° Cn 21'
Lunar Eclipse	Jul 5 2020	04:44	13° Cp 37'
Mon Cnj Sun	Jul 20 2020	17:33	28° Cn 26'
Mon Cnj Sun	Aug 19 2020	02:42	26° Le 35'
Mon Cnj Sun	Sep 17 2020	11:00	25° Vi 00'
Mon Cnj Sun	Oct 16 2020	19:31	23° Li 53'
Mon Cnj Sun	Nov 15 2020	05:07	23° Sc 17'
Lunar Eclipse	Nov 30 2020	09:30	08° Ge 38'
Solar Eclipse	Dec 14 2020	16:17	23° Sg 08'
Mon Cnj Sun	Jan 13 2021	05:00	23° Cp 13'

Event	Date	Time	Position
Mon Cnj Sun	Feb 11 2021	19:06	23° Aq 16'
Mon Cnj Sun	Mar 13 2021	10:21	23° Pi 03'
Mon Cnj Sun	Apr 12 2021	02:31	22° Ar 24'
Mon Cnj Sun	May 11 2021	19:00	21° Ta 17'
Lunar Eclipse	May 26 2021	11:14	05° Sg 25'
Solar Eclipse	Jun 10 2021	10:53	19° Ge 47'
Mon Cnj Sun	Jul 10 2021	01:17	18° Cn 01'
Mon Cnj Sun	Aug 8 2021	13:50	16° Le 14'
Mon Cnj Sun	Sep 7 2021	00:52	14° Vi 38'
Mon Cnj Sun	Oct 6 2021	11:05	13° Li 24'
Mon Cnj Sun	Nov 4 2021	21:15	12° Sc 40'
Lunar Eclipse	Nov 19 2021	08:57	27° Ta 14'
Solar Eclipse	Dec 4 2021	07:43	12° Sg 22'
Mon Cnj Sun	Jan 2 2022	18:34	12° Cp 20'
Mon Cnj Sun	Feb 1 2022	05:46	12° Aq 19'
Mon Cnj Sun	Mar 2 2022	17:35	12° Pi 06'
Mon Cnj Sun	Apr 1 2022	06:24	11° Ar 30'
Solar Eclipse	Apr 30 2022	20:28	10° Ta 28'
Lunar Eclipse	May 16 2022	04:14	25° Sc 17'
Mon Cnj Sun	May 30 2022	11:30	09° Ge 03'
Mon Cnj Sun	Jun 29 2022	02:52	07° Cn 22'
Mon Cnj Sun	Jul 28 2022	17:55	05° Le 38'
Mon Cnj Sun	Aug 27 2022	08:17	04° Vi 03'
Mon Cnj Sun	Sep 25 2022	21:55	02° Li 48'
Solar Eclipse	Oct 25 2022	10:49	02° Sc 00'
Lunar Eclipse	Nov 8 2022	11:02	16° Ta 00'
Mon Cnj Sun	Nov 23 2022	22:57	01° Sg 37'
Mon Cnj Sun	Dec 23 2022	10:17	01° Cp 32'
Mon Cnj Sun	Jan 21 2023	20:53	01° Aq 32'
Mon Cnj Sun	Feb 20 2023	07:06	01° Pi 22'
Mon Cnj Sun	Mar 21 2023	17:23	00° Ar 49'
Solar Eclipse	Apr 20 2023	04:13	29° Ar 50'
Lunar Eclipse	May 5 2023	17:34	14° Sc 58'
Mon Cnj Sun	May 19 2023	15:53	28° Ta 25'
Mon Cnj Sun	Jun 18 2023	04:37	26° Ge 43'
Mon Cnj Sun	Jul 17 2023	18:32	24° Cn 56'
Mon Cnj Sun	Aug 16 2023	09:38	23° Le 17'
Mon Cnj Sun	Sep 15 2023	01:40	21° Vi 58'
Solar Eclipse	Oct 14 2023	17:55	21° Li 07'
Lunar Eclipse	Oct 28 2023	20:24	05° Ta 09'
Mon Cnj Sun	Nov 13 2023	09:27	20° Sc 43'
Mon Cnj Sun	Dec 12 2023	23:32	20° Sg 40'
Mon Cnj Sun	Jan 11 2024	11:57	20° Cp 44'
Mon Cnj Sun	Feb 9 2024	22:59	20° Aq 40'

Appendix I • *New Moons + Solar & Lunar Eclipses 1920 to 2120*

Mon Cnj Sun	Mar 10 2024	09:00	20° Pi 16'
Lunar Eclipse	Mar 25 2024	07:00	05° Li 07'
Solar Eclipse	Apr 8 2024	18:21	19° Ar 24'
Mon Cnj Sun	May 8 2024	03:22	18° Ta 02'
Mon Cnj Sun	Jun 6 2024	12:38	16° Ge 17'
Mon Cnj Sun	Jul 5 2024	22:57	14° Cn 23'
Mon Cnj Sun	Aug 4 2024	11:13	12° Le 34'
Mon Cnj Sun	Sep 3 2024	01:56	11° Vi 04'
Lunar Eclipse	Sep 18 2024	02:34	25° Pi 40'
Solar Eclipse	Oct 2 2024	18:49	10° Li 03'
Mon Cnj Sun	Nov 1 2024	12:47	09° Sc 35'
Mon Cnj Sun	Dec 1 2024	06:21	09° Sg 32'
Mon Cnj Sun	Dec 30 2024	22:27	09° Cp 43'
Mon Cnj Sun	Jan 29 2025	12:36	09° Aq 51'
Mon Cnj Sun	Feb 28 2025	00:45	09° Pi 40'
Lunar Eclipse	Mar 14 2025	06:55	23° Vi 56'
Solar Eclipse	Mar 29 2025	10:58	09° Ar 00'
Mon Cnj Sun	Apr 27 2025	19:31	07° Ta 46'
Mon Cnj Sun	May 27 2025	03:02	06° Ge 05'
Mon Cnj Sun	Jun 25 2025	10:32	04° Cn 07'
Mon Cnj Sun	Jul 24 2025	19:11	02° Le 08'
Mon Cnj Sun	Aug 23 2025	06:07	00° Vi 23'
Lunar Eclipse	Sep 7 2025	18:09	15° Pi 22'
Solar Eclipse	Sep 21 2025	19:54	29° Vi 05'
Mon Cnj Sun	Oct 21 2025	12:25	28° Li 21'
Mon Cnj Sun	Nov 20 2025	06:47	28° Sc 11'
Mon Cnj Sun	Dec 20 2025	01:43	28° Sg 24'
Mon Cnj Sun	Jan 18 2026	19:52	28° Cp 43'
Solar Eclipse	Feb 17 2026	12:01	28° Aq 49'
Lunar Eclipse	Mar 3 2026	11:38	12° Vi 53'
Mon Cnj Sun	Mar 19 2026	01:23	28° Pi 27'
Mon Cnj Sun	Apr 17 2026	11:52	27° Ar 28'
Mon Cnj Sun	May 16 2026	20:01	25° Ta 57'
Mon Cnj Sun	Jun 15 2026	02:54	24° Ge 03'
Mon Cnj Sun	Jul 14 2026	09:44	21° Cn 59'
Solar Eclipse	Aug 12 2026	17:37	20° Le 01'
Lunar Eclipse	Aug 28 2026	04:18	04° Pi 54'
Mon Cnj Sun	Sep 11 2026	03:27	18° Vi 25'
Mon Cnj Sun	Oct 10 2026	15:50	17° Li 21'
Mon Cnj Sun	Nov 9 2026	07:02	16° Sc 53'
Mon Cnj Sun	Dec 9 2026	00:52	16° Sg 56'
Mon Cnj Sun	Jan 7 2027	20:24	17° Cp 18'
Solar Eclipse	Feb 6 2027	15:56	17° Aq 37'
Lunar Eclipse	Feb 20 2027	23:24	02° Vi 05'

Mon Cnj Sun	Mar 8 2027	09:29	17° Pi 34'
Mon Cnj Sun	Apr 6 2027	23:51	16° Ar 57'
Mon Cnj Sun	May 6 2027	10:59	15° Ta 42'
Mon Cnj Sun	Jun 4 2027	19:40	13° Ge 58'
Mon Cnj Sun	Jul 4 2027	03:02	11° Cn 57'
Lunar Eclipse	Jul 18 2027	15:45	25° Cp 48'
Solar Eclipse	Aug 2 2027	10:05	09° Le 55'
Lunar Eclipse	Aug 17 2027	07:29	24° Aq 11'
Mon Cnj Sun	Aug 31 2027	17:41	08° Vi 06'
Mon Cnj Sun	Sep 30 2027	02:36	06° Li 43'
Mon Cnj Sun	Oct 29 2027	13:37	05° Sc 54'
Mon Cnj Sun	Nov 28 2027	03:24	05° Sg 39'
Mon Cnj Sun	Dec 27 2027	20:12	05° Cp 50'
Lunar Eclipse	Jan 12 2028	04:03	21° Cn 27'
Solar Eclipse	Jan 26 2028	15:12	06° Aq 11'
Mon Cnj Sun	Feb 25 2028	10:37	06° Pi 20'
Mon Cnj Sun	Mar 26 2028	04:31	06° Ar 02'
Mon Cnj Sun	Apr 24 2028	19:47	05° Ta 08'
Mon Cnj Sun	May 24 2028	08:16	03° Ge 41'
Mon Cnj Sun	Jun 22 2028	18:28	01° Cn 50'
Lunar Eclipse	Jul 6 2028	18:11	15° Cp 11'
Solar Eclipse	Jul 22 2028	03:02	29° Cn 50'
Mon Cnj Sun	Aug 20 2028	10:44	27° Le 56'
Mon Cnj Sun	Sep 18 2028	18:24	26° Vi 21'
Mon Cnj Sun	Oct 18 2028	02:57	25° Li 15'
Mon Cnj Sun	Nov 16 2028	13:18	24° Sc 43'
Mon Cnj Sun	Dec 16 2028	02:06	24° Sg 38'
Lunar Eclipse	Dec 31 2028	16:48	10° Cn 32'
Solar Eclipse	Jan 14 2029	17:24	24° Cp 50'
Mon Cnj Sun	Feb 13 2029	10:31	25° Aq 00'
Mon Cnj Sun	Mar 15 2029	04:19	24° Pi 52'
Mon Cnj Sun	Apr 13 2029	21:40	24° Ar 14'
Mon Cnj Sun	May 13 2029	13:42	23° Ta 04'
Solar Eclipse	Jun 12 2029	03:50	21° Ge 29'
Lunar Eclipse	Jun 26 2029	03:22	04° Cp 49'
Solar Eclipse	Jul 11 2029	15:51	19° Cn 37'
Mon Cnj Sun	Aug 10 2029	01:56	17° Le 44'
Mon Cnj Sun	Sep 8 2029	10:44	16° Vi 04'
Mon Cnj Sun	Oct 7 2029	19:15	14° Li 48'
Mon Cnj Sun	Nov 6 2029	04:24	14° Sc 02'
Solar Eclipse	Dec 5 2029	14:52	13° Sg 45'
Lunar Eclipse	Dec 20 2029	22:46	29° Ge 20'
Mon Cnj Sun	Jan 4 2030	02:50	13° Cp 46'
Mon Cnj Sun	Feb 2 2030	16:07	13° Aq 51'

Appendix I • *New Moons + Solar & Lunar Eclipses 1920 to 2120*

Mon Cnj Sun	Mar 4 2030	06:35	13° Pi 43'
Mon Cnj Sun	Apr 2 2030	22:02	13° Ar 12'
Mon Cnj Sun	May 2 2030	14:12	12° Ta 13'
Solar Eclipse	Jun 1 2030	06:21	10° Ge 49'
Lunar Eclipse	Jun 15 2030	18:41	24° Sg 43'
Mon Cnj Sun	Jun 30 2030	21:34	09° Cn 08'
Mon Cnj Sun	Jul 30 2030	11:11	07° Le 21'
Mon Cnj Sun	Aug 28 2030	23:07	05° Vi 41'
Mon Cnj Sun	Sep 27 2030	09:55	04° Li 20'
Mon Cnj Sun	Oct 26 2030	20:17	03° Sc 27'
Solar Eclipse	Nov 25 2030	06:46	03° Sg 02'
Lunar Eclipse	Dec 9 2030	22:40	17° Ge 53'
Mon Cnj Sun	Dec 24 2030	17:32	02° Cp 56'
Mon Cnj Sun	Jan 23 2031	04:31	02° Aq 57'
Mon Cnj Sun	Feb 21 2031	15:49	02° Pi 48'
Mon Cnj Sun	Mar 23 2031	03:49	02° Ar 19'
Mon Cnj Sun	Apr 21 2031	16:57	01° Ta 24'
Lunar Eclipse	May 7 2031	03:40	16° Sc 24'
Solar Eclipse	May 21 2031	07:17	00° Ge 04'
Lunar Eclipse	Jun 5 2031	11:58	14° Sg 39'
Mon Cnj Sun	Jun 19 2031	22:25	28° Ge 27'
Mon Cnj Sun	Jul 19 2031	13:40	26° Cn 43'
Mon Cnj Sun	Aug 18 2031	04:32	25° Le 04'
Mon Cnj Sun	Sep 16 2031	18:47	23° Vi 42'
Mon Cnj Sun	Oct 16 2031	08:21	22° Li 46'
Lunar Eclipse	Oct 30 2031	07:33	06° Ta 40'
Solar Eclipse	Nov 14 2031	21:10	22° Sc 17'
Mon Cnj Sun	Dec 14 2031	09:06	22° Sg 09'
Mon Cnj Sun	Jan 12 2032	20:07	22° Cp 10'
Mon Cnj Sun	Feb 11 2032	06:24	22° Aq 04'
Mon Cnj Sun	Mar 11 2032	16:25	21° Pi 39'
Mon Cnj Sun	Apr 10 2032	02:39	20° Ar 47'
Lunar Eclipse	Apr 25 2032	15:10	05° Sc 58'
Solar Eclipse	May 9 2032	13:36	19° Ta 29'
Mon Cnj Sun	Jun 8 2032	01:32	17° Ge 50'
Mon Cnj Sun	Jul 7 2032	14:41	16° Cn 02'
Mon Cnj Sun	Aug 6 2032	05:12	14° Le 18'
Mon Cnj Sun	Sep 4 2032	20:57	12° Vi 52'
Mon Cnj Sun	Oct 4 2032	13:26	11° Li 52'
Lunar Eclipse	Oct 18 2032	18:58	25° Ar 56'
Solar Eclipse	Nov 3 2032	05:45	11° Sc 21'
Mon Cnj Sun	Dec 2 2032	08:53	11° Sg 14'
Mon Cnj Sun	Jan 1 2033	10:17	11° Cp 18'
Mon Cnj Sun	Jan 30 2033	22:00	11° Aq 19'

Mon Cnj Sun	Mar 1 2033	08:23	11° Pi 03'
Solar Eclipse	Mar 30 2033	17:52	10° Ar 20'
Lunar Eclipse	Apr 14 2033	19:17	25° Li 09'
Mon Cnj Sun	Apr 29 2033	02:46	09° Ta 07'
Mon Cnj Sun	May 28 2033	11:37	07° Ge 27'
Mon Cnj Sun	Jun 26 2033	21:07	05° Cn 34'
Mon Cnj Sun	Jul 26 2033	08:13	03° Le 40'
Mon Cnj Sun	Aug 24 2033	21:40	02° Vi 02'
Solar Eclipse	Sep 23 2033	13:40	00° Li 50'
Lunar Eclipse	Oct 8 2033	10:58	15° Ar 28'
Mon Cnj Sun	Oct 23 2033	07:28	00° Sc 12'
Mon Cnj Sun	Nov 22 2033	01:39	00° Sg 03'
Mon Cnj Sun	Dec 21 2033	18:46	00° Cp 12'
Mon Cnj Sun	Jan 20 2034	10:02	00° Aq 24'
Mon Cnj Sun	Feb 18 2034	23:10	00° Pi 21'
Solar Eclipse	Mar 20 2034	10:15	29° Pi 52'
Lunar Eclipse	Apr 3 2034	19:19	14° Li 06'
Mon Cnj Sun	Apr 18 2034	19:26	28° Ar 50'
Mon Cnj Sun	May 18 2034	03:13	27° Ta 16'
Mon Cnj Sun	Jun 16 2034	10:26	25° Ge 22'
Mon Cnj Sun	Jul 15 2034	18:15	23° Cn 20'
Mon Cnj Sun	Aug 14 2034	03:53	21° Le 27'
Solar Eclipse	Sep 12 2034	16:14	19° Vi 58'
Lunar Eclipse	Sep 28 2034	02:57	05° Ar 04'
Mon Cnj Sun	Oct 12 2034	07:33	19° Li 03'
Mon Cnj Sun	Nov 11 2034	01:16	18° Sc 42'
Mon Cnj Sun	Dec 10 2034	20:14	18° Sg 50'
Mon Cnj Sun	Jan 9 2035	15:03	19° Cp 10'
Mon Cnj Sun	Feb 8 2035	08:22	19° Aq 23'
Lunar Eclipse	Feb 22 2035	08:54	03° Vi 33'
Solar Eclipse	Mar 9 2035	23:09	19° Pi 12'
Mon Cnj Sun	Apr 8 2035	10:58	18° Ar 26'
Mon Cnj Sun	May 7 2035	20:04	17° Ta 06'
Mon Cnj Sun	Jun 6 2035	03:21	15° Ge 17'
Mon Cnj Sun	Jul 5 2035	09:59	13° Cn 15'
Mon Cnj Sun	Aug 3 2035	17:12	11° Le 13'
Lunar Eclipse	Aug 19 2035	01:00	25° Aq 55'
Solar Eclipse	Sep 2 2035	01:59	09° Vi 27'
Mon Cnj Sun	Oct 1 2035	13:07	08° Li 11'
Mon Cnj Sun	Oct 31 2035	02:59	07° Sc 30'
Mon Cnj Sun	Nov 29 2035	19:38	07° Sg 24'
Mon Cnj Sun	Dec 29 2035	14:31	07° Cp 41'
Mon Cnj Sun	Jan 28 2036	10:17	08° Aq 03'
Lunar Eclipse	Feb 11 2036	22:09	22° Le 45'

Appendix I • *New Moons + Solar & Lunar Eclipses 1920 to 2120*

Solar Eclipse	Feb 27 2036	04:59	08° Pi 10'
Mon Cnj Sun	Mar 27 2036	20:57	07° Ar 45'
Mon Cnj Sun	Apr 26 2036	09:33	06° Ta 44'
Mon Cnj Sun	May 25 2036	19:17	05° Ge 09'
Mon Cnj Sun	Jun 24 2036	03:10	03° Cn 12'
Solar Eclipse	Jul 23 2036	10:17	01° Le 09'
Lunar Eclipse	Aug 7 2036	02:49	15° Aq 11'
Solar Eclipse	Aug 21 2036	17:35	29° Le 14'
Mon Cnj Sun	Sep 20 2036	01:52	27° Vi 41'
Mon Cnj Sun	Oct 19 2036	11:50	26° Li 40'
Mon Cnj Sun	Nov 18 2036	00:14	26° Sc 14'
Mon Cnj Sun	Dec 17 2036	15:34	26° Sg 16'
Solar Eclipse	Jan 16 2037	09:34	26° Cp 35'
Lunar Eclipse	Jan 31 2037	14:04	12° Le 02'
Mon Cnj Sun	Feb 15 2037	04:54	26° Aq 50'
Mon Cnj Sun	Mar 16 2037	23:36	26° Pi 42'
Mon Cnj Sun	Apr 15 2037	16:08	26° Ar 01'
Mon Cnj Sun	May 15 2037	05:54	24° Ta 45'
Mon Cnj Sun	Jun 13 2037	17:10	23° Ge 01'
Solar Eclipse	Jul 13 2037	02:32	21° Cn 03'
Lunar Eclipse	Jul 27 2037	04:15	04° Aq 29'
Mon Cnj Sun	Aug 11 2037	10:42	19° Le 06'
Mon Cnj Sun	Sep 9 2037	18:25	17° Vi 24'
Mon Cnj Sun	Oct 9 2037	02:34	16° Li 09'
Mon Cnj Sun	Nov 7 2037	12:03	15° Sc 25'
Mon Cnj Sun	Dec 6 2037	23:38	15° Sg 11'
Solar Eclipse	Jan 5 2038	13:41	15° Cp 18'
Lunar Eclipse	Jan 21 2038	04:00	01° Le 11'
Mon Cnj Sun	Feb 4 2038	05:52	15° Aq 29'
Mon Cnj Sun	Mar 5 2038	23:15	15° Pi 28'
Mon Cnj Sun	Apr 4 2038	16:43	15° Ar 00'
Mon Cnj Sun	May 4 2038	09:20	14° Ta 01'
Mon Cnj Sun	Jun 3 2038	00:24	12° Ge 33'
Lunar Eclipse	Jun 17 2038	02:30	26° Sg 02'
Solar Eclipse	Jul 2 2038	13:32	10° Cn 47'
Lunar Eclipse	Jul 16 2038	11:48	24° Cp 04'
Mon Cnj Sun	Aug 1 2038	00:40	08° Le 54'
Mon Cnj Sun	Aug 30 2038	10:13	07° Vi 09'
Mon Cnj Sun	Sep 28 2038	18:58	05° Li 45'
Mon Cnj Sun	Oct 28 2038	03:53	04° Sc 49'
Mon Cnj Sun	Nov 26 2038	13:47	04° Sg 23'
Lunar Eclipse	Dec 11 2038	17:30	19° Ge 45'
Solar Eclipse	Dec 26 2038	01:02	04° Cp 19'
Mon Cnj Sun	Jan 24 2039	13:36	04° Aq 24'

Mon Cnj Sun	Feb 23 2039	03:17	04° Pi 20'
Mon Cnj Sun	Mar 24 2039	17:59	03° Ar 56'
Mon Cnj Sun	Apr 23 2039	09:35	03° Ta 06'
Mon Cnj Sun	May 23 2039	01:38	01° Ge 49'
Lunar Eclipse	Jun 6 2039	18:48	15° Sg 56'
Solar Eclipse	Jun 21 2039	17:21	00° Cn 12'
Mon Cnj Sun	Jul 21 2039	07:54	28° Cn 27'
Mon Cnj Sun	Aug 19 2039	20:51	26° Le 44'
Mon Cnj Sun	Sep 18 2039	08:23	25° Vi 17'
Mon Cnj Sun	Oct 17 2039	19:09	24° Li 16'
Mon Cnj Sun	Nov 16 2039	05:46	23° Sc 43'
Lunar Eclipse	Nov 30 2039	16:50	08° Ge 19'
Solar Eclipse	Dec 15 2039	16:32	23° Sg 32'
Mon Cnj Sun	Jan 14 2040	03:25	23° Cp 33'
Mon Cnj Sun	Feb 12 2040	14:24	23° Aq 28'
Mon Cnj Sun	Mar 13 2040	01:46	23° Pi 05'
Mon Cnj Sun	Apr 11 2040	14:00	22° Ar 17'
Solar Eclipse	May 11 2040	03:28	21° Ta 03'
Lunar Eclipse	May 26 2040	11:47	05° Sg 50'
Mon Cnj Sun	Jun 9 2040	18:03	19° Ge 30'
Mon Cnj Sun	Jul 9 2040	09:15	17° Cn 46'
Mon Cnj Sun	Aug 8 2040	00:26	16° Le 05'
Mon Cnj Sun	Sep 6 2040	15:14	14° Vi 38'
Mon Cnj Sun	Oct 6 2040	05:26	13° Li 34'
Solar Eclipse	Nov 4 2040	18:56	12° Sc 58'
Lunar Eclipse	Nov 18 2040	19:06	27° Ta 03'
Mon Cnj Sun	Dec 4 2040	07:33	12° Sg 45'
Mon Cnj Sun	Jan 2 2041	19:08	12° Cp 45'
Mon Cnj Sun	Feb 1 2041	05:43	12° Aq 43'
Mon Cnj Sun	Mar 2 2041	15:39	12° Pi 25'
Mon Cnj Sun	Apr 1 2041	01:29	11° Ar 41'
Solar Eclipse	Apr 30 2041	11:46	10° Ta 30'
Lunar Eclipse	May 16 2041	00:52	25° Sc 32'
Mon Cnj Sun	May 29 2041	22:56	08° Ge 55'
Mon Cnj Sun	Jun 28 2041	11:17	07° Cn 08'
Mon Cnj Sun	Jul 28 2041	01:02	05° Le 21'
Mon Cnj Sun	Aug 26 2041	16:16	03° Vi 48'
Mon Cnj Sun	Sep 25 2041	08:41	02° Li 39'
Solar Eclipse	Oct 25 2041	01:30	02° Sc 00'
Lunar Eclipse	Nov 8 2041	04:43	16° Ta 08'
Mon Cnj Sun	Nov 23 2041	17:37	01° Sg 48'
Mon Cnj Sun	Dec 23 2041	08:06	01° Cp 51'
Mon Cnj Sun	Jan 21 2042	20:42	01° Aq 56'
Mon Cnj Sun	Feb 20 2042	07:39	01° Pi 47'

Appendix I • *New Moons + Solar & Lunar Eclipses 1920 to 2120*

Mon Cnj Sun	Mar 21 2042	17:23	01° Ar 13'
Lunar Eclipse	Apr 5 2042	14:16	15° Li 55'
Solar Eclipse	Apr 20 2042	02:19	00° Ta 08'
Mon Cnj Sun	May 19 2042	10:55	28° Ta 36'
Mon Cnj Sun	Jun 17 2042	19:48	26° Ge 45'
Mon Cnj Sun	Jul 17 2042	05:52	24° Cn 49'
Mon Cnj Sun	Aug 15 2042	18:01	23° Le 03'
Mon Cnj Sun	Sep 14 2042	08:50	21° Vi 41'
Lunar Eclipse	Sep 29 2042	10:34	06° Ar 25'
Solar Eclipse	Oct 14 2042	02:03	20° Li 51'
Lunar Eclipse	Oct 28 2042	19:48	05° Ta 31'
Mon Cnj Sun	Nov 12 2042	20:28	20° Sc 35'
Mon Cnj Sun	Dec 12 2042	14:30	20° Sg 41'
Mon Cnj Sun	Jan 11 2043	06:53	20° Cp 55'
Mon Cnj Sun	Feb 9 2043	21:08	21° Aq 00'
Mon Cnj Sun	Mar 11 2043	09:09	20° Pi 41'
Lunar Eclipse	Mar 25 2043	14:26	04° Li 50'
Solar Eclipse	Apr 9 2043	19:07	19° Ar 49'
Mon Cnj Sun	May 9 2043	03:21	18° Ta 25'
Mon Cnj Sun	Jun 7 2043	10:35	16° Ge 36'
Mon Cnj Sun	Jul 6 2043	17:51	14° Cn 34'
Mon Cnj Sun	Aug 5 2043	02:23	12° Le 36'
Mon Cnj Sun	Sep 3 2043	13:17	10° Vi 57'
Lunar Eclipse	Sep 19 2043	01:47	26° Pi 02'
Solar Eclipse	Oct 3 2043	03:12	09° Li 48'
Mon Cnj Sun	Nov 1 2043	19:57	09° Sc 16'
Mon Cnj Sun	Dec 1 2043	14:37	09° Sg 16'
Mon Cnj Sun	Dec 31 2043	09:48	09° Cp 35'
Mon Cnj Sun	Jan 30 2044	04:04	09° Aq 53'
Solar Eclipse	Feb 28 2044	20:12	09° Pi 53'
Lunar Eclipse	Mar 13 2044	19:41	23° Vi 52'
Mon Cnj Sun	Mar 29 2044	09:26	09° Ar 20'
Mon Cnj Sun	Apr 27 2044	19:42	08° Ta 11'
Mon Cnj Sun	May 27 2044	03:40	06° Ge 30'
Mon Cnj Sun	Jun 25 2044	10:24	04° Cn 30'
Mon Cnj Sun	Jul 24 2044	17:10	02° Le 26'
Solar Eclipse	Aug 23 2044	01:06	00° Vi 34'
Lunar Eclipse	Sep 7 2044	11:24	15° Pi 29'
Mon Cnj Sun	Sep 21 2044	11:03	29° Vi 06'
Mon Cnj Sun	Oct 20 2044	23:36	28° Li 13'
Mon Cnj Sun	Nov 19 2044	14:58	27° Sc 55'
Mon Cnj Sun	Dec 19 2044	08:53	28° Sg 05'
Mon Cnj Sun	Jan 18 2045	04:25	28° Cp 28'
Solar Eclipse	Feb 16 2045	23:51	28° Aq 42'

Lunar Eclipse	Mar 3 2045	07:53	13° Vi 08'
Mon Cnj Sun	Mar 18 2045	17:15	28° Pi 30'
Mon Cnj Sun	Apr 17 2045	07:27	27° Ar 42'
Mon Cnj Sun	May 16 2045	18:27	26° Ta 17'
Mon Cnj Sun	Jun 15 2045	03:05	24° Ge 26'
Mon Cnj Sun	Jul 14 2045	10:28	22° Cn 24'
Solar Eclipse	Aug 12 2045	17:39	20° Le 25'
Lunar Eclipse	Aug 27 2045	14:08	04° Pi 43'
Mon Cnj Sun	Sep 11 2045	01:28	18° Vi 44'
Mon Cnj Sun	Oct 10 2045	10:37	17° Li 32'
Mon Cnj Sun	Nov 8 2045	21:49	16° Sc 53'
Mon Cnj Sun	Dec 8 2045	11:41	16° Sg 46'
Mon Cnj Sun	Jan 7 2046	04:24	17° Cp 01'
Lunar Eclipse	Jan 22 2046	12:51	02° Le 39'
Solar Eclipse	Feb 5 2046	23:10	17° Aq 18'
Mon Cnj Sun	Mar 7 2046	18:15	17° Pi 20'
Mon Cnj Sun	Apr 6 2046	11:52	16° Ar 51'
Mon Cnj Sun	May 6 2046	02:56	15° Ta 46'
Mon Cnj Sun	Jun 4 2046	15:22	14° Ge 11'
Mon Cnj Sun	Jul 4 2046	01:39	12° Cn 17'
Lunar Eclipse	Jul 18 2046	00:55	25° Cp 37'
Solar Eclipse	Aug 2 2046	10:25	10° Le 19'
Mon Cnj Sun	Aug 31 2046	18:25	08° Vi 31'
Mon Cnj Sun	Sep 30 2046	02:25	07° Li 06'
Mon Cnj Sun	Oct 29 2046	11:17	06° Sc 12'
Mon Cnj Sun	Nov 27 2046	21:50	05° Sg 48'
Mon Cnj Sun	Dec 27 2046	10:39	05° Cp 49'
Lunar Eclipse	Jan 12 2047	01:21	21° Cn 44'
Solar Eclipse	Jan 26 2047	01:44	06° Aq 00'
Mon Cnj Sun	Feb 24 2047	18:26	06° Pi 03'
Mon Cnj Sun	Mar 26 2047	11:44	05° Ar 44'
Mon Cnj Sun	Apr 25 2047	04:40	04° Ta 55'
Mon Cnj Sun	May 24 2047	20:28	03° Ge 36'
Solar Eclipse	Jun 23 2047	10:36	01° Cn 55'
Lunar Eclipse	Jul 7 2047	10:34	15° Cp 16'
Solar Eclipse	Jul 22 2047	22:49	00° Le 04'
Mon Cnj Sun	Aug 21 2047	09:16	28° Le 16'
Mon Cnj Sun	Sep 19 2047	18:31	26° Vi 45'
Mon Cnj Sun	Oct 19 2047	03:28	25° Li 40'
Mon Cnj Sun	Nov 17 2047	12:59	25° Sc 05'
Solar Eclipse	Dec 16 2047	23:38	24° Sg 55'
Lunar Eclipse	Jan 1 2048	06:57	10° Cn 31'
Mon Cnj Sun	Jan 15 2048	11:32	24° Cp 58'
Mon Cnj Sun	Feb 14 2048	00:31	24° Aq 58'

Appendix I • *New Moons + Solar & Lunar Eclipses 1920 to 2120*

Mon Cnj Sun	Mar 14 2048	14:28	24° Pi 41'
Mon Cnj Sun	Apr 13 2048	05:20	23° Ar 57'
Mon Cnj Sun	May 12 2048	20:58	22° Ta 48'
Solar Eclipse	Jun 11 2048	12:50	21° Ge 16'
Lunar Eclipse	Jun 26 2048	02:08	05° Cp 10'
Mon Cnj Sun	Jul 11 2048	04:04	19° Cn 33'
Mon Cnj Sun	Aug 9 2048	17:59	17° Le 49'
Mon Cnj Sun	Sep 8 2048	06:25	16° Vi 17'
Mon Cnj Sun	Oct 7 2048	17:45	15° Li 08'
Mon Cnj Sun	Nov 6 2048	04:38	14° Sc 26'
Solar Eclipse	Dec 5 2048	15:30	14° Sg 10'
Lunar Eclipse	Dec 20 2048	06:39	29° Ge 03'
Mon Cnj Sun	Jan 4 2049	02:24	14° Cp 09'
Mon Cnj Sun	Feb 2 2049	13:16	14° Aq 07'
Mon Cnj Sun	Mar 4 2049	00:11	13° Pi 51'
Mon Cnj Sun	Apr 2 2049	11:39	13° Ar 10'
Mon Cnj Sun	May 2 2049	00:11	12° Ta 02'
Lunar Eclipse	May 17 2049	11:14	26° Sc 59'
Solar Eclipse	May 31 2049	14:00	10° Ge 33'
Lunar Eclipse	Jun 15 2049	19:27	25° Sg 08'
Mon Cnj Sun	Jun 30 2049	04:50	08° Cn 52'
Mon Cnj Sun	Jul 29 2049	20:07	07° Le 08'
Mon Cnj Sun	Aug 28 2049	11:19	05° Vi 36'
Mon Cnj Sun	Sep 27 2049	02:05	04° Li 25'
Mon Cnj Sun	Oct 26 2049	16:15	03° Sc 41'
Lunar Eclipse	Nov 9 2049	15:38	17° Ta 40'
Solar Eclipse	Nov 25 2049	05:36	03° Sg 22'
Mon Cnj Sun	Dec 24 2049	17:52	03° Cp 21'
Mon Cnj Sun	Jan 23 2050	04:57	03° Aq 22'
Mon Cnj Sun	Feb 21 2050	15:03	03° Pi 10'
Mon Cnj Sun	Mar 23 2050	00:41	02° Ar 34'
Mon Cnj Sun	Apr 21 2050	10:26	01° Ta 31'
Lunar Eclipse	May 6 2050	22:26	16° Sc 35'
Solar Eclipse	May 20 2050	20:51	00° Ge 02'
Mon Cnj Sun	Jun 19 2050	08:22	28° Ge 16'
Mon Cnj Sun	Jul 18 2050	21:17	26° Cn 27'
Mon Cnj Sun	Aug 17 2050	11:47	24° Le 47'
Mon Cnj Sun	Sep 16 2050	03:49	23° Vi 30'
Mon Cnj Sun	Oct 15 2050	20:49	22° Li 41'
Lunar Eclipse	Oct 30 2050	03:16	06° Ta 53'
Solar Eclipse	Nov 14 2050	13:41	22° Sc 22'
Mon Cnj Sun	Dec 14 2050	05:18	22° Sg 23'
Mon Cnj Sun	Jan 12 2051	18:58	22° Cp 30'

Mon Cnj Sun	Feb 11 2051	06:42	22° Aq 28'
Mon Cnj Sun	Mar 12 2051	16:53	22° Pi 03'
Solar Eclipse	Apr 11 2051	01:59	21° Ar 09'
Lunar Eclipse	Apr 26 2051	02:19	05° Sc 50'
Mon Cnj Sun	May 10 2051	10:29	19° Ta 44'
Mon Cnj Sun	Jun 8 2051	18:57	17° Ge 57'
Mon Cnj Sun	Jul 8 2051	04:09	16° Cn 00'
Mon Cnj Sun	Aug 6 2051	15:05	14° Le 08'
Mon Cnj Sun	Sep 5 2051	04:33	12° Vi 36'
Solar Eclipse	Oct 4 2051	20:47	11° Li 35'
Lunar Eclipse	Oct 19 2051	19:13	26° Ar 21'
Mon Cnj Sun	Nov 3 2051	14:59	11° Sc 08'
Mon Cnj Sun	Dec 3 2051	09:37	11° Sg 09'
Mon Cnj Sun	Jan 2 2052	03:06	11° Cp 24'
Mon Cnj Sun	Jan 31 2052	18:30	11° Aq 34'
Mon Cnj Sun	Mar 1 2052	07:36	11° Pi 25'
Solar Eclipse	Mar 30 2052	18:27	10° Ar 45'
Lunar Eclipse	Apr 14 2052	02:29	24° Li 51'
Mon Cnj Sun	Apr 29 2052	03:21	09° Ta 31'
Mon Cnj Sun	May 28 2052	10:50	07° Ge 49'
Mon Cnj Sun	Jun 26 2052	17:50	05° Cn 49'
Mon Cnj Sun	Jul 26 2052	01:31	03° Le 47'
Mon Cnj Sun	Aug 24 2052	11:07	01° Vi 59'
Solar Eclipse	Sep 22 2052	23:33	00° Li 39'
Lunar Eclipse	Oct 8 2052	10:55	15° Ar 52'
Mon Cnj Sun	Oct 22 2052	15:03	29° Li 55'
Mon Cnj Sun	Nov 21 2052	09:03	29° Sc 45'
Mon Cnj Sun	Dec 21 2052	04:15	29° Sg 59'
Mon Cnj Sun	Jan 19 2053	23:12	00° Aq 20'
Mon Cnj Sun	Feb 18 2053	16:32	00° Pi 29'
Lunar Eclipse	Mar 4 2053	17:10	14° Vi 35'
Solar Eclipse	Mar 20 2053	07:11	00° Ar 08'
Mon Cnj Sun	Apr 18 2053	18:48	29° Ar 11'
Mon Cnj Sun	May 18 2053	03:43	27° Ta 41'
Mon Cnj Sun	Jun 16 2053	10:51	25° Ge 46'
Mon Cnj Sun	Jul 15 2053	17:27	23° Cn 41'
Mon Cnj Sun	Aug 14 2053	00:41	21° Le 43'
Lunar Eclipse	Aug 29 2053	07:53	06° Pi 27'
Solar Eclipse	Sep 12 2053	09:36	20° Vi 06'
Mon Cnj Sun	Oct 11 2053	20:54	19° Li 00'
Mon Cnj Sun	Nov 10 2053	10:56	18° Sc 30'
Mon Cnj Sun	Dec 10 2053	03:41	18° Sg 32'
Mon Cnj Sun	Jan 8 2054	22:34	18° Cp 52'
Mon Cnj Sun	Feb 7 2054	18:14	19° Aq 11'

Appendix I • *New Moons + Solar & Lunar Eclipses 1920 to 2120*

Lunar Eclipse	Feb 22 2054	06:47	03° Vi 51'
Solar Eclipse	Mar 9 2054	12:46	19° Pi 09'
Mon Cnj Sun	Apr 8 2054	04:33	18° Ar 34'
Mon Cnj Sun	May 7 2054	17:01	17° Ta 22'
Mon Cnj Sun	Jun 6 2054	02:40	15° Ge 39'
Mon Cnj Sun	Jul 5 2054	10:34	13° Cn 39'
Solar Eclipse	Aug 3 2054	17:48	11° Le 38'
Lunar Eclipse	Aug 18 2054	09:22	25° Aq 41'
Solar Eclipse	Sep 2 2054	01:18	09° Vi 49'
Mon Cnj Sun	Oct 1 2054	09:50	08° Li 27'
Mon Cnj Sun	Oct 30 2054	20:02	07° Sc 37'
Mon Cnj Sun	Nov 29 2054	08:34	07° Sg 19'
Mon Cnj Sun	Dec 28 2054	23:52	07° Cp 27'
Solar Eclipse	Jan 27 2055	17:39	07° Aq 45'
Lunar Eclipse	Feb 11 2055	22:49	23° Le 10'
Mon Cnj Sun	Feb 26 2055	12:39	07° Pi 53'
Mon Cnj Sun	Mar 28 2055	07:01	07° Ar 35'
Mon Cnj Sun	Apr 26 2055	23:17	06° Ta 42'
Mon Cnj Sun	May 26 2055	12:57	05° Ge 17'
Mon Cnj Sun	Jun 25 2055	00:16	03° Cn 29'
Solar Eclipse	Jul 24 2055	09:48	01° Le 31'
Lunar Eclipse	Aug 7 2055	10:57	14° Aq 57'
Mon Cnj Sun	Aug 22 2055	18:15	29° Le 39'
Mon Cnj Sun	Sep 21 2055	02:20	28° Vi 06'
Mon Cnj Sun	Oct 20 2055	10:50	27° Li 01'
Mon Cnj Sun	Nov 18 2055	20:34	26° Sc 28'
Mon Cnj Sun	Dec 18 2055	08:16	26° Sg 21'
Solar Eclipse	Jan 16 2056	22:11	26° Cp 30'
Lunar Eclipse	Feb 1 2056	12:36	12° Le 22'
Mon Cnj Sun	Feb 15 2056	14:00	26° Aq 36'
Mon Cnj Sun	Mar 16 2056	06:53	26° Pi 25'
Mon Cnj Sun	Apr 14 2056	23:51	25° Ar 45'
Mon Cnj Sun	May 14 2056	16:06	24° Ta 35'
Mon Cnj Sun	Jun 13 2056	07:04	23° Ge 01'
Lunar Eclipse	Jun 27 2056	09:48	06° Cp 29'
Solar Eclipse	Jul 12 2056	20:20	21° Cn 12'
Lunar Eclipse	Jul 26 2056	18:55	04° Aq 31'
Mon Cnj Sun	Aug 11 2056	07:48	19° Le 23'
Mon Cnj Sun	Sep 9 2056	17:48	17° Vi 46'
Mon Cnj Sun	Oct 9 2056	03:01	16° Li 33'
Mon Cnj Sun	Nov 7 2056	12:21	15° Sc 49'
Mon Cnj Sun	Dec 6 2056	22:31	15° Sg 32'
Lunar Eclipse	Dec 22 2056	01:34	00° Cn 55'
Solar Eclipse	Jan 5 2057	09:50	15° Cp 32'

Mon Cnj Sun	Feb 3 2057	22:11	15° Aq 34'
Mon Cnj Sun	Mar 5 2057	11:25	15° Pi 22'
Mon Cnj Sun	Apr 4 2057	01:32	14° Ar 46'
Mon Cnj Sun	May 3 2057	16:32	13° Ta 44'
Mon Cnj Sun	Jun 2 2057	08:11	12° Ge 18'
Lunar Eclipse	Jun 17 2057	02:19	26° Sg 25'
Solar Eclipse	Jul 1 2057	23:48	10° Cn 37'
Mon Cnj Sun	Jul 31 2057	14:32	08° Le 53'
Mon Cnj Sun	Aug 30 2057	03:55	07° Vi 17'
Mon Cnj Sun	Sep 28 2057	16:01	06° Li 01'
Mon Cnj Sun	Oct 28 2057	03:19	05° Sc 11'
Mon Cnj Sun	Nov 26 2057	14:23	04° Sg 48'
Lunar Eclipse	Dec 11 2057	00:46	19° Ge 26'
Solar Eclipse	Dec 26 2057	01:23	04° Cp 44'
Mon Cnj Sun	Jan 24 2058	12:14	04° Aq 44'
Mon Cnj Sun	Feb 22 2058	22:57	04° Pi 33'
Mon Cnj Sun	Mar 24 2058	09:50	04° Ar 00'
Mon Cnj Sun	Apr 22 2058	21:29	03° Ta 00'
Solar Eclipse	May 22 2058	10:24	01° Ge 36'
Lunar Eclipse	Jun 6 2058	19:16	16° Sg 20'
Solar Eclipse	Jun 21 2058	00:35	29° Ge 56'
Mon Cnj Sun	Jul 20 2058	15:40	28° Cn 12'
Mon Cnj Sun	Aug 19 2058	07:04	26° Le 35'
Mon Cnj Sun	Sep 17 2058	22:18	25° Vi 17'
Mon Cnj Sun	Oct 17 2058	13:05	24° Li 25'
Solar Eclipse	Nov 16 2058	03:10	24° Sc 00'
Lunar Eclipse	Nov 30 2058	03:17	08° Ge 09'
Mon Cnj Sun	Dec 15 2058	16:12	23° Sg 55'
Mon Cnj Sun	Jan 14 2059	03:57	23° Cp 57'
Mon Cnj Sun	Feb 12 2059	14:28	23° Aq 52'
Mon Cnj Sun	Mar 14 2059	00:06	23° Pi 24'
Mon Cnj Sun	Apr 12 2059	09:29	22° Ar 29'
Solar Eclipse	May 11 2059	19:16	21° Ta 07'
Lunar Eclipse	May 27 2059	08:04	06° Sg 05'
Mon Cnj Sun	Jun 10 2059	05:57	19° Ge 25'
Mon Cnj Sun	Jul 9 2059	17:59	17° Cn 34'
Mon Cnj Sun	Aug 8 2059	07:38	15° Le 48'
Mon Cnj Sun	Sep 6 2059	23:01	14° Vi 22'
Mon Cnj Sun	Oct 6 2059	15:50	13° Li 24'
Solar Eclipse	Nov 5 2059	09:12	12° Sc 57'
Lunar Eclipse	Nov 19 2059	13:10	27° Ta 11'
Mon Cnj Sun	Dec 5 2059	01:50	12° Sg 54'
Mon Cnj Sun	Jan 3 2060	16:41	13° Cp 03'
Mon Cnj Sun	Feb 2 2060	05:23	13° Aq 06'

Appendix I • *New Moons + Solar & Lunar Eclipses 1920 to 2120*

Mon Cnj Sun	Mar 2 2060	16:12	12° Pi 50'
Mon Cnj Sun	Apr 1 2060	01:38	12° Ar 05'
Lunar Eclipse	Apr 15 2060	21:22	26° Li 39'
Solar Eclipse	Apr 30 2060	10:11	10° Ta 49'
Mon Cnj Sun	May 29 2060	18:24	09° Ge 08'
Mon Cnj Sun	Jun 28 2060	02:58	07° Cn 12'
Mon Cnj Sun	Jul 27 2060	12:50	05° Le 15'
Mon Cnj Sun	Aug 26 2060	00:57	03° Vi 34'
Mon Cnj Sun	Sep 24 2060	15:54	02° Li 22'
Lunar Eclipse	Oct 9 2060	18:42	17° Ar 14'
Solar Eclipse	Oct 24 2060	09:26	01° Sc 44'
Lunar Eclipse	Nov 8 2060	04:18	16° Ta 31'
Mon Cnj Sun	Nov 23 2060	04:16	01° Sg 38'
Mon Cnj Sun	Dec 22 2060	22:40	01° Cp 51'
Mon Cnj Sun	Jan 21 2061	15:17	02° Aq 06'
Mon Cnj Sun	Feb 20 2061	05:32	02° Pi 05'
Mon Cnj Sun	Mar 21 2061	17:24	01° Ar 36'
Lunar Eclipse	Apr 4 2061	21:48	15° Li 38'
Solar Eclipse	Apr 20 2061	03:05	00° Ta 34'
Mon Cnj Sun	May 19 2061	11:03	29° Ta 00'
Mon Cnj Sun	Jun 17 2061	18:03	27° Ge 04'
Mon Cnj Sun	Jul 17 2061	01:11	25° Cn 01'
Mon Cnj Sun	Aug 15 2061	09:40	23° Le 06'
Mon Cnj Sun	Sep 13 2061	20:38	21° Vi 35'
Lunar Eclipse	Sep 29 2061	09:33	06° Ar 46'
Solar Eclipse	Oct 13 2061	10:42	20° Li 37'
Mon Cnj Sun	Nov 12 2061	03:40	20° Sc 16'
Mon Cnj Sun	Dec 11 2061	22:33	20° Sg 24'
Mon Cnj Sun	Jan 10 2062	17:53	20° Cp 45'
Mon Cnj Sun	Feb 9 2062	12:11	21° Aq 00'
Solar Eclipse	Mar 11 2062	04:14	20° Pi 52'
Lunar Eclipse	Mar 25 2062	03:36	04° Li 46'
Mon Cnj Sun	Apr 9 2062	17:17	20° Ar 08'
Mon Cnj Sun	May 9 2062	03:23	18° Ta 49'
Mon Cnj Sun	Jun 7 2062	11:12	17° Ge 01'
Mon Cnj Sun	Jul 6 2062	17:53	14° Cn 58'
Mon Cnj Sun	Aug 5 2062	00:41	12° Le 55'
Solar Eclipse	Sep 3 2062	08:43	11° Vi 09'
Lunar Eclipse	Sep 18 2062	18:37	26° Pi 08'
Mon Cnj Sun	Oct 2 2062	18:50	09° Li 52'
Mon Cnj Sun	Nov 1 2062	07:33	09° Sc 09'
Mon Cnj Sun	Nov 30 2062	23:01	09° Sg 01'
Mon Cnj Sun	Dec 30 2062	16:57	09° Cp 15'
Mon Cnj Sun	Jan 29 2063	12:23	09° Aq 37'

Solar Eclipse	Feb 28 2063	07:38	09° Pi 44'
Lunar Eclipse	Mar 14 2063	16:15	24° Vi 07'
Mon Cnj Sun	Mar 30 2063	00:50	09° Ar 22'
Mon Cnj Sun	Apr 28 2063	14:52	08° Ta 22'
Mon Cnj Sun	May 28 2063	01:47	06° Ge 49'
Mon Cnj Sun	Jun 26 2063	10:26	04° Cn 54'
Mon Cnj Sun	Jul 25 2063	17:56	02° Le 52'
Solar Eclipse	Aug 24 2063	01:18	00° Vi 58'
Lunar Eclipse	Sep 7 2063	20:53	15° Pi 17'
Mon Cnj Sun	Sep 22 2063	09:22	29° Vi 26'
Mon Cnj Sun	Oct 21 2063	18:47	28° Li 25'
Mon Cnj Sun	Nov 20 2063	06:10	27° Sc 57'
Mon Cnj Sun	Dec 19 2063	20:04	27° Sg 57'
Mon Cnj Sun	Jan 18 2064	12:37	28° Cp 12'
Lunar Eclipse	Feb 2 2064	21:37	13° Le 49'
Solar Eclipse	Feb 17 2064	07:03	28° Aq 24'
Mon Cnj Sun	Mar 18 2064	01:45	28° Pi 15'
Mon Cnj Sun	Apr 16 2064	19:02	27° Ar 35'
Mon Cnj Sun	May 16 2064	09:55	26° Ta 20'
Mon Cnj Sun	Jun 14 2064	22:21	24° Ge 39'
Mon Cnj Sun	Jul 14 2064	08:46	22° Cn 43'
Lunar Eclipse	Jul 28 2064	07:41	06° Aq 02'
Solar Eclipse	Aug 12 2064	17:50	20° Le 49'
Mon Cnj Sun	Sep 11 2064	02:11	19° Vi 09'
Mon Cnj Sun	Oct 10 2064	10:34	17° Li 55'
Mon Cnj Sun	Nov 8 2064	19:45	17° Sc 12'
Mon Cnj Sun	Dec 8 2064	06:29	16° Sg 57'
Mon Cnj Sun	Jan 6 2065	19:15	17° Cp 01'
Lunar Eclipse	Jan 22 2065	09:54	02° Le 55'
Solar Eclipse	Feb 5 2065	10:03	17° Aq 09'
Mon Cnj Sun	Mar 7 2065	02:16	17° Pi 03'
Mon Cnj Sun	Apr 5 2065	19:01	16° Ar 33'
Mon Cnj Sun	May 5 2065	11:31	15° Ta 32'
Mon Cnj Sun	Jun 4 2065	03:05	14° Ge 05'
Solar Eclipse	Jul 3 2065	17:16	12° Cn 20'
Lunar Eclipse	Jul 17 2065	17:46	25° Cp 43'
Solar Eclipse	Aug 2 2065	05:47	10° Le 31'
Mon Cnj Sun	Aug 31 2065	16:40	08° Vi 50'
Mon Cnj Sun	Sep 30 2065	02:25	07° Li 30'
Mon Cnj Sun	Oct 29 2065	11:49	06° Sc 37'
Mon Cnj Sun	Nov 27 2065	21:40	06° Sg 12'
Solar Eclipse	Dec 27 2065	08:28	06° Cp 07'
Lunar Eclipse	Jan 11 2066	15:08	21° Cn 42'
Mon Cnj Sun	Jan 25 2066	20:15	06° Aq 10'

Appendix I • *New Moons + Solar & Lunar Eclipses 1920 to 2120*

Mon Cnj Sun	Feb 24 2066	08:51	06° Pi 03'
Mon Cnj Sun	Mar 25 2066	22:14	05° Ar 34'
Mon Cnj Sun	Apr 24 2066	12:30	04° Ta 39'
Mon Cnj Sun	May 24 2066	03:39	03° Ge 19'
Solar Eclipse	Jun 22 2066	19:16	01° Cn 42'
Lunar Eclipse	Jul 7 2066	09:35	15° Cp 37'
Mon Cnj Sun	Jul 22 2066	10:34	29° Cn 58'
Mon Cnj Sun	Aug 21 2066	00:50	28° Le 19'
Mon Cnj Sun	Sep 19 2066	13:48	26° Vi 57'
Mon Cnj Sun	Oct 19 2066	01:43	25° Li 59'
Mon Cnj Sun	Nov 17 2066	13:07	25° Sc 29'
Solar Eclipse	Dec 17 2066	00:18	25° Sg 21'
Lunar Eclipse	Dec 31 2066	14:41	10° Cn 13'
Mon Cnj Sun	Jan 15 2067	11:18	25° Cp 22'
Mon Cnj Sun	Feb 13 2067	21:58	25° Aq 16'
Mon Cnj Sun	Mar 15 2067	08:29	24° Pi 50'
Mon Cnj Sun	Apr 13 2067	19:24	23° Ar 57'
Mon Cnj Sun	May 13 2067	07:21	22° Ta 39'
Lunar Eclipse	May 28 2067	18:42	07° Sg 32'
Solar Eclipse	Jun 11 2067	20:42	21° Ge 02'
Lunar Eclipse	Jun 27 2067	02:53	05° Cp 36'
Mon Cnj Sun	Jul 11 2067	11:17	19° Cn 17'
Mon Cnj Sun	Aug 10 2067	02:37	17° Le 36'
Mon Cnj Sun	Sep 8 2067	18:10	16° Vi 11'
Mon Cnj Sun	Oct 8 2067	09:29	15° Li 11'
Mon Cnj Sun	Nov 7 2067	00:15	14° Sc 39'
Lunar Eclipse	Nov 20 2067	23:50	28° Ta 43'
Solar Eclipse	Dec 6 2067	14:05	14° Sg 30'
Mon Cnj Sun	Jan 5 2068	02:39	14° Cp 33'
Mon Cnj Sun	Feb 3 2068	13:45	14° Aq 32'
Mon Cnj Sun	Mar 3 2068	23:38	14° Pi 13'
Mon Cnj Sun	Apr 2 2068	08:52	13° Ar 27'
Mon Cnj Sun	May 1 2068	18:08	12° Ta 12'
Lunar Eclipse	May 17 2068	05:35	27° Sc 10'
Solar Eclipse	May 31 2068	04:04	10° Ge 33'
Mon Cnj Sun	Jun 29 2068	15:12	08° Cn 43'
Mon Cnj Sun	Jul 29 2068	03:55	06° Le 53'
Mon Cnj Sun	Aug 27 2068	18:29	05° Vi 19'
Mon Cnj Sun	Sep 26 2068	10:49	04° Li 11'
Mon Cnj Sun	Oct 26 2068	04:18	03° Sc 35'
Lunar Eclipse	Nov 9 2068	11:41	17° Ta 54'
Solar Eclipse	Nov 24 2068	21:43	03° Sg 26'
Mon Cnj Sun	Dec 24 2068	13:45	03° Cp 34'
Mon Cnj Sun	Jan 23 2069	03:37	03° Aq 42'

Mon Cnj Sun	Feb 21 2069	15:18	03° Pi 34'
Mon Cnj Sun	Mar 23 2069	01:14	03° Ar 00'
Solar Eclipse	Apr 21 2069	09:59	01° Ta 53'
Lunar Eclipse	May 6 2069	09:12	16° Sc 27'
Solar Eclipse	May 20 2069	18:07	00° Ge 19'
Mon Cnj Sun	Jun 19 2069	02:15	28° Ge 25'
Mon Cnj Sun	Jul 18 2069	11:14	26° Cn 26'
Mon Cnj Sun	Aug 16 2069	22:04	24° Le 38'
Mon Cnj Sun	Sep 15 2069	11:36	23° Vi 14'
Solar Eclipse	Oct 15 2069	04:04	22° Li 24'
Lunar Eclipse	Oct 30 2069	03:36	07° Ta 18'
Mon Cnj Sun	Nov 13 2069	22:38	22° Sc 08'
Mon Cnj Sun	Dec 13 2069	17:39	22° Sg 17'
Mon Cnj Sun	Jan 12 2070	11:23	22° Cp 35'
Mon Cnj Sun	Feb 11 2070	02:53	22° Aq 42'
Mon Cnj Sun	Mar 12 2070	15:53	22° Pi 24'
Solar Eclipse	Apr 11 2070	02:31	21° Ar 34'
Lunar Eclipse	Apr 25 2070	09:32	05° Sc 32'
Mon Cnj Sun	May 10 2070	11:09	20° Ta 10'
Mon Cnj Sun	Jun 8 2070	18:25	18° Ge 20'
Mon Cnj Sun	Jul 8 2070	01:15	16° Cn 17'
Mon Cnj Sun	Aug 6 2070	08:52	14° Le 17'
Mon Cnj Sun	Sep 4 2070	18:29	12° Vi 35'
Solar Eclipse	Oct 4 2070	07:02	11° Li 25'
Lunar Eclipse	Oct 19 2070	19:00	26° Ar 44'
Mon Cnj Sun	Nov 2 2070	22:43	10° Sc 51'
Mon Cnj Sun	Dec 2 2070	16:54	10° Sg 50'
Mon Cnj Sun	Jan 1 2071	12:16	11° Cp 09'
Mon Cnj Sun	Jan 31 2071	07:16	11° Aq 29'
Mon Cnj Sun	Mar 2 2071	00:32	11° Pi 30'
Lunar Eclipse	Mar 16 2071	01:18	25° Vi 33'
Solar Eclipse	Mar 31 2071	15:04	11° Ar 00'
Mon Cnj Sun	Apr 30 2071	02:31	09° Ta 53'
Mon Cnj Sun	May 29 2071	11:17	08° Ge 14'
Mon Cnj Sun	Jun 27 2071	18:21	06° Cn 14'
Mon Cnj Sun	Jul 27 2071	00:57	04° Le 10'
Mon Cnj Sun	Aug 25 2071	08:17	02° Vi 16'
Lunar Eclipse	Sep 9 2071	14:52	17° Pi 03'
Solar Eclipse	Sep 23 2071	17:22	00° Li 48'
Mon Cnj Sun	Oct 23 2071	04:50	29° Li 53'
Mon Cnj Sun	Nov 21 2071	19:00	29° Sc 33'
Mon Cnj Sun	Dec 21 2071	11:48	29° Sg 41'
Mon Cnj Sun	Jan 20 2072	06:36	00° Aq 02'
Mon Cnj Sun	Feb 19 2072	02:04	00° Pi 16'

Appendix I • *New Moons + Solar & Lunar Eclipses 1920 to 2120*

Lunar Eclipse	Mar 4 2072	15:18	14° Vi 54'
Solar Eclipse	Mar 19 2072	20:22	00° Ar 04'
Mon Cnj Sun	Apr 18 2072	11:57	29° Ar 18'
Mon Cnj Sun	May 18 2072	00:19	27° Ta 56'
Mon Cnj Sun	Jun 16 2072	09:58	26° Ge 07'
Mon Cnj Sun	Jul 15 2072	17:57	24° Cn 06'
Mon Cnj Sun	Aug 14 2072	01:22	22° Le 08'
Lunar Eclipse	Aug 28 2072	16:00	06° Pi 12'
Solar Eclipse	Sep 12 2072	09:08	20° Vi 28'
Mon Cnj Sun	Oct 11 2072	17:56	19° Li 16'
Mon Cnj Sun	Nov 10 2072	04:22	18° Sc 37'
Mon Cnj Sun	Dec 9 2072	17:00	18° Sg 28'
Mon Cnj Sun	Jan 8 2073	08:12	18° Cp 38'
Solar Eclipse	Feb 7 2073	01:41	18° Aq 52'
Lunar Eclipse	Feb 22 2073	07:27	04° Vi 16'
Mon Cnj Sun	Mar 8 2073	20:16	18° Pi 51'
Mon Cnj Sun	Apr 7 2073	14:15	18° Ar 22'
Mon Cnj Sun	May 7 2073	06:16	17° Ta 19'
Mon Cnj Sun	Jun 5 2073	19:52	15° Ge 46'
Mon Cnj Sun	Jul 5 2073	07:17	13° Cn 55'
Solar Eclipse	Aug 3 2073	17:05	11° Le 59'
Lunar Eclipse	Aug 17 2073	17:46	25° Aq 27'
Mon Cnj Sun	Sep 2 2073	01:53	10° Vi 14'
Mon Cnj Sun	Oct 1 2073	10:22	08° Li 52'
Mon Cnj Sun	Oct 30 2073	19:14	07° Sc 58'
Mon Cnj Sun	Nov 29 2073	05:13	07° Sg 35'
Mon Cnj Sun	Dec 28 2073	16:56	07° Cp 33'
Solar Eclipse	Jan 27 2074	06:38	07° Aq 40'
Lunar Eclipse	Feb 11 2074	21:06	23° Le 29'
Mon Cnj Sun	Feb 25 2074	22:01	07° Pi 39'
Mon Cnj Sun	Mar 27 2074	14:20	07° Ar 17'
Mon Cnj Sun	Apr 26 2074	06:48	06° Ta 25'
Mon Cnj Sun	May 25 2074	22:45	05° Ge 06'
Mon Cnj Sun	Jun 24 2074	13:39	03° Cn 26'
Lunar Eclipse	Jul 8 2074	17:06	16° Cp 56'
Solar Eclipse	Jul 24 2074	03:08	01° Le 38'
Lunar Eclipse	Aug 7 2074	02:07	14° Aq 59'
Mon Cnj Sun	Aug 22 2074	15:00	29° Le 55'
Mon Cnj Sun	Sep 21 2074	01:29	28° Vi 28'
Mon Cnj Sun	Oct 20 2074	11:12	27° Li 26'
Mon Cnj Sun	Nov 18 2074	20:57	26° Sc 53'
Mon Cnj Sun	Dec 18 2074	07:21	26° Sg 43'
Lunar Eclipse	Jan 2 2075	09:40	12° Cn 06'
Solar Eclipse	Jan 16 2075	18:38	26° Cp 44'

Mon Cnj Sun	Feb 15 2075	06:42	26° Aq 41'
Mon Cnj Sun	Mar 16 2075	19:26	26° Pi 20'
Mon Cnj Sun	Apr 15 2075	08:56	25° Ar 32'
Mon Cnj Sun	May 14 2075	23:23	24° Ta 18'
Mon Cnj Sun	Jun 13 2075	14:40	22° Ge 45'
Lunar Eclipse	Jun 28 2075	09:47	06° Cp 52'
Solar Eclipse	Jul 13 2075	06:12	21° Cn 02'
Mon Cnj Sun	Aug 11 2075	21:12	19° Le 21'
Mon Cnj Sun	Sep 10 2075	11:03	17° Vi 53'
Mon Cnj Sun	Oct 9 2075	23:44	16° Li 49'
Mon Cnj Sun	Nov 8 2075	11:36	16° Sc 11'
Mon Cnj Sun	Dec 7 2075	23:04	15° Sg 57'
Lunar Eclipse	Dec 22 2075	08:49	00° Cn 36'
Solar Eclipse	Jan 6 2076	10:15	15° Cp 57'
Mon Cnj Sun	Feb 4 2076	21:02	15° Aq 55'
Mon Cnj Sun	Mar 5 2076	07:25	15° Pi 36'
Mon Cnj Sun	Apr 3 2076	17:48	14° Ar 51'
Mon Cnj Sun	May 3 2076	04:53	13° Ta 39'
Solar Eclipse	Jun 1 2076	17:15	12° Ge 05'
Lunar Eclipse	Jun 17 2076	02:39	26° Sg 49'
Solar Eclipse	Jul 1 2076	07:05	10° Cn 21'
Mon Cnj Sun	Jul 30 2076	22:06	08° Le 37'
Mon Cnj Sun	Aug 29 2076	13:44	07° Vi 06'
Mon Cnj Sun	Sep 28 2076	05:28	05° Li 59'
Mon Cnj Sun	Oct 27 2076	20:51	05° Sc 19'
Solar Eclipse	Nov 26 2076	11:29	05° Sg 05'
Lunar Eclipse	Dec 10 2076	11:36	19° Ge 17'
Mon Cnj Sun	Dec 26 2076	00:54	05° Cp 07'
Mon Cnj Sun	Jan 24 2077	12:46	05° Aq 10'
Mon Cnj Sun	Feb 22 2077	22:08	04° Pi 58'
Mon Cnj Sun	Mar 24 2077	08:25	04° Ar 20'
Mon Cnj Sun	Apr 22 2077	17:21	03° Ta 13'
Solar Eclipse	May 22 2077	02:39	01° Ge 40'
Lunar Eclipse	Jun 6 2077	15:08	16° Sg 34'
Mon Cnj Sun	Jun 20 2077	12:56	29° Ge 51'
Mon Cnj Sun	Jul 20 2077	00:42	27° Cn 59'
Mon Cnj Sun	Aug 18 2077	14:18	26° Le 17'
Mon Cnj Sun	Sep 17 2077	05:54	25° Vi 00'
Mon Cnj Sun	Oct 16 2077	23:08	24° Li 13'
Solar Eclipse	Nov 15 2077	17:01	23° Sc 58'
Lunar Eclipse	Nov 29 2077	21:44	08° Ge 18'
Mon Cnj Sun	Dec 15 2077	10:07	24° Sg 03'
Mon Cnj Sun	Jan 14 2078	01:15	24° Cp 15'
Mon Cnj Sun	Feb 12 2078	14:00	24° Aq 14'

Appendix I • New Moons + Solar & Lunar Eclipses 1920 to 2120

Mon Cnj Sun	Mar 14 2078	00:39	23° Pi 50'
Mon Cnj Sun	Apr 12 2078	09:46	22° Ar 54'
Lunar Eclipse	Apr 27 2078	04:20	07° Sc 20'
Solar Eclipse	May 11 2078	17:57	21° Ta 27'
Mon Cnj Sun	Jun 10 2078	01:50	19° Ge 38'
Mon Cnj Sun	Jul 9 2078	10:10	17° Cn 38'
Mon Cnj Sun	Aug 7 2078	19:53	15° Le 44'
Mon Cnj Sun	Sep 6 2078	8:00	14° Vi 09'
Mon Cnj Sun	Oct 5 2078	23:07	13° Li 06'
Lunar Eclipse	Oct 21 2078	02:56	28° Ar 07'
Solar Eclipse	Nov 4 2078	16:57	12° Sc 40'
Lunar Eclipse	Nov 19 2078	12:53	27° Ta 34'
Mon Cnj Sun	Dec 4 2078	12:09	12° Sg 43'
Mon Cnj Sun	Jan 3 2079	06:51	13° Cp 01'
Mon Cnj Sun	Feb 1 2079	23:37	13° Aq 15'
Mon Cnj Sun	Mar 3 2079	13:50	13° Pi 08'
Mon Cnj Sun	Apr 2 2079	01:31	12° Ar 29'
Lunar Eclipse	Apr 16 2079	05:04	26° Li 23'
Solar Eclipse	May 1 2079	10:58	11° Ta 15'
Mon Cnj Sun	May 30 2079	18:42	09° Ge 33'
Mon Cnj Sun	Jun 29 2079	01:32	07° Cn 32'
Mon Cnj Sun	Jul 28 2079	08:34	05° Le 29'
Mon Cnj Sun	Aug 26 2079	17:04	03° Vi 39'
Mon Cnj Sun	Sep 25 2079	04:07	02° Li 16'
Lunar Eclipse	Oct 10 2079	17:25	17° Ar 34'
Solar Eclipse	Oct 24 2079	18:20	01° Sc 30'
Mon Cnj Sun	Nov 23 2079	11:30	01° Sg 19'
Mon Cnj Sun	Dec 23 2079	06:32	01° Cp 33'
Mon Cnj Sun	Jan 22 2080	01:57	01° Aq 56'
Mon Cnj Sun	Feb 20 2080	20:12	02° Pi 06'
Solar Eclipse	Mar 21 2080	12:07	01° Ar 47'
Lunar Eclipse	Apr 4 2080	11:25	15° Li 37'
Mon Cnj Sun	Apr 20 2080	01:01	00° Ta 53'
Mon Cnj Sun	May 19 2080	10:58	29° Ta 23'
Mon Cnj Sun	Jun 17 2080	18:41	27° Ge 29'
Mon Cnj Sun	Jul 17 2080	01:22	25° Cn 25'
Mon Cnj Sun	Aug 15 2080	08:14	23° Le 26'
Solar Eclipse	Sep 13 2080	16:26	21° Vi 48'
Lunar Eclipse	Sep 29 2080	01:55	06° Ar 51'
Mon Cnj Sun	Oct 13 2080	02:45	20° Li 41'
Mon Cnj Sun	Nov 11 2080	15:38	20° Sc 09'
Mon Cnj Sun	Dec 11 2080	07:11	20° Sg 08'
Mon Cnj Sun	Jan 10 2081	01:03	20° Cp 26'
Mon Cnj Sun	Feb 8 2081	20:18	20° Aq 44'

Solar Eclipse	Mar 10 2081	15:18	20° Pi 43'
Lunar Eclipse	Mar 25 2081	00:30	05° Li 02'
Mon Cnj Sun	Apr 9 2081	08:16	20° Ar 10'
Mon Cnj Sun	May 8 2081	22:10	19° Ta 00'
Mon Cnj Sun	Jun 7 2081	09:03	17° Ge 19'
Mon Cnj Sun	Jul 6 2081	17:45	15° Cn 21'
Mon Cnj Sun	Aug 5 2081	01:25	13° Le 21'
Solar Eclipse	Sep 3 2081	09:03	11° Vi 34'
Lunar Eclipse	Sep 18 2081	03:47	25° Pi 56'
Mon Cnj Sun	Oct 2 2081	17:24	10° Li 12'
Mon Cnj Sun	Nov 1 2081	03:05	09° Sc 22'
Mon Cnj Sun	Nov 30 2081	14:37	09° Sg 03'
Mon Cnj Sun	Dec 30 2081	04:29	09° Cp 07'
Mon Cnj Sun	Jan 28 2082	20:48	09° Aq 21'
Lunar Eclipse	Feb 13 2082	06:18	24° Le 57'
Solar Eclipse	Feb 27 2082	14:50	09° Pi 26'
Mon Cnj Sun	Mar 29 2082	09:06	09° Ar 06'
Mon Cnj Sun	Apr 28 2082	02:03	08° Ta 15'
Mon Cnj Sun	May 27 2082	16:48	06° Ge 51'
Mon Cnj Sun	Jun 26 2082	05:17	05° Cn 05'
Mon Cnj Sun	Jul 25 2082	15:55	03° Le 11'
Lunar Eclipse	Aug 8 2082	14:34	16° Aq 31'
Solar Eclipse	Aug 24 2082	01:19	01° Vi 22'
Mon Cnj Sun	Sep 22 2082	10:05	29° Vi 51'
Mon Cnj Sun	Oct 21 2082	18:52	28° Li 49'
Mon Cnj Sun	Nov 20 2082	04:21	28° Sc 16'
Mon Cnj Sun	Dec 19 2082	15:12	28° Sg 08'
Mon Cnj Sun	Jan 18 2083	03:51	28° Cp 13'
Lunar Eclipse	Feb 2 2083	18:21	14° Le 05'
Solar Eclipse	Feb 16 2083	18:16	28° Aq 15'
Mon Cnj Sun	Mar 18 2083	09:58	28° Pi 00'
Mon Cnj Sun	Apr 17 2083	02:11	27° Ar 17'
Mon Cnj Sun	May 16 2083	18:15	26° Ta 06'
Mon Cnj Sun	Jun 15 2083	09:39	24° Ge 32'
Solar Eclipse	Jul 14 2083	23:56	22° Cn 46'
Lunar Eclipse	Jul 29 2083	01:02	06° Aq 11'
Solar Eclipse	Aug 13 2083	12:46	21° Le 00'
Mon Cnj Sun	Sep 12 2083	00:08	19° Vi 28'
Mon Cnj Sun	Oct 11 2083	10:24	18° Li 18'
Mon Cnj Sun	Nov 9 2083	20:16	17° Sc 37'
Mon Cnj Sun	Dec 9 2083	06:26	17° Sg 21'
Solar Eclipse	Jan 7 2084	17:18	17° Cp 20'
Lunar Eclipse	Jan 22 2084	23:16	02° Le 52'
Mon Cnj Sun	Feb 6 2084	04:54	17° Aq 19'

Appendix I • *New Moons + Solar & Lunar Eclipses 1920 to 2120*

Mon Cnj Sun	Mar 6 2084	17:05	17° Pi 04'
Mon Cnj Sun	Apr 5 2084	05:53	16° Ar 24'
Mon Cnj Sun	May 4 2084	19:34	15° Ta 17'
Mon Cnj Sun	Jun 3 2084	10:14	13° Ge 48'
Solar Eclipse	Jul 3 2084	01:39	12° Cn 07'
Lunar Eclipse	Jul 17 2084	17:03	26° Cp 05'
Mon Cnj Sun	Aug 1 2084	17:05	10° Le 25'
Mon Cnj Sun	Aug 31 2084	07:46	08° Vi 53'
Mon Cnj Sun	Sep 29 2084	21:18	07° Li 41'
Mon Cnj Sun	Oct 29 2084	09:48	06° Sc 55'
Mon Cnj Sun	Nov 27 2084	21:40	06° Sg 35'
Solar Eclipse	Dec 27 2084	09:08	06° Cp 33'
Lunar Eclipse	Jan 10 2085	22:43	21° Cn 24'
Mon Cnj Sun	Jan 25 2085	20:08	06° Aq 33'
Mon Cnj Sun	Feb 24 2085	06:33	06° Pi 21'
Mon Cnj Sun	Mar 25 2085	16:38	05° Ar 44'
Mon Cnj Sun	Apr 24 2085	03:00	04° Ta 39'
Mon Cnj Sun	May 23 2085	14:24	03° Ge 11'
Lunar Eclipse	Jun 8 2085	02:03	18° Sg 02'
Solar Eclipse	Jun 22 2085	03:19	01° Cn 27'
Lunar Eclipse	Jul 7 2085	10:16	16° Cp 02'
Mon Cnj Sun	Jul 21 2085	17:44	29° Cn 41'
Mon Cnj Sun	Aug 20 2085	09:12	28° Le 05'
Mon Cnj Sun	Sep 19 2085	01:08	26° Vi 50'
Mon Cnj Sun	Oct 18 2085	17:01	26° Li 02'
Mon Cnj Sun	Nov 17 2085	08:22	25° Sc 41'
Lunar Eclipse	Dec 1 2085	08:11	09° Ge 50'
Solar Eclipse	Dec 16 2085	22:39	25° Sg 40'
Mon Cnj Sun	Jan 15 2086	11:25	25° Cp 45'
Mon Cnj Sun	Feb 13 2086	22:28	25° Aq 40'
Mon Cnj Sun	Mar 15 2086	08:05	25° Pi 12'
Mon Cnj Sun	Apr 13 2086	16:54	24° Ar 14'
Mon Cnj Sun	May 13 2086	01:42	22° Ta 48'
Lunar Eclipse	May 28 2086	12:36	07° Sg 41'
Solar Eclipse	Jun 11 2086	11:14	21° Ge 02'
Mon Cnj Sun	Jul 10 2086	22:03	19° Cn 08'
Mon Cnj Sun	Aug 9 2086	10:39	17° Le 21'
Mon Cnj Sun	Sep 8 2086	01:18	15° Vi 54'
Mon Cnj Sun	Oct 7 2086	17:58	14° Li 57'
Mon Cnj Sun	Nov 6 2086	11:55	14° Sc 32'
Lunar Eclipse	Nov 20 2086	20:13	28° Ta 58'
Solar Eclipse	Dec 6 2086	05:49	14° Sg 33'
Mon Cnj Sun	Jan 4 2087	22:12	14° Cp 45'
Mon Cnj Sun	Feb 3 2087	12:12	14° Aq 52'

Mon Cnj Sun	Mar 4 2087	23:46	14° Pi 37'
Mon Cnj Sun	Apr 3 2087	09:27	13° Ar 51'
Solar Eclipse	May 2 2087	17:52	12° Ta 34'
Lunar Eclipse	May 17 2087	15:56	27° Sc 00'
Solar Eclipse	Jun 1 2087	01:40	10° Ge 51'
Mon Cnj Sun	Jun 30 2087	09:32	08° Cn 52'
Mon Cnj Sun	Jul 29 2087	18:22	06° Le 54'
Mon Cnj Sun	Aug 28 2087	05:09	05° Vi 10'
Mon Cnj Sun	Sep 26 2087	06:48	03° Li 55'
Solar Eclipse	Oct 26 2087	11:30	03° Sc 16'
Lunar Eclipse	Nov 10 2087	12:06	18° Ta 19'
Mon Cnj Sun	Nov 25 2087	06:25	03° Sg 11'
Mon Cnj Sun	Dec 25 2087	01:44	03° Cp 27'
Mon Cnj Sun	Jan 23 2088	19:40	03° Aq 45'
Mon Cnj Sun	Feb 22 2088	11:10	03° Pi 47'
Mon Cnj Sun	Mar 23 2088	00:02	03° Ar 20'
Solar Eclipse	Apr 21 2088	10:26	02° Ta 18'
Lunar Eclipse	May 5 2088	16:26	16° Sc 09'
Mon Cnj Sun	May 20 2088	18:50	00° Ge 44'
Mon Cnj Sun	Jun 19 2088	01:55	28° Ge 48'
Mon Cnj Sun	Jul 18 2088	08:40	26° Cn 43'
Mon Cnj Sun	Aug 16 2088	16:17	24° Le 47'
Mon Cnj Sun	Sep 15 2088	01:59	23° Vi 13'
Solar Eclipse	Oct 14 2088	14:41	22° Li 14'
Lunar Eclipse	Oct 30 2088	03:11	07° Ta 40'
Mon Cnj Sun	Nov 13 2088	06:33	21° Sc 51'
Mon Cnj Sun	Dec 13 2088	00:53	21° Sg 58'
Mon Cnj Sun	Jan 11 2089	20:19	22° Cp 20'
Mon Cnj Sun	Feb 10 2089	15:17	22° Aq 37'
Mon Cnj Sun	Mar 12 2089	08:25	22° Pi 29'
Lunar Eclipse	Mar 26 2089	09:21	06° Li 27'
Solar Eclipse	Apr 10 2089	22:47	21° Ar 48'
Mon Cnj Sun	May 10 2089	10:05	20° Ta 30'
Mon Cnj Sun	Jun 8 2089	18:46	18° Ge 43'
Mon Cnj Sun	Jul 8 2089	01:49	16° Cn 41'
Mon Cnj Sun	Aug 6 2089	08:29	14° Le 39'
Mon Cnj Sun	Sep 4 2089	15:59	12° Vi 52'
Lunar Eclipse	Sep 19 2089	21:57	27° Pi 42'
Solar Eclipse	Oct 4 2089	01:16	11° Li 34'
Mon Cnj Sun	Nov 2 2089	12:56	10° Sc 50'
Mon Cnj Sun	Dec 2 2089	03:13	10° Sg 39'
Mon Cnj Sun	Dec 31 2089	19:58	10° Cp 52'
Mon Cnj Sun	Jan 30 2090	14:35	11° Aq 11'
Mon Cnj Sun	Mar 1 2090	09:48	11° Pi 17'

Appendix I • *New Moons + Solar & Lunar Eclipses 1920 to 2120*

Lunar Eclipse	Mar 15 2090	23:43	25° Vi 52'
Solar Eclipse	Mar 31 2090	03:49	10° Ar 56'
Mon Cnj Sun	Apr 29 2090	19:13	09° Ta 58'
Mon Cnj Sun	May 29 2090	07:31	08° Ge 28'
Mon Cnj Sun	Jun 27 2090	17:12	06° Cn 35'
Mon Cnj Sun	Jul 27 2090	01:20	04° Le 34'
Mon Cnj Sun	Aug 25 2090	09:00	02° Vi 41'
Lunar Eclipse	Sep 8 2090	22:46	16° Pi 47'
Solar Eclipse	Sep 23 2090	17:04	01° Li 11'
Mon Cnj Sun	Oct 23 2090	02:11	00° Sc 10'
Mon Cnj Sun	Nov 21 2090	12:50	29° Sc 41'
Mon Cnj Sun	Dec 21 2090	01:31	29° Sg 39'
Mon Cnj Sun	Jan 19 2091	16:32	29° Cp 50'
Solar Eclipse	Feb 18 2091	09:40	29° Aq 58'
Lunar Eclipse	Mar 5 2091	16:00	15° Vi 19'
Mon Cnj Sun	Mar 20 2091	03:47	29° Pi 47'
Mon Cnj Sun	Apr 18 2091	21:21	29° Ar 06'
Mon Cnj Sun	May 18 2091	13:08	27° Ta 53'
Mon Cnj Sun	Jun 17 2091	02:42	26° Ge 14'
Mon Cnj Sun	Jul 16 2091	14:17	24° Cn 21'
Solar Eclipse	Aug 15 2091	00:23	22° Le 29'
Lunar Eclipse	Aug 29 2091	00:41	05° Pi 59'
Mon Cnj Sun	Sep 13 2091	09:36	20° Vi 53'
Mon Cnj Sun	Oct 12 2091	18:30	19° Li 41'
Mon Cnj Sun	Nov 11 2091	03:43	18° Sc 59'
Mon Cnj Sun	Dec 10 2091	13:55	18° Sg 44'
Mon Cnj Sun	Jan 9 2092	01:38	18° Cp 45'
Solar Eclipse	Feb 7 2092	15:04	18° Aq 49'
Lunar Eclipse	Feb 23 2092	05:31	04° Vi 35'
Mon Cnj Sun	Mar 8 2092	05:58	18° Pi 40'
Mon Cnj Sun	Apr 6 2092	21:43	18° Ar 05'
Mon Cnj Sun	May 6 2092	13:40	17° Ta 02'
Mon Cnj Sun	Jun 5 2092	05:19	15° Ge 35'
Mon Cnj Sun	Jul 4 2092	20:12	13° Cn 52'
Lunar Eclipse	Jul 19 2092	00:25	27° Cp 23'
Solar Eclipse	Aug 3 2092	09:56	12° Le 05'
Lunar Eclipse	Aug 17 2092	09:24	25° Aq 30'
Mon Cnj Sun	Sep 1 2092	22:15	10° Vi 29'
Mon Cnj Sun	Oct 1 2092	09:17	09° Li 12'
Mon Cnj Sun	Oct 30 2092	19:30	08° Sc 23'
Mon Cnj Sun	Nov 29 2092	05:37	07° Sg 59'
Mon Cnj Sun	Dec 28 2092	16:12	07° Cp 55'
Lunar Eclipse	Jan 12 2093	17:45	23° Cn 16'
Solar Eclipse	Jan 27 2093	03:24	07° Aq 56'

Mon Cnj Sun	Feb 25 2093	15:07	07° Pi 46'
Mon Cnj Sun	Mar 27 2093	03:19	07° Ar 13'
Mon Cnj Sun	Apr 25 2093	16:14	06° Ta 13'
Mon Cnj Sun	May 25 2093	06:09	04° Ge 50'
Mon Cnj Sun	Jun 23 2093	21:06	03° Cn 10'
Lunar Eclipse	Jul 8 2093	17:15	17° Cp 19'
Solar Eclipse	Jul 23 2093	12:37	01° Le 27'
Mon Cnj Sun	Aug 22 2093	03:55	29° Le 51'
Mon Cnj Sun	Sep 20 2093	18:18	28° Vi 33'
Mon Cnj Sun	Oct 20 2093	07:35	27° Li 40'
Mon Cnj Sun	Nov 18 2093	19:59	27° Sc 14'
Mon Cnj Sun	Dec 18 2093	07:49	27° Sg 08'
Lunar Eclipse	Jan 1 2094	16:53	11° Cn 46'
Solar Eclipse	Jan 16 2094	19:07	27° Cp 09'
Mon Cnj Sun	Feb 15 2094	05:45	27° Aq 02'
Mon Cnj Sun	Mar 16 2094	15:46	26° Pi 34'
Mon Cnj Sun	Apr 15 2094	01:39	25° Ar 38'
Mon Cnj Sun	May 14 2094	12:11	24° Ta 15'
Solar Eclipse	Jun 13 2094	00:05	22° Ge 34'
Lunar Eclipse	Jun 28 2094	10:00	07° Cp 17'
Solar Eclipse	Jul 12 2094	13:38	20° Cn 46'
Mon Cnj Sun	Aug 11 2094	04:38	19° Le 05'
Mon Cnj Sun	Sep 9 2094	20:33	17° Vi 42'
Mon Cnj Sun	Oct 9 2094	12:46	16° Li 45'
Mon Cnj Sun	Nov 8 2094	04:44	16° Sc 17'
Solar Eclipse	Dec 7 2094	19:52	16° Sg 12'
Lunar Eclipse	Dec 21 2094	19:57	00° Cn 27'
Mon Cnj Sun	Jan 6 2095	09:35	16° Cp 18'
Mon Cnj Sun	Feb 4 2095	21:30	16° Aq 19'
Mon Cnj Sun	Mar 6 2095	07:40	16° Pi 00'
Mon Cnj Sun	Apr 4 2095	16:37	15° Ar 11'
Mon Cnj Sun	May 4 2095	01:07	13° Ta 53'
Solar Eclipse	Jun 2 2095	09:59	12° Ge 12'
Lunar Eclipse	Jun 17 2095	22:07	27° Sg 02'
Mon Cnj Sun	Jul 1 2095	19:56	10° Cn 18'
Mon Cnj Sun	Jul 31 2095	07:30	08° Le 26'
Mon Cnj Sun	Aug 29 2095	21:07	06° Vi 50'
Mon Cnj Sun	Sep 28 2095	12:56	05° Li 42'
Mon Cnj Sun	Oct 28 2095	06:34	05° Sc 07'
Solar Eclipse	Nov 27 2095	00:56	05° Sg 02'
Lunar Eclipse	Dec 11 2095	06:23	19° Ge 27'
Mon Cnj Sun	Dec 26 2095	18:26	05° Cp 14'
Mon Cnj Sun	Jan 25 2096	09:46	05° Aq 25'
Mon Cnj Sun	Feb 23 2096	22:30	05° Pi 19'

Appendix I • New Moons + Solar & Lunar Eclipses 1920 to 2120

Mon Cnj Sun	Mar 24 2096	08:56	04° Ar 45'
Mon Cnj Sun	Apr 22 2096	17:45	03° Ta 37'
Lunar Eclipse	May 7 2096	11:08	17° Sc 56'
Solar Eclipse	May 22 2096	01:37	02° Ge 01'
Lunar Eclipse	Jun 6 2096	03:00	16° Sg 28'
Mon Cnj Sun	Jun 20 2096	09:13	00° Cn 06'
Mon Cnj Sun	Jul 19 2096	17:22	28° Cn 05'
Mon Cnj Sun	Aug 18 2096	03:02	26° Le 14'
Mon Cnj Sun	Sep 16 2096	15:12	24° Vi 48'
Mon Cnj Sun	Oct 16 2096	06:30	23° Li 56'
Lunar Eclipse	Oct 31 2096	11:18	09° Ta 04'
Solar Eclipse	Nov 15 2096	00:37	23° Sc 40'
Lunar Eclipse	Nov 29 2096	21:35	08° Ge 41'
Mon Cnj Sun	Dec 14 2096	20:07	23° Sg 51'
Mon Cnj Sun	Jan 13 2097	15:02	24° Cp 12'
Mon Cnj Sun	Feb 12 2097	07:51	24° Aq 22'
Mon Cnj Sun	Mar 13 2097	21:58	24° Pi 06'
Mon Cnj Sun	Apr 12 2097	09:28	23° Ar 16'
Lunar Eclipse	Apr 26 2097	12:10	07° Sc 04'
Solar Eclipse	May 11 2097	18:42	21° Ta 52'
Mon Cnj Sun	Jun 10 2097	02:15	20° Ge 02'
Mon Cnj Sun	Jul 9 2097	09:00	17° Cn 59'
Mon Cnj Sun	Aug 7 2097	16:01	15° Le 58'
Mon Cnj Sun	Sep 6 2097	00:35	14° Vi 15'
Mon Cnj Sun	Oct 5 2097	11:47	13° Li 03'
Lunar Eclipse	Oct 21 2097	01:24	28° Ar 27'
Solar Eclipse	Nov 4 2097	02:10	12° Sc 27'
Mon Cnj Sun	Dec 3 2097	19:28	12° Sg 25'
Mon Cnj Sun	Jan 2 2098	14:34	12° Cp 43'
Mon Cnj Sun	Feb 1 2098	09:56	13° Aq 04'
Mon Cnj Sun	Mar 3 2098	04:04	13° Pi 07'
Solar Eclipse	Apr 1 2098	19:49	12° Ar 38'
Lunar Eclipse	Apr 15 2098	19:06	26° Li 22'
Mon Cnj Sun	May 1 2098	08:33	11° Ta 33'
Mon Cnj Sun	May 30 2098	18:24	09° Ge 55'
Mon Cnj Sun	Jun 29 2098	02:08	07° Cn 57'
Mon Cnj Sun	Jul 28 2098	08:52	05° Le 53'
Mon Cnj Sun	Aug 26 2098	15:54	04° Vi 00'
Solar Eclipse	Sep 25 2098	00:18	02° Li 31'
Lunar Eclipse	Oct 10 2098	09:22	17° Ar 38'
Solar Eclipse	Oct 24 2098	10:51	01° Sc 35'
Mon Cnj Sun	Nov 22 2098	23:53	01° Sg 13'
Mon Cnj Sun	Dec 22 2098	15:26	01° Cp 19'
Mon Cnj Sun	Jan 21 2099	09:09	01° Aq 36'

Mon Cnj Sun	Feb 20 2099	04:07	01° Pi 49'
Solar Eclipse	Mar 21 2099	22:48	01° Ar 38'
Lunar Eclipse	Apr 5 2099	08:39	15° Li 53'
Mon Cnj Sun	Apr 20 2099	15:31	00° Ta 53'
Mon Cnj Sun	May 20 2099	05:18	29° Ta 33'
Mon Cnj Sun	Jun 18 2099	16:12	27° Ge 47'
Mon Cnj Sun	Jul 18 2099	01:02	25° Cn 48'
Mon Cnj Sun	Aug 16 2099	08:56	23° Le 51'
Solar Eclipse	Sep 14 2099	16:52	22° Vi 13'
Lunar Eclipse	Sep 29 2099	10:47	06° Ar 38'
Mon Cnj Sun	Oct 14 2099	01:34	21° Li 02'
Mon Cnj Sun	Nov 12 2099	11:31	20° Sc 23'
Mon Cnj Sun	Dec 11 2099	23:11	20° Sg 12'
Mon Cnj Sun	Jan 10 2100	12:57	20° Cp 19'
Mon Cnj Sun	Feb 9 2100	04:57	20° Aq 29'
Lunar Eclipse	Feb 24 2100	14:53	06° Vi 03'
Solar Eclipse	Mar 10 2100	22:30	20° Pi 25'
Mon Cnj Sun	Apr 9 2100	16:18	19° Ar 54'
Mon Cnj Sun	May 9 2100	08:55	18° Ta 51'
Mon Cnj Sun	Jun 7 2100	23:33	17° Ge 20'
Mon Cnj Sun	Jul 7 2100	12:08	15° Cn 31'
Mon Cnj Sun	Aug 5 2100	23:03	13° Le 38'
Lunar Eclipse	Aug 19 2100	21:31	27° Aq 01'
Solar Eclipse	Sep 4 2100	08:51	11° Vi 57'
Mon Cnj Sun	Oct 3 2100	18:04	10° Li 37'
Mon Cnj Sun	Nov 2 2100	03:16	09° Sc 46'
Mon Cnj Sun	Dec 1 2100	13:02	09° Sg 23'
Mon Cnj Sun	Dec 30 2100	23:58	09° Cp 20'
Mon Cnj Sun	Jan 29 2101	12:26	09° Aq 24'
Lunar Eclipse	Feb 14 2101	02:44	25° Le 12'
Solar Eclipse	Feb 28 2101	02:26	09° Pi 18'
Mon Cnj Sun	Mar 29 2101	17:32	08° Ar 52'
Mon Cnj Sun	Apr 28 2101	09:11	07° Ta 57'
Mon Cnj Sun	May 28 2101	00:51	06° Ge 36'
Mon Cnj Sun	Jun 26 2101	04:07	04° Cn 57'
Mon Cnj Sun	Jul 26 2101	06:33	03° Le 11'
Lunar Eclipse	Aug 9 2101	08:21	16° Aq 39'
Solar Eclipse	Aug 24 2101	19:48	01° Vi 32'
Mon Cnj Sun	Sep 23 2101	07:42	00° Li 09'
Mon Cnj Sun	Oct 22 2101	18:31	29° Li 11'
Mon Cnj Sun	Nov 21 2101	04:50	28° Sc 41'
Mon Cnj Sun	Dec 20 2101	15:16	28° Sg 32'
Solar Eclipse	Jan 19 2102	02:09	28° Cp 32'
Lunar Eclipse	Feb 3 2102	07:21	14° Le 01'

Appendix I • *New Moons + Solar & Lunar Eclipses 1920 to 2120*

Mon Cnj Sun	Feb 17 2102	13:30	28° Aq 27'
Mon Cnj Sun	Mar 19 2102	01:13	28° Pi 02'
Mon Cnj Sun	Apr 17 2102	13:26	27° Ar 09'
Mon Cnj Sun	May 17 2102	02:32	25° Ta 52'
Mon Cnj Sun	Jun 15 2102	16:47	24° Ge 15'
Solar Eclipse	Jul 15 2102	08:03	22° Cn 32'
Lunar Eclipse	Jul 30 2102	00:32	06° Aq 33'
Mon Cnj Sun	Aug 13 2102	23:39	20° Le 53'
Mon Cnj Sun	Sep 12 2102	14:46	19° Vi 29'
Mon Cnj Sun	Oct 12 2102	04:53	18° Li 28'
Mon Cnj Sun	Nov 10 2102	17:58	17° Sc 55'
Mon Cnj Sun	Dec 10 2102	06:17	17° Sg 44'
Solar Eclipse	Jan 8 2103	17:58	17° Cp 45'
Lunar Eclipse	Jan 23 2103	06:45	02° Le 33'
Mon Cnj Sun	Feb 7 2103	04:56	17° Aq 43'
Mon Cnj Sun	Mar 8 2103	15:04	17° Pi 23'
Mon Cnj Sun	Apr 7 2103	00:42	16° Ar 35'
Mon Cnj Sun	May 6 2103	10:33	15° Ta 19'
Mon Cnj Sun	Jun 4 2103	21:26	13° Ge 41'
Lunar Eclipse	Jun 20 2103	09:21	28° Sg 30'
Solar Eclipse	Jul 4 2103	09:59	11° Cn 53'
Lunar Eclipse	Jul 19 2103	17:39	26° Cp 30'
Mon Cnj Sun	Aug 3 2103	00:15	10° Le 08'
Mon Cnj Sun	Sep 1 2103	15:52	08° Vi 38'
Mon Cnj Sun	Oct 1 2103	08:13	07° Li 32'
Mon Cnj Sun	Oct 31 2103	00:39	06° Sc 56'
Mon Cnj Sun	Nov 29 2103	16:33	06° Sg 46'
Lunar Eclipse	Dec 13 2103	16:37	20° Ge 58'
Solar Eclipse	Dec 29 2103	07:15	06° Cp 52'
Mon Cnj Sun	Jan 27 2104	20:09	06° Aq 57'
Mon Cnj Sun	Feb 26 2104	07:06	06° Pi 46'
Mon Cnj Sun	Mar 26 2104	16:26	06° Ar 07'
Mon Cnj Sun	Apr 25 2104	00:51	04° Ta 58'
Mon Cnj Sun	May 24 2104	09:13	03° Ge 22'
Lunar Eclipse	Jun 8 2104	19:30	18° Sg 10'
Solar Eclipse	Jun 22 2104	18:22	01° Cn 30'
Mon Cnj Sun	Jul 22 2104	04:56	29° Cn 34'
Mon Cnj Sun	Aug 20 2104	17:28	27° Le 51'
Mon Cnj Sun	Sep 19 2104	08:15	26° Vi 32'
Mon Cnj Sun	Oct 19 2104	01:14	25° Li 46'
Mon Cnj Sun	Nov 17 2104	19:38	25° Sc 32'
Lunar Eclipse	Dec 2 2104	04:51	10° Ge 05'
Solar Eclipse	Dec 17 2104	13:58	25° Sg 42'
Mon Cnj Sun	Jan 16 2105	06:38	25° Cp 57'

Mon Cnj Sun	Feb 14 2105	20:42	25° Aq 59'
Mon Cnj Sun	Mar 16 2105	08:08	25° Pi 36'
Mon Cnj Sun	Apr 14 2105	17:32	24° Ar 39'
Solar Eclipse	May 14 2105	01:39	23° Ta 12'
Lunar Eclipse	May 28 2105	22:34	07° Sg 31'
Solar Eclipse	Jun 12 2105	09:10	21° Ge 21'
Mon Cnj Sun	Jun 12 2105	09:10	21° Ge 21'
Mon Cnj Sun	Jul 11 2105	16:51	19° Cn 19'
Mon Cnj Sun	Aug 10 2105	01:35	17° Le 23'
Mon Cnj Sun	Sep 8 2105	12:24	15° Vi 46'
Mon Cnj Sun	Oct 8 2105	02:10	14° Li 41'
Solar Eclipse	Nov 6 2105	19:06	14° Sc 13'
Lunar Eclipse	Nov 21 2105	20:42	29° Ta 23'
Mon Cnj Sun	Dec 6 2105	14:16	14° Sg 17'
Mon Cnj Sun	Jan 5 2106	09:49	14° Cp 37'
Mon Cnj Sun	Feb 4 2106	03:50	14° Aq 54'
Mon Cnj Sun	Mar 5 2106	19:18	14° Pi 49'
Mon Cnj Sun	Apr 4 2106	08:00	14° Ar 11'
Solar Eclipse	May 3 2106	18:13	12° Ta 58'
Lunar Eclipse	May 17 2106	23:15	26° Sc 43'
Mon Cnj Sun	Jun 2 2106	02:26	11° Ge 16'
Mon Cnj Sun	Jul 1 2106	09:25	09° Cn 16'
Mon Cnj Sun	Jul 30 2106	16:08	07° Le 12'
Mon Cnj Sun	Aug 28 2106	23:49	05° Vi 21'
Mon Cnj Sun	Sep 27 2106	09:39	03° Li 57'
Solar Eclipse	Oct 26 2106	22:30	03° Sc 08'
Lunar Eclipse	Nov 11 2106	11:30	18° Ta 41'
Mon Cnj Sun	Nov 25 2106	14:30	02° Sg 55'
Mon Cnj Sun	Dec 25 2106	08:55	03° Cp 08'
Mon Cnj Sun	Jan 24 2107	04:19	03° Aq 30'
Mon Cnj Sun	Feb 22 2107	23:10	03° Pi 41'
Mon Cnj Sun	Mar 24 2107	16:08	03° Ar 24'
Lunar Eclipse	Apr 7 2107	17:17	17° Li 17'
Solar Eclipse	Apr 23 2107	06:20	02° Ta 31'
Lunar Eclipse	May 7 2107	04:45	16° Sc 04'
Mon Cnj Sun	May 22 2107	17:31	01° Ge 04'
Mon Cnj Sun	Jun 21 2107	02:10	29° Ge 12'
Mon Cnj Sun	Jul 20 2107	09:17	27° Cn 09'
Mon Cnj Sun	Aug 18 2107	16:05	25° Le 10'
Mon Cnj Sun	Sep 16 2107	23:48	23° Vi 32'
Lunar Eclipse	Oct 2 2107	05:08	08° Ar 25'
Solar Eclipse	Oct 16 2107	09:19	22° Li 24'
Mon Cnj Sun	Nov 14 2107	21:10	21° Sc 51'
Mon Cnj Sun	Dec 14 2107	11:30	21° Sg 48'

Appendix I • New Moons + Solar & Lunar Eclipses 1920 to 2120

Mon Cnj Sun	Jan 13 2108	04:09	22° Cp 03'
Mon Cnj Sun	Feb 11 2108	22:31	22° Aq 18'
Mon Cnj Sun	Mar 12 2108	17:23	22° Pi 15'
Lunar Eclipse	Mar 27 2108	08:01	06° Li 47'
Solar Eclipse	Apr 11 2108	11:06	21° Ar 42'
Mon Cnj Sun	May 11 2108	02:19	20° Ta 35'
Mon Cnj Sun	Jun 9 2108	14:35	18° Ge 57'
Mon Cnj Sun	Jul 9 2108	00:24	17° Cn 01'
Mon Cnj Sun	Aug 7 2108	08:45	15° Le 03'
Mon Cnj Sun	Sep 5 2108	16:43	13° Vi 18'
Lunar Eclipse	Sep 20 2108	05:40	27° Pi 26'
Solar Eclipse	Oct 5 2108	01:08	11° Li 57'
Mon Cnj Sun	Nov 3 2108	10:34	11° Sc 08'
Mon Cnj Sun	Dec 2 2108	21:24	10° Sg 48'
Mon Cnj Sun	Jan 1 2109	10:04	10° Cp 50'
Mon Cnj Sun	Jan 31 2109	00:50	10° Aq 59'
Solar Eclipse	Mar 1 2109	17:31	11° Pi 00'
Lunar Eclipse	Mar 17 2109	00:24	26° Vi 18'
Mon Cnj Sun	Mar 31 2109	11:07	10° Ar 38'
Mon Cnj Sun	Apr 30 2109	04:16	09° Ta 45'
Mon Cnj Sun	May 29 2109	19:51	08° Ge 23'
Mon Cnj Sun	Jun 28 2109	09:27	06° Cn 39'
Mon Cnj Sun	Jul 27 2109	21:15	04° Le 47'
Solar Eclipse	Aug 26 2109	07:45	03° Vi 02'
Lunar Eclipse	Sep 9 2109	07:44	16° Pi 34'
Mon Cnj Sun	Sep 24 2109	17:26	01° Li 35'
Mon Cnj Sun	Oct 24 2109	02:47	00° Sc 35'
Mon Cnj Sun	Nov 22 2109	12:21	00° Sg 04'
Mon Cnj Sun	Dec 21 2109	22:43	29° Sg 55'
Mon Cnj Sun	Jan 20 2110	10:20	29° Cp 57'
Solar Eclipse	Feb 18 2110	23:25	29° Aq 55'
Lunar Eclipse	Mar 6 2110	13:47	15° Vi 37'
Mon Cnj Sun	Mar 20 2110	13:46	29° Pi 36'
Mon Cnj Sun	Apr 19 2110	04:56	28° Ar 49'
Mon Cnj Sun	May 18 2110	20:24	27° Ta 36'
Mon Cnj Sun	Jun 17 2110	11:48	26° Ge 01'
Mon Cnj Sun	Jul 17 2110	02:43	24° Cn 17'
Solar Eclipse	Aug 15 2110	16:46	22° Le 35'
Lunar Eclipse	Aug 29 2110	16:48	06° Pi 03'
Mon Cnj Sun	Sep 14 2110	05:36	21° Vi 07'
Mon Cnj Sun	Oct 13 2110	17:11	20° Li 02'
Mon Cnj Sun	Nov 12 2110	03:55	19° Sc 23'
Mon Cnj Sun	Dec 11 2110	14:23	19° Sg 09'
Mon Cnj Sun	Jan 10 2111	01:04	19° Cp 08'

Lunar Eclipse	Jan 25 2111	01:48	04° Le 26'
Solar Eclipse	Feb 8 2111	12:07	19° Aq 05'
Mon Cnj Sun	Mar 9 2111	23:27	18° Pi 47'
Mon Cnj Sun	Apr 8 2111	11:06	18° Ar 03'
Mon Cnj Sun	May 7 2111	23:26	16° Ta 51'
Mon Cnj Sun	Jun 6 2111	12:51	15° Ge 19'
Mon Cnj Sun	Jul 6 2111	03:31	13° Cn 35'
Lunar Eclipse	Jul 21 2111	00:43	27° Cp 47'
Solar Eclipse	Aug 4 2111	19:05	11° Le 53'
Mon Cnj Sun	Sep 3 2111	10:43	10° Vi 24'
Mon Cnj Sun	Oct 3 2111	01:39	09° Li 17'
Mon Cnj Sun	Nov 1 2111	15:32	08° Sc 36'
Mon Cnj Sun	Dec 1 2111	04:28	08° Sg 20'
Mon Cnj Sun	Dec 30 2111	16:37	08° Cp 20'
Lunar Eclipse	Jan 14 2112	00:59	22° Cn 57'
Solar Eclipse	Jan 29 2112	03:58	08° Aq 21'
Mon Cnj Sun	Feb 27 2112	14:23	08° Pi 08'
Mon Cnj Sun	Mar 28 2112	00:00	07° Ar 28'
Mon Cnj Sun	Apr 26 2112	09:23	06° Ta 20'
Mon Cnj Sun	May 25 2112	19:24	04° Ge 47'
Solar Eclipse	Jun 24 2112	06:52	03° Cn 00'
Lunar Eclipse	Jul 9 2112	17:17	17° Cp 43'
Solar Eclipse	Jul 23 2112	20:11	01° Le 11'
Mon Cnj Sun	Aug 22 2112	11:13	29° Le 34'
Mon Cnj Sun	Sep 21 2112	03:27	28° Vi 21'
Mon Cnj Sun	Oct 20 2112	20:11	27° Li 36'
Mon Cnj Sun	Nov 19 2112	12:43	27° Sc 19'
Solar Eclipse	Dec 19 2112	04:19	27° Sg 23'
Lunar Eclipse	Jan 2 2113	04:24	11° Cn 38'
Mon Cnj Sun	Jan 17 2113	18:17	27° Cp 31'
Mon Cnj Sun	Feb 16 2113	06:11	27° Aq 27'
Mon Cnj Sun	Mar 17 2113	16:07	26° Pi 58'
Mon Cnj Sun	Apr 16 2113	00:42	25° Ar 59'
Mon Cnj Sun	May 15 2113	08:48	24° Ta 30'
Solar Eclipse	Jun 13 2113	17:17	22° Ge 41'
Lunar Eclipse	Jun 29 2113	05:01	07° Cp 28'
Mon Cnj Sun	Jul 13 2113	02:56	20° Cn 44'
Mon Cnj Sun	Aug 11 2113	14:23	18° Le 54'
Mon Cnj Sun	Sep 10 2113	04:03	17° Vi 25'
Mon Cnj Sun	Oct 9 2113	20:07	16° Li 28'
Mon Cnj Sun	Nov 8 2113	14:08	16° Sc 04'
Solar Eclipse	Dec 8 2113	08:56	16° Sg 09'
Lunar Eclipse	Dec 22 2113	15:06	00° Cn 38'
Mon Cnj Sun	Jan 7 2114	02:46	16° Cp 25'

Appendix I • *New Moons + Solar & Lunar Eclipses 1920 to 2120*

Mon Cnj Sun	Feb 5 2114	18:14	16° Aq 35'
Mon Cnj Sun	Mar 7 2114	06:53	16° Pi 21'
Mon Cnj Sun	Apr 5 2114	17:06	15° Ar 36'
Mon Cnj Sun	May 5 2114	01:38	14° Ta 18'
Lunar Eclipse	May 19 2114	17:50	28° Sc 29'
Solar Eclipse	Jun 3 2114	09:13	12° Ge 33'
Lunar Eclipse	Jun 18 2114	09:33	26° Sg 55'
Mon Cnj Sun	Jul 2 2114	16:37	10° Cn 34'
Mon Cnj Sun	Aug 1 2114	00:39	08° Le 33'
Mon Cnj Sun	Aug 30 2114	10:18	06° Vi 47'
Mon Cnj Sun	Sep 28 2114	22:34	05° Li 30'
Mon Cnj Sun	Oct 28 2114	14:03	04° Sc 49'
Lunar Eclipse	Nov 12 2114	19:46	20° Ta 05'
Solar Eclipse	Nov 27 2114	08:25	04° Sg 44'
Lunar Eclipse	Dec 12 2114	06:22	19° Ge 51'
Mon Cnj Sun	Dec 27 2114	04:08	05° Cp 01'
Mon Cnj Sun	Jan 25 2115	23:10	05° Aq 22'
Mon Cnj Sun	Feb 24 2115	15:59	05° Pi 27'
Mon Cnj Sun	Mar 26 2115	05:59	05° Ar 01'
Mon Cnj Sun	Apr 24 2115	17:18	04° Ta 00'
Lunar Eclipse	May 8 2115	19:13	17° Sc 41'
Solar Eclipse	May 24 2115	02:20	02° Ge 27'
Mon Cnj Sun	Jun 22 2115	09:46	00° Cn 31'
Mon Cnj Sun	Jul 21 2115	16:28	28° Cn 27'
Mon Cnj Sun	Aug 19 2115	23:33	26° Le 29'
Mon Cnj Sun	Sep 18 2115	08:14	24° Vi 54'
Mon Cnj Sun	Oct 17 2115	19:35	23° Li 52'
Lunar Eclipse	Nov 2 2115	09:30	09° Ta 23'
Solar Eclipse	Nov 16 2115	10:07	23° Sc 27'
Mon Cnj Sun	Dec 16 2115	03:31	23° Sg 33'
Mon Cnj Sun	Jan 14 2116	22:36	23° Cp 54'
Mon Cnj Sun	Feb 13 2116	17:51	24° Aq 11'
Mon Cnj Sun	Mar 14 2116	11:49	24° Pi 05'
Solar Eclipse	Apr 13 2116	03:22	23° Ar 25'
Lunar Eclipse	Apr 27 2116	02:42	07° Sc 04'
Mon Cnj Sun	May 12 2116	15:59	22° Ta 10'
Mon Cnj Sun	Jun 11 2116	01:47	20° Ge 25'
Mon Cnj Sun	Jul 10 2116	09:32	18° Cn 24'
Mon Cnj Sun	Aug 8 2116	16:25	16° Le 23'
Mon Cnj Sun	Sep 6 2116	23:39	14° Vi 36'
Solar Eclipse	Oct 6 2116	08:19	13° Li 18'
Lunar Eclipse	Oct 21 2116	16:55	28° Ar 29'
Solar Eclipse	Nov 4 2116	19:04	12° Sc 33'
Mon Cnj Sun	Dec 4 2116	08:13	12° Sg 20'

Mon Cnj Sun	Jan 2 2117	23:43	12° Cp 29'
Mon Cnj Sun	Feb 1 2117	17:12	12° Aq 45'
Mon Cnj Sun	Mar 3 2117	11:49	12° Pi 50'
Solar Eclipse	Apr 2 2117	06:08	12° Ar 28'
Lunar Eclipse	Apr 16 2117	16:39	26° Li 40'
Mon Cnj Sun	May 1 2117	22:37	11° Ta 32'
Mon Cnj Sun	May 31 2117	12:19	10° Ge 04'
Mon Cnj Sun	Jun 29 2117	23:17	08° Cn 14'
Mon Cnj Sun	Jul 29 2117	08:20	06° Le 15'
Mon Cnj Sun	Aug 27 2117	16:32	04° Vi 25'
Solar Eclipse	Sep 26 2117	00:49	02° Li 56'
Lunar Eclipse	Oct 10 2117	17:57	17° Ar 24'
Mon Cnj Sun	Oct 25 2117	09:52	01° Sc 56'
Mon Cnj Sun	Nov 23 2117	20:04	01° Sg 27'
Mon Cnj Sun	Dec 23 2117	07:48	01° Cp 23'
Mon Cnj Sun	Jan 21 2118	21:24	01° Aq 30'
Mon Cnj Sun	Feb 20 2118	13:00	01° Pi 34'
Lunar Eclipse	Mar 7 2118	23:21	17° Vi 05'
Solar Eclipse	Mar 22 2118	06:02	01° Ar 19'
Mon Cnj Sun	Apr 20 2118	23:21	00° Ta 37'
Mon Cnj Sun	May 20 2118	15:40	29° Ta 24'
Mon Cnj Sun	Jun 19 2118	06:14	27° Ge 47'
Mon Cnj Sun	Jul 18 2118	18:59	25° Cn 57'
Mon Cnj Sun	Aug 17 2118	06:15	24° Le 09'
Lunar Eclipse	Aug 31 2118	04:37	07° Pi 34'
Solar Eclipse	Sep 15 2118	16:30	22° Vi 36'
Mon Cnj Sun	Oct 15 2118	02:11	21° Li 27'
Mon Cnj Sun	Nov 13 2118	11:47	20° Sc 47'
Mon Cnj Sun	Dec 12 2118	21:47	20° Sg 32'
Mon Cnj Sun	Jan 11 2119	08:44	20° Cp 32'
Mon Cnj Sun	Feb 9 2119	20:57	20° Aq 32'
Lunar Eclipse	Feb 25 2119	10:59	06° Vi 16'
Solar Eclipse	Mar 11 2119	10:28	20° Pi 18'
Mon Cnj Sun	Apr 10 2119	01:00	19° Ar 40'
Mon Cnj Sun	May 9 2119	16:05	18° Ta 34'
Mon Cnj Sun	Jun 8 2119	07:24	17° Ge 05'
Mon Cnj Sun	Jul 7 2119	22:34	15° Cn 22'
Mon Cnj Sun	Aug 6 2119	13:13	13° Le 39'
Lunar Eclipse	Aug 20 2119	15:46	27° Aq 11'
Solar Eclipse	Sep 5 2119	02:55	12° Vi 06'
Mon Cnj Sun	Oct 4 2119	15:23	10° Li 54'
Mon Cnj Sun	Nov 3 2119	02:45	10° Sc 08'
Mon Cnj Sun	Dec 2 2119	13:29	09° Sg 48'
Mon Cnj Sun	Jan 1 2120	00:07	09° Cp 44'

Appendix II • *Sun-Mercury Inferior + Superior Conjunctions 1920 to 2120*

Solar Eclipse	Jan 30 2120	10:57	09° Aq 43'
Lunar Eclipse	Feb 14 2120	15:20	25° Le 07'
Mon Cnj Sun	Feb 28 2120	22:00	09° Pi 31'
Mon Cnj Sun	Mar 29 2120	09:13	08° Ar 55'
Mon Cnj Sun	Apr 27 2120	20:51	07° Ta 51'
Mon Cnj Sun	May 27 2120	09:24	06° Ge 23'
Mon Cnj Sun	Jun 25 2120	23:17	04° Cn 40'
Solar Eclipse	Jul 25 2120	14:27	02° Le 56'
Lunar Eclipse	Aug 9 2120	08:04	17° Aq 02'
Mon Cnj Sun	Aug 24 2120	06:16	01° Vi 23'
Mon Cnj Sun	Sep 22 2120	21:53	00° Li 09'
Mon Cnj Sun	Oct 22 2120	12:36	29° Li 20'
Mon Cnj Sun	Nov 21 2120	02:15	28° Sc 58'
Mon Cnj Sun	Dec 20 2120	14:58	28° Sg 55'

Appendix II

Sun-Mercury Inferior (R) + Superior (D) Conjunctions 1920 to 2120

Sun Cnj Mer	Feb 5 1920	20:46	15° Aq 46' D
Sun Cnj Mer	Mar 20 1920	07:59	29° Pi 25' R
Sun Cnj Mer	May 26 1920	01:53	04° Ge 30' D
Sun Cnj Mer	Jul 27 1920	07:21	03° Le 55' R
Sun Cnj Mer	Sep 9 1920	01:55	16° Vi 04' D
Sun Cnj Mer	Nov 16 1920	06:09	23° Sc 36' R
Sun Cnj Mer	Jan 16 1921	19:32	26° Cp 10' D
Sun Cnj Mer	Mar 3 1921	02:16	11° Pi 58' R
Sun Cnj Mer	May 10 1921	11:38	19° Ta 15' D
Sun Cnj Mer	Jul 8 1921	05:17	15° Cn 29' R
Sun Cnj Mer	Aug 23 1921	10:42	29° Le 44' D
Sun Cnj Mer	Oct 31 1921	10:34	07° Sc 28' R
Sun Cnj Mer	Dec 27 1921	16:10	05° Cp 23' D
Sun Cnj Mer	Feb 14 1922	10:09	24° Aq 57' R
Sun Cnj Mer	Apr 24 1922	17:45	03° Ta 44' D
Sun Cnj Mer	Jun 18 1922	08:46	26° Ge 18' R
Sun Cnj Mer	Aug 7 1922	06:28	13° Le 57' D
Sun Cnj Mer	Oct 15 1922	10:40	21° Li 17' R
Sun Cnj Mer	Dec 6 1922	19:00	13° Sg 53' D
Sun Cnj Mer	Jan 29 1923	03:53	08° Aq 13' R
Sun Cnj Mer	Apr 8 1923	18:04	17° Ar 52' D
Sun Cnj Mer	May 29 1923	02:52	06° Ge 43' R
Sun Cnj Mer	Jul 22 1923	09:47	28° Cn 33' D
Sun Cnj Mer	Sep 29 1923	04:19	04° Li 59' R
Sun Cnj Mer	Nov 16 1923	00:32	22° Sc 37' D
Sun Cnj Mer	Jan 13 1924	04:24	21° Cp 43' R

Sun Cnj Mer	Mar 22 1924	09:49	01° Ar 30' D
Sun Cnj Mer	May 8 1924	01:37	17° Ta 11' R
Sun Cnj Mer	Jul 5 1924	17:57	13° Cn 23' D
Sun Cnj Mer	Sep 11 1924	12:55	18° Vi 29' R
Sun Cnj Mer	Oct 26 1924	03:00	02° Sc 25' D
Sun Cnj Mer	Dec 27 1924	09:13	05° Cp 22' R
Sun Cnj Mer	Mar 5 1925	13:34	14° Pi 28' D
Sun Cnj Mer	Apr 18 1925	17:10	28° Ar 08' R
Sun Cnj Mer	Jun 20 1925	04:51	28° Ge 19' D
Sun Cnj Mer	Aug 25 1925	09:20	01° Vi 38' R
Sun Cnj Mer	Oct 7 1925	08:42	13° Li 33' D
Sun Cnj Mer	Dec 11 1925	16:14	19° Sg 07' R
Sun Cnj Mer	Feb 16 1926	00:43	26° Aq 36' D
Sun Cnj Mer	Mar 31 1926	06:03	09° Ar 46' R
Sun Cnj Mer	Jun 4 1926	16:40	13° Ge 17' D
Sun Cnj Mer	Aug 7 1926	14:03	14° Le 17' R
Sun Cnj Mer	Sep 19 1926	14:41	25° Vi 53' D
Sun Cnj Mer	Nov 25 1926	23:40	02° Sg 57' R
Sun Cnj Mer	Jan 28 1927	14:00	07° Aq 39' D
Sun Cnj Mer	Mar 13 1927	14:42	22° Pi 01' R
Sun Cnj Mer	May 20 1927	03:40	28° Ta 08' D
Sun Cnj Mer	Jul 19 1927	23:41	26° Cn 16' R
Sun Cnj Mer	Sep 2 1927	15:11	09° Vi 08' D
Sun Cnj Mer	Nov 10 1927	05:42	16° Sc 49' R
Sun Cnj Mer	Jan 9 1928	01:28	17° Cp 32' D
Sun Cnj Mer	Feb 24 1928	15:15	04° Pi 46' R
Sun Cnj Mer	May 3 1928	12:06	12° Ta 47' D
Sun Cnj Mer	Jun 29 1928	13:14	07° Cn 30' R
Sun Cnj Mer	Aug 16 1928	05:05	23° Le 03' D
Sun Cnj Mer	Oct 24 1928	08:33	00° Sc 41' R
Sun Cnj Mer	Dec 18 1928	12:47	26° Sg 22' D
Sun Cnj Mer	Feb 7 1929	03:42	17° Aq 53' R
Sun Cnj Mer	Apr 17 1929	16:00	27° Ar 08' D
Sun Cnj Mer	Jun 9 1929	11:04	18° Ge 06' R
Sun Cnj Mer	Jul 31 1929	04:24	07° Le 27' D
Sun Cnj Mer	Oct 8 1929	06:13	14° Li 28' R
Sun Cnj Mer	Nov 27 1929	14:02	04° Sg 51' D
Sun Cnj Mer	Jan 22 1930	00:40	01° Aq 16' R
Sun Cnj Mer	Apr 1 1930	13:00	11° Ar 04' D
Sun Cnj Mer	May 20 1930	05:09	28° Ta 27' R
Sun Cnj Mer	Jul 15 1930	10:02	22° Cn 10' D
Sun Cnj Mer	Sep 21 1930	20:21	28° Vi 06' R
Sun Cnj Mer	Nov 7 1930	02:49	13° Sc 58' D
Sun Cnj Mer	Jan 6 1931	03:20	14° Cp 50' R
Sun Cnj Mer	Mar 16 1931	00:09	24° Pi 26' D

Appendix II • *Sun-Mercury Inferior + Superior Conjunctions 1920 to 2120*

Sun Cnj Mer	Apr 30 1931	10:08	09° Ta 06' R
Sun Cnj Mer	Jun 29 1931	19:38	07° Cn 04' D
Sun Cnj Mer	Sep 5 1931	00:09	11° Vi 28' R
Sun Cnj Mer	Oct 18 1931	16:52	24° Li 20' D
Sun Cnj Mer	Dec 21 1931	09:21	28° Sg 33' R
Sun Cnj Mer	Feb 26 1932	21:26	07° Pi 05' D
Sun Cnj Mer	Apr 10 1932	10:42	20° Ar 20' R
Sun Cnj Mer	Jun 13 1932	07:09	22° Ge 02' D
Sun Cnj Mer	Aug 17 1932	14:00	24° Le 25' R
Sun Cnj Mer	Sep 29 1932	09:29	06° Li 01' D
Sun Cnj Mer	Dec 4 1932	16:47	12° Sg 21' R
Sun Cnj Mer	Feb 8 1933	00:03	18° Aq 47' D
Sun Cnj Mer	Mar 23 1933	08:22	02° Ar 15' R
Sun Cnj Mer	May 28 1933	18:49	06° Ge 57' D
Sun Cnj Mer	Jul 30 1933	11:11	06° Le 48' R
Sun Cnj Mer	Sep 11 1933	23:56	18° Vi 45' D
Sun Cnj Mer	Nov 18 1933	23:47	26° Sc 12' R
Sun Cnj Mer	Jan 20 1934	02:41	29° Cp 22' D
Sun Cnj Mer	Mar 6 1934	00:16	14° Pi 44' R
Sun Cnj Mer	May 13 1934	04:56	21° Ta 44' D
Sun Cnj Mer	Jul 11 1934	12:12	18° Cn 29' R
Sun Cnj Mer	Aug 26 1934	06:43	02° Vi 20' D
Sun Cnj Mer	Nov 3 1934	04:40	10° Sc 04' R
Sun Cnj Mer	Dec 31 1934	02:54	08° Cp 44' D
Sun Cnj Mer	Feb 17 1935	06:21	27° Aq 40' R
Sun Cnj Mer	Apr 27 1935	11:41	06° Ta 17' D
Sun Cnj Mer	Jun 21 1935	18:04	29° Ge 25' R
Sun Cnj Mer	Aug 10 1935	01:06	16° Le 29' D
Sun Cnj Mer	Oct 18 1935	05:32	23° Li 54' R
Sun Cnj Mer	Dec 10 1935	07:28	17° Sg 18' D
Sun Cnj Mer	Jan 31 1936	22:51	10° Aq 54' R
Sun Cnj Mer	Apr 10 1936	13:01	20° Ar 28' D
Sun Cnj Mer	May 31 1936	12:37	09° Ge 51' R
Sun Cnj Mer	Jul 24 1936	03:28	01° Le 02' D
Sun Cnj Mer	Oct 1 1936	00:19	07° Li 38' R
Sun Cnj Mer	Nov 18 1936	11:06	25° Sc 56' D
Sun Cnj Mer	Jan 14 1937	22:32	24° Cp 22' R
Sun Cnj Mer	Mar 25 1937	06:16	04° Ar 11' D
Sun Cnj Mer	May 11 1937	09:44	20° Ta 16' R
Sun Cnj Mer	Jul 8 1937	11:05	15° Cn 50' D
Sun Cnj Mer	Sep 14 1937	10:30	21° Vi 10' R
Sun Cnj Mer	Oct 29 1937	09:48	05° Sc 33' D
Sun Cnj Mer	Dec 30 1937	02:52	08° Cp 00' R
Sun Cnj Mer	Mar 8 1938	12:02	17° Pi 16' D
Sun Cnj Mer	Apr 21 1938	22:22	01° Ta 08' R

Sun Cnj Mer	Jun 22 1938	21:41	00° Cn 46' D
Sun Cnj Mer	Aug 28 1938	08:57	04° Vi 23' R
Sun Cnj Mer	Oct 10 1938	11:33	16° Li 30' D
Sun Cnj Mer	Dec 14 1938	09:42	21° Sg 44' R
Sun Cnj Mer	Feb 19 1939	01:59	29° Aq 31' D
Sun Cnj Mer	Apr 3 1939	08:07	12° Ar 40' R
Sun Cnj Mer	Jun 7 1939	09:29	15° Ge 44' D
Sun Cnj Mer	Aug 10 1939	16:10	17° Le 07' R
Sun Cnj Mer	Sep 22 1939	14:11	28° Vi 40' D
Sun Cnj Mer	Nov 28 1939	17:10	05° Sg 34' R
Sun Cnj Mer	Jan 31 1940	18:54	10° Aq 45' D
Sun Cnj Mer	Mar 15 1940	13:58	24° Pi 50' R
Sun Cnj Mer	May 21 1940	20:41	00° Ge 36' D
Sun Cnj Mer	Jul 22 1940	04:47	29° Cn 12' R
Sun Cnj Mer	Sep 4 1940	12:13	11° Vi 47' D
Sun Cnj Mer	Nov 11 1940	23:30	19° Sc 26' R
Sun Cnj Mer	Jan 11 1941	10:20	20° Cp 49' D
Sun Cnj Mer	Feb 26 1941	12:24	07° Pi 31' R
Sun Cnj Mer	May 6 1941	05:36	15° Ta 17' D
Sun Cnj Mer	Jul 2 1941	21:11	10° Cn 33' R
Sun Cnj Mer	Aug 19 1941	00:23	25° Le 37' D
Sun Cnj Mer	Oct 27 1941	02:56	03° Sc 18' R
Sun Cnj Mer	Dec 22 1941	00:35	29° Sg 46' D
Sun Cnj Mer	Feb 9 1942	23:20	20° Aq 35' R
Sun Cnj Mer	Apr 20 1942	10:20	29° Ar 42' D
Sun Cnj Mer	Jun 12 1942	20:49	21° Ge 13' R
Sun Cnj Mer	Aug 2 1942	22:35	09° Le 58' D
Sun Cnj Mer	Oct 11 1942	01:31	17° Li 06' R
Sun Cnj Mer	Dec 1 1942	01:57	08° Sg 14' D
Sun Cnj Mer	Jan 24 1943	19:15	03° Aq 56' R
Sun Cnj Mer	Apr 4 1943	08:34	13° Ar 42' D
Sun Cnj Mer	May 23 1943	14:34	01° Ge 34' R
Sun Cnj Mer	Jul 18 1943	03:30	24° Cn 38' D
Sun Cnj Mer	Sep 24 1943	16:57	00° Li 45' R
Sun Cnj Mer	Nov 10 1943	11:56	17° Sc 12' D
Sun Cnj Mer	Jan 8 1944	21:14	17° Cp 29' R
Sun Cnj Mer	Mar 17 1944	21:25	27° Pi 10' D
Sun Cnj Mer	May 2 1944	17:10	12° Ta 09' R
Sun Cnj Mer	Jul 1 1944	12:38	09° Cn 31' D
Sun Cnj Mer	Sep 6 1944	22:30	14° Vi 10' R
Sun Cnj Mer	Oct 20 1944	21:53	27° Li 23' D
Sun Cnj Mer	Dec 23 1944	02:53	01° Cp 10' R
Sun Cnj Mer	Feb 28 1945	21:01	09° Pi 55' D
Sun Cnj Mer	Apr 13 1945	14:30	23° Ar 17' R
Sun Cnj Mer	Jun 15 1945	23:57	24° Ge 28' D

Appendix II • *Sun-Mercury Inferior + Superior Conjunctions 1920 to 2120*

Sun Cnj Mer	Aug 20 1945	14:57	27° Le 12' R
Sun Cnj Mer	Oct 2 1945	10:46	08° Li 52' D
Sun Cnj Mer	Dec 7 1945	10:12	14° Sg 57' R
Sun Cnj Mer	Feb 11 1946	02:43	21° Aq 46' D
Sun Cnj Mer	Mar 26 1946	09:06	05° Ar 06' R
Sun Cnj Mer	May 31 1946	11:39	09° Ge 24' D
Sun Cnj Mer	Aug 2 1946	14:37	09° Le 40' R
Sun Cnj Mer	Sep 14 1946	22:19	21° Vi 28' D
Sun Cnj Mer	Nov 21 1946	17:22	28° Sc 48' R
Sun Cnj Mer	Jan 23 1947	09:13	02° Aq 31' D
Sun Cnj Mer	Mar 8 1947	22:34	17° Pi 31' R
Sun Cnj Mer	May 15 1947	22:08	24° Ta 13' D
Sun Cnj Mer	Jul 14 1947	18:36	21° Cn 27' R
Sun Cnj Mer	Aug 29 1947	03:00	04° Vi 56' D
Sun Cnj Mer	Nov 5 1947	22:41	12° Sc 40' R
Sun Cnj Mer	Jan 3 1948	13:15	12° Cp 04' D
Sun Cnj Mer	Feb 20 1948	02:50	00° Pi 23' R
Sun Cnj Mer	Apr 29 1948	05:32	08° Ta 48' D
Sun Cnj Mer	Jun 24 1948	03:00	02° Cn 29' R
Sun Cnj Mer	Aug 11 1948	19:55	19° Le 00' D
Sun Cnj Mer	Oct 20 1948	00:19	26° Li 31' R
Sun Cnj Mer	Dec 12 1948	19:50	20° Sg 43' D
Sun Cnj Mer	Feb 2 1949	18:01	13° Aq 35' R
Sun Cnj Mer	Apr 13 1949	07:50	23° Ar 03' D
Sun Cnj Mer	Jun 3 1949	22:28	12° Ge 58' R
Sun Cnj Mer	Jul 26 1949	21:17	03° Le 31' D
Sun Cnj Mer	Oct 3 1949	20:11	10° Li 16' R
Sun Cnj Mer	Nov 21 1949	22:10	29° Sc 16' D
Sun Cnj Mer	Jan 17 1950	16:48	27° Cp 01' R
Sun Cnj Mer	Mar 28 1950	02:28	06° Ar 51' D
Sun Cnj Mer	May 14 1950	18:17	23° Ta 22' R
Sun Cnj Mer	Jul 11 1950	04:17	18° Cn 18' D
Sun Cnj Mer	Sep 17 1950	07:47	23° Vi 51' R
Sun Cnj Mer	Nov 1 1950	17:12	08° Sc 42' D
Sun Cnj Mer	Jan 1 1951	20:34	10° Cp 37' R
Sun Cnj Mer	Mar 11 1951	10:10	20° Pi 01' D
Sun Cnj Mer	Apr 25 1951	04:02	04° Ta 09' R
Sun Cnj Mer	Jun 25 1951	14:33	03° Cn 13' D
Sun Cnj Mer	Aug 31 1951	08:09	07° Vi 07' R
Sun Cnj Mer	Oct 13 1951	14:52	19° Li 27' D
Sun Cnj Mer	Dec 17 1951	03:09	24° Sg 21' R
Sun Cnj Mer	Feb 22 1952	02:47	02° Pi 25' D
Sun Cnj Mer	Apr 5 1952	10:33	15° Ar 35' R
Sun Cnj Mer	Jun 9 1952	02:15	18° Ge 11' D
Sun Cnj Mer	Aug 12 1952	17:51	19° Le 55' R

Sun Cnj Mer	Sep 24 1952	14:03	01° Li 27' D
Sun Cnj Mer	Nov 30 1952	10:37	08° Sg 10' R
Sun Cnj Mer	Feb 2 1953	23:11	13° Aq 50' D
Sun Cnj Mer	Mar 18 1953	13:36	27° Pi 39' R
Sun Cnj Mer	May 24 1953	13:39	03° Ge 04' D
Sun Cnj Mer	Jul 25 1953	09:27	02° Le 07' R
Sun Cnj Mer	Sep 7 1953	09:35	14° Vi 27' D
Sun Cnj Mer	Nov 14 1953	17:15	22° Sc 03' R
Sun Cnj Mer	Jan 14 1954	18:33	24° Cp 04' D
Sun Cnj Mer	Mar 1 1954	09:51	10° Pi 16' R
Sun Cnj Mer	May 8 1954	23:03	17° Ta 47' D
Sun Cnj Mer	Jul 6 1954	04:48	13° Cn 35' R
Sun Cnj Mer	Aug 21 1954	20:01	28° Le 12' D
Sun Cnj Mer	Oct 29 1954	21:15	05° Sc 55' R
Sun Cnj Mer	Dec 25 1954	12:07	03° Cp 10' D
Sun Cnj Mer	Feb 12 1955	19:12	23° Aq 18' R
Sun Cnj Mer	Apr 23 1955	04:35	02° Ta 15' D
Sun Cnj Mer	Jun 16 1955	06:26	24° Ge 20' R
Sun Cnj Mer	Aug 5 1955	16:57	12° Le 29' D
Sun Cnj Mer	Oct 13 1955	20:41	19° Li 43' R
Sun Cnj Mer	Dec 4 1955	14:09	11° Sg 38' D
Sun Cnj Mer	Jan 27 1956	13:59	06° Aq 37' R
Sun Cnj Mer	Apr 6 1956	03:55	16° Ar 19' D
Sun Cnj Mer	May 26 1956	00:11	04° Ge 43' R
Sun Cnj Mer	Jul 19 1956	21:01	27° Cn 07' D
Sun Cnj Mer	Sep 26 1956	13:20	03° Li 25' R
Sun Cnj Mer	Nov 12 1956	21:36	20° Sc 29' D
Sun Cnj Mer	Jan 10 1957	15:12	20° Cp 08' R
Sun Cnj Mer	Mar 20 1957	18:19	29° Pi 52' D
Sun Cnj Mer	May 6 1957	00:34	15° Ta 13' R
Sun Cnj Mer	Jul 4 1957	05:37	11° Cn 58' D
Sun Cnj Mer	Sep 9 1957	20:32	16° Vi 52' R
Sun Cnj Mer	Oct 24 1957	03:28	00° Sc 27' D
Sun Cnj Mer	Dec 25 1957	20:25	03° Cp 48' R
Sun Cnj Mer	Mar 3 1958	20:12	12° Pi 45' D
Sun Cnj Mer	Apr 16 1958	18:45	26° Ar 15' R
Sun Cnj Mer	Jun 18 1958	16:43	26° Ge 55' D
Sun Cnj Mer	Aug 23 1958	15:10	29° Le 58' R
Sun Cnj Mer	Oct 5 1958	12:31	11° Li 45' D
Sun Cnj Mer	Dec 10 1958	03:36	17° Sg 34' R
Sun Cnj Mer	Feb 14 1959	04:54	24° Aq 45' D
Sun Cnj Mer	Mar 29 1959	10:17	07° Ar 58' R
Sun Cnj Mer	Jun 3 1959	04:30	11° Ge 52' D
Sun Cnj Mer	Aug 5 1959	17:33	12° Le 32' R
Sun Cnj Mer	Sep 17 1959	21:05	24° Vi 12' D

Appendix II • *Sun-Mercury Inferior + Superior Conjunctions 1920 to 2120*

Sun Cnj Mer	Nov 24 1959	10:56	01° Sg 24' R
Sun Cnj Mer	Jan 26 1960	15:10	05° Aq 40' D
Sun Cnj Mer	Mar 10 1960	21:16	20° Pi 19' R
Sun Cnj Mer	May 17 1960	15:17	26° Ta 42' D
Sun Cnj Mer	Jul 17 1960	00:34	24° Cn 25' R
Sun Cnj Mer	Aug 30 1960	23:33	07° Vi 33' D
Sun Cnj Mer	Nov 7 1960	16:40	15° Sc 16' R
Sun Cnj Mer	Jan 5 1961	23:06	15° Cp 23' D
Sun Cnj Mer	Feb 21 1961	23:35	03° Pi 07' R
Sun Cnj Mer	May 1 1961	23:17	11° Ta 19' D
Sun Cnj Mer	Jun 27 1961	11:42	05° Cn 34' R
Sun Cnj Mer	Aug 14 1961	14:56	21° Le 33' D
Sun Cnj Mer	Oct 22 1961	18:59	29° Li 08' R
Sun Cnj Mer	Dec 16 1961	08:04	24° Sg 08' D
Sun Cnj Mer	Feb 5 1962	13:19	16° Aq 16' R
Sun Cnj Mer	Apr 16 1962	02:29	25° Ar 37' D
Sun Cnj Mer	Jun 7 1962	08:22	16° Ge 06' R
Sun Cnj Mer	Jul 29 1962	15:14	06° Le 00' D
Sun Cnj Mer	Oct 6 1962	15:49	12° Li 54' R
Sun Cnj Mer	Nov 25 1962	09:36	02° Sg 38' D
Sun Cnj Mer	Jan 20 1963	11:07	29° Cp 40' R
Sun Cnj Mer	Mar 30 1963	22:25	09° Ar 29' D
Sun Cnj Mer	May 18 1963	03:11	26° Ta 28' R
Sun Cnj Mer	Jul 13 1963	21:31	20° Cn 45' D
Sun Cnj Mer	Sep 20 1963	04:47	26° Vi 30' R
Sun Cnj Mer	Nov 5 1963	01:08	11° Sc 53' D
Sun Cnj Mer	Jan 4 1964	14:17	13° Cp 15' R
Sun Cnj Mer	Mar 13 1964	07:57	22° Pi 46' D
Sun Cnj Mer	Apr 27 1964	10:10	07° Ta 10' R
Sun Cnj Mer	Jun 27 1964	07:25	05° Cn 39' D
Sun Cnj Mer	Sep 2 1964	07:02	09° Vi 49' R
Sun Cnj Mer	Oct 15 1964	18:44	22° Li 26' D
Sun Cnj Mer	Dec 18 1964	20:36	26° Sg 58' R
Sun Cnj Mer	Feb 24 1965	03:07	05° Pi 17' D
Sun Cnj Mer	Apr 8 1965	13:26	18° Ar 29' R
Sun Cnj Mer	Jun 11 1965	19:02	20° Ge 37' D
Sun Cnj Mer	Aug 15 1965	19:11	22° Le 43' R
Sun Cnj Mer	Sep 27 1965	14:27	04° Li 15' D
Sun Cnj Mer	Dec 3 1965	04:05	10° Sg 47' R
Sun Cnj Mer	Feb 6 1966	02:54	16° Aq 52' D
Sun Cnj Mer	Mar 21 1966	13:38	00° Ar 29' R
Sun Cnj Mer	May 27 1966	06:38	05° Ge 31' D
Sun Cnj Mer	Jul 28 1966	13:43	05° Le 01' R
Sun Cnj Mer	Sep 10 1966	07:22	17° Vi 08' D
Sun Cnj Mer	Nov 17 1966	10:58	24° Sc 38' R

Sun Cnj Mer	Jan 18 1967	02:11	27° Cp 17' D
Sun Cnj Mer	Mar 4 1967	07:36	13° Pi 02' R
Sun Cnj Mer	May 11 1967	16:25	20° Ta 17' D
Sun Cnj Mer	Jul 9 1967	12:02	16° Cn 35' R
Sun Cnj Mer	Aug 24 1967	15:51	00° Vi 47' D
Sun Cnj Mer	Nov 1 1967	15:28	08° Sc 31' R
Sun Cnj Mer	Dec 28 1967	23:18	06° Cp 32' D
Sun Cnj Mer	Feb 15 1968	15:16	26° Aq 00' R
Sun Cnj Mer	Apr 24 1968	22:36	04° Ta 47' D
Sun Cnj Mer	Jun 18 1968	15:48	27° Ge 26' R
Sun Cnj Mer	Aug 7 1968	11:25	14° Le 59' D
Sun Cnj Mer	Oct 15 1968	15:40	22° Li 20' R
Sun Cnj Mer	Dec 7 1968	02:31	15° Sg 03' D
Sun Cnj Mer	Jan 29 1969	08:49	09° Aq 17' R
Sun Cnj Mer	Apr 8 1969	23:00	18° Ar 55' D
Sun Cnj Mer	May 29 1969	09:50	07° Ge 50' R
Sun Cnj Mer	Jul 22 1969	14:34	29° Cn 35' D
Sun Cnj Mer	Sep 29 1969	09:29	06° Li 03' R
Sun Cnj Mer	Nov 16 1969	07:47	23° Sc 47' D
Sun Cnj Mer	Jan 13 1970	09:15	22° Cp 46' R
Sun Cnj Mer	Mar 23 1970	14:58	02° Ar 33' D
Sun Cnj Mer	May 9 1970	08:21	18° Ta 17' R
Sun Cnj Mer	Jul 6 1970	22:39	14° Cn 25' D
Sun Cnj Mer	Sep 12 1970	18:18	19° Vi 33' R
Sun Cnj Mer	Oct 27 1970	09:40	03° Sc 33' D
Sun Cnj Mer	Dec 28 1970	14:01	06° Cp 25' R
Sun Cnj Mer	Mar 6 1971	19:03	15° Pi 33' D
Sun Cnj Mer	Apr 19 1971	23:34	29° Ar 15' R
Sun Cnj Mer	Jun 21 1971	09:32	29° Ge 22' D
Sun Cnj Mer	Aug 26 1971	15:01	02° Vi 43' R
Sun Cnj Mer	Oct 8 1971	14:46	14° Li 39' D
Sun Cnj Mer	Dec 12 1971	21:02	20° Sg 11' R
Sun Cnj Mer	Feb 17 1972	06:38	27° Aq 42' D
Sun Cnj Mer	Mar 31 1972	12:00	10° Ar 52' R
Sun Cnj Mer	Jun 4 1972	21:21	14° Ge 19' D
Sun Cnj Mer	Aug 7 1972	20:03	15° Le 22' R
Sun Cnj Mer	Sep 19 1972	20:15	26° Vi 58' D
Sun Cnj Mer	Nov 26 1972	04:28	04° Sg 01' R
Sun Cnj Mer	Jan 28 1973	20:31	08° Aq 47' D
Sun Cnj Mer	Mar 13 1973	20:16	23° Pi 07' R
Sun Cnj Mer	May 20 1973	08:24	29° Ta 10' D
Sun Cnj Mer	Jul 20 1973	06:05	27° Cn 22' R
Sun Cnj Mer	Sep 2 1973	20:24	10° Vi 12' D
Sun Cnj Mer	Nov 10 1973	10:32	17° Sc 53' R
Sun Cnj Mer	Jan 9 1974	08:22	18° Cp 41' D

Appendix II • *Sun-Mercury Inferior + Superior Conjunctions 1920 to 2120*

Sun Cnj Mer	Feb 24 1974	20:30	05° Pi 51' R
Sun Cnj Mer	May 4 1974	16:55	13° Ta 50' D
Sun Cnj Mer	Jun 30 1974	20:06	08° Cn 38' R
Sun Cnj Mer	Aug 17 1974	10:07	24° Le 07' D
Sun Cnj Mer	Oct 25 1974	13:28	01° Sc 45' R
Sun Cnj Mer	Dec 19 1974	20:02	27° Sg 32' D
Sun Cnj Mer	Feb 8 1975	08:43	18° Aq 57' R
Sun Cnj Mer	Apr 18 1975	20:55	28° Ar 12' D
Sun Cnj Mer	Jun 10 1975	18:14	19° Ge 14' R
Sun Cnj Mer	Aug 1 1975	09:17	08° Le 30' D
Sun Cnj Mer	Oct 9 1975	11:15	15° Li 32' R
Sun Cnj Mer	Nov 28 1975	21:20	06° Sg 01' D
Sun Cnj Mer	Jan 23 1976	05:33	02° Aq 20' R
Sun Cnj Mer	Apr 1 1976	18:06	12° Ar 08' D
Sun Cnj Mer	May 20 1976	12:15	29° Ta 35' R
Sun Cnj Mer	Jul 15 1976	14:50	23° Cn 13' D
Sun Cnj Mer	Sep 22 1976	01:34	29° Vi 10' R
Sun Cnj Mer	Nov 7 1976	09:44	15° Sc 06' D
Sun Cnj Mer	Jan 6 1977	08:07	15° Cp 54' R
Sun Cnj Mer	Mar 16 1977	05:25	25° Pi 30' D
Sun Cnj Mer	Apr 30 1977	16:44	10° Ta 12' R
Sun Cnj Mer	Jun 30 1977	00:22	08° Cn 06' D
Sun Cnj Mer	Sep 5 1977	05:41	12° Vi 33' R
Sun Cnj Mer	Oct 18 1977	23:16	25° Li 27' D
Sun Cnj Mer	Dec 21 1977	14:08	29° Sg 36' R
Sun Cnj Mer	Feb 27 1978	03:03	08° Pi 09' D
Sun Cnj Mer	Apr 11 1978	16:49	21° Ar 26' R
Sun Cnj Mer	Jun 14 1978	11:50	23° Ge 04' D
Sun Cnj Mer	Aug 18 1978	20:11	25° Le 31' R
Sun Cnj Mer	Sep 30 1978	15:22	07° Li 06' D
Sun Cnj Mer	Dec 5 1978	21:33	13° Sg 24' R
Sun Cnj Mer	Feb 9 1979	06:06	19° Aq 53' D
Sun Cnj Mer	Mar 24 1979	14:05	03° Ar 20' R
Sun Cnj Mer	May 29 1979	23:31	07° Ge 59' D
Sun Cnj Mer	Jul 31 1979	17:27	07° Le 54' R
Sun Cnj Mer	Sep 13 1979	05:25	19° Vi 50' D
Sun Cnj Mer	Nov 20 1979	04:36	27° Sc 15' R
Sun Cnj Mer	Jan 21 1980	09:15	00° Aq 29' D
Sun Cnj Mer	Mar 6 1980	05:39	15° Pi 48' R
Sun Cnj Mer	May 13 1980	09:40	22° Ta 46' D
Sun Cnj Mer	Jul 11 1980	18:45	19° Cn 35' R
Sun Cnj Mer	Aug 26 1980	11:52	03° Vi 22' D
Sun Cnj Mer	Nov 3 1980	09:32	11° Sc 07' R
Sun Cnj Mer	Dec 31 1980	10:04	09° Cp 53' D
Sun Cnj Mer	Feb 17 1981	11:31	28° Aq 43' R

Sun Cnj Mer	Apr 27 1981	16:30	07° Ta 18' D
Sun Cnj Mer	Jun 22 1981	00:57	00° Cn 31' R
Sun Cnj Mer	Aug 10 1981	06:01	17° Le 31' D
Sun Cnj Mer	Oct 18 1981	10:31	24° Li 57' R
Sun Cnj Mer	Dec 10 1981	14:54	18° Sg 28' D
Sun Cnj Mer	Feb 1 1982	03:49	11° Aq 57' R
Sun Cnj Mer	Apr 11 1982	17:58	21° Ar 30' D
Sun Cnj Mer	Jun 1 1982	19:42	10° Ge 58' R
Sun Cnj Mer	Jul 25 1982	08:17	02° Le 04' D
Sun Cnj Mer	Oct 2 1982	05:28	08° Li 41' R
Sun Cnj Mer	Nov 19 1982	18:23	27° Sc 05' D
Sun Cnj Mer	Jan 16 1983	03:24	25° Cp 25' R
Sun Cnj Mer	Mar 26 1983	11:26	05° Ar 14' D
Sun Cnj Mer	May 12 1983	16:37	21° Ta 23' R
Sun Cnj Mer	Jul 9 1983	15:49	16° Cn 52' D
Sun Cnj Mer	Sep 15 1983	15:49	22° Vi 14' R
Sun Cnj Mer	Oct 30 1983	16:29	06° Sc 40' D
Sun Cnj Mer	Dec 31 1983	07:41	09° Cp 03' R
Sun Cnj Mer	Mar 8 1984	17:32	18° Pi 20' D
Sun Cnj Mer	Apr 22 1984	04:49	02° Ta 14' R
Sun Cnj Mer	Jun 23 1984	02:23	01° Cn 48' D
Sun Cnj Mer	Aug 28 1984	14:32	05° Vi 27' R
Sun Cnj Mer	Oct 10 1984	17:36	17° Li 35' D
Sun Cnj Mer	Dec 14 1984	14:28	22° Sg 47' R
Sun Cnj Mer	Feb 19 1985	07:49	00° Pi 37' D
Sun Cnj Mer	Apr 3 1985	14:05	13° Ar 45' R
Sun Cnj Mer	Jun 7 1985	14:10	16° Ge 45' D
Sun Cnj Mer	Aug 10 1985	10:08	18° Le 11' R
Sun Cnj Mer	Sep 22 1985	07:49	29° Vi 44' D
Sun Cnj Mer	Nov 28 1985	09:56	06° Sg 37' R
Sun Cnj Mer	Feb 1 1986	01:11	11° Aq 52' D
Sun Cnj Mer	Mar 16 1986	19:34	25° Pi 55' R
Sun Cnj Mer	May 23 1986	01:24	01° Ge 38' D
Sun Cnj Mer	Jul 23 1986	11:10	00° Le 18' R
Sun Cnj Mer	Sep 5 1986	17:32	12° Vi 51' D
Sun Cnj Mer	Nov 13 1986	04:19	20° Sc 29' R
Sun Cnj Mer	Jan 12 1987	17:06	21° Cp 57' D
Sun Cnj Mer	Feb 27 1987	17:40	08° Pi 35' R
Sun Cnj Mer	May 7 1987	10:25	16° Ta 20' D
Sun Cnj Mer	Jul 4 1987	04:03	11° Cn 40' R
Sun Cnj Mer	Aug 20 1987	05:29	26° Le 40' D
Sun Cnj Mer	Oct 28 1987	07:50	04° Sc 21' R
Sun Cnj Mer	Dec 23 1987	07:52	00° Cp 56' D
Sun Cnj Mer	Feb 11 1988	04:23	21° Aq 39' R
Sun Cnj Mer	Apr 20 1988	15:14	00° Ta 45' D

Appendix II • *Sun-Mercury Inferior + Superior Conjunctions 1920 to 2120*

Sun Cnj Mer	Jun 13 1988	03:55	22° Ge 21' R
Sun Cnj Mer	Aug 3 1988	03:29	11° Le 00' D
Sun Cnj Mer	Oct 11 1988	06:33	18° Li 09' R
Sun Cnj Mer	Dec 1 1988	09:23	09° Sg 24' D
Sun Cnj Mer	Jan 25 1989	00:11	05° Aq 00' R
Sun Cnj Mer	Apr 4 1989	13:36	14° Ar 45' D
Sun Cnj Mer	May 23 1989	21:35	02° Ge 42' R
Sun Cnj Mer	Jul 18 1989	08:16	25° Cn 41' D
Sun Cnj Mer	Sep 24 1989	22:11	01° Li 49' R
Sun Cnj Mer	Nov 10 1989	18:56	18° Sc 21' D
Sun Cnj Mer	Jan 9 1990	02:04	18° Cp 32' R
Sun Cnj Mer	Mar 19 1990	02:39	28° Pi 13' D
Sun Cnj Mer	May 3 1990	23:49	13° Ta 16' R
Sun Cnj Mer	Jul 2 1990	17:21	10° Cn 33' D
Sun Cnj Mer	Sep 8 1990	04:00	15° Vi 15' R
Sun Cnj Mer	Oct 22 1990	04:21	28° Li 30' D
Sun Cnj Mer	Dec 24 1990	07:39	02° Cp 13' R
Sun Cnj Mer	Mar 2 1991	02:35	11° Pi 00' D
Sun Cnj Mer	Apr 14 1991	20:42	24° Ar 23' R
Sun Cnj Mer	Jun 17 1991	04:38	25° Ge 31' D
Sun Cnj Mer	Aug 21 1991	20:42	28° Le 17' R
Sun Cnj Mer	Oct 3 1991	16:40	09° Li 58' D
Sun Cnj Mer	Dec 8 1991	14:58	16° Sg 01' R
Sun Cnj Mer	Feb 12 1992	08:43	22° Aq 53' D
Sun Cnj Mer	Mar 26 1992	14:55	06° Ar 12' R
Sun Cnj Mer	May 31 1992	16:21	10° Ge 26' D
Sun Cnj Mer	Aug 2 1992	20:43	10° Le 46' R
Sun Cnj Mer	Sep 15 1992	03:48	22° Vi 33' D
Sun Cnj Mer	Nov 21 1992	22:09	29° Sc 51' R
Sun Cnj Mer	Jan 23 1993	15:42	03° Aq 39' D
Sun Cnj Mer	Mar 9 1993	04:01	18° Pi 35' R
Sun Cnj Mer	May 16 1993	02:51	25° Ta 15' D
Sun Cnj Mer	Jul 15 1993	01:08	22° Cn 34' R
Sun Cnj Mer	Aug 29 1993	08:12	06° Vi 00' D
Sun Cnj Mer	Nov 6 1993	03:33	13° Sc 44' R
Sun Cnj Mer	Jan 3 1994	20:20	13° Cp 14' D
Sun Cnj Mer	Feb 20 1994	08:01	01° Pi 27' R
Sun Cnj Mer	Apr 30 1994	10:21	09° Ta 50' D
Sun Cnj Mer	Jun 25 1994	09:57	03° Cn 37' R
Sun Cnj Mer	Aug 13 1994	00:54	20° Le 04' D
Sun Cnj Mer	Oct 21 1994	05:17	27° Li 34' R
Sun Cnj Mer	Dec 14 1994	03:16	21° Sg 53' D
Sun Cnj Mer	Feb 3 1995	23:00	14° Aq 39' R
Sun Cnj Mer	Apr 14 1995	12:49	24° Ar 06' D
Sun Cnj Mer	Jun 5 1995	05:38	14° Ge 07' R

Sun Cnj Mer	Jul 28 1995	02:09	04° Le 33' D
Sun Cnj Mer	Oct 5 1995	01:17	11° Li 20' R
Sun Cnj Mer	Nov 23 1995	05:26	00° Sg 26' D
Sun Cnj Mer	Jan 18 1996	21:40	28° Cp 04' R
Sun Cnj Mer	Mar 28 1996	07:37	07° Ar 54' D
Sun Cnj Mer	May 15 1996	01:12	24° Ta 29' R
Sun Cnj Mer	Jul 11 1996	09:01	19° Cn 19' D
Sun Cnj Mer	Sep 17 1996	13:05	24° Vi 54' R
Sun Cnj Mer	Nov 1 1996	23:55	09° Sc 50' D
Sun Cnj Mer	Jan 2 1997	01:22	11° Cp 41' R
Sun Cnj Mer	Mar 11 1997	15:34	21° Pi 06' D
Sun Cnj Mer	Apr 25 1997	10:32	05° Ta 15' R
Sun Cnj Mer	Jun 25 1997	19:14	04° Cn 14' D
Sun Cnj Mer	Aug 31 1997	13:43	08° Vi 11' R
Sun Cnj Mer	Oct 13 1997	21:00	20° Li 33' D
Sun Cnj Mer	Dec 17 1997	07:53	25° Sg 24' R
Sun Cnj Mer	Feb 22 1998	08:29	03° Pi 30' D
Sun Cnj Mer	Apr 6 1998	16:35	16° Ar 40' R
Sun Cnj Mer	Jun 10 1998	06:57	19° Ge 12' D
Sun Cnj Mer	Aug 13 1998	23:48	21° Le 00' R
Sun Cnj Mer	Sep 25 1998	19:50	02° Li 32' D
Sun Cnj Mer	Dec 1 1998	15:23	09° Sg 13' R
Sun Cnj Mer	Feb 4 1999	05:20	14° Aq 55' D
Sun Cnj Mer	Mar 19 1999	19:14	28° Pi 44' R
Sun Cnj Mer	May 25 1999	18:22	04° Ge 06' D
Sun Cnj Mer	Jul 26 1999	15:48	03° Le 13' R
Sun Cnj Mer	Sep 8 1999	14:58	15° Vi 31' D
Sun Cnj Mer	Nov 15 1999	22:04	23° Sc 05' R
Sun Cnj Mer	Jan 16 2000	01:19	25° Cp 12' D
Sun Cnj Mer	Mar 1 2000	15:00	11° Pi 20' R
Sun Cnj Mer	May 9 2000	03:49	18° Ta 49' D
Sun Cnj Mer	Jul 6 2000	11:35	14° Cn 41' R
Sun Cnj Mer	Aug 22 2000	01:05	29° Le 14' D
Sun Cnj Mer	Oct 30 2000	02:09	06° Sc 57' R
Sun Cnj Mer	Dec 25 2000	19:23	04° Cp 19' D
Sun Cnj Mer	Feb 13 2001	00:17	24° Aq 21' R
Sun Cnj Mer	Apr 23 2001	09:24	03° Ta 17' D
Sun Cnj Mer	Jun 16 2001	13:26	25° Ge 27' R
Sun Cnj Mer	Aug 5 2001	21:51	13° Le 31' D
Sun Cnj Mer	Oct 14 2001	01:43	20° Li 46' R
Sun Cnj Mer	Dec 4 2001	21:36	12° Sg 48' D
Sun Cnj Mer	Jan 27 2002	18:55	07° Aq 39' R
Sun Cnj Mer	Apr 7 2002	08:55	17° Ar 21' D
Sun Cnj Mer	May 27 2002	07:09	05° Ge 49' R
Sun Cnj Mer	Jul 21 2002	01:47	28° Cn 09' D

Appendix II • *Sun-Mercury Inferior + Superior Conjunctions 1920 to 2120*

Sun Cnj Mer	Sep 27 2002	18:31	04° Li 28' R
Sun Cnj Mer	Nov 14 2002	04:39	21° Sc 37' D
Sun Cnj Mer	Jan 11 2003	20:02	21° Cp 10' R
Sun Cnj Mer	Mar 21 2003	23:34	00° Ar 56' D
Sun Cnj Mer	May 7 2003	07:21	16° Ta 20' R
Sun Cnj Mer	Jul 5 2003	10:20	13° Cn 00' D
Sun Cnj Mer	Sep 11 2003	01:57	17° Vi 56' R
Sun Cnj Mer	Oct 25 2003	09:58	01° Sc 34' D
Sun Cnj Mer	Dec 27 2003	01:11	04° Cp 50' R
Sun Cnj Mer	Mar 4 2004	01:43	13° Pi 49' D
Sun Cnj Mer	Apr 17 2004	01:05	27° Ar 21' R
Sun Cnj Mer	Jun 18 2004	21:24	27° Ge 56' D
Sun Cnj Mer	Aug 23 2004	20:51	01° Vi 02' R
Sun Cnj Mer	Oct 5 2004	18:29	12° Li 50' D
Sun Cnj Mer	Dec 10 2004	08:21	18° Sg 37' R
Sun Cnj Mer	Feb 14 2005	10:50	25° Aq 50' D
Sun Cnj Mer	Mar 29 2005	16:11	09° Ar 03' R
Sun Cnj Mer	Jun 3 2005	09:12	12° Ge 53' D
Sun Cnj Mer	Aug 5 2005	23:36	13° Le 37' R
Sun Cnj Mer	Sep 18 2005	02:38	25° Vi 17' D
Sun Cnj Mer	Nov 24 2005	15:43	02° Sg 27' R
Sun Cnj Mer	Jan 26 2006	21:34	06° Aq 47' D
Sun Cnj Mer	Mar 12 2006	02:44	21° Pi 23' R
Sun Cnj Mer	May 18 2006	20:02	27° Ta 44' D
Sun Cnj Mer	Jul 18 2006	07:07	25° Cn 32' R
Sun Cnj Mer	Sep 1 2006	04:49	08° Vi 37' D
Sun Cnj Mer	Nov 8 2006	21:30	16° Sc 20' R
Sun Cnj Mer	Jan 7 2007	06:05	16° Cp 32' D
Sun Cnj Mer	Feb 23 2007	04:45	04° Pi 11' R
Sun Cnj Mer	May 3 2007	04:05	12° Ta 21' D
Sun Cnj Mer	Jun 28 2007	18:40	06° Cn 41' R
Sun Cnj Mer	Aug 15 2007	19:56	22° Le 36' D
Sun Cnj Mer	Oct 23 2007	23:55	00° Sc 11' R
Sun Cnj Mer	Dec 17 2007	15:27	25° Sg 18' D
Sun Cnj Mer	Feb 6 2008	18:19	17° Aq 20' R
Sun Cnj Mer	Apr 16 2008	07:24	26° Ar 41' D
Sun Cnj Mer	Jun 7 2008	15:27	17° Ge 14' R
Sun Cnj Mer	Jul 29 2008	20:00	07° Le 03' D
Sun Cnj Mer	Oct 6 2008	20:53	13° Li 58' R
Sun Cnj Mer	Nov 25 2008	16:52	03° Sg 47' D
Sun Cnj Mer	Jan 20 2009	15:59	00° Aq 44' R
Sun Cnj Mer	Mar 31 2009	03:29	10° Ar 33' D
Sun Cnj Mer	May 18 2009	10:02	27° Ta 36' R
Sun Cnj Mer	Jul 14 2009	02:16	21° Cn 47' D
Sun Cnj Mer	Sep 20 2009	10:05	27° Vi 35' R

Sun Cnj Mer	Nov 5 2009	08:02	13° Sc 02' D
Sun Cnj Mer	Jan 4 2010	19:06	14° Cp 19' R
Sun Cnj Mer	Mar 14 2010	13:16	23° Pi 50' D
Sun Cnj Mer	Apr 28 2010	16:44	08° Ta 17' R
Sun Cnj Mer	Jun 28 2010	12:07	06° Cn 42' D
Sun Cnj Mer	Sep 3 2010	12:35	10° Vi 54' R
Sun Cnj Mer	Oct 17 2010	01:05	23° Li 33' D
Sun Cnj Mer	Dec 20 2010	01:23	28° Sg 02' R
Sun Cnj Mer	Feb 25 2011	08:48	06° Pi 23' D
Sun Cnj Mer	Apr 9 2011	19:36	19° Ar 36' R
Sun Cnj Mer	Jun 12 2011	23:44	21° Ge 39' D
Sun Cnj Mer	Aug 17 2011	01:04	23° Le 48' R
Sun Cnj Mer	Sep 28 2011	20:16	05° Li 21' D
Sun Cnj Mer	Dec 4 2011	08:52	11° Sg 50' R
Sun Cnj Mer	Feb 7 2012	09:02	17° Aq 59' D
Sun Cnj Mer	Mar 21 2012	19:21	01° Ar 34' R
Sun Cnj Mer	May 27 2012	11:19	06° Ge 34' D
Sun Cnj Mer	Jul 28 2012	19:57	06° Le 07' R
Sun Cnj Mer	Sep 10 2012	12:44	18° Vi 12' D
Sun Cnj Mer	Nov 17 2012	15:47	25° Sc 42' R
Sun Cnj Mer	Jan 18 2013	08:56	28° Cp 26' D
Sun Cnj Mer	Mar 4 2013	12:58	14° Pi 06' R
Sun Cnj Mer	May 11 2013	21:10	21° Ta 19' D
Sun Cnj Mer	Jul 9 2013	18:41	17° Cn 42' R
Sun Cnj Mer	Aug 24 2013	20:56	01° Vi 50' D
Sun Cnj Mer	Nov 1 2013	20:19	09° Sc 34' R
Sun Cnj Mer	Dec 29 2013	06:27	07° Cp 41' D
Sun Cnj Mer	Feb 15 2014	20:22	27° Aq 04' R
Sun Cnj Mer	Apr 26 2014	03:27	05° Ta 49' D
Sun Cnj Mer	Jun 19 2014	22:50	28° Ge 34' R
Sun Cnj Mer	Aug 8 2014	16:21	16° Le 03' D
Sun Cnj Mer	Oct 16 2014	20:40	23° Li 24' R
Sun Cnj Mer	Dec 8 2014	09:51	16° Sg 13' D
Sun Cnj Mer	Jan 30 2015	13:45	10° Aq 20' R
Sun Cnj Mer	Apr 10 2015	04:00	19° Ar 58' D
Sun Cnj Mer	May 30 2015	16:56	08° Ge 58' R
Sun Cnj Mer	Jul 23 2015	19:24	00° Le 37' D
Sun Cnj Mer	Sep 30 2015	14:38	07° Li 07' R
Sun Cnj Mer	Nov 17 2015	14:53	24° Sc 55' D
Sun Cnj Mer	Jan 14 2016	14:05	23° Cp 49' R
Sun Cnj Mer	Mar 23 2016	20:11	03° Ar 37' D
Sun Cnj Mer	May 9 2016	15:12	19° Ta 25' R
Sun Cnj Mer	Jul 7 2016	03:24	15° Cn 27' D
Sun Cnj Mer	Sep 12 2016	23:40	20° Vi 37' R
Sun Cnj Mer	Oct 27 2016	16:16	04° Sc 40' D

Appendix II • *Sun-Mercury Inferior + Superior Conjunctions 1920 to 2120*

Sun Cnj Mer	Dec 28 2016	18:47	07° Cp 28' R
Sun Cnj Mer	Mar 7 2017	00:29	16° Pi 37' D
Sun Cnj Mer	Apr 20 2017	05:54	00° Ta 20' R
Sun Cnj Mer	Jun 21 2017	14:14	00° Cn 23' D
Sun Cnj Mer	Aug 26 2017	20:42	03° Vi 47' R
Sun Cnj Mer	Oct 8 2017	20:54	15° Li 45' D
Sun Cnj Mer	Dec 13 2017	01:49	21° Sg 14' R
Sun Cnj Mer	Feb 17 2018	12:27	28° Aq 47' D
Sun Cnj Mer	Apr 1 2018	17:53	11° Ar 56' R
Sun Cnj Mer	Jun 6 2018	02:02	15° Ge 20' D
Sun Cnj Mer	Aug 9 2018	02:06	16° Le 27' R
Sun Cnj Mer	Sep 21 2018	01:52	28° Vi 02' D
Sun Cnj Mer	Nov 27 2018	09:15	05° Sg 03' R
Sun Cnj Mer	Jan 30 2019	02:52	09° Aq 54' D
Sun Cnj Mer	Mar 15 2019	01:48	24° Pi 11' R
Sun Cnj Mer	May 21 2019	13:07	00° Ge 12' D
Sun Cnj Mer	Jul 21 2019	12:34	28° Cn 28' R
Sun Cnj Mer	Sep 4 2019	01:40	11° Vi 15' D
Sun Cnj Mer	Nov 11 2019	15:22	18° Sc 55' R
Sun Cnj Mer	Jan 10 2020	15:19	19° Cp 49' D
Sun Cnj Mer	Feb 26 2020	01:45	06° Pi 55' R
Sun Cnj Mer	May 4 2020	21:41	14° Ta 52' D
Sun Cnj Mer	Jul 1 2020	02:53	09° Cn 44' R
Sun Cnj Mer	Aug 17 2020	15:07	25° Le 09' D
Sun Cnj Mer	Oct 25 2020	18:23	02° Sc 47' R
Sun Cnj Mer	Dec 20 2020	03:26	28° Sg 42' D
Sun Cnj Mer	Feb 8 2021	13:48	20° Aq 01' R
Sun Cnj Mer	Apr 19 2021	01:50	29° Ar 14' D
Sun Cnj Mer	Jun 11 2021	01:13	20° Ge 21' R
Sun Cnj Mer	Aug 1 2021	14:08	09° Le 32' D
Sun Cnj Mer	Oct 9 2021	16:18	16° Li 35' R
Sun Cnj Mer	Nov 29 2021	04:39	07° Sg 10' D
Sun Cnj Mer	Jan 23 2022	10:28	03° Aq 22' R
Sun Cnj Mer	Apr 2 2022	23:11	13° Ar 11' D
Sun Cnj Mer	May 21 2022	19:18	00° Ge 43' R
Sun Cnj Mer	Jul 16 2022	19:38	24° Cn 15' D
Sun Cnj Mer	Sep 23 2022	06:50	00° Li 14' R
Sun Cnj Mer	Nov 8 2022	16:43	16° Sc 15' D
Sun Cnj Mer	Jan 7 2023	12:57	16° Cp 56' R
Sun Cnj Mer	Mar 17 2023	10:45	26° Pi 34' D
Sun Cnj Mer	May 1 2023	23:28	11° Ta 19' R
Sun Cnj Mer	Jul 1 2023	05:06	09° Cn 08' D
Sun Cnj Mer	Sep 6 2023	11:09	13° Vi 36' R
Sun Cnj Mer	Oct 20 2023	05:38	26° Li 34' D
Sun Cnj Mer	Dec 22 2023	18:54	00° Cp 39' R

Sun Cnj Mer	Feb 28 2024	08:43	09° Pi 14' D
Sun Cnj Mer	Apr 11 2024	23:03	22° Ar 32' R
Sun Cnj Mer	Jun 14 2024	16:32	24° Ge 06' D
Sun Cnj Mer	Aug 19 2024	01:58	26° Le 35' R
Sun Cnj Mer	Sep 30 2024	21:09	08° Li 11' D
Sun Cnj Mer	Dec 6 2024	02:18	14° Sg 27' R
Sun Cnj Mer	Feb 9 2025	12:08	20° Aq 59' D
Sun Cnj Mer	Mar 24 2025	19:48	04° Ar 24' R
Sun Cnj Mer	May 30 2025	04:13	09° Ge 01' D
Sun Cnj Mer	Jul 31 2025	23:41	09° Le 00' R
Sun Cnj Mer	Sep 13 2025	10:52	20° Vi 54' D
Sun Cnj Mer	Nov 20 2025	09:23	28° Sc 18' R
Sun Cnj Mer	Jan 21 2026	15:49	01° Aq 36' D
Sun Cnj Mer	Mar 7 2026	11:02	16° Pi 52' R
Sun Cnj Mer	May 14 2026	14:24	23° Ta 48' D
Sun Cnj Mer	Jul 13 2026	01:26	20° Cn 42' R
Sun Cnj Mer	Aug 27 2026	17:04	04° Vi 26' D
Sun Cnj Mer	Nov 4 2026	14:24	12° Sc 10' R
Sun Cnj Mer	Jan 1 2027	17:07	11° Cp 02' D
Sun Cnj Mer	Feb 18 2027	16:39	29° Aq 47' R
Sun Cnj Mer	Apr 28 2027	21:22	08° Ta 21' D
Sun Cnj Mer	Jun 23 2027	08:00	01° Cn 39' R
Sun Cnj Mer	Aug 11 2027	11:02	18° Le 34' D
Sun Cnj Mer	Oct 19 2027	15:31	26° Li 01' R
Sun Cnj Mer	Dec 11 2027	22:17	19° Sg 38' D
Sun Cnj Mer	Feb 2 2028	08:47	13° Aq 01' R
Sun Cnj Mer	Apr 11 2028	22:56	22° Ar 34' D
Sun Cnj Mer	Jun 2 2028	02:46	12° Ge 06' R
Sun Cnj Mer	Jul 25 2028	13:07	03° Le 06' D
Sun Cnj Mer	Oct 2 2028	10:37	09° Li 45' R
Sun Cnj Mer	Nov 20 2028	01:40	28° Sc 15' D
Sun Cnj Mer	Jan 16 2029	08:16	26° Cp 29' R
Sun Cnj Mer	Mar 26 2029	16:34	06° Ar 18' D
Sun Cnj Mer	May 12 2029	23:27	22° Ta 30' R
Sun Cnj Mer	Jul 9 2029	20:32	17° Cn 54' D
Sun Cnj Mer	Sep 15 2029	21:11	23° Vi 18' R
Sun Cnj Mer	Oct 30 2029	23:14	07° Sc 49' D
Sun Cnj Mer	Dec 31 2029	12:28	10° Cp 06' R
Sun Cnj Mer	Mar 9 2030	22:54	19° Pi 24' D
Sun Cnj Mer	Apr 23 2030	11:14	03° Ta 21' R
Sun Cnj Mer	Jun 24 2030	07:04	02° Cn 50' D
Sun Cnj Mer	Aug 29 2030	20:11	06° Vi 32' R
Sun Cnj Mer	Oct 11 2030	23:48	18° Li 42' D
Sun Cnj Mer	Dec 15 2030	19:14	23° Sg 51' R
Sun Cnj Mer	Feb 20 2031	13:36	01° Pi 42' D

Appendix II • *Sun-Mercury Inferior + Superior Conjunctions 1920 to 2120*

Sun Cnj Mer	Apr 4 2031	20:02	14° Ar 51' R
Sun Cnj Mer	Jun 8 2031	18:50	17° Ge 47' D
Sun Cnj Mer	Aug 12 2031	04:05	19° Le 17' R
Sun Cnj Mer	Sep 24 2031	01:27	00° Li 49' D
Sun Cnj Mer	Nov 30 2031	02:43	07° Sg 40' R
Sun Cnj Mer	Feb 2 2032	07:32	13° Aq 00' D
Sun Cnj Mer	Mar 17 2032	01:11	27° Pi 00' R
Sun Cnj Mer	May 23 2032	06:07	02° Ge 40' D
Sun Cnj Mer	Jul 23 2032	17:31	01° Le 24' R
Sun Cnj Mer	Sep 5 2032	22:48	13° Vi 54' D
Sun Cnj Mer	Nov 13 2032	09:08	21° Sc 32' R
Sun Cnj Mer	Jan 12 2033	23:56	23° Cp 06' D
Sun Cnj Mer	Feb 27 2033	23:00	09° Pi 40' R
Sun Cnj Mer	May 7 2033	15:11	17° Ta 22' D
Sun Cnj Mer	Jul 4 2033	10:48	12° Cn 47' R
Sun Cnj Mer	Aug 20 2033	10:33	27° Le 43' D
Sun Cnj Mer	Oct 28 2033	12:45	05° Sc 24' R
Sun Cnj Mer	Dec 23 2033	15:09	02° Cp 05' D
Sun Cnj Mer	Feb 11 2034	09:29	22° Aq 42' R
Sun Cnj Mer	Apr 21 2034	20:08	01° Ta 47' D
Sun Cnj Mer	Jun 14 2034	10:59	23° Ge 28' R
Sun Cnj Mer	Aug 4 2034	08:24	12° Le 03' D
Sun Cnj Mer	Oct 12 2034	11:35	19° Li 13' R
Sun Cnj Mer	Dec 2 2034	16:45	10° Sg 34' D
Sun Cnj Mer	Jan 26 2035	05:06	06° Aq 03' R
Sun Cnj Mer	Apr 5 2035	18:42	15° Ar 48' D
Sun Cnj Mer	May 25 2035	04:45	03° Ge 50' R
Sun Cnj Mer	Jul 19 2035	13:05	26° Cn 43' D
Sun Cnj Mer	Sep 26 2035	03:22	02° Li 53' R
Sun Cnj Mer	Nov 12 2035	01:56	19° Sc 29' D
Sun Cnj Mer	Jan 10 2036	06:52	19° Cp 35' R
Sun Cnj Mer	Mar 19 2036	07:54	29° Pi 17' D
Sun Cnj Mer	May 4 2036	06:34	14° Ta 23' R
Sun Cnj Mer	Jul 2 2036	22:04	11° Cn 35' D
Sun Cnj Mer	Sep 8 2036	09:26	16° Vi 18' R
Sun Cnj Mer	Oct 22 2036	10:46	29° Li 37' D
Sun Cnj Mer	Dec 24 2036	12:25	03° Cp 16' R
Sun Cnj Mer	Mar 2 2037	08:09	12° Pi 04' D
Sun Cnj Mer	Apr 15 2037	02:56	25° Ar 29' R
Sun Cnj Mer	Jun 17 2037	09:18	26° Ge 32' D
Sun Cnj Mer	Aug 22 2037	02:28	29° Le 21' R
Sun Cnj Mer	Oct 3 2037	22:34	11° Li 03' D
Sun Cnj Mer	Dec 8 2037	19:42	17° Sg 03' R
Sun Cnj Mer	Feb 12 2038	14:40	23° Aq 58' D
Sun Cnj Mer	Mar 27 2038	20:41	07° Ar 16' R

Sun Cnj Mer	Jun 1 2038	21:04	11° Ge 28' D
Sun Cnj Mer	Aug 4 2038	02:55	11° Le 52' R
Sun Cnj Mer	Sep 16 2038	09:22	23° Vi 37' D
Sun Cnj Mer	Nov 23 2038	02:57	00° Sg 54' R
Sun Cnj Mer	Jan 24 2039	22:09	04° Aq 46' D
Sun Cnj Mer	Mar 10 2039	09:27	19° Pi 39' R
Sun Cnj Mer	May 17 2039	07:36	26° Ta 17' D
Sun Cnj Mer	Jul 16 2039	07:43	23° Cn 40' R
Sun Cnj Mer	Aug 30 2039	13:26	07° Vi 03' D
Sun Cnj Mer	Nov 7 2039	08:26	14° Sc 46' R
Sun Cnj Mer	Jan 5 2040	03:23	14° Cp 22' D
Sun Cnj Mer	Feb 21 2040	13:13	02° Pi 30' R
Sun Cnj Mer	Apr 30 2040	15:10	10° Ta 52' D
Sun Cnj Mer	Jun 25 2040	16:53	04° Cn 43' R
Sun Cnj Mer	Aug 13 2040	05:53	21° Le 06' D
Sun Cnj Mer	Oct 21 2040	10:16	28° Li 37' R
Sun Cnj Mer	Dec 14 2040	10:39	23° Sg 03' D
Sun Cnj Mer	Feb 4 2041	03:59	15° Aq 42' R
Sun Cnj Mer	Apr 14 2041	17:42	25° Ar 08' D
Sun Cnj Mer	Jun 5 2041	12:39	15° Ge 13' R
Sun Cnj Mer	Jul 28 2041	06:58	05° Le 35' D
Sun Cnj Mer	Oct 5 2041	06:24	12° Li 23' R
Sun Cnj Mer	Nov 23 2041	12:49	01° Sg 35' D
Sun Cnj Mer	Jan 19 2042	02:32	29° Cp 07' R
Sun Cnj Mer	Mar 29 2042	12:42	08° Ar 57' D
Sun Cnj Mer	May 16 2042	08:04	25° Ta 36' R
Sun Cnj Mer	Jul 12 2042	13:43	20° Cn 21' D
Sun Cnj Mer	Sep 18 2042	18:23	25° Vi 58' R
Sun Cnj Mer	Nov 3 2042	06:45	10° Sc 58' D
Sun Cnj Mer	Jan 3 2043	06:10	12° Cp 44' R
Sun Cnj Mer	Mar 12 2043	20:58	22° Pi 10' D
Sun Cnj Mer	Apr 26 2043	17:04	06° Ta 22' R
Sun Cnj Mer	Jun 26 2043	23:56	05° Cn 16' D
Sun Cnj Mer	Sep 1 2043	19:17	09° Vi 15' R
Sun Cnj Mer	Oct 15 2043	03:13	21° Li 39' D
Sun Cnj Mer	Dec 18 2043	12:40	26° Sg 27' R
Sun Cnj Mer	Feb 23 2044	14:16	04° Pi 36' D
Sun Cnj Mer	Apr 6 2044	22:40	17° Ar 46' R
Sun Cnj Mer	Jun 10 2044	11:38	20° Ge 14' D
Sun Cnj Mer	Aug 14 2044	05:41	22° Le 05' R
Sun Cnj Mer	Sep 26 2044	01:32	03° Li 37' D
Sun Cnj Mer	Dec 1 2044	20:11	10° Sg 17' R
Sun Cnj Mer	Feb 4 2045	11:36	16° Aq 03' D
Sun Cnj Mer	Mar 20 2045	00:56	29° Pi 49' R
Sun Cnj Mer	May 25 2045	23:06	05° Ge 08' D

Appendix II • *Sun-Mercury Inferior + Superior Conjunctions 1920 to 2120*

Sun Cnj Mer	Jul 26 2045	22:05	04° Le 19' R
Sun Cnj Mer	Sep 8 2045	20:20	16° Vi 35' D
Sun Cnj Mer	Nov 16 2045	02:54	24° Sc 09' R
Sun Cnj Mer	Jan 16 2046	08:02	26° Cp 20' D
Sun Cnj Mer	Mar 2 2046	20:31	12° Pi 25' R
Sun Cnj Mer	May 10 2046	08:38	19° Ta 52' D
Sun Cnj Mer	Jul 7 2046	18:23	15° Cn 49' R
Sun Cnj Mer	Aug 23 2046	06:14	00° Vi 18' D
Sun Cnj Mer	Oct 31 2046	07:02	08° Sc 01' R
Sun Cnj Mer	Dec 27 2046	02:35	05° Cp 28' D
Sun Cnj Mer	Feb 14 2047	05:22	25° Aq 25' R
Sun Cnj Mer	Apr 24 2047	14:17	04° Ta 20' D
Sun Cnj Mer	Jun 17 2047	20:34	26° Ge 35' R
Sun Cnj Mer	Aug 7 2047	02:46	14° Le 34' D
Sun Cnj Mer	Oct 15 2047	06:42	21° Li 50' R
Sun Cnj Mer	Dec 6 2047	04:59	13° Sg 58' D
Sun Cnj Mer	Jan 28 2048	23:50	08° Aq 43' R
Sun Cnj Mer	Apr 7 2048	13:55	18° Ar 25' D
Sun Cnj Mer	May 27 2048	14:15	06° Ge 58' R
Sun Cnj Mer	Jul 21 2048	06:35	29° Cn 11' D
Sun Cnj Mer	Sep 27 2048	23:41	05° Li 32' R
Sun Cnj Mer	Nov 14 2048	11:42	22° Sc 46' D
Sun Cnj Mer	Jan 12 2049	00:50	22° Cp 14' R
Sun Cnj Mer	Mar 22 2049	04:45	01° Ar 59' D
Sun Cnj Mer	May 7 2049	14:01	17° Ta 27' R
Sun Cnj Mer	Jul 5 2049	15:04	14° Cn 02' D
Sun Cnj Mer	Sep 11 2049	07:24	19° Vi 01' R
Sun Cnj Mer	Oct 25 2049	16:33	02° Sc 42' D
Sun Cnj Mer	Dec 27 2049	05:58	05° Cp 54' R
Sun Cnj Mer	Mar 5 2050	07:13	14° Pi 54' D
Sun Cnj Mer	Apr 18 2050	07:21	28° Ar 27' R
Sun Cnj Mer	Jun 20 2050	02:06	28° Ge 59' D
Sun Cnj Mer	Aug 25 2050	02:36	02° Vi 07' R
Sun Cnj Mer	Oct 7 2050	00:31	13° Li 57' D
Sun Cnj Mer	Dec 11 2050	13:09	19° Sg 40' R
Sun Cnj Mer	Feb 15 2051	16:45	26° Aq 56' D
Sun Cnj Mer	Mar 30 2051	22:05	10° Ar 09' R
Sun Cnj Mer	Jun 4 2051	13:55	13° Ge 55' D
Sun Cnj Mer	Aug 7 2051	05:43	14° Le 43' R
Sun Cnj Mer	Sep 19 2051	08:14	26° Vi 22' D
Sun Cnj Mer	Nov 25 2051	20:32	03° Sg 30' R
Sun Cnj Mer	Jan 28 2052	03:59	07° Aq 54' D
Sun Cnj Mer	Mar 12 2052	08:15	22° Pi 27' R
Sun Cnj Mer	May 19 2052	00:45	28° Ta 46' D
Sun Cnj Mer	Jul 18 2052	13:34	26° Cn 38' R

Sun Cnj Mer	Sep 1 2052	10:03	09° Vi 41' D
Sun Cnj Mer	Nov 9 2052	02:22	17° Sc 23' R
Sun Cnj Mer	Jan 7 2053	13:08	17° Cp 41' D
Sun Cnj Mer	Feb 23 2053	09:59	05° Pi 14' R
Sun Cnj Mer	May 3 2053	08:53	13° Ta 23' D
Sun Cnj Mer	Jun 29 2053	01:28	07° Cn 48' R
Sun Cnj Mer	Aug 16 2053	00:54	23° Le 39' D
Sun Cnj Mer	Oct 24 2053	04:50	01° Sc 14' R
Sun Cnj Mer	Dec 17 2053	22:50	26° Sg 27' D
Sun Cnj Mer	Feb 6 2054	23:19	18° Aq 23' R
Sun Cnj Mer	Apr 17 2054	12:19	27° Ar 43' D
Sun Cnj Mer	Jun 8 2054	22:35	18° Ge 22' R
Sun Cnj Mer	Jul 31 2054	00:55	08° Le 05' D
Sun Cnj Mer	Oct 8 2054	01:57	15° Li 01' R
Sun Cnj Mer	Nov 27 2054	00:12	04° Sg 57' D
Sun Cnj Mer	Jan 21 2055	20:53	01° Aq 47' R
Sun Cnj Mer	Apr 1 2055	08:36	11° Ar 36' D
Sun Cnj Mer	May 19 2055	17:03	28° Ta 43' R
Sun Cnj Mer	Jul 15 2055	07:01	22° Cn 49' D
Sun Cnj Mer	Sep 21 2055	15:20	28° Vi 38' R
Sun Cnj Mer	Nov 6 2055	14:52	14° Sc 09' D
Sun Cnj Mer	Jan 5 2056	23:55	15° Cp 22' R
Sun Cnj Mer	Mar 14 2056	18:41	24° Pi 55' D
Sun Cnj Mer	Apr 28 2056	23:22	09° Ta 23' R
Sun Cnj Mer	Jun 28 2056	16:51	07° Cn 43' D
Sun Cnj Mer	Sep 3 2056	18:06	11° Vi 58' R
Sun Cnj Mer	Oct 17 2056	07:20	24° Li 39' D
Sun Cnj Mer	Dec 20 2056	06:09	29° Sg 04' R
Sun Cnj Mer	Feb 25 2057	14:29	07° Pi 28' D
Sun Cnj Mer	Apr 10 2057	01:44	20° Ar 41' R
Sun Cnj Mer	Jun 13 2057	04:28	22° Ge 41' D
Sun Cnj Mer	Aug 17 2057	06:58	24° Le 53' R
Sun Cnj Mer	Sep 29 2057	02:07	06° Li 26' D
Sun Cnj Mer	Dec 4 2057	13:39	12° Sg 53' R
Sun Cnj Mer	Feb 7 2058	15:08	19° Aq 04' D
Sun Cnj Mer	Mar 23 2058	01:03	02° Ar 38' R
Sun Cnj Mer	May 28 2058	16:03	07° Ge 35' D
Sun Cnj Mer	Jul 30 2058	02:16	07° Le 13' R
Sun Cnj Mer	Sep 11 2058	18:11	19° Vi 16' D
Sun Cnj Mer	Nov 18 2058	20:35	26° Sc 45' R
Sun Cnj Mer	Jan 19 2059	15:33	29° Cp 33' D
Sun Cnj Mer	Mar 5 2059	18:20	15° Pi 10' R
Sun Cnj Mer	May 13 2059	01:56	22° Ta 21' D
Sun Cnj Mer	Jul 11 2059	01:27	18° Cn 49' R
Sun Cnj Mer	Aug 26 2059	02:06	02° Vi 53' D

Appendix II • *Sun-Mercury Inferior + Superior Conjunctions 1920 to 2120*

Sun Cnj Mer	Nov 3 2059	01:12	10° Sc 37' R
Sun Cnj Mer	Dec 30 2059	13:39	08° Cp 50' D
Sun Cnj Mer	Feb 17 2060	01:28	28° Aq 07' R
Sun Cnj Mer	Apr 26 2060	08:17	06° Ta 51' D
Sun Cnj Mer	Jun 20 2060	05:49	29° Ge 41' R
Sun Cnj Mer	Aug 8 2060	21:17	17° Le 05' D
Sun Cnj Mer	Oct 17 2060	01:40	24° Li 27' R
Sun Cnj Mer	Dec 8 2060	17:20	17° Sg 23' D
Sun Cnj Mer	Jan 30 2061	18:43	11° Aq 23' R
Sun Cnj Mer	Apr 10 2061	08:59	21° Ar 00' D
Sun Cnj Mer	May 30 2061	23:57	10° Ge 05' R
Sun Cnj Mer	Jul 24 2061	00:11	01° Le 39' D
Sun Cnj Mer	Sep 30 2061	19:49	08° Li 10' R
Sun Cnj Mer	Nov 17 2061	22:03	26° Sc 04' D
Sun Cnj Mer	Jan 14 2062	18:57	24° Cp 53' R
Sun Cnj Mer	Mar 25 2062	01:23	04° Ar 40' D
Sun Cnj Mer	May 10 2062	22:02	20° Ta 32' R
Sun Cnj Mer	Jul 8 2062	08:09	16° Cn 29' D
Sun Cnj Mer	Sep 14 2062	05:06	21° Vi 41' R
Sun Cnj Mer	Oct 28 2062	22:57	05° Sc 48' D
Sun Cnj Mer	Dec 29 2062	23:36	08° Cp 31' R
Sun Cnj Mer	Mar 8 2063	05:58	17° Pi 42' D
Sun Cnj Mer	Apr 21 2063	12:19	01° Ta 27' R
Sun Cnj Mer	Jun 22 2063	18:56	01° Cn 25' D
Sun Cnj Mer	Aug 28 2063	02:21	04° Vi 52' R
Sun Cnj Mer	Oct 10 2063	02:58	16° Li 51' D
Sun Cnj Mer	Dec 14 2063	06:35	22° Sg 17' R
Sun Cnj Mer	Feb 18 2064	18:20	29° Aq 53' D
Sun Cnj Mer	Apr 1 2064	23:51	13° Ar 02' R
Sun Cnj Mer	Jun 6 2064	06:43	16° Ge 22' D
Sun Cnj Mer	Aug 9 2064	08:03	17° Le 32' R
Sun Cnj Mer	Sep 21 2064	07:27	29° Vi 07' D
Sun Cnj Mer	Nov 27 2064	14:01	06° Sg 07' R
Sun Cnj Mer	Jan 30 2065	09:10	11° Aq 01' D
Sun Cnj Mer	Mar 15 2065	07:19	25° Pi 16' R
Sun Cnj Mer	May 21 2065	17:49	01° Ge 14' D
Sun Cnj Mer	Jul 21 2065	18:59	29° Cn 35' R
Sun Cnj Mer	Sep 4 2065	06:56	12° Vi 19' D
Sun Cnj Mer	Nov 11 2065	20:11	19° Sc 59' R
Sun Cnj Mer	Jan 10 2066	22:13	20° Cp 59' D
Sun Cnj Mer	Feb 26 2066	06:59	07° Pi 59' R
Sun Cnj Mer	May 6 2066	02:28	15° Ta 54' D
Sun Cnj Mer	Jul 2 2066	09:45	10° Cn 52' R
Sun Cnj Mer	Aug 18 2066	20:09	26° Le 13' D
Sun Cnj Mer	Oct 26 2066	23:18	03° Sc 51' R

Sun Cnj Mer	Dec 21 2066	10:47	29° Sg 52' D
Sun Cnj Mer	Feb 9 2067	18:51	21° Aq 05' R
Sun Cnj Mer	Apr 20 2067	06:46	00° Ta 17' D
Sun Cnj Mer	Jun 12 2067	08:22	21° Ge 29' R
Sun Cnj Mer	Aug 2 2067	19:03	10° Le 35' D
Sun Cnj Mer	Oct 10 2067	21:22	17° Li 39' R
Sun Cnj Mer	Nov 30 2067	12:01	08° Sg 20' D
Sun Cnj Mer	Jan 24 2068	15:23	04° Aq 27' R
Sun Cnj Mer	Apr 3 2068	04:17	14° Ar 15' D
Sun Cnj Mer	May 22 2068	02:17	01° Ge 50' R
Sun Cnj Mer	Jul 17 2068	00:25	25° Cn 17' D
Sun Cnj Mer	Sep 23 2068	12:06	01° Li 18' R
Sun Cnj Mer	Nov 8 2068	23:41	17° Sc 24' D
Sun Cnj Mer	Jan 7 2069	17:48	18° Cp 00' R
Sun Cnj Mer	Mar 17 2069	16:04	27° Pi 38' D
Sun Cnj Mer	May 2 2069	06:07	12° Ta 26' R
Sun Cnj Mer	Jul 1 2069	09:48	10° Cn 10' D
Sun Cnj Mer	Sep 6 2069	16:40	14° Vi 41' R
Sun Cnj Mer	Oct 20 2069	12:03	27° Li 41' D
Sun Cnj Mer	Dec 22 2069	23:40	01° Cp 42' R
Sun Cnj Mer	Feb 28 2070	14:18	10° Pi 19' D
Sun Cnj Mer	Apr 13 2070	05:16	23° Ar 38' R
Sun Cnj Mer	Jun 15 2070	21:15	25° Ge 08' D
Sun Cnj Mer	Aug 20 2070	07:48	27° Le 40' R
Sun Cnj Mer	Oct 2 2070	03:04	09° Li 17' D
Sun Cnj Mer	Dec 7 2070	07:04	15° Sg 30' R
Sun Cnj Mer	Feb 10 2071	18:09	22° Aq 05' D
Sun Cnj Mer	Mar 26 2071	01:33	05° Ar 29' R
Sun Cnj Mer	May 31 2071	08:54	10° Ge 03' D
Sun Cnj Mer	Aug 2 2071	05:52	10° Le 06' R
Sun Cnj Mer	Sep 14 2071	16:19	21° Vi 58' D
Sun Cnj Mer	Nov 21 2071	14:11	29° Sc 21' R
Sun Cnj Mer	Jan 22 2072	22:27	02° Aq 44' D
Sun Cnj Mer	Mar 7 2072	16:27	17° Pi 57' R
Sun Cnj Mer	May 14 2072	19:09	24° Ta 50' D
Sun Cnj Mer	Jul 13 2072	08:03	21° Cn 48' R
Sun Cnj Mer	Aug 27 2072	22:12	05° Vi 29' D
Sun Cnj Mer	Nov 4 2072	19:16	13° Sc 13' R
Sun Cnj Mer	Jan 2 2073	00:15	12° Cp 11' D
Sun Cnj Mer	Feb 18 2073	21:49	00° Pi 51' R
Sun Cnj Mer	Apr 29 2073	02:11	09° Ta 23' D
Sun Cnj Mer	Jun 23 2073	14:58	02° Cn 46' R
Sun Cnj Mer	Aug 11 2073	16:01	19° Le 37' D
Sun Cnj Mer	Oct 19 2073	20:31	27° Li 04' R
Sun Cnj Mer	Dec 12 2073	05:42	20° Sg 47' D

Appendix II • *Sun-Mercury Inferior + Superior Conjunctions 1920 to 2120*

Sun Cnj Mer	Feb 2 2074	13:47	14° Aq 04' R
Sun Cnj Mer	Apr 13 2074	03:55	23° Ar 36' D
Sun Cnj Mer	Jun 3 2074	09:51	13° Ge 13' R
Sun Cnj Mer	Jul 26 2074	17:59	04° Le 08' D
Sun Cnj Mer	Oct 3 2074	15:46	10° Li 49' R
Sun Cnj Mer	Nov 21 2074	08:53	29° Sc 24' D
Sun Cnj Mer	Jan 17 2075	13:09	27° Cp 31' R
Sun Cnj Mer	Mar 27 2075	21:46	07° Ar 21' D
Sun Cnj Mer	May 14 2075	06:24	23° Ta 37' R
Sun Cnj Mer	Jul 11 2075	01:18	18° Cn 56' D
Sun Cnj Mer	Sep 17 2075	02:31	24° Vi 22' R
Sun Cnj Mer	Nov 1 2075	05:56	08° Sc 56' D
Sun Cnj Mer	Jan 1 2076	17:15	11° Cp 09' R
Sun Cnj Mer	Mar 10 2076	04:19	20° Pi 28' D
Sun Cnj Mer	Apr 23 2076	17:43	04° Ta 27' R
Sun Cnj Mer	Jun 24 2076	11:45	03° Cn 51' D
Sun Cnj Mer	Aug 30 2076	01:46	07° Vi 35' R
Sun Cnj Mer	Oct 12 2076	05:58	19° Li 48' D
Sun Cnj Mer	Dec 16 2076	00:00	24° Sg 54' R
Sun Cnj Mer	Feb 20 2077	19:22	02° Pi 47' D
Sun Cnj Mer	Apr 5 2077	02:02	15° Ar 56' R
Sun Cnj Mer	Jun 8 2077	23:30	18° Ge 49' D
Sun Cnj Mer	Aug 12 2077	10:01	20° Le 21' R
Sun Cnj Mer	Sep 24 2077	07:09	01° Li 53' D
Sun Cnj Mer	Nov 30 2077	07:29	08° Sg 43' R
Sun Cnj Mer	Feb 2 2078	13:46	14° Aq 06' D
Sun Cnj Mer	Mar 18 2078	06:45	28° Pi 04' R
Sun Cnj Mer	May 24 2078	10:51	03° Ge 42' D
Sun Cnj Mer	Jul 24 2078	23:57	02° Le 30' R
Sun Cnj Mer	Sep 7 2078	04:09	14° Vi 58' D
Sun Cnj Mer	Nov 14 2078	13:59	22° Sc 35' R
Sun Cnj Mer	Jan 14 2079	06:48	24° Cp 14' D
Sun Cnj Mer	Mar 1 2079	04:17	10° Pi 43' R
Sun Cnj Mer	May 8 2079	19:59	18° Ta 24' D
Sun Cnj Mer	Jul 5 2079	17:37	13° Cn 54' R
Sun Cnj Mer	Aug 21 2079	15:38	28° Le 46' D
Sun Cnj Mer	Oct 29 2079	17:41	06° Sc 27' R
Sun Cnj Mer	Dec 24 2079	22:29	03° Cp 15' D
Sun Cnj Mer	Feb 12 2080	14:36	23° Aq 47' R
Sun Cnj Mer	Apr 22 2080	01:03	02° Ta 50' D
Sun Cnj Mer	Jun 14 2080	18:01	24° Ge 36' R
Sun Cnj Mer	Aug 4 2080	13:17	13° Le 05' D
Sun Cnj Mer	Oct 12 2080	16:38	20° Li 16' R
Sun Cnj Mer	Dec 3 2080	00:06	11° Sg 43' D
Sun Cnj Mer	Jan 26 2081	10:02	07° Aq 06' R

Sun Cnj Mer	Apr 5 2081	23:43	16° Ar 51' D
Sun Cnj Mer	May 25 2081	11:44	04° Ge 58' R
Sun Cnj Mer	Jul 19 2081	17:52	27° Cn 45' D
Sun Cnj Mer	Sep 26 2081	08:36	03° Li 57' R
Sun Cnj Mer	Nov 12 2081	09:02	20° Sc 39' D
Sun Cnj Mer	Jan 10 2082	11:42	20° Cp 38' R
Sun Cnj Mer	Mar 20 2082	13:09	00° Ar 21' D
Sun Cnj Mer	May 5 2082	13:17	15° Ta 30' R
Sun Cnj Mer	Jul 4 2082	02:46	12° Cn 37' D
Sun Cnj Mer	Sep 9 2082	14:51	17° Vi 23' R
Sun Cnj Mer	Oct 23 2082	17:16	00° Sc 44' D
Sun Cnj Mer	Dec 25 2082	17:11	04° Cp 20' R
Sun Cnj Mer	Mar 3 2083	13:44	13° Pi 10' D
Sun Cnj Mer	Apr 16 2083	09:15	26° Ar 36' R
Sun Cnj Mer	Jun 18 2083	14:00	27° Ge 34' D
Sun Cnj Mer	Aug 23 2083	08:13	00° Vi 26' R
Sun Cnj Mer	Oct 5 2083	04:29	12° Li 09' D
Sun Cnj Mer	Dec 10 2083	00:28	18° Sg 06' R
Sun Cnj Mer	Feb 13 2084	20:40	25° Aq 05' D
Sun Cnj Mer	Mar 28 2084	02:32	08° Ar 22' R
Sun Cnj Mer	Jun 2 2084	01:46	12° Ge 30' D
Sun Cnj Mer	Aug 4 2084	09:04	12° Le 58' R
Sun Cnj Mer	Sep 16 2084	14:52	24° Vi 42' D
Sun Cnj Mer	Nov 23 2084	07:46	01° Sg 57' R
Sun Cnj Mer	Jan 25 2085	04:43	05° Aq 54' D
Sun Cnj Mer	Mar 10 2085	14:57	20° Pi 44' R
Sun Cnj Mer	May 17 2085	12:22	27° Ta 19' D
Sun Cnj Mer	Jul 16 2085	14:17	24° Cn 47' R
Sun Cnj Mer	Aug 30 2085	18:39	08° Vi 07' D
Sun Cnj Mer	Nov 7 2085	13:18	15° Sc 50' R
Sun Cnj Mer	Jan 5 2086	10:24	15° Cp 31' D
Sun Cnj Mer	Feb 21 2086	18:25	03° Pi 35' R
Sun Cnj Mer	May 1 2086	20:02	11° Ta 55' D
Sun Cnj Mer	Jun 26 2086	23:54	05° Cn 52' R
Sun Cnj Mer	Aug 14 2086	10:56	22° Le 10' D
Sun Cnj Mer	Oct 22 2086	15:14	29° Li 41' R
Sun Cnj Mer	Dec 15 2086	18:00	24° Sg 13' D
Sun Cnj Mer	Feb 5 2087	08:59	16° Aq 45' R
Sun Cnj Mer	Apr 15 2087	22:40	26° Ar 12' D
Sun Cnj Mer	Jun 6 2087	19:48	16° Ge 22' R
Sun Cnj Mer	Jul 29 2087	11:49	06° Le 38' D
Sun Cnj Mer	Oct 6 2087	11:30	13° Li 27' R
Sun Cnj Mer	Nov 24 2087	20:04	02° Sg 45' D
Sun Cnj Mer	Jan 20 2088	07:23	00° Aq 11' R
Sun Cnj Mer	Mar 29 2088	17:49	10° Ar 01' D

Appendix II • *Sun-Mercury Inferior + Superior Conjunctions 1920 to 2120*

Sun Cnj Mer	May 16 2088	15:01	26° Ta 44' R
Sun Cnj Mer	Jul 12 2088	18:28	21° Cn 23' D
Sun Cnj Mer	Sep 18 2088	23:40	27° Vi 02' R
Sun Cnj Mer	Nov 3 2088	13:34	12° Sc 06' D
Sun Cnj Mer	Jan 3 2089	10:56	13° Cp 47' R
Sun Cnj Mer	Mar 13 2089	02:17	23° Pi 14' D
Sun Cnj Mer	Apr 26 2089	23:33	07° Ta 28' R
Sun Cnj Mer	Jun 27 2089	04:38	06° Cn 18' D
Sun Cnj Mer	Sep 2 2089	00:52	10° Vi 20' R
Sun Cnj Mer	Oct 15 2089	09:33	22° Li 46' D
Sun Cnj Mer	Dec 18 2089	17:27	27° Sg 31' R
Sun Cnj Mer	Feb 23 2090	19:59	05° Pi 41' D
Sun Cnj Mer	Apr 8 2090	04:42	18° Ar 51' R
Sun Cnj Mer	Jun 11 2090	16:19	21° Ge 16' D
Sun Cnj Mer	Aug 15 2090	11:38	23° Le 10' R
Sun Cnj Mer	Sep 27 2090	07:18	04° Li 42' D
Sun Cnj Mer	Dec 3 2090	00:59	11° Sg 20' R
Sun Cnj Mer	Feb 5 2091	17:51	17° Aq 10' D
Sun Cnj Mer	Mar 21 2091	06:37	00° Ar 54' R
Sun Cnj Mer	May 27 2091	03:50	06° Ge 10' D
Sun Cnj Mer	Jul 28 2091	04:27	05° Le 25' R
Sun Cnj Mer	Sep 10 2091	01:42	17° Vi 38' D
Sun Cnj Mer	Nov 17 2091	07:44	25° Sc 11' R
Sun Cnj Mer	Jan 17 2092	14:50	27° Cp 28' D
Sun Cnj Mer	Mar 3 2092	01:53	13° Pi 29' R
Sun Cnj Mer	May 10 2092	13:24	20° Ta 54' D
Sun Cnj Mer	Jul 8 2092	01:03	16° Cn 55' R
Sun Cnj Mer	Aug 23 2092	11:20	01° Vi 21' D
Sun Cnj Mer	Oct 31 2092	11:57	09° Sc 04' R
Sun Cnj Mer	Dec 27 2092	09:52	06° Cp 38' D
Sun Cnj Mer	Feb 14 2093	10:30	26° Aq 28' R
Sun Cnj Mer	Apr 24 2093	19:10	05° Ta 22' D
Sun Cnj Mer	Jun 18 2093	03:31	27° Ge 42' R
Sun Cnj Mer	Aug 7 2093	07:40	15° Le 36' D
Sun Cnj Mer	Oct 15 2093	11:42	22° Li 53' R
Sun Cnj Mer	Dec 6 2093	12:23	15° Sg 07' D
Sun Cnj Mer	Jan 29 2094	04:46	09° Aq 46' R
Sun Cnj Mer	Apr 8 2094	18:56	19° Ar 28' D
Sun Cnj Mer	May 28 2094	21:25	08° Ge 05' R
Sun Cnj Mer	Jul 22 2094	11:23	00° Le 13' D
Sun Cnj Mer	Sep 29 2094	04:51	06° Li 35' R
Sun Cnj Mer	Nov 15 2094	18:50	23° Sc 55' D
Sun Cnj Mer	Jan 13 2095	05:40	23° Cp 17' R
Sun Cnj Mer	Mar 23 2095	09:59	03° Ar 03' D
Sun Cnj Mer	May 8 2095	20:53	18° Ta 34' R

Sun Cnj Mer	Jul 6 2095	19:48	15° Cn 04' D
Sun Cnj Mer	Sep 12 2095	12:47	20° Vi 04' R
Sun Cnj Mer	Oct 26 2095	23:05	03° Sc 48' D
Sun Cnj Mer	Dec 28 2095	10:45	06° Cp 57' R
Sun Cnj Mer	Mar 5 2096	12:47	15° Pi 58' D
Sun Cnj Mer	Apr 18 2096	13:43	29° Ar 33' R
Sun Cnj Mer	Jun 20 2096	06:49	00° Cn 00' D
Sun Cnj Mer	Aug 25 2096	08:18	03° Vi 11' R
Sun Cnj Mer	Oct 7 2096	06:30	15° Li 02' D
Sun Cnj Mer	Dec 11 2096	17:54	20° Sg 43' R
Sun Cnj Mer	Feb 15 2097	22:39	28° Aq 02' D
Sun Cnj Mer	Mar 31 2097	03:56	11° Ar 14' R
Sun Cnj Mer	Jun 4 2097	18:38	14° Ge 57' D
Sun Cnj Mer	Aug 7 2097	11:50	15° Le 48' R
Sun Cnj Mer	Sep 19 2097	13:50	27° Vi 26' D
Sun Cnj Mer	Nov 26 2097	01:19	04° Sg 33' R
Sun Cnj Mer	Jan 28 2098	10:21	09° Aq 01' D
Sun Cnj Mer	Mar 13 2098	13:44	23° Pi 31' R
Sun Cnj Mer	May 20 2098	05:29	29° Ta 47' D
Sun Cnj Mer	Jul 19 2098	20:07	27° Cn 44' R
Sun Cnj Mer	Sep 2 2098	15:20	10° Vi 44' D
Sun Cnj Mer	Nov 10 2098	07:13	18° Sc 26' R
Sun Cnj Mer	Jan 8 2099	20:03	18° Cp 50' D
Sun Cnj Mer	Feb 24 2099	15:12	06° Pi 18' R
Sun Cnj Mer	May 4 2099	13:41	14° Ta 26' D
Sun Cnj Mer	Jun 30 2099	08:24	08° Cn 55' R
Sun Cnj Mer	Aug 17 2099	05:57	24° Le 42' D
Sun Cnj Mer	Oct 25 2099	09:47	02° Sc 18' R
Sun Cnj Mer	Dec 19 2099	06:11	27° Sg 37' D
Sun Cnj Mer	Feb 8 2100	04:20	19° Aq 26' R
Sun Cnj Mer	Apr 18 2100	17:12	28° Ar 46' D
Sun Cnj Mer	Jun 10 2100	05:36	19° Ge 29' R
Sun Cnj Mer	Aug 1 2100	05:46	09° Le 07' D
Sun Cnj Mer	Oct 9 2100	07:03	16° Li 05' R
Sun Cnj Mer	Nov 28 2100	07:39	06° Sg 07' D
Sun Cnj Mer	Jan 23 2101	01:47	02° Aq 50' R
Sun Cnj Mer	Apr 2 2101	13:40	12° Ar 39' D
Sun Cnj Mer	May 20 2101	23:59	29° Ta 50' R
Sun Cnj Mer	Jul 16 2101	11:45	23° Cn 51' D
Sun Cnj Mer	Sep 22 2101	20:37	29° Vi 42' R
Sun Cnj Mer	Nov 7 2101	21:50	15° Sc 18' D
Sun Cnj Mer	Jan 7 2102	04:46	16° Cp 25' R
Sun Cnj Mer	Mar 17 2102	00:01	25° Pi 59' D
Sun Cnj Mer	May 1 2102	05:59	10° Ta 31' R
Sun Cnj Mer	Jun 30 2102	21:34	08° Cn 46' D

Appendix II • *Sun-Mercury Inferior + Superior Conjunctions 1920 to 2120*

Sun Cnj Mer	Sep 5 2102	23:40	13° Vi 03' R
Sun Cnj Mer	Oct 19 2102	13:41	25° Li 46' D
Sun Cnj Mer	Dec 22 2102	10:58	00° Cp 08' R
Sun Cnj Mer	Feb 27 2103	20:13	08° Pi 34' D
Sun Cnj Mer	Apr 12 2103	07:53	21° Ar 48' R
Sun Cnj Mer	Jun 15 2103	09:09	23° Ge 43' D
Sun Cnj Mer	Aug 19 2103	12:48	25° Le 58' R
Sun Cnj Mer	Oct 1 2103	07:53	07° Li 31' D
Sun Cnj Mer	Dec 6 2103	18:26	13° Sg 57' R
Sun Cnj Mer	Feb 9 2104	21:20	20° Aq 12' D
Sun Cnj Mer	Mar 24 2104	06:49	03° Ar 44' R
Sun Cnj Mer	May 29 2104	20:46	08° Ge 38' D
Sun Cnj Mer	Jul 31 2104	08:28	08° Le 19' R
Sun Cnj Mer	Sep 12 2104	23:33	20° Vi 20' D
Sun Cnj Mer	Nov 20 2104	01:22	27° Sc 48' R
Sun Cnj Mer	Jan 20 2105	22:10	00° Aq 41' D
Sun Cnj Mer	Mar 6 2105	23:43	16° Pi 15' R
Sun Cnj Mer	May 14 2105	06:42	23° Ta 24' D
Sun Cnj Mer	Jul 12 2105	08:07	19° Cn 56' R
Sun Cnj Mer	Aug 27 2105	07:14	03° Vi 57' D
Sun Cnj Mer	Nov 4 2105	06:04	11° Sc 41' R
Sun Cnj Mer	Dec 31 2105	20:47	10° Cp 00' D
Sun Cnj Mer	Feb 18 2106	06:36	29° Aq 11' R
Sun Cnj Mer	Apr 28 2106	13:08	07° Ta 54' D
Sun Cnj Mer	Jun 22 2106	12:55	00° Cn 49' R
Sun Cnj Mer	Aug 11 2106	02:15	18° Le 08' D
Sun Cnj Mer	Oct 19 2106	06:39	25° Li 31' R
Sun Cnj Mer	Dec 11 2106	00:45	18° Sg 33' D
Sun Cnj Mer	Feb 1 2107	23:41	12° Aq 27' R
Sun Cnj Mer	Apr 12 2107	14:00	22° Ar 04' D
Sun Cnj Mer	Jun 2 2107	07:09	11° Ge 14' R
Sun Cnj Mer	Jul 26 2107	05:03	02° Le 42' D
Sun Cnj Mer	Oct 3 2107	00:59	09° Li 14' R
Sun Cnj Mer	Nov 20 2107	05:14	27° Sc 14' D
Sun Cnj Mer	Jan 16 2108	23:48	25° Cp 56' R
Sun Cnj Mer	Mar 26 2108	06:35	05° Ar 44' D
Sun Cnj Mer	May 12 2108	04:52	21° Ta 39' R
Sun Cnj Mer	Jul 9 2108	12:54	17° Cn 31' D
Sun Cnj Mer	Sep 15 2108	10:20	22° Vi 45' R
Sun Cnj Mer	Oct 30 2108	05:37	06° Sc 56' D
Sun Cnj Mer	Dec 31 2108	04:24	09° Cp 35' R
Sun Cnj Mer	Mar 9 2109	11:26	18° Pi 46' D
Sun Cnj Mer	Apr 22 2109	18:41	02° Ta 33' R
Sun Cnj Mer	Jun 23 2109	23:38	02° Cn 27' D
Sun Cnj Mer	Aug 29 2109	08:03	05° Vi 56' R

Sun Cnj Mer	Oct 11 2109	09:05	17° Li 57' D
Sun Cnj Mer	Dec 15 2109	11:21	23° Sg 20' R
Sun Cnj Mer	Feb 20 2110	00:08	00° Pi 58' D
Sun Cnj Mer	Apr 4 2110	05:47	14° Ar 07' R
Sun Cnj Mer	Jun 8 2110	11:25	17° Ge 24' D
Sun Cnj Mer	Aug 11 2110	14:07	18° Le 38' R
Sun Cnj Mer	Sep 23 2110	13:09	00° Li 12' D
Sun Cnj Mer	Nov 29 2110	18:48	07° Sg 10' R
Sun Cnj Mer	Feb 1 2111	15:28	12° Aq 07' D
Sun Cnj Mer	Mar 17 2111	12:52	26° Pi 20' R
Sun Cnj Mer	May 23 2111	22:32	02° Ge 16' D
Sun Cnj Mer	Jul 24 2111	01:23	00° Le 40' R
Sun Cnj Mer	Sep 6 2111	12:14	13° Vi 22' D
Sun Cnj Mer	Nov 14 2111	01:02	21° Sc 02' R
Sun Cnj Mer	Jan 13 2112	05:09	22° Cp 07' D
Sun Cnj Mer	Feb 28 2112	12:16	09° Pi 03' R
Sun Cnj Mer	May 7 2112	07:15	16° Ta 56' D
Sun Cnj Mer	Jul 3 2112	16:33	11° Cn 58' R
Sun Cnj Mer	Aug 20 2112	01:10	27° Le 15' D
Sun Cnj Mer	Oct 28 2112	04:14	04° Sc 54' R
Sun Cnj Mer	Dec 22 2112	18:08	01° Cp 01' D
Sun Cnj Mer	Feb 10 2113	23:54	22° Aq 08' R
Sun Cnj Mer	Apr 21 2113	11:38	01° Ta 19' D
Sun Cnj Mer	Jun 13 2113	15:26	22° Ge 36' R
Sun Cnj Mer	Aug 3 2113	23:55	11° Le 37' D
Sun Cnj Mer	Oct 12 2113	02:27	18° Li 42' R
Sun Cnj Mer	Dec 1 2113	19:29	09° Sg 29' D
Sun Cnj Mer	Jan 25 2114	20:19	05° Aq 30' R
Sun Cnj Mer	Apr 5 2114	09:21	15° Ar 17' D
Sun Cnj Mer	May 24 2114	09:18	02° Ge 57' R
Sun Cnj Mer	Jul 19 2114	05:11	26° Cn 19' D
Sun Cnj Mer	Sep 25 2114	17:20	02° Li 21' R
Sun Cnj Mer	Nov 11 2114	06:39	18° Sc 32' D
Sun Cnj Mer	Jan 9 2115	22:38	19° Cp 03' R
Sun Cnj Mer	Mar 19 2115	21:26	28° Pi 42' D
Sun Cnj Mer	May 4 2115	12:50	13° Ta 33' R
Sun Cnj Mer	Jul 3 2115	14:32	11° Cn 12' D
Sun Cnj Mer	Sep 8 2115	22:08	15° Vi 45' R
Sun Cnj Mer	Oct 22 2115	18:23	28° Li 47' D
Sun Cnj Mer	Dec 25 2115	04:27	02° Cp 45' R
Sun Cnj Mer	Mar 1 2116	19:57	11° Pi 24' D
Sun Cnj Mer	Apr 14 2116	11:30	24° Ar 44' R
Sun Cnj Mer	Jun 17 2116	01:56	26° Ge 09' D
Sun Cnj Mer	Aug 21 2116	13:35	28° Le 45' R
Sun Cnj Mer	Oct 3 2116	08:56	10° Li 22' D

Appendix III • *Sun-Venus Inferior + Superior Conjunctions 1920 to 2120*

Sun Cnj Mer	Dec 8 2116	11:50	16° Sg 33' R
Sun Cnj Mer	Feb 12 2117	00:12	23° Aq 11' D
Sun Cnj Mer	Mar 27 2117	07:22	06° Ar 35' R
Sun Cnj Mer	Jun 1 2117	13:37	11° Ge 05' D
Sun Cnj Mer	Aug 3 2117	12:03	11° Le 11' R
Sun Cnj Mer	Sep 15 2117	21:48	23° Vi 02' D
Sun Cnj Mer	Nov 22 2117	18:58	00° Sg 24' R
Sun Cnj Mer	Jan 24 2118	04:58	03° Aq 51' D
Sun Cnj Mer	Mar 9 2118	21:53	19° Pi 01' R
Sun Cnj Mer	May 16 2118	23:57	25° Ta 53' D
Sun Cnj Mer	Jul 15 2118	14:46	22° Cn 55' R
Sun Cnj Mer	Aug 30 2118	03:26	06° Vi 33' D
Sun Cnj Mer	Nov 7 2118	00:09	14° Sc 17' R
Sun Cnj Mer	Jan 4 2119	07:22	13° Cp 20' D
Sun Cnj Mer	Feb 21 2119	02:58	01° Pi 55' R
Sun Cnj Mer	May 1 2119	07:03	10° Ta 26' D
Sun Cnj Mer	Jun 25 2119	22:02	03° Cn 54' R
Sun Cnj Mer	Aug 13 2119	21:00	20° Le 40' D
Sun Cnj Mer	Oct 22 2119	01:30	28° Li 08' R
Sun Cnj Mer	Dec 14 2119	13:08	21° Sg 58' D
Sun Cnj Mer	Feb 4 2120	18:47	15° Aq 08' R
Sun Cnj Mer	Apr 14 2120	08:54	24° Ar 39' D
Sun Cnj Mer	Jun 4 2120	16:58	14° Ge 21' R
Sun Cnj Mer	Jul 27 2120	22:48	05° Le 11' D
Sun Cnj Mer	Oct 4 2120	20:55	11° Li 53' R
Sun Cnj Mer	Nov 22 2120	16:05	00° Sg 33' D

Appendix III

Sun-Venus Inferior (R) + Superior (D) Conjunctions 1920 to 2120

Sun Cnj Ven	Jul 3 1920	20:51	11° Cn 33' D
Sun Cnj Ven	Apr 22 1921	17:37	02° Ta 02' R
Sun Cnj Ven	Feb 9 1922	07:16	19° Aq 46' D
Sun Cnj Ven	Nov 25 1922	05:57	02° Sg 11' R
Sun Cnj Ven	Sep 10 1923	11:01	16° Vi 42' D
Sun Cnj Ven	Jul 1 1924	12:20	09° Cn 21' R
Sun Cnj Ven	Apr 24 1925	01:11	03° Ta 20' D
Sun Cnj Ven	Feb 7 1926	15:08	18° Aq 06' R
Sun Cnj Ven	Nov 21 1926	12:27	28° Sc 26' D
Sun Cnj Ven	Sep 10 1927	17:51	17° Vi 00' R
Sun Cnj Ven	Jul 1 1928	15:31	09° Cn 30' D
Sun Cnj Ven	Apr 20 1929	09:25	29° Ar 48' R
Sun Cnj Ven	Feb 6 1930	17:39	17° Aq 13' D

Sun Cnj Ven	Nov 22 1930	18:16	29° Sc 44' R
Sun Cnj Ven	Sep 8 1931	04:11	14° Vi 33' D
Sun Cnj Ven	Jun 29 1932	04:39	07° Cn 12' R
Sun Cnj Ven	Apr 21 1933	16:20	01° Ta 05' D
Sun Cnj Ven	Feb 5 1934	04:23	15° Aq 41' R
Sun Cnj Ven	Nov 19 1934	00:19	25° Sc 59' D
Sun Cnj Ven	Sep 8 1935	08:48	14° Vi 46' R
Sun Cnj Ven	Jun 29 1936	09:42	07° Cn 26' D
Sun Cnj Ven	Apr 18 1937	01:13	27° Ar 35' R
Sun Cnj Ven	Feb 4 1938	04:04	14° Aq 41' D
Sun Cnj Ven	Nov 20 1938	06:30	27° Sc 16' R
Sun Cnj Ven	Sep 5 1939	21:14	12° Vi 23' D
Sun Cnj Ven	Jun 26 1940	21:13	05° Cn 04' R
Sun Cnj Ven	Apr 19 1941	07:34	28° Ar 50' D
Sun Cnj Ven	Feb 2 1942	17:32	13° Aq 15' R
Sun Cnj Ven	Nov 16 1942	12:09	23° Sc 30' D
Sun Cnj Ven	Sep 6 1943	00:05	12° Vi 32' R
Sun Cnj Ven	Jun 27 1944	03:57	05° Cn 21' D
Sun Cnj Ven	Apr 15 1945	16:44	25° Ar 20' R
Sun Cnj Ven	Feb 1 1946	15:19	12° Aq 08' D
Sun Cnj Ven	Nov 17 1946	19:01	24° Sc 50' R
Sun Cnj Ven	Sep 3 1947	14:23	10° Vi 14' D
Sun Cnj Ven	Jun 24 1948	13:37	02° Cn 55' R
Sun Cnj Ven	Apr 16 1949	22:48	26° Ar 36' D
Sun Cnj Ven	Jan 31 1950	06:40	10° Aq 49' R
Sun Cnj Ven	Nov 13 1950	23:59	21° Sc 02' D
Sun Cnj Ven	Sep 3 1951	15:08	10° Vi 18' R
Sun Cnj Ven	Jun 24 1952	22:17	03° Cn 18' D
Sun Cnj Ven	Apr 13 1953	08:15	23° Ar 06' R
Sun Cnj Ven	Jan 30 1954	00:17	09° Aq 34' D
Sun Cnj Ven	Nov 15 1954	07:26	22° Sc 23' R
Sun Cnj Ven	Sep 1 1955	07:57	08° Vi 06' D
Sun Cnj Ven	Jun 22 1956	06:09	00° Cn 47' R
Sun Cnj Ven	Apr 14 1957	13:38	24° Ar 20' D
Sun Cnj Ven	Jan 28 1958	19:47	08° Aq 24' R
Sun Cnj Ven	Nov 11 1958	12:20	18° Sc 36' D
Sun Cnj Ven	Sep 1 1959	06:23	08° Vi 04' R
Sun Cnj Ven	Jun 22 1960	16:24	01° Cn 13' D
Sun Cnj Ven	Apr 10 1961	23:51	20° Ar 51' R
Sun Cnj Ven	Jan 27 1962	10:19	07° Aq 00' D
Sun Cnj Ven	Nov 12 1962	20:06	19° Sc 57' R
Sun Cnj Ven	Aug 30 1963	01:30	05° Vi 58' D
Sun Cnj Ven	Jun 19 1964	22:40	28° Ge 38' R
Sun Cnj Ven	Apr 12 1965	04:21	22° Ar 03' D

Appendix III • Sun-Venus Inferior + Superior Conjunctions 1920 to 2120

Sun Cnj Ven	Jan 26 1966	08:37	05° Aq 56' R
Sun Cnj Ven	Nov 9 1966	00:40	16° Sc 09' D
Sun Cnj Ven	Aug 29 1967	21:40	05° Vi 50' R
Sun Cnj Ven	Jun 20 1968	10:22	29° Ge 07' D
Sun Cnj Ven	Apr 8 1969	15:10	18° Ar 36' R
Sun Cnj Ven	Jan 24 1970	20:27	04° Aq 27' D
Sun Cnj Ven	Nov 10 1970	08:49	17° Sc 32' R
Sun Cnj Ven	Aug 27 1971	18:54	03° Vi 50' D
Sun Cnj Ven	Jun 17 1972	15:09	26° Ge 30' R
Sun Cnj Ven	Apr 9 1973	19:13	19° Ar 47' D
Sun Cnj Ven	Jan 23 1974	21:20	03° Aq 30' R
Sun Cnj Ven	Nov 6 1974	13:09	13° Sc 44' D
Sun Cnj Ven	Aug 27 1975	13:11	03° Vi 38' R
Sun Cnj Ven	Jun 18 1976	04:36	27° Ge 03' D
Sun Cnj Ven	Apr 6 1977	06:29	16° Ar 20' R
Sun Cnj Ven	Jan 22 1978	06:15	01° Aq 52' D
Sun Cnj Ven	Nov 7 1978	21:34	15° Sc 07' R
Sun Cnj Ven	Aug 25 1979	12:38	01° Vi 43' D
Sun Cnj Ven	Jun 15 1980	07:27	24° Ge 20' R
Sun Cnj Ven	Apr 7 1981	09:22	17° Ar 28' D
Sun Cnj Ven	Jan 21 1982	10:06	01° Aq 02' R
Sun Cnj Ven	Nov 4 1982	02:02	11° Sc 19' D
Sun Cnj Ven	Aug 25 1983	04:35	01° Vi 25' R
Sun Cnj Ven	Jun 15 1984	22:32	24° Ge 58' D
Sun Cnj Ven	Apr 3 1985	22:00	14° Ar 05' R
Sun Cnj Ven	Jan 19 1986	16:05	29° Cp 17' D
Sun Cnj Ven	Nov 5 1986	10:16	12° Sc 42' R
Sun Cnj Ven	Aug 23 1987	06:25	29° Le 36' D
Sun Cnj Ven	Jun 13 1988	00:00	22° Ge 12' R
Sun Cnj Ven	Apr 4 1989	23:29	15° Ar 09' D
Sun Cnj Ven	Jan 18 1990	22:42	28° Cp 35' R
Sun Cnj Ven	Nov 1 1990	15:15	08° Sc 56' D
Sun Cnj Ven	Aug 22 1991	20:21	29° Le 14' R
Sun Cnj Ven	Jun 13 1992	16:30	22° Ge 53' D
Sun Cnj Ven	Apr 1 1993	13:11	11° Ar 49' R
Sun Cnj Ven	Jan 17 1994	02:04	26° Cp 43' D
Sun Cnj Ven	Nov 2 1994	23:12	10° Sc 18' R
Sun Cnj Ven	Aug 21 1995	00:04	27° Le 29' D
Sun Cnj Ven	Jun 10 1996	16:19	20° Ge 02' R
Sun Cnj Ven	Apr 2 1997	13:45	12° Ar 51' D
Sun Cnj Ven	Jan 16 1998	11:18	26° Cp 07' R
Sun Cnj Ven	Oct 30 1998	04:22	06° Sc 32' D
Sun Cnj Ven	Aug 20 1999	11:58	27° Le 02' R
Sun Cnj Ven	Jun 11 2000	10:31	20° Ge 48' D

Sun Cnj Ven	Mar 30 2001	04:17	09° Ar 31' R
Sun Cnj Ven	Jan 14 2002	11:32	24° Cp 07' D
Sun Cnj Ven	Oct 31 2002	12:06	07° Sc 53' R
Sun Cnj Ven	Aug 18 2003	18:05	25° Le 23' D
Sun Cnj Ven	Jun 8 2004	08:43	17° Ge 53' R
Sun Cnj Ven	Mar 31 2005	03:30	10° Ar 31' D
Sun Cnj Ven	Jan 13 2006	23:59	23° Cp 40' R
Sun Cnj Ven	Oct 27 2006	17:50	04° Sc 10' D
Sun Cnj Ven	Aug 18 2007	03:41	24° Le 50' R
Sun Cnj Ven	Jun 9 2008	04:18	18° Ge 42' D
Sun Cnj Ven	Mar 27 2009	19:24	07° Ar 15' R
Sun Cnj Ven	Jan 11 2010	21:06	21° Cp 32' D
Sun Cnj Ven	Oct 29 2010	01:10	05° Sc 30' R
Sun Cnj Ven	Aug 16 2011	12:08	23° Le 17' D
Sun Cnj Ven	Jun 6 2012	01:09	15° Ge 44' R
Sun Cnj Ven	Mar 28 2013	17:05	08° Ar 10' D
Sun Cnj Ven	Jan 11 2014	12:24	21° Cp 11' R
Sun Cnj Ven	Oct 25 2014	07:31	01° Sc 48' D
Sun Cnj Ven	Aug 15 2015	19:22	22° Le 39' R
Sun Cnj Ven	Jun 6 2016	21:49	16° Ge 35' D
Sun Cnj Ven	Mar 25 2017	10:17	04° Ar 57' R
Sun Cnj Ven	Jan 9 2018	07:02	18° Cp 57' D
Sun Cnj Ven	Oct 26 2018	14:16	03° Sc 06' R
Sun Cnj Ven	Aug 14 2019	06:07	21° Le 11' D
Sun Cnj Ven	Jun 3 2020	17:44	13° Ge 35' R
Sun Cnj Ven	Mar 26 2021	06:58	05° Ar 50' D
Sun Cnj Ven	Jan 9 2022	00:48	18° Cp 43' R
Sun Cnj Ven	Oct 22 2022	21:17	29° Li 26' D
Sun Cnj Ven	Aug 13 2023	11:16	20° Le 28' R
Sun Cnj Ven	Jun 4 2024	15:33	14° Ge 29' D
Sun Cnj Ven	Mar 23 2025	01:07	02° Ar 39' R
Sun Cnj Ven	Jan 6 2026	16:36	16° Cp 22' D
Sun Cnj Ven	Oct 24 2026	03:44	00° Sc 45' R
Sun Cnj Ven	Aug 12 2027	00:21	19° Le 06' D
Sun Cnj Ven	Jun 1 2028	10:00	11° Ge 26' R
Sun Cnj Ven	Mar 23 2029	20:12	03° Ar 28' D
Sun Cnj Ven	Jan 6 2030	13:18	16° Cp 15' R
Sun Cnj Ven	Oct 20 2030	11:12	27° Li 06' D
Sun Cnj Ven	Aug 11 2031	03:01	18° Le 17' R
Sun Cnj Ven	Jun 2 2032	09:07	12° Ge 23' D
Sun Cnj Ven	Mar 20 2033	16:05	00° Ar 21' R
Sun Cnj Ven	Jan 4 2034	02:10	13° Cp 46' D
Sun Cnj Ven	Oct 21 2034	17:04	28° Li 22' R
Sun Cnj Ven	Aug 9 2035	18:40	17° Le 01' D

Appendix III • *Sun-Venus Inferior + Superior Conjunctions 1920 to 2120*

Sun Cnj Ven	May 30 2036	02:25	09° Ge 16' R
Sun Cnj Ven	Mar 21 2037	09:16	01° Ar 05' D
Sun Cnj Ven	Jan 4 2038	01:27	13° Cp 46' R
Sun Cnj Ven	Oct 18 2038	01:41	24° Li 46' D
Sun Cnj Ven	Aug 8 2039	19:02	16° Le 06' R
Sun Cnj Ven	May 31 2040	02:25	10° Ge 15' D
Sun Cnj Ven	Mar 18 2041	06:46	28° Pi 02' R
Sun Cnj Ven	Jan 1 2042	12:17	11° Cp 12' D
Sun Cnj Ven	Oct 19 2042	06:29	26° Li 00' R
Sun Cnj Ven	Aug 7 2043	12:40	14° Le 55' D
Sun Cnj Ven	May 27 2044	18:42	07° Ge 06' R
Sun Cnj Ven	Mar 18 2045	22:23	28° Pi 43' D
Sun Cnj Ven	Jan 1 2046	13:36	11° Cp 17' R
Sun Cnj Ven	Oct 15 2046	16:02	22° Li 28' D
Sun Cnj Ven	Aug 6 2047	11:04	13° Le 56' R
Sun Cnj Ven	May 28 2048	19:51	08° Ge 09' D
Sun Cnj Ven	Mar 15 2049	21:30	25° Pi 43' R
Sun Cnj Ven	Dec 29 2049	21:53	08° Cp 37' D
Sun Cnj Ven	Oct 16 2050	20:02	23° Li 39' R
Sun Cnj Ven	Aug 5 2051	06:57	12° Le 51' D
Sun Cnj Ven	May 25 2052	11:00	04° Ge 56' R
Sun Cnj Ven	Mar 16 2053	11:05	26° Pi 19' D
Sun Cnj Ven	Dec 30 2053	02:00	08° Cp 49' R
Sun Cnj Ven	Oct 13 2054	06:45	20° Li 09' D
Sun Cnj Ven	Aug 4 2055	03:14	11° Le 46' R
Sun Cnj Ven	May 26 2056	13:19	06° Ge 01' D
Sun Cnj Ven	Mar 13 2057	12:10	23° Pi 24' R
Sun Cnj Ven	Dec 27 2057	07:31	06° Cp 01' D
Sun Cnj Ven	Oct 14 2058	09:40	21° Li 18' R
Sun Cnj Ven	Aug 3 2059	01:22	10° Le 46' D
Sun Cnj Ven	May 23 2060	03:13	02° Ge 46' R
Sun Cnj Ven	Mar 13 2061	23:35	23° Pi 54' D
Sun Cnj Ven	Dec 27 2061	14:12	06° Cp 20' R
Sun Cnj Ven	Oct 10 2062	21:45	17° Li 52' D
Sun Cnj Ven	Aug 1 2063	19:16	09° Le 36' R
Sun Cnj Ven	May 24 2064	06:20	03° Ge 53' D
Sun Cnj Ven	Mar 11 2065	02:38	21° Pi 04' R
Sun Cnj Ven	Dec 24 2065	17:33	03° Cp 27' D
Sun Cnj Ven	Oct 11 2066	23:20	18° Li 57' R
Sun Cnj Ven	Jul 31 2067	19:38	08° Le 42' D
Sun Cnj Ven	May 20 2068	19:36	00° Ge 37' R
Sun Cnj Ven	Mar 11 2069	12:14	21° Pi 30' D
Sun Cnj Ven	Dec 25 2069	02:24	03° Cp 51' R
Sun Cnj Ven	Oct 8 2070	12:45	15° Li 35' D

Sun Cnj Ven	Jul 30 2071	11:31	07° Le 27' R
Sun Cnj Ven	May 21 2072	23:22	01° Ge 45' D
Sun Cnj Ven	Mar 8 2073	16:53	18° Pi 43' R
Sun Cnj Ven	Dec 22 2073	03:24	00° Cp 52' D
Sun Cnj Ven	Oct 9 2074	13:18	16° Li 37' R
Sun Cnj Ven	Jul 29 2075	13:56	06° Le 37' D
Sun Cnj Ven	May 18 2076	11:46	28° Ta 25' R
Sun Cnj Ven	Mar 9 2077	00:35	19° Pi 04' D
Sun Cnj Ven	Dec 22 2077	14:41	01° Cp 23' R
Sun Cnj Ven	Oct 6 2078	03:43	13° Li 18' D
Sun Cnj Ven	Jul 28 2079	03:35	05° Le 17' R
Sun Cnj Ven	May 19 2080	16:25	29° Ta 37' D
Sun Cnj Ven	Mar 6 2081	07:12	16° Pi 23' R
Sun Cnj Ven	Dec 19 2081	13:16	28° Sg 17' D
Sun Cnj Ven	Oct 7 2082	03:17	14° Li 18' R
Sun Cnj Ven	Jul 27 2083	08:38	04° Le 34' D
Sun Cnj Ven	May 16 2084	04:05	26° Ta 16' R
Sun Cnj Ven	Mar 6 2085	12:36	16° Pi 38' D
Sun Cnj Ven	Dec 20 2085	02:45	28° Sg 54' R
Sun Cnj Ven	Oct 3 2086	19:23	11° Li 04' D
Sun Cnj Ven	Jul 25 2087	19:47	03° Le 08' R
Sun Cnj Ven	May 17 2088	09:01	27° Ta 27' D
Sun Cnj Ven	Mar 3 2089	21:26	14° Pi 01' R
Sun Cnj Ven	Dec 16 2089	23:45	25° Sg 45' D
Sun Cnj Ven	Oct 4 2090	17:23	11° Li 59' R
Sun Cnj Ven	Jul 25 2091	02:58	02° Le 29' D
Sun Cnj Ven	May 13 2092	20:19	24° Ta 05' R
Sun Cnj Ven	Mar 4 2093	00:38	14° Pi 11' D
Sun Cnj Ven	Dec 17 2093	14:50	26° Sg 24' R
Sun Cnj Ven	Oct 1 2094	10:52	08° Li 48' D
Sun Cnj Ven	Jul 23 2095	12:03	00° Le 58' R
Sun Cnj Ven	May 15 2096	01:42	25° Ta 17' D
Sun Cnj Ven	Mar 1 2097	11:33	11° Pi 39' R
Sun Cnj Ven	Dec 14 2097	09:54	23° Sg 11' D
Sun Cnj Ven	Oct 2 2098	07:40	09° Li 41' R
Sun Cnj Ven	Jul 22 2099	21:24	00° Le 25' D
Sun Cnj Ven	May 12 2100	12:23	21° Ta 53' R
Sun Cnj Ven	Mar 2 2101	12:28	11° Pi 44' D
Sun Cnj Ven	Dec 16 2101	03:02	23° Sg 56' R
Sun Cnj Ven	Sep 30 2102	02:32	06° Li 34' D
Sun Cnj Ven	Jul 22 2103	04:24	28° Cn 50' R
Sun Cnj Ven	May 13 2104	18:29	23° Ta 08' D
Sun Cnj Ven	Feb 28 2105	01:36	09° Pi 18' R
Sun Cnj Ven	Dec 12 2105	20:10	20° Sg 38' D

Appendix IV • *Sun-Mars Conjunctions + Oppositions 1920 to 2120*

Sun Cnj Ven	Sep 30 2106	21:53	07° Li 23' R
Sun Cnj Ven	Jul 21 2107	15:53	28° Cn 22' D
Sun Cnj Ven	May 10 2108	04:19	19° Ta 41' R
Sun Cnj Ven	Feb 27 2109	23:52	09° Pi 15' D
Sun Cnj Ven	Dec 13 2109	15:05	21° Sg 27' R
Sun Cnj Ven	Sep 27 2110	18:37	04° Li 20' D
Sun Cnj Ven	Jul 19 2111	20:42	26° Cn 40' R
Sun Cnj Ven	May 11 2112	10:49	20° Ta 57' D
Sun Cnj Ven	Feb 25 2113	15:39	06° Pi 56' R
Sun Cnj Ven	Dec 10 2113	06:43	18° Sg 05' D
Sun Cnj Ven	Sep 28 2114	12:10	05° Li 05' R
Sun Cnj Ven	Jul 19 2115	10:17	26° Cn 17' D
Sun Cnj Ven	May 7 2116	20:31	17° Ta 30' R
Sun Cnj Ven	Feb 25 2117	11:15	06° Pi 46' D
Sun Cnj Ven	Dec 11 2117	03:19	18° Sg 59' R
Sun Cnj Ven	Sep 25 2118	10:52	02° Li 08' D
Sun Cnj Ven	Jul 17 2119	13:12	24° Cn 32' R
Sun Cnj Ven	May 9 2120	03:05	18° Ta 46' D

Table IV

Sun-Mars Conjunctions (D) + Oppositions (R) 1920 to 2120

(Zodiac degree shown is for Mars; e.g., Sun is 180° opposite @ "R")

Sun Opp Mar	Apr 21 1920	08:43	00° Sc 56' R
Sun Cnj Mar	Jun 29 1921	06:26	06° Cn 56' D
Sun Opp Mar	Jun 10 1922	14:10	18° Sg 53' R
Sun Cnj Mar	Aug 8 1923	19:35	15° Le 12' D
Sun Opp Mar	Aug 23 1924	17:02	00° Pi 15' R
Sun Cnj Mar	Sep 13 1925	11:30	20° Vi 08' D
Sun Opp Mar	Nov 4 1926	09:30	11° Ta 12' R
Sun Cnj Mar	Oct 21 1927	02:09	26° Li 40' D
Sun Opp Mar	Dec 21 1928	13:35	29° Ge 28' R
Sun Cnj Mar	Dec 3 1929	07:11	10° Sg 39' D
Sun Opp Mar	Jan 27 1931	19:06	06° Le 53' R
Sun Cnj Mar	Feb 1 1932	05:31	11° Aq 09' D
Sun Opp Mar	Mar 1 1933	20:28	10° Vi 49' R
Sun Cnj Mar	Apr 14 1934	13:54	23° Ar 55' D
Sun Opp Mar	Apr 6 1935	17:34	15° Li 59' R
Sun Cnj Mar	Jun 11 1936	00:01	19° Ge 52' D
Sun Opp Mar	May 19 1937	18:37	28° Sc 20' R
Sun Cnj Mar	Jul 24 1938	19:08	01° Le 12' D
Sun Opp Mar	Jul 23 1939	08:03	29° Cp 34' R

Sun Cnj Mar	Aug 30 1940	08:30	06° Vi 48' D
Sun Opp Mar	Oct 10 1941	12:47	16° Ar 49' R
Sun Cnj Mar	Oct 6 1942	00:06	12° Li 06' D
Sun Opp Mar	Dec 5 1943	18:31	12° Ge 45' R
Sun Cnj Mar	Nov 14 1944	18:28	22° Sc 16' D
Sun Opp Mar	Jan 14 1946	00:52	23° Cn 15' R
Sun Cnj Mar	Jan 6 1947	07:15	15° Cp 08' D
Sun Opp Mar	Feb 17 1948	16:16	27° Le 55' R
Sun Cnj Mar	Mar 17 1949	10:14	26° Pi 29' D
Sun Opp Mar	Mar 23 1950	05:44	02° Li 01' R
Sun Cnj Mar	May 22 1951	13:22	00° Ge 38' D
Sun Opp Mar	May 1 1952	01:31	10° Sc 37' R
Sun Cnj Mar	Jul 8 1953	21:00	16° Cn 22' D
Sun Opp Mar	Jun 24 1954	17:21	02° Cp 38' R
Sun Cnj Mar	Aug 17 1955	02:46	23° Le 26' D
Sun Opp Mar	Sep 10 1956	21:58	18° Pi 08' R
Sun Cnj Mar	Sep 21 1957	14:29	28° Vi 19' D
Sun Opp Mar	Nov 16 1958	14:32	23° Ta 44' R
Sun Cnj Mar	Oct 30 1959	01:46	05° Sc 53' D
Sun Opp Mar	Dec 30 1960	10:21	08° Cn 44' R
Sun Cnj Mar	Dec 14 1961	18:29	22° Sg 32' D
Sun Opp Mar	Feb 4 1963	11:57	14° Le 57' R
Sun Cnj Mar	Feb 17 1964	02:57	27° Aq 28' D
Sun Opp Mar	Mar 9 1965	12:29	18° Vi 43' R
Sun Cnj Mar	Apr 29 1966	05:29	08° Ta 27' D
Sun Opp Mar	Apr 15 1967	11:30	24° Li 48' R
Sun Cnj Mar	Jun 21 1968	15:47	00° Cn 18' D
Sun Opp Mar	May 31 1969	15:51	09° Sg 59' R
Sun Cnj Mar	Aug 2 1970	12:01	09° Le 46' D
Sun Opp Mar	Aug 10 1971	06:53	17° Aq 00' R
Sun Cnj Mar	Sep 7 1972	10:57	14° Vi 54' D
Sun Opp Mar	Oct 25 1973	03:27	01° Ta 34' R
Sun Cnj Mar	Oct 14 1974	12:56	20° Li 47' D
Sun Opp Mar	Dec 15 1975	13:58	22° Ge 58' R
Sun Cnj Mar	Nov 25 1976	01:20	02° Sg 54' D
Sun Opp Mar	Jan 22 1978	00:11	01° Le 36' R
Sun Cnj Mar	Jan 20 1979	12:17	29° Cp 50' D
Sun Opp Mar	Feb 25 1980	05:43	05° Vi 46' R
Sun Cnj Mar	Apr 2 1981	14:13	12° Ar 44' D
Sun Opp Mar	Mar 31 1982	10:13	10° Li 22' R
Sun Cnj Mar	Jun 3 1983	11:21	12° Ge 19' D
Sun Opp Mar	May 11 1984	08:52	20° Sc 50' R
Sun Cnj Mar	Jul 18 1985	02:41	25° Cn 25' D
Sun Opp Mar	Jul 10 1986	05:28	17° Cp 40' R

Appendix IV • *Sun-Mars Conjunctions + Oppositions 1920 to 2120*

Sun Cnj Mar	Aug 25 1987	07:32	01° Vi 34' D
Sun Opp Mar	Sep 28 1988	03:31	05° Ar 13' R
Sun Cnj Mar	Sep 29 1989	19:00	06° Li 36' D
Sun Opp Mar	Nov 27 1990	20:33	05° Ge 20' R
Sun Cnj Mar	Nov 8 1991	09:16	15° Sc 27' D
Sun Opp Mar	Jan 7 1993	22:42	17° Cn 39' R
Sun Cnj Mar	Dec 27 1993	02:28	05° Cp 20' D
Sun Opp Mar	Feb 12 1995	02:31	22° Le 54' R
Sun Cnj Mar	Mar 4 1996	14:02	14° Pi 17' D
Sun Opp Mar	Mar 17 1997	07:55	26° Vi 46' R
Sun Cnj Mar	May 12 1998	19:46	21° Ta 52' D
Sun Opp Mar	Apr 24 1999	17:37	04° Sc 05' R
Sun Cnj Mar	Jul 1 2000	15:50	10° Cn 05' D
Sun Opp Mar	Jun 13 2001	17:46	22° Sg 45' R
Sun Cnj Mar	Aug 10 2002	22:17	18° Le 06' D
Sun Opp Mar	Aug 28 2003	17:59	05° Pi 01' R
Sun Cnj Mar	Sep 15 2004	12:55	23° Vi 00' D
Sun Opp Mar	Nov 7 2005	07:57	15° Ta 00' R
Sun Cnj Mar	Oct 23 2006	06:46	29° Li 43' D
Sun Opp Mar	Dec 24 2007	19:47	02° Cn 36' R
Sun Cnj Mar	Dec 5 2008	22:04	14° Sg 09' D
Sun Opp Mar	Jan 29 2010	19:43	09° Le 47' R
Sun Cnj Mar	Feb 4 2011	16:40	15° Aq 30' D
Sun Opp Mar	Mar 3 2012	20:10	13° Vi 39' R
Sun Cnj Mar	Apr 18 2013	00:20	28° Ar 08' D
Sun Opp Mar	Apr 8 2014	21:04	18° Li 56' R
Sun Cnj Mar	Jun 14 2015	15:56	23° Ge 17' D
Sun Opp Mar	May 22 2016	11:17	01° Sg 47' R
Sun Cnj Mar	Jul 27 2017	00:57	04° Le 12' D
Sun Opp Mar	Jul 27 2018	05:13	04° Aq 08' R
Sun Cnj Mar	Sep 2 2019	10:42	09° Vi 41' D
Sun Opp Mar	Oct 13 2020	23:26	21° Ar 04' R
Sun Cnj Mar	Oct 8 2021	04:01	15° Li 05' D
Sun Opp Mar	Dec 8 2022	05:42	16° Ge 05' R
Sun Cnj Mar	Nov 18 2023	05:42	25° Sc 36' D
Sun Opp Mar	Jan 16 2025	02:39	26° Cn 12' R
Sun Cnj Mar	Jan 9 2026	11:41	19° Cp 12' D
Sun Opp Mar	Feb 19 2027	15:51	00° Vi 46' R
Sun Cnj Mar	Mar 21 2028	02:36	01° Ar 00' D
Sun Opp Mar	Mar 25 2029	07:49	04° Li 57' R
Sun Cnj Mar	May 25 2030	10:50	04° Ge 17' D
Sun Opp Mar	May 4 2031	12:04	13° Sc 50' R
Sun Cnj Mar	Jul 11 2032	05:16	19° Cn 28' D

Sun Opp Mar	Jun 28 2033	01:30	06° Cp 41' R
Sun Cnj Mar	Aug 19 2034	05:22	26° Le 19' D
Sun Opp Mar	Sep 15 2035	19:39	22° Pi 48' R
Sun Cnj Mar	Sep 23 2036	15:45	01° Li 11' D
Sun Opp Mar	Nov 19 2037	09:10	27° Ta 22' R
Sun Cnj Mar	Nov 1 2038	07:00	08° Sc 57' D
Sun Opp Mar	Jan 2 2040	15:27	11° Cn 49' R
Sun Cnj Mar	Dec 17 2040	12:49	26° Sg 11' D
Sun Opp Mar	Feb 6 2042	12:05	17° Le 49' R
Sun Cnj Mar	Feb 20 2043	17:46	01° Pi 58' D
Sun Opp Mar	Mar 11 2044	12:50	21° Vi 35' R
Sun Cnj Mar	May 2 2045	10:42	12° Ta 26' D
Sun Opp Mar	Apr 17 2046	18:07	27° Li 54' R
Sun Cnj Mar	Jun 25 2047	02:56	03° Cn 32' D
Sun Opp Mar	Jun 3 2048	14:51	13° Sg 42' R
Sun Cnj Mar	Aug 4 2049	15:16	12° Le 41' D
Sun Opp Mar	Aug 14 2050	07:52	21° Aq 45' R
Sun Cnj Mar	Sep 10 2051	12:24	17° Vi 46' D
Sun Opp Mar	Oct 28 2052	06:34	05° Ta 33' R
Sun Cnj Mar	Oct 16 2053	16:59	23° Li 47' D
Sun Opp Mar	Dec 17 2054	22:15	26° Ge 11' R
Sun Cnj Mar	Nov 28 2055	13:52	06° Sg 17' D
Sun Opp Mar	Jan 24 2057	01:32	04° Le 32' R
Sun Cnj Mar	Jan 23 2058	20:23	04° Aq 04' D
Sun Opp Mar	Feb 27 2059	05:31	08° Vi 37' R
Sun Cnj Mar	Apr 6 2060	03:55	17° Ar 07' D
Sun Opp Mar	Apr 2 2061	12:53	13° Li 18' R
Sun Cnj Mar	Jun 6 2062	06:05	15° Ge 51' D
Sun Opp Mar	May 14 2063	22:22	24° Sc 10' R
Sun Cnj Mar	Jul 20 2064	10:03	28° Cn 30' D
Sun Opp Mar	Jul 13 2065	21:03	22° Cp 02' R
Sun Cnj Mar	Aug 27 2066	09:58	04° Vi 28' D
Sun Opp Mar	Oct 2 2067	19:55	09° Ar 42' R
Sun Cnj Mar	Oct 1 2068	21:51	09° Li 33' D
Sun Opp Mar	Nov 30 2069	10:20	08° Ge 47' R
Sun Cnj Mar	Nov 10 2070	18:26	18° Sc 42' D
Sun Opp Mar	Jan 11 2072	01:05	20° Cn 37' R
Sun Cnj Mar	Dec 30 2072	02:55	09° Cp 14' D
Sun Opp Mar	Feb 14 2074	01:59	25° Le 43' R
Sun Cnj Mar	Mar 9 2075	06:51	18° Pi 49' D
Sun Opp Mar	Mar 19 2076	08:56	29° Vi 38' R
Sun Cnj Mar	May 15 2077	20:35	25° Ta 39' D
Sun Opp Mar	Apr 27 2078	01:39	07° Sc 13' R
Sun Cnj Mar	Jul 5 2079	01:19	13° Cn 15' D

Appendix IV • *Sun-Mars Conjunctions + Oppositions 1920 to 2120*

Sun Opp Mar	Jun 16 2080	20:28	26° Sg 36' R
Sun Cnj Mar	Aug 13 2081	01:26	21° Le 01' D
Sun Opp Mar	Sep 1 2082	17:40	09° Pi 45' R
Sun Cnj Mar	Sep 18 2083	14:21	25° Vi 53' D
Sun Opp Mar	Nov 10 2084	06:07	18° Ta 48' R
Sun Cnj Mar	Oct 25 2085	11:04	02° Sc 45' D
Sun Opp Mar	Dec 27 2086	02:38	05° Cn 46' R
Sun Cnj Mar	Dec 9 2087	13:24	17° Sg 40' D
Sun Opp Mar	Jan 31 2089	20:23	12° Le 41' R
Sun Cnj Mar	Feb 8 2090	05:29	19° Aq 55' D
Sun Opp Mar	Mar 6 2091	20:15	16° Vi 30' R
Sun Cnj Mar	Apr 21 2092	09:37	02° Ta 18' D
Sun Opp Mar	Apr 11 2093	02:21	21° Li 58' R
Sun Cnj Mar	Jun 17 2094	05:46	26° Ge 37' D
Sun Opp Mar	May 26 2095	06:27	05° Sg 20' R
Sun Cnj Mar	Jul 29 2096	05:28	07° Le 10' D
Sun Opp Mar	Jul 31 2097	03:39	08° Aq 46' R
Sun Cnj Mar	Sep 4 2098	12:04	12° Vi 33' D
Sun Opp Mar	Oct 18 2099	08:04	25° Ar 16' R
Sun Cnj Mar	Oct 11 2100	06:57	18° Li 03' D
Sun Opp Mar	Dec 11 2101	15:43	19° Ge 24' R
Sun Cnj Mar	Nov 21 2102	15:52	28° Sc 54' D
Sun Opp Mar	Jan 20 2104	04:16	29° Cn 09' R
Sun Cnj Mar	Jan 13 2105	15:07	23° Cp 15' D
Sun Opp Mar	Feb 22 2106	15:34	03° Vi 36' R
Sun Cnj Mar	Mar 26 2107	17:45	05° Ar 27' D
Sun Opp Mar	Mar 28 2108	09:13	07° Li 50' R
Sun Cnj Mar	May 29 2109	08:18	07° Ge 55' D
Sun Opp Mar	May 7 2110	22:18	17° Sc 03' R
Sun Cnj Mar	Jul 15 2111	13:35	22° Cn 34' D
Sun Opp Mar	Jul 2 2112	11:07	10° Cp 48' R
Sun Cnj Mar	Aug 22 2113	08:09	29° Le 13' D
Sun Opp Mar	Sep 20 2114	16:34	27° Pi 26' R
Sun Cnj Mar	Sep 27 2115	18:19	04° Li 07' D
Sun Opp Mar	Nov 23 2116	02:09	00° Ge 57' R
Sun Cnj Mar	Nov 4 2117	14:39	12° Sc 07' D
Sun Opp Mar	Jan 5 2119	19:13	14° Cn 52' R
Sun Cnj Mar	Dec 22 2119	10:01	29° Sg 58' D

Appendix V
Sun-Jupiter Conjunctions (D) + Oppositions (R) 1920 to 2020
(Zodiac degree shown is for Jupiter; e.g., Sun is 180° opposite @ "R")

Sun Opp Jup	Feb 3 1920	06:30	13° Le 08' R
Sun Cnj Jup	Aug 22 1920	09:01	28° Le 56' D
Sun Opp Jup	Mar 5 1921	02:15	13° Vi 58' R
Sun Cnj Jup	Sep 22 1921	22:12	29° Vi 20' D
Sun Opp Jup	Apr 4 1922	13:44	14° Li 00' R
Sun Cnj Jup	Oct 23 1922	11:25	29° Li 16' D
Sun Opp Jup	May 5 1923	14:40	14° Sc 04' R
Sun Cnj Jup	Nov 22 1923	22:24	29° Sc 36' D
Sun Opp Jup	Jun 6 1924	00:50	15° Sg 01' R
Sun Cnj Jup	Dec 23 1924	05:34	01° Cp 08' D
Sun Opp Jup	Jul 10 1925	10:24	17° Cp 37' R
Sun Cnj Jup	Jan 25 1926	05:41	04° Aq 30' D
Sun Opp Jup	Aug 15 1926	20:07	22° Aq 12' R
Sun Cnj Jup	Mar 1 1927	10:53	09° Pi 51' D
Sun Opp Jup	Sep 22 1927	12:37	28° Pi 30' R
Sun Cnj Jup	Apr 6 1928	14:41	16° Ar 32' D
Sun Opp Jup	Oct 29 1928	00:41	05° Ta 21' R
Sun Cnj Jup	May 14 1929	12:59	23° Ta 13' D
Sun Opp Jup	Dec 3 1929	23:02	11° Ge 19' R
Sun Cnj Jup	Jun 20 1930	15:34	28° Ge 33' D
Sun Opp Jup	Jan 6 1931	17:54	15° Cn 27' R
Sun Cnj Jup	Jul 25 1931	19:49	01° Le 53' D
Sun Opp Jup	Feb 7 1932	15:08	17° Le 38' R
Sun Cnj Jup	Aug 26 1932	21:08	03° Vi 22' D
Sun Opp Jup	Mar 9 1933	08:39	18° Vi 20' R
Sun Cnj Jup	Sep 27 1933	05:43	03° Li 39' D
Sun Opp Jup	Apr 8 1934	20:32	18° Li 18' R
Sun Cnj Jup	Oct 27 1934	16:52	03° Sc 35' D
Sun Opp Jup	May 10 1935	00:20	18° Sc 25' R
Sun Cnj Jup	Nov 27 1935	04:44	04° Sg 00' D
Sun Opp Jup	Jun 10 1936	16:02	19° Sg 33' R
Sun Cnj Jup	Dec 27 1936	16:15	05° Cp 45' D
Sun Opp Jup	Jul 15 1937	08:15	22° Cp 24' R
Sun Cnj Jup	Jan 29 1938	23:22	09° Aq 25' D
Sun Opp Jup	Aug 21 1938	00:21	27° Aq 17' R
Sun Cnj Jup	Mar 6 1939	12:15	15° Pi 02' D
Sun Opp Jup	Sep 27 1939	19:06	03° Ar 46' R
Sun Cnj Jup	Apr 11 1940	21:35	21° Ar 50' D
Sun Opp Jup	Nov 3 1940	04:19	10° Ta 36' R

Appendix V • *Sun-Jupiter Conjunctions + Oppositions 1920 to 2120*

Sun Cnj Jup	May 19 1941	19:59	28° Ta 25' D
Sun Opp Jup	Dec 8 1941	20:12	16° Ge 21' R
Sun Cnj Jup	Jun 25 1942	16:43	03° Cn 28' D
Sun Opp Jup	Jan 11 1943	07:12	20° Cn 11' R
Sun Cnj Jup	Jul 30 1943	12:53	06° Le 29' D
Sun Opp Jup	Feb 11 1944	22:12	22° Le 04' R
Sun Cnj Jup	Aug 31 1944	06:22	07° Vi 42' D
Sun Opp Jup	Mar 13 1945	12:32	22° Vi 34' R
Sun Cnj Jup	Oct 1 1945	09:53	07° Li 51' D
Sun Opp Jup	Apr 13 1946	00:33	22° Li 29' R
Sun Cnj Jup	Oct 31 1946	19:28	07° Sc 46' D
Sun Opp Jup	May 14 1947	08:16	22° Sc 41' R
Sun Cnj Jup	Dec 1 1947	09:59	08° Sg 21' D
Sun Opp Jup	Jun 15 1948	06:56	24° Sg 04' R
Sun Cnj Jup	Jan 1 1949	03:34	10° Cp 24' D
Sun Opp Jup	Jul 20 1949	08:07	27° Cp 15' R
Sun Cnj Jup	Feb 3 1950	19:41	14° Aq 25' D
Sun Opp Jup	Aug 26 1950	07:13	02° Pi 29' R
Sun Cnj Jup	Mar 11 1951	17:24	20° Pi 19' D
Sun Opp Jup	Oct 3 1951	04:07	09° Ar 08' R
Sun Cnj Jup	Apr 17 1952	07:21	27° Ar 13' D
Sun Opp Jup	Nov 8 1952	09:09	15° Ta 54' R
Sun Cnj Jup	May 25 1953	03:38	03° Ge 38' D
Sun Opp Jup	Dec 13 1953	16:41	21° Ge 23' R
Sun Cnj Jup	Jun 30 1954	17:39	08° Cn 22' D
Sun Opp Jup	Jan 15 1955	20:01	24° Cn 54' R
Sun Cnj Jup	Aug 4 1955	05:31	11° Le 04' D
Sun Opp Jup	Feb 16 1956	05:38	26° Le 31' R
Sun Cnj Jup	Sep 4 1956	16:18	12° Vi 05' D
Sun Opp Jup	Mar 17 1957	18:01	26° Vi 53' R
Sun Cnj Jup	Oct 5 1957	16:00	12° Li 08' D
Sun Opp Jup	Apr 17 1958	07:32	26° Li 47' R
Sun Cnj Jup	Nov 5 1958	01:13	12° Sc 06' D
Sun Opp Jup	May 18 1959	20:00	27° Sc 07' R
Sun Cnj Jup	Dec 5 1959	18:30	12° Sg 52' D
Sun Opp Jup	Jun 20 1960	01:57	28° Sg 44' R
Sun Cnj Jup	Jan 5 1961	18:25	15° Cp 11' D
Sun Opp Jup	Jul 25 1961	10:37	02° Aq 14' R
Sun Cnj Jup	Feb 8 1962	18:08	19° Aq 30' D
Sun Opp Jup	Aug 31 1962	14:48	07° Pi 42' R
Sun Cnj Jup	Mar 16 1963	22:23	25° Pi 36' D
Sun Opp Jup	Oct 8 1963	10:59	14° Ar 26' R
Sun Cnj Jup	Apr 22 1964	14:20	02° Ta 28' D
Sun Opp Jup	Nov 13 1964	09:35	21° Ta 02' R

Sun Cnj Jup	May 30 1965	07:12	08° Ge 39' D
Sun Opp Jup	Dec 18 1965	09:08	26° Ge 14' R
Sun Cnj Jup	Jul 5 1966	14:05	13° Cn 05' D
Sun Opp Jup	Jan 20 1967	05:17	29° Cn 27' R
Sun Cnj Jup	Aug 8 1967	18:49	15° Le 31' D
Sun Opp Jup	Feb 20 1968	11:02	00° Vi 52' R
Sun Cnj Jup	Sep 9 1968	00:26	16° Vi 23' D
Sun Opp Jup	Mar 21 1969	22:53	01° Li 08' R
Sun Cnj Jup	Oct 9 1969	21:38	16° Li 24' D
Sun Opp Jup	Apr 21 1970	15:14	01° Sc 05' R
Sun Cnj Jup	Nov 9 1970	07:21	16° Sc 28' D
Sun Opp Jup	May 23 1971	08:59	01° Sg 35' R
Sun Cnj Jup	Dec 10 1971	04:10	17° Sg 26' D
Sun Opp Jup	Jun 24 1972	21:43	03° Cp 26' R
Sun Cnj Jup	Jan 10 1973	09:19	20° Cp 00' D
Sun Opp Jup	Jul 30 1973	12:49	07° Aq 12' R
Sun Cnj Jup	Feb 13 1974	15:53	24° Aq 34' D
Sun Opp Jup	Sep 5 1974	20:18	12° Pi 52' R
Sun Cnj Jup	Mar 22 1975	01:41	00° Ar 48' D
Sun Opp Jup	Oct 13 1975	14:59	19° Ar 39' R
Sun Cnj Jup	Apr 27 1976	19:35	07° Ta 39' D
Sun Opp Jup	Nov 18 1976	08:16	26° Ta 07' R
Sun Cnj Jup	Jun 4 1977	09:35	13° Ge 38' D
Sun Opp Jup	Dec 23 1977	00:40	01° Cn 04' R
Sun Cnj Jup	Jul 10 1978	10:38	17° Cn 49' D
Sun Opp Jup	Jan 24 1979	15:18	04° Le 02' R
Sun Cnj Jup	Aug 13 1979	09:12	20° Le 02' D
Sun Opp Jup	Feb 24 1980	18:02	05° Vi 17' R
Sun Cnj Jup	Sep 13 1980	09:55	20° Vi 45' D
Sun Opp Jup	Mar 26 1981	05:54	05° Li 29' R
Sun Cnj Jup	Oct 14 1981	04:46	20° Li 45' D
Sun Opp Jup	Apr 26 1982	00:28	05° Sc 27' R
Sun Cnj Jup	Nov 13 1982	14:15	20° Sc 52' D
Sun Opp Jup	May 27 1983	22:29	06° Sg 03' R
Sun Cnj Jup	Dec 14 1983	12:48	21° Sg 57' D
Sun Opp Jup	Jun 29 1984	16:12	08° Cp 04' R
Sun Cnj Jup	Jan 14 1985	22:20	24° Cp 42' D
Sun Opp Jup	Aug 4 1985	11:41	12° Aq 01' R
Sun Cnj Jup	Feb 18 1986	10:06	29° Aq 27' D
Sun Opp Jup	Sep 10 1986	21:15	17° Pi 51' R
Sun Cnj Jup	Mar 27 1987	00:55	05° Ar 49' D
Sun Opp Jup	Oct 18 1987	14:32	24° Ar 40' R
Sun Cnj Jup	May 2 1988	20:59	12° Ta 39' D
Sun Opp Jup	Nov 23 1988	03:04	01° Ge 02' R

Appendix V • *Sun-Jupiter Conjunctions + Oppositions 1920 to 2120*

Sun Cnj Jup	Jun 9 1989	09:10	18° Ge 30' D
Sun Opp Jup	Dec 27 1989	14:16	05° Cn 48' R
Sun Cnj Jup	Jul 15 1990	05:32	22° Cn 29' D
Sun Opp Jup	Jan 29 1991	00:26	08° Le 35' R
Sun Cnj Jup	Aug 17 1991	22:24	24° Le 30' D
Sun Opp Jup	Feb 29 1992	00:37	09° Vi 40' R
Sun Cnj Jup	Sep 17 1992	18:31	25° Vi 06' D
Sun Opp Jup	Mar 30 1993	12:01	09° Li 47' R
Sun Cnj Jup	Oct 18 1993	10:16	25° Li 03' D
Sun Opp Jup	Apr 30 1994	08:55	09° Sc 47' R
Sun Cnj Jup	Nov 17 1994	19:48	25° Sc 14' D
Sun Opp Jup	Jun 1 1995	11:22	10° Sg 30' R
Sun Cnj Jup	Dec 18 1995	21:43	26° Sg 29' D
Sun Opp Jup	Jul 4 1996	11:41	12° Cp 45' R
Sun Cnj Jup	Jan 19 1997	13:07	29° Cp 30' D
Sun Opp Jup	Aug 9 1997	13:39	16° Aq 59' R
Sun Cnj Jup	Feb 23 1998	08:51	04° Pi 31' D
Sun Opp Jup	Sep 16 1998	03:02	23° Pi 03' R
Sun Cnj Jup	Apr 1 1999	06:10	11° Ar 04' D
Sun Opp Jup	Oct 23 1999	19:04	29° Ar 55' R
Sun Cnj Jup	May 8 2000	04:08	17° Ta 52' D
Sun Opp Jup	Nov 28 2000	02:12	06° Ge 09' R
Sun Cnj Jup	Jun 14 2001	12:38	23° Ge 30' D
Sun Opp Jup	Jan 1 2002	05:53	10° Cn 38' R
Sun Cnj Jup	Jul 20 2002	01:18	27° Cn 10' D
Sun Opp Jup	Feb 2 2003	09:12	13° Le 06' R
Sun Cnj Jup	Aug 22 2003	10:08	28° Le 54' D
Sun Opp Jup	Mar 4 2004	05:05	13° Vi 57' R
Sun Cnj Jup	Sep 21 2004	23:48	29° Vi 19' D
Sun Opp Jup	Apr 3 2005	15:30	13° Li 58' R
Sun Cnj Jup	Oct 22 2005	12:54	29° Li 13' D
Sun Opp Jup	May 4 2006	14:36	13° Sc 59' R
Sun Cnj Jup	Nov 21 2006	21:15	29° Sc 30' D
Sun Opp Jup	Jun 5 2007	23:13	14° Sg 54' R
Sun Cnj Jup	Dec 23 2007	05:56	01° Cp 00' D
Sun Opp Jup	Jul 9 2008	07:39	17° Cp 28' R
Sun Cnj Jup	Jan 24 2009	05:44	04° Aq 22' D
Sun Opp Jup	Aug 14 2009	17:53	22° Aq 04' R
Sun Cnj Jup	Feb 28 2010	10:44	09° Pi 44' D
Sun Opp Jup	Sep 21 2010	11:36	28° Pi 23' R
Sun Cnj Jup	Apr 6 2011	14:40	16° Ar 27' D
Sun Opp Jup	Oct 29 2011	01:42	05° Ta 17' R
Sun Cnj Jup	May 13 2012	13:23	23° Ta 10' D
Sun Opp Jup	Dec 3 2012	01:45	11° Ge 17' R

Sun Cnj Jup	Jun 19 2013	16:11	28° Ge 32' D
Sun Opp Jup	Jan 5 2014	21:11	15° Cn 27' R
Sun Cnj Jup	Jul 24 2014	20:44	01° Le 52' D
Sun Opp Jup	Feb 6 2015	18:20	17° Le 37' R
Sun Cnj Jup	Aug 26 2015	22:02	03° Vi 21' D
Sun Opp Jup	Mar 8 2016	10:57	18° Vi 18' R
Sun Cnj Jup	Sep 26 2016	07:00	03° Li 37' D
Sun Opp Jup	Apr 7 2017	21:39	18° Li 15' R
Sun Cnj Jup	Oct 26 2017	18:09	03° Sc 31' D
Sun Opp Jup	May 9 2018	00:39	18° Sc 21' R
Sun Cnj Jup	Nov 26 2018	06:33	03° Sg 56' D
Sun Opp Jup	Jun 10 2019	15:28	19° Sg 28' R
Sun Cnj Jup	Dec 27 2019	18:25	05° Cp 41' D
Sun Opp Jup	Jul 14 2020	07:58	22° Cp 20' R
Sun Cnj Jup	Jan 29 2021	01:40	09° Aq 21' D
Sun Opp Jup	Aug 20 2021	00:28	27° Aq 13' R
Sun Cnj Jup	Mar 5 2022	14:06	14° Pi 58' D
Sun Opp Jup	Sep 26 2022	19:33	03° Ar 41' R
Sun Cnj Jup	Apr 11 2023	22:07	21° Ar 45' D
Sun Opp Jup	Nov 3 2023	05:02	10° Ta 30' R
Sun Cnj Jup	May 18 2024	18:45	28° Ta 18' D
Sun Opp Jup	Dec 7 2024	20:58	16° Ge 15' R
Sun Cnj Jup	Jun 24 2025	15:17	03° Cn 21' D
Sun Opp Jup	Jan 10 2026	08:42	20° Cn 06' R
Sun Cnj Jup	Jul 29 2026	12:18	06° Le 24' D
Sun Opp Jup	Feb 11 2027	00:29	22° Le 02' R
Sun Cnj Jup	Aug 31 2027	07:29	07° Vi 41' D
Sun Opp Jup	Mar 12 2028	15:37	22° Vi 35' R
Sun Cnj Jup	Sep 30 2028	12:51	07° Li 53' D
Sun Opp Jup	Apr 12 2029	04:05	22° Li 32' R
Sun Cnj Jup	Oct 30 2029	23:57	07° Sc 50' D
Sun Opp Jup	May 13 2030	11:33	22° Sc 46' R
Sun Cnj Jup	Nov 30 2030	14:43	08° Sg 25' D
Sun Opp Jup	Jun 15 2031	09:20	24° Sg 06' R
Sun Cnj Jup	Jan 1 2032	07:41	10° Cp 25' D
Sun Opp Jup	Jul 19 2032	08:34	27° Cp 14' R
Sun Cnj Jup	Feb 2 2033	21:30	14° Aq 21' D
Sun Opp Jup	Aug 25 2033	05:40	02° Pi 21' R
Sun Cnj Jup	Mar 10 2034	16:17	20° Pi 09' D
Sun Opp Jup	Oct 2 2034	00:58	08° Ar 55' R
Sun Cnj Jup	Apr 17 2035	03:13	26° Ar 57' D
Sun Opp Jup	Nov 8 2035	05:42	15° Ta 38' R
Sun Cnj Jup	May 23 2036	22:33	03° Ge 21' D
Sun Opp Jup	Dec 12 2036	14:42	21° Ge 09' R

Appendix V • *Sun-Jupiter Conjunctions + Oppositions 1920 to 2120*

Sun Cnj Jup	Jun 29 2037	13:43	08° Cn 09' D
Sun Opp Jup	Jan 14 2038	19:58	24° Cn 44' R
Sun Cnj Jup	Aug 3 2038	04:07	10° Le 57' D
Sun Opp Jup	Feb 15 2039	08:02	26° Le 28' R
Sun Cnj Jup	Sep 4 2039	18:03	12° Vi 04' D
Sun Opp Jup	Mar 16 2040	21:58	26° Vi 55' R
Sun Cnj Jup	Oct 4 2040	20:24	12° Li 13' D
Sun Opp Jup	Apr 16 2041	12:21	26° Li 52' R
Sun Cnj Jup	Nov 4 2041	06:33	12° Sc 12' D
Sun Opp Jup	May 17 2042	23:55	27° Sc 12' R
Sun Cnj Jup	Dec 4 2042	23:05	12° Sg 55' D
Sun Opp Jup	Jun 20 2043	02:36	28° Sg 42' R
Sun Cnj Jup	Jan 5 2044	19:38	15° Cp 06' D
Sun Opp Jup	Jul 24 2044	06:55	02° Aq 02' R
Sun Cnj Jup	Feb 7 2045	14:43	19° Aq 13' D
Sun Opp Jup	Aug 30 2045	07:02	07° Pi 19' R
Sun Cnj Jup	Mar 15 2046	14:31	25° Pi 10' D
Sun Opp Jup	Oct 7 2046	01:29	13° Ar 57' R
Sun Cnj Jup	Apr 22 2047	04:37	01° Ta 59' D
Sun Opp Jup	Nov 13 2047	02:11	20° Ta 36' R
Sun Cnj Jup	May 28 2048	22:54	08° Ge 16' D
Sun Opp Jup	Dec 17 2048	05:33	25° Ge 57' R
Sun Cnj Jup	Jul 4 2049	09:46	12° Cn 52' D
Sun Opp Jup	Jan 19 2050	05:57	29° Cn 20' R
Sun Cnj Jup	Aug 7 2050	18:55	15° Le 28' D
Sun Opp Jup	Feb 19 2051	14:40	00° Vi 53' R
Sun Cnj Jup	Sep 9 2051	03:41	16° Vi 26' D
Sun Opp Jup	Mar 21 2052	03:58	01° Li 14' R
Sun Cnj Jup	Oct 9 2052	02:34	16° Li 31' D
Sun Opp Jup	Apr 20 2053	19:41	01° Sc 11' R
Sun Cnj Jup	Nov 8 2053	12:00	16° Sc 32' D
Sun Opp Jup	May 22 2054	11:03	01° Sg 36' R
Sun Cnj Jup	Dec 9 2054	06:30	17° Sg 23' D
Sun Opp Jup	Jun 24 2055	19:51	03° Cp 18' R
Sun Cnj Jup	Jan 10 2056	08:18	19° Cp 47' D
Sun Opp Jup	Jul 29 2056	06:47	06° Aq 54' R
Sun Cnj Jup	Feb 12 2057	10:36	24° Aq 11' D
Sun Opp Jup	Sep 4 2057	11:29	12° Pi 26' R
Sun Cnj Jup	Mar 20 2058	17:43	00° Ar 21' D
Sun Opp Jup	Oct 12 2058	06:38	19° Ar 11' R
Sun Cnj Jup	Apr 27 2059	11:17	07° Ta 13' D
Sun Opp Jup	Nov 18 2059	03:01	25° Ta 45' R
Sun Cnj Jup	Jun 3 2060	03:47	13° Ge 21' D
Sun Opp Jup	Dec 21 2060	23:27	00° Cn 52' R

Sun Cnj Jup	Jul 9 2061	08:24	17° Cn 40' D
Sun Opp Jup	Jan 23 2062	16:51	03° Le 57' R
Sun Cnj Jup	Aug 12 2062	09:06	19° Le 58' D
Sun Opp Jup	Feb 23 2063	20:35	05° Vi 15' R
Sun Cnj Jup	Sep 13 2063	11:01	20° Vi 43' D
Sun Opp Jup	Mar 25 2064	07:21	05° Li 26' R
Sun Cnj Jup	Oct 13 2064	05:37	20° Li 41' D
Sun Opp Jup	Apr 25 2065	00:17	05° Sc 22' R
Sun Cnj Jup	Nov 12 2065	14:21	20° Sc 45' D
Sun Opp Jup	May 26 2066	20:10	05° Sg 54' R
Sun Cnj Jup	Dec 13 2066	12:19	21° Sg 47' D
Sun Opp Jup	Jun 29 2067	12:23	07° Cp 53' R
Sun Cnj Jup	Jan 14 2068	21:10	24° Cp 31' D
Sun Opp Jup	Aug 3 2068	07:45	11° Aq 49' R
Sun Cnj Jup	Feb 17 2069	08:57	29° Aq 16' D
Sun Opp Jup	Sep 9 2069	18:52	17° Pi 41' R
Sun Cnj Jup	Mar 26 2070	00:10	05° Ar 41' D
Sun Opp Jup	Oct 17 2070	14:18	24° Ar 33' R
Sun Cnj Jup	May 2 2071	20:58	12° Ta 34' D
Sun Opp Jup	Nov 23 2071	05:15	01° Ge 00' R
Sun Cnj Jup	Jun 8 2072	09:55	18° Ge 28' D
Sun Opp Jup	Dec 26 2072	17:41	05° Cn 48' R
Sun Cnj Jup	Jul 14 2073	06:35	22° Cn 28' D
Sun Opp Jup	Jan 28 2074	03:54	08° Le 34' R
Sun Cnj Jup	Aug 16 2074	23:36	24° Le 29' D
Sun Opp Jup	Feb 28 2075	03:11	09° Vi 38' R
Sun Cnj Jup	Sep 17 2075	19:24	25° Vi 03' D
Sun Opp Jup	Mar 29 2076	13:21	09° Li 44' R
Sun Cnj Jup	Oct 17 2076	11:15	24° Li 58' D
Sun Opp Jup	Apr 29 2077	08:40	09° Sc 41' R
Sun Cnj Jup	Nov 16 2077	20:42	25° Sc 08' D
Sun Opp Jup	May 31 2078	10:15	10° Sg 24' R
Sun Cnj Jup	Dec 17 2078	22:48	26° Sg 23' D
Sun Opp Jup	Jul 4 2079	10:06	12° Cp 39' R
Sun Cnj Jup	Jan 19 2080	14:38	29° Cp 25' D
Sun Opp Jup	Aug 8 2080	12:58	16° Aq 54' R
Sun Cnj Jup	Feb 22 2081	10:23	04° Pi 27' D
Sun Opp Jup	Sep 15 2081	03:14	22° Pi 59' R
Sun Cnj Jup	Mar 31 2082	07:13	11° Ar 00' D
Sun Opp Jup	Oct 22 2082	20:05	29° Ar 51' R
Sun Cnj Jup	May 8 2083	04:06	17° Ta 48' D
Sun Opp Jup	Nov 28 2083	03:43	06° Ge 04' R
Sun Cnj Jup	Jun 13 2084	11:39	23° Ge 26' D
Sun Opp Jup	Dec 31 2084	07:37	10° Cn 34' R

Appendix V • *Sun-Jupiter Conjunctions + Oppositions 1920 to 2120*

Sun Cnj Jup	Jul 19 2085	00:53	27° Cn 07' D
Sun Opp Jup	Feb 1 2086	11:41	13° Le 03' R
Sun Cnj Jup	Aug 21 2086	10:43	28° Le 53' D
Sun Opp Jup	Mar 4 2087	08:08	13° Vi 57' R
Sun Cnj Jup	Sep 22 2087	02:15	29° Vi 20' D
Sun Opp Jup	Apr 2 2088	18:45	14° Li 00' R
Sun Cnj Jup	Oct 21 2088	16:40	29° Li 16' D
Sun Opp Jup	May 3 2089	18:05	14° Sc 03' R
Sun Cnj Jup	Nov 21 2089	03:53	29° Sc 33' D
Sun Opp Jup	Jun 5 2090	01:52	14° Sg 57' R
Sun Cnj Jup	Dec 22 2090	10:23	01° Cp 02' D
Sun Opp Jup	Jul 9 2091	09:04	17° Cp 28' R
Sun Cnj Jup	Jan 24 2092	08:42	04° Aq 20' D
Sun Opp Jup	Aug 13 2092	17:27	21° Aq 59' R
Sun Cnj Jup	Feb 27 2093	11:05	09° Pi 36' D
Sun Opp Jup	Sep 20 2093	09:38	28° Pi 12' R
Sun Cnj Jup	Apr 5 2094	12:20	16° Ar 14' D
Sun Opp Jup	Oct 27 2094	23:04	05° Ta 03' R
Sun Cnj Jup	May 13 2095	09:02	22° Ta 55' D
Sun Opp Jup	Dec 2 2095	23:44	11° Ge 03' R
Sun Cnj Jup	Jun 18 2096	12:09	28° Ge 18' D
Sun Opp Jup	Jan 4 2097	20:53	15° Cn 17' R
Sun Cnj Jup	Jul 23 2097	18:36	01° Le 43' D
Sun Opp Jup	Feb 5 2098	19:51	17° Le 33' R
Sun Cnj Jup	Aug 25 2098	22:40	03° Vi 18' D
Sun Opp Jup	Mar 8 2099	14:17	18° Vi 19' R
Sun Cnj Jup	Sep 26 2099	10:15	03° Li 40' D
Sun Opp Jup	Apr 8 2100	02:08	18° Li 20' R
Sun Cnj Jup	Oct 26 2100	23:27	03° Sc 37' D
Sun Opp Jup	May 9 2101	04:58	18° Sc 27' R
Sun Cnj Jup	Nov 26 2101	11:47	04° Sg 02' D
Sun Opp Jup	Jun 10 2102	18:02	19° Sg 31' R
Sun Cnj Jup	Dec 27 2102	21:46	05° Cp 41' D
Sun Opp Jup	Jul 15 2103	06:37	22° Cp 14' R
Sun Cnj Jup	Jan 30 2104	00:53	09° Aq 11' D
Sun Opp Jup	Aug 19 2104	19:01	26° Aq 57' R
Sun Cnj Jup	Mar 5 2105	08:45	14° Pi 37' D
Sun Opp Jup	Sep 26 2105	11:22	03° Ar 16' R
Sun Cnj Jup	Apr 11 2106	13:28	21° Ar 18' D
Sun Opp Jup	Nov 2 2106	21:09	10° Ta 04' R
Sun Cnj Jup	May 19 2107	10:09	27° Ta 53' D
Sun Opp Jup	Dec 8 2107	16:19	15° Ge 54' R
Sun Cnj Jup	Jun 24 2108	09:36	03° Cn 05' D
Sun Opp Jup	Jan 10 2109	07:45	19° Cn 55' R

Sun Cnj Jup	Jul 29 2109	10:49	06° Le 17' D
Sun Opp Jup	Feb 11 2110	03:10	22° Le 00' R
Sun Cnj Jup	Aug 31 2110	09:38	07° Vi 42' D
Sun Opp Jup	Mar 13 2111	20:09	22° Vi 38' R
Sun Cnj Jup	Oct 1 2111	17:24	07° Li 58' D
Sun Opp Jup	Apr 12 2112	08:49	22° Li 37' R
Sun Cnj Jup	Oct 31 2112	04:57	07° Sc 55' D
Sun Opp Jup	May 13 2113	14:54	22° Sc 49' R
Sun Cnj Jup	Nov 30 2113	18:29	08° Sg 26' D
Sun Opp Jup	Jun 15 2114	09:19	24° Sg 03' R
Sun Cnj Jup	Jan 1 2115	08:26	10° Cp 18' D
Sun Opp Jup	Jul 20 2115	04:33	27° Cp 01' R
Sun Cnj Jup	Feb 3 2116	18:29	14° Aq 04' D
Sun Opp Jup	Aug 24 2116	22:22	01° Pi 59' R
Sun Cnj Jup	Mar 10 2117	09:34	19° Pi 45' D
Sun Opp Jup	Oct 1 2117	16:40	08° Ar 29' R
Sun Cnj Jup	Apr 16 2118	19:21	26° Ar 32' D
Sun Opp Jup	Nov 7 2118	23:42	15° Ta 16' R
Sun Cnj Jup	May 24 2119	16:03	03° Ge 02' D
Sun Opp Jup	Dec 13 2119	12:24	20° Ge 55' R
Sun Cnj Jup	Jun 29 2120	10:27	07° Cn 59' D

Appendix VI

Sun-Saturn Conjunctions (D) + Oppositions (R) 1920 to 2120

(Zodiac degree shown is for Saturn; e.g., Sun is 180° opposite @ "R")

Sun Opp Sat	Feb 28 1920	04:04	08° Vi 17' R
Sun Cnj Sat	Sep 7 1920	23:43	15° Vi 00' D
Sun Opp Sat	Mar 12 1921	13:06	21° Vi 25' R
Sun Cnj Sat	Sep 21 1921	13:21	28° Vi 00' D
Sun Opp Sat	Mar 25 1922	16:47	04° Li 15' R
Sun Cnj Sat	Oct 4 1922	16:56	10° Li 40' D
Sun Opp Sat	Apr 7 1923	15:09	16° Li 46' R
Sun Cnj Sat	Oct 17 1923	11:05	23° Li 02' D
Sun Opp Sat	Apr 19 1924	08:52	29° Li 01' R
Sun Cnj Sat	Oct 28 1924	20:35	05° Sc 09' D
Sun Opp Sat	May 1 1925	22:26	11° Sc 00' R
Sun Cnj Sat	Nov 9 1925	22:29	17° Sc 00' D
Sun Opp Sat	May 14 1926	08:20	22° Sc 46' R
Sun Cnj Sat	Nov 21 1926	17:52	28° Sc 40' D
Sun Opp Sat	May 26 1927	15:24	04° Sg 22' R
Sun Cnj Sat	Dec 3 1927	08:15	10° Sg 10' D
Sun Opp Sat	Jun 6 1928	20:18	15° Sg 50' R

Appendix VI • *Sun-Saturn Conjunctions + Oppositions 1920 to 2120*

Sun Cnj Sat	Dec 13 1928	19:16	21° Sg 33' D
Sun Opp Sat	Jun 19 1929	00:05	27° Sg 13' R
Sun Cnj Sat	Dec 25 1929	04:21	02° Cp 54' D
Sun Opp Sat	Jul 1 1930	03:38	08° Cp 34' R
Sun Cnj Sat	Jan 5 1931	13:10	14° Cp 14' D
Sun Opp Sat	Jul 13 1931	07:57	19° Cp 57' R
Sun Cnj Sat	Jan 16 1932	23:20	25° Cp 38' D
Sun Opp Sat	Jul 24 1932	14:12	01° Aq 25' R
Sun Cnj Sat	Jan 27 1933	12:28	07° Aq 08' D
Sun Opp Sat	Aug 5 1933	23:05	13° Aq 01' R
Sun Cnj Sat	Feb 8 1934	06:21	18° Aq 48' D
Sun Opp Sat	Aug 18 1934	11:22	24° Aq 49' R
Sun Cnj Sat	Feb 20 1935	06:15	00° Pi 41' D
Sun Opp Sat	Aug 31 1935	04:14	06° Pi 50' R
Sun Cnj Sat	Mar 3 1936	13:30	12° Pi 49' D
Sun Opp Sat	Sep 12 1936	02:04	19° Pi 07' R
Sun Cnj Sat	Mar 16 1937	05:43	25° Pi 14' D
Sun Opp Sat	Sep 25 1937	04:58	01° Ar 42' R
Sun Cnj Sat	Mar 29 1938	07:39	07° Ar 57' D
Sun Opp Sat	Oct 8 1938	13:16	14° Ar 35' R
Sun Cnj Sat	Apr 11 1939	19:32	21° Ar 00' D
Sun Opp Sat	Oct 22 1939	02:50	27° Ar 48' R
Sun Cnj Sat	Apr 24 1940	17:37	04° Ta 22' D
Sun Opp Sat	Nov 3 1940	21:01	11° Ta 18' R
Sun Cnj Sat	May 9 1941	01:11	18° Ta 01' D
Sun Opp Sat	Nov 17 1941	19:19	25° Ta 03' R
Sun Cnj Sat	May 23 1942	17:03	01° Ge 55' D
Sun Opp Sat	Dec 1 1942	20:43	09° Ge 02' R
Sun Cnj Sat	Jun 7 1943	15:23	15° Ge 59' D
Sun Opp Sat	Dec 15 1943	23:52	23° Ge 08' R
Sun Cnj Sat	Jun 21 1944	17:39	00° Cn 11' D
Sun Opp Sat	Dec 29 1944	03:25	07° Cn 18' R
Sun Cnj Sat	Jul 6 1945	20:47	14° Cn 22' D
Sun Opp Sat	Jan 12 1946	05:49	21° Cn 26' R
Sun Cnj Sat	Jul 21 1946	21:39	28° Cn 29' D
Sun Opp Sat	Jan 26 1947	05:49	05° Le 26' R
Sun Cnj Sat	Aug 5 1947	17:24	12° Le 26' D
Sun Opp Sat	Feb 9 1948	02:13	19° Le 14' R
Sun Cnj Sat	Aug 19 1948	05:56	26° Le 08' D
Sun Opp Sat	Feb 21 1949	18:01	02° Vi 47' R
Sun Cnj Sat	Sep 2 1949	09:28	09° Vi 34' D
Sun Opp Sat	Mar 7 1950	04:49	16° Vi 03' R
Sun Cnj Sat	Sep 16 1950	02:58	22° Vi 40' D
Sun Opp Sat	Mar 20 1951	10:11	28° Vi 59' R

321

Sun Cnj Sat	Sep 29 1951	10:33	05° Li 28' D
Sun Opp Sat	Apr 1 1952	10:11	11° Li 37' R
Sun Cnj Sat	Oct 11 1952	08:17	17° Li 57' D
Sun Opp Sat	Apr 14 1953	05:25	23° Li 58' R
Sun Cnj Sat	Oct 23 1953	20:38	00° Sc 08' D
Sun Opp Sat	Apr 26 1954	20:07	06° Sc 02' R
Sun Cnj Sat	Nov 5 1954	01:02	12° Sc 04' D
Sun Opp Sat	May 9 1955	06:40	17° Sc 52' R
Sun Cnj Sat	Nov 16 1955	22:40	23° Sc 48' D
Sun Opp Sat	May 20 1956	14:16	29° Sc 31' R
Sun Cnj Sat	Nov 27 1956	14:43	05° Sg 20' D
Sun Opp Sat	Jun 1 1957	19:40	11° Sg 01' R
Sun Cnj Sat	Dec 9 1957	02:46	16° Sg 46' D
Sun Opp Sat	Jun 13 1958	23:27	22° Sg 25' R
Sun Cnj Sat	Dec 20 1958	12:17	28° Sg 07' D
Sun Opp Sat	Jun 26 1959	02:46	03° Cp 46' R
Sun Cnj Sat	Dec 31 1959	20:51	09° Cp 26' D
Sun Opp Sat	Jul 7 1960	06:25	15° Cp 07' R
Sun Cnj Sat	Jan 11 1961	06:10	20° Cp 47' D
Sun Opp Sat	Jul 19 1961	11:24	26° Cp 32' R
Sun Cnj Sat	Jan 22 1962	17:39	02° Aq 13' D
Sun Opp Sat	Jul 31 1962	18:49	08° Aq 04' R
Sun Cnj Sat	Feb 3 1963	09:03	13° Aq 48' D
Sun Opp Sat	Aug 13 1963	05:32	19° Aq 45' R
Sun Cnj Sat	Feb 15 1964	06:00	25° Aq 35' D
Sun Opp Sat	Aug 24 1964	20:18	01° Pi 39' R
Sun Cnj Sat	Feb 26 1965	09:49	07° Pi 35' D
Sun Opp Sat	Sep 6 1965	15:39	13° Pi 49' R
Sun Cnj Sat	Mar 10 1966	21:51	19° Pi 52' D
Sun Opp Sat	Sep 19 1966	16:02	26° Pi 15' R
Sun Cnj Sat	Mar 23 1967	19:01	02° Ar 27' D
Sun Opp Sat	Oct 2 1967	22:03	09° Ar 00' R
Sun Cnj Sat	Apr 5 1968	02:08	15° Ar 21' D
Sun Opp Sat	Oct 15 1968	09:25	22° Ar 05' R
Sun Cnj Sat	Apr 18 1969	19:48	28° Ar 35' D
Sun Opp Sat	Oct 29 1969	01:42	05° Ta 27' R
Sun Cnj Sat	May 2 1970	23:25	12° Ta 07' D
Sun Opp Sat	Nov 11 1970	22:34	19° Ta 07' R
Sun Cnj Sat	May 17 1971	11:53	25° Ta 56' D
Sun Opp Sat	Nov 25 1971	23:05	03° Ge 01' R
Sun Cnj Sat	May 31 1972	07:55	09° Ge 57' D
Sun Opp Sat	Dec 9 1972	01:52	17° Ge 05' R
Sun Cnj Sat	Jun 15 1973	09:00	24° Ge 06' D
Sun Opp Sat	Dec 23 1973	05:51	01° Cn 15' R

Appendix VI • *Sun-Saturn Conjunctions + Oppositions 1920 to 2120*

Sun Cnj Sat	Jun 30 1974	12:11	08° Cn 19' D
Sun Opp Sat	Jan 6 1975	09:25	15° Cn 25' R
Sun Cnj Sat	Jul 15 1975	14:46	22° Cn 30' D
Sun Opp Sat	Jan 20 1976	11:00	29° Cn 30' R
Sun Cnj Sat	Jul 29 1976	13:49	06° Le 33' D
Sun Opp Sat	Feb 2 1977	09:36	13° Le 26' R
Sun Cnj Sat	Aug 13 1977	06:28	20° Le 23' D
Sun Opp Sat	Feb 16 1978	04:08	27° Le 07' R
Sun Cnj Sat	Aug 27 1978	14:53	03° Vi 58' D
Sun Opp Sat	Mar 1 1979	17:42	10° Vi 32' R
Sun Cnj Sat	Sep 10 1979	13:40	17° Vi 15' D
Sun Opp Sat	Mar 14 1980	02:02	23° Vi 38' R
Sun Cnj Sat	Sep 23 1980	02:08	00° Li 12' D
Sun Opp Sat	Mar 27 1981	04:53	06° Li 26' R
Sun Cnj Sat	Oct 6 1981	04:30	12° Li 50' D
Sun Opp Sat	Apr 9 1982	02:30	18° Li 55' R
Sun Cnj Sat	Oct 18 1982	21:24	25° Li 10' D
Sun Opp Sat	Apr 21 1983	19:27	01° Sc 07' R
Sun Cnj Sat	Oct 31 1983	05:56	07° Sc 14' D
Sun Opp Sat	May 3 1984	08:21	13° Sc 04' R
Sun Cnj Sat	Nov 11 1984	07:01	19° Sc 04' D
Sun Opp Sat	May 15 1985	17:57	24° Sc 49' R
Sun Cnj Sat	Nov 23 1985	01:45	00° Sg 42' D
Sun Opp Sat	May 28 1986	00:42	06° Sg 24' R
Sun Cnj Sat	Dec 4 1986	15:56	12° Sg 12' D
Sun Opp Sat	Jun 9 1987	05:20	17° Sg 52' R
Sun Cnj Sat	Dec 16 1987	02:53	23° Sg 35' D
Sun Opp Sat	Jun 20 1988	09:13	29° Sg 15' R
Sun Cnj Sat	Dec 26 1988	11:57	04° Cp 56' D
Sun Opp Sat	Jul 2 1989	13:08	10° Cp 37' R
Sun Cnj Sat	Jan 6 1990	21:02	16° Cp 17' D
Sun Opp Sat	Jul 14 1990	17:44	22° Cp 01' R
Sun Cnj Sat	Jan 18 1991	07:45	27° Cp 42' D
Sun Opp Sat	Jul 27 1991	00:21	03° Aq 30' R
Sun Cnj Sat	Jan 29 1992	21:33	09° Aq 14' D
Sun Opp Sat	Aug 7 1992	09:53	15° Aq 08' R
Sun Cnj Sat	Feb 9 1993	16:10	20° Aq 55' D
Sun Opp Sat	Aug 19 1993	23:01	26° Aq 57' R
Sun Cnj Sat	Feb 21 1994	17:03	02° Pi 50' D
Sun Opp Sat	Sep 1 1994	16:40	09° Pi 00' R
Sun Cnj Sat	Mar 6 1995	01:32	15° Pi 00' D
Sun Opp Sat	Sep 14 1995	15:19	21° Pi 20' R
Sun Cnj Sat	Mar 17 1996	19:04	27° Pi 28' D
Sun Opp Sat	Sep 26 1996	19:11	03° Ar 57' R

Sun Cnj Sat	Mar 30 1997	22:20	10° Ar 14' D
Sun Opp Sat	Oct 10 1997	04:26	16° Ar 54' R
Sun Cnj Sat	Apr 13 1998	11:41	23° Ar 20' D
Sun Opp Sat	Oct 23 1998	18:49	00° Ta 09' R
Sun Cnj Sat	Apr 27 1999	11:04	06° Ta 45' D
Sun Opp Sat	Nov 6 1999	13:53	13° Ta 41' R
Sun Cnj Sat	May 10 2000	19:45	20° Ta 26' D
Sun Opp Sat	Nov 19 2000	12:41	27° Ta 29' R
Sun Cnj Sat	May 25 2001	12:33	04° Ge 21' D
Sun Opp Sat	Dec 3 2001	14:13	11° Ge 28' R
Sun Cnj Sat	Jun 9 2002	11:24	18° Ge 27' D
Sun Opp Sat	Dec 17 2002	17:28	25° Ge 35' R
Sun Cnj Sat	Jun 24 2003	13:39	02° Cn 38' D
Sun Opp Sat	Dec 31 2003	20:57	09° Cn 45' R
Sun Cnj Sat	Jul 8 2004	16:38	16° Cn 49' D
Sun Opp Sat	Jan 13 2005	23:06	23° Cn 52' R
Sun Cnj Sat	Jul 23 2005	17:01	00° Le 55' D
Sun Opp Sat	Jan 27 2006	22:48	07° Le 51' R
Sun Cnj Sat	Aug 7 2006	11:54	14° Le 50' D
Sun Opp Sat	Feb 10 2007	18:42	21° Le 38' R
Sun Cnj Sat	Aug 21 2007	23:28	28° Le 31' D
Sun Opp Sat	Feb 24 2008	09:48	05° Vi 09' R
Sun Cnj Sat	Sep 4 2008	02:00	11° Vi 55' D
Sun Opp Sat	Mar 8 2009	19:53	18° Vi 22' R
Sun Cnj Sat	Sep 17 2009	18:22	24° Vi 59' D
Sun Opp Sat	Mar 22 2010	00:37	01° Li 17' R
Sun Cnj Sat	Oct 1 2010	00:42	07° Li 44' D
Sun Opp Sat	Apr 3 2011	23:56	13° Li 52' R
Sun Cnj Sat	Oct 13 2011	21:13	20° Li 11' D
Sun Opp Sat	Apr 15 2012	18:26	26° Li 10' R
Sun Cnj Sat	Oct 25 2012	08:32	02° Sc 20' D
Sun Opp Sat	Apr 28 2013	08:27	08° Sc 12' R
Sun Cnj Sat	Nov 6 2013	12:01	14° Sc 14' D
Sun Opp Sat	May 10 2014	18:28	20° Sc 01' R
Sun Cnj Sat	Nov 18 2014	08:50	25° Sc 55' D
Sun Opp Sat	May 23 2015	01:35	01° Sg 38' R
Sun Cnj Sat	Nov 30 2015	00:16	07° Sg 27' D
Sun Opp Sat	Jun 3 2016	06:37	13° Sg 07' R
Sun Cnj Sat	Dec 10 2016	11:51	18° Sg 51' D
Sun Opp Sat	Jun 15 2017	10:18	24° Sg 30' R
Sun Cnj Sat	Dec 21 2017	21:09	00° Cp 11' D
Sun Opp Sat	Jun 27 2018	13:28	05° Cp 51' R
Sun Cnj Sat	Jan 2 2019	05:50	11° Cp 31' D
Sun Opp Sat	Jul 9 2019	17:07	17° Cp 12' R

Appendix VI • *Sun-Saturn Conjunctions + Oppositions 1920 to 2120*

Sun Cnj Sat	Jan 13 2020	15:16	22° Cp 53' D
Sun Opp Sat	Jul 20 2020	22:28	28° Cp 38' R
Sun Cnj Sat	Jan 24 2021	03:01	04° Aq 20' D
Sun Opp Sat	Aug 2 2021	06:14	10° Aq 11' R
Sun Cnj Sat	Feb 4 2022	19:05	15° Aq 56' D
Sun Opp Sat	Aug 14 2022	17:11	21° Aq 54' R
Sun Cnj Sat	Feb 16 2023	16:48	27° Aq 44' D
Sun Opp Sat	Aug 27 2023	08:28	03° Pi 50' R
Sun Cnj Sat	Feb 28 2024	21:25	09° Pi 46' D
Sun Opp Sat	Sep 8 2024	04:35	16° Pi 01' R
Sun Cnj Sat	Mar 12 2025	10:29	22° Pi 05' D
Sun Opp Sat	Sep 21 2025	05:46	28° Pi 30' R
Sun Cnj Sat	Mar 25 2026	08:55	04° Ar 43' D
Sun Opp Sat	Oct 4 2026	12:29	11° Ar 18' R
Sun Cnj Sat	Apr 7 2027	17:18	17° Ar 40' D
Sun Opp Sat	Oct 18 2027	00:36	24° Ar 24' R
Sun Cnj Sat	Apr 20 2028	12:10	00° Ta 56' D
Sun Opp Sat	Oct 30 2028	17:34	07° Ta 49' R
Sun Cnj Sat	May 4 2029	16:57	14° Ta 30' D
Sun Opp Sat	Nov 13 2029	15:00	21° Ta 31' R
Sun Cnj Sat	May 19 2030	06:22	28° Ta 20' D
Sun Opp Sat	Nov 27 2030	15:55	05° Ge 26' R
Sun Cnj Sat	Jun 3 2031	02:59	12° Ge 22' D
Sun Opp Sat	Dec 11 2031	19:00	19° Ge 31' R
Sun Cnj Sat	Jun 17 2032	04:23	26° Ge 33' D
Sun Opp Sat	Dec 24 2032	22:55	03° Cn 41' R
Sun Cnj Sat	Jul 2 2033	07:39	10° Cn 45' D
Sun Opp Sat	Jan 8 2034	02:12	17° Cn 50' R
Sun Cnj Sat	Jul 17 2034	09:49	24° Cn 55' D
Sun Opp Sat	Jan 22 2035	03:25	01° Le 54' R
Sun Cnj Sat	Aug 1 2035	08:03	08° Le 56' D
Sun Opp Sat	Feb 5 2036	01:32	15° Le 48' R
Sun Cnj Sat	Aug 14 2036	23:53	22° Le 45' D
Sun Opp Sat	Feb 17 2037	19:27	29° Le 28' R
Sun Cnj Sat	Aug 29 2037	07:12	06° Vi 18' D
Sun Opp Sat	Mar 3 2038	08:33	12° Vi 51' R
Sun Cnj Sat	Sep 12 2038	04:43	19° Vi 32' D
Sun Opp Sat	Mar 16 2039	16:13	25° Vi 55' R
Sun Cnj Sat	Sep 25 2039	16:08	02° Li 27' D
Sun Opp Sat	Mar 28 2040	18:15	08° Li 40' R
Sun Cnj Sat	Oct 7 2040	17:26	15° Li 03' D
Sun Opp Sat	Apr 10 2041	15:12	21° Li 07' R
Sun Cnj Sat	Oct 20 2041	09:07	27° Li 21' D
Sun Opp Sat	Apr 23 2042	07:28	03° Sc 17' R

Sun Cnj Sat	Nov 1 2042	16:31	09° Sc 22' D
Sun Opp Sat	May 5 2043	19:38	15° Sc 12' R
Sun Cnj Sat	Nov 13 2043	16:40	21° Sc 11' D
Sun Opp Sat	May 17 2044	04:37	26° Sc 56' R
Sun Cnj Sat	Nov 24 2044	10:46	02° Sg 48' D
Sun Opp Sat	May 29 2045	10:58	08° Sg 29' R
Sun Cnj Sat	Dec 6 2045	00:30	14° Sg 16' D
Sun Opp Sat	Jun 10 2046	15:22	19° Sg 56' R
Sun Cnj Sat	Dec 17 2046	11:07	25° Sg 39' D
Sun Opp Sat	Jun 22 2047	19:09	01° Cp 18' R
Sun Cnj Sat	Dec 28 2047	20:03	06° Cp 59' D
Sun Opp Sat	Jul 3 2048	23:05	12° Cp 40' R
Sun Cnj Sat	Jan 8 2049	05:16	18° Cp 21' D
Sun Opp Sat	Jul 16 2049	03:51	24° Cp 05' R
Sun Cnj Sat	Jan 19 2050	16:18	29° Cp 46' D
Sun Opp Sat	Jul 28 2050	10:43	05° Aq 35' R
Sun Cnj Sat	Jan 31 2051	06:37	11° Aq 19' D
Sun Opp Sat	Aug 9 2051	20:41	17° Aq 14' R
Sun Cnj Sat	Feb 12 2052	01:53	23° Aq 02' D
Sun Opp Sat	Aug 21 2052	10:32	29° Aq 04' R
Sun Cnj Sat	Feb 23 2053	03:41	04° Pi 59' D
Sun Opp Sat	Sep 3 2053	04:53	11° Pi 10' R
Sun Cnj Sat	Mar 7 2054	13:26	17° Pi 11' D
Sun Opp Sat	Sep 16 2054	04:11	23° Pi 32' R
Sun Cnj Sat	Mar 20 2055	08:11	29° Pi 41' D
Sun Opp Sat	Sep 29 2055	09:02	06° Ar 12' R
Sun Cnj Sat	Apr 1 2056	12:41	12° Ar 31' D
Sun Opp Sat	Oct 11 2056	19:20	19° Ar 12' R
Sun Cnj Sat	Apr 15 2057	03:34	25° Ar 40' D
Sun Opp Sat	Oct 25 2057	10:40	02° Ta 30' R
Sun Cnj Sat	Apr 29 2058	04:29	09° Ta 07' D
Sun Opp Sat	Nov 8 2058	06:38	16° Ta 06' R
Sun Cnj Sat	May 13 2059	14:28	22° Ta 51' D
Sun Opp Sat	Nov 22 2059	06:10	29° Ta 55' R
Sun Cnj Sat	May 27 2060	08:21	06° Ge 49' D
Sun Opp Sat	Dec 5 2060	08:05	13° Ge 56' R
Sun Cnj Sat	Jun 11 2061	07:52	20° Ge 56' D
Sun Opp Sat	Dec 19 2061	11:35	28° Ge 04' R
Sun Cnj Sat	Jun 26 2062	10:18	05° Cn 07' D
Sun Opp Sat	Jan 2 2063	15:08	12° Cn 14' R
Sun Cnj Sat	Jul 11 2063	13:06	19° Cn 18' D
Sun Opp Sat	Jan 16 2064	17:08	° Cn 21' R
Sun Cnj Sat	Jul 25 2064	13:06	03° Le 23' D
Sun Opp Sat	Jan 29 2065	16:28	10° Le 19' R

Appendix VI • *Sun-Saturn Conjunctions + Oppositions 1920 to 2120*

Sun Cnj Sat	Aug 9 2065	07:20	17° Le 17' D
Sun Opp Sat	Feb 12 2066	11:51	24° Le 04' R
Sun Cnj Sat	Aug 23 2066	17:55	00° Vi 56' D
Sun Opp Sat	Feb 26 2067	02:20	07° Vi 33' R
Sun Cnj Sat	Sep 6 2067	19:20	14° Vi 17' D
Sun Opp Sat	Mar 10 2068	11:45	20° Vi 44' R
Sun Cnj Sat	Sep 19 2068	10:34	27° Vi 19' D
Sun Opp Sat	Mar 23 2069	15:48	03° Li 36' R
Sun Cnj Sat	Oct 2 2069	15:34	10° Li 02' D
Sun Opp Sat	Apr 5 2070	14:27	16° Li 09' R
Sun Cnj Sat	Oct 15 2070	10:44	22° Li 26' D
Sun Opp Sat	Apr 18 2071	08:06	28° Li 24' R
Sun Cnj Sat	Oct 27 2071	21:01	04° Sc 32' D
Sun Opp Sat	Apr 29 2072	21:15	10° Sc 24' R
Sun Cnj Sat	Nov 7 2072	22:30	16° Sc 24' D
Sun Opp Sat	May 12 2073	06:46	22° Sc 10' R
Sun Cnj Sat	Nov 19 2073	19:18	28° Sc 04' D
Sun Opp Sat	May 24 2074	13:21	03° Sg 46' R
Sun Cnj Sat	Dec 1 2074	10:00	09° Sg 34' D
Sun Opp Sat	Jun 5 2075	17:47	15° Sg 13' R
Sun Cnj Sat	Dec 12 2075	21:08	20° Sg 57' D
Sun Opp Sat	Jun 16 2076	21:10	26° Sg 36' R
Sun Cnj Sat	Dec 23 2076	06:09	02° Cp 17' D
Sun Opp Sat	Jun 29 2077	00:15	07° Cp 56' R
Sun Cnj Sat	Jan 3 2078	14:44	13° Cp 36' D
Sun Opp Sat	Jul 11 2078	03:54	19° Cp 18' R
Sun Cnj Sat	Jan 15 2079	00:17	24° Cp 58' D
Sun Opp Sat	Jul 23 2079	09:24	00° Aq 44' R
Sun Cnj Sat	Jan 26 2080	12:22	06° Aq 26' D
Sun Opp Sat	Aug 3 2080	17:25	12° Aq 18' R
Sun Cnj Sat	Feb 6 2081	04:55	18° Aq 03' D
Sun Opp Sat	Aug 16 2081	04:39	24° Aq 02' R
Sun Cnj Sat	Feb 18 2082	03:15	29° Aq 53' D
Sun Opp Sat	Aug 28 2082	20:23	05° Pi 59' R
Sun Cnj Sat	Mar 2 2083	08:39	11° Pi 57' D
Sun Opp Sat	Sep 10 2083	17:09	18° Pi 13' R
Sun Cnj Sat	Mar 13 2084	22:41	24° Pi 18' D
Sun Opp Sat	Sep 22 2084	19:03	00° Ar 44' R
Sun Cnj Sat	Mar 26 2085	22:19	06° Ar 57' D
Sun Opp Sat	Oct 6 2085	02:25	13° Ar 33' R
Sun Cnj Sat	Apr 9 2086	07:59	19° Ar 56' D
Sun Opp Sat	Oct 19 2086	15:07	26° Ar 42' R
Sun Cnj Sat	Apr 23 2087	03:56	03° Ta 15' D
Sun Opp Sat	Nov 2 2087	08:49	10° Ta 09' R

Sun Cnj Sat	May 6 2088	09:42	16° Ta 51' D
Sun Opp Sat	Nov 15 2088	06:50	23° Ta 53' R
Sun Cnj Sat	May 21 2089	00:09	00° Ge 43' D
Sun Opp Sat	Nov 29 2089	08:04	07° Ge 49' R
Sun Cnj Sat	Jun 4 2090	21:24	14° Ge 46' D
Sun Opp Sat	Dec 13 2090	11:21	21° Ge 55' R
Sun Cnj Sat	Jun 19 2091	23:03	28° Ge 57' D
Sun Opp Sat	Dec 27 2091	15:15	06° Cn 05' R
Sun Cnj Sat	Jul 4 2092	02:25	13° Cn 09' D
Sun Opp Sat	Jan 9 2093	18:17	20° Cn 14' R
Sun Cnj Sat	Jul 19 2093	04:17	27° Cn 18' D
Sun Opp Sat	Jan 23 2094	19:17	04° Le 17' R
Sun Cnj Sat	Aug 3 2094	01:43	11° Le 18' D
Sun Opp Sat	Feb 6 2095	17:00	18° Le 09' R
Sun Cnj Sat	Aug 17 2095	16:39	25° Le 05' D
Sun Opp Sat	Feb 20 2096	10:22	01° Vi 47' R
Sun Cnj Sat	Aug 30 2096	22:59	08° Vi 36' D
Sun Opp Sat	Mar 4 2097	22:53	15° Vi 08' R
Sun Cnj Sat	Sep 13 2097	19:25	21° Vi 49' D
Sun Opp Sat	Mar 18 2098	05:58	28° Vi 11' R
Sun Cnj Sat	Sep 27 2098	05:49	04° Li 42' D
Sun Opp Sat	Mar 31 2099	07:22	10° Li 54' R
Sun Cnj Sat	Oct 10 2099	06:09	17° Li 16' D
Sun Opp Sat	Apr 13 2100	03:46	23° Li 19' R
Sun Cnj Sat	Oct 22 2100	20:47	29° Li 32' D
Sun Opp Sat	Apr 25 2101	19:28	05° Sc 27' R
Sun Cnj Sat	Nov 4 2101	03:05	11° Sc 31' D
Sun Opp Sat	May 8 2102	06:57	17° Sc 20' R
Sun Cnj Sat	Nov 16 2102	02:22	23° Sc 18' D
Sun Opp Sat	May 20 2103	15:15	29° Sc 02' R
Sun Cnj Sat	Nov 27 2103	19:52	04° Sg 53' D
Sun Opp Sat	May 31 2104	21:10	10° Sg 34' R
Sun Cnj Sat	Dec 8 2104	09:01	16° Sg 20' D
Sun Opp Sat	Jun 13 2105	01:25	22° Sg 00' R
Sun Cnj Sat	Dec 19 2105	19:10	27° Sg 42' D
Sun Opp Sat	Jun 25 2106	04:57	03° Cp 22' R
Sun Cnj Sat	Dec 31 2106	04:00	09° Cp 02' D
Sun Opp Sat	Jul 7 2107	08:39	14° Cp 43' R
Sun Cnj Sat	Jan 11 2108	13:17	20° Cp 23' D
Sun Opp Sat	Jul 18 2108	13:34	26° Cp 08' R
Sun Cnj Sat	Jan 22 2109	00:23	01° Aq 49' D
Sun Opp Sat	Jul 30 2109	20:40	07° Aq 38' R
Sun Cnj Sat	Feb 2 2110	15:04	13° Aq 22' D
Sun Opp Sat	Aug 12 2110	06:49	19° Aq 18' R

Sun Cnj Sat	Feb 14 2111	10:53	25° Aq 07' D
Sun Opp Sat	Aug 24 2111	21:02	01° Pi 10' R
Sun Cnj Sat	Feb 26 2112	13:21	07° Pi 05' D
Sun Opp Sat	Sep 5 2112	15:50	13° Pi 17' R
Sun Cnj Sat	Mar 9 2113	23:59	19° Pi 19' D
Sun Opp Sat	Sep 18 2113	15:38	25° Pi 41' R
Sun Cnj Sat	Mar 22 2114	19:39	01° Ar 51' D
Sun Opp Sat	Oct 1 2114	21:09	08° Ar 23' R
Sun Cnj Sat	Apr 5 2115	01:11	14° Ar 43' D
Sun Opp Sat	Oct 15 2115	08:14	21° Ar 25' R
Sun Cnj Sat	Apr 17 2116	17:17	27° Ar 55' D
Sun Opp Sat	Oct 28 2116	00:17	04° Ta 46' R
Sun Cnj Sat	May 1 2117	19:32	11° Ta 25' D
Sun Opp Sat	Nov 10 2117	21:56	18° Ta 24' R
Sun Cnj Sat	May 16 2118	06:42	25° Ta 11' D
Sun Opp Sat	Nov 24 2118	21:08	02° Ge 16' R
Sun Cnj Sat	May 31 2119	01:29	09° Ge 10' D
Sun Opp Sat	Dec 8 2119	23:35	16° Ge 19' R
Sun Cnj Sat	Jun 14 2120	01:36	23° Ge 18' D
Sun Opp Sat	Dec 22 2120	03:20	00° Cn 27' R

Appendix VII
Sun-Uranus Conjunctions 1920 to 2120

Sun Cnj Ura	Feb 21 1920	14:07	01° Pi 39'
Sun Cnj Ura	Feb 24 1921	18:36	05° Pi 37'
Sun Cnj Ura	Feb 28 1922	23:01	09° Pi 35'
Sun Cnj Ura	Mar 5 1923	03:32	13° Pi 32'
Sun Cnj Ura	Mar 8 1924	08:11	17° Pi 30'
Sun Cnj Ura	Mar 12 1925	13:12	21° Pi 27'
Sun Cnj Ura	Mar 16 1926	18:30	25° Pi 25'
Sun Cnj Ura	Mar 21 1927	00:14	29° Pi 23'
Sun Cnj Ura	Mar 24 1928	06:07	03° Ar 21'
Sun Cnj Ura	Mar 28 1929	12:36	07° Ar 20'
Sun Cnj Ura	Apr 1 1930	19:20	11° Ar 20'
Sun Cnj Ura	Apr 6 1931	02:22	15° Ar 19'
Sun Cnj Ura	Apr 9 1932	09:53	19° Ar 20'
Sun Cnj Ura	Apr 13 1933	18:02	23° Ar 21'
Sun Cnj Ura	Apr 18 1934	02:37	27° Ar 22'
Sun Cnj Ura	Apr 22 1935	11:56	01° Ta 25'
Sun Cnj Ura	Apr 25 1936	21:45	05° Ta 29'
Sun Cnj Ura	Apr 30 1937	08:38	09° Ta 34'
Sun Cnj Ura	May 4 1938	20:09	13° Ta 41'

Sun Cnj Ura	May 9 1939	08:33	17° Ta 49'
Sun Cnj Ura	May 12 1940	21:53	21° Ta 59'
Sun Cnj Ura	May 17 1941	12:18	26° Ta 11'
Sun Cnj Ura	May 22 1942	03:18	00° Ge 24'
Sun Cnj Ura	May 26 1943	19:18	04° Ge 39'
Sun Cnj Ura	May 30 1944	11:58	08° Ge 55'
Sun Cnj Ura	Jun 4 1945	05:43	13° Ge 13'
Sun Cnj Ura	Jun 9 1946	00:04	17° Ge 33'
Sun Cnj Ura	Jun 13 1947	19:16	21° Ge 55'
Sun Cnj Ura	Jun 17 1948	15:24	26° Ge 18'
Sun Cnj Ura	Jun 22 1949	12:33	00° Cn 44'
Sun Cnj Ura	Jun 27 1950	10:17	05° Cn 11'
Sun Cnj Ura	Jul 2 1951	09:07	09° Cn 41'
Sun Cnj Ura	Jul 6 1952	08:50	14° Cn 12'
Sun Cnj Ura	Jul 11 1953	09:23	18° Cn 46'
Sun Cnj Ura	Jul 16 1954	10:42	23° Cn 21'
Sun Cnj Ura	Jul 21 1955	12:34	27° Cn 58'
Sun Cnj Ura	Jul 25 1956	15:14	02° Le 37'
Sun Cnj Ura	Jul 30 1957	18:16	07° Le 17'
Sun Cnj Ura	Aug 4 1958	21:36	11° Le 58'
Sun Cnj Ura	Aug 10 1959	01:17	16° Le 41'
Sun Cnj Ura	Aug 14 1960	05:24	21° Le 24'
Sun Cnj Ura	Aug 19 1961	09:21	26° Le 08'
Sun Cnj Ura	Aug 24 1962	13:40	00° Vi 54'
Sun Cnj Ura	Aug 29 1963	17:53	05° Vi 40'
Sun Cnj Ura	Sep 2 1964	22:17	10° Vi 26'
Sun Cnj Ura	Sep 8 1965	02:30	15° Vi 13'
Sun Cnj Ura	Sep 13 1966	06:31	20° Vi 01'
Sun Cnj Ura	Sep 18 1967	10:26	24° Vi 49'
Sun Cnj Ura	Sep 22 1968	14:01	29° Vi 36'
Sun Cnj Ura	Sep 27 1969	17:02	04° Li 24'
Sun Cnj Ura	Oct 2 1970	19:32	09° Li 11'
Sun Cnj Ura	Oct 7 1971	21:33	13° Li 57'
Sun Cnj Ura	Oct 11 1972	22:36	18° Li 42'
Sun Cnj Ura	Oct 16 1973	23:00	23° Li 26'
Sun Cnj Ura	Oct 21 1974	22:20	28° Li 08'
Sun Cnj Ura	Oct 26 1975	21:04	02° Sc 49'
Sun Cnj Ura	Oct 30 1976	18:48	07° Sc 28'
Sun Cnj Ura	Nov 4 1977	15:41	12° Sc 06'
Sun Cnj Ura	Nov 9 1978	11:42	16° Sc 43'
Sun Cnj Ura	Nov 14 1979	07:02	21° Sc 18'
Sun Cnj Ura	Nov 18 1980	01:14	25° Sc 51'
Sun Cnj Ura	Nov 22 1981	18:49	00° Sg 23'

Appendix VII • Sun-Uranus Conjunctions 1920 to 2120

Sun Cnj Ura	Nov 27 1982	11:23	04° Sg 53'
Sun Cnj Ura	Dec 2 1983	03:09	09° Sg 21'
Sun Cnj Ura	Dec 5 1984	17:57	13° Sg 47'
Sun Cnj Ura	Dec 10 1985	07:47	18° Sg 11'
Sun Cnj Ura	Dec 14 1986	20:43	22° Sg 33'
Sun Cnj Ura	Dec 19 1987	08:45	26° Sg 54'
Sun Cnj Ura	Dec 22 1988	19:47	01° Cp 12'
Sun Cnj Ura	Dec 27 1989	06:12	05° Cp 28'
Sun Cnj Ura	Dec 31 1990	15:51	09° Cp 42'
Sun Cnj Ura	Jan 5 1992	00:45	13° Cp 55'
Sun Cnj Ura	Jan 8 1993	09:09	18° Cp 06'
Sun Cnj Ura	Jan 12 1994	16:59	22° Cp 16'
Sun Cnj Ura	Jan 17 1995	00:22	26° Cp 24'
Sun Cnj Ura	Jan 21 1996	07:21	00° Aq 31'
Sun Cnj Ura	Jan 24 1997	13:53	04° Aq 37'
Sun Cnj Ura	Jan 28 1998	20:08	08° Aq 42'
Sun Cnj Ura	Feb 2 1999	01:59	12° Aq 45'
Sun Cnj Ura	Feb 6 2000	07:14	16° Aq 47'
Sun Cnj Ura	Feb 9 2001	12:19	20° Aq 49'
Sun Cnj Ura	Feb 13 2002	17:06	24° Aq 49'
Sun Cnj Ura	Feb 17 2003	21:38	28° Aq 48'
Sun Cnj Ura	Feb 22 2004	02:07	02° Pi 47'
Sun Cnj Ura	Feb 25 2005	06:33	06° Pi 45'
Sun Cnj Ura	Mar 1 2006	11:02	10° Pi 43'
Sun Cnj Ura	Mar 5 2007	15:39	14° Pi 40'
Sun Cnj Ura	Mar 8 2008	20:19	18° Pi 38'
Sun Cnj Ura	Mar 13 2009	01:27	22° Pi 36'
Sun Cnj Ura	Mar 17 2010	06:50	26° Pi 34'
Sun Cnj Ura	Mar 21 2011	12:24	00° Ar 32'
Sun Cnj Ura	Mar 24 2012	18:20	04° Ar 30'
Sun Cnj Ura	Mar 29 2013	00:38	08° Ar 29'
Sun Cnj Ura	Apr 2 2014	07:08	12° Ar 28'
Sun Cnj Ura	Apr 6 2015	14:08	16° Ar 27'
Sun Cnj Ura	Apr 9 2016	21:27	20° Ar 27'
Sun Cnj Ura	Apr 14 2017	05:30	24° Ar 27'
Sun Cnj Ura	Apr 18 2018	14:00	28° Ar 29'
Sun Cnj Ura	Apr 22 2019	23:07	02° Ta 31'
Sun Cnj Ura	Apr 26 2020	09:01	06° Ta 35'
Sun Cnj Ura	Apr 30 2021	19:54	10° Ta 40'
Sun Cnj Ura	May 5 2022	07:21	14° Ta 47'
Sun Cnj Ura	May 9 2023	19:56	18° Ta 56'
Sun Cnj Ura	May 13 2024	09:13	23° Ta 06'
Sun Cnj Ura	May 17 2025	23:32	27° Ta 17'
Sun Cnj Ura	May 22 2026	14:26	01° Ge 30'

Sun Cnj Ura	May 27 2027	06:12	05° Ge 45'
Sun Cnj Ura	May 30 2028	22:47	10° Ge 01'
Sun Cnj Ura	Jun 4 2029	16:23	14° Ge 19'
Sun Cnj Ura	Jun 9 2030	10:27	18° Ge 39'
Sun Cnj Ura	Jun 14 2031	05:43	23° Ge 00'
Sun Cnj Ura	Jun 18 2032	01:46	27° Ge 24'
Sun Cnj Ura	Jun 22 2033	22:49	01° Cn 49'
Sun Cnj Ura	Jun 27 2034	20:38	06° Cn 16'
Sun Cnj Ura	Jul 2 2035	19:30	10° Cn 46'
Sun Cnj Ura	Jul 6 2036	19:19	15° Cn 17'
Sun Cnj Ura	Jul 11 2037	19:59	19° Cn 51'
Sun Cnj Ura	Jul 16 2038	21:10	24° Cn 26'
Sun Cnj Ura	Jul 21 2039	23:10	29° Cn 03'
Sun Cnj Ura	Jul 26 2040	01:49	03° Le 42'
Sun Cnj Ura	Jul 31 2041	04:40	08° Le 22'
Sun Cnj Ura	Aug 5 2042	08:06	13° Le 03'
Sun Cnj Ura	Aug 10 2043	11:44	17° Le 46'
Sun Cnj Ura	Aug 14 2044	15:48	22° Le 29'
Sun Cnj Ura	Aug 19 2045	19:54	27° Le 14'
Sun Cnj Ura	Aug 25 2046	00:11	01° Vi 59'
Sun Cnj Ura	Aug 30 2047	04:35	06° Vi 46'
Sun Cnj Ura	Sep 3 2048	09:10	11° Vi 33'
Sun Cnj Ura	Sep 8 2049	13:22	16° Vi 20'
Sun Cnj Ura	Sep 13 2050	17:41	21° Vi 08'
Sun Cnj Ura	Sep 18 2051	21:43	25° Vi 56'
Sun Cnj Ura	Sep 23 2052	01:19	00° Li 44'
Sun Cnj Ura	Sep 28 2053	04:30	05° Li 31'
Sun Cnj Ura	Oct 3 2054	07:00	10° Li 18'
Sun Cnj Ura	Oct 8 2055	08:58	15° Li 04'
Sun Cnj Ura	Oct 12 2056	10:04	19° Li 48'
Sun Cnj Ura	Oct 17 2057	10:20	24° Li 32'
Sun Cnj Ura	Oct 22 2058	09:48	29° Li 14'
Sun Cnj Ura	Oct 27 2059	08:38	03° Sc 56'
Sun Cnj Ura	Oct 31 2060	06:20	08° Sc 35'
Sun Cnj Ura	Nov 5 2061	03:27	13° Sc 14'
Sun Cnj Ura	Nov 9 2062	23:35	17° Sc 51'
Sun Cnj Ura	Nov 14 2063	18:59	22° Sc 26'
Sun Cnj Ura	Nov 18 2064	13:24	27° Sc 00'
Sun Cnj Ura	Nov 23 2065	19:01	01° Sg 32'
Sun Cnj Ura	Nov 27 2066	23:40	06° Sg 02'
Sun Cnj Ura	Dec 2 2067	15:32	10° Sg 30'
Sun Cnj Ura	Dec 6 2068	06:11	14° Sg 56'
Sun Cnj Ura	Dec 10 2069	20:06	19° Sg 20'

Appendix VII • Sun-Uranus Conjunctions 1920 to 2120

Sun Cnj Ura	Dec 15 2070	08:58	23° Sg 42'
Sun Cnj Ura	Dec 19 2071	20:55	28° Sg 02'
Sun Cnj Ura	Dec 23 2072	08:05	02° Cp 20'
Sun Cnj Ura	Dec 27 2073	18:31	06° Cp 36'
Sun Cnj Ura	Jan 1 2075	04:10	10° Cp 50'
Sun Cnj Ura	Jan 5 2076	13:16	15° Cp 03'
Sun Cnj Ura	Jan 8 2077	21:40	19° Cp 15'
Sun Cnj Ura	Jan 13 2078	05:41	23° Cp 25'
Sun Cnj Ura	Jan 17 2079	13:12	27° Cp 33'
Sun Cnj Ura	Jan 21 2080	20:10	01° Aq 41'
Sun Cnj Ura	Jan 25 2081	02:49	05° Aq 47'
Sun Cnj Ura	Jan 29 2082	08:58	09° Aq 52'
Sun Cnj Ura	Feb 2 2083	14:36	13° Aq 55'
Sun Cnj Ura	Feb 6 2084	19:54	17° Aq 57'
Sun Cnj Ura	Feb 10 2085	00:53	21° Aq 58'
Sun Cnj Ura	Feb 14 2086	05:40	25° Aq 58'
Sun Cnj Ura	Feb 18 2087	10:17	29° Aq 58'
Sun Cnj Ura	Feb 22 2088	14:42	03° Pi 56'
Sun Cnj Ura	Feb 25 2089	19:16	07° Pi 55'
Sun Cnj Ura	Mar 1 2090	23:50	11° Pi 53'
Sun Cnj Ura	Mar 6 2091	04:25	15° Pi 50'
Sun Cnj Ura	Mar 9 2092	09:21	19° Pi 48'
Sun Cnj Ura	Mar 13 2093	14:34	23° Pi 46'
Sun Cnj Ura	Mar 17 2094	19:56	27° Pi 44'
Sun Cnj Ura	Mar 22 2095	01:35	01° Ar 42'
Sun Cnj Ura	Mar 25 2096	07:23	05° Ar 40'
Sun Cnj Ura	Mar 29 2097	13:36	09° Ar 39'
Sun Cnj Ura	Apr 2 2098	20:05	13° Ar 38'
Sun Cnj Ura	Apr 7 2099	02:51	17° Ar 37'
Sun Cnj Ura	Apr 11 2100	10:16	21° Ar 37'
Sun Cnj Ura	Apr 15 2101	18:17	25° Ar 38'
Sun Cnj Ura	Apr 20 2102	02:42	29° Ar 39'
Sun Cnj Ura	Apr 24 2103	12:00	03° Ta 42'
Sun Cnj Ura	Apr 27 2104	21:59	07° Ta 46'
Sun Cnj Ura	May 2 2105	08:55	11° Ta 52'
Sun Cnj Ura	May 6 2106	20:33	15° Ta 59'
Sun Cnj Ura	May 11 2107	09:03	20° Ta 07'
Sun Cnj Ura	May 14 2108	22:23	24° Ta 17'
Sun Cnj Ura	May 19 2109	12:36	28° Ta 28'
Sun Cnj Ura	May 24 2110	03:16	02° Ge 41'
Sun Cnj Ura	May 28 2111	19:03	06° Ge 56'
Sun Cnj Ura	Jun 1 2112	11:33	11° Ge 12'
Sun Cnj Ura	Jun 6 2113	04:59	15° Ge 29'
Sun Cnj Ura	Jun 10 2114	23:08	19° Ge 49'

Sun Cnj Ura	Jun 15 2115	18:23	24° Ge 10'
Sun Cnj Ura	Jun 19 2116	14:29	28° Ge 34'
Sun Cnj Ura	Jun 24 2117	11:42	03° Cn 00'
Sun Cnj Ura	Jun 29 2118	09:33	07° Cn 27'
Sun Cnj Ura	Jul 4 2119	08:41	11° Cn 57'
Sun Cnj Ura	Jul 8 2120	08:34	16° Cn 29'

Appendix VIII
Sun-Neptune Conjunctions 1920 to 2120

Sun Cnj Nep	Aug 3 1920	23:31	11° Le 16'
Sun Cnj Nep	Aug 6 1921	12:49	13° Le 29'
Sun Cnj Nep	Aug 9 1922	02:07	15° Le 41'
Sun Cnj Nep	Aug 11 1923	15:09	17° Le 54'
Sun Cnj Nep	Aug 13 1924	04:09	20° Le 06'
Sun Cnj Nep	Aug 15 1925	17:03	22° Le 18'
Sun Cnj Nep	Aug 18 1926	05:33	24° Le 31'
Sun Cnj Nep	Aug 20 1927	18:18	26° Le 42'
Sun Cnj Nep	Aug 22 1928	06:53	28° Le 54'
Sun Cnj Nep	Aug 24 1929	19:28	01° Vi 06'
Sun Cnj Nep	Aug 27 1930	07:56	03° Vi 19'
Sun Cnj Nep	Aug 29 1931	20:28	05° Vi 31'
Sun Cnj Nep	Aug 31 1932	08:58	07° Vi 43'
Sun Cnj Nep	Sep 2 1933	21:21	09° Vi 55'
Sun Cnj Nep	Sep 5 1934	09:30	12° Vi 07'
Sun Cnj Nep	Sep 7 1935	21:35	14° Vi 19'
Sun Cnj Nep	Sep 9 1936	09:41	16° Vi 30'
Sun Cnj Nep	Sep 11 1937	21:18	18° Vi 41'
Sun Cnj Nep	Sep 14 1938	09:02	20° Vi 53'
Sun Cnj Nep	Sep 16 1939	20:34	23° Vi 04'
Sun Cnj Nep	Sep 18 1940	08:07	25° Vi 14'
Sun Cnj Nep	Sep 20 1941	19:33	27° Vi 25'
Sun Cnj Nep	Sep 23 1942	06:49	29° Vi 36'
Sun Cnj Nep	Sep 25 1943	18:16	01° Li 47'
Sun Cnj Nep	Sep 27 1944	05:37	03° Li 59'
Sun Cnj Nep	Sep 29 1945	16:54	06° Li 10'
Sun Cnj Nep	Oct 2 1946	04:03	08° Li 21'
Sun Cnj Nep	Oct 4 1947	15:18	10° Li 32'
Sun Cnj Nep	Oct 6 1948	02:12	12° Li 43'
Sun Cnj Nep	Oct 8 1949	13:05	14° Li 54'
Sun Cnj Nep	Oct 10 1950	23:41	17° Li 05'
Sun Cnj Nep	Oct 13 1951	10:16	19° Li 16'
Sun Cnj Nep	Oct 14 1952	20:53	21° Li 26'

Appendix VIII • *Sun-Neptune Conjunctions 1920 to 2120*

Sun Cnj Nep	Oct 17 1953	07:08	23° Li 37'
Sun Cnj Nep	Oct 19 1954	17:38	25° Li 47'
Sun Cnj Nep	Oct 22 1955	03:58	27° Li 58'
Sun Cnj Nep	Oct 23 1956	14:21	00° Sc 09'
Sun Cnj Nep	Oct 26 1957	00:39	02° Sc 20'
Sun Cnj Nep	Oct 28 1958	10:55	04° Sc 31'
Sun Cnj Nep	Oct 30 1959	21:10	06° Sc 41'
Sun Cnj Nep	Nov 1 1960	07:18	08° Sc 52'
Sun Cnj Nep	Nov 3 1961	17:14	11° Sc 02'
Sun Cnj Nep	Nov 6 1962	03:02	13° Sc 13'
Sun Cnj Nep	Nov 8 1963	12:56	15° Sc 23'
Sun Cnj Nep	Nov 9 1964	22:28	17° Sc 33'
Sun Cnj Nep	Nov 12 1965	08:12	19° Sc 44'
Sun Cnj Nep	Nov 14 1966	17:43	21° Sc 54'
Sun Cnj Nep	Nov 17 1967	03:19	24° Sc 04'
Sun Cnj Nep	Nov 18 1968	12:57	26° Sc 15'
Sun Cnj Nep	Nov 20 1969	22:25	28° Sc 26'
Sun Cnj Nep	Nov 23 1970	08:07	00° Sg 37'
Sun Cnj Nep	Nov 25 1971	17:43	02° Sg 48'
Sun Cnj Nep	Nov 27 1972	03:17	04° Sg 58'
Sun Cnj Nep	Nov 29 1973	12:42	07° Sg 09'
Sun Cnj Nep	Dec 1 1974	22:08	09° Sg 20'
Sun Cnj Nep	Dec 4 1975	07:20	11° Sg 30'
Sun Cnj Nep	Dec 5 1976	16:36	13° Sg 41'
Sun Cnj Nep	Dec 8 1977	01:48	15° Sg 51'
Sun Cnj Nep	Dec 10 1978	11:00	18° Sg 01'
Sun Cnj Nep	Dec 12 1979	20:21	20° Sg 12'
Sun Cnj Nep	Dec 14 1980	05:26	22° Sg 23'
Sun Cnj Nep	Dec 16 1981	14:53	24° Sg 34'
Sun Cnj Nep	Dec 19 1982	00:14	26° Sg 45'
Sun Cnj Nep	Dec 21 1983	09:41	28° Sg 56'
Sun Cnj Nep	Dec 22 1984	19:10	01° Cp 08'
Sun Cnj Nep	Dec 25 1985	04:35	03° Cp 19'
Sun Cnj Nep	Dec 27 1986	14:04	05° Cp 31'
Sun Cnj Nep	Dec 29 1987	23:20	07° Cp 42'
Sun Cnj Nep	Dec 31 1988	08:39	09° Cp 53'
Sun Cnj Nep	Jan 2 1990	17:55	12° Cp 05'
Sun Cnj Nep	Jan 5 1991	03:22	14° Cp 16'
Sun Cnj Nep	Jan 7 1992	12:35	16° Cp 27'
Sun Cnj Nep	Jan 8 1993	22:03	18° Cp 39'
Sun Cnj Nep	Jan 11 1994	07:32	20° Cp 51'
Sun Cnj Nep	Jan 13 1995	17:06	23° Cp 02'
Sun Cnj Nep	Jan 16 1996	02:54	25° Cp 14'
Sun Cnj Nep	Jan 17 1997	12:34	27° Cp 26'

Sun Cnj Nep	Jan 19 1998	22:34	29° Cp 39'
Sun Cnj Nep	Jan 22 1999	08:22	01° Aq 51'
Sun Cnj Nep	Jan 24 2000	18:08	04° Aq 03'
Sun Cnj Nep	Jan 26 2001	03:55	06° Aq 15'
Sun Cnj Nep	Jan 28 2002	13:45	08° Aq 27'
Sun Cnj Nep	Jan 30 2003	23:34	10° Aq 39'
Sun Cnj Nep	Feb 2 2004	09:29	12° Aq 52'
Sun Cnj Nep	Feb 3 2005	07:29	15° Aq 04'
Sun Cnj Nep	Feb 6 2006	05:33	17° Aq 17'
Sun Cnj Nep	Feb 8 2007	15:52	19° Aq 29'
Sun Cnj Nep	Feb 11 2008	02:03	21° Aq 42'
Sun Cnj Nep	Feb 12 2009	12:41	23° Aq 56'
Sun Cnj Nep	Feb 14 2010	23:19	26° Aq 09'
Sun Cnj Nep	Feb 17 2011	09:56	28° Aq 22'
Sun Cnj Nep	Feb 19 2012	20:41	00° Pi 36'
Sun Cnj Nep	Feb 21 2013	07:19	02° Pi 49'
Sun Cnj Nep	Feb 23 2014	18:11	05° Pi 02'
Sun Cnj Nep	Feb 26 2015	04:55	07° Pi 15'
Sun Cnj Nep	Feb 28 2016	15:47	09° Pi 29'
Sun Cnj Nep	Mar 2 2017	02:44	11° Pi 42'
Sun Cnj Nep	Mar 4 2018	13:54	13° Pi 55'
Sun Cnj Nep	Mar 7 2019	01:00	16° Pi 09'
Sun Cnj Nep	Mar 8 2020	12:23	18° Pi 23'
Sun Cnj Nep	Mar 11 2021	00:01	20° Pi 37'
Sun Cnj Nep	Mar 13 2022	11:43	22° Pi 52'
Sun Cnj Nep	Mar 15 2023	23:39	25° Pi 06'
Sun Cnj Nep	Mar 17 2024	11:22	27° Pi 21'
Sun Cnj Nep	Mar 19 2025	23:25	29° Pi 36'
Sun Cnj Nep	Mar 22 2026	11:19	01° Ar 50'
Sun Cnj Nep	Mar 24 2027	23:13	04° Ar 05'
Sun Cnj Nep	Mar 26 2028	11:16	06° Ar 19'
Sun Cnj Nep	Mar 28 2029	23:25	08° Ar 33'
Sun Cnj Nep	Mar 31 2030	11:39	10° Ar 48'
Sun Cnj Nep	Apr 2 2031	23:55	13° Ar 02'
Sun Cnj Nep	Apr 4 2032	12:24	15° Ar 17'
Sun Cnj Nep	Apr 7 2033	01:02	17° Ar 32'
Sun Cnj Nep	Apr 9 2034	13:57	19° Ar 47'
Sun Cnj Nep	Apr 12 2035	02:40	22° Ar 02'
Sun Cnj Nep	Apr 13 2036	15:47	24° Ar 17'
Sun Cnj Nep	Apr 16 2037	04:50	26° Ar 32'
Sun Cnj Nep	Apr 18 2038	17:48	28° Ar 47'
Sun Cnj Nep	Apr 21 2039	06:52	01° Ta 02'
Sun Cnj Nep	Apr 22 2040	19:53	03° Ta 17'

Appendix VIII • Sun-Neptune Conjunctions 1920 to 2120

Sun Cnj Nep	Apr 25 2041	09:09	05° Ta 32'
Sun Cnj Nep	Apr 27 2042	22:15	07° Ta 46'
Sun Cnj Nep	Apr 30 2043	11:28	10° Ta 01'
Sun Cnj Nep	May 2 2044	00:49	12° Ta 16'
Sun Cnj Nep	May 4 2045	14:27	14° Ta 32'
Sun Cnj Nep	May 7 2046	03:59	16° Ta 47'
Sun Cnj Nep	May 9 2047	17:47	19° Ta 02'
Sun Cnj Nep	May 11 2048	07:41	21° Ta 18'
Sun Cnj Nep	May 13 2049	21:33	23° Ta 33'
Sun Cnj Nep	May 16 2050	11:29	25° Ta 48'
Sun Cnj Nep	May 19 2051	01:09	28° Ta 03'
Sun Cnj Nep	May 20 2052	15:09	00° Ge 18'
Sun Cnj Nep	May 23 2053	05:00	02° Ge 33'
Sun Cnj Nep	May 25 2054	18:48	04° Ge 47'
Sun Cnj Nep	May 28 2055	08:41	07° Ge 02'
Sun Cnj Nep	May 29 2056	22:42	09° Ge 17'
Sun Cnj Nep	Jun 1 2057	12:45	11° Ge 31'
Sun Cnj Nep	Jun 4 2058	02:51	13° Ge 46'
Sun Cnj Nep	Jun 6 2059	17:04	16° Ge 01'
Sun Cnj Nep	Jun 8 2060	07:23	18° Ge 17'
Sun Cnj Nep	Jun 10 2061	21:49	20° Ge 32'
Sun Cnj Nep	Jun 13 2062	11:51	22° Ge 47'
Sun Cnj Nep	Jun 16 2063	02:10	25° Ge 01'
Sun Cnj Nep	Jun 17 2064	16:19	27° Ge 16'
Sun Cnj Nep	Jun 20 2065	06:24	29° Ge 31'
Sun Cnj Nep	Jun 22 2066	20:22	01° Cn 45'
Sun Cnj Nep	Jun 25 2067	10:17	03° Cn 59'
Sun Cnj Nep	Jun 27 2068	00:23	06° Cn 13'
Sun Cnj Nep	Jun 29 2069	14:19	08° Cn 27'
Sun Cnj Nep	Jul 2 2070	04:17	10° Cn 41'
Sun Cnj Nep	Jul 4 2071	18:18	12° Cn 55'
Sun Cnj Nep	Jul 6 2072	08:34	15° Cn 09'
Sun Cnj Nep	Jul 8 2073	22:31	17° Cn 23'
Sun Cnj Nep	Jul 11 2074	12:36	19° Cn 36'
Sun Cnj Nep	Jul 14 2075	02:30	21° Cn 50'
Sun Cnj Nep	Jul 15 2076	16:24	24° Cn 04'
Sun Cnj Nep	Jul 18 2077	06:10	26° Cn 17'
Sun Cnj Nep	Jul 20 2078	19:35	28° Cn 31'
Sun Cnj Nep	Jul 23 2079	09:14	00° Le 44'
Sun Cnj Nep	Jul 24 2080	22:40	02° Le 57'
Sun Cnj Nep	Jul 27 2081	12:03	05° Le 10'
Sun Cnj Nep	Jul 30 2082	01:21	07° Le 23'
Sun Cnj Nep	Aug 1 2083	14:40	09° Le 36'
Sun Cnj Nep	Aug 3 2084	04:13	11° Le 49'

Sun Cnj Nep	Aug 5 2085	17:38	14° Le 02'
Sun Cnj Nep	Aug 8 2086	06:52	16° Le 14'
Sun Cnj Nep	Aug 10 2087	20:09	18° Le 27'
Sun Cnj Nep	Aug 12 2088	09:25	20° Le 40'
Sun Cnj Nep	Aug 14 2089	22:14	22° Le 52'
Sun Cnj Nep	Aug 17 2090	11:11	25° Le 04'
Sun Cnj Nep	Aug 19 2091	23:54	27° Le 17'
Sun Cnj Nep	Aug 21 2092	12:36	29° Le 28'
Sun Cnj Nep	Aug 24 2093	01:07	01° Vi 40'
Sun Cnj Nep	Aug 26 2094	13:33	03° Vi 52'
Sun Cnj Nep	Aug 29 2095	02:04	06° Vi 04'
Sun Cnj Nep	Aug 30 2096	14:30	08° Vi 16'
Sun Cnj Nep	Sep 2 2097	02:50	10° Vi 28'
Sun Cnj Nep	Sep 4 2098	15:06	12° Vi 40'
Sun Cnj Nep	Sep 7 2099	03:31	14° Vi 52'
Sun Cnj Nep	Sep 9 2100	15:34	17° Vi 04'
Sun Cnj Nep	Sep 12 2101	03:41	19° Vi 16'
Sun Cnj Nep	Sep 14 2102	15:28	21° Vi 27'
Sun Cnj Nep	Sep 17 2103	03:16	23° Vi 39'
Sun Cnj Nep	Sep 18 2104	14:52	25° Vi 50'
Sun Cnj Nep	Sep 21 2105	02:10	28° Vi 01'
Sun Cnj Nep	Sep 23 2106	13:39	00° Li 11'
Sun Cnj Nep	Sep 26 2107	00:59	02° Li 22'
Sun Cnj Nep	Sep 27 2108	12:17	04° Li 33'
Sun Cnj Nep	Sep 29 2109	23:28	06° Li 44'
Sun Cnj Nep	Oct 2 2110	10:46	08° Li 55'
Sun Cnj Nep	Oct 4 2111	21:54	11° Li 06'
Sun Cnj Nep	Oct 6 2112	09:02	13° Li 17'
Sun Cnj Nep	Oct 8 2113	19:53	15° Li 28'
Sun Cnj Nep	Oct 11 2114	06:42	17° Li 39'
Sun Cnj Nep	Oct 13 2115	17:30	19° Li 50'
Sun Cnj Nep	Oct 15 2116	03:52	22° Li 00'
Sun Cnj Nep	Oct 17 2117	14:24	24° Li 11'
Sun Cnj Nep	Oct 20 2118	00:43	26° Li 21'
Sun Cnj Nep	Oct 22 2119	11:05	28° Li 31'
Sun Cnj Nep	Oct 23 2120	21:19	00° Sc 42'

Appendix IX

Sun-Pluto Conjunctions 1920 to 2120

Sun Cnj Plu	Jun 29 1920	09:00	07° Cn 17'
Sun Cnj Plu	Jun 30 1921	19:35	08° Cn 25'
Sun Cnj Plu	Jul 2 1922	06:13	09° Cn 34'

Appendix IX • *Sun-Pluto Conjunctions 1920 to 2120*

Sun Cnj Plu	Jul 3 1923	17:05	10° Cn 43'
Sun Cnj Plu	Jul 4 1924	04:14	11° Cn 53'
Sun Cnj Plu	Jul 5 1925	15:45	13° Cn 04'
Sun Cnj Plu	Jul 7 1926	03:23	14° Cn 15'
Sun Cnj Plu	Jul 8 1927	15:24	15° Cn 27'
Sun Cnj Plu	Jul 9 1928	03:58	16° Cn 40'
Sun Cnj Plu	Jul 10 1929	16:46	17° Cn 54'
Sun Cnj Plu	Jul 12 1930	06:03	19° Cn 09'
Sun Cnj Plu	Jul 13 1931	19:34	20° Cn 25'
Sun Cnj Plu	Jul 14 1932	09:33	21° Cn 42'
Sun Cnj Plu	Jul 15 1933	23:59	22° Cn 59'
Sun Cnj Plu	Jul 17 1934	14:25	24° Cn 18'
Sun Cnj Plu	Jul 19 1935	05:29	25° Cn 37'
Sun Cnj Plu	Jul 19 1936	20:52	26° Cn 57'
Sun Cnj Plu	Jul 21 1937	12:39	28° Cn 18'
Sun Cnj Plu	Jul 23 1938	04:55	29° Cn 40'
Sun Cnj Plu	Jul 24 1939	21:29	01° Le 04'
Sun Cnj Plu	Jul 25 1940	14:52	02° Le 28'
Sun Cnj Plu	Jul 27 1941	08:39	03° Le 54'
Sun Cnj Plu	Jul 29 1942	02:55	05° Le 21'
Sun Cnj Plu	Jul 30 1943	21:52	06° Le 50'
Sun Cnj Plu	Jul 31 1944	17:22	08° Le 20'
Sun Cnj Plu	Aug 2 1945	13:26	09° Le 51'
Sun Cnj Plu	Aug 4 1946	09:53	11° Le 24'
Sun Cnj Plu	Aug 6 1947	06:59	12° Le 58'
Sun Cnj Plu	Aug 7 1948	04:37	14° Le 34'
Sun Cnj Plu	Aug 9 1949	02:54	16° Le 11'
Sun Cnj Plu	Aug 11 1950	01:37	17° Le 49'
Sun Cnj Plu	Aug 13 1951	01:05	19° Le 29'
Sun Cnj Plu	Aug 14 1952	01:27	21° Le 11'
Sun Cnj Plu	Aug 16 1953	02:16	22° Le 55'
Sun Cnj Plu	Aug 18 1954	04:03	24° Le 40'
Sun Cnj Plu	Aug 20 1955	06:26	26° Le 28'
Sun Cnj Plu	Aug 21 1956	09:43	28° Le 17'
Sun Cnj Plu	Aug 23 1957	13:43	00° Vi 08'
Sun Cnj Plu	Aug 25 1958	18:12	02° Vi 01'
Sun Cnj Plu	Aug 27 1959	23:42	03° Vi 56'
Sun Cnj Plu	Aug 29 1960	05:47	05° Vi 52'
Sun Cnj Plu	Aug 31 1961	12:38	07° Vi 51'
Sun Cnj Plu	Sep 2 1962	20:10	09° Vi 51'
Sun Cnj Plu	Sep 5 1963	04:39	11° Vi 54'
Sun Cnj Plu	Sep 6 1964	13:55	13° Vi 59'
Sun Cnj Plu	Sep 9 1965	00:01	16° Vi 06'
Sun Cnj Plu	Sep 11 1966	10:54	18° Vi 15'

Sun Cnj Plu	Sep 13 1967	22:41	20° Vi 26'
Sun Cnj Plu	Sep 15 1968	11:27	22° Vi 40'
Sun Cnj Plu	Sep 18 1969	00:40	24° Vi 55'
Sun Cnj Plu	Sep 20 1970	14:53	27° Vi 13'
Sun Cnj Plu	Sep 23 1971	05:41	29° Vi 32'
Sun Cnj Plu	Sep 24 1972	21:12	01° Li 54'
Sun Cnj Plu	Sep 27 1973	13:15	04° Li 17'
Sun Cnj Plu	Sep 30 1974	05:51	06° Li 41'
Sun Cnj Plu	Oct 2 1975	23:13	09° Li 07'
Sun Cnj Plu	Oct 4 1976	17:06	11° Li 35'
Sun Cnj Plu	Oct 7 1977	11:28	14° Li 05'
Sun Cnj Plu	Oct 10 1978	06:21	16° Li 35'
Sun Cnj Plu	Oct 13 1979	01:56	19° Li 08'
Sun Cnj Plu	Oct 14 1980	21:40	21° Li 41'
Sun Cnj Plu	Oct 17 1981	17:57	24° Li 16'
Sun Cnj Plu	Oct 20 1982	14:16	26° Li 51'
Sun Cnj Plu	Oct 23 1983	10:55	29° Li 27'
Sun Cnj Plu	Oct 25 1984	07:35	02° Sc 04'
Sun Cnj Plu	Oct 28 1985	04:04	04° Sc 40'
Sun Cnj Plu	Oct 31 1986	00:38	07° Sc 17'
Sun Cnj Plu	Nov 2 1987	21:02	09° Sc 54'
Sun Cnj Plu	Nov 4 1988	17:16	12° Sc 30'
Sun Cnj Plu	Nov 7 1989	13:14	15° Sc 06'
Sun Cnj Plu	Nov 10 1990	09:05	17° Sc 42'
Sun Cnj Plu	Nov 13 1991	04:30	20° Sc 17'
Sun Cnj Plu	Nov 14 1992	23:47	22° Sc 52'
Sun Cnj Plu	Nov 17 1993	18:25	25° Sc 25'
Sun Cnj Plu	Nov 20 1994	12:52	27° Sc 58'
Sun Cnj Plu	Nov 23 1995	06:45	00° Sg 29'
Sun Cnj Plu	Nov 24 1996	23:56	02° Sg 59'
Sun Cnj Plu	Nov 27 1997	16:35	05° Sg 28'
Sun Cnj Plu	Nov 30 1998	08:26	07° Sg 55'
Sun Cnj Plu	Dec 2 1999	23:39	10° Sg 20'
Sun Cnj Plu	Dec 4 2000	14:05	12° Sg 44'
Sun Cnj Plu	Dec 7 2001	03:55	15° Sg 06'
Sun Cnj Plu	Dec 9 2002	16:57	17° Sg 26'
Sun Cnj Plu	Dec 12 2003	05:28	19° Sg 45'
Sun Cnj Plu	Dec 13 2004	17:05	22° Sg 02'
Sun Cnj Plu	Dec 16 2005	04:12	24° Sg 18'
Sun Cnj Plu	Dec 18 2006	14:40	26° Sg 31'
Sun Cnj Plu	Dec 21 2007	00:17	28° Sg 44'
Sun Cnj Plu	Dec 22 2008	09:23	00° Cp 54'
Sun Cnj Plu	Dec 24 2009	17:32	03° Cp 02'

Appendix IX • Sun-Pluto Conjunctions 1920 to 2120

Sun Cnj Plu	Dec 27 2010	01:04	05° Cp 09'
Sun Cnj Plu	Dec 29 2011	07:43	07° Cp 13'
Sun Cnj Plu	Dec 30 2012	13:38	09° Cp 16'
Sun Cnj Plu	Jan 1 2014	18:57	11° Cp 17'
Sun Cnj Plu	Jan 3 2015	23:34	13° Cp 16'
Sun Cnj Plu	Jan 6 2016	03:28	15° Cp 13'
Sun Cnj Plu	Jan 7 2017	06:45	17° Cp 09'
Sun Cnj Plu	Jan 9 2018	09:33	19° Cp 03'
Sun Cnj Plu	Jan 11 2019	11:38	20° Cp 56'
Sun Cnj Plu	Jan 13 2020	13:20	22° Cp 48'
Sun Cnj Plu	Jan 14 2021	14:19	24° Cp 38'
Sun Cnj Plu	Jan 16 2022	14:51	26° Cp 26'
Sun Cnj Plu	Jan 18 2023	14:44	28° Cp 13'
Sun Cnj Plu	Jan 20 2024	13:46	29° Cp 59'
Sun Cnj Plu	Jan 21 2025	12:29	01° Aq 42'
Sun Cnj Plu	Jan 23 2026	10:28	03° Aq 25'
Sun Cnj Plu	Jan 25 2027	08:01	05° Aq 06'
Sun Cnj Plu	Jan 27 2028	05:03	06° Aq 46'
Sun Cnj Plu	Jan 28 2029	01:33	08° Aq 24'
Sun Cnj Plu	Jan 29 2030	21:46	10° Aq 02'
Sun Cnj Plu	Jan 31 2031	17:27	11° Aq 38'
Sun Cnj Plu	Feb 2 2032	12:47	13° Aq 13'
Sun Cnj Plu	Feb 3 2033	07:42	14° Aq 47'
Sun Cnj Plu	Feb 5 2034	02:19	16° Aq 20'
Sun Cnj Plu	Feb 6 2035	20:18	17° Aq 51'
Sun Cnj Plu	Feb 8 2036	13:53	19° Aq 22'
Sun Cnj Plu	Feb 9 2037	07:03	20° Aq 51'
Sun Cnj Plu	Feb 10 2038	23:45	22° Aq 20'
Sun Cnj Plu	Feb 12 2039	16:13	23° Aq 47'
Sun Cnj Plu	Feb 14 2040	08:04	25° Aq 13'
Sun Cnj Plu	Feb 14 2041	23:46	26° Aq 39'
Sun Cnj Plu	Feb 16 2042	15:11	28° Aq 04'
Sun Cnj Plu	Feb 18 2043	06:05	29° Aq 28'
Sun Cnj Plu	Feb 19 2044	21:01	00° Pi 51'
Sun Cnj Plu	Feb 20 2045	11:31	02° Pi 14'
Sun Cnj Plu	Feb 22 2046	01:54	03° Pi 35'
Sun Cnj Plu	Feb 23 2047	15:53	04° Pi 56'
Sun Cnj Plu	Feb 25 2048	05:21	06° Pi 16'
Sun Cnj Plu	Feb 25 2049	18:45	07° Pi 35'
Sun Cnj Plu	Feb 27 2050	07:39	08° Pi 54'
Sun Cnj Plu	Feb 28 2051	20:19	10° Pi 11'
Sun Cnj Plu	Mar 1 2052	08:43	11° Pi 28'
Sun Cnj Plu	Mar 2 2053	20:53	12° Pi 44'
Sun Cnj Plu	Mar 4 2054	08:53	13° Pi 59'

Sun Cnj Plu	Mar 5 2055	20:33	15° Pi 14'
Sun Cnj Plu	Mar 6 2056	08:08	16° Pi 29'
Sun Cnj Plu	Mar 7 2057	19:33	17° Pi 43'
Sun Cnj Plu	Mar 9 2058	06:50	18° Pi 56'
Sun Cnj Plu	Mar 10 2059	17:44	20° Pi 09'
Sun Cnj Plu	Mar 11 2060	04:24	21° Pi 21'
Sun Cnj Plu	Mar 12 2061	14:56	22° Pi 32'
Sun Cnj Plu	Mar 14 2062	01:03	23° Pi 43'
Sun Cnj Plu	Mar 15 2063	11:04	24° Pi 54'
Sun Cnj Plu	Mar 15 2064	20:47	26° Pi 03'
Sun Cnj Plu	Mar 17 2065	06:21	27° Pi 13'
Sun Cnj Plu	Mar 18 2066	15:52	28° Pi 21'
Sun Cnj Plu	Mar 20 2067	00:55	29° Pi 30'
Sun Cnj Plu	Mar 20 2068	10:10	00° Ar 38'
Sun Cnj Plu	Mar 21 2069	19:17	01° Ar 45'
Sun Cnj Plu	Mar 23 2070	04:11	02° Ar 52'
Sun Cnj Plu	Mar 24 2071	13:03	03° Ar 59'
Sun Cnj Plu	Mar 24 2072	21:29	05° Ar 05'
Sun Cnj Plu	Mar 26 2073	05:59	06° Ar 11'
Sun Cnj Plu	Mar 27 2074	14:09	07° Ar 16'
Sun Cnj Plu	Mar 28 2075	22:00	08° Ar 21'
Sun Cnj Plu	Mar 29 2076	05:58	09° Ar 25'
Sun Cnj Plu	Mar 30 2077	13:40	10° Ar 29'
Sun Cnj Plu	Mar 31 2078	21:17	11° Ar 33'
Sun Cnj Plu	Apr 2 2079	04:46	12° Ar 37'
Sun Cnj Plu	Apr 2 2080	12:11	13° Ar 40'
Sun Cnj Plu	Apr 3 2081	19:43	14° Ar 43'
Sun Cnj Plu	Apr 5 2082	03:00	15° Ar 46'
Sun Cnj Plu	Apr 6 2083	10:12	16° Ar 49'
Sun Cnj Plu	Apr 6 2084	17:17	17° Ar 51'
Sun Cnj Plu	Apr 8 2085	00:16	18° Ar 53'
Sun Cnj Plu	Apr 9 2086	07:02	19° Ar 54'
Sun Cnj Plu	Apr 10 2087	13:36	20° Ar 55'
Sun Cnj Plu	Apr 10 2088	20:13	21° Ar 56'
Sun Cnj Plu	Apr 12 2089	02:40	22° Ar 56'
Sun Cnj Plu	Apr 13 2090	09:01	23° Ar 56'
Sun Cnj Plu	Apr 14 2091	15:13	24° Ar 56'
Sun Cnj Plu	Apr 14 2092	21:26	25° Ar 56'
Sun Cnj Plu	Apr 16 2093	03:50	26° Ar 56'
Sun Cnj Plu	Apr 17 2094	09:54	27° Ar 55'
Sun Cnj Plu	Apr 18 2095	16:05	28° Ar 55'
Sun Cnj Plu	Apr 18 2096	22:10	29° Ar 54'
Sun Cnj Plu	Apr 20 2097	04:02	00° Ta 53'
Sun Cnj Plu	Apr 21 2098	09:55	01° Ta 51'

Appendix IX • *Sun-Pluto Conjunctions 1920 to 2120*

Sun Cnj Plu	Apr 22 2099	15:25	02° Ta 50'
Sun Cnj Plu	Apr 23 2100	21:08	03° Ta 48'
Sun Cnj Plu	Apr 25 2101	02:46	04° Ta 46'
Sun Cnj Plu	Apr 26 2102	08:06	05° Ta 44'
Sun Cnj Plu	Apr 27 2103	13:41	06° Ta 42'
Sun Cnj Plu	Apr 27 2104	19:07	07° Ta 39'
Sun Cnj Plu	Apr 29 2105	00:42	08° Ta 37'
Sun Cnj Plu	Apr 30 2106	06:16	09° Ta 34'
Sun Cnj Plu	May 1 2107	11:36	10° Ta 32'
Sun Cnj Plu	May 1 2108	17:12	11° Ta 29'
Sun Cnj Plu	May 2 2109	22:33	12° Ta 26'
Sun Cnj Plu	May 4 2110	03:44	13° Ta 23'
Sun Cnj Plu	May 5 2111	09:00	14° Ta 20'
Sun Cnj Plu	May 5 2112	14:09	15° Ta 17'
Sun Cnj Plu	May 6 2113	19:24	16° Ta 13'
Sun Cnj Plu	May 8 2114	00:27	17° Ta 10'
Sun Cnj Plu	May 9 2115	05:33	18° Ta 06'
Sun Cnj Plu	May 9 2116	10:50	19° Ta 03'
Sun Cnj Plu	May 10 2117	16:04	20° Ta 00'
Sun Cnj Plu	May 11 2118	21:21	20° Ta 57'
Sun Cnj Plu	May 13 2119	02:38	21° Ta 53'
Sun Cnj Plu	May 13 2120	08:02	22° Ta 50'

Solstice Point Degrees of the Zodiac (Antiscion)

♑		♐		♒		♏		♓		♎		♈		♍		♉		♌		♊		♋
1	30	1	30	1	30	1	30	1	30	1	30
2	29	2	29	2	29	2	29	2	29	2	29
3	28	3	28	3	28	3	28	3	28	3	28
4	27	4	27	4	27	4	27	4	27	4	27
5	26	5	26	5	26	5	26	5	26	5	26
6	25	6	25	6	25	6	25	6	25	6	25
7	24	7	24	7	24	7	24	7	24	7	24
8	23	8	23	8	23	8	23	8	23	8	23
9	22	9	22	9	22	9	22	9	22	9	22
10	21	10	21	10	21	10	21	10	21	10	21
11	20	11	20	11	20	11	20	11	20	11	20
12	19	12	19	12	19	12	19	12	19	12	19
13	18	13	18	13	18	13	18	13	18	13	18
14	17	14	17	14	17	14	17	14	17	14	17
15	16	15	16	15	16	15	16	15	16	15	16
16	15	16	15	16	15	16	15	16	15	16	15
17	14	17	14	17	14	17	14	17	14	17	14
18	13	18	13	18	13	18	13	18	13	18	13
19	12	19	12	19	12	19	12	19	12	19	12
20	11	20	11	20	11	20	11	20	11	20	11
21	10	21	10	21	10	21	10	21	10	21	10
22	9	22	9	22	9	22	9	22	9	22	9
23	8	23	8	23	8	23	8	23	8	23	8
24	7	24	7	24	7	24	7	24	7	24	7
25	6	25	6	25	6	25	6	25	6	25	6
26	5	26	5	26	5	26	5	26	5	26	5
27	4	27	4	27	4	27	4	27	4	27	4
28	3	28	3	28	3	28	3	28	3	28	3
29	2	29	2	29	2	29	2	29	2	29	2
30	1	30	1	30	1	30	1	30	1	30	1

Appendix XI • *Equinox Point Degrees of the Zodiac (Contrascion)*

Equinox Point Degrees of the Zodiac (Contrascion)

♈	♓	♉	♒	♊	♑	♋	♐	♌	♍	♍	♎
1	30	1	30	1	30	1	30	1	30	1	30
2	29	2	29	2	29	2	29	2	29	2	29
3	28	3	28	3	28	3	28	3	28	3	28
4	27	4	27	4	27	4	27	4	27	4	27
5	26	5	26	5	26	5	26	5	26	5	26
6	25	6	25	6	25	6	25	6	25	6	25
7	24	7	24	7	24	7	24	7	24	7	24
8	23	8	23	8	23	8	23	8	23	8	23
9	22	9	22	9	22	9	22	9	22	9	22
10	21	10	21	10	21	10	21	10	21	10	21
11	20	11	20	11	20	11	20	11	20	11	20
12	19	12	19	12	19	12	19	12	19	12	19
13	18	13	18	13	18	13	18	13	18	13	18
14	17	14	17	14	17	14	17	14	17	14	17
15	16	15	16	15	16	15	16	15	16	15	16
16	15	16	15	16	15	16	15	16	15	16	15
17	14	17	14	17	14	17	14	17	14	17	14
18	13	18	13	18	13	18	13	18	13	18	13
19	12	19	12	19	12	19	12	19	12	19	12
20	11	20	11	20	11	20	11	20	11	20	11
21	10	21	10	21	10	21	10	21	10	21	10
22	9	22	9	22	9	22	9	22	9	22	9
23	8	23	8	23	8	23	8	23	8	23	8
24	7	24	7	24	7	24	7	24	7	24	7
25	6	25	6	25	6	25	6	25	6	25	6
26	5	26	5	26	5	26	5	26	5	26	5
27	4	27	4	27	4	27	4	27	4	27	4
28	3	28	3	28	3	28	3	28	3	28	3
29	2	29	2	29	2	29	2	29	2	29	2
30	1	30	1	30	1	30	1	30	1	30	1

Notes

1. The transit of Uranus in opposition to its natal position occurs between ages 39 to 43. The secondary progressed Moon opposes the natal Moon at age 40 ½ years.
2. A diurnal horoscope is cast for the date of an event using the time of birth.
3. *Cycles of Becoming* is available from the publisher of this book. [*Editors note: It is still available from the publisher of the second edition at www.revelore.press!*]
4. One of the best definitions of the specific influence of the transiting planets can be found in *The Principles of Astrology* by Charles E.O. Carter.
5. Stationary transits can form two exact aspects on either side of the planet's station while remaining within a 1° orb.
6. The author's mother died at a progressed Moon-Jupiter opposition in 7° Taurus-Scorpio, the exact degrees of his progressed horizon. She passed away at a third progressed Moon return three days before her 82nd birthday.
7. The inferior planets of Mercury and Venus lie within the orbit of the Earth, whereas the superior planets of Mars, Jupiter, Saturn, Uranus, Neptune, and Pluto orbit beyond Earth.
8. Astronomical facts from: *The Astrologer's Astronomical Handbook* by Jeff Mayo. Distance from Sun is mean distance.
9. An inferior planet's synodic cycle begins with its retrograde conjunction with the Sun.
10. The *soul groups*, determined by the pre-natal synodic cycle, are detailed in later chapters. The degree symbols shown on page 21 are the 1931 Sabian Symbols from Marc Jones.
11. To reference the relevant symbol, one must round up to the next higher degree.
12. Author Celeste Teal proposes that this 'erasure' occurs at the prenatal Lunar Eclipse. To research the degree symbols for your pre-natal Lunar Eclipse, see Appendix I.
13. In addition, the more frequent lunar holographic transits are calculated. See page 33.
14. Holographic transits, also known as Phase Angle Return charts, are calculated using the latitude and longitude for the current place of residence.
15. Transits in the outer wheel are calculated for 29 March 2006, with Pluto stationary Rx.
16. The author has repeatedly observed that individuals with 12th-house South Nodes lose their spouses to a co-worker. In the derivative houses, the 12th is the 6th from the 7th.
17. Natal distance arcs and Phase Angle Return charts were calculated with *Janus* software. This program calculates distance arcs in a 0° to 360° value. Displayed horoscopes were recalculated with the [now defunct] *Io Edition* program for the Macintosh.
18. Throughout this book, three sets of degree symbols will be referenced: 1. Sabian Symbols from Marc Jones' 1931 *Lecture-Lessons*; 2. Charubel's symbols from *The Degrees of the Zodiac Symbolised*, published in 1898 by Alan Leo; and 3. Sepharial's translation of *La Volasfera*, also published in that 1898 Astrological Manuals No. 8 by Alan Leo.
19. Only a few of the software programs can do the more precise calculations. *Solar Fire*™

Notes

only does Sun-Moon phase angle returns, but not for the Sun and the other planets. Many astrologers already use the Sun-Moon phase angle to help women who wish to conceive. These charts are accurate for timing ovulation. The *Janus* program from New Zealand, *Winstar* from Matrix, and *Nova Chartwheels* from Astrolabe can calculate all of the phase angle returns between the Sun and the other planets. Additionally, these programs can also calculate the lunar-planet and the interplanetary phase angle returns. Two combined programs from Halloran Software can calculate phase angle returns.

[20] The Sun-Moon phase angle return is the trickiest to "eyeball," because of the rapid lunar motion. However, with meticulous scrutiny one can even find these monthly dates.

[21] From *The Principles of Astrology*, C.E.O. Carter's Law of Excitation: *"If at the time that a progressed body is in aspect to another by direction, either of these bodies forms an aspect by transit with either of the two directional bodies, then this transit will excite the direction into immediate operation."*

[22] Her return to school in order to pursue a new career was to become a pharmacologist, a profession ruled by Neptune.

[23] Further contributing to the dissolution of an old ego identity and to the formation of a new one is the transit of Neptune making seven conjunctions to the progressed Sun between April 2004 and December 2006. The Sun in a woman's horoscope symbolizes the husband; the astrologer sees how the repeating transit of Neptune produced the affair.

[24] The eight lunation cycle phases are: New 0° to 45°; Crescent 45° to 90°; First Quarter 90° to 135°; Gibbous 135° to 180°; Full 180° to 225°; Disseminating 225° to 270°; Last Quarter 270° to 315°; Balsamic 315° to 360°. The eight lunar phases have been psychologically and spiritually defined as: 1) the impulse to evolve; 2) heeding the call; 3) overcoming external resistance; 4) searching for illumination; 5) achieving awareness and objective understanding; 6) assimilation and synthesis; 7) facing internal resistance; and 8) mastery, release and seeding of the next cycle.

[25] Some astrology software programs, such as *Solar Fire*™, allow the user to insert the glyph for the Earth into a Tropical nativity. Other programs, such as *Io Edition* for Macintosh, only allow the Earth glyph to be inserted into Heliocentric nativities. In this case, the astrologer can hand draw the Earth glyph in the sign and degree opposite the Sun.

[26] This technique places the Sun as if it were at 0° Aries and then measures the distance arc to the Moon. 103° to 104° into the Zodiac equates with the 14th degree of Cancer.

[27] A Table of Solstice Points can be found on page 344. Most astrology software programs can measure the distance arcs in a nativity. In *Solar Fire*™, once the chart is displayed, click the "Reports" button; then select "Difference Listing" in the upper right window.

28 These charts are *not* effective as a birth control method.
29 Perihelion occurs when a planet is closest to the Sun during its elliptical orbit.
30 Maximum daily movement occurs at the inferior conjunction of Mercury and the Sun.
31 See table of inferior conjunctions and synodic cycle durations on page 50.
32 The retrograde Mercury period that the author was born into lasted 20 days. Mercury had stationed retrograde at 00° Sagittarius 41' on 3 November 1953, and stationed direct at 14° Scorpio 36' on 23 November 1953. The degree travel between stations was 16°. On the day of his birth, Mercury had a 24-hour degree movement of 01° 20', its maximum.
33 See *Cycles of Becoming* by Alexander Ruperti, p. 111.
34 Duration and degree movement of retrogradation is found in *Progressions*, where in Appendix I there is Table 15–Planet Stations 1920–2120 (Revelore, ed., pp. 97–153).
35 Website address [was]: http://206.130.120.5/mm5/merchant.mvc?Screen=PROD&Store_Code=A&Product_Code=B-MMEphemVM&Category_Code=
36 The author, who was born at the inferior conjunction, has a superior conjunction of the Sun and Mercury in the chart for his astrology business, Earthwalk School of Astrology (12 February 1992; Noon; Lake Oswego, OR). The conjunction is in 23° Aquarius.
37 A *cazimi* conjunction is a planet within 00° 17' of the Sun. *Partile* is exact to the minute.
38 *Profiles in Courage* was written while the then Senator Kennedy was recovering from lower back surgery (Libra rising). President Kennedy's health was unstable for most of his life, a testament to his ruler, Venus, in square to the Moon, an aspect that produces periodic and returning diseases or illness.
39 Charles E.O. Carter, *An Encyclopcedia of Psychological Astrology* (L.N. Fowler, 1924).
40 To order a "Letter Progressions" lifetime report for $15 postpaid in the US, contact Mr Munkasey at StarFlash12@cs.com. Name, mailing address, and birth data are required.
41 Some readers may wonder just how to ascertain from which "mental matrix" on the causal plane one's individual hologram of thought has emerged, and from which "previous eras that affected the thinking of those living during that time" is the soul in this lifetime connected to from past lives? Sun-Mercury inferior conjunctions recur in the same degree of the Zodiac on an alternating basis after 79 years, next after 125 years, and then back to 79 years, and so on. Occasionally, the inferior conjunction recurs in the same degree after 204 years. The math behind this is as follows: 79 years × 365.26 days per year = 28,855.54 days. Divide this product of days by the length of a Sun-Mercury synodic cycle: 28,855.54 days ÷ 115.88 days/cycle = 249. Thus, 249 synodic cycles of Mercury = exactly 79 years. In the longer periodicity, 394 synodic cycles of Mercury = exactly 125 years (125 × 365.26 = 45,657.5 ÷ 115.88 = 394). It is the author's belief that these numbers of years are reincarnation cycles. Soul groups

with the same pre-natal Sun-Mercury inferior conjunction degree reincarnate when the Mercury synodic cycle originates in that exact same degree, with either 79, 125, or 204 years between births. For example, the author's 1953 soul group has a pre-natal Sun-Mercury inferior conjunction degree of Scorpio 23. Sun-Mercury inferior conjunctions also occurred in this degree in 1874, 1670, 1591, 1466, 1387, 1262, 1183, 1058, and so on. These years in history are when his soul group had previously incarnated. The next inferior conjunction in Scorpio 23 will occur in 2078, and this soul group would reincarnate at that time.

[42] It is of interest that this progressed inferior conjunction was in fact rising for Mr Lincoln, exactly mirroring the symbolism. Saturn, conjoining the pre-natal inferior conjunction and solar eclipse, is his chart ruler.

[43] A Table of Equinox Points can be found on page 345.

[44] A quincunx is a 150° aspect between planets in cardinal and mutable signs. Inconjuncts are formed when one of the two planets in a 150° aspect is in a fixed sign. The latter is the more difficult of these two aspects. A Yod with a fixed sign apex planet is the worst.

[45] Meiji Constitution of Japan; 11 February 1889; 12:00 PM LMT; Tokyo (BWH #171).

[46] This technique can also be applied to Mundane Astrology forecasts. On 8 October 1929, for example, there was an inferior conjunction of the Sun and Mercury in 14° Libra 29', exactly conjunct the US Saturn. The stock market crash followed shortly thereafter.

[47] Venus in this Sun-Mercury phase angle return was conjunct the author's progressed Moon in 06° Aquarius, exact to 06' of arc, confirming what the author wrote about in Chapter One on "Secondary Progressions Interacting with Phase Angle Returns." The Sun-Mercury inferior conjunction had occurred the day before in Pisces 22, conjunct the author's Descendant to the degree, showing that relationship concerns would weigh heavily on his mind during the entire length of this personal Sun-Mercury synodic cycle.

[48] If the secondary progressed Sun-Venus cycle reverses polarity; *i.e.*, from having been a morning star, then reaching progressed superior conjunction and becoming an evening star, one will experience a complete transformation in their approach to relationship.

[49] Oprah Winfrey has a dignified Mars which is the sole and final dispositor of her nativity.

[50] As a further testimony to the work of Charles E.O. Carter, wherein *An Encyclopædia of Psychological Astrology* he wrote about Enteric Fever (Typhoid), he listed Virgo rising, Mars and Saturn in affliction, and 10° of the mutables—all of which Modigliani had.

[51] It was unintended by the author, yet ironic, that both case studies have Virgo 11 rising.

[52] The author's secondary progressions will become Oprah Winfrey's nativity then!

[53] Exceptionally astute astrologers will have observed that the North Node in Aquarius

10 at the time of inferior conjunction is in the precise degree of the superior conjunction of 29 January 1954, when Oprah Winfrey was born. It is also not lost on this astrologer that Uranus at the inferior conjunction was exactly opposite his natal Sun/Moon midpoint, and that Saturn at the inferior conjunction was in the degree of his natal Neptune.

54 Some of these karmic relationships are getting a little familiar by now, wouldn't you say?

55 The phase angle return chart was cast for Lake City, Washington, the author's residence.

56 This phase angle return was cast for Lake Oswego, Oregon, his residence in June 1995. One observes that the transit North Node was also exactly conjunct the author's Venus.

57 It is of note that the Sun conjoined the co-rulers of his 7th house of second children. This phase angle return was cast for Arch Cape, Oregon, his residence in January 1997.

58 Carter, *The Principles of Astrology*.

59 The synodic cycle of Mars varies from 762 to 819 days in length. The average is 779 days.

60 The retrograde station of Mars on 18 March 1999 was in 12° Scorpio 12'. The Sun was in 27° Pisces 30', forming a 135° sesquiquadrate, exact to 18' of arc.

61 The Mars cycle fluctuates wildly in its individual phase lengths. The author researched 308 synodic cycles of Mars from 1448–2105 calculated by astrologer Michael Munkasey and found that, for example, from heliacal rising of Mars to waxing square can vary from 199 to 297 days. Similarly, from the waning square to heliacal setting of Mars varies from 212 to 292 days. Because of the elliptical nature of Mars' orbit, and its proximity to Earth at either its aphelion or perihelion, the oriental and occidental phase lengths of Mars are in a binary pattern. When one is shorter, the other is longer and vice versa. One has to speculate, of course, about vast waves of independent souls incarnating during oriental phase, and likewise those with the karma to work for others during the occidental phase.

62 Astrologers should bear in mind that this occurs at the progressed-to-progressed aspects of the Sun and Mars, and not at the progressed-to-natal aspects.

63 In another portentous aspect of magnitude, Saturn had perfected a progressed square with his Sun. This, of course, was a progressed-to-natal aspect, separating by only 06'. His secondary progressed Mars was also forming an inconjunct to the natal Sun; all bodies being in 11°. A slight rectification of FDR's nativity would have placed his progressed Descendant in 13° Taurus at the time of Pearl Harbor, and in exact conjunction with Neptune. The 7th house rules open enemies, and here we see the sneak attack by the Japanese on Hawaii. It is of note that his ruler, Mercury, is in 27° Aquarius, conjunct the US Sibly chart's Moon, exact to 01'. FDR's Moon is conjunct the US Jupiter,

Notes

attesting to his widespread popularity with the American people, both Democrat and Republican.

64 His progressed Sun-Mars opposition occurred at 08° Cancer-Capricorn 45', exactly on his Venus/Jupiter midpoint. Both his wife and his sister-in-law died in the crash with him.

65 Capone had a highly visible scar on his face, hence his nickname, from a switchblade cut to the right cheek suffered during a violent fight when he was a bartender. He made a pass at a woman, and was attcked by her brother in an Italian neighborhood in Brooklyn.

66 The author's Vertex in 00° Pisces 35' formed a synastric Grand Cross with the mother's Lunar Nodes and Pluto.

67 There can be unrelated strings of synodic cycle conjunctions falling in the same degree. In 804 and 1009 AD, for example, Sun-Mars conjunctions also occurred in Leo 24. This phenomenon may explain large gaps of time between incarnations; *i.e.*, from 1009 to 1955.

68 Also born during this synodic cycle was the French mathematician and astronomer, Pierre-Simon, Marquis de Laplace, on 23 March 1749.

69 When one is trying to hold to a vision, despite all obstacles, these aspects are worth gold. His partner has her Chiron in 5° Aquarius, degree of the Sun in the phase angle return.

70 In a remarkable twist of fate, the Midheaven for this Sun-Mars holographic transit is in the precise degree, Cancer 17, of the author's pre-natal Sun-Mars conjunction.

71 Astrologers see that the author's natal Moon-Mars distance arc of 148° 05' has replicated itself in the heavens. The author has found that, of the 25 to 27 Moon-Mars phase angle subcycles occurring during the life of one's 25–26 month Sun-Mars holographic transit, the lunar phase angle which repeats the natal signs, *i.e.*, Libra-Pisces, is quite revealing.

72 An inconjunct aspect occurs when one of the two bodies in 150° relationship is in a fixed sign. If the bodies in the 150° aspect are in cardinal and mutable signs, it is a quincunx. The same applies to the 30° aspect. If one body is in a fixed sign, it is an inconjunct. If the bodies in the 30° aspect are in cardinal and mutable signs, it is a semisextile.

73 Perhaps one can attribute this to an afflicted Jupiter on an angle. In detriment in Gemini and retrograde, the author's Jupiter is weak. However, on the MC, some good resulted. Some of his colleagues have teased him over the years about his private life being public knowledge. With the ruler of the IC conjunct the MC, it is impossible to keep a personal life private instead of public, so the author has learned to become transparent about his foibles and character defects. *If one cannot beat them, join them* ... as the saying goes.

74 It is of interest that Irène Curie was born less than two months after Amelia Earhart,

and both of these unconventional women had the Saturn-Uranus conjunction in Scorpio.

75 The two degrees derived from the short and long arcs are Contrascia, or Equinox Points.

76 In another example of astrological time twins, Carl Lewis, the US Olympic champion sprinter and long jumper, was born on the same day as Diana. Diana's two distance arcs share both a geometric and a harmonic relationship. Whereas arc *A* is a close triseptile, arc *B* forms a close semiseptile aspect of 25° 43'. Thus, $1/14 + 3/7 = 1/2$, or 180°.

77 In another example of both a geometric and a harmonic relationship, Cobain's distance arc *B* is a tenth harmonic aspect, the decile, or semiquintile. Thus, $2/5 + 1/10 = 1/2$.

78 It is of interest that the Sabian Symbol for Taurus 7 is known as the "Jesus" degree: *Out of the past comes the "woman of Samaria" to draw water from Jacob's well.* The dying man in Charubel's astral vision could indeed have been Jesus Christ expiring on the cross.

79 Saturn is in *partile* (exact to the minute of arc) conjunction with his 2nd cusp.

80 Kant also wrote extensively on the sciences during his life.

81 The first of the following two symbols is from *La Volasfera*; the second from Charubel.

82 On 10 January 1973, a Sun-Jupiter conjunction occurred in 20° Capricorn 00'. In the use of degree symbols, this would be read as Capricorn 20, whereas 20° 01' is Capricorn 21.

83 The author has a special affinity with Kant; his pre-natal Sun-Jupiter conjunction also includes Mercury in a three-planet formation. An extensive research project, to see how frequently and regularly this phenomenon occurs, will have to wait. It is clear, however, that the heavenly realms operate in divine cyclic and geometric beauty and perfection. With Mercury, either 249 synodic cycles of 116 days each recur in a 79-year pattern, or 394 synodic cycles of 116 days each recur in a 125-year pattern. With Venus, 157 synodic cycles of 584 days each recur in a 251-year pattern. With Mars, 96 synodic cycles of 779 days each repeat in a 205-year periodicity. With Jupiter, 76 synodic cycles of 399 days each recur in an 83-year pattern. And with Saturn, 142 synodic cycles of 378 days each recur in an 147-year pattern.

84 This is a historical pattern of US presidents dying in office, or being assassinated, when elected during Jupiter-Saturn conjunctions in Earth signs, dating back to 1840.

85 The Sun is conjunct the US Sibly chart Moon in 27° Aquarius.

86 Carter, *The Principles of Astrology*, p. 31.

87 Bush took office with progressed Sun conjunct Mars and progressed Mars square Sun.

88 The tropical year of 365 days 5 hours 48.75 minutes is about midway between the lunar year of 354 days and the Sun-Saturn synodic cycle of 378 days.

89 One presumes that with a progressed Sun-Saturn opposition, she suffered depression. It is also clear that with a recent progressed First Quarter square, her life was in crisis.

90 A portcullis is a grating that can be lowered to prevent entrance to a fortified place.

91 This experience occurred at his transit Uranus opposition to natal Uranus.

Notes

[92] Saturn remains retrograde for 4½ months a year, traveling 6°–7° in the Zodiac during retrogression, and about 37.5% of the population is therefore born with this placement. Saturn orbits approximately 18°–21° through the Zodiac each year when direct, and thus about 62.5% of souls possess this horoscopic condition.

[93] This aspect is also called a sesquiquintile.

[94] The quadriundecile of 130° 55', quadrinovile of 160°, quinqueundecile of 163° 38', and the contraquindecile of 165° also fall into this class of aspects from the Sun to Saturn Rx.

[95] Saturn had stationed direct just 4 ½ hours before her birth.

[96] Wilson's progressed Venus was forming a Yod with his natal Neptune-Pluto sextile.

[97] Charles E.O. Carter *The Astrology of Accidents* (L.N. Fowler, 1932).

[98] Drowning is caused by the lungs (Mercury) filling with fluids, causing suffocation (Saturn).

[99] These *five* sidereal cycles reflect the exaltation of Saturn in Venus-ruled Libra. It is also of interest that more conjunctions fall in Saturn's dignity (13 in Capricorn and Aquarius), and fewer conjunctions fall in Saturn's detriment (11 each in Cancer and Leo).

[100] It is possible that the chart ruler for this incarnation and the recurring periodicity of its synodic cycle determines the length of time until the subsequent incarnation.

[101] A planet is out-of-bounds if its declination exceeds 23° 27', the obliquity of the ecliptic. The Moon's maximum declination is about 28° 35'.

[102] Virgo 29 from *La Volasfera*.

[103] A 12-year pattern of Jupiter in Pisces producing political scandals in the United States has been going on for some time; *e.g.* 1998 = Lewinsky scandal; 1986 = Iran-Contra Affair 1974 = Watergate; 1962 = Bay of Pigs Invasion in Cuba, etc.

[104] Bill Clinton was impeached as President of the United States on 19 December 1998 by the House of Representatives. He was subsequently acquitted by the Senate on 12 February 1999, the very day of Jupiter's ingress into Aries.

[105] A householder is a family man or woman; *i.e.*, a husband and wife with children.

[106] Sepharial was the gifted Theosophical astrologer, Walter Old (a.k.a. Gornold; 1864–1929).

[107] These two degrees are Contrascia, or Equinox Points of one another.

[108] This distance arc is equal to the triseptile aspect of 154 $2/7$°.

[109] For the three outer planets, the author recommends referring to the local Midheaven and its degree symbol, rather than the rising degree, as these universal energies are less personal, and more of an expression of one's life work and professional reputation.

[110] This Sun-Uranus conjunction was joined by Mars, adding to its power and energy. The Moon was in the exact degree of the author's natal Uranus, and trine to his Sun, making him a true child of these celestial energies.

[111] The illusory glamour of maintaining one's "celebrity image" in New York City, as Scott and Zelda Fitzgerald attempted in the 1920s, despite being unable to keep up

financially with their wealthier friends, was a manifestation of the Neptune in Leo era (1914–1929). Fitzgerald's 3rd-house ruler, Mars, is exactly conjunct his Neptune, and this allowed him to first perceive, and then articulate the hedonistic pursuit of glamour by his generation.

[112] The rising degree in the author's pre-natal Sun-Neptune conjunction chart is the exact degree of his South Node, implying that his spiritual work from past lives is continuing.

[113] Besides mental discomfort of feeling like he was overreaching in his attempts to define and describe relationships between free will and fate within the space-time continuum, the author also experienced what can be described as an *astral vibration* while writing.

[114] See page 142.

[115] At the moment that the author finished writing, Pisces 23 was rising. From *La Volasfera*:

> *A warrior in helmet drawing a long bow to which the fletch is duly set.*

> This symbol is capable of two renderings, the first of which points to a strong character, a set purpose, a lofty aim and in some particular sense the gift of prophecy and knowledge of future events. On the other hand, there is the weakness which depends on the hazard of life, the carelessness or indifference which arises from lack of interest and finds expression in vanity and self-inflation. At its best it signifies the higher indifference which affects the mind secure of its achievements, in the worst case it denotes improvidence and carelessness, a life set upon a hazard. It is a degree of SPECULATION.

Bibliography

Arroyo, Stephen. *Astrology, Karma & Transformation*. CRCS, 1978.
———. *Relationships & Life Cycles*. CRCS, 1979.
Blaschke, Robert P. *Astrology: A Language of Life; Volume I – Progressions*. Earthwalk School of Astrology, 1998.
———. *Astrology: A Language of Life; Volume II – Sabian Aspect Orbs*. Earthwalk School of Astrology, 2000.
———. *Astrology: A Language of Life; Volume III – A Handbook for the Self-Employed Astrologer*. Earthwalk School of Astrology, 2002.
———. *Astrology: A Language of Life; Volume IV – Relationship Analysis*. Earthwalk School of Astrology, 2004.
Campion, Nicholas. *The Book of World Horoscopes* (BWH). Wessex Astrologer, 2004.
Carter, Charles E.O. *An Encyclopædia of Psychological Astrology*. L.N. Fowler, 1924.
———. *The Principles of Astrology*. L.N. Fowler, 1925.
———. *The Seven Great Problems of Astrology*. L.N. Fowler, 1927.
———. *The Zodiac and the Soul*. L.N. Fowler, 1928.
———. *Symbolic Directions in Modern Astrology*. L.N. Fowler, 1929.
———. *The Astrological Aspects*. L.N. Fowler, 1930.
———. *The Astrology of Accidents*. L.N. Fowler, 1932.
———. *Some Principles of Horoscopic Delineation*. L.N. Fowler, 1934.
———. *Essays on the Foundations of Astrology*. L.N. Fowler, 1947.
———. *An Introduction to Political Astrology*. L.N. Fowler, 1951.
Charubel. *The Degrees of the Zodiac Symbolised*. Astrology Classics, 2005. (Includes a translation by Sepharial of a smiliar series of degree symbols found in La Volasfera)
Cleaver, Eldridge. *Soul on Ice*. Dell Publishing, 1968.
Copernicus, Nicolaus. *De revolutionibus orbium coelestium*. 1543.
Fitzgerald, F. Scott. *This Side of Paradise*. Charles Scribner & Son, 1920.
———. *The Great Gatsby*. Charles Scribner & Son, 1925.
Hand, Robert. *Planets in Transit*. Whitford Press, 1976.
Jones, Marc Edmund. *Lecture-Lessons*. Sabian Assembly, 1931.
Kant, Immanuel. *Critique of Pure Reason*. Prometheus Books, 1990.
Kennedy, John F. *Profiles in Courage*. Harper & Row, 1956.
Leo, Alan. *The Progressed Horoscope*. L.N. Fowler, 1906.
Mayo, Jeff. *The Astrologer's Astronomical Handbook*. L.N. Fowler, 1965.
Munkasey, Michael. *Ephemerides: Cycles and Phases of Venus & Mercury*. NCGR, 2003.
Rodden, Lois M. *Modern Transits*. AFA, 1978.
Rudhyar, Dane. *An Astrological Mandala: The Cycle of Transformations and its 360 Symbolic Phases*. Random House, 1973.
Ruperti, Alexander. *Cycles of Becoming*. Earthwalk School of Astrology, 2005.
Sepharial. *Sepharial's Manual of Astrology*. Sterling Publishing Co., 1962.
———. *Transits and Planetary Periods*. Samuel Weiser, 1973.
Sullivan, Erin. *Retrograde Planets: Traversing the Inner Sky*. Samuel Weiser, 2000.
Teal, Celeste. *Eclipses*. Llewellyn, 2006.
The Holy Bible. King James Version. 1611.

www.ingramcontent.com/pod-product-compliance
Lightning Source LLC
Chambersburg PA
CBHW070242090526
44586CB00035B/1517